Apple Pro Training Series

Optimizing Your Final Cut Pro System

Sean Cullen, Matthew Geller, Charles Roberts, and Adam Wilt

Apple
Certified

Apple Pro Training Series: Optimizing Your Final Cut Pro System
Sean Cullen, Matthew Geller, Charles Roberts, and Adam Wilt
Copyright © 2006 by Sean Cullen, Matthew Geller, Charles Roberts, and Adam Wilt

Published by Peachpit Press. For information on Peachpit Press books, contact:

Peachpit Press
1249 Eighth Street
Berkeley, CA 94710
(510) 524-2178
Fax: (510) 524-2221
http://www.peachpit.com
To report errors, please send a note to errata@peachpit.com
Peachpit Press is a division of Pearson Education

Editor: Nancy Peterson
Contributing Writers: Estelle McGechie, Jonathan Tyrrell
Series Editor: Serena Herr
Managing Editor: Kristin Kalning
Production Coordinator: Laurie Stewart, Happenstance Type-O-Rama
Technical Editors: Scot Barbour, Adam Green, Conrad Klahn, Mark Leabo, Ken Stone
Technical Reviewers: Brendan Boykin and Eric Geoffroy
Copy Editor: Darren Meiss
Compositor: Chris Gillespie, Happenstance Type-O-Rama
Indexer: Joy Dean Lee
Cover Art Direction: Charlene Charles-Will
Cover Illustration: Alicia Buelow
Cover Production: George Mattingly / GMD
Front Cover Photos: Claudio Miranda

ISBN 0-321-26871-7
9 8 7 6 5 4 3 2 1
Printed and bound in the United States of America

The authors dedicate this book to Charles McConathy, who was busy optimizing Final Cut Pro—and the working lives of FCP users— from the day Final Cut Pro started to the day Charles died. Charles, you are missed.

Contributing Writers

 Sean Cullen has worked as Assistant Editor to acclaimed film editor Walter Murch on such films as *Apocalypse Now Redux* and *The English Patient*. For Anthony Minghella's Civil War epic *Cold Mountain*, Sean was responsible for the first implementation of Final Cut Pro on a large-scale feature film. Most recently he was the Associate Editor of the film *Jarhead*, a film edited by Murch and directed by Sam Mendes.

 Matthew Geller is a Chicago-based systems integrator, consultant, and all-around technology therapist specializing in digital video post-production installations for organizations ranging from independent boutiques to international broadcast facilities. He is a certified instructor and courseware author for Apple and helped form the Chicago Final Cut Pro Users Group.

 Estelle McGechie was awarded a specialist visa by the U.S. Government for outstanding achievement in the field of editing. Her editing and 2D animation work has included short narrative, documentary, advertising, lifestyle, and music videos. She consults for various broadcast and film companies, including VH1, MTV, Nickelodeon, World Wrestling Entertainment, ABC, NBC, and The Motion Picture Editors Guild.

 Charles Roberts is an assistant professor of post-production in the Film and Video Department at Fitchburg State College. He is also a member of the summer faculty at the International Film Workshops in Rockport, Maine, and a system consultant of post-production environments for the University of Massachusetts and other higher education institutions.

Jonathan Eric Tyrrell is an independent filmmaker and digital artist living in Vancouver, British Columbia. His work has been exhibited at a wide range of venues in the UK and North America. He emigrated to Canada after completing an MA in Film and Television Studies at Warwick University in England. Jonathan is an Assistant Professor in the Media Arts area at Emily Carr Institute.

Adam Wilt is a video systems and software engineer for companies such as Abekas, Pinnacle, and Louth Automation (now Accom, Avid, and Harris, respectively); CBS and ABC; Circuit Studios; and Omneon Video Networks. In his spare time, he writes for *DV* magazine, teaches technology to a wide variety of groups, speaks at industry events like NAB, IBC, and DV Expo, and freelances as a cameraman, sound recordist, and editor. He doesn't sleep much. His Web site is www.adamwilt.com.

Contents at a Glance

Table of Contents

Using Final Cut Pro in Real World Workflows

Fundamentals of Video Standards and Hardware Primer

Troubleshooting Final Cut Pro

Getting Started

Welcome to the official training course for optimizing Final Cut Pro systems. This book is a guide to installing, configuring, managing, and troubleshooting Final Cut Pro in real-world post-production workflows. It is intended for independent, commercial, and corporate video editors as well as post-production houses and system integrators—anyone who wants to move beyond a simple Final Cut Pro installation and make the most of his or her professional nonlinear editing system.

The Methodology

Like all Apple Pro Training titles, this book emphasizes hands-on training. Where appropriate, it includes real-world, step-by-step exercises, so you can learn by doing. Some sections of the book, such as "Fundamentals of Video Standards and Hardware," are primarily reference information, and do not include detailed exercises. Each lesson builds on previous ones, but you can start with any section and focus on that topic.

Course Structure

This book is designed to help you set up, optimize, and maintain an effective FCP editing system. It is divided into five sections:

Lessons 1–6: Using Final Cut Pro in Real World Workflows

This section starts with a birds-eye view of common editing workflows for DV and film projects, and then uses exercises to walk you through the details of online and offline editing and distribution workflows.

Lessons 7–9: Fundamentals of Video Standards and Hardware Primer

This is a primer on the technology behind an editing system. It covers video standards and formats, plus all the hardware that goes along with them— including capture cards, decks, and storage systems.

Lessons 10–12: Configuring Final Cut Pro and Managing Your System

In this section you'll learn to install, set up, configure, optimize, and maintain a professional Final Cut Pro editing system.

Lessons 13–15: Integrating Your System

Aimed primarily at systems integrators, this section shows you how to incorporate high-end capture cards, storage systems, and Xsan into an industry-standard Final Cut Pro installation.

Lessons 16–18: Troubleshooting Final Cut Pro

The final section of the book covers troubleshooting. Chapter 16 gives an overview of basic troubleshooting methodology. Chapters 17 and 18 are symptom-and-solution guides to help you identify and solve the most common errors and issues encountered by video editors.

System Requirements

The book assumes a working level of familiarity with the Mac OS X operating system and Final Cut Pro. It was written for Final Cut Pro 5 and Mac OS X 10.4 (Tiger), but notes are included throughout referencing earlier versions of the software and the OS. Basic system requirements for Final Cut Pro 5 are:

► Macintosh computer with a PowerPC G4 (500 MHz or faster) or G5 processor; HD features require 1 GHz or faster single or dual processors

► 1 GB of RAM (2 GB recommended for HD)

► AGP Quartz Extreme graphics card

► Mac OS X v10.3.9 or Mac OS X v10.4 (or later)

► QuickTime 7.0 or later

► 1 GB of disk space

► DVD-ROM drive

Copying the Lesson Files

This book includes an APTS_OptimizingFCP DVD, which holds all the files you will need to complete the lessons. All files are contained in the Opt FCP Book Files folder. Within that folder, there is a Lessons folder and a Media folder containing the applicable project and media files for those lessons that include exercises.

While installing these files on your computer, it's important to keep all of the numbered Lesson folders together in the main Lessons folder on your hard drive. If you copy the Opt FCP Book Files folder directly from the DVD to your hard drive, you should not have to reconnect your project files to the media.

Installing the Lesson Files

You will need approximately 4.5 GB of free disk space on either your hard drive or a separate media drive to copy all the project and media files for this book.

1   Put the APTS_OptimizingFCP DVD into your computer's DVD drive.

2   Drag the Opt FCP Book Files folder to your media drive or your computer's hard drive.

3   Eject the disk. Do not launch the project files from your hard drive until you have ejected the disk.

Reconnecting Broken Media Links

In the process of copying the media from this book's DVD, you may break a link between the project file and the media file. If this happens, the next time you open a project file, a window will appear saying that it can't find a file and asking you to reconnect the project files. Reconnecting the project files is a simple process. Just follow these steps:

1   If the Can't Find File window appears, click the Find File button.

2   Navigate to where the Lessons folder resides on your hard drive or media drive, then go to the specific Projects or Media subfolder for the current lesson.

3   Select the media file you wish to reconnect from the File Browser. Click the Use Selected Path to Reconnect Other Missing Files box. Click the Choose button. This should reconnect all the media for that project.

4   Repeat steps 2 and 3 until all the project files have been reconnected.

Companion Web Site

This book stays current. As Final Cut Pro is updated, check for revised lessons and additional content, such as hardware-specific setup guides, at www.peachpit.com/apts.optfcp.

About the Apple Training Series

Optimizing Your Final Cut Pro System is part of the official training series for Apple Pro applications developed by experts in the field and certified by Apple Computer. The lessons are designed to let you learn at your own pace, and are also the approved curriculum for Apple Certified training centers worldwide. For more information and a complete listing of Apple Pro Training titles, please see the series product guide at the back of this book.

Apple Pro Certification Program

The Apple Pro Training and Certification Programs are designed to keep you at the forefront of Apple's digital media technology while giving you a competitive edge in today's ever-changing job market.

Upon completing the course material in this book, you can become a Certified Apple Pro by taking the online certification exam through an Apple Authorized Training Center. Certification is offered in Final Cut Pro, DVD Studio Pro, Motion, SoundTrack Pro, Shake, and Logic. Successful certification as an Apple Pro gives you official recognition of your knowledge of Apple's professional applications while allowing you to market yourself to employers and clients as a skilled, pro-level user of Apple products.

For those who prefer to learn in an instructor-led setting, Apple also offers training courses at Apple Authorized Training Centers worldwide. These courses, which use the Apple Pro Training Series books as their curriculum, are taught by Apple Certified Trainers and balance concepts and lectures with hands-on labs and exercises. Apple Authorized Training Centers have been carefully selected and have met Apple's highest standards in all areas, including facilities, instructors, course delivery, and infrastructure. The goal of the program is to offer Apple customers, from beginners to the most seasoned professionals, the highest quality training experience.

To find an Authorized Training Center near you, go to www.apple.com/software/pro/training.

Resources

Apple Pro Training Series: Optimizing Your Final Cut Pro System is not intended to be a comprehensive reference manual, nor does it replace the documentation that comes with the application. For comprehensive information about application features, refer to these resources:

▶ The FCP Reference Guide. Accessed through the Final Cut Pro's Help menu, the FCP Reference Guide contains a complete description of all features.

▶ Apple's Web site: www.apple.com.

Using Final Cut Pro in Real World Workflows

Sean Cullen | Estelle McGechie

1

Lesson Files	None
Media	None
Time	This lesson takes approximately 20 minutes to complete.
Goals	Understand the principles of online editing
	Understand the principles of offline editing
	Choose an editing method for your project

Introduction to Online and Offline Editing

There are many ways to approach editing your project in Final Cut Pro. Choosing your method early will help you understand the scope of your project. By taking these first steps, you will lay down a foundation for equipment requirements and make an outline of where your project will begin and end.

The versatility of Final Cut Pro allows a variety of editing approaches. Projects can originate and end in either film or video; they can involve multiple formats, such as tapes, DVDs, or film negative. However, despite the myriad ways you can approach a project, the basic methods of editing break down into just two categories: online editing and offline editing.

Each of these methods has a direct impact on the many choices you will have to make when determining how to complete your project. In this lesson, we will focus on defining the two editing workflow approaches: offline and online. You'll learn the basic principles of each method, and their advantages and disadvantages, as well as the possibility of switching between methods if your situation demands it. You can then decide which workflow works best for each of your projects.

In Lesson 2, we will look at determining storage and hardware components based on your online or offline workflow. In Lessons 3 through 6, you will complete exercises based on editing and finishing either video or film. During this process, you will acquire a general idea of what each workflow entails.

After these lessons, we'll delve into terminology, with a hardware and video standards primer in order to prepare for configuring and integrating a system. Video cards, monitors, decks, and all the flexibility that a Final Cut Pro system offers is explained and examined prior to the system setup. We will then examine how the system is configured and integrated into a working environment. And finally, we'll discuss troubleshooting the most common problems that Final Cut Pro users encounter.

Basic Principles of Offline and Online Editing

In an offline workflow, you use temporary low-resolution clips during the creative editing process. Once you have locked picture, you recapture the edited sequence at a higher resolution for final output. Whenever you are editing with clips at your project's final output resolution, you are using an online workflow. Many projects will begin with low-resolution clips, edit using an offline workflow, and move to an online workflow for the final finishing process. Some genres—such as documentary, film, and episodic television—begin with an offline workflow and finish with an online workflow. Other genres, such as news and live television, use online workflows exclusively.

> **NOTE ▶** *Locked picture* means that the edit is final. The edited sequence is complete; no changes will be made to the edited sequence after this point.

A typical online and offline workflow sample path would look similar to this:

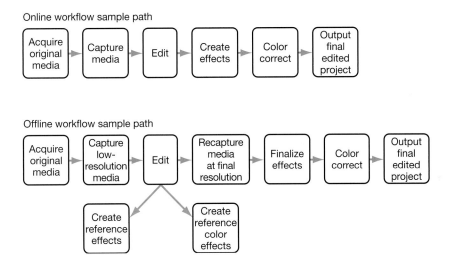

Online workflow sample path

Acquire original media → Capture media → Edit → Create effects → Color correct → Output final edited project

Offline workflow sample path

Acquire original media → Capture low-resolution media → Edit → Recapture media at final resolution → Finalize effects → Color correct → Output final edited project

Edit → Create reference effects / Create reference color effects

With an online or linear path, once you have completed a task, you use the result of *that* task as a basis for the next. For instance, once you have captured your clips, you edit and create the very effects and color corrections you will use in your final output.

In an offline path, you refer back to your original media prior to final delivery, whether it's a film or video project. Keep in mind that there are technical differences between film and video in the offline path. The offline workflow example in the preceding image illustrates the general concept. (See Lesson 4 for a film workflow sample.)

The fundamental principle that distinguishes offline editing is that you use stand-in or proxy media to make creative decisions instead of using the final media.

Online Editing in SD and HD

Of the two editing methods with Final Cut Pro, online editing is more straightforward. A typical online workflow path is to capture media from a video tape, edit the material, create effects, color correct, and finally, output the edited sequence from your computer.

Because video is the basic medium for online editing, the most common video formats used for online editing are standard definition (SD) and high definition (HD).

Because you use final media in an online workflow, you can immediately see the result of a given task. If you make a change in color, you are directly affecting what will end up on the final output. For instance, in an online workflow, you can concentrate on making an effect look perfect on your screen, because what you see on *your* screen is exactly what others will see when viewing your material. In theory, in an online workflow the effect is treated only once.

Offline Editing

When you edit using an offline workflow, you use low-resolution media to create effects and re-create that effect prior to the final output. Typically, an offline project will include captured material at a relatively low resolution. Prior to final output, you will either recapture the media from at a higher resolution (for SD/HD video projects), or you will conform the negative to match the edited sequence in Final Cut Pro (for film projects).

In an offline project, every frame of low-resolution media represents a frame of the original source media. Since you will need to refer back to the original source media at the end of the project, tracking and maintaining the links between the low-resolution media and the original source media is vitally important. For offline video projects, you maintain the links between the low-resolution media and original media by using timecode. For offline film projects, you maintain the links through a database in Cinema Tools by using the film's edge numbers, key numbers, and timecode. (See Lesson 4 for more information on film.)

> **NOTE** ► A conform refers to the final step in the editing process, where a project is completed in the final resolution. For example, after a film is edited in Final Cut Pro, you will export film lists for a negative cutter to "conform" the negative.

Window burn showing timecode of current clip

DAT timecode

Key number

Window burn showing film key number. DAT timecode is on clapboard.

The primary principle in designing an offline workflow is that all media in the system must have a one-to-one correlation to the original source media—be it a frame of video or a frame of film. Your primary task is to maintain the link to your source media because the delivery of your project depends on that link being accurate. So when designing an offline workflow, you will need to be especially careful about capturing the original source media in Final Cut Pro in an accurate manner. In an offline workflow, you can spend less time concentrating on how the image looks, provided you maintain the link between low-resolution media and the original source media. For example, in an offline workflow project, since you are using low-resolution media, a dissolve or color correction that you create in Final Cut Pro will not necessarily reflect how it will look in the final high resolution. Since you are using low-resolution media, any effects or color corrections you create during the creative editing are essentially visual guides and will be used as a reference for the final conform. Your effects or color corrections created with low-resolution media will ultimately need to be either tweaked or re-created during the finishing process.

Choosing Between Online and Offline Workflows

Given these two very different approaches to editing with Final Cut Pro, which should you choose? In general, an online workflow tends to benefit short projects, whereas an offline workflow tends to favor longer projects. Online workflows are ideal for projects with quick turnarounds; offline workflows are ideal for projects with longer turnarounds.

Advantages of an Online Workflow

▶ Final Effects and color correction—Because you are editing with your final resolution, you are aware of how your effect or color correction will look in your final output. You will not need to use a temporary effect or color correction.

▶ Simplicity—Once you have captured your media, there is no need to recapture the media at a higher resolution prior to your output.

▶ Efficiency—Because an online workflow tends to require fewer steps, the final project takes less time.

Disadvantages of an Online Workflow

▶ Resolution—Some resolutions—such as film—are still beyond the technical capability of desktop computers. However, with advances in technology, this will change, and a true film online workflow will become possible. But for now, the only way to cut film on a computer is to edit using an offline workflow.

▶ Storage—For longer shows, online workflow resolutions can be too unwieldy during the creative editing process. For instance, if you were editing a 1-hour documentary with a 10:1 shooting ratio (600 minutes of raw footage) using one of the high definition online resolutions, if you captured the entire 600 minutes of raw material, the hard drive space required would be in the terabytes (that's thousands of gigabytes). However, if you captured the entire 600 minutes of raw footage using an offline resolution of Photo JPEG, the hard drive space required would be greatly reduced.

NOTE ▶ A shooting ratio is the comparison of shot footage to edited footage. For example, if someone is editing a film with a final duration of 2 hours, and the shooting ratio is 3:1, then for every edited minute the person shot three times the amount needed.

Consider an online workflow if

▶   Your project length is short (30 minutes or under).

▶   Your shooting ratio does not exceed 3:1.

▶   You have limited time to complete your project.

▶   You have adequate drive capacity to store raw media files at your final resolution.

Generally, news, short-form broadcast (30 minutes or less), sports, commercials, and tight-deadline projects are well known for their online workflow.

Advantages of an Offline Workflow

▶   Flexibility—Editing using an offline workflow allows for lower hardware requirements. Using an offline workflow allows you to edit large amounts of work on a system as streamlined and portable as a laptop.

▶   Storage—Editing using an offline workflow allows you greater storage choices. You can edit low-resolution media on drives as basic as a FireWire drive. In an offline workflow, the lower media resolutions place fewer demands on the technical capabilities of your storage device. Using an offline workflow also allows you to copy larger sections of work—in less time—to smaller drives. For example, when using an offline workflow, you could copy a greater amount of your media, in less time than it would take to copy the same media files at a higher resolution—and you could potentially use a small FireWire drive, such as an iPod, as the transport.

▶ Real-time performance—Working with lower-resolution copies of your media files will allow you to view a greater number of effects and composites in real time without the need for rendering.

Disadvantages of an Offline Workflow

▶ Complexity—There's no doubt that an offline workflow is more challenging. Because you will need to recapture or conform your video or film to your original source media, you will need to be meticulous about maintaining an accurate relationship between your low-resolution media files and your original source media. It's essential that you enter the correct source data pertaining to the numbers—tape, reel, key, edge, and so on—that you are using. Keep track of *all* your assets—you need to be a stickler for detail!

▶ Time—You need to dedicate more time to an offline workflow. You will usually spend more time in the beginning, entering the data; in the middle, keeping track of the media; and in the end, finishing the project. Editing offline is a detailed process, and preparing to complete a project requires significant attention because you need to either recapture the tapes (for video), or output various cut lists (for film). If you cannot dedicate an appropriate amount of time to your project, an offline workflow may not be your best solution.

Consider an online workflow if

▶ Your project length is long (45 minutes or more).

▶ Your shooting ratio exceeds 3:1.

▶ You have adequate time to complete your project.

▶ You have limited drive capacity or lower drive technical specifications.

Documentary, long-form broadcast (45+ minute duration), and film are common choices for offline workflow.

Switching Between Offline and Online Workflows

In a traditional offline workflow, you begin your project at low-resolution, then edit, lock picture, prepare your sequence, and increase resolution as a part of your finishing process, essentially switching to an online workflow prior to final output. However, many times you may find that you need to decrease resolution, thereby switching from an online workflow to an offline workflow. Final Cut Pro is extremely flexible. Using the Media Manager, you can seamlessly switch between online and offline workflows. (See Lessons 3 and 5 for exercises using the Media Manager.) It's common to consider decreasing resolution to edit on a laptop or if you find you have a longer time to complete your project, or a greater amount of raw material. Because it's easy enough to decrease and increase resolution, you can switch between using an offline and online workflows to reassess your project workflow, adjusting your choices according to your equipment and project parameters at any time.

Lesson Review

1. What are the two basic editing workflow modes?
2. Describe the main steps in offline workflow.
3. When editing with clips at your project's final output resolution, are you working online or offline?
4. Why is it important to track and maintain the links between the low-resolution and original source media?
5. What Final Cut Pro tool do you use to switch between an online and offline workflow?

Answers

1. Online and offline.
2. You use temporary low-resolution clips during the editing process. Once you have locked picture, you recapture the edited sequence at a higher resolution for final output.

3. Online.

4. Because you will need to refer back to the original source media at the end of the project.

5. The Media Manager.

2

Lesson Files   None

Media   None

Time   This lesson takes approximately 40 minutes to complete.

Goals   Review basic specifications for the three common formats: standard definition video (SD), high definition video (HD), and data files from a film scanner

Learn common picture- and sound-acquisition media

Learn common picture-transfer media

Determine capture codecs

Choose storage, exchange, and archive media for your project

Choose hardware components for your project

Setting Up for Online and Offline Workflows

Setting up your project involves making a few basic decisions, yet setting up correctly can make the difference between a smooth workflow or one that is fraught with difficulty. By taking the time to investigate each component of your system and the ramifications of your choices, you can avoid problems. For instance, working through all the tape requirements of your project might save you from using an inappropriate tape format and let you avoid having to transfer everything from, say, DV to BetaSP.

Online and offline editing share many basic editing principles, and it's advantageous to examine both workflows when determining your project requirements.

The first step in learning how to set up your project is to understand the basic editing formats: standard definition video (SD), high definition video (HD), and data files. You also need to understand the various components of your project, which can be broken down into two different categories: media (the tapes and hard drives you'll use to store your picture and sound) and hardware (computers and displays; the more permanent aspect of your project). This lesson lists the most common forms of a given component as well as factors that will influence your choices. With this in mind, your task of selecting the components will boil down to a few straight-forward decisions.

Typical Formats

In the world of nonlinear editing, a large and ever-growing number of formats are available for both online and offline editing. However, they can be broken down into three groups: standard definition video (SD), high definition video (HD), and data files from a film scanner.

Standard Definition (SD)

Standard definition video is the bulk of the transmission or delivery infrastruc-ture into our homes–for example, cable TV or antennae. In North America and Japan, this analog format is known as NTSC (National Television Standards Committee); in most other regions, it's known as PAL (Phase Alternating Line); and in France and Russia, it's known as SECAM (SEquential Couleur Avec Mémoire). For the purposes of these chapters, we will discuss NTSC and PAL because these transmissions constitute the majority. (See the section on frame rates and standards in Lesson 7 for more information.)

PAL and NTSC have different aspect ratios and frame rates. Arming yourself with detailed technical information about the broadcast standards of each of these formats and understanding their differences will greatly assist you in the design of your project workflow. NTSC analog video, when translated or encoded into its digital uncompressed format (referred to as D1), has a frame size of 720 x 486 pixels running at 29.97 frames per second (fps) non-drop frame (NDF), and it is also known as 30 fps drop-frame (DF). (See the section on timecode DF versus NDF in Lesson 7 for more information). PAL and its uncompressed digital format has a frame size of 720 x 576 pixels run-ning at 25 fps.

Assuming a 10-bit sample depth, the D1 NTSC video data rate is 27 MB/second (megabytes per second) and can be considered unwieldy because of its large file size. As a consequence, codecs (**co**mpression **de**compression) were developed to compress this data rate with varying degrees of artifacts (depending on the specific codec in use). One of the most common codecs is DV25, otherwise referred to as digital video (DV). You find this codec on consumer and pro-sumer mini DV tape formats. DV25 codec was developed in conjunction with IEEE-1394, or FireWire, and takes advantage of the FireWire architecture. (For more on codecs and compression, see Lesson 7, and for more on FireWire, see Lesson 9.) Many Final Cut Pro users will work with some form of DV via FireWire; it's fast becoming the de facto standard for nonlinear editing.

High Definition (HD)

High definition is increasingly available to residential consumers via satellite TV, digital cable TV, and over antennae. Although HD TV comes in many forms and formats, the two most common formats are 720p and 1080i. 720p has a frame size of 1280 x 720 running at 24, 30, or 60 fps progressive scan; 1080i has a frame size of 1920 x 1080 running at 59.94 fps interlaced scan. (See Lesson 7 for more details.)

Although HD formats offer increased spatial resolution over SD, it's increas-ingly common that 720p 24 replaces film acquisition for video delivery due to its film-like qualities (progressive scan and film frame rate). 1080i 59.94 with its increased temporal resolution is more appropriate for fast motion sporting events acquisition.

Final Cut Pro supports many established HD formats and will probably sup-port new formats as they are introduced. HD formats come in a vast array, so prior to making your final acquisition or post-facility decision (whichever may come first), make sure that all the post-production facilities you plan to use are compatible. Remember that not *all* formats are supported in *all* locations, and a particular format may require specific playback equipment.

Data Files

Data files are created when you scan a film negative with a film scanner. These data files are most often used in a process called a digital intermediate, or DI.

The term comes from the process of transferring a film project from a film negative (analog) to hard drives (digital) then back onto film negative (analog) for distribution; hence the name *digital intermediate*.

You can generate data files at any point in your process, but timing determines if you work online or offline. If you scan the negative and use the scanned files as your media, never to return to the original negative, and output using the same scanned files, then your workflow is online. The important aspect of using data files in an online workflow is that once you have converted the image on the negative to a digital format, you no longer need to maintain any reference to the original negative. The data files have such a high resolution that instead of going back to the film negative for release, a new negative is created using the files. By using data files to capture your film negative, you can adjust color and create transitions, as well as add visual effects without compromising the quality of the original image.

If you scan the negative and use the scanned files as a "reference" to the original negative, and you plan to return to the original negative for final output, then your workflow is offline.

There are many flavors of film formats, but data files generally come in two standard resolutions for 35mm full camera aperture scanning: 2K (2048 x 1536 pixels) and 4K (4096 x 3072 pixels). 2K scans are considered roughly equal to film resolution; 4K scans are usually reserved for visual effects shots and shots that require extra sharp focus.

Even though the resolution of online formats varies from 720 x 480 to 4096 x 3072, the common thread is that they are all used in online workflows. Therefore, we can consider all these formats roughly equal when designing a workflow. The real difference is how much quality you want and how much equipment you can afford. The online 2K and 4K resolutions are outside the capabilities of the current version of Final Cut Pro. However, offline workflows for 2 K and 4 K resolutions can always be designed with lower resolution media; you can create and edit resolutions lower than 2K and 4K and return them in the form of an EDL (edit decision list) or cut list for your negative cutter to complete the finished film. (See Lessons 4 and 6 for more information.)

Selecting a Medium

When you begin a project, you need to determine which of the various media you will use to store your picture and audio. A poorly chosen medium can easily sap time away from the art of editing.

We will cover the major media that you'll need to consider, and we'll discuss the factors that will influence your selection. You need to think about each of these workflow components carefully, and keep in mind that any component you leave undetermined could easily cause problems later in the project.

For each medium category, we'll cover the traditional considerations of selecting a medium and the general advantages and disadvantages of each one.

Picture Capture Medium

Typically, you have to accept the picture capture medium you are given, because the producer, director, and the director of photography (DP) usually choose the camera and the camera format. However, if you have an opportunity for some early input, knowing the basic strengths and weaknesses of each medium may help you influence the choice of picture capture medium.

In general, tapes are traditional for video projects, film is traditional for high-end capture for both TV and films, and hard-disk cameras are gaining favor in all industries that can afford them. Tape works well for shows that need integration with other facilities, but it can become cumbersome and inefficient as a show grows larger. Digital files are fast and easy to exchange, but properly configuring the workflow requires expertise and time. Film has superior resolution and aesthetic qualities, but in an online workflow, the image quality will be limited by the medium you transfer the image to. This is because, although you can capture your material on film negative, you can't edit film directly in Final Cut Pro, so you must transfer the image to another format such as video or data files.

▶ Tapes—Tapes are traditional and safe. They provide a good backup for your media and are the most widely transferable format. The quality of the picture on the tape depends on the camera and its format, so you can easily capture all but the highest quality material on tape.

▶ Files—Another option for capture is digital recording directly to a hard disk using a direct-to-disk camera. Although this is new technology, and some are limited by storage capacity, direct-to-disk cameras are coming down in price and going up in their storage capacity. Direct-to-disk cameras have two main advantages over other media: you never have to reload the camera with a tape, and you can review your material in full resolution just moments after you shoot it. Additionally, the media arrives as files and not on tape or film, so you do not need to capture the material; you simply transfer files to your storage medium.

▶ Film negative—A form of high-quality capture is to expose a 35mm negative and then transfer the image to a videotape in a telecine session, or to create data files by scanning the negative on a film scanner. (See the "Performing a Telecine" section in Lesson 4 for more information.) However, since we're discussing only picture capture media for Final Cut Pro integration, you would consider using film as a capture medium only if you intended to transfer the media to videotape or data files that could be edited in Final Cut Pro.

Many variables are involved in choosing a picture capture medium, but sometimes your project's genre and delivery format will help you decide. For example, if you're shooting a sports program that contains fast action and requires quick turnaround and delivery for broadcast, you might choose 1080i (digital HD tape). Perhaps you're shooting a feature film and can't afford film acquisition, yet you want a similar feel to film, and your delivery involves a transfer to film and DVD. Then you might choose 720p 24 (digital HD tape). If your project is special effects–dominated, receiving digital files might suit you best, so you might choose direct-to-tape.

Regardless of choice, remember to make sure your system is compatible. For example, if you choose direct-to-tape, check to see if the digital files are easily imported into Final Cut Pro. If you choose a tape format, check for access to an appropriate deck in order to capture the material.

Picture Transfer Medium

For a variety of reasons, online and offline workflows often include a transfer from the original capture medium to a tape, hard drive, or work print. Usually this is an integral part of converting a format, for example converting HD 1080i 59.97 fps to SD NTSC 29.97 fps.

In an online workflow, you might perform a transfer if the source material of a project were originally acquired with film; film must be converted for a non-linear system. In an offline workflow, the availability and format of a deck might influence which transfer format you use.

For a typical film project, before you choose the transfer format, you need to decide if you will process and print either selected takes from the camera nega-tive or the camera negatives in their entirety. In short, if you print selectively, the processing lab breaks down the camera rolls into lab rolls. The processing lab will produce two sets of lab rolls: "A" rolls for printing (the selected scenes) and "B" rolls for archive (the excluded scenes). Selective scene printing will help you cut down on processing fees, but your key numbers will jump wher-ever you excluded scenes. (See Lesson 4 for more information.) A less common method is to opt for processing and printing all takes, by camera roll. Printing the entire film material provides continuous key numbers but is more expen-sive, and you will need additional organizational time to break down the cam-era rolls, depending on how much material you have.

The choice of transfer medium can impact your budget and efficiency. The medium decision is dependent on one or a number of factors.

In an offline workflow, your transfer medium often depends on what format and tape machine you can afford, or for film what the telecine room can trans-fer to and which format looks reasonable during the editing process. You do need to be sure that your tape medium is perfectly frame accurate and time-code controlled. Since you want to maintain all forms of metadata that link your low-resolution material back to the source, place window burns on your tapes. For film, you should also check with telecine to provide consistent flex files and also ask that the "A" frames of the film fall on *even* seconds of time-code. (See Lessons 4 and 6 for more information.)

In an online workflow, you can determine the transfer medium using the same criteria you use for an offline workflow: what format and tape machine you can afford, what format looks reasonable during the editing process or, for film, what the telecine room can transfer to. However, you need to consider more than the aesthetic look of the format. In an online workflow, you begin and finish with the same format, so you need to consider carefully what format quality is reasonable for the finishing process. In an online workflow, generally you try to maintain high resolutions, so you should choose a transfer format based on the higher-resolution formats, including digital Betacam and various flavors of HD.

▶ SD tapes—This medium is good for offline workflows because it's generally a low-cost way to store proxy media. Decks for SD tapes are usually cheaper than HD, and most editing facilities have a wide range of SD decks available. The disadvantage of using SD tapes is they have a lower spatial resolution than HD, and since SD tapes are NTSC 29.97 fps and PAL 25 fps, respectively, the process of conforming to an original format of 24 fps requires additional attention to ensure frame accuracy during an online conform. (For a list of SD tape formats, see the section on frame rates and standards in Lesson 7; and for 24p SD conversion, see Lesson 8.)

▶ HD tapes—This format works well for online *and* offline workflow transfers. HD offers superior quality compared to SD, but HD tapes can be more expensive. The advantages of using HD tapes in an offline workflow on a film project is that you can choose a progressive 24 fps frame rate format and thus achieve a one-to-one frame correlation between the video and film frames. Also, the progressive frame rate will emulate the film aesthetic. (For a list of HD tape formats, see the section on frame rates and standards in Lesson 7.)

Keep in mind that timecode is the only metadata that links media to tapes. So, if you are using a transfer as a means of format conversion (not online), common practice is to ask for window burns on the video picture so that when you look at a frame of video, you know which frame of film/HD you're looking at. If you are transferring film to HD tapes for offline capture, and you also plan to use the HD tapes in some form of

final output or for an online workflow, then you should consider making
either an additional transfer of the HD tape—one with window burn of
keycode and timecode and one without (clean). Or, if possible, place the
window burns below the picture. When you place window burns below or
above the picture you can use either a widescreen filter or crop your clips
to eliminate the window burn display prior to your final output.

Timecode window burn

Timecode and keycode window burn below the piocture.

Sound-Capture Medium

You usually have more freedom when planning for the sound medium than the picture medium as long as you can talk to the sound recordist ahead of time. The sound medium is more flexible, and you usually choose it later in the pre-production process.

Most recordists have experience on timecode DAT (digital audio tape) or Nagra (analog tape) machines, and many are comfortable on a variety of machines. Although they may prefer to record sound on a particular recording device, most professionals will agree to use any professional-level equipment. When the sound is recorded on a different medium from the picture, it is often referred to as "dual-system production" or "double system sound." In any dual-system production, you will need to sync the sound back to the picture during your post production.

The most common digital field recording devices are timecode DAT recorders. The advantage of a timecode DAT is that it can generate timecode for a video camera to record. The picture and sound then have the same timecode, which makes synching sound a snap. If you need to capture directly from the source medium, DAT players are readily available for purchase or rental, and you can easily connect one to your Final Cut Pro station. (See the section on DAT in Lesson 8 for more information.) If you capture sound during production on a dual system, and you do not have access to an appropriate audio deck, you can have a lab capture the sound material overnight and deliver sound files to you in the morning. In this case, talk to the lab to be sure they have the capabilities to capture your sound medium and deliver compatible files.

New technology has been introduced in the form of direct-to-disk or hard disk sound recorders. Several on the market now provide files instead of tape. One unique feature of hard disk recorders is that they continuously record to a small RAM buffer once you turn them on. This means that the recordist rarely misses the sound at the head of a shot. Traditionally with DAT, a sound recordist had to begin recording in advance of the director calling action. This meant running extra tape and, as a consequence, we as editors had more material to wade through. Hard disk recorders are advantageous because they save time. However you do need to confirm that the file delivered by the direct-to-disk device is compatible with your system. (See the section on audio in Lesson 8 for more information.)

If your sound is delivered along with the picture, there is no need to sync. If the sound was captured via the camera mic, the sound you receive may be less than ideal because the quality of most cameras' built-in microphones is generally low. However, if the sound was captured with the use of an external professional microphone and mixer, operated by a sound recordist and recorded onto the tape through the camera, then the sound quality will be high. Remember that if you have no recordist, keep a close eye on the sound when capturing. Is it distorted? One of your roles as editor is to identify technical issues as they arise, so speak up right away.

A less conventional method used by some adventurous sound recordists is to record sound directly into a laptop. You can use any number of sound applications, but use a professional application so that you can capture timecode, or at least be sure that the timebase of the computer is perfectly accurate.

▶   DAT tapes—DAT tapes are commonly used for capturing sound on a film set. Whenever you use dual-system production, you will need to sync with the picture during post-production. (See the "Sync Techniques" section in this lesson for tips on identifying sync points when recording onto discrete picture and sound media.)

▶   Hard disk recorder—Many new devices make recording direct-to-disk a real possibility for all types of projects. Since a recording device may use one of many available audio file formats, be sure Final Cut Pro can import the audio file format the device creates. The great advantage of hard disk recorders is that you reduce the time spent capturing your audio; you simply load the file onto your storage medium and import it into your project.

▶   Picture tapes—It's common to record the final sound directly onto the picture tapes , and for many projects that originate on tape this can be advantageous since there is no need for syncing. However, try to avoid using the camera mic as your only sound recording device. You'll obtain superior results by using a high-quality external mic and a good sound recordist.

▶   Files—Whenever you're considering delivery of digital files, always check for compatibility. Although Final Cut Pro can import many audio formats, make sure you check exactly which file formats the lab or the sound recordist plan to use and run a quick import test. (See Lesson 8 for compatible file formats.)

Sync Techniques

▶ Using timecode—Many cameras have a timecode input that attaches directly to the timecode output of a DAT or other sound recording device. By recording the DAT recorder's timecode, the picture tapes and the sound tapes have the same timecode stamp, making it very easy to sync them up. It's also common to have both the sound recording device and the camera run time-of-day timecode. This allows the machines to stay in sync while disconnected, provided the sound recordist enforces sync between them once or twice a day.

▶ Using a timecode, or SMPTE, clapboard—The clapboard has a timecode display that allows you to look at a frame of picture and read the sound timecode that relates to it. Although it involves looking at the image and doing some work by hand, this is an easy way to determine sync.

SMPTE clapboard

NOTE ▸ SMPTE is the Society of Motion Picture and Television Engineers, a technical society devoted to advancing the theory, application, and standardization of motion-imaging technology. See www.smpte.org for more information.

▸ Using event sync—Event sync is an effective alternative for syncing audio to video. It's a manual method involving an event that occurs simultaneously on the picture and sound track, such as the clap from a clapboard. When the clapboard is struck, the visual of the clap is recorded by picture, and the sound of the clap is recorded by sound. In order to put the two back into sync, you have to match the event on each medium. The benefit of this method is that you can use just about anything to create the event, such as two paperback books placed spine to spine. This method is effective although syncing using event sync can be quite time-consuming; there is no timecode reference, so you must rely on manually finding each event.

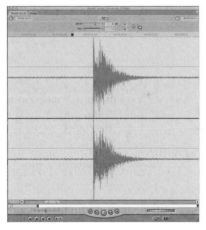

Event sync using a hand clap. The video of the closed hand matches the audio peak of the clap, allowing you to use the clap as a visual and audible reference.

Capture Codec

Codec is an acronym for **co**mpression **dec**ompression. Basically a codec is an extension that QuickTime can read allowing Final Cut Pro to work with different formats of digital video.

You'll need to consider source tape format, workflow, capture card, storage medium, and storage size to decide on a picture codec. You can choose among numerous codecs; some are dependent on third-party capture cards with installed drivers. However, for the purposes of this discussion, we will break down the codecs into two categories: low and high data rates. For comparison, the following chart lists a small range of the available codecs and their respective data rates. (See also the section on codecs and compression in Lesson 7.)

Format	Typical Data Rate	Typical Consideration
Offline RT (using Photo JPEG)	Varies between 300 and 500 KB/sec	Low data rate, offline workflow
25:1 compressed M-JPEG	1 MB/sec	Low data rate, offline workflow
DV-25	3.6 MB/sec	Low data rate, offline workflow
DVCPRO-50	7.2 MB/sec	Low data rate, offline/ online workflow
2:1 compressed M-JPEG	12 MB/sec	High data rate, offline/ online workflow
Uncompressed standard definition video	24 MB/sec	High data rate, online workflow
Uncompressed 8-bit HD 1080 29.97i	124.29 MB/sec	High data rate, online workflow
Uncompressed 10-bit HD 1080 29.97i	165.72 MB/sec	High data rate, online workflow

An editor using an online workflow will frequently capture at the codec resolution of the original tape format, provided there is adequate storage. For example, the online project *New England Aquarium*, a 30-second television commercial was shot DVCPRO HD 720p 24 and was captured at the native DVCPRO HD 720p 24 codec. The data rate was 7.38 MB/second. The project was short, and the raw material did not exceed the available storage.

In an offline workflow, generally the choice of codec falls within the low data rate range; editors will choose a codec based on what they perceive as a reasonable resolution for the footage. The editors of *The Magic Hour*, a comedy mock-documentary, used a DV25 codec for their offline workflow, and the DV25 low data rate of 3.6 MB/second meant that not only did the resolution of their project look reasonable during their creative editing stage, but also their storage requirements were minimal.

When considering an offline workflow codec at a low data rate, you should first run some tests. Select representative shots for your project as best you can. Try to pick a variety of shots: bright and dark, close-up and a long shot, and so on. Then try capturing your selection of shots with various codecs. Do some side-by-side comparisons of the media. The resolution and clarity of an image can vary depending on the codec, so be sure that you can see everything you need to see during the offline edit, such as the direction that someone's eyes are looking or action in the distance.

Consider your codec and storage together since one will likely influence the other. (See Lesson 9 for more information on data rate calculations.)

Storage Medium

How to store your media is perhaps the most important decision you can make when setting up your workflow. An offline workflow storage requirement may exceed those of an online workflow. This might seem counterintuitive, since an individual offline workflow media file is usually smaller, requiring less bandwidth. But the number of files in an offline workflow can be excessive.

Do some quick codec math before deciding on your storage medium. Whichever storage medium you choose needs to have sustained transfer speeds that are fast enough to keep up with the data rate. Generally, in an online workflow, if you are capturing video using a codec that is 12 MB/second or higher, (including any codec of uncompressed video), then you should consider a higher-performance storage device such as a RAID. If you are capturing low data rates, you can probably use lower-bandwidth hard drives such as FireWire drives. (See the section on performance and capacity in Lesson 9 for more information.)

Remember, when you're calculating your storage needs, you should take into account all the files you may create or receive from other sources, such as an animation facility. Files may include renders, graphics, animation, and tests. As a guideline, add 20 percent to your data rate calculations, and use that figure as your minimum storage requirement.

Keep in mind also that the media requirements of your project may increase unpredictably (due to additional shooting, for example). Depending on your budget and project, allow for at least 10 percent and preferably as much as 50 percent extra storage.

Using a single internal hard drive may be sufficient if the project is small, straightforward, and remains on the same machine for the life of the project.

If two or three people are working together, FireWire drives may be adequate since they provide more portability than internal drives at a relatively low cost. Using FireWire drives for a small editing team can be sufficient, especially for low data rate projects. (See the section on FireWire in Lesson 9 for more information.)

An Xserve RAID will give you a greater amount of storage. High transfer speeds and a much larger bandwidth allow you to edit with high data rates. An Xserve RAID can be beneficial for online and offline workflows, especially if your offline workflow has large storage requirements. (See the RAID section in Lesson 9 for more information.)

If you have four or more machines, and if you need to access higher bandwidth, as in a 12+MB/second data rate, then you may consider investing in a SAN (storage area network) solution. A SAN allows multiple users to access the same data simultaneously just as you would if you were using a file server. Although a SAN is more complex and requires greater granular management than FireWire or Xserve RAIDs, its advantages can be enormous for an editor. A SAN provides the most transparent use of your media files and, along with an Xserve RAID, it is the most expandable system available. So even for offline workflows with as little as two editors, it's often the best choice. With the introduction of Apple's Xsan software (see Lesson 15), you can now set up a file-based SAN for a relatively low cost.

▶ Internal drives—For a project that exists on a single-machine, if the project does not exceed the internal drive storage capacity, and the bandwidth required for the data rate is commensurate with the speed of the drive, then this storage method is convenient and adequate. You can keep all the media on internal drives, but for optimal performance, you need to keep all media off the drive that runs the operating system. In the case of a desktop machine, use at least two physical drives, one for your operating system and applications and the other for storing your media. A laptop contains only one internal drive, so use an external FireWire drive when editing with a laptop.

▶ External FireWire drives—FireWire drives deliver good performance for low data rate/low bandwidth projects and allow for great portability. For example, with a FireWire drive, you can easily move your project from a desktop machine to a laptop. It's common to have multiple identical FireWire drives as the backbone of a small editing project. The media is captured to one drive and then copied to all the other drives. Replicate all media file structures and their locations on the drives so that you can avoid reconnecting media files whenever projects are moved between machines. This allows you to transfer a project between machines without having to transfer the media each time.

▶   Xserve RAID—An Xserve RAID is an excellent storage medium for single-editor online or offline projects. Expandable, high bandwidth, high data transfer means that Xserve RAIDs offer superior performance to FireWire or internal drives. However, a RAID is less portable than its FireWire counterpart.

▶   XSAN   XSAN allows multiple users to access the same media simultaneously. Typically, file transfers are done over a dedicated Fibre Channel network, and since a SAN is hardware-based and requires configuration, it does cost more than a FireWire-based storage solution. However, SANs provide much greater bandwidth, allow the use of high data rate codecs, and are extremely flexible. They can be scaled from a fairly small two-client installation to a large team of editors. Any laptops on the network will need to connect via Ethernet to the SAN instead of high-speed Fibre Channel.

If you're planning to take the show on the road, and you don't have a team of roadies to move your RAID or SAN and desktop machines, and the codec you've chosen is appropriate for FireWire (under 10 MB/second), consider external FireWire drives.

If you know that you and the majority of your facility will need simultaneous access to the media, a SAN solution will serve you best. In all of these options, and if your budget allows, consider having the ultimate of all scenarios—Xsan and FireWire—which lets you easily share *and* travel. (See the media storage overview section in Lesson 9, for further technical details.)

Exchange Medium

The essence of exchanging media files is when you send a media file to another person, that person makes changes to it, and then sends the modified media file back to you. This is different from sending someone a preview of your project, say on a DVD, since that is for viewing purposes only. Therefore, in an exchange medium you absolutely must be able to give *and* receive media files in a frame-accurate manner, with minimal hassle and negligible quality loss. The two main media file exchange methods are tapes and files.

Tapes are a traditional medium for exchange and are platform agnostic. However, when using tapes to exchange media files, the image quality commonly deteriorates. If you exchange media only a couple of times, and you use a professional quality tape format, this may not be a problem. In addition to the loss of quality, another disadvantage to exchanging media files with tapes is that the transfer needs to be done on both ends with the physical tape, not to mention the time it takes to output, then load and capture, the media itself. These issues are magnified if you need to post the tape to the other side of the country, for example. Additionally, the cost of tapes can quickly add up over the life of a project.

On the other hand, using the media files directly to exchange media is very streamlined, and this alone makes the use of file exchange very attractive. Another significant advantage is that you don't need a physical tape, therefore allowing an editor to send one or more data files through a server or via File Transport Protocol (FTP). For example, if an editor is working in New York, and the special effects facility is located in California, the editor can upload the media file to the facility's server and skip posting the tape! The California effects facility can make changes to the media file and upload the altered file to a transfer site; the editor downloads the media file and incorporates it back into the project.

▶ Tapes—The traditional form of exchange is to send tapes back and forth. It is an excellent method for systems with limited capability to share QuickTime codecs. The disadvantage is that you need to output the media onto the tape, make sure the integrity of your picture and timecode are intact, use professional formats, and physically send the tapes to their destination. Tape stock can also quickly increase a project's budget.

▶ Files—A convenient way to exchange media is to send the QuickTime media files back and forth. The advantage is that you can exchange media much faster than with the traditional tape method. You need to be sure the person you are exchanging a file with can both import and export the file in a similarly efficient manner. If the other person is running Final Cut Pro, the exchange will be seamless. If the other person is running another professional application, find out that person's preferred file format since Final Cut Pro can export a number of different formats. (See the section on wrappers and file formats in Lesson 7 for more information.)

In any exchange scenario, whether you use tape or file, you need to watch for degradation in quality and check timecode accuracy. Run a few tests before relying on an accumulative process of exchange. Attempt to limit the amount any *one* file is exchanged during the course of your project.

Preview Medium

Generally, a project will use multiple preview media so that everyone involved in the post-production can readily see the various stages of the edit. An editor may be required in both online and offline workflows to output previews of an edit using any number of media. For example, the *New England Aquarium* editors exported QuickTime files to send to the sound department for review; *The Magic Hour* editors output an edit on DVD for the directors to preview at home.

Professional format tapes are a traditional preview medium because you can reference timecode to communicate a specific shot. For instance, during special effects design, the director may need to discuss a shot with the special effects team on the other side of the country. The director and the special effects team can both reference timecode to ensure they're discussing the same thing. DVDs are useful not only for viewing at home but also on laptops, and occasionally you may even use the editing workstation as a preview medium. Traditional analog methods involve previewing an edit by conforming a work print of the original film negative. This method is becoming less popular, especially because it's usually more expensive and time consuming. Essentially, your preview medium is all about convenience, both for you and the people on the receiving end.

▶   Tapes—Tapes are the most traditional form of preview medium. Provided you have access to an appropriate tape deck, it is common to output to VHS tape with some form of timecode reference usually through a Timeline window burn. If you need timecode precision, an output to a timecode-accurate professional tape format such as Betacam or HD may be necessary. If you need multiple copies, it's common to output to a professional tape format and send the preview master to a duplication house for copies onto the appropriate medium. Tapes can become time consuming and expensive depending on the number of copies you are required to create.

▶ DVD—DVDs are fast becoming the standard preview medium because they're small and easy to navigate, and the SD DVDs offer reasonably high-quality picture and sound. In addition to authoring SD DVDs, DVD Studio Pro 4 now supports authoring of HD DVDs. This makes it possible for you to take advantage of the superior quality of HD. You can make DVDs of your material in two ways: using a computer or a DVD recorder. With a computer, you can use an application such as Apple's DVD Studio Pro to program a DVD, or you can purchase a DVD recorder and output your edited sequence directly to the DVD. The advantage of using your computer to program a DVD is that you can customize the DVD, and duplicates are efficient once you've programmed the first. The advantage of a DVD recorder is that you can record your edit without any additional setup time. Duplicates of your output using a DVD recorder are, however, a challenge because you need to re-output the edit from the Timeline or duplicate the original recorded DVD. You can make duplicates from the original output to a DVD recorder, however, the DVD duplicate will lose image quality.

▶ Computer—You can always use Final Cut Pro or even QuickTime Player to preview the project. This method involves little or no setup time although the hitch is that for portability you may need a laptop. You can even export a file from Final Cut Pro and view it using the QuickTime Player. Since Final Cut Pro doesn't use proprietary formats, you can output a QuickTime or QuickTime compatible format for any modern computer. You can also use a computer in a timecode-sensitive environment such as a sound mix stage. Several products, such as Gallery UK's VirtualVTR (www.virtualvtr.com), can open any QuickTime movie and synchronize playback chasing timecode. You can control VirtualVTR via

Midi, Sony 9-pin, or TCP/IP. This is extremely useful because you can shuttle and change locations in the QuickTime file more readily than you can by tape.

▶ Work print—A bulky but traditional preview medium for film. The advantage of using a work print is that the aesthetic quality of the image is closer to the final film image that audiences will watch on the screen at a cinema. The disadvantage is that it takes a few days to conform a work print; it's usually more expensive, and although the aesthetic is film, the work print image usually contains many distracting scratches and grease pencil marks.

Consider the amount of previews you need to deliver. If you're screening an edit for a small group of people, using a computer and projector would be sensible. If you're screening for a larger audience, it may be more convenient to consider an output to a professional quality tape format. If your audience is scattered, VHS tapes or DVDs will be a good option. Remember, tapes are output in real time, so if you don't have the luxury of a duplication facility, DVD burning may be the most efficient and convenient method.

Archive Medium

When you archive a project, look for a storage medium that will not only last a long time but can be recovered quickly if the project starts up again. (One of the most common reasons for restarting a project is for DVD release.) The factors to consider when choosing an archive medium are the same for both online and offline projects. When you archive a project, you will save two different categories of information: the Final Cut Pro project and some media files.

The Final Cut Pro project you archive should contain all the sequences (edited Timelines) or versions you create during the editing process. When you archive a project, you should save both the Final Cut Pro project containing the edited sequences and an output of each sequence for a visual record of the edit.

Professional videotape formats are the traditional medium for archiving the output of each sequence, but you should consider archiving the sequences electronically as well. To do this, simply export each sequence as a self-contained QuickTime movie. The editors of the *New England Aquarium* project exported a QuickTime movie of the completed commercial as part of their archive process and included the QT file on their archive DVD along with the Final Cut Pro project file, music, and graphic files.

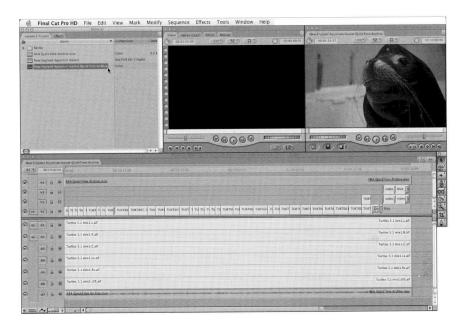

Look at the placement of the archive clip in the above image. The editors of the New England Aquarium project output a QuickTime of the finished commercial. They then duplicated the master sequence and placed the QuickTime, low-resolution output of the master sequence into the new sequence above the offline clips.

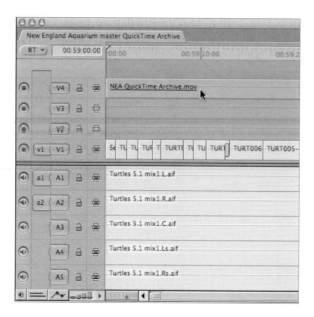

The benefit of exporting a QT file of your final edit is that you can view your cut immediately without needing to recapture your entire media. The QT file doesn't need to be high resolution; low-compression formats such as MPEG are fine, as long as you can get a sense of your edit visually. After you export the QT file, duplicate the edited sequence and place the reference QT file into a new track above the edited clips in the duplicated sequence. This way you can play back the movie and see the clips that created it without needing to reload or reconnect the original media files.

The ideal archive medium for your project and/or media depends on the size of storage required, ranging from CDs and DVDs for small projects to video-tapes, tape drives, or hard drives for longer projects.

▶   CDs and DVDs—This medium is an ideal way to back up projects and preferences, as well as graphics and any small elements that did not origi-nate on tape. Because it's safer to keep the project archive off the active machine and in a secure environment, data CDs and DVDs are good storage solutions. Realistically, you will probably be able to use CDs for your projects and graphics, and DVDs will be suitable for projects, graphics, and small amounts of media. Blu-ray disc technology (www.blu-ray.com) will allow even greater data storage options. The Blu-ray format was initially developed to enable HD DVD solutions, and it also enables large data storage. A single layer Blu-ray disc can hold 25 GB and a dual layer 50 GB. Currently there are even prototypes of single layer 100 GB Blu-ray discs in development.

▶ Videotapes—Tapes are a good medium for archiving linear incremental cuts of the project. Tapes provide an ideal way to preserve a slice in time and are application-independent, therefore you can view your edit without a computer. In addition to archiving incremental cuts, editors usually output several final masters of an edit onto professional videotape and keep one master with the Final Cut Pro project file archive and source tapes for storage. Because videotape is linear, be sure to save the project file containing the progress of the cuts in conjunction with the tape; you can always recapture an archived project as long as you save the source tapes. The best way to archive the source material is to save the original tapes. If you choose to archive edits using tapes, remember to also output any media not represented on source tapes, such as visual effects originating on computer.

▶ Hard drives—Archiving the Final Cut Pro project and media on a hard drive is straightforward, and it's becoming less expensive as the prices of hard drives fall. The main advantage of archiving the Final Cut Pro project file and all the media files themselves is that you can reopen a project without needing to recapture from tapes.

▶ Tape drives—Tape drives are a traditional way to back up media files for large projects. A tape drive allows you to store large amounts of data (multiple terabytes) for possibly less money than hard drives. The disadvantage is that you need a separate device to store or recover the media. It can also take several days to archive or recover a complete show.

Generally, you can archive the Final Cut Pro project file and small elements onto data CD or DVD and save visual cut references on videotape. Blu-ray disc technology developments will enable more options for project and media file archive in the future. QuickTime archives of sequences are an excellent and efficient method of viewing edited versions, and usually the QuickTime reference file can be saved onto a DVD. Purchasing a hard drive for media archive storage is possibly the most convenient and time-efficient method, and combining CD/DVD, QuickTime references, tapes, and hard drives is the most thorough. (For detailed steps on archiving your project, see Lesson 12.)

Selecting Hardware

Selecting hardware for online and offline projects involves many factors, including budget, convenience, and flexibility. When you make any choices about hardware, take into account the other components in the system to avoid conflicts. A helpful reseller can make the difference between a smooth and rough first day, so choose your supplier based not only on price but also support and experience.

Computer

Selecting your computer setup is relatively straightforward. Basically, when it comes to speed and RAM, the more you have, the greater the power and flexibility. Final Cut Pro is amazingly flexible, and it can run on a variety of CPU and laptop configurations. You can find the current minimum system requirements for Final Cut Pro on the Apple Web site (www.apple.com/finalcutpro/specs.html). However, if you want an optimal system, you must go beyond the minimum requirements. Generally the computer equation depends on your needs: project size + media codec + media storage + additional components + portability + budget = correct choice.

For the offline workflow of *The Magic Hour* project, the media codec was within the low data rate range, the storage requirements were modest (under a terabyte), it did not require capture cards, and it involved editing while traveling. The decision: laptop.

Project Size and Capture Codec	Workflow Type	Computer Options
Short or small section of long project; low data rates and bandwidth	Offline	PowerBook G4* Power Mac G4 w/min. FCP setup Power Mac G5 w/min. FCP setup
Mid-length; low data rates and bandwidth	Offline	Power Mac G5 w/min setup
Large; low to medium data rates and bandwidth	Offline and some online projects	Power Mac G5** w/extra RAM
Large; high data rates and bandwidth	Offline and any online project	Power Mac G5 w/Fibre and video cards and extra RAM

*A laptop offers no expandability, but it allows portability.

**The G5 can be expanded with additional drives, external FireWire, RAID, and SAN.

► Laptop—Laptops are great for field editing and mobile presentations. And they can be fantastic for more than just mobile editing stations. When they're not on the road, the post-production team can utilize a laptop for everything from creating graphics and titles to logging and organizing. As a stand-alone system, a small project can often work well on a laptop, but the scalability is limited. Laptops provide tremendous portability but may not provide enough options for every project.

► Desktop—Desktop machines are the workhorse machines for Final Cut Pro. With a desktop machine, you can increase your edit suite options and upgrade internal components as your project requirements grow. Generally, desktop machines are more powerful and expandable than laptops although not nearly as portable.

If you're working on a small offline workflow project with a tight budget, a single desktop computer with minimum Final Cut Pro requirements is the way to go. If you're working on a large project, beginning with an offline workflow and finishing with an online resolution, a higher-end system will be the best option. An offline workflow project that requires a team of editors working on individual components of a larger project might consider multiple Power Mac G5s with extra RAM. If the same team of editors needed simultaneous access to their media, they could install the necessary cards and components to run Xsan.

Apple offers many configurations. Because you can interchange hardware components, like upgrading the video card, increasing the factory installed RAM, and installing Fibre cards, in many ways your decision boils down to how much computer horsepower you need for a given set of project parameters. Keep in mind that *more* is better when it comes to computer systems, so always aim for a little more power than you anticipate needing.

Selecting a Picture and Sound I/O Device

Adding a video card to your system will provide additional video horsepower within Final Cut Pro and let you connect to external devices such as monitors, tape decks, and serial control cables. Generally, the input/output (I/O) device, whether external or internal, is dictated by your project workflow and deck interface. Offline workflows will often use external I/O devices connecting via a basic FireWire device and capturing lower data rates; online workflows regularly use internal video cards that enable the capture of uncompressed 8-bit and 10-bit SD and HD through a professional deck. An exception to the external I/O for offline and internal I/O for online norm is AJA's (www.aja.com) I/O FireWire interfaces, which allow online workflow projects the option of capturing D1 10-bit uncompressed video *without* the need for an internal video card.

For offline workflows or simple projects with straightforward capture and common effects, an external I/O device is usually ample. However, if your project is using an online workflow, *and* you plan to use a large number of effects, consider a powerful internal card to make your render times shorter.

► External I/O device—You can use a number of external devices to capture picture from a variety of sources. An example of a common external I/O device is a DV camera or deck controlled over FireWire. Although an internal device doesn't require additional hardware for capture or machine control, currently there are few I/O devices capable of delivering uncompressed video through a FireWire interface. External I/O devices are best suited to offline workflows with the exception of AJA's I/O FireWire interface. (See Lesson 8 for technical details.)

► Internal video card—The benefit of an internal video card is that it lets you capture both analog and digital SD or HD (depending on the capture card), with genlock and RS-422 control. Internal capture cards interface with most professional decks, and although an internal video card requires some initial configuration, most provide capture to uncompressed 8-bit and 10-bit codecs in addition to several compressed formats. Some manufacturers also provide hardware acceleration of the most common effects and filters, alleviating some of the CPU render burden. (See the PCI cards section in Lesson 8 for more information.)

NOTE ► *Genlock* is short for generator locking device, and it is also referred to as *blackburst*. In simple terms, it's a composite signal, commonly containing black video that allows the synchronization of two video signals so that the chroma levels in your video remain consistent and stable.

RS-422 is a serial connector commonly used by professional decks for timecode and control.

DeckLink high definition capture card

The most important factors for choosing external/internal devices are your project workflow and deck interface requirements. An online workflow can benefit greatly from an internal card, especially one that can handle some of the render processing. The Apple Web site lists a number of qualified devices, and the Apple support pages (www.apple.com/finalcutpro/qualification.html) contain pertinent information on compatible I/O devices.

Selecting a VTR or Video Deck

Your VTR (videotape recorder) will likely follow your picture acquisition format in a video online workflow or the picture transfer format in an offline workflow. For example, the online *New England Aquarium* project was shot with a Panasonic Varicam camera and captured via a Panasonic AJ-HD1200A deck. The Cohen brothers' film *Intolerable Cruelty* was shot on film and transferred to HD 24p then down converted to DVCAM for the offline ingest via a DVCAM deck.

There are a variety of decks and a wide range of functionality for each format, so check all the options and models prior to making your final decision. (See the video recording formats section in Lesson 7 for more information.) Occasionally a small, low-budget DV project will use the shooting camera itself as a tape deck to capture media. However, you should avoid using video cameras as a deck since they aren't designed for the wear and tear of constantly shuttling and playing back. If you do use the camera as your capture device, you can limit the wear and tear on the heads by either capturing the entire tape or by using Capture Now in Final Cut Pro. On professional projects, you should use a professional VTR to capture your media.

▶ Video camera—For short DV projects, you can use the video camera to shoot and capture material, but make sure you minimize the wear and tear on the record heads by limiting unnecessary shuttling of the tape.

▶ FireWire controlled VTR—Many VTR decks allow deck control over FireWire. A VTR controlled over FireWire is specifically designed to be used as a capture device. Using a FireWire-controlled VTR is always a better option than capturing via a camera because the components are more robust. For longer projects or for future investment, try to opt for the professional models, which are intended for the rigors of constant use.

▶ Serial controlled VTR—Editors use a serial controlled VTR in professional environments. Many allow genlock, component, balanced audio input/output, and greater signal stability. Because there is no latency in the serial bus (because you use timecode to sync the deck to the computer), these decks are also more responsive. The sync control is delivered through a serial port called RS-422, which connects your computer to the deck. If you are using an internal video card, chances are it comes with the serial port adapter. If not, you will need to purchase a high-speed USB serial adapter. (See the machine control section in Lesson 8 for more information.) Depending on the deck model, you will discover a number of options, such as large timecode display, audio meters, and controls to adjust audio input and output. Professional serial controlled decks have many technical benefits (see the section on capturing video and audio in Lesson 8 for more information); in addition, they generally offer greater performance and reliability.

Usually the deck format will be predicated by your picture acquisition or transfer format and budget. However, within one category you'll find many deck models with options ranging from basic to advanced. Since the Cohen Brothers transferred the raw footage of *Intolerable Cruelty* to DVCAM, they could have captured their footage via a basic Sony DSR-11 deck with minimal deck options. However, if they needed additional options such as an LCD monitor for viewing content directly on the deck face panel, audio levels, and RS-422 control, they could have opted for the Sony DSR-45.

Sony DSR-11 DVCAM deck

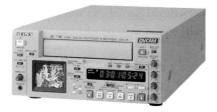

Sony DSR-45 DVCAM deck

Regardless of workflow, a professional deck is robust and technically superior to using a camera or a consumer/prosumer deck. If you can't afford a professional deck for your project, consider renting one for capture ingest and output of your project.

Selecting a Playback Monitor

Most projects use a mix of monitors for playback. You can choose from a wide variety of devices for flexibility and performance. A small, low-budget project may use a consumer TV—which is readily available and generally less expensive than the professional equivalent—for viewing cuts. Offline and online workflow projects benefit from using professional reference monitors because the color calibration between Final Cut Pro and external venues is important. Let's assume for stylistic reasons you decide to saturate the blue tones in your clips, and you base your color decisions on a consumer uncalibrated TV monitor. If the screening venue for your edit is professionally calibrated, you may discover that your saturated blues on the consumer TV are flat and drab at the screening venue. Monitor calibration is important to ensure that the colors you see when viewing and correcting your project are the same colors that your audience will see when they view the final product.

The same output can look strikingly different on different displays, so you need to understand the technical specifications for color variance of the monitor you choose. (See the sections on monitoring environment and setting up a video monitor in Lesson 8 for more information.)

▶ Consumer TV—A plain old TV can be a great addition to any cutting room, especially during the offline process. TVs are cheap and often help you look at your material through the eyes of your final audience. However, a consumer TV is not color-accurate and should not be used as your final color reference.

▶ Professional reference monitor—Professional monitors are more expensive but much more accurate. They range in options from standard to advanced. Standard professional monitors allow basic color calibration options such as hue and contrast, which allow you to perform rough calibration using SMPTE video bars. The more advanced professional monitors are accurately calibrated via various bias and gain components using a probe. You should always view your material on an accurately calibrated professional reference monitor for color correction or prior to duplication or broadcast.

Sony BVM-14H5U broadcast multiformat monitor

▶ LCD display—An LCD display provides a sharp, rich-colored image from your computer. You can't connect an LCD display to a VTR though, so they are limited to playback from within Final Cut Pro using Digital Cinema Desktop. An LCD display is not as accurate in color or quality as a professional reference monitor, so again check your final output prior to color correction, duplication, or broadcast.

▶ Plasma screen—A plasma screen provides a spectacular image on a large surface. Currently, plasma displays are costly, but they tend to have a high contrast ratio that mimics the look of film quite well, making them a good option for a film project.

▶ Video projector—Video projectors are available in a range of sizes and costs. In a controlled environment, like a darkened room, a video projector provides a large image for many people to view. In general, the more money you spend, the greater the brightness and sharpness. Because all new Macs can output DVI (Digital Video Interface), they are convenient. Again, as with any uncalibrated device, projectors should not be the basis for a color correction.

In most cases, choose a playback monitor that mimics your material as closely as possible. A professional, calibrated monitor is probably going to be your best choice. Keep in mind that the gamma response of each of the displays we listed varies significantly. (See the section on measurement and control in Lesson 8 for more information.)

You might also consider your final output. If, for example, you are cutting a film, you might use a plasma display because it can replicate the look of film quite well. However, if you're cutting a documentary destined for video, and your budget is tight, you may choose a consumer TV for the offline workflow phase. Whenever you're considering a consumer playback monitor—whether it's a TV, video projector, or plasma display—remember to perform only temporary color corrections, because the choices you make while using an uncalibrated device may not be accurate. Prior to completing a project, allow time for final color corrections using a professionally calibrated monitor as your reference.

Lesson Review

1. What factors should you consider when choosing a picture codec?
2. Why is doing codec math useful in choosing one storage medium over another?
3. Why does the exchange medium need to be frame accurate?
4. What factors should you consider when selecting computers?
5. Why is a professionally calibrated monitor the best gauge of image quality and precision?

Answers

1. Source tape format, workflow, capture card, storage medium, and storage size.

2. A storage medium needs to have sustained transfer speeds that are fast enough to keep up with the data rate. Also, you can calculate your storage requirements.

3. So you can maintain timecode integrity.

4. Project requirements and size, media codec, media storage, additional components, portability, and budget.

5. LCD displays, projectors, and plasma screens don't display colors or brightness as accurately or as well.

3

Lesson Files   Lessons > Lesson 03 > Lesson 03 Project.fcp

Media   Media > Lesson 03 Media

Time   This lesson takes approximately 90 minutes to complete.

Goals   Plan and organize your project

Capturo your projoot in onc piccc or by individual scene

Synchronize your video and audio if your sources are separate media

Increase resolution by recapturing entire source content

Increase resolution by recapturing selected source content

Decrease resolution by using the Media Manager

Gathering and Editing Video

With the advent of nonlinear editing systems, editing is as much a technical art as it is aesthetic. Understanding some basic video approaches will not only improve your technical aptitude but also allow you the freedom to concentrate on the *art* of editing. You will learn how to organize an online or offline video project, gather project content, and convert offline content to online resolutions and online content to offline resolutions.

In this lesson, you'll observe the workflow of a typical video. Your project specifications may vary, but the principles of video workflow still hold. And since Final Cut Pro is adaptable, it will accommodate different approaches seamlessly.

Organizing Projects

Before you begin, you need to establish a framework for your project—a clear path from beginning to end. This will streamline your process and identify and help you overcome obstacles. You'll learn how to plan an efficient workflow, determine sound specifications and timecode, and decide when to switch between resolutions.

Planning an Online or Offline Video Workflow

When you receive your project specifications, it's best to plan the complete workflow you expect to use. Planning will identify possible problems, and early detection will allow you time to alter your route. For example, the *New England Aquarium* online project content came from six one-hour source tapes. The editor initially planned to capture each tape in its entirety at an online resolution of DVCPRO HD 720p with the resulting data rate of 13.8 Mb/sec. However, a calculation of storage requirements revealed there wasn't sufficient storage capacity for 6 hours of content. As a result, early in the process, the editor decided to capture only those clips that would become the basis for the edit.

The *New England Aquarium* project was relatively short and the variables therefore contained. However, for longer online projects like the documentary *Spellbound,* the planning process might be more involved. Because *Spellbound* is a documentary, you might have expected the workflow to begin offline, but it didn't. There were 160 hours of footage shot on DV, captured at DV25 resolution. The planning process for *Spellbound* may have included how best to sync the multicamera shoots during the national spelling competitions, or whether selected scenes or entire tapes were to be captured.

Blocking days or planning for particular tasks can also be useful. If you need to color correct every shot, and you have estimated that your color corrections take, on average, 1 hour per edited minute, then your projection needs to allow for 8 hours of color correcting and extra time for rendering. Plan to use your daytime hours for editing, and save rendering or exporting until you take a lunch break or until after you have finished for the day.

The Magic Hour offline workflow planning involved an extra time allotment for syncing DAT tapes. During the planning stage, this preparation allowed the editor to realistically identify a start date for creative editing. Time was also calculated for recapturing the low-resolution files at a higher resolution for color correction and output to tape.

Micro preparation can result in time-saving and provide an estimate of expected delivery. Your project may deviate from your plan, but you will be better prepared to accommodate changes as a result of your initial forecast.

Determining Sound Specifications

If your sound is delivered on a medium separate from the picture tapes, either by DAT (digital audio tapes) or data files, then before you begin capturing material, take time to discuss the original sound settings with your sound recordist.

Discuss the original frame rate of the source sound recordings. Generally, if you are planning on syncing during a telecine session, you will ask that the sound frame rate be recorded so that it matches your video transfer rate.

If your audio is delivered as data files, check the sample rate and bit depth. Final Cut Pro currently accepts sample rates up to 96 kHz and bit depths of 24. If the audio data file sample rates and bit depths are higher, you'll need to convert the audio files via an audio software application program such as Soundtrack Pro or a converter program such as Compressor.

Keeping Track of Timecode

Timecode is a critical part of any workflow. Typically, you will use two types of timecode: source and sequence. Source timecode numerically identifies one frame of information from another on the source tapes or source file. The source timecode is captured or imported with the picture and links the captured media to the identical time on the tape or file. When you begin editing, you will reference sequence timecode. Sequence timecode is timecode that numerically differentiates one frame of *edited* material from another.

Check the timecode of your captured material against your source tape, especially since, at some stage (for example, during a recapture), you may need to reference the original source timecode. You can check your captured media timecode against the source tape in the Log and Capture window. Load a clip in the Viewer, launch the Log and Capture window, pause the tape at the timecode matching the clip in the Viewer, and compare timecodes and picture to see that they match. If you captured discrete picture and audio material (say your audio was delivered on DAT), you may need to keep track of at least two source timecodes: one for picture and one or more for sound.

Final Cut Pro allows you to modify a media file and source timecode. This is recommended only if the timecode of your source media clip is wrong, or if you need to create auxiliary timecodes. Altering the source timecodes for any other reason may cause a mismatch between video and sound during recapture.

Since the sequence timecode represents a numerical value of a frame of *edited* material, you can modify it more liberally. During the editing phase, you may decide to modify your sequence timecode to suit your editing style. You might change it to begin at the zero hour, for example. During the editing phase, the sequence timecode has little consequence for your project and is useful for reference purposes. Conversely, for output, the sequence timecode takes a more prominent role because standards for picture start have been established within the industry. (See "Outputting Your Project" in Lesson 5 for further details.)

Occasionally, your source tapes or files will have no timecode track. This is usually a result of file transfer from a special-effects house or music imported from CD. Keep data backups of nontimecoded sources, or transfer them to timecoded tapes and capture from the transferred tape.

Organizing Media

Some basic rules will help you organize and manage your material. Some of these conventions are unique to Final Cut Pro, but most are pertinent for *all* nonlinear systems.

Before you begin to capture material, think about your naming conventions. In Final Cut Pro, the name you assign the captured QuickTime file becomes the name of the media file at the Finder level. Final Cut Pro does allow you the option of changing the clip name in the Browser while maintaining the media link to the clip in the Finder. Altering a clip name in the Browser will not alter the QuickTime media file at the Finder level. However, don't change the name of a clip in the Browser of Final Cut Pro, because other methods, such as marking or subclipping, can elegantly achieve a clip name change while maintaining the name reference at the Finder level. (See the "Marking Sync Points" section later in this lesson.)

Consider carefully where you will set your scratch disks, and be consistent. Keep your media structure organized and thoughtful. Create separate folders for materials that are not captured via tape, such as music and graphics. Consistency throughout a project will enhance efficiency.

▶ Unique tape names—Numbering is the best tape-naming method. If your tapes do not have numbers, take an indelible pen and begin numbering each tape and case immediately. Where duplicate numbers already exist, mark one with an alphabetical appendage. For example, two tapes numbered 101 would become 101 and 101a. A tape name is your reference to the timecode on that particular tape. So, if you had two tapes, each beginning with timecode 01:00:00;00, the only means of distinguishing one timecode from the other is the tape name. Any nonlinear system knows only numbers, so it is your job to make the distinction clear.

▶ Unique names—Keep all clip names unique. Remember, on any computer, files that live in the same folder must have unique names. Since the name you assign a clip, once captured, is the same as the QuickTime media file created at the Finder level, you need to preserve unique names. Even if you create two discrete folders, this convention is still pertinent because it's important to be able to distinguish one content file from another, especially when relinking.

NOTE ▶ In the OS language Unix, the location of a folder named *Example* on a Desktop would be expressed as /Users/Estelle/Desktop/Example. *Example* is the folder, and everything prior to the folder name is the path.

► Names that make sense—Think librarian! If you're working on a project that has more of a script convention, naming media clips using scenes, takes, and camera angles might make sense. If you are working on a documentary, you might name clips by subject or interview. If your project follows the progress of an event, perhaps a date-naming scheme will be useful. Another method is to name a clip by the tape number, and break it down with subclips or markers after the media is captured.

► Consistent naming—Be consistent! Once you've chosen a naming convention, follow it closely. On any computer, the more consistent you are with your naming convention, the better the results for searches or sorting. Final Cut Pro has some powerful search capabilities that are enhanced through consistent clip naming. You can search for every clip containing any number of field values, including names in either the Browser or sequence. Final Cut Pro can also sort hierarchically in the Browser. For example, you can perform a primary sort by clicking a Browser heading, and then you can perform a secondary sort by holding down the Shift key and clicking another heading. You'll be able to sort more accurately if you keep these names consistent.

► Safe characters—For any filename on any computer, avoid characters that are used as commands in the operating system. Safe characters include letters, numbers, and underscores (_). Avoid characters such as forward slashes (/), colons (:), asterisks (*), and so on. All symbols are used as instructions by the operating system and must not be used to form a filename.

► Leading zeros to sort numbers correctly—Use leading zeros to make your sorting numerically and alphabetically correct. For instance, without leading zeros your clip named *25* will be listed after your clip named *125*, not before it. (25 is alphabetically sorted before 125, but numerically after it.) If you use a leading zero (025), Final Cut Pro will place the clips named 025 and 125 in numerical as well as alphabetical order.

Organizing Final Cut Pro Projects

Generally, an online workflow will have a shorter turnaround than an offline workflow. However, you need to clearly structure and organize a project regardless of length, size, or workflow. There are many organizational techniques, including personal preference. However, you should organize a project using common sense so that others could easily identify your project structure.

Organize your clips logically into bins, or use multiple bins to organize the same media in different ways. For example, one bin could organize clips by the date they were shot; another could have the same material organized by scene; and yet another could be organized by location.

The editors of *The Magic Hour* organized clips by character *and* location. Each bin was clearly named, and sequences were labeled by editor, version, and date. For example, the master sequence was labeled TMH_MASTER_EM_03282005.

Consider saving sequences incrementally. One method is to save a sequence prior to a major revision. Although you can view a Browser heading named *Last Modified*, you may want to consider adding a date appendage to saved sequences, like in the preceding example. Adding date values to any file is a useful tool.

Archive old bins and sequences. Since Final Cut Pro will let you open multiple projects at once, you can have all your material open at the same time. However, for efficiency and simplicity, you'll want to archive old bins and sequences. Archiving also reduces project load times. (See Lesson 12 for more information on archiving.)

Gathering Media

Before you begin to capture material, consider your project specifications. Determine what you will capture, by complete tape or by selection.

Determine the codec, and remember to calculate the storage space requirements. (See Lesson 9 for more information on these calculations.) Also, test the first captured media files to ensure they are at the quality and resolution you intended.

The following strategies have been gathered through experience and discussions as common practices. There are numerous variations and personal preferences to the steps listed. Some of the following methods may work best when your project has specific circumstances, but use these examples as starting points and veer from the steps as appropriate.

Planning and Capturing

Source material may arrive on two different media—for instance, video tapes and DAT tapes. This is an area where many people make small mistakes that adversely impact the final delivery, so we will first detail the process of capturing picture and sound separately, then cover synching them in Final Cut Pro.

Source material may also arrive on a single medium—for example, when picture and sound were recorded simultaneously on tape or if sync was achieved during the telecine process. Toward the end of this lesson, we will cover single-source capture.

New Project Settings

When you create a new project, you can either use an appropriate Easy Setup, or you can independently set the sequence, capture, and device control presets along with the video/audio playback. A preset in Final Cut Pro is a preconfigured group of settings. For example, the device control preset has 12 settings that control your video deck. When you select a device control preset, all 12 settings are automatically configured. When you select an Easy Setup, Final Cut Pro automatically configures the settings of *all* the presets. The Easy Setup stores the sequence, capture, device control, and audio/video settings.

The Easy Setup is a great shortcut for many of the standard project configurations. However, if you need more granular control, and you configure an alternate sequence preset, save the modified setup as an Easy Setup so you can recall the settings in other areas of Final Cut Pro, such as the Sequence Settings window.

Here's how to modify an Easy Setup preset:

1 Choose Final Cut Pro > Audio/Video Settings, or press Option-Cmd-Q.

2 In the Summary tab, select the mix of presets that suit your project.

3   Click Create Easy Setup.

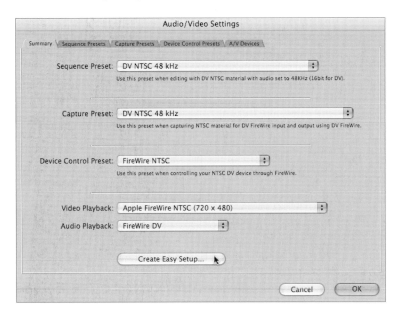

4   Type a name and description for your Easy Setup.

Click the Enable Verification Of Device Control In First Start Dialog check box if you want Final Cut Pro to check for device control at application launch.

5   Click Create.

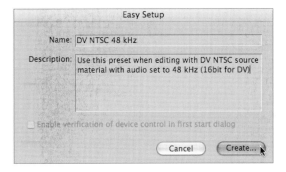

6   Enter a filename and location if you do not want to use the default location.

The default location for new Easy Setups is /Library/Application Support/ Final Cut Pro System Support/Custom Settings.

7   Click Save.

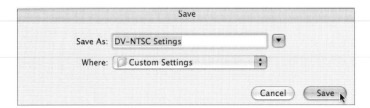

Your new Easy Setup is selected and will now be available as an option in all Setup windows.

Capture Media by Complete Tape

If your picture and sound are recorded on different media, you will need to capture each one separately. (See Lesson 2 for information on sound capture mediums.) Often, the easiest method for syncing picture and sound can be logging and capturing an entire source tape.

When you capture an entire source tape, you will capture one long clip instead of logging and capturing a tape as individual clips. Syncing picture and audio from an entire tape clip is sometimes easier and faster because the sync points in smaller clips can be unclear. This is especially true if you are not supplied with any sound recording location notes. Sound recording location notes will often identify start/stop timecodes and scene or take numbers along with general comments about the quality of a recording. Without this information, capturing the entire tape and breaking it down inside Final Cut Pro is often easier, especially since you will have the audio waveform to assist you visually. The same applies to picture. If there are no location notes or SMPTE clapboards, finding the sync points by capturing an entire tape will often be easier.

After capturing entire tapes, the long clips will be broken into more manageable lengths through marking, subclipping, and merging.

Here's how to log and capture an entire tape:

1   Turn on and connect your capture device to your computer.

For example, if you are using FireWire control, connect the FireWire cable between your camera or deck and your computer.

2   From the Browser, click to select the Logging bin.

3   Choose File > Set Logging Bin.

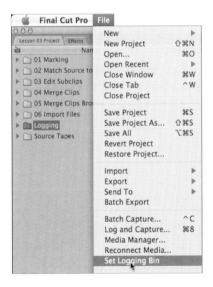

All captured or logged clips will now be placed into this bin.

> **TIP** You can change the size of your Browser text. Ctrl-click in the Browser and choose Text Size > Medium from the pop-up menu.

4   Press Cmd-8 to open the Log and Capture window.

5   Type the Reel number of your tape and leave Prompt checked.

6   Use the J, K, and L keys to locate the start of the tape, and set the In point.

Remember to allow some tape run from the head of the tape for pre-roll. The amount of pre-roll you require is dependent on your configuration and deck settings.

7   Use the J, K, and L keys to find the picture or sound end point of the tape, and set the Out point.

8   Click the Clip Settings tab and select the Video and Audio check boxes. Or capture video or audio only by deselecting either the Video or Audio check box.

9   Choose the appropriate number of audio channels per clip from the Input
Channels pop-up menu. Provided you have the appropriate third-party
hardware, you can capture up to 24 audio channels in one clip.

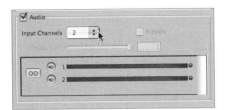

10   Choose how the audio channels are grouped by clicking the Stereo/Mono
toggle. QuickTime 7 also supports discrete audio channels.

11   Click the Logging tab.

12   Click the Clip button to capture from the marked In to Out points.

For picture or audio delivered as files, see the "Importing Media" section later
in this lesson.

Speed Clip Logging

If your final sound is recorded with picture or transferred and synced during
the telecine, preparing your media is much easier.

Even though your audio and picture are synced on tape, whether to capture
your media as one long clip or smaller clips is more a matter of personal

preference. Generally, editors will log a pre-synced tape prior to capture. The following exercise will increase your logging speed.

1   Press Cmd-8 to open the Log and Capture window, if it's not already open.

> **TIP** To speed through your logging, enable the handy default Media Logging button bar, which includes buttons for all the commands you'd expect to use during logging and capturing. Simply choose Tools > Button Bars > Media Logging.

2   Type the Reel number of your tape, and deselect the Prompt check box.

When you deselect Prompt, you will not be prompted to enter a name when you log or capture a clip.

3   Deselect the Description check box.

4   Select the check box for Scene, and make sure Shot/Take and Angle are selected also.

5   Enter a Scene.

6   Enter a Shot/Take number.

The Shot/Take number will automatically increase after you log each clip.

7   Set your audio Channel grouping and number of audio tracks.

Provided that you choose to maintain the same settings throughout an entire logging session, you will only need to set this for the first logged clip.

TIP▸ Before capture, you can modify a logged clip's audio format in the Browser, and after capture you can modify a clip in the Timeline. In the Browser, simply select the offline clip you want to modify and choose Modify > Clip Settings. Then choose your modifications and continue to capture. From the Timeline, you can change a clip between stereo and channels 1+2. To toggle this option, simply choose Modify > Stereo Pair.

8   Set your In and Out points for the clip.

9   Press F2 to log the clip.

10 When you're finished logging all your clips, click the Batch button.

TIP▸ It's a good idea to get into the habit of saving your project. Press Cmd-S to save your project before and after capturing.

The Batch Capture dialog opens.

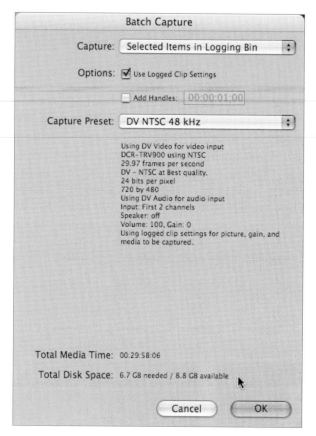

From the Batch Capture dialog, you can verify your capture settings and capture multiple clips at once. The Batch Capture dialog is useful because it allows you to view the total media time and disk space required based on the duration of the selected clips and the codec setting in your capture preset.

Marking Sync Points

If you have captured the entire source tape, each clip is one long file. In order to make it manageable for editing and syncing, you need to break it down into smaller segments. The segments can be scenes, like cinéma vérité, or individual takes a lá script style. The beginning of either a scene or a take is a natural place to begin syncing because the picture and audio probably began roughly at the same place. The method of location recording will determine how you identify sync. If the location sound was recorded with a SMPTE clapboard, or the timecode of the source video matches the timecode of the audio, then your syncing process will be more straightforward.

If your picture was recorded with a clapboard, you would identify the sync point as the moment the clapboard closed. If your picture was recorded with event sync, like a hand clap, you would identify the sync point as the moment the hand closed. If your location sound was recorded without identifiable sync references like timecode or event sync, then your sync point will vary depending on your given set of circumstances. However, the goal is to find a moment in the picture that will be easily identifiable in the audio.

The best way to begin is to load the master clip into the Viewer and use markers. Markers allow you to easily add a new name value to a clip. If a marker is used in a sequence or copied to another location in the Browser, it becomes a subclip. A subclip made from a marker keeps the name of the marker and adds the name of the master clip as an appendage.

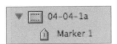

A marker placed on a master clip

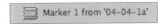

After you move or copy the marker, it maintains a name reference to the master clip.

NOTE ▶ Remember, Final Cut Pro can link a clip to its QuickTime file on the hard drive even if you change the clip name in the project file after capturing.

You need to mark only the head of each take. The end of a marker is either the frame before the next marker or the end of the clip, whichever comes first. If you have any material you don't want, such as a long tail at the end of the tape, simply place a marker at the head of the unused portion, and name it something like *long tail*.

Let's cut down a single video and audio clip by applying a marker to the closed clapboard in the picture and find the audio event that matches. If you had captured an entire tape, you would continue to place markers on the long clip to identify all the sync points.

1   Choose File > Open > **Lesson 03 Project.fcp**.

2   Open the bin named 01 Marking.

3   Double-click the **Reel 04** video clip to load it into the Viewer.

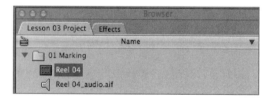

4   Use the J, K, and L keys to find the frame where the clapper is fully closed.

5   Press M once to set the marker at the playhead location.

6   Press M a second time to open the Edit Marker dialog.

7   Name the marker the name of the scene or take. In this example, name the marker *04-04-1a*.

8   Double-click the **Reel 04_audio.aif** audio clip to load it into the Viewer.

9   Use the J, K, and L keys to find the frame where you hear the clapper is closed. The audio waveform will be identified as a solid block.

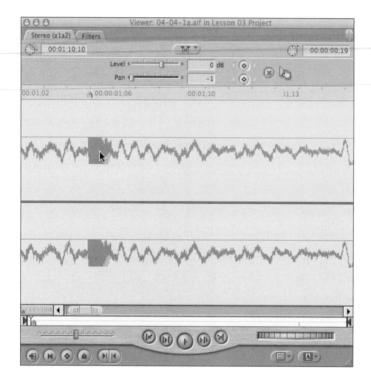

10   Press Cmd-+ to zoom into the audio waveform at the playhead position.

11   Place the playhead at the first frame of the audio waveform when the clapper closes and press M once to set the marker at the playhead location.

12   Press M a second time to open the Edit Marker dialog.

13 Name the marker the name of the scene or take. In this example, name the marker *04-04-1a_audio*. Click OK.

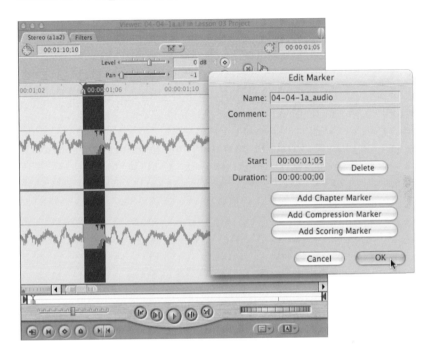

Prepare a Sequence for Combining Picture and Audio

After marking the clips, you will create a sequence that can act as a base for both the picture and audio clips.

Often, editors will match the video source-tape timecode to their sequence timecode to visually help identify a loss of sync. You can check the integrity of your clip timecode by placing the playhead over any given frame of video and make sure the sequence timecode matches the clip timecode.

Follow these steps to match the video source to sequence timecode:

1   Click the disclosure triangle to the left of the 02 Match Source to Sequence Timecode bin.

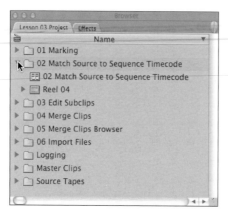

2   Click the disclosure triangle next to the **Reel 04** video clip icon to see the markers. (Make sure your Browser or bin is in List view.)

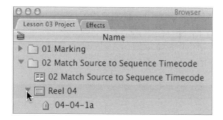

3   Double-click the 04-04-1a marker to load it into the Viewer.

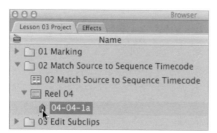

Once a marker is loaded into the Viewer, it assumes subclip attributes.

4   Press the Home key to go to the first frame of the subclip in the Viewer.

5   In the upper-right corner of the Viewer, click the Current Timecode field to highlight the entire timecode number, and press Cmd-C to copy the timecode.

6   Select the Timeline to make it the active window.

7   Choose Sequence > Settings.

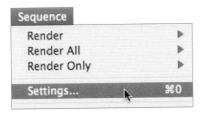

8 Click the Timeline Options tab.

9 The Starting Timecode field should already be highlighted. Press Cmd-V to paste the clip timecode.

The clip timecode now matches the sequence Timecode. You will find this useful if you use the sequence in the Viewer and turn on the timecode overlays. To show the timecode overlays for the Viewer, make the Viewer active, then press Option-Z. You can quickly scrub along all your selected scenes that originated from the same tape. It's also a very quick way, while you're syncing, to identify that your video is in sync.

TIP It's common to name the sync sequence by the source tape name. This is especially useful if you plan to use the sequence not just as a means of syncing the clips but also as an assembly of synced clips. The sequence then quickly identifies the original tape.

Edit Subclips

Once you have prepared a sequence, you are ready to edit the marked clips.
Final Cut Pro will automatically create subclips from the markers.

1   Click the disclosure triangle to the left of the 03 Edit Subclips bin.

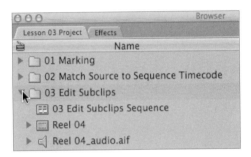

2   Double-click *03 Edit Subclips Sequence* to load it into the Timeline.

3   In the Browser, click the disclosure triangle to the left of the Reel 04 video
clip to reveal the marker.

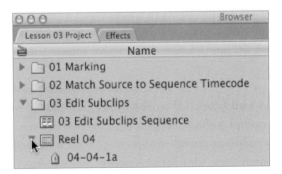

4   Drag the 04-04-1a video marker to the Canvas Overwrite overlay to edit
the marker into *03 Edit Subclips Sequence.*

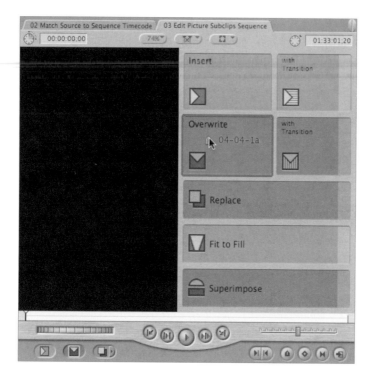

The marker is edited into the sequence. Although we just edited the single
marker into the sequence, if you had a number of markers on a clip, you
could lasso and drag all your markers to edit them into the sequence
simultaneously.

5   Press the Home key to jump the playhead to the beginning of *03 Edit
Subclips Sequence.*

6   In the Browser, click the disclosure triangle to the left of the **Reel
04_audio.aif** audio clip to reveal the marker.

7   Drag the 04-04-1a_audio marker to the Canvas Overwrite overlay to edit
the marker into *03 Edit Subclips Sequence.*

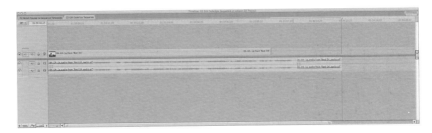

8   Press Shift-Z in the Timeline to fit the contents of the sequence to the
window.

Once you've edited the picture and audio into the sequence, check the synchronized result. Checking sync will require you to play some, if not all, of
every scene. Play the sequence, find dialogue or an identifiable picture and
audio event, and make sure it looks and sounds correct. If you recognize a loss
of sync, simply slip the video or audio by one frame at a time and play back
the result. Continue slipping the video or audio until the clips look in sync.

Merged Clips

Merged clips are a fantastic resource because they can link to multiple
QuickTime media files while maintaining a single clip icon inside Final Cut
Pro. You can merge 1 video clip with up to 24 audio clips. This is a perfect
solution for projects shot on dual recording systems such as film and DAT.

Before actually merging two or more clips, you first need to decide your
method. You have five options: merge by lining up the In or Out points,
Timecode, Auxiliary Timecode 1, or Auxiliary Timecode 2. If you slated all
your shots at the beginning with a clapboard, you could use the In points to

line up the shots. If you tail slated the shots, you could use the Out points. If the timecode of your video and audio clips was synchronized during the shoot, you would choose timecode to merge *and* sync. The method you choose depends on your project conditions; in this example, you will merge using the In points.

> **TIP** If you merge using In or Out points, trim your clips in the Timeline or Viewer as needed to make sure you line up the In or Out points so that the merge will work appropriately.

Here's how to merge clips from the Timeline:

1   Click the disclosure triangle to the left of the 04 Merge Clips bin.

2   Double-click *04 Merge Clips Sequence* to load it into the Timeline.

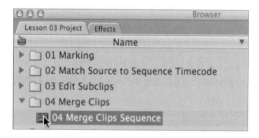

3   Hold down Shift and click to highlight the video and audio clips in the sequence.

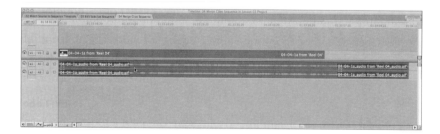

NOTE ▶ If you have more than one synced video and audio clip in your sequence, you'll need to link your video to your synced audio clips one group at a time.

4   Press Cmd-L to link the video and audio clips.

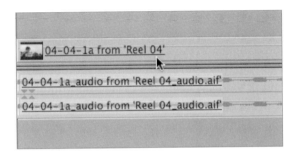

Linked clips' names have an underline.

5   Drag the linked clip from the Timeline to the Browser, and release it into the 04 Merge Clips bin.

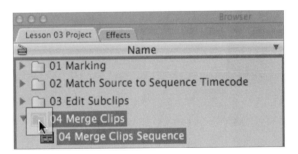

Merging clips directly from the Timeline is convenient, but there will be times when you will need to merge clips directly from the Browser. Merging clips from the Browser allows you to choose from multiple sync points.

1   Click the disclosure triangle to the left of the 05 Merge Clips Browser bin.

2   Hold down Shift and click the icon of video clip and audio clip to select them.

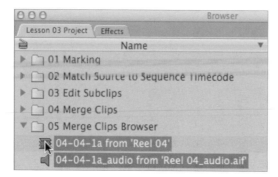

3   Choose Modify > Merge Clips.

4   The Merge Clips dialog opens; by default, In Points is selected. Leave In Points selected and click OK.

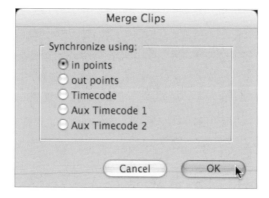

The video and audio clips have been merged, and the new clip is named after the video clip with the appendage *Merged*. If you want to merge audio clips without video, the top-most selected audio clip will form the new clip name.

04-04-1a from 'Reel 04' Merged

All merged clips maintain their relationship to the individual QuickTime files, source tape, and timecode.

Importing Media

There may be instances when you can import some, if not all, of your media directly from files. If you're fortunate, a lab or post facility will do the capturing for you overnight, and you will simply import the files. You can import individual files, multiple files, an entire folder or a group of folders. Alternately, you can drag files or folders from the Finder window directly to the Final Cut Pro Browser or bin.

1 Click the disclosure triangle to the left of the 06 Import Files bin.

2 Double-click the *06 Import to Timeline* sequence to load it into the Timeline.

3 Press and hold the Command key. Tap the Tab key, and release all keys when you see the Finder icon highlighted.

Pressing Cmd-Tab navigates you through open applications.

TIP Use Exposé to clear all Windows from your screen to reveal your Desktop. To change the settings for Exposé, see the section on customizing Exposé in Lesson 10.

4 Press Cmd-N to open a new Finder window.

5 Click the Column icon to display the Finder contents in columns.

6 Navigate to the Lesson 03 Media folder.

7 Select the **Reel 04** media file.

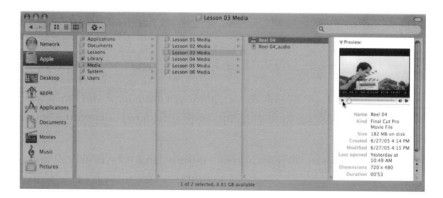

The benefit of viewing a Finder window in Column view is that you can preview your files.

8 In the title bar of the Finder window, click and hold directly over the Lesson 03 Media icon (don't let go of the mouse until instructed) and press Cmd-Tab to navigate back to Final Cut Pro.

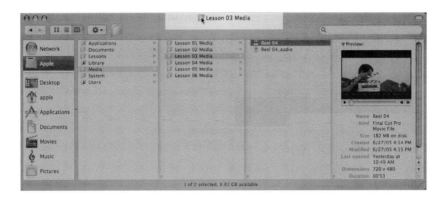

9   Drag the mouse to the Browser window and release the mouse when you
     see the Browser window highlighted.

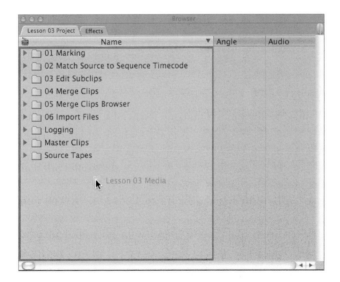

This is an efficient way to import files. You can also import LiveType and
Motion projects using the same method.

Import Files by Other Methods:

▶   Open a Finder window, and leave the Browser of the Final Cut Pro interface visible. Locate the files you want to import, and drag the files directly to the Browser.

▶   Open a Finder window, and leave the Timeline of the Final Cut Pro interface visible. Locate the files you want to import, and drag the files directly to the Timeline.

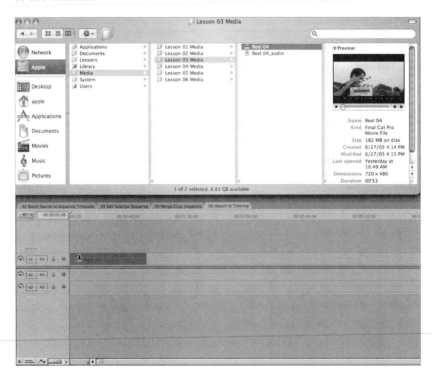

▶   Press Cmd-I, locate the files you want to import, and click Choose.

▸ Choose File > Import > Folder, locate the folder you want to import, and click Choose.

NOTE ▸ If you import files from any removable storage media (CD, DVD), make sure you first copy the files to your media hard drive. If you don't, the clips will become offline when you remove the CD or DVD from your drive.

Changing Resolutions

Traditionally, it was common practice to only increase resolution towards the end of your nonlinear project. However, the Media Manager in Final Cut Pro makes it possible to decrease project resolutions with ease. This provides you with great flexibility—you can move your project effortlessly between low and high resolutions.

Increasing Resolution

Generally, the editor of an offline project will lock picture, and proceed to recapture the original source material at a higher resolution in preparation for color correction and output. This standard will depend on your project requirements and can range from increasing resolutions for export to an effects facility to previewing an edit during postproduction of a film

> **NOTE** ▸ *Lock picture* means to complete editing. No major editing revisions of the project will be undertaken after picture lock.

During post-production of the Cohen brothers' film, *Intolerable Cruelty*, Joel and Ethan Cohen increased the resolution of their work-in-progress for previews. They shot film, transferred to HD and DVCAM, captured at DV25 from the DVCAM tapes and recaptured at higher HD resolution for previews. The HD online was used for the preview screening only and was not used for the final film release. A traditional film preview screening involves a matchback to the negative workprint viewed through a projector. However, this HD online allowed Joel and Ethan to keep their preview screening looking closer to the high-quality film aesthetic minus the scratching of grease pencil, dirt, and splice tape normally viewed during standard preview screenings that matchback to a film workprint.

Paul Ziller, the director and editor of the film *Firefight*, incorporated over 250 visual effects. Adam Stern, president of Artifex Studios Ltd and five other digital artists created the visual effects for *Firefight*. The artists needed the clips at a high resolution. Adam and his team sent the clips via QuickTime across the network to one of the Macs, where another artist worked on them, applying special effects, then sent them back onto the Final Cut Pro system. Paul then cut the affected clips right back into his edit.

The Magic Hour editors locked picture and recaptured only the edited clips in their final sequence, then discarded the low-resolution media. Although this is a common process during high-resolution recapture, the editors may have chosen an alternate path like Joel and Ethan Cohen. Joel and Ethan's editing assistants kept the captured DV25 media on their system concurrently recapturing at the HD resolution. Joel and Ethan were continuing to edit the film, and they increased resolution for preview purposes, whereas *The Magic Hour* editors had completed their editing process and increased resolution for color correction and output.

Your reasons and timing for increasing resolution may differ, but your basic approach will remain the same. There are essentially two methods of recapturing media: selected and complete. If you decide to recapture the entire source file at a higher resolution, you can achieve the recapture through the Batch Capture window. However, if you require selected or partial clip recapture, you will need to leverage the power of the Media Manager in Final Cut Pro.

Recapture Entire Source File

You can recapture files directly through the Batch Capture window. Recapturing this way pulls in the entire source duration regardless of how much is used in a sequence or marked on a clip.

If you need to keep the low-resolution media files, simply save a copy of your project with the Save Project As (Shift-Cmd-S) function in Final Cut Pro. Add an appendage to the name of your project, perhaps something like *High Resolution*. Use your current project if you want to delete the low-resolution version.

> **TIP** Change your audio/video settings to your new resolution. The easiest way is to change the Easy Setup (Ctrl-Q). If you have existing sequences, you'll need to change their settings. Open the existing sequence, press Cmd-0 (Cmd-zero), click the Load Sequence Preset button, and alter the sequence setting to reflect your new resolution.

1   Select the elements you want to recapture.

You can choose sequences, bins, or clips.

2   Choose Modify > Make Offline.

3   Select one of the three options in the Make Offline dialog, and then
click OK:

   ▶   Leave Them on the Disk—Media remains in the current location.

   ▶   Move Them to the Trash—Moves the media files to the Trash but
does not delete them.

   ▶   Delete Them from the Disk—Moves the selected media files to the
Trash and deletes them from the disk.

4 Choose File > Batch Capture to open the Batch Capture window.

5 From the Capture drop-down, choose All Selected Items.

You will have three options in this drop-down if you have made no selections in your project: All Selected Items, Offline Items, and All Items.

6 Check Use Logged Clip Settings if you want to maintain the clip settings you specified for each clip during the log and capture process. If you deselect this option, the clips will be captured using the current settings in the Clip Settings tab.

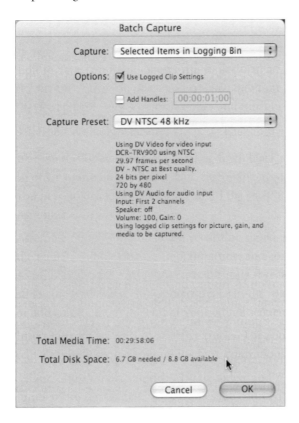

7   Leave Add Handles deselected.

If you have time-remapped clips or clips with speed effects, it's best not to add handles because the new source media duration can affect the time remap and speed effect.

8   From the Capture Preset drop-down, choose your new resolution and then click OK.

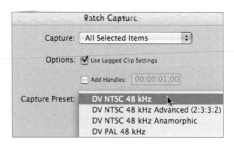

9   The recapture dialog opens and prompts you for tapes. Select and load your tape at the prompt, then click Continue.

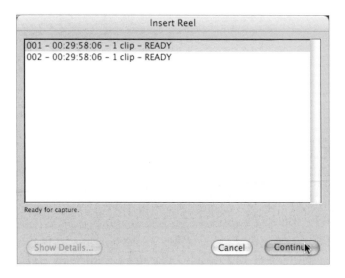

Recapture Selected Source Media

If you want to recapture only your selected or marked clips, you will use the Media Manager. Final Cut Pro's Media Manager is a powerful tool with many uses, one of which is to help streamline your workflow during the capture or recapture process.

We will focus on using the Media Manager prior to recapturing selected clips. The scope of the Media Manager is extremely flexible, and you can us it on one or more clips, one or many sequences, or even an entire project. The affected elements of your project depend on what was selected in your Browser, Timeline, or Viewer prior to opening the Media Manager.

> **TIP** ▶ Since functions of the Media Manager read clip relationships, you need to understand the difference between master and affiliate clips. A master clip is a first instance of a clip in the Browser. The first instance could be from a logged, captured, imported, or merged clip. An affiliate clip is any clip edited, subclipped, or copied throughout your project. An affiliate clip shares properties of the master clip, which allows for powerful manipulation. You can reconnect or change the properties of a master clip and affect all copies (also called affiliates).

If you have enough space, and if you deem it necessary, you can keep your low-resolution clips on your system while also increasing the resolution. See the option in step 6 in the following exercise.

Here's how to increase resolution for selected source media using Media Manager:

1   Select the elements that you need to recapture.

    You can choose sequences, bins, or clips.

2   Choose File > Media Manager. The Media Manager dialog opens.

3 Choose Create Offline from the Media pop-up menu.

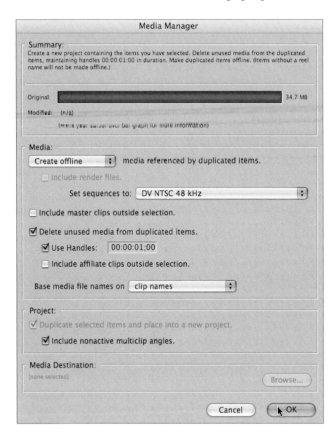

4 Select your new settings for the copied sequence in the Set Sequences To pop-up menu.

You can choose from your installed sequence presets, or the current sequence setting, or you can choose Custom to create your own. Any custom sequence setting modified through the Media Manager is for immediate use only and will not be saved as a sequence preset.

5   Deselect the check box for Include Master Clips Outside Selection.

With this option deselected, the master clips in your new project will only be based on the In and Out points of the selected items.

6   Select the check box Delete Unused Media From Duplicated Items.

With this option selected, any media files that are outside your selection will be deleted.

This step is optional and dependent on whether you choose to keep your low- and high-resolution media simultaneously. If you choose to keep your low-resolution media, deselect this check box and skip ahead to step 9.

7   Select the check box for Use Handles if you require handles on your media files. Define the number of handles you require.

8   Deselect the check box Include Affiliate Clips Outside Selection.

With this option deselected, you are ensuring that any media affiliated with your selection is *not* included. This includes affiliate clips.

9   From the Base Media File Names On pop-up menu, choose Clip Names.

You can choose either existing filenames or clip names. Existing filenames will maintain the names of the original media files; clip names will change your media names to the names you assigned to your clips during the editing process. This is relevant especially since you may have marked and subclipped your clips. If you have changed the names of your clips, set this option to Clip Names. If you have not altered the clip names in any way, or you want to maintain your original naming convention, set this option to Existing Filenames.

10   Click OK.

A dialog opens, prompting you to save your new project file.

11 Navigate to where you want to save your project. Perhaps keep the original project name and add the appendage of your resolution—for example, *Joe_Bloggs_Feature_Film-DV50_NTSC*.

Final Cut Pro scans your selected elements and reconstructs the project.

12 If Final Cut Pro prompts you for additional information, you have three options: Add, Continue, or Abort.

If the Media Manager detects that a currently open project references the same media, an Additional Items Found dialog appears.

▶ Click Add if you want Media Manager to consider any additional portions of media files referenced by any currently *open* projects.

▶ Click Continue if you don't want Media Manager to consider other referenced media files.

▶ Click Abort to stop the Media Manager operation so that you can modify a Media Manager setting.

A Confirm Media Modifications dialog appears if the Media Manager is going to permanently change or delete any media files.

13 Click Continue to confirm the change, and Media Manager will complete the process.

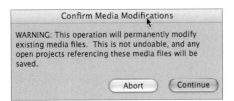

NOTE ▶ If your media has no source timecode track or reel name, the media file will not be affected by the Media Manager. This is a precautionary feature in Final Cut Pro to prevent altering a media file that you may not be able to recapture.

Decreasing Resolution

Sometimes you'll need to convert your project from high to low resolution—for example, the project may be on hiatus, your storage or bandwidth requirements may have decreased, or maybe it's time to archive. During post-production of *Cold Mountain*, the assistant editors wanted to prepare scenes on their laptops so they decreased the resolution of the media files in order to accommodate smaller bandwidths and file sizes. After the assistants prepped a scene on a laptop, they copied their project file to the main editing station, changed the sequence setup to match the higher-resolution media files, and reconnected the clips to the higher-resolution media files. This process gave everyone involved in the post-production of *Cold Mountain* greater flexibility.

1   Select the elements that you need to decrease in resolution.

2   Choose File > Media Manager to open the Media Manager dialog.

3   Choose Recompress from the Media pop-up menu.

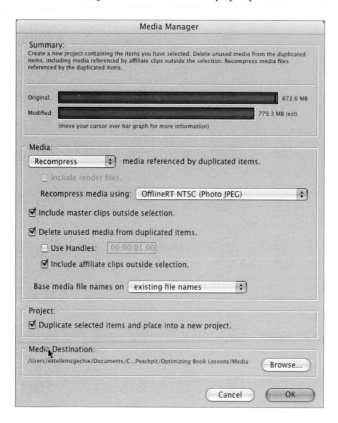

When you select the Recompress option, you can recompress your media files with a different codec and frame size. The Recompress option affects only QuickTime movies; other file types, such as Photoshop, are simply copied.

> **TIP** ▶ Use the Batch Export feature in Final Cut Pro to recompress any temporal compressed files, such as Cinepak, Sorenson, or H.264 because these files are not suited to recompressing through the Media Manager.

> **NOTE** ▶ If your clips have motion attributes, the attributes will be changed to match the new frame size of the setting you choose.

4   Select your new settings for the copied sequence in the Recompress Media Using pop-up menu.

5   Select the check box for Include Master Clips Outside Selection.

With this option selected, the master clips in your new project will be included.

6   Select the check box Delete Unused Media From Duplicated Items.

With this option selected, any media files that are outside your selection will be deleted.

This step is optional and dependent on whether you choose to keep your low- and high-resolution media simultaneously. If you choose to keep your high-resolution media, deselect this check box and skip ahead to step 9.

7   Select the check box for Use Handles if you require handles on your media files. Define the number of handles you require.

8   Select the check box Include Affiliate Clips Outside Selection.

With this option selected, you ensure that any media affiliated with your selection will be included.

9   From the Base Media File Names On pop-up menu, choose Existing File
     Names.

10   Click OK.

     A dialog opens, prompting you to save your new project file.

11   Navigate to where you want to save your project. Perhaps keep the original
     project name and add the appendage of your new compression, for example
     Joe_Bloggs_Feature_Film-PhotoJPEG.

     Final Cut Pro scans your selected elements and reconstructs the project.

     NOTE ▸ The Media Manager is not designed to convert frame rates. To
     convert frame rates, the most elegant solution is to use Compressor.

Reconnect Clips

You can reconnect clips at any time during your editing process. Doing so
establishes a relationship between the clip in the Browser and the project file
located on your drive. The file path of a connected clip is stored in the clip's
Source property.

In addition to the usual reconnecting of clips after you modify, move, or delete
media files in the Finder, you may also find it useful to reconnect media files
when you switch between resolutions. Throughout the previews of *Intolerable
Cruelty,* Joel and Ethan Cohen's assistants reconnected clips between low and high
resolutions. During the post-production of *Cold Mountain,* the assistant editors
reconnected clips from the low-resolution media they used while they were editing on laptops to the higher-resolution media they used when they were editing
on the main editing systems.

1   Select the elements you want to reconnect.

2   Choose File > Reconnect Media.

The Reconnect Files dialog appears.

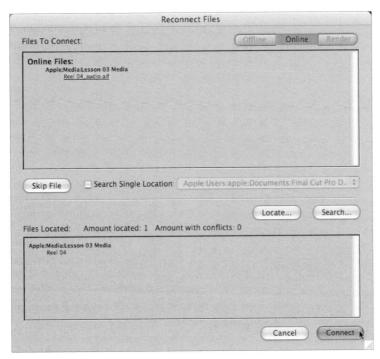

Final Cut Pro automatically searches for the first clip to reconnect. A clip that is ready for connection is highlighted in the Files To Connect list.

3   Click Skip File if you want to remove the currently highlighted clip while continuing to reconnect other clips in the list.

4   Choose a path from the Search Folders pop-up menu, then select the Single Search Location option. This limits where Final Cut Pro searches for media files, and it streamlines the reconnection process.

   If you need to widen your search, deselect the Single Search Location option so that all folders in the Search Folders pop-up menu are searched. Final Cut Pro will search through every folder on every connected volume.

5   Click Search, and Final Cut Pro will search files automatically. Once a match for a file is found, the Reconnect dialog appears. If a match is not found, click the Locate button and manually navigate to the location of the media file.

You have several options to help you find your clip:

▶   Show pop-up menu—To limit the kind of files Final Cut Pro will search, you can specify Video Files, Sound Files, or Still Image Files.

▶   Matched Name Only—Leave this option checked, and Final Cut Pro will restrict the search to the file whose name matches the filename in the clip's Source property. If you need to reconnect to a media file whose name differs, deselect this check box.

TIP ▶ If Final Cut Pro is unable to locate a file that matches the filename in the clip's Source property, it will search for a file whose name matches the clip name.

▶ Search—Shows the path of the file. If more than one match is found, you can use this pop-up menu to choose which file you want. This is especially useful if you have low-resolution and high-resolution files available.

▶ Reconnect All Files in Relative Path—Select this check box, and Final Cut Pro will automatically reconnect all remaining clips whose files are located in this folder. This is especially useful when you are reconnecting a lot of clips; it will speed up the reconnection process considerably.

6 Click Choose to add the correct file to the Files Located area in the Reconnect Files dialog.

If any attributes of the selected file do not match the clip you're reconnecting, the File Attribute Mismatch dialog appears. This dialog is a useful guide listing the mismatched attributes.

7 Click Try Again to search for another file to connect, or click Continue to reconnect the file to the current clip, even though attributes may not match.

Any clips connected with mismatched attributes will appear in italics in the Files Located area, and a total number of clip–media file mismatches will be displayed next to Amount With Conflicts.

All located media files appear in a list in the Files Located area of the Reconnect Files dialog.

8   Click Connect, and all files located in the Files Located area will connect to their media files.

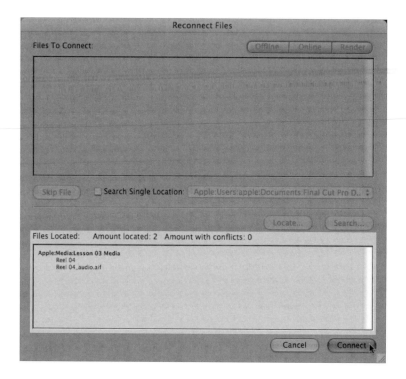

TIP ▶ You can click Connect at any time, even if there are still clips listed in the Files To Connect list.

NOTE ▶ Understanding reconnecting in Final Cut Pro is important. Final Cut Pro will check that media files correspond to the clips in your project. Final Cut Pro confirms connections for clips to media files when you open a project file and when you switch from any application to Final Cut Pro. If Final Cut Pro detects a missing media file, or if you have altered a media file at the Finder level, Final Cut Pro will display an Offline Files dialog. If you see this dialog, select the appropriate option; if you choose to reconnect, follow the reconnection guides in the preceding steps.

Playback and Performance

The flexibility of Final Cut Pro allows multiple resolutions in a project or sequence. If you kept the low-resolution media files, you may find it useful to view both the low- and high-resolution media files in the same project. Simply open both low- and high-resolution projects, and drag, or copy and paste, the elements into a project Browser.

> **TIP** For clarity, save a mixed-resolution project with an identifiable appendage, perhaps something like *mixres*. Identify sequences or bins containing low- or high-resolution clips in the same way. Using colored labels may also be useful.

Sequences may contain mixed-resolution clips. Set the sequence setting to the codec value of the majority of the clips in your sequence. For example, if your project contained an edited 40-minute sequence with clips captured at DV50, yet a special-effects company sent you three MOV files at 8-bit uncompressed, it would make the most sense to set your sequence settings to DV50 since the DV50 codec forms the majority. Prior to final output, you will usually need to render those clips whose codec differs from the sequence setting.

Final Cut Pro will always attempt to play back, in real time, any codec that does not correspond to the sequence settings. How Final Cut Pro will treat an element that requires rendering depends on the Real-Time Playback settings of your sequence. You can change the Real-Time Playback (often referred to as RT Playback) to access more playback options. However, the performance of the RT Playback is dependent on your system capabilities. A high CPU speed, multiple processors, maximum RAM, and increased Level 2 and Level 3 processor cache all serve to increase RT Playback in the Timeline. In addition, fast hard drives, fast bus speed, and an accelerated graphics card will also assist maximum RT Playback.

> **TIP** You will access more real-time performance if you disable external video monitoring. Use the shortcut Cmd-F12 to toggle external video monitoring on and off.

There are many useful configurations of RT settings and options. However, as a rule you can obtain a good balance of performance and quality by Ctrl-clicking the RT pop-up menu from your sequence and choosing the following options:

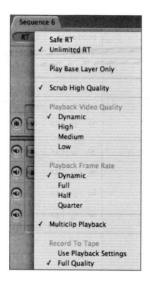

▶ Unlimited RT—Choosing this option tells Final Cut Pro to play as many effects as possible when the number of effects exceeds the processing capabilities of your system. You may experience dropped frames; however, this option is excellent for previewing your more complex composites. Also, activating Unlimited RT is the only way to view third-party FXScript filters and transitions that were built for playback utilizing the Final Cut Pro Real-Time Playback performance.

▶ Scrub High Quality—Choosing this option enables video displayed in the Canvas to be shown at full quality when you scrub or park the playhead. Although this can be useful for checking the image quality or colors of a clip, you may want to toggle it on and off. Consider deselecting this option if you are working with CPU-intensive video codecs such as HD.

▶ Playback Video Quality: Dynamic—Choosing Dynamic allows Final Cut Pro to automatically change between high, medium, and low video playback quality. Enabling this option allows you to view more real-time effects.

> ▶ Playback Frame Rate: Dynamic—Final Cut Pro will automatically reduce or increase the frame rate so that you can view the most possible real-time effects. Although this is useful, toggle this option back to Full after you have finished viewing your effects or composites. Choosing Full will return the frame rate play back to the editing timebase set in your sequence settings.

These options allow for increased RT playback. Toggle among the RT playback options to find settings that will work best with your project.

Lesson Review

1. It's always helpful to talk with your sound recordist, but in one situation it's vital. When is that?

2. What are the two types of timecode called?

3. Describe a simple and effective way to keep your media structure organized.

4. What makes using markers so handy?

5. When can you reconnect media during the editing process?

6. Technically, what are you doing when you reconnect clips in your project?

7. Where is the file path of a connected clip stored?

Answers

1. If your sound is delivered on a medium separate from the picture tapes, you must discuss the original sound recording settings.

2. Source and sequence.

3. Creating separate folders for materials that are not captured via tape, such as music and graphics.

4. It's an effective way to sync video and audio and to break down long clips.

5. Whenever you want to.

6. You are establishing a relationship between the clip in the Browser and the media file located on your drive.

7. In the clip's Source property.

4

Lesson Files   Lessons > Lesson 04 > Lesson 04 Project.fcp, Lesson 04 Database, Lesson 04 Connect Clips, Lesson 04 Manual Database, Lesson 04 Conform Database, Lesson 04 Reverse Telecine

Media   Media > Lesson 04 Media

Time   This lesson takes approximately 90 minutes to complete.

Goals   Learn the traditional film workflow and terminology

Plan a film workflow

Determine film, sound, and telecine specifications

Create and export a Cinema Tools database

Connect clips to the database

Prepare the clips for editing in Final Cut Pro

Set up a Cinema Tools project in Final Cut Pro

Determine how to effectively use effects, transitions, and filters

Visually identify duplicate frames

Gathering and Editing Film

In the previous chapter, you learned the principles of gathering and editing video, which shaped an important foundation for working with film.

If your project was shot on 35mm or 16mm film, and you plan to finish on film, you need to design a workflow that allows you to generate an accurate cut list so that you can conform your original film. This type of project, which originates and finishes on film, requires an offline workflow in Final Cut Pro that incorporates Cinema Tools.

There are many variations of professional film workflows; for the purposes of these exercises, you'll observe an example of a typical film workflow. Your film project specifications may vary, but the principles of film workflow will still apply. In this lesson, you will learn how to plan and organize a film project, gather media, and leverage Cinema Tools to track your original film and audio sources.

Traditional Film Workflow

In order to gain a greater understanding of your Final Cut Pro film workflow, let's first look at a conventional film-nonlinear-film workflow:

▶ Expose the negative on a series of camera rolls on the film set.

▶ Record sound on the film set.

▶ Develop camera roll negatives at a lab, and join them to form lab rolls for printing.

  NOTE ▶ The lab rolls of the processed negative are what a negative cutter uses to create the final cut negative once you have locked the cut.

▶ Transfer sound to a tape format, or deliver it as data files.

▶ Print lab rolls to create a work print.

▶ Cut the work print into daily rolls.

▶ Sync daily rolls with sound, and then project them.

▶ Send daily rolls and sound to the telecine bay to be transferred to tape.

▶ Import a flex file using Cinema Tools, and create a database.

  NOTE ▶ A flex file contains all the metadata that is added during a telecine session: tape name, start timecode, duration, daily roll, ink number, and key number.

▶ Export a batch list or XML file from Cinema Tools.

  MORE INFO ▶ See the XML section in Lesson 5 for more details on XML files.

▶ Capture the source clips with Final Cut Pro.

▶ Connect the clips to the database.

▶ Edit the clips in Final Cut Pro.

▶ Create cut lists and change lists with Cinema Tools.

▶ Once the edit is complete, conform the work print to match the cut from Final Cut Pro. Screen a preview from the conformed work print.

▶ Make final changes in the edit, and lock it.

▶ Make a final change list in Cinema Tools, and conform a final work print.

▶ Send the sound files, a duplicate of the work print, cut lists, and change lists to the sound department.

▶ Send the work print, along with detailed cut lists and change lists, to the negative cutter. The negative cutter conforms the negative and matches the cut to the Cinema Tools cut list.

▶ Create an answer print from the conformed negative and final sound. This print is used for final color correction.

▶ Once the answer print is made, make multiple prints for distribution to theaters.

This breakdown is very general, but it helps clarify where Final Cut Pro and Cinema Tools fit within the entire film workflow.

Film Terminology Primer

A brief film primer will help you understand the film workflow process.

Film

Perhaps the most significant feature of editing with the physical medium of film is that editing requires specially equipped film cutting rooms; film must be viewed in a nonlinear fashion, and it requires a large amount of physical space to store. Film has traditionally been used in offline workflows because the proxy image (the work print) is aesthetically close to the source image (the negative).

Creating a Work Print

When you expose the negative in the camera on set, you create source media. Remember that film negative is not necessarily fragile, it's just very valuable. You want the negative to look as pristine as possible when you conform your final film, and so rather than edit with the negative, in traditional film workflows you create another print of the film, commonly referred to as a *work print*.

Key Numbers

Your negative has a unique set of coding on the edge of the film. This code is called a *key number*. It's also referred to as a *key code* or an *edge number*. Key numbers do not appear on every frame. For 35mm film, they appear every 64 perforations; for 16mm film, they appear every 20 or 40 frames (depending on film stock). However, you will notice that key numbers have a numerical extension that is added when the negative is developed. For example, *+04* at the end of a key number indicates that you are viewing the fourth frame from the original key number. When you make a work print, these numbers are transferred onto the work print, thereby creating a numerical link between the negative and the work print.

Lab Rolls

When the lab processes the negative, it combines the relatively short camera rolls into larger reels called *lab rolls*. Lab rolls can become quite large, and they are usually assembled by camera-order. However, you'll commonly view your material in take-order, so many people choose to create *daily rolls*.

Daily Rolls

To make daily rolls, you cut up the lab rolls and reassemble the material into the order you prefer. Generally, a daily roll contains an entire day of shot material. The primary function of daily rolls is to structure the material so that it is easy for you to find, watch, and store.

Ink Numbers

Once you have assembled the daily rolls, you code the frames with *ink numbers*. This number is also referred to as an *ink code, edge code,* or *Acmade code*. Ink numbers are added to the edge of the work print and sound reel to maintain sync. This is a second set of tracking information on the film; *key numbers* relate to the negative, and *ink numbers* relate to the work print.

Screening Dailies

The daily rolls are typically screened for the director, the DP, and other department heads. As a rule, dailies are screened daily during the shooting phase of a film production, so the name *dailies* became the term for the first screening of the assembled material. Dailies serve many purposes, from allowing the department heads to review their work to checking the quality of the negative or sound.

Performing a Telecine

Once you are done viewing dailies, you have the daily rolls and the corresponding sound files transferred to videotape. This process is called *telecine*.

> **NOTE ▶** The term *telecine* can be a verb, as in "can you telecine this for me?" It can also be a noun, as in "can you bring the film to telecine?"

When you perform a telecine, the primary goal is to transfer the image from film to video, and it's also important to transfer as much of the film metadata as possible. The film metadata is recorded in a data file and on the image itself, in timecode window burns. You can record all manner of metadata, but the primary metadata for most film projects is the key number, ink number, daily roll number (stored in the ink number prefix), timecode, videotape reel number, and often the name of the production. In general, the key numbers are automatically read from the film; the ink numbers are input by the telecine operator; and the timecode is automatically generated during the telecine process.

SMPTE clapboard (or smart slate)   DAT timecode

Tape timecode   Key number

When you perform a telecine, the operator will produce an electronic file describing the metadata accumulated during the telecine. Each record in the telecine electronic file is commonly referred to as an *event*. By recording an event at the start of each take or camera roll, you combine the metadata that correlates the timecode, ink number, and the key number for each record. Basically, the electronic file is what you will load into Cinema Tools to form your database, and subsequently you will export the metadata to batch capture in Final Cut Pro.

Telecine Paperwork

Be prepared to deliver a list of shots to the telecine operator prior to your session. It's common to generate a shot list in some form of database program such as FileMaker Pro or Excel. Your shot list should contain as much information as possible, including at least the shot names and start key numbers and ink numbers of each shot. Most telecine machines can preload information contained in a shot list to a telecine log file. Providing the telecine log file ahead of time will allow the operator to be more precise, and you will get back greater detail for your Cinema Tools database.

> **TIP** ▶ Some telecine machines still use a floppy disk drive. Call the facility prior to your session to check what ejectable devices they can support.

Most telecine machines have a feature that will automatically capture a new event for every change in key numbers. This method is accurate, but if there are two consecutive shots with continuous key numbers, it doesn't record an event for the second shot. You can manually enter the information for the second shot in Cinema Tools, but you can save considerable time if you prepare your paperwork prior to your telecine session.

Organizing Film Projects

As with a video project, before you begin, you need to establish a framework for your project—a clear path from beginning to end. Planning is beneficial for any project, and taking time to organize your post-production process during the pre-production of a film will help you determine your best approach.

Planning a Film Workflow

To ensure success, begin your planning early. When you edit film on a nonlinear system there are many considerations. You will need to decide which film format to use, which frame rate to use for the telecine transfer, which editing timebase you will use, what sound recorder and sound timebase to use, and how to sync the sound with the film.

Aside from the technical preparation, you need to have an idea of who's who. Introduce yourself to everyone involved in the production process. Make sure to introduce yourself to the personnel at the facility who will develop your film, work prints, and release prints; the telecine operator; the negative cutter; and the audio post-production team. An early dialogue with anyone directly involved in handling your film will establish communication and help you streamline your process.

Determining Film Specifications

Consider which film format you use. Cinema Tools supports 35mm 4-perf, 35mm 3-perf, and 16mm-20 film formats.

Determining Telecine Specifications

You must decide on video frame rates, how and what to transfer, and what aesthetic look to apply to your film. Telecine machines are expensive and have to be used in a facility that provides a trained operator. Any decisions regarding your transfer process should be made prior to your session, so you should run a couple of tests prior to committing to an entire process.

When deciding how much to transfer during a telecine session, you will need to choose between transferring by complete *camera roll* or selectively by *scene-and-take*:

▶   Camera roll—If you decide to transfer an entire roll of film continuously, you need only one event for Cinema Tools to establish the metadata link between the film and video. Although Cinema Tools will generate an accurate cut list from a camera-roll clip with a single event, if you prefer, you can create additional records in Cinema Tools at any time during the course of your project. Camera-roll transfer has its drawbacks, however. Syncing the audio onto the videotape during the telecine can be difficult. When a film is shot, typically you will begin the audio recording before and after the film starts and stops rolling, which means you won't be able to maintain sync from the beginning of the camera roll through the end. In the case of transferring by camera roll, you will need to sync the audio in Final Cut Pro. (See Lesson 3 for sync steps.)

▶   Scene-and-take—If you decide to transfer only the scenes and takes you need, your telecine can be a little more expensive than if you telecine the camera roll. The benefit of transferring scene-and-take is that your audio is easier to sync during the telecine. Also, an event will be logged for each clip, minimizing your manual data entry in Cinema Tools.

Film runs at a frame rate of 24 fps. Video runs at 29.97 fps NTSC; 25 fps PAL; or 24 fps (24p)—depending on your video standard. You can choose among a number of options for the distribution of film's 24 fps among the frame rates of NTSC and PAL.

▶ NTSC—Performing a 3:2 pull-down is the most common way to transfer film to NTSC video. This is also known as a pull-down pattern of 2:3:2:3. (See the section on 24p in Lesson 7 for further technical details.) Since there is no neat calculation for squeezing 24 frames of film into 30 frames of video, the 3:2 pull-down gives you the right equation to transfer the film.

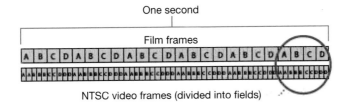

One second

Film frames

NTSC video frames (divided into fields)

NOTE ▶ In the preceding illustration, the A frame is a complete frame of film in a video frame, which makes it a perfect frame to begin a video clip. For simplification, you will usually ask the telecine operator to set the A frames to start at non-drop-frame timecode numbers ending in 5 or 0.

With the 3:2 pull-down, a film frame is added or subtracted to the video frames in order to make them match.

In order to edit film at it's native frame rate of 24 fps, you can use the Reverse Telecine feature in Cinema Tools. The Reverse Telecine feature restores a one-to-one correlation between the film and video.

▶ PAL—Because PAL is 25 fps and closer to the film frame rate, the calculation is more straightforward. You can either transfer the film by running the film at 25 fps, commonly referred to as the 24@25 method, or by using the 24&1 method. The 24&1 method adds two extra fields per second. One extra field is added to the 12th and 24th film frame.

▶   24p—This is the ideal frame rate because it has a one-to-one correlation with film. Other factors make 24p an ideal format: its progressive frame rate and high spatial quality replicate film's aesthetic. You will need the right hardware (24p VTR) to capture 24p.

You need to bring a variety of materials to your telecine sessions—typically, the work print, sound files, paperwork, and an electronic file that contains a list of all the events you want the telecine operator to record. You will also need to consider how you want to adjust the color and contrast of each scene. During the telecine session, you will set your basic color and contrast, and after your picture edit is complete, you will fine-tune your color adjustments with a colorist.

When you complete your telecine, you'll receive two critical pieces of material: your videotapes and an electronic file called a telecine log file, which contains the metadata recorded during your telecine session. You should also ask for a printout of the telecine log file. Be sure to check your information as soon as possible. Make sure you have the correct tapes, files, and number of events, and that your sound is in sync.

Determining Sound Specifications
When you begin a film project, the task of defining your sound specifications is similar to that of a video project. For film, sound is recorded on separate media, so the main factors you need to be concerned with are frame rate, sync, and final mix.

During the film shoot, you will usually have your choice of timecode standards: 30 fps, 29.97 fps (non-drop-frame and drop-frame), 25 fps, or 24 fps. Ideally, you should choose your recording timecode standard based on your video transfer timecode standard. Matching the audio timebase to the video transfer timebase is standard practice because the sync process is easier. This standard is especially true if you are syncing during the telecine.

TIP ▶ If you are editing in NTSC, use non-drop frame timebase for both video and audio.

When you achieve sync through the telecine transfer, you need to maintain the original audio timecode records. Capturing your original audio timecode information will be imperative if you plan to export the audio information in an EDL for a professional audio mix. Check that your original audio timecode is recorded in the event log during your telecine session. You may also need to compensate for a particular format; NTSC and PAL transfers can alter how you transfer your audio in order to maintain correct sync.

▶ NTSC audio transfer—During a telecine session, film must be slowed down 0.1 percent (from 24 fps to 23.967 fps) in order to compensate for the NTSC actual frame rate of 29.97 fps. If the film must be slowed, audio must be slowed down also to maintain sync.

▶ PAL audio transfer—If you use the 24@25 method of video transfer, you will speed up the video from 24 fps to 25 fps. Your audio will need to be sped up by the same amount. However, if you are using the 24&1 method of video transfer, you should run your audio at 25 fps.

If you do not sync during the telecine process, you will capture separate video and audio files and sync your clips directly in Final Cut Pro. (See the exercise in the "Capture Media By Complete Tape" section of Lesson 3.)

TIP ▶ Using the Conform feature in Cinema Tools will let you achieve a change in audio frame rate. You can also modify the speed of an audio clip directly in Final Cut Pro. To achieve a speed change in Final Cut Pro, simply select the clips you wish to change, choose Modify > Speed, and apply the appropriate speed change. For example, for NTSC you will apply a speed change of 99.9%. This will slow down the audio by 0.1%.

Organizing Media

Film projects share the same rules of media organization as video. (See the section on organizing media in Lesson 3.) However, because the clip names in Final Cut Pro film projects are a result of your Cinema Tools database, you need to consider the appropriate film clip naming conventions:

▶ Scene and take—Cinema Tools creates a clip name by using the scene and take number. If your clip is from scene 50, take 1, it will be named 50-1.

▶ Reel and timecode—Where no scene and take number exist, Cinema Tools will use the reel number and timecode of a clip. Therefore, a clip with a reel number of 003 and timecode of 01:01:01;01 would be named 003-01.01.01.01.

▶ Unique names—Cinema Tools identifies clips with identical names, which may be created when you are shooting with multiple cameras. In these cases, Cinema Tools adds the roll or reel number to the end of the clip. If you have multiple angles, let's say you've shot roll 3A and roll 3B that both captured scene 23 take 2, then your clips will be named 23-2 and 23-2B. Where no roll identifiers exist, a number will be added to index the second clip. For example, the second occurrence of the identical clip name 23-2B would become 23-2_1.

▶ Database accuracy—Always check your database before exporting it to Final Cut Pro. In List view, sort by Slate, and ensure your clip names are unique. If you find any duplicate names, modify the record in the Scene or Take fields. Do not modify clip names once they are captured.

▶ Burn-in accuracy—Check the accuracy of your window burns. You're relying on this information throughout your project, so it's important that the information is correct. Spot-check each record against your logs, and compare the displayed video timecode against the timecode displayed on your deck.

Cinema Tools

Cinema Tools is your metadata tracking database, which allows you to edit film transferred to video and return to film to conform the work print and negative. Cinema Tools works closely with Final Cut Pro to track more than your film metadata; it also tracks duplicate frames, opticals, and titles.

NOTE ▶ *Duplicate frames* are any additional frames of negative that must be optically reproduced. *Opticals* include transitions and motion effects. You need to account for duplicate frames, opticals, and titles in the final film conform because they can increase the budget.

Although you can create a new database and enter information manually in Cinema Tools, you will usually work with a telecine event log to kick-start your database. Your typical workflow with Cinema Tools and Final Cut Pro will include the following steps:

▶   Create and export a Cinema Tools database.

▶   Capture the source clips in Final Cut Pro.

▶   Connect the clips to the database.

▶   Prepare and edit the clips in Final Cut Pro.

▶   Create cut, duplicate, optical, and title lists with Cinema Tools. (See Lesson 6.)

The Database

The Cinema Tools database is at the center of your project. You'll use it to track all your elements. Your database must include the camera roll, daily roll or lab roll numbers, and the edge code. And it must have a clip connected to it or have video reel or video timecode numbers. Cinema Tools uses these values to produce a cut list. If a record is inadequate, Cinema Tools will flag it in the cut list as <missing >; you can produce a missing elements list through Cinema Tools. After you identify missing elements, you can update your database within Cinema Tools.

Your Cinema Tools database can be detailed or streamlined. You can work in many different ways, by scene-and-take or camera roll. You can add, delete, and merge databases. In the next section of this lesson, you will work with a detailed database. You'll use a project of your own to practice importing a log from a telecine session and add new records.

Import a Telecine Log

Cinema Tools supports the telecine log formats of ALE, FTL, FLX, and ATN. Although you can import a telecine log directly into Cinema Tools, importing the log through Final Cut Pro is easier because the offline clips from the telecine log will be imported into Final Cut Pro simultaneously.

1   From your own Final Cut Pro project, choose File > Import > Cinema Tools Telecine Log.

2   Click the Choose Database button.

> **TIP**▶ If you are working with multiple camera angles, and you need to add a camera letter, then choose the Add Camera Letter option, and choose the applicable camera letter from the pop-up menu.

3   Navigate to your telecine log, and click Choose.

Your offline clips will appear in Final Cut Pro ready for batch capturing.

You can also import your telecine log directly from Cinema Tools:

1   Choose Database > New Database.

2   From the pop-up menu, choose all your settings: Film Standard, Video TC Rate, Audio TC Rate, and TK Speed.

3   Name the database, and choose a location to save the file.

> **TIP**▶ Save all your databases together in a folder titled by project name (for example, SU&FR_Project_databases). Be methodical and organized; back up your databases together with your Final Cut Pro projects daily.

Although you can export a standard batch list, export an XML batch list instead. An XML batch list is incredibly useful because it gives you access to all the film metadata that's viewable in Final Cut Pro. (See Lesson 5 for more information on XML, eXtensible Markup Language.)

1   In Cinema Tools, choose Database > Open Database.

2   Navigate to the Lessons folder. Click to select **Lesson 04 Database**, then click Open.

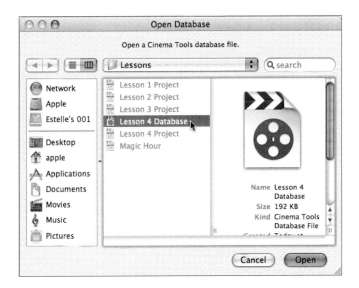

The database opens, displaying a List view and a Detail view. No clips are connected to this database.

TIP ➤ You cannot export an XML batch list from a database that has clips connected. You must first disconnect the clips prior to the export.

3   Choose File > Export > XML Batch List.

4   Save the export XML batch list as *Lesson 4 XML export*, and click Save.

5   Open the **Lesson 04 Project.fcp** file to launch Final Cut Pro.

6   Choose File > Import > XML.

7 Navigate to the Lesson 4 XML export file, click to select it, then click
Choose to import.

The Import XML dialog opens.

You have the flexibility to choose a number of settings, from importing a
new project to including markers and effects.

8   In the Destination pop-up menu, choose **Lesson 04 Project**.

9   For the Sequence Settings, choose DV NTSC 48 kHz, and select the Override With Settings From XML check box.

10   Deselect all of the check boxes in the Options section of the dialog, and click OK.

Your offline clips are imported into your project, ready for batch capturing. They all contain the film metadata and are linked to your Cinema Tools database.

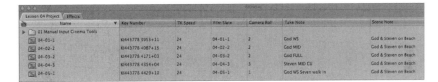

TIP ▶ You can view the film metadata directly in the Browser or through the clip Properties window.

Manual Database Input

If you have no transfer logs, you can manually enter information into your Cinema Tools database. You will need a record for every clip that has either non-continuous timecode or key numbers. For scene-and-take, since each take may jump key numbers, you create a record for every take. For camera-roll transfers, since the key number runs continuously, you need one record for the entire clip. Although it can be tedious, entering information manually into a Cinema Tools database is easy, especially if you have the key numbers and video timecode burned into the frame.

NOTE ▶ In these steps, you are viewing the clips directly in Cinema Tools. Typically, entering information into a Cinema Tools database would be done prior to capture, and you would use a deck to view your footage. However, it's useful to know that you can create a database no matter what approach you use.

1   From Cinema Tools, close **Lesson 04 Database**.

2   Choose Database > New Database.

3   Select the following settings: Film Standard = 35mm 4p, Video TC Rate = 30 NDF, Audio TC Rate = 30 NDF, and TK Speed = 24. Then click OK.

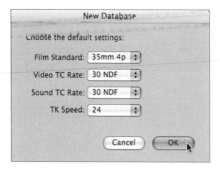

4   Navigate to the Lessons folder, name your new database *Lesson 4 Manual Entry Database*, and click Save.

Two database windows open—List View and Detail View. You will enter information in the Detail View window.

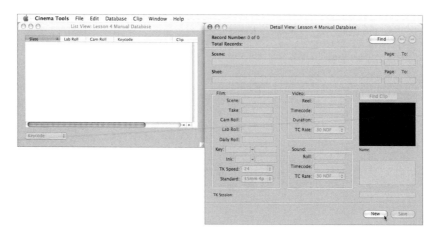

5   Choose File > Open Clip.

6   Navigate to Media > Lesson 04 Media > CT Manual File Entry folder. Select the clip named **04-04-1**, and click Choose to open it.

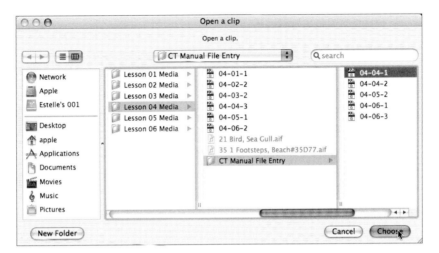

7   Arrange the Detail View window and clip window so that you can see each side by side.

8   In the Clip window, click the Enter In DB box.

9   Enter *Scene: 04, Take: 04*, and click OK.

> **NOTE** ▶ In film language, the clip name *04-04-1* represents scene-take-angle.

The video information is automatically entered into your database, and the clip is connected.

> **NOTE** ▶ You could also enter the scene and shot information manually and connect the clip afterwards. Once you have entered the scene and shot information, in the Detail View window you can connect the clip of the record by clicking Connect Clip. If you make a mistake, in the Clip window simply disconnect the clip by clicking Disconnect.

10   Enter the Scene description.

This scene is from Jesse Costello's film *Straighten Up and Fly Right*. It's a beach scene between two characters, God and Steven, so name the scene *God & Steven on Beach*.

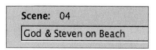

11   Enter the Key number. Look on the Clip window and make sure you are parked on the first frame of video.

The key number is the number that begins with a K.

12 Play the clip in the Clip window, and when you see a frame that is representative of the entire clip, pause the playback, and click Poster Frame.

13 Enter an appropriate take note under the poster frame in the Detail View window.

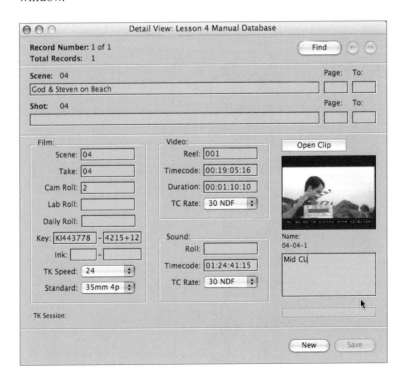

Once you have finished entering information in the database, close the Clip window and repeat steps 5 through 13 to complete the remaining clips.

14 After you have completed the exercise, press Cmd-W to close **Lesson 04 Manual Database.**

In this exercise, you manually entered minimum information. Of course, there are many details you left out that you would normally enter, such as the Camera, Daily, Lab, and Sound Roll numbers. The sound timecode information could also be entered from the clapboard timecode. Entering additional information enables greater tracking capabilities and increases your conform accuracy.

> **NOTE ▶** If you are only working with film negative, you won't need to enter the Daily Roll or Ink numbers. Entering a Daily Roll and Ink number applies only to film projects that print a work print.

> **TIP ▶** If you want to include the sound roll and timecode information in the preceding exercise, you can do so by adding it to each record. The sound roll number for these clips is 01. Add the sound timecode from the clapboard timecode reading at the head of each clip.

Connect Clips on Command

You can connect multiple clips to your database by using the Connect Clips command. This is especially useful because you can automate the process of connecting. You can use the Find command to find selected records to connect, or you can use it to show all records.

1 Choose Database > Open Database.

2 Navigate to the Lessons folder, click the **Lesson 04 Connect Clips** database, and click Open.

3 Click the List View window to activate it.

4 Choose Keycode from the pop-up menu to view the keycode information.

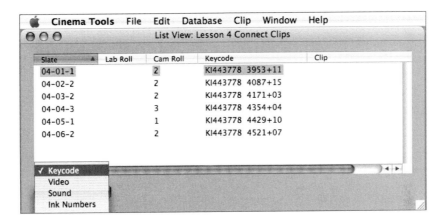

5 Press Cmd-F to display the Find dialog window.

6 Click the Find All button to display all records in the database.

> **NOTE** ▶ Activate the Find feature in the Detail view by clicking the Find button. You can search for scene and take by exact and similar values. You can replace or add to an existing list or show the entire database. This is useful when you're searching for particular scenes or records, especially once a database contains a lot of records.

7 Choose Database > Connect Clips.

8 Navigate to the Lesson 04 Media folder, and select the clip named 04-01-1.

Every record that matches a clip name in the same directory will be connected to the database.

9   After you have completed the exercise, press Cmd-W to close **Lesson 04 Connect Clips** database.

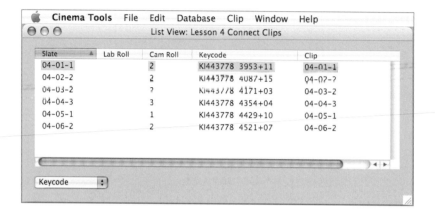

TIP ▶ You should not rename or move a clip once it is connected. If you do, the clip-to-database link is broken. As long as you have not renamed a clip, you can fix a broken link by using the Reconnect Clips command. The Reconnect Clips command works in the same way as the Connect Clips command: choose Database > Reconnect Clips, and navigate to the location of your clips.

Prepping the Clips

Prior to editing, you need to decide exactly how you will treat your footage. You have two Cinema Tools features to consider: Conform and Reverse Telecine.

Conform

The Conform feature provides a great way to correct video clip frame duration errors or change the frame rate of a clip. Every QuickTime file has a frame duration setting that tells each frame how long to display, such as 1/25th of a second for PAL. Occasionally, this frame duration during capture is set to inconsistent values. On playback, visually you will not notice the difference in the clip. However, if the clip has inconsistent frame durations, you will get errors in your cut list or errors during a reverse telecine. In these cases, you would simply reapply a clip's frame rate to reset the frame duration.

> **TIP** ▶ You can check and mark long frames in Final Cut Pro. From the Browser, simply select the clip or clips you wish to check and choose Tools > Long Frames > Mark. Any clips that have long frames will be marked, and you can correct them by using the Cinema Tools Conform feature. Once you have completed the conform, you can clear the marked long frames by choosing Tools > Long Frames > Clear.

You can also use the Conform feature to *change* a clip's frame rate, choosing among 23.98, 24, 25, 29.97, and 30 fps. If your clip contains video and audio, the audio rate will be adjusted to maintain sync. You can apply the Conform feature to a clip with or without a database record.

1   Choose Database > Open Database.

2   Navigate to the Lessons folder. Click the **Lesson 04 Database**, and click Open.

3   In the Detail View window, click Open.

4   In the clip window, click Conform.

5   From the Conform To pop-up menu, choose the frame rate you want to conform to, then click Conform.

TIP ▶ You can batch conform all files in the same directory. Choose File > Batch Conform, navigate to the directory containing the clips you want to conform, select a single clip, and click Choose. The batch conform will be applied to all clips contained in the same directory.

TIP ▶ Using Final Cut Pro 5, you can conform 25 fps to 24 fps directly from Final Cut Pro. From the Browser, simply select the clip you wish to conform from 25 fps to 24 fps and choose Tools > Conform 25 to 24.

Reverse Telecine

During your telecine, you converted your 24 fps film to 30 fps video. If you're planning to edit your project at 24 fps, you need to apply the Reverse Telecine feature. This feature, which reverses the 3:2 pull-down, applies to NTSC transfers only. It works by removing the extra fields that were applied during your telecine transfer.

TIP ▶ Allow for processing time when performing a reverse telecine in Cinema Tools. For a large number of clips, set up a batch reverse telecine and let your computer run overnight.

1   Choose Database > Open Database.

2   Navigate to the Lessons folder, select **Lesson 04 Reverse Telecine** and click Open.

3   In the Detail View window, click Open Clip.

4   Press the right arrow key on your keyboard to step through the clip frame by frame, and park the playhead on an A frame.

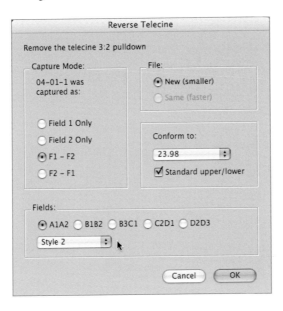

Pay particular attention to the key number frame indicators at the end of the key number. Notice that the key number pattern on these clips is A1A2, B1B2, B3C1, C2D1, D2D3. Also note that there seems to be two fields displayed simultaneously, indicated by the number displayed at the end of the timecode number.

Identifying your film pattern is important. You will need to establish the sequence of your film frame numbers and fields in order to enter them into the Reverse Telecine dialog box. Cinema Tools needs this information to reverse telecine your footage correctly.

5   In the clip window, click Reverse Telecine to display the Reverse Telecine dialog box.

6   In the Capture Mode area, select F1 – F2.

We established our field and key number pattern for these tutorial clips, and based on that information, you can select the appropriate actions in the dialog. Here is how the patterns break down:

Key Number Pattern	Field Pattern	Capture Mode
AA, BB, BC, CD, DD or A1A2, B1B2, B3C1, C2D1, D2D3	Both fields with field 1 dominance	F1 – F2
AB, BB, CC, DD, DA, or A2B1, B2B3, C1C2, D1D2, D3A1	Both fields with field 2 dominance	F2 – F1
A, B, B, C, D or A1, B1, B3, C2, D1	One field with field 1 dominance	Field 1 Only
A, B, C, D, D or A2, B2, C1, D1, D3	One field with field 2 dominance	Field 2 Only

7   Choose Style 2 from the Style Type pop-up menu. You also need to select the frame type corresponding to the frame currently displayed in the clip window. You parked the playhead on the A frame so you can select A1A2 from the Fields options.

8   In the File area, select New (Smaller).

If you reverse telecine a single field (Field 1 *or* Field 2 only), you have the option of selecting either a New or Same file. The New option creates a new file in the same directory as your source and applies a .rev file extension after the name. A New file is smaller than the source. The Same option applies changes to the original clip; no data is removed, it simply does not display the extra frames in the editing system.

TIP ▶ If you are creating new files, you have already performed a test to check that your settings are correct, and you no longer need the original file. Simply remove the .rev extension when prompted, and replace the original file with the New clip.

9 Choose 23.98 from the Conform To pop-up menu.

The benefit of choosing 23.98 fps is that you can use the Final Cut Pro pull-down feature to output your 23.98 fps video sequence as 29.97 fps. Choose 24 if you output tapes with a 24 fps video deck.

10 Select the Standard Upper/Lower check box.

11 Click OK to begin the process.

TIP ▶ Before you apply your reverse telecine settings on the entire film, check your results on a single clip to make sure there are no errors. After your first clip has finished processing, step through it frame by frame. You should clearly see the A, B, C, D sequence. Each frame should be fully visible, legible, and sequential. If this is not the case, disconnect the clip from your database, and reconnect the record to the original clip. Try applying a different style from the Field Style pop-up menu or deselecting the Standard Upper/Lower check box.

Once you have successfully performed a reverse telecine on a single clip, you can batch telecine the remaining clips. This is useful because you'll be able to apply your settings to an entire directory of clips. Choose File > Batch Reverse Telecine, navigate to the directory containing your clips, check your Reverse Telecine settings, and click OK. You will notice that Cinema Tools will place three new folders and one text file in the original directory: one folder containing your original clips, one folder containing your reversed clips, one folder containing any skipped clips, and a text file containing a log report. Once the batch reverse telecine is complete, you will need to reconnect your database records to the new reversed clips.

TIP Using Final Cut Pro 5, you can perform a Cinema Tools reverse telecine directly from your Final Cut Pro project. Simply select the clip you wish to reverse telecine and choose Tools > Cinema Tools Reverse Telecine.

Film in Final Cut Pro

Since your final medium is film, every decision you make to your final edit will have direct implications on your final film conform. When editing a film-based project in Final Cut Pro, you need to be aware of your editing timebase, video and audio track limitations, film effects, transitions, filters, and duplicate frames.

Setting Up Your Project

There are many methods of configuring a Final Cut Pro film project. Your project specifications may differ from the ones we use in this lesson, but you can use these exercises as a general guide. For the purposes of this section, we'll focus on the most important project settings.

The Editing Timebase

Make sure you set the editing timebase of your project to match the frame rate of your clips. You can set the timebase manually through the Audio/Video Settings or directly in the Sequence Settings or choose from a number of pre-installed Easy Setups. You have a number of Easy Setups to choose from that are designed specifically for use with Cinema Tools.

1   Navigate to the Lessons folder, and double click **Lesson 04 Project.fcp** to launch Final Cut Pro.

2   Choose Final Cut Pro > Easy Setup.

3 Select the Show All check box.

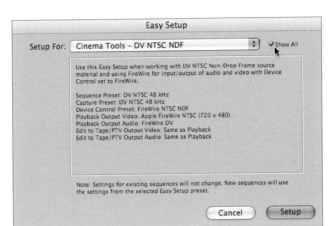

4 Select Cinema Tools – DV NTSC NDF from the Setup For pop-up menu.

Multiple Tracks

While editing a film project, you can edit as you would for a video project. However, for the final sequences, you need to follow the film conform rules:

▶ In your final sequences, use tracks 1 and 2 only. Other tracks will be ignored in the Cinema Tools cut list.

▶ Video edits and transitions must be on video track 1.

▶ Titles and superimposed effects must be on video track 2.

▶ If you plan to export an audio EDL, use only the first eight audio tracks.

Film Effects and Transitions

Final Cut Pro has many effects and transitions, which you'll need to create for your final film. It's great to use Final Cut Pro to experiment with transition type or timing, and choosing an effect is more cost efficient in Final Cut Pro than printing and experimenting on film. While you edit, keep in mind that effects fall into two categories:

▶ Basic effects—Basic transitions and effects include dissolves, wipes, titles, and motion effects. Talk to your effects lab to find out exactly what effects it offers and how much the effects will cost. Your effects lab will use the instructions you supplied in the Cinema Tools list to create the effects. Basic effects are usually created through contact printing or optical printing.

▶ Complex effects—Any effect that requires a composite, blue screen, animation, or detailed motion is produced by scanning film digitally. By scanning the negative, restoring, and reprinting, you also remove scratches, dirt, or hair from your negative.

NOTE ▶ In contact printing, you use the original negative. Optical printing requires printing a new negative.

Filters

You can apply filters, including color corrections, to your clips in Final Cut Pro, but they will not be tracked in your Cinema Tools cut list. It's an excellent idea to envision a film color correction or filter by applying them during your editing process, although a color corrector (also called a color timer) will complete the process for your finished film. Output a QuickTime file or tape as a visual reference.

Duplicate Frames

Since every duplicate frame means duplicating the original negative, which will increase the cost of your final film, keeping track of duplicate frames is important. You can display duplicate frames in Final Cut Pro, which gives you a visual aid for identifying duplicate frames. You can set duplicate frames to display in every new sequence, or toggle it on and off in your current sequence.

1   Open the Duplicate Frames sequence.

2   Choose Show Duplicate Frames from the Track Layout pop-up menu in the Timeline.

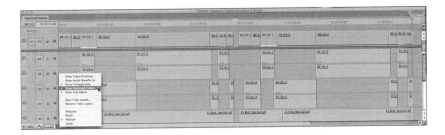

Notice the colored bars that appear at the bottom of each clip. These are the duplicate frame indicators. Each color set corresponds to the matching duplicate. Where duplicate frames fall within a transition you will see the duplicates indicated as white dots.

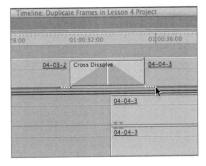

3   Choose Final Cut Pro > User Preferences.

4   Click the Timeline Options tab.

5   Select the Show Duplicate Frames check box.

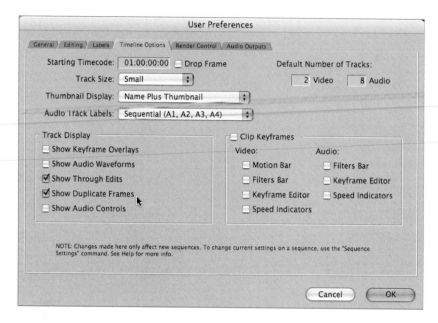

Setting Timeline Options in the User Preferences makes changes applicable to every *new* sequence.

The Cutback

When editing film, you need to allow for extra frames so that the negative cutter can make a splice. This is commonly referred to as a *cutback frame*. The negative cutter actually uses a portion of a frame (generally ½ to 1½ frames from the ingoing and outgoing clip) in order to cement two edited frames together. You should attempt to allow for this during your editing. The rule is that you should not cut back to the very next frame, because *that* frame needs to be preserved for the negative cutter to cut and cement the negative.

For 35mm film, allow 2 frames; for 16mm, allow 3 frames. Due to the smaller gauge, 16mm film requires a greater amount of cutback frames for the negative cutter.

Because you're editing on a nonlinear system, it's easy to forget about one or two frames. You can control your duplicate handle size and threshold frames in the Editing tab of User Preferences.

1   Choose Final Cut Pro > User Preferences.

2   Select the Editing tab.

3   Enter *2* in the Dupe Detection Handle Size field.

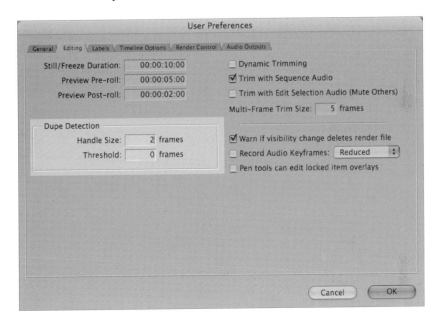

In this lesson, we have been using 35mm film. Enter *3* as your minimum in the Dupe Detection Handle Size frame entry box for 16mm film.

The Threshold field allows you to set a number for the minimum frames that must be duplicated prior to a frame indicator appearing in your sequence. This is very useful. For instance, if you set the handle size for cutback frames to 2, but your film budget allowed you the option of choosing to optically reproduce any frames that equaled 24 consecutively duplicated frames, you would enter 24 in the Threshold field. What this would do is limit the duplicate frame indicator in your Timeline. In this case, you will not see a duplicate frame indicator appearing in your Timeline whenever you hit 24 consecutive duplicate frames, because anything above that number will be optically reproduced. Basically, these options allow you to visually control how your duplicate frames are indicated in your Timeline.

Check, Change, and Synchronize

From time to time, you will need to access the film metadata of your clips. For instance, you may want to check the key number or ink number associated with a particular clip, or perhaps view the shot notes or scene notes. You can see this information directly in Final Cut Pro in the Item Properties Film tab.

1   Double click the *Scene 4* sequence in your Browser to open it into your Timeline.

2   Ctrl-click any video clip contained in the sequence.

3   Choose Item Properties > Film from the contextual menu.

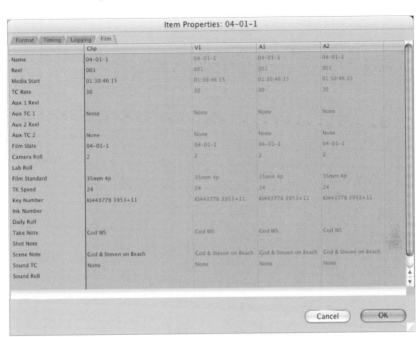

The Item Properties Film tab opens to reveal all the film metadata associated with the clip.

If you add or change information in your Cinema Tools database, you can update your film metadata directly from Final Cut Pro using the Synchronize with Cinema Tools command.

1   From Cinema Tools, make changes to your Cinema Tools database.

2   From the Browser, select the clips you wish to update.

3   Choose Tools > Synchronize with Cinema Tools.

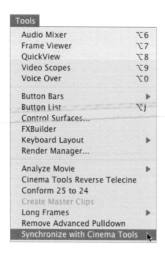

4   Choose your Cinema Tools database, or create a new database, then click OK.

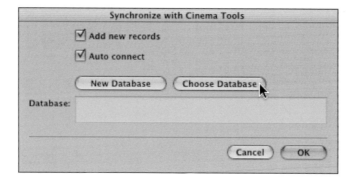

If you select Add New Records and Auto Connect and click New Database, you will export your Final Cut Pro clip metadata, create new records, connect the clips, and create a new database. This is an excellent option when you want to export film metadata from Final Cut Pro.

If you click Choose Database, navigate to your altered database, and then your clips in Final Cut Pro will be updated with the database additions.

Lesson Review

1. What film formats does Cinema Tools support?

2. What are the two main ways of transferring film during a telecine session?

3. How should the telecine operator set the A frames to start?

4. Why is it better to match the audio timebase to the video transfer time-base than the reverse?

5. What's the advantage of detailing or streamlining your Cinema Tools database?

6. What makes an XML batch list so useful?

7. What's a good way to correct video clip frame duration errors or change the frame rate of a clip?

8. For NTSC projects, what must you do if you are planning to edit your project at 24 fps?

Answers

1. Cinema Tools supports 35mm 4-perf and 16mm-20 film formats.

2. By complete camera roll or selectively by scene and take.

3. The A frames should start at non-drop-frame timecode numbers ending in 5 or 0.

4. The sync is easier to achieve that way.

5. You can work in many different ways, and you can add, delete, and merge databases.

6. It gives you access to all the film metadata that is viewable in Final Cut Pro.

7. Using the Conform feature.

8. You will need to apply Reverse Telecine.

5

Lesson Files   Lessons > Lesson 05 Project.fcp

Media   Media > Lesson 01 Media > The Magic Hour Media; Lesson 04 Media; Lesson 05 Media

Time   This lesson takes approximately 90 minutes to complete.

Goals   Share projects between Final Cut Pro users

Learn methods of exchanging information with other Apple Pro video applications

Define EDL, OMF, and XML and learn to export these files

Prepare your sequence for output

Output with Print to Video and Edit to Tape

Export your sequence using QuickTime movie and conversion

Batch export multiple elements

Lesson 5
Distributing Video Projects

Final Cut Pro is extremely flexible, and it is designed to enable the smooth exchange of information. You can share everything from projects, bins, sequences, and preferences to exports of OMF, EDL, and XML files. Beyond outputting to tape, Final Cut Pro easily integrates with Apple's family of professional applications. With third-party software like Automatic Duck, you can even exchange a complete project including edited sequences with other nonlinear editing systems.

In this lesson, you will learn traditional techniques of preparation for final output and organization of your project prior to delivery for an online session. You will examine methods of sharing your projects and sequences, and you will learn how to output video with an academy leader and exchange information with Apple's other Pro applications.

Sharing Projects

As with all workflow-related solutions, consider your sharing methods from the outset. Communicate with everyone involved on your project to determine how they will retrieve and send project information to ensure a successful approach.

Sharing in Final Cut Pro

It's a good idea to set up a clear method for exchanging sequences and projects between Final Cut Pro workstations. During the course of a project, you may exchange your project, sequences, and bins with other members of your production team, so you need to keep track of current versions and perhaps even who created them.

During the course of *The Magic Hour* project, there were a number of editors involved in the post-production who exchanged sequences, bins, and even filters. Since they worked as a team, it was important to determine an elegant system of exchange.

A variety of editors contributed the following techniques, which you can use to design your own method of organization:

▶ Include your initials and date at the end of your project name, bins, or sequences, such as *ProjectName_em_05262005* or *SequenceName_em_05262005*. This makes the process of identification clearer.

▶ Save a project named *Transfer* for transferring individual sequences or bins. When transferring individual elements, also label the elements with initials and date.

▶ Save a project named *FiltersandEffects* for saving and sharing your effects and filters.

> **TIP** You can save groups of filters on a video generator, like a color matte. Give the video generator an appropriate name, and use the copy and paste attributes option to place multiple filters on a clip. This is a very effective method because you don't need to apply the individual filters, and you don't need to remember the filter order.

▶ Use Media Manager to share a project and media in the same or different resolutions. (See Lesson 3 for details.)

NOTE ▶ If you are sharing projects that are using different resolutions, for example if you are sharing sequences between an OfflineRT and DVCPRO HD project, remember that you will need to reset the sequence settings.

NOTE ▶ When sharing Final Cut Pro projects, bins, and sequences, unless you're working with an identical media file structure, you may need to reconnect your media.

Exchanging with Pro Video Applications

Perhaps the most flexible and time-saving task you can accomplish with Final Cut Pro is the seamless exchange of information among the Apple Pro video applications. For instance, let's say you want to remove a city skyline in the background of a clip; you can send the clip directly to Shake from Final Cut Pro. You can easily exchange information with LiveType, Cinema Tools, Compressor, Soundtrack Pro, Logic, Motion, DVD Studio Pro, and Shake.

In Final Cut Pro, the Send To command lets you exchange information with Motion, Soundtrack Pro, and Shake.

You can also use the External Editor feature in Final Cut Pro to open the media file of a clip in another application. When you assign an application to a media file type, you can open a clip's media file through Final Cut Pro and automatically launch the assigned application. So for example, if you assigned Adobe Photoshop as your still-image external editor, you could open the still clip in Photoshop using External Editor, alter the file, save, return to Final Cut Pro, and the still image would be updated automatically.

1   Press Shift-Q to launch the System Settings dialog.

2   Click the External Editors tab.

3   Click Set, and then navigate to the Applications folder.

4   Click Preview, and then click Choose.

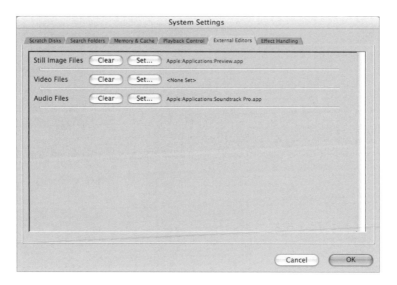

5   Click OK.

NOTE ▶ LiveType and Motion assign their own Creator property. A clip's Creator property determines what application will open it.

Here, you'll open the PICT file directly from the Final Cut Pro sequence. Preview will launch automatically since you assigned it to open still images in the External Editors tab of the User Preferences.

1   Open **Lesson 05 Project.fcp**.

2   Ctrl-click the **2 magicians bw.pct** clip from *01 External Editors Sequence.*

3   Choose Open In Editor from the contextual menu.

The PICT will launch in Preview.

4 In Preview, choose Tools > Flip Horizontal.

5 Press Cmd-S to save the file.

6 Press Cmd-Tab to return to Final Cut Pro.

The PICT is updated automatically in your Final Cut Pro project.

Before   After

You can assign any application, and it will work in the same manner. If you are working on titles or lower thirds created in Adobe Illustrator, assign Illustrator as the still image files external editor. It might be useful to assign Adobe After Effects as your video files external editor if you are time remapping your video. There are endless possibilities, and since any application can be set as an external editor, you can easily share, open, and edit your media files while you work from within Final Cut Pro.

For more information on assigning external editors, see the section on preferences in Lesson 11. For more information on other Apple Pro video and audio applications, refer to the Apple Pro Training Series books.

Exporting an EDL

The most basic interchange format you can use for sharing projects is an edit decision list (EDL). An EDL represents edits from a single sequence, and you can use it to exchange information with older editing systems that don't recognize other formats like XML. An EDL contains a description of your sequence as text, which describes each clip and its placement in your sequence, but EDLs include only basic transitions.

In order to export a successful EDL, you must avoid nested sequences, clips on tracks above video track 2, and non-SMPTE standard transitions. Video and audio filters, motion parameters and keyframes, although not applied, are listed in the EDL for your reference.

1   Open *02 Export EDL Sequence* and make sure your Timeline is the active window.

2   Choose File > Export > EDL.

3   Enter *02_Export_EDL_Sequence* as your EDL title.

This is the name of the EDL that is embedded in the text file.

TIP To help easily recognize your EDLs, give your EDL the same name as your sequence and include the date or version number.

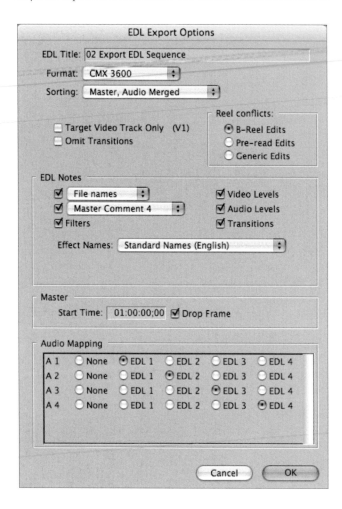

TIP ▶ You can export your Master Comment columns and Comment A/B columns to the EDL for assistance with the online. For example, these comments could include effect notes, or they could be used to communicate color correction notes.

There are a number of settings and options in the EDL dialog. Base your settings on what your recipient requires. The format you need to supply may change the options.

4   Leave all the settings at their defaults, and click OK.

The second name in the Save As entry in the Save dialog is the filename that will appear on your Mac HD.

5   Navigate to the Lessons folder and click Save.

6   When prompted, save the second EDL in the same location.

NOTE ▶ The second EDL is the b Reel EDL. Since an EDL is essentially read to a linear A/B roll suite, transition events from the same reel are not possible. The B reel is compiled by copying all the conflicting shots to a new tape. By default, Final Cut Pro automatically detects reel conflicts and creates a second EDL with a *B* at the end of the EDL name.

7   Choose File > Open.

8   Navigate to the Lessons folder and open the **02_Export_EDL_Sequence .edl** file.

Scroll down the file and read the EDL dialog. You can read your entire cut! You can even read where reel names were changed and what they were changed to. You will see what filters were applied, where transitions occurred, the video opacity, and audio levels.

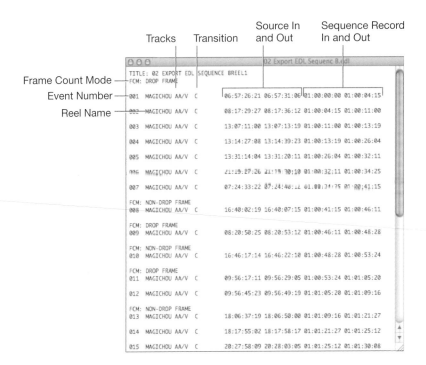

- The Tracks field determines which tracks are used. V=video, A=audio, A2=audio 2, AA=both audio channels.

- The Transition field represents the type of edit. C=cut, D=dissolve, W=wipe, K=key.

MORE INFO ▶ For more information see "Importing and Exporting EDLs" in the Final Cut Pro 5 user's manual.

Exporting an OMF

Traditionally, you would expect to export an OMF for your audio mixer. This is because an Open Media Framework (OMF) can store more information than a traditional EDL. An OMF export contains your audio clips, their placement within a sequence, and the media files themselves. There are no track limitations, you can maintain linear cross-fade information, and you can add handles if desired.

Before you export an OMF, keep in mind that if you have applied a speed effect, those clips will be permanently changed. If your sequence contains any nested sequences, the nests will become a single media file. Any levels, pan, or filters you applied will not be exported. The Final Cut Pro OMF export has a two-gigabyte limit. (Automatic Duck's new Pro Export resolves the two-gigabit limitation.)

If you see a two-gigabit error message, simply duplicate your sequence, creating a part 1 and part 2. Export each part separately; this way you can split your OMF export in half. Un-nest nested sequences and include original media clips with their speed-affected counterparts. Keep a written log of filters, levels, and pans if you want to communicate those to your audio mixer.

1   Open *03 Export OMF Sequence*.

2   Enable track visibility for all audio tracks you want to export.

3   Choose File > Export > Audio to OMF.

4   In the OMF Audio Export dialog, set Rate to 48 kHz, Depth to 16-bit,
    Handle Length to 1 sec, and select Include Crossfade Transitions.
    Click OK.

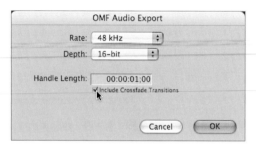

NOTE ▶ You can choose from the following sample rates: 32 kHz, 44.1 kHz,
48 kHz, 88.2 kHz, and 96 kHz. You can also choose between a 16-bit and
24-bit rate.

TIP ▶ Find out your audio post facility's preferred settings prior to your
OMF export.

5   Create a new folder named *OMF Export*, enter your sequence name as a
    filename, and click Save.

TIP ▶ You can import your final mixed OMF audio using Automatic
Duck's Pro Import FCP.

Exporting an XML File

XML, eXtensible Markup Language, is a unique language that allows you to
create, translate, exchange, and read any single element or an entire Final Cut
Pro project file in a text editor. Using XML allows you to export all your project information into a database, such as FileMaker, or translate your entire
final sequence along with your filters to another nonlinear editor.

Since you can view an XML file in a text editor, you can also learn to read, construct, and edit a Final Cut Pro project directly in a text editor. The most basic example of how you can leverage XML is the ability to change multiple clips at once. For example, if your project contains hundreds of titles and graphics that have been positioned for a 4:3 aspect ratio, but you need to deliver a 16:9 project, you could export the sequence using XML and modify all the position parameters of each clip simultaneously. This is a very basic example of how you can leverage a Final Cut Pro XML interchange. To learn more, read Chapter 12 of the Final Cut Pro user's manual.

Here, you'll export a sequence as an XML file, modify the font of the lower thirds, and import the XML file back to Final Cut Pro.

1 Select *04 Export XML Sequence.*

2 Choose File > Export > XML.

The Export XML dialog appears.

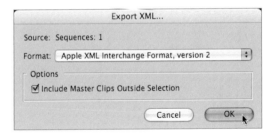

3 Choose Apple XML Interchange Format, Version 2 from the Format pop-up menu.

> **TIP** ▶ Choose an older version of the Final Cut Pro XML Interchange Format to make a current project backward compatible. This means that a Final Cut Pro 5 project file could be read with an older version of Final Cut Pro.

4   Select Include Master Clips Outside Selection if you want to include the master clips in the XML export that are associated with the selection.

5   Click OK.

6   Navigate to the Lessons folder, and name your file *04_Export_XML_Sequence_Arial.xml*.

The XML file stores the attributes of each sequence, the name and location of the all clips, and all other information such as timecode, frame rate, and media source location.

Here's how to take a look at the XML file in TextEdit:

1   In the Finder, navigate to the XML file you exported.

2   Ctrl-click the XML file and from the contextual menu choose Open With > Other.

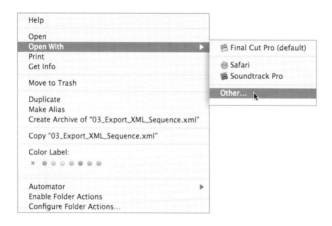

3   Choose TextEdit from the Applications folder.

4   Look at the text file to see what XML Interchange Format language text looks like.

The file is similar in appearance to an HTML document, except XML language has more descriptions. This file contains the text values of your entire sequence. You're going to change the font of every lower third.

5   Press Cmd-F to launch the Find dialog.

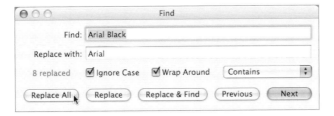

6   Type *Arial Black* in the Find field, type *Arial* in the Replace With field, and then click Replace All.

Eight instances of Arial Black are replaced with Arial.

7   Press Cmd-S to save the XML text document.

8   From the Finder, navigate to the XML file and double-click it to launch it.

By default, your XML file will launch a Final Cut Pro Import XML dialog.

9 Choose Lesson 05 Project from the Destination pop-up menu.

> **NOTE ▸** You can include the XML sequence in your currently open project, or you can create a new project. Simply choose your option from the Destination pop-up menu.

10 Choose OfflineRT NTSC (Photo JPEG) as your Sequence Setting and click OK.

> **NOTE ▸** If an error warning dialog appears, you can choose to view the log to check for errors by clicking Yes. You can then locate the error and delete it from your sequence or the XML file.

11 Select Reconnect To Media Files, Include Markers, and Include Audio/Video Effects before clicking OK.

12 Double-click your imported sequence to load it in the Timeline.

13 Press Shift-M or Option-M to navigate to the Timeline markers and view your font changes.

Before

After

Click between the original sequence and your modified sequence to see the changes.

Changing a font is just one example of the Apple XML Interchange Format capabilities. To learn more, see the "Importing and Exporting Final Cut Pro XML" chapter in the Final Cut Pro user's manual.

XML Developers

Automatic Duck (www.automaticduck.com) uses XML to translate project and sequence information between Final Cut Pro and other professional applications. Automatic Duck allows you to exchange project and sequence information between Final Cut Pro, Motion, Avid, Pro Tools, Adobe After Effects, Premiere Pro, and Discreet Combustion. They also offer a free XML Exporter plug-in for Final Cut Pro designed to make exporting XML faster and easier.

Using an Automatic Duck plug-in, you can start a project on one platform and finish on another. During post-production at a broadcast facility, I frequently sent OMFs to the audio department; they mixed the audio and sent it back for me to include in my final output and archive. Automatic Duck's Pro Import FCP allowed me to import the OMF composition directly into Final Cut Pro. This plug-in also allowed me to share projects with Avid editing systems.

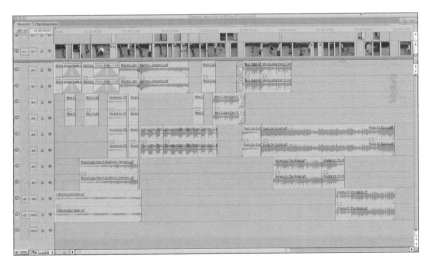

Final Cut Pro Timeline

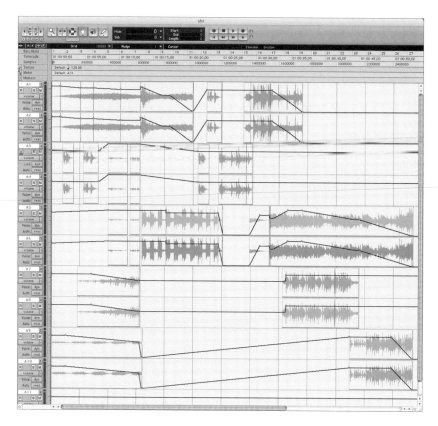

Audio from the Final Cut Pro Timeline exported to a Pro Tools session; all the levels are retained, as is the pan information.

Other companies, such as Spherico (www.spherico.com) and Digital Heaven (www.digital-heaven.co.uk), also make some elegant XML solutions for Final Cut Pro.

Outputting Your Project

After your edit is final, it's good practice to prep your sequence. You will prepare your sequence for either output to tape or an online session.

Depending on your workflow, you will typically finish your picture and audio edit then take your finished project, XML or EDL, elements, and source media, including a final output of your edit, to an online editing facility for finishing. Your booked time at a specialized online editing facility is commonly called an *online session.* Your online session may include increasing resolution, color correction, transition and filter manipulation, and preserving broadcast video specifications. Depending on the length and detail of your project, an online session will take from 1 to 10 days. Since your online session is utilizing sophisticated broadcast equipment, highly trained personnel, and limited time, you need to be well prepared. Organize your sequence before your online session.

You'll probably output your sequence during various stages of your project with little need for strict preparation. However, if you're responsible for your final output, you will benefit greatly by following the same principles of preparation as those of an online session. Traditionally, you output your finished sequence to a high-quality tape format and this becomes your master. You may also output a QuickTime movie or create a DVD.

Preparing for Your Online Session

Communicate with your online editor or the online facility coordinator to learn their preferred delivery specifications. Ask what format they need for your sequence. Do they require an XML or EDL export? If your online facility is running Final Cut Pro, you'll simply bring your Final Cut Pro project. In this case, ask what version of Final Cut Pro they are running. How is your session booked? Is it booked for an increase in resolution, titles, *and* color correction, or is it booked for just color correction? Determining these aspects prior to your session will make your time more productive and reduce costs. Use the following checklist as a rough guide:

Ask Questions

▶   What is the preferred sequence format (such as EDL-CMX 3600, XML-Version 2, or Final Cut Pro)?

▶   What information should my cut list include (levels, pan, transitions, filters, and so on)?

▶   What is the preferred format for the guide output? (Include window burns of your sequence timecode in your output guide.)

What You Should Bring

▶ All your source tapes and copies of any media you created without source timecode, including stills, music, effects, and titles

▶ EDL, XML, or Final Cut Pro project file

▶ An output of your final sequence with sequence timecode burned in

▶ An output of your sequence with timecode window burn

▶ A detailed list of which clips you want to affect and at what timecode they appear in the sequence; these could include titles, transitions, color correction, filters, and credits

▶ A detailed list of any text. Supply this as an electronic file, and make sure you save it as a Simple Text document. Check spelling prior to your session.

> **TIP** ▶ If you're completing your online session on another Final Cut Pro system, and your media drives are portable, as a precaution you could take them with you to the session. If you have difficulty locating an element of your project, doing so may save time.

Prepping Your Sequence

There are many methods of preparing a sequence for an online session and final output, but we'll focus on the most common aspects of organization.

Organizing Your Clips

Now that you have your final sequence, it's a good idea to duplicate it and add an identity. Add the word *master* and a date to the end of the name. At a glance you should be able to recognize which sequence is your final locked version.

Play through your sequence and place all your video clips onto the lowest tracks. For example, if you have an interview on video track 1 and some cutaways on video track 2 then move those clips on track 2 to track 1.

1 Select *05 Organize Your Clips Sequence* and press Return to load it in the Timeline.

2 In the Timecode field of the Timeline, type *10.* to move the playhead 10 seconds forward in the Timeline to position 01:00:10;00.

3 Press Cmd-+ to zoom into the Timeline at the playhead position.

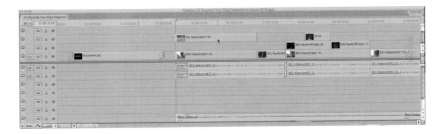

4 Press the spacebar to play the sequence. Play just a few clips.

Notice that the cutaway clips are on video tracks 2 and 3? During the offline editing workflow, it was easier to experiment and make editing decisions using a number of tracks. However, now that you are tidying up, you'll begin to move the clips from the higher tracks down into position on the lower tracks. The goal is to reduce the number of tracks and clean up the sequence so that only the necessary clips are represented in the final edit.

5   Click to select the **001 RoyParkEXT 09** clip, hold down the Shift key to constrain the clip's movement, and click and drag the clip down to video track 1.

You will overwrite the video clip on video track 1.

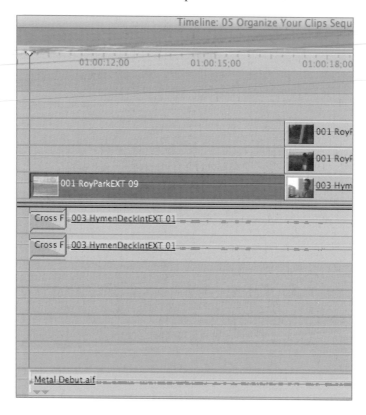

6   Press Cmd-Shift-A to deselect all clips in the Timeline.

7   Press the down arrow on your keyboard twice to navigate the playhead to the first frame of the next group of clips you will affect. The timecode should read 01:00:19;09.

8 Click to select the clip named **comp** on video track 3, hold down the Shift key to constrain the clip's movement, and click and drag the clip down to video track 2.

9 Press Cmd-Shift-A to deselect all clips in the Timeline.

10 Lasso the three clips on video track 2 to select them.

11 Hold down the Shift key to constrain the clips' movement, and click and drag them all down to video track 1.

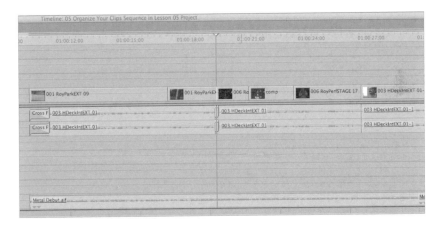

Your sequence is beginning to be much more concise. It's also easier to see exactly what clips constitute your edit.

You can continue to reduce the number of video tracks and then delete any empty tracks once you have finished. Remember to watch for composites and titles. If you are preparing your sequence for an EDL, you'll need to re-create any composites that appear above video track 2.

TIP To delete tracks, choose Sequence > Delete Tracks. Select Video Tracks, then select All Empty Tracks.

As with video, you need to arrange your audio so that it's clear and organized. You will usually prep your audio tracks either prior to your audio mix or online session, depending on what comes first. The goal with audio is to arrange the audio clips in a logical order. Discuss the order of your audio tracks with your audio mixer or online editor. Depending on preferred practices and the genre of your edit, the arrangement of audio can sway from simple to detailed. Use the following checklist as a rough guide:

▶ Dialogue: sync audio. Audio tracks 1 and 2

▶ Narration/voiceover: Audio track 3

▶ Ambience: Room tone, background tones. Audio track 4

▶ Sound effects: including sound effects you recorded or made or those captured from a sound effects library. Audio tracks 5 and 6

▶ Music: Audio tracks 7 and 8

▶ Foley: Audio tracks 9 and 10

The number of audio tracks for each group depends on the complexity of your project. The placement of each group may also vary, but the traditional arrangement is the order listed previously: dialog, narration, ambience, effects, music, and foley.

> **NOTE** ▶ The individual tracks that contain the dialog, music, and effects of the soundtrack are called *leaves*. Each group of leaves that comprise final mixdown audio is often called a *stem*. A final mixdown includes stems of dialog, music, and effects (DME or ME).

Take a look at the arranged audio tracks in *05 Organize Your Clips Sequence.*

1   Select *05 Organize Your Clips Sequence* and press Return to load it in the
    Timeline if it's not already open.

2   Press Shift-Z to fit the contents of the sequence in the window.

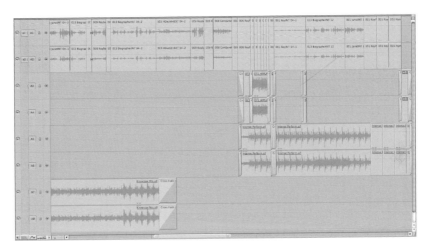

The audio tracks have already been organized. Dialog is on audio tracks 1
and 2, sound effects are on 3 and 4, and the music is on 5, 6, 7, and 8.

Prepare Clips for Recapture

Prior to exporting your XML or EDL, or delivering your Final Cut Pro project, you will need to use the Create Offline option in the Media Manager to
prepare your clips for recapture during an online session. The goal in using
the Create Offline option is to trim the clips, reducing the amount you will
need to recapture; to change your sequence settings to a higher resolution

(if required); to duplicate your sequence; and to save the duplicated sequence in a new project.

1   Click to select any sequence from the Browser.

2   Choose File > Media Manager. The Media Manager dialog opens.

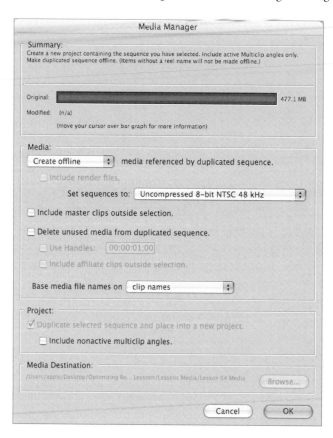

3   Choose Create Offline from the Media pop-up menu.

4   Choose your new sequence settings in the Set Sequences To pop-up menu.

5   Deselect the check box for Include Master Clips Outside Selection.

6   Deselect the check box Delete Unused Media From Duplicated Sequence.

With this option deselected, your original media files will not be affected, and you will have the choice of adding handles.

TIP When you're prepping your sequence for recapture, you do not need to create handles in the Create Offline dialog. Generally, you'll have the ability to add handles during recapture. Of course, check with your online facility if you are unsure of their process.

7   From the Base Media File Names On pop-up menu, choose Clip Names.

You can choose either existing filenames or clip names. Existing filenames will maintain the names of the original media files; clip names will change your media names to the names you assigned to your clips during the editing process.

8   Deselect Include Nonactive Multiclip Angles.

9   Click OK.

A dialog opens, prompting you to save your new project file.

10 Navigate to where you want to save your project, enter a name, and click Save.

TIP You could keep the original project name and add as an appendage your resolution or the word *Master* or *Final*, for example, *TMH_Master_052805-8bit*.

Final Cut Pro scans your selected elements and reconstructs the project.

> **NOTE** ▶ If your media has no source timecode track or reel name, the media file will not be affected by the Media Manager. This is a useful precautionary feature in Final Cut Pro to prevent you from altering a media file that you may not be able to recapture.

Your sequence is now ready to export a cut list, recapture in Final Cut Pro at a higher resolution, or to take to your online session.

For additional details about the Create Offline option in Media Manager, see the "Recapture Selected Source Media" section in Lesson 3.

Timecode Filters

Whenever you output a reference tape, file, or still image, it's a great idea to include a timecode window burn, which will help you identify or reference a frame of video. Depending on the purpose of your output, you will want to include a window burn of either the sequence or clip timecode. For example, if you are sending a reference output of your edit to your director for approval, include a sequence window burn by applying a Timecode Generator filter.

If you are creating a reference output of your edit for your online session, you may want to apply a window burn indicating the timecode of each clip. In this case, you will need to apply a Timecode Reader filter. The purpose of applying a window burn of either the sequence or clip timecode is to make referencing easier. Depending on which filter you apply, it'll be easy to see where a clip occurs within your sequence or know what the clip timecode is by looking at the output. This is especially important if you are outputting to a DVD, VHS, or QuickTime movie. For extra benefit, consider applying both filters.

1   Double-click *06 Timecode Window Burn Sequence* to load it in the Timeline.

2   Click to select the first clip in the sequence: **04-01-1**.

3   Choose Effects > Video Filters > Video > Timecode Reader.

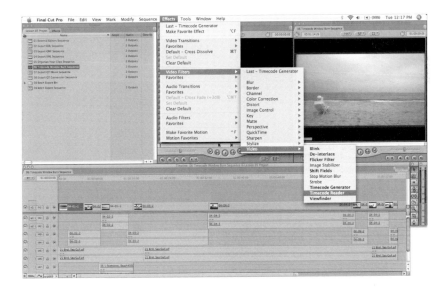

The Timecode Reader filter, which visually identifies the clip's timecode, is applied.

4   Double-click the **04-01-1** clip to load it into the Viewer.

Make sure you place your playhead over the **04-01-1** clip in the Timeline so you can see the changes you make to the filter as they update in the Canvas.

5   Click the Filters tab to view the filters.

6   Choose Show Title Safe from the View pop-up menu on the Canvas.

By choosing Show Title Safe, you can ensure that you are placing your timecode filters within the viewable field.

7   In the Timecode Reader filter, choose the following settings: Size: 15; Center: 175, 176; and Opacity: 0. Deselect the Ignore Opacity check box.

8   Select the **04-01-1** clip in the Timeline and press Cmd-C to copy.

9   Lasso all other clips in the Timeline.

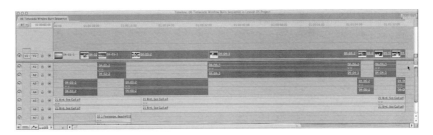

10 Ctrl-click the selected clips and choose Paste Attributes from the short-
    cut menu.

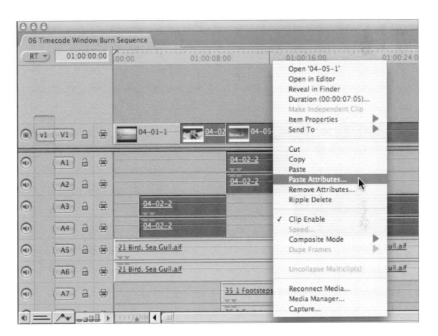

11 Select Filters from the Paste Attributes dialog and click OK.

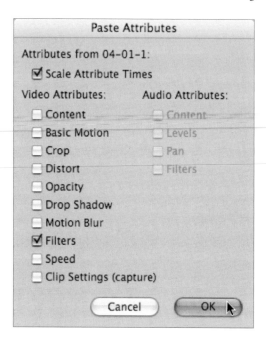

The Timecode Reader filter is applied to all clips in the Timeline with the same settings and parameters you applied on the first clip.

Now add the Timecode Generator filter, first nesting the original sequence so the Timecode Generator reads continuously.

1 Press Cmd-N to create a new sequence. Name it *06 Timecode Generator.*

2 Double-click the *06 Timecode Generator* sequence to load it in the Timeline.

3 Select *06 Timecode Window Burn Sequence* and drag it to the Edit Overlay in the Canvas and choose Overwrite.

4   Click to select the nested sequence.

5   Choose Effects > Video Filters > Video > Timecode Generator.

6   In the Timeline, select *06 Timecode Window Burn Sequence* and press Return to load it in the Viewer.

7   Click the Filters tab.

8   Enter *06 TWBS* in the Label field. This identifies the sequence.

9   Make the following adjustments to the filter: Format: 30fps; Hour Offset: 1; Size: 15; Center: –123, 175; and Opacity: 0. Deselect the Ignore Opacity check box.

   NOTE ▶ You should set the format to your video source. Normally, this would be 29.97 for NTSC and 25 fps for PAL.

TIP You can use the keyboard shortcut Option-C to nest clips. To ensure success, when nesting a sequence for a Timecode Generator make sure you match your nested sequence settings and sequence timecode to your original sequence.

Your output now identifies the sequence timecode and the timecode of each source clip.

Outputting to Tape

Perhaps the most common form of outputting information is to make a tape. You can edit to tape (ETT), print to video (PTV), or record directly from the Timeline. Whenever you master to tape, you should place bars with tone, slate, and countdown at the beginning of the tape. This is used for calibration and to identify a tape. You can either use the built-in leader accessible from the PTV or ETT windows, or you can edit a leader directly into your sequence.

> **TIP** ▶ Keep a copy of the sequence you used to make an output to ensure you have a record of what's on the tape. Duplicate your original sequence and add *Output* and a date to the end of the sequence name. Make sure you also identify the corresponding tape with the name of the project and sequence.

Leader

A leader consists of SMPTE color bars and 1 kHz reference tone, slate (also called a title card), and SMPTE countdown. Although the arrangement and duration of color bars, slate, and countdown can vary (depending on the delivery specifications of your client), the general rule is 1 minute color bars and tone, 10 seconds title card, 10 seconds black, 8 seconds countdown, 2 seconds black, then picture start.

For output, change your sequence timecode so that the first frame of edited picture begins at the first hour: 01:00:00;00. All bars, tone, slate, and countdown begin prior to the first hour frame. Traditionally, the leader will begin at 00:58:30;00. Always ask for delivery specifications and when none are given, you can use the following chart of traditional standards.

Timecode	Leader/Trailer	Duration
00:58:00;00	Black/slug	30 seconds
00:58:30;00	Color bars and tone	60 seconds
00:59:30;00	Black	10 seconds
00:59:40;00	Slate/title card	10 seconds
00:59:50;00	Countdown	10 seconds, includes 2-pop at 00:59:58;00
01:00:00;00	Picture start	Program duration
End of program	Black	60 seconds

NOTE ▶ Although a countdown can be useful for any output, traditionally it's used for tapes that are delivered for broadcast or to the audio
mixer responsible for your final audio mix. When delivering a tape for
duplication, you will usually leave the countdown black.

If you have no delivery specifications requiring the inclusion of particular
information on your slate, use the following checklist as a rough guide:

▶ Name: program title (or project name, sequence name, version)

▶ Production credits: producer, director, editor, post facility

▶ Total run time: (TRT) program duration

▶ Picture start: timecode of picture start and timebase (such as, PAL, NTSC
NDF, or NTSC DF)

▶ Date: output date

▶ Transmission date: (TX) date of broadcast transmission

▶ Output purpose: preview, master, rough edit

▶ Audio channels: stereo, mono, or unmixed

TIP ▶ Sometimes it's useful to identify the edited clip resolution on the title card, especially during a review of effects, credit scrolls, and titles. You can pinpoint the source of a problem that's due to the resolution of your effect or the effect itself.

Built-In Leader/Trailer

Final Cut Pro has built-in leader elements accessible through the Print to Video dialog and in the Edit to Tape dialog from the Mastering Settings tab. The built-in leader/trailer options are great for basic presentation, single-instance output. If you require your sequence to show visually in the Timeline, edit your slate or your entire leader directly into your sequence.

NOTE ▶ Slug and bars and tone (NTSC, PAL, and HD) are available from the Video Generators drop-down menu on the Viewer.

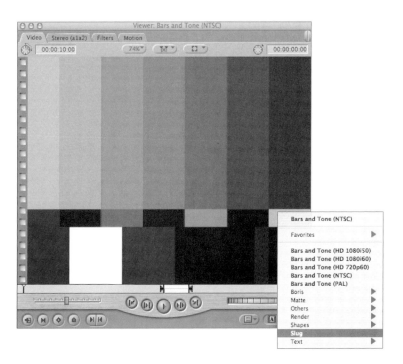

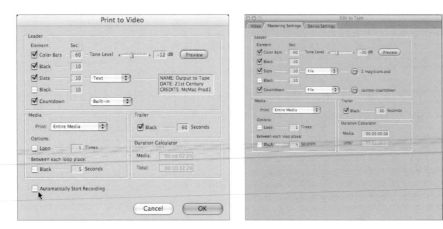

Print to Video   Edit to Tape

TIP ▶ You can use the clip name or a text, PICT, or QuickTime file as your slate. You can also choose the built-in or QuickTime file as your countdown.

Print to Video

The Print to Video command does not allow you to set In and Out points on the tape, and you do not have control over the destination timecode on the tape, so recording will start wherever the tape is currently cued. You will use the Print to Video command if you are editing HDV or if video equipment does not support device control. The most common noncontrollable devices are VCRs or DVD recorders.

Of course, you can also record directly from the Timeline, but the Print to Video command gives you more control and options. From the Print to Video window, you can insert leader and trailer elements, select to record the In to Out points from your sequence, loop, or record the entire duration.

If your deck has remote device control, either RS-422 or FireWire, you can set the Print to Video command to begin recording automatically. Simply select the Automatically Start Recording check box in the Print to Video dialog.

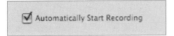

> **MORE INFO** ▶ For further details on the Print to Video command, see the "Printing to Video and Output from the Timeline" section in the Final Cut Pro user's manual.

Edit to Tape

The Edit to Tape command allows you to perform an Assemble edit and an Insert edit, and it lets you black and code a tape. Your equipment must support device control (FireWire or RS-422) and must be capable of performing an Insert edit.

▶ Black and code is a process of laying down black and timecode on a tape. In order to use Edit to Tape, your video tape needs continuous timecode. You need to black and code only up to the start of your program for an Assemble edit.

▶ Assemble Edit allows consistent recording signal. It records all tracks on the tape including video, audio, timecode, and control track. With an Assemble Edit, the Out point ends abruptly (breaking control track), so add some trailer black to your sequence in the Mastering Settings dialog or add some slug to the end of your edited sequence.

▶ Insert Edit allows edits of selective tracks. The control track is not replaced. Both In and Out points have continuous control track.

Insert editing allows you to set frame-accurate In and Out points while also allowing you to edit video, individual audio tracks, and timecode. Most professional editing facilities black and code all their tapes, and most use the Insert editing command exclusively.

1   Choose File > Edit to Tape

2   Choose the Mastering mode from the pop-up menu.

This mode is useful if you want to output your sequence with the built-in leaders accessible through the Mastering Settings tab. If you choose the Mastering mode, you only need to set an In point on the tape; the Out point will be automatically set.

Choose the Editing mode when you are Insert editing one clip. The Mastering Settings built-in leader and trailer elements will not be available.

TIP The Edit to Tape window appears over the Canvas and is sized proportionate to the Canvas window. If you want to increase the size of your Edit to Tape window, increase the size of your Canvas prior to choosing the Edit to Tape command.

3 Set In and Out points on your clip or sequence if you don't need to output the entire duration.

4 Select your edited sequence or clip from the Browser.

5 Type the timecode in the Timecode field to set the destination In point on the tape.

6 Select to enable video and timecode and choose your audio tracks from the pop-up menu.

NOTE ▶ When a destination video, audio, or timecode track is enabled, it is yellow.

NOTE ▶ Final Cut Pro can output up to eight tracks of audio when performing an Insert edit. The number of tracks available is dependent on the number of available tracks on your VTR. You also need to set the audio output presets in your sequence. For more information, see the "Working with Multiple Audio Output Channels" section in the Final Cut Pro user's manual.

7   Click the Mastering Settings tab and enable the options you want to include, and disable the options you don't want to include.

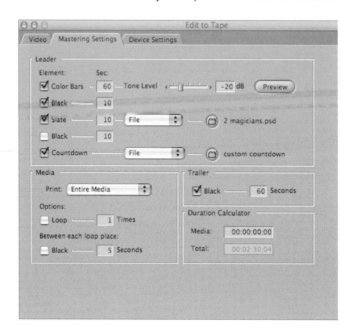

8   Click the Preview button to preview your edit.

This is useful if you are Insert editing onto a preexisting edited tape.

9   Select your edited sequence or clip in the Browser, then click the Insert Edit button on the Edit to Tape window.

10 Click OK to begin recording.

`TIP` Press Escape to cancel the preview or record to tape.

`TIP` Although any element that requires rendering will be rendered automatically, it's an excellent idea to render and save your sequence or clip prior to your edit to tape. For quick access, you can set the render quality in the Real-Time pop-up menu in the Timeline. All audio is automatically rendered at high quality.

Exporting Media

You can export your sequence or clip as a self-contained or reference QuickTime movie, choose from all the available sequence presets, or perform a QuickTime conversion and choose from a number of QuickTime compatible formats such as MPEG-2 or AVI. You can include your markers for use in other applications such as Motion, DVD Studio Pro, Soundtrack, and Soundtrack Pro.

Export QuickTime Movie

The Export QuickTime Movie command is streamlined when you simply want to export a QT movie using one of the available sequence presets. You can export two kinds of QuickTime movies: self-contained and reference.

In self-contained movies, every frame of your original sequence is reproduced to create an independent QuickTime movie. The resulting movie file is larger than a reference movie, and the total size depends on the sequence setting and length. Use a self-contained QT movie if you plan to deliver or share your sequence with someone else, or for archive purposes.

Reference movies reference the original source media. Like a clip in a Browser, a reference movie is a pointer to the original sequence clip's QuickTime media files. In order to view a reference movie, all original QT files must be available on the same system. The resulting file size of a reference movie is very small since it contains no media. Use a reference QT movie if you are planning to use the QT movie with another application on the same machine. For example, you could use a QT reference movie in Motion, Shake, or another application. You can even share a QT reference movie with another colleague on your XSAN, as long as that person has access to the original QT source media.

1   Select *07 Export QT Movie Sequence* from the Browser.

2   Choose File > Export > QuickTime Movie.

3   Choose a location, and name your movie.

4   Choose a sequence setting from the Setting pop-up menu.

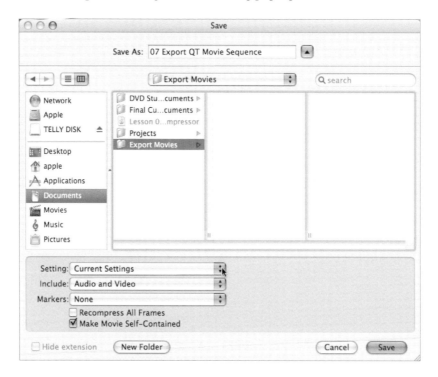

Current Settings uses the sequence or clip setting you selected. If you want, choose another setting from the pop-up menu.

If you choose to export a self-contained movie, you have the option of choosing to recompress the media in your export. Selecting the Recompress All Frames option is useful if you choose a codec setting lower than your current sequence setting. If you choose a setting equal or higher than your current sequence setting, deselect the Recompress All Frames option so that you can export your media without exposing it to unnecessary recompression artifacts.

5 Choose what you need to include from the Include pop-up menu. You can choose Video or Audio only, and Video and Audio both.

6 If you have set markers in your clip or sequence for export, identify which markers you want to export or choose All from the Markers pop-up menu.

7 Select the Make Movie Self-Contained check box and click Save.

TIP ▶ Export a QuickTime reference movie and use Compressor to convert your file to another QuickTime-compatible format.

Export QuickTime Conversion

If you need to export any QuickTime compatible file format such as AIFF, AVI, MPEG-2, or still image sequences, you will use the Export QuickTime Conversion command. You can export 3G, AIFF, QuickTime movie, AU, AVI, WAVE, DV stream, still image, image sequence, MPEG-2, and MPEG-4.

There are too many configurations and choices to cover in this lesson, so the focus here is on exporting for the Web. Of course, there are many reasons to use QuickTime conversion, so for more detailed information see the "Exporting QuickTime-Compatible Files" section in the Final Cut Pro user's manual.

In this exercise, you'll export a compressed QuickTime movie file for Web distribution. This kind of compressed file is perfect for posting on an FTP site for editorial approval.

1 Double-click *08 Export QT Conversion Sequence* to load it in the Timeline.

2 Choose File > Export > Using QuickTime Conversion.

3 Choose a location and name for your movie.

4 Choose QuickTime Movie from the Format pop-up menu.

5 Choose Broadband – Medium from the Use pop-up menu.

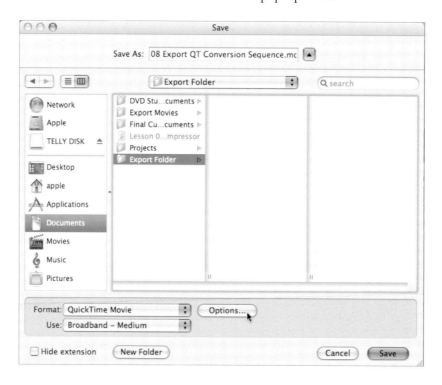

TIP ▶ Base this Internet setting on who you're delivering the file to. If your director has dial-up access, choose the Dial-Up preset or simply output a low and high compression.

6 Click Options.

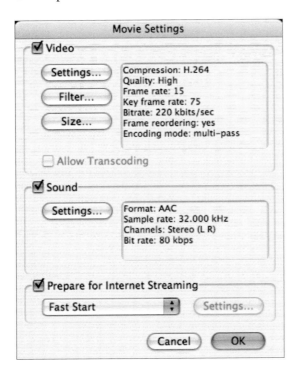

These are the default settings for Broadband – Medium compression with QuickTime 7. You will find that all the default settings produce excellent results. However, if you want to create your own, you can use the default settings as a jumping off point.

7 Click OK when you have finished viewing or selecting your options.

8 Click Save to export your file.

Export Still

For many reasons, you may find it useful to export a still or still image. You might want to use them for press kits, storyboard, scene stills, log book images, or graphics. Nearly all still image formats are supported in Final Cut Pro. Two common image formats are JPEG, which is a good compression compromise with a small resulting file size but good image detail, and TIFF. (You can choose to save a TIFF file with no compression.)

> **TIP** ▶ Exported still images are 72 dpi. For still images that are intended for print, change the dpi in Adobe Photoshop.

Here's how to export an uncompressed still image:

1 Open *08 Export QT Conversion Sequence.*

2 In the Timeline, find a frame you want to export.

3 Choose File > Export > Using QuickTime Conversion.

4 Choose a location and name for your still image.

5 Choose Still Image from the Format pop-up window.

6 Click Options.

7 In the Export Image Sequence Settings dialog, choose TIFF from the Format pop-up menu.

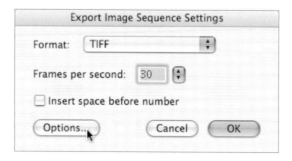

8   Ignore the Frames Per Second pop-up menu; it does not apply to still images.

9   Deselect the check box for Insert Space Before Number. Click Options.

10 In the TIFF Options dialog, choose Millions of Colors from the pop-up menu.

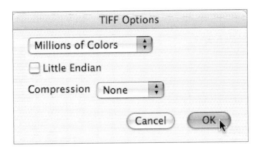

11 Choose None from the Compression pop-up menu. Click OK.

12 In the Export Image Sequence Settings dialog, click OK and then click Save.

> **TIP** ▶ You may find it useful to place a De-interlace filter on your clip or sequence prior to export. (Choose Effects > Video Filters > Video > De-interlace.) Since video is a combination of two interlaced fields, you can sometimes notice flickering in the image. Use the De-interlace filter to remove the upper (odd) or lower (even) field, and the remaining field is duplicated to create a whole image. This filter is especially useful if your exported QuickTime movie is intended for playback on a computer since computer screens display lines progressively.

Batch Export

You can export multiple elements with various codecs, formats, and settings by using the Batch Export command. This is a great feature that will save you time, especially if you need to export a number of clips, sequences, or bins.

Here's how to export some clips to AIFF using standard settings.

1   Hold down Shift and select 09 Batch Export Bin and *09 Batch Export Sequence.*

2   Choose File > Batch Export.

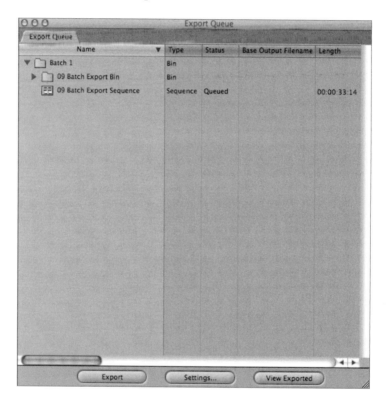

The Export Queue window launches. By default, your batch export elements are placed in a bin named Batch 1. You can rename or create new bins, and you can move, delete, and add to the Batch Queue window just like a Browser window.

TIP You can also add to the Export Queue by dragging and dropping elements from the Browser.

NOTE ▶ Make sure you export your items in the Export Queue, because anything in the Export Queue will be deleted after you quit Final Cut Pro.

3   Select a batch folder and click Settings.

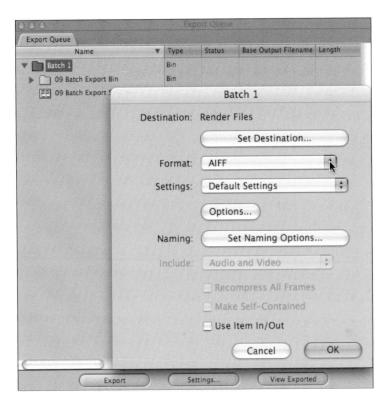

In the dialog, set your Destination, Format, Settings, Naming conventions, and options for including audio and video, item In and Out, reference or self-contained movie, and recompress frames.

4   Click Set Destination to set your export destination.

5   Choose AIFF from the Format pop-up menu.

6   Click Options.

7   Choose 48.000 kHz from the Rate pop-up menu in the Sound Settings dialog.

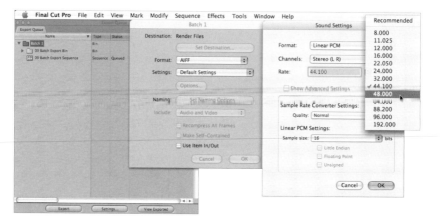

8   Click OK in the Sound Settings and Batch dialogs.

9   Click Export.

10   Click View Exported to open your exported files in separate windows in Final Cut Pro.

Lesson Review

1.   What do these applications have in common: LiveType, Cinema Tools, Compressor, SoundTrack Pro, Logic, Motion, DVD Studio Pro, and Shake?

2.   What is the most basic interchange format?

3.   Name an advantage Open Media Framework (OMF) has over a traditional EDL.

4.   What is OMF most commonly used for?

5. What is XML and what does it do?

6. What might you be doing while working at a specialized online editing facility?

7. What should you do before you output your online session?

8. Name four possible reasons for using the Create Offline option.

9. When should you include a window burn of the sequence or clip timecode?

10. What should appear at the beginning of any master tape?

11. What does the Batch Export command let you do?

Answers

1. They can all seamlessly exchange information.

2. Edit decision list (EDL).

3. OMF can store more information than EDL.

4. Audio export.

5. XML, or eXtensible Markup Language, lets you create, translate, exchange, and read any single element or an entire Final Cut Pro project file.

6. Increasing resolution, color correction, transition and filter manipulation, and preserving broadcast video specifications.

7. Play through your sequence and arrange all your video clips onto the lowest possible tracks.

8. Trim the clips to reduce the amount you will need to recapture; change your sequence settings to another resolution; duplicate your sequence; and save the duplicated sequence in a new project.

9. Whenever you create a reference output.

10. Bars and tone, slate, and countdown.

11. It lets you export multiple elements with various codecs, formats, and settings.

6

Lesson Files

Media

Time

Goals

Lessons > Lesson 06 > Lesson 06 Project.fcp, Lesson 06 Database

Media > Lesson 06 Media

This lesson takes approximately 90 minutes to complete.

Learn how Cinema Tools searches and matches records

Export a Cinema Tools film list

Open and compare a film list to your edited sequence

Recognize how to find and fix missing elements

Export a change list

Learn how to rebalance reels in a film project

Export a Cinema Tools audio EDL

Distributing Film Projects

You edit a film project in Final Cut Pro much the same way you would a video project. Once you have completed your edit, you're ready to begin the process of cutting your work print and then your film. In order to conform your work print and negative, you need to give your negative cutter a number of lists that contain the information about how to cut your film.

In this lesson, you will learn how to generate cut lists and change lists in Cinema Tools. We'll also look at a variety of other lists, including dupe, optical, pull, and scene lists. You will learn how to balance a reel and how to resolve common issues relating to missing elements.

Cinema Tools Lists

When you conform a work print or negative, you need to provide a list that describes your film sequence in much the same way an EDL describes edits in a video sequence.

The first time you export a conform list, it's generally referred to as a *cut list*. Any subsequent changes to your project are based on changes to the previous cut, so all subsequent conform lists that you provide are called *change lists*— lists that detail changes made since the first cut list.

It's important to know how Cinema Tools searches and matches records, because it can only produce a cut list if it can locate a record that matches the Final Cut Pro sequence clip. Cinema Tools uses clip-based and timecode-based methods to locate and match records from Final Cut Pro:

▶ Clip-based—Cinema Tools acquires the clip name from Final Cut Pro, then checks the clip name against the database. It searches for the clip by using the same pathname that was assigned in Final Cut Pro. If that fails, Cinema Tools searches for the clip by name and modification date. Once it locates the clip in the database, it can locate the corresponding record, because each clip is linked to a record.

▶ Timecode-based—If Cinema Tools can't locate a clip using the clip-based method, it will attempt to check the video reel and timecode against the database.

Cinema Tools tries the clip-based method first, then the timecode-based one. If both methods fail, the record will appear in the film list as <missing >. See the "Finding and Fixing Missing Elements" section later in this lesson.

> **NOTE** ▶ If you conform the frame rate of the clips, for example from 30 fps to 24 fps, Cinema Tools can only produce accurate find results with the clip-based method. This is because when you conform a clip, Cinema Tools will produce new timecode for that clip based on the new frame rate. However, with clips that are reverse-telecined, for example from 30 fps to 24 fps, both the clip- and timecode-based methods will produce accurate results, since Cinema Tools tracks the original timecode.

Film Lists

Cinema Tools can create a variety of lists from your edited project. These exported lists are all called *film lists*, and they include the following lists: cut, missing elements, dupe, optical, pull, scene, and change. You export the lists you need using the Film Lists dialog.

Let's export a Cinema Tools film list from FCP. While the Film List dialog is open, you'll learn about each setting and take an in-depth look at the types of lists available.

1   Open the **Lesson 06 Project.fcp** Final Cut Pro project file.

2   Select the *Scene 4* sequence in the Timeline.

3   Click the Timeline Layout pop-up and enable Show Duplicate Frames.

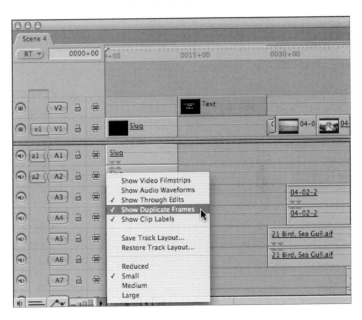

You will notice that there are two transitions and some duplicate frames showing in this sequence. Later in the exercise, you will see how these elements are displayed in the film list.

4   Choose File > Export > Cinema Tools Film Lists.

5   Leave Scene 4 as the Title for this list.

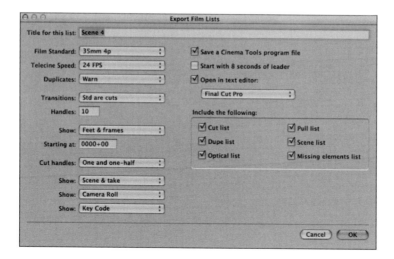

Leaving the name of the sequence as the title will help you identify which sequence you exported this cut list from.

6   Choose 35mm 4p as your Film Standard.

This is the same standard you entered for the database you created in Lesson 4.

NOTE ▶ Cinema Tools uses the film standard you choose here to calculate the footage counts in the cut list, so it's important that it matches. If any of the database record film standards differ, you will see a film-standard warning message. If in doubt, open your original source database and double-check.

7   Choose 24 fps from the Telecine Speed pop-up menu.

This is the speed at which you transferred the footage.

8   Choose Warn from the Duplicates pop-up menu.

With this option selected, you will see a warning message in your cut list every time a duplicate frame occurs. The message will tell you exactly which frames have been used and where they occur in the sequence. You will also see these details in a double usage warnings list.

NOTE ▶ Double usage warnings lists are especially useful if you want to go back to your edit and revise the duplicated frames within your sequence. For example, you may want to export a cut list with this warning, see where the duplicated instances occur, obtain a cost estimate from the lab, and either absorb the costs or re-edit the sequence.

9   Choose Std Are Cuts from the Transitions pop-up menu.

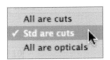

The three options in this list define whether transitions are listed for contact printing or optical printing:

▶ All Are Cuts—Choose this option if you are exporting a list for conforming a work print. This option will place a cut in the middle of a transition, regardless of whether the transition has an equal amount of frames on either side or if it is a standard-length transition. In the list, you will see notes indicating the start and end of the transition for the outgoing and incoming clips, and you will use the notes as a guide so that you can mark the transitions on the conformed work print.

▶ Std Are Cuts—Choose this option if you are going to have your transitions printed on a contact printer. In this option, standard-length transitions are listed as cuts and will appear in the cut list, and nonstandard transitions are described as opticals.

▶ All Are Opticals—Choose this option if you are having *all* your transitions printed optically. This option will place all clips that form part of a fade or dissolve in the optical list.

NOTE ▶ Always ask your contact printer how they define standard-length durations and how many handles they want you to set. The regular standard-length transitions for 23.98 fps and 24 fps projects are identified as durations of 16, 24, 32, 48, 64, and 96 frames. For 29.97 fps and 30 fps, standard-length are identified as 20, 30, 40, 60, 80, and 120 frames in duration.

10 Enter *10* in the Handles field.

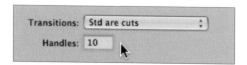

These handles are applied to transitions only. You will enter a number between 0 and 32. Cinema Tools will apply the number you indicate in this setting plus half a frame to the head and tail of each incoming and outgoing clip.

11 Choose Feet & Frames from the Show pop-up menu.

The Show pop-up options allow you to count your footage using either feet and frames, timecode, or frames. You can use any of these options to verify the accuracy of your cut list against your edited sequence.

Feet and frames is useful when conforming to a film work print because it allows you to check your sync using a synchronizer block. You can also set your edited sequence to show feet and frames and use this option to verify the accuracy of the sequence running time against the cut list.

NOTE ▶ A synchronizer block has a counter connected to several rotating wheels with sprockets and a footage counter. When working with film, you can interlock the film onto the sprockets and check the position of the film by footage and frame number. You can then check the footage and frame against your list and verify that the readings match.

Time is useful if you want to compare running times in the cut list with the timecode shown in the sequence. Set your sequence to timecode, and compare the cut list to the timecode in your edited sequence.

NOTE ▶ You may notice that the timecode shown in the cut list may not match the timecode shown in the sequence. This is because you need to calculate from the film frame number.

Count is useful if you are printing opticals because you will know how many frames are used between the beginning and the end of an effect.

12 Enter *0000+00* in the Starting At field.

This is where you will enter a starting location for the cut list. For example, if you're exporting the second scene from a film, you would begin the count from the starting position of that scene within the film. If you're generating a cut list with time, enter the starting timecode of your edited sequence in the Starting At field.

13 Choose One And One-Half from the Cut Handles pop-up menu.

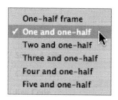

Find out what allowances your negative cutter prefers with cut handles. You can select to allow for up to five and one-half frames of cut handles. Cinema Tools assumes that at least one-half of a frame is destroyed. This allowance is essential information, and is included in the duplicate list and double usage warning list.

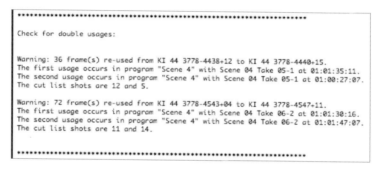

This is an example of a double usage warning list.

14 Choose Scene & Take from the Show pop-up menu.

Showing scene and take is more useful than showing clip name because it relates directly to the Cinema Tools database.

TIP Consider naming your clips by scene and take names. This will be especially useful when comparing your clips to the cut list and your Cinema Tools database.

15 Choose Camera Roll from the Show pop-up menu.

Choose the option that matches how your film is stored. If you're unsure, ask your negative or work print cutter which type of roll they want to see displayed.

16 Choose Key Code from the Show pop-up menu.

You only have the option to choose Ink Numbers when the film standard is 35mm 4 perf.

17 Select the Save A Cinema Tools Program File check box.

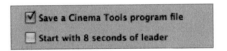

You need a program file if you plan to make changes to your Final Cut Pro sequence or if you want to export an audio EDL from Cinema Tools.

18 Deselect Start With 8 Seconds Of Leader.

This option inserts 8 seconds of leader before the start of the sequence. It's best to insert the leader directly into your sequence to maintain sequence timecode accuracy.

19 Select Open In Text Editor so that the film list opens immediately in the specified text editor.

20 Choose Other from the pop-up menu.

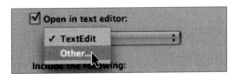

21 Select Final Cut Pro from the Applications folder, and click Open.

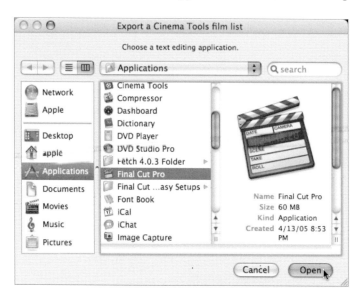

It's easier to view and compare the film list in a Final Cut Pro window. Although you can't print or save changes to the list, you can edit the document and then copy and paste the text to a text application.

22 Select Cut List.

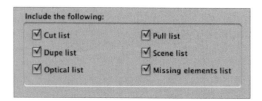

A cut list is also known as your assembly list. It contains all the information you need to cut your film negative or work print. If your edited sequence contains any titles or superimposed images, you will see two lists, a cut list and a foreground layer list. The foreground layer list contains only the title and superimposed image information contained on video track 2.

```
*************************************************************

The cut list in construction order:

Shot Footage  Length   Keycode      In Frame  Out Frame  Roll    Scene   Take

001  0000+00  0012+00      Slug                          leader

002  0012+00  0015+00      fill                          leader

     0027+00 to 0028+07 Fade-in of 24 frames (01+08)
     In-coming KI 44 3778 from 4017+12 to 4019+03

003  0027+00  0008+06   KI 44 3778  4017+12   4026+01    1       04      01-1

004  0035+06  0005+10   KI 44 3778  4116+06   4121+15    1       04      02-2

     Note -- this shot has a duplicate usage.
005  0041+00  0010+12   KI 44 3778  4438+13   4449+08    2       04      05-1

006  0051+12  0024+14   KI 44 3778  4183+10   4208+07    1       04      03-2

007  0076+10  0047+06   KI 44 3778  4360+08   4407+13    2       04      04-3

008  0124+00  0000+01      fill                          leader

009  0124+01  0005+05   KI 44 3778  4528+15   4534+03    2       04      06-2

010  0129+06  0006+11   KI 44 3778  4411+14   4418+08    2       04      04-3

     Note -- this shot has a duplicate usage.
011  0136+01  0004+05   KI 44 3778  4543+05   4547+09    2       04      06-2

     Note -- this shot has a duplicate usage.
012  0140+06  0004+06   KI 44 3778  4435+15   4440+04    2       04      05-1

     0143+04 to 0144+11 Fade-out of 24 frames (01+08)
     Out-going KI 44 3778 from 4438+13 to 4440+04

013  0144+12  0016+04      fill                          leader

     Note -- this shot has a duplicate usage.
014  0161+00  0004+05   KI 44 3778  4543+05   4547+09    2       04      06-2

000  0165+05               Length

*************************************************************
```

This is an example of a cut list, also called an assembly list.

```
*************************************************************

The foreground layer cut list:

     The foreground layer, or layer 2, is for supers and titles
     which overlay the background layer.

Shot Footage  Length   Keycode      In Frame  Out Frame  Roll    Scene   Take

001  0000+00  0012+00      fill                          leader

002  0012+00  0015+00

000  0027+00               Length

*************************************************************
```

This is an example of a foreground layer cut list.

23 Select Dupe List.

You must give your lab the dupe list so the technicians can pull shots from your negative rolls and make duplicates.

```
The dupe list:

Scene          Take          Roll          Keycode

04             06-2          2             KI 44 3778  4521+08      shots 11, 14
```

This is an example of a dupe list.

24 Select Optical List.

The optical list is the master list for all transition and motion effects. This list describes how the effects shots are assembled. If you have motion effects or transitions in your edited sequence, you will also get a motion effects and a transition effects list.

```
The Optical List:

There are 1 items in the optical list.

--------------------------------------------------------------------
Optical 1, Shot 012, Start = 0140+06, End = 0144+11, Length = 0004+06

Shot      Footage  Length

012.1     0000+00  0004+06   Transition Effect 1

          0004+05            Last Frame of Picture.
```

This is an example of an optical list.

```
••••••••••••••••••••••••••••••••••••••••••••••••••••••••••••••

The Transition Effects List:

There are a total of 1 transition effects.

---------------------------------------------------------------
Transition Effect 1, Shot number 012.1

Start = 0000+00, End = 0004+05, Length = 0004+06


            +---------------------------+
0000+00 | KI 44 3778  4435+15        |                     0000+00
        |                           |
        | Scene 04  Take 05-1       |
        |                           |
        |- - - - - - - - - - - | -->  +---------------------------+
0002+14 | KI 44 3778  4438+13        |  | Black                   | 0002+14
        |                           |  |                         |
        | Edge Wipe 1 second        |  | Edge Wipe 24 fr (01+08) |
        |                           |  |                         |
0004+05 | KI 44 3778  4440+04        |  |                         | 0004+05
            +---------------------------+ --> +---------------------------+



••••••••••••••••••••••••••••••••••••••••••••••••••••••••••••••
```

This is an example of a transition effects list.

25 Select Pull List.

The pull list and the cut list both show the shots contained in the edited sequence. Where the cut list defines the sequence order of the shots, the pull list defines the order in which the shots can be found on the negative rolls.

```
••••••••••••••••••••••••••••••••••••••••••••••••••••••••••••••

The pull list:

Shot Length   Keycode    In Frame  Out Frame  Roll    Scene   Take

003  0007+10  KI 44 3778  4018+08   4026+01    1       04      01-1

004  0005+10  KI 44 3778  4116+06   4121+15    1       04      02-2

006  0024+14  KI 44 3778  4183+10   4208+07    1       04      03-2

007  0047+06  KI 44 3778  4360+08   4407+13    2       04      04-3

010  0006+11  KI 44 3778  4411+14   4418+08    2       04      04-3

005  0010+12  KI 44 3778  4438+13   4449+08    2       04      05-1

009  0005+05  KI 44 3778  4528+15   4534+03    2       04      06-2

011  0004+05  KI 44 3778  4543+05   4547+09    2       04      06-2

014  0004+05  KI 44 3778  4543+05   4547+09    2       04      06-2


••••••••••••••••••••••••••••••••••••••••••••••••••••••••••••••
```

This is an example of a pull list.

26 Select Scene List.

The scene list contains each shot that is listed in the cut list, except each shot is only listed once. You can also use this list to order prints of the clips in your program so that you can conform a work print.

```
••••••••••••••••••••••••••••••••••••••••••••••••••••••••••••••••

The scene list:

Scene          Take          Roll          Keycode                Length

04             01-1          1             KI 44 3778  4014+12     0070+13
04             02-2          1             KI 44 3778  4095+12     0038+05
04             03-2          1             KI 44 3778  4178+04     0044+08
04             04-3          2             KI 44 3778  4357+00     0075+08
04             05-1          2             KI 44 3778  4435+12     0029+13
04             06-2          2             KI 44 3778  4521+08     0031+13

••••••••••••••••••••••••••••••••••••••••••••••••••••••••••••••••
```

This is an example of a scene list.

```
••••••••••••••••••••••••••••••••••••••••••••••••••••••••••••••••

The optical scene list:

Scene          Take          Roll          Keycode                Length

04             05-1          2             KI 44 3778  4435+12     0029+13

```

This is an example of an optical scene list.

NOTE ▶ If you selected Optical List and Scene List, you will see an optical scene list included in the cut list. An optical scene list contains a description of all the shots used in all the opticals and motion effects. Each shot is only listed once. The lab uses the list to pull the negative shots needed to make the opticals.

27 Select Missing Elements List.

This essential list shows all the clips that lack the information that the negative cutter will need to conform the negative. The list is useful because the missing information is shown for each missing element.

Each source clip must be connected to a record unless you use the time-code-based method for cut list generation. Generally, this relates only to camera-roll transfers, since you capture an entire camera roll and enter one database record for each complete clip. If you use the timecode-based method, each record must include a video reel, timecode, and duration.

28 Click OK.

29 Enter *SUFR_FilmList_version01* in the Save As dialog.

30 Click Choose Database.

31 Navigate to the Lesson 06 folder, choose **Lesson 06 Database**, and click Open.

32 In the Save The Film List As dialog, click Save.

33 Enter *SUFR_Cinema ToolsFL_version01* in the Cinema Tools Program File Save As dialog box, and click Save.

The film list opens in a Viewer window in Final Cut Pro. It is a read-only file, but you can copy and paste the text file into a text application and save and print it.

> **TIP** ▶ Information in the lists must be very easy to read, so always use a monospaced font such as Arial or Courier for printing and displaying information. Your negative cutter needs to easily distinguish between letters and numbers.

Compare and Review

Whenever you export your film list, compare the window burns of your key or ink numbers to those in the film list. This is an extremely important step, because it helps you catch errors in the film list. Double-check the codes with special care if you don't plan on conforming a work print.

If your sequence includes speed changes, make sure you check the keycode numbers assigned in the motion effects list against the window burn. Where a number is inaccurate, update the film list and save the changes.

Open the exported cut list you just made and compare the keycode numbers listed in the cut list against those in the *Scene 4* edited sequence. Since you have the Timeline displaying feet and frames, you can also check the running time of your sequence against the cut list.

1 Scroll down *SUFR_FilmList_version01* in Final Cut Pro until you see the heading showing the cut list in construction order.

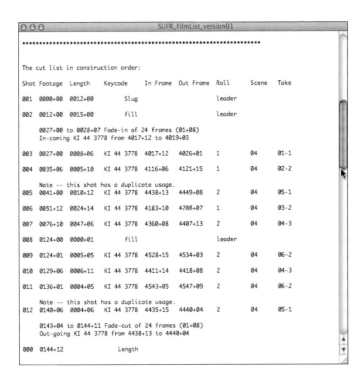

Compare each shot in the *Scene 4* Timeline to the shots and information in the cut list.

2 Place your playhead at the beginning of the Timeline.

3 Look at the Shot 001 in the cut list, then look at shot 1 in the *Scene 4* sequence.

Does your footage counter in the sequence and in the cut list begin at 0000+00?

4 In the Timeline, press the down arrow key to jump the playhead to the beginning of the next clip.

Is the Timeline feet and frames displaying 0012+00? That should match the length of the first event in the cut list.

5   Continue comparing the events in the cut list to those in your Timeline.

6   Look at the keycode numbers on the window burns of the clips in the Canvas.

Do they match the keycode numbers displayed in your list?

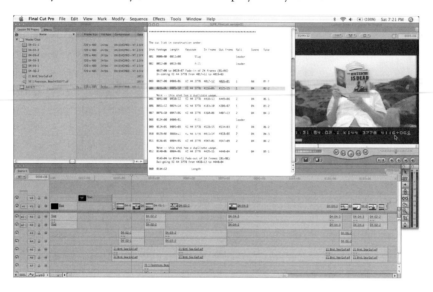

This type of error checking may seem tedious, but it will ensure a successful conform.

Finding and Fixing Missing Elements

If you encounter missing elements in your cut list, you will need to find and enter the missing information. To find the database record, look at your clips in the List View window, and click the Clip name field to sort by the name of the clip, if the clip name appeared in the missing elements list. If your clip names include the scene identifier, you will be able to use Slate to search for the record, as well as use the Find command in Cinema Tools.

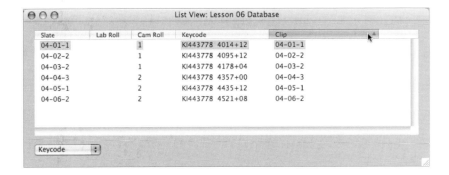

You can use reel and timecode to look for a record. In List view, choose Video from the pop-up window. The timecode in the missing elements list may not match the timecode in the database because the timecode in the database lists the first frame of timecode, but don't worry about it. Just make sure the time-code fits within the range from the In point and doesn't exceed the duration of the clip.

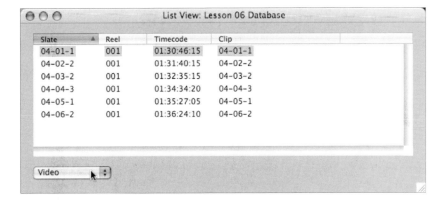

If no database record exists, you will need to create a new record and connect the clip. Just open it in a clip window, click Identify, and enter the information for that clip.

Change Lists

In a traditional film workflow, you export an initial film list, assemble a work print, screen the conformed film, and finally decide what changes to the film are needed. In Final Cut Pro, the process is reversed. The edited sequence is changed to reflect the decisions made during the screening, and a change list is exported from the edited sequence. The negative cutter or film assistant then makes changes to the work print. Another screening take places, and further changes to the conformed film are decided on. This process continues until the film is finally locked.

The changes made to your edited sequence since your initial film list export appear in the change list. You can also use a change list to generate a *change pull list* and a *discard list*. A change list compares the first video track from a previously exported list to the first video track of the changed sequence. It doesn't look at any other track. You will see optical effects and gaps described as *leaders* in a change list. This description is useful and enables you to keep sync while an optical is being made.

> **TIP** If you need to alter a Cinema Tools database between exporting lists, make sure you re-export the list from which you had seen the errors. That way you will ensure your change list integrity. For example, if you exported an initial cut list, found database errors, and fixed the errors in the database, you would need to re-export the cut list again. That way your cut list will include the database fixes, and all subsequent change lists will be accurate.

1   Duplicate the *Scene 4* sequence, and name the duplicated sequence *Scene 4 Version 02*.

2   Trim some of the edited clips in the duplicated sequence. Exactly what you do isn't important; the goal here is just to make some changes.

3   Type *0161+00* in the feet and frame counter in the Timeline, and press Return.

4   Delete the extra clip at the playhead position.

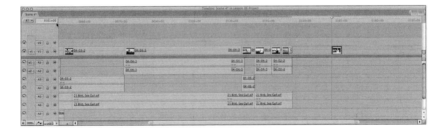

5   Choose File > Export > Cinema Tools Change List.

6   Select the *SUFR_Cinema ToolsFL_version01* Cinema Tools program file you created earlier.

The Change List dialog opens.

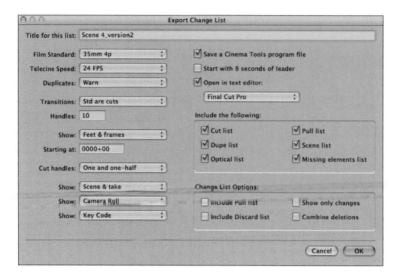

NOTE ▶ Keep the Film Standard, Telecine Speed, Show Key Code, and Start With 8 Seconds Of Leader values the same as your original cut list. This is essential to exporting an accurate change list.

7   Choose All Are Cuts from the Transitions pop-up menu.

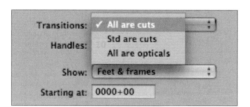

When you export a change list, choose All Are Cuts whether the transitions are of standard length or not. Cinema Tools will insert notes describing the transitions. These notes will include where and how the transitions should be represented on the work print.

Remember, this is a change list; it doesn't need to describe every event that led up to the changes.

8   Deselect the Dupe List and Optical List check boxes from the list selections.

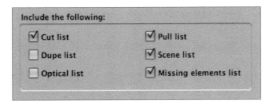

9   Select *all* check boxes in the Change List Options:

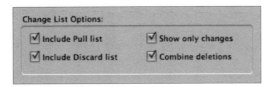

> ▶   Include Pull List—This will include any new shots that need to be added.

> ▶   Include Discard List—This will list any shots that need to be removed.

> ▶   Show Only Changes—Select this option to display new edits only. However, if the Cut List check box is selected, the original cut list is included in the Show Only Changes list file. This means all footage from the sequence, both changed and unchanged, will be included.

> ▶   Combine Deletions—This is a very useful option because it will regard footage deletions that are continuous as one shot instead of a series. A film assistant will remove a series of pieces as one piece and store them intact. This saves you time because you won't need to store a series of shots.

10   Click OK, and enter *SUFR_ChangeList_version01* for the change list name.

11   Enter *SUFR_Cinema ToolsFL_version02* for the Cinema Tools program file name.

Remember, this is the second version of your Cinema Tools program file.

12   Click Save.

13 Scroll down the change list, and stop when you reach the heading labeled The Cut List In Construction Order.

14 Compare your cut list construction order against your new sequence. Check that everything is correct.

15 Scroll up to the statistics heading. You will see figures for original length and new length.

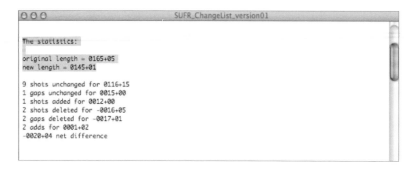

16 Compare the new length to the length of your sequence.

> **TIP** ▶ As long as you have the exported Cinema Tools program files (.pgm), you can export a change list directly from Cinema Tools. The dialog in the change list from Cinema Tools is more straightforward and only includes Change List options specifically applicable to changes. This is useful if another editor or assistant is working on your Final Cut Pro project, or if you need to re-export a change list without opening FCP.

Reel Balance

You may need to reapportion the footage on your reels to ensure the length of each reel is in the correct range. For 35mm film, the range is 10- and 20-minute reels, which translates into 1,000- to 2,000-foot reels. In 16 mm film, you will work with 10-minute, 400-foot reels. Always ask what length the negative cutter prefers. Whenever you reel balance, you are deleting and adding equal amounts of footage. To maintain an accurate cut list, you need to perform the reel balancing edits separately from other changes you may make.

Let's say that during your changes you discover that you need to make a reel adjustment and reel balance. Here is how to move a scene from the tail of one reel to the head of another:

1   Complete your initial changes, and conform the film on the two reels to the change lists exported from their associated sequences.

2   In Final Cut Pro, delete the scene from the tail of sequence 1, and move it to the head of sequence 2.

3   Export new change and cut lists for both sequences.

4   Use the new change and cut lists as guides for balancing the two reels.

Exporting

Once you've completed your edit and locked picture, you may want to export a QuickTime movie or conversion, the audio, or an audio EDL.

> **NOTE ►** If you are exporting a QuickTime movie, OMF, or EDL directly from Final Cut Pro, see the sections on exporting media, EDL, and OMF in Lesson 5.

Cinema Tools Audio EDL

If your audio is synced during telecine, your telecine log will usually contain the audio information. If no audio information was given in the telecine log, you could manually add information to the records in Cinema Tools. If a smart slate was used during production, you could add information from the smart slate reading. Either way you can produce an audio EDL directly from your Cinema Tools database.

To produce an accurate audio EDL from Cinema Tools, you need an audio timecode and reel number for each record. As with key code numbers, it's important that the audio timecode correlates to the first frame of the clip.

1   Select the *Scene 4* sequence.

2   Choose File > Export > Cinema Tools Audio EDL.

The Cinema Tools Export Audio EDL dialog opens.

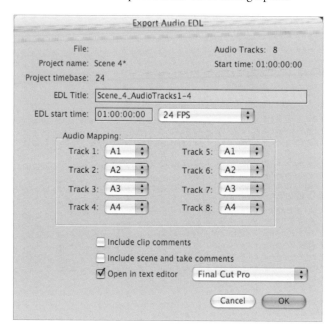

3   Enter *Scene_4_AudioTracks1-4* for the EDL Title.

TIP ▶ Keep the EDL name consistent with the sequence that produced it.

4   Enter *01:00:00:00* for the sequence start time. This should match the Final Cut Pro sequence start time.

5 Choose 24 fps from the timecode type pop-up menu. This should match your project timebase.

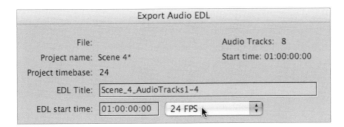

6 Select your Audio Mapping preferences for Tracks 1 through 4. In this example, leave them at their default settings.

7 Turn Audio Mapping for Tracks 5 through 8 to Off.

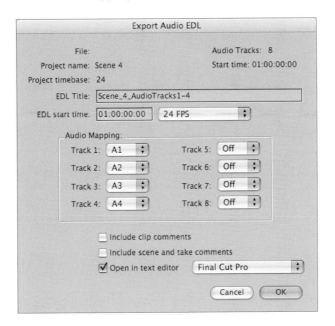

TIP ▶ Since EDLs support only four audio tracks, you can export your EDL four tracks at a time. Just identify which tracks you are including in your EDL name.

8   Click OK.

9   Select **Lesson 06 Database**, and click Choose. This is the database that contains the audio and clip information for this sequence.

10 Enter *Scene_4_AudioTracks1-4* for the Save the Audio EDL As dialog, and click Save.

You selected Final Cut Pro earlier as your text editor, so the EDL file will open in a Final Cut Pro window.

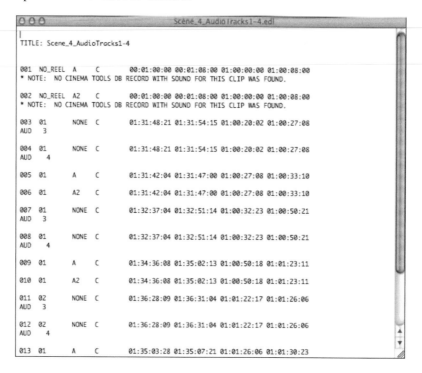

11 Repeat steps 1 through 5.

> **NOTE** ▶ For Step 3, enter "Scene_4_AudioTracks5-8" for the EDL title.

12 Turn Audio Mapping preferences to Off for Tracks 1 through 4.

13 Map audio Track 5 to A1, Track 6 to A2, Track 7 to A3, and Track 8 to A4.

You can choose to include clip, scene, and take comments.

14 Click OK.

15 Select **Lesson 06 Database**, and click Choose. This is the database that contains the audio and clip information for this sequence.

16 Enter *Scene_4_AudioTracks5-8* for the Save The Audio EDL dialog.

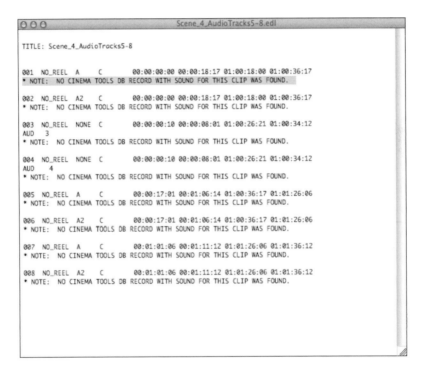

Notice that the EDL of the audio tracks contains a note alerting you that there is no Cinema Tools database record for the audio clip. This is because this audio clip came from an effects CD so there is no record of the clip in the database. Cinema Tools will alert you if there is no existing record, which is a very useful feature.

Always ask your audio mixers their preferred EDL export method; some prefer a separate EDL per audio track. Whatever the method, remember to identify clearly which track you are including in your export.

> **TIP** ▶ When you copy an audio clip that has no reel number associated with it—as in the preceding example where the audio originated from an effects CD—use the CD name as the reel name and enter the title of the CD in Final Cut Pro. It's also a good idea to include the track number. This way you can give your audio department an accurate list and maintain a good record in your project.

> **NOTE** ▶ Cinema Tools creates two files during the EDL export: a text (.txt) file and a CMX 3600 EDL (.edl) file.

The Final Conform

As with an online session for video, there are a number of elements you should deliver so a negative cutter can successfully assemble the film. Early on, ask what form the cutter wants to get the information in, from the film lists to the delivery of elements. For example, does the cutter require only the film lists in a file, or should you include a printed list? What tape format can they support for the reference tapes of the film?

What you deliver will depend on the circumstances, but you can use the following list as a rough guide:

- ▶   Delivery of elements
- ▶   Conformed work print
- ▶   Tape output of the assembled film
- ▶   Tape output of each sequence matching the cut list for that sequence
- ▶   Film lists of each sequence, printed, and text file
- ▶   Telecine tapes
- ▶   Negative

Lesson Review

1. What do you call the two methods Cinema Tools uses to locate records from Final Cut Pro?

2. Name the kinds of film lists that Cinema Tools can create.

3. How are standard transitions for 23.98 fps and 24 fps projects identified?

4. If you select Optical List and Scene List in the Export Film Lists dialog, what will you see in the cut list?

5. What should you do whenever you export your film list?

6. What does a change list do?

7. What do you need in order to produce an accurate audio EDL from Cinema Tools?

Answers

1. Clip-based and timecode-based.

2. Cut, missing elements, dupe, optical, pull, scene, and change.

3. As durations of 16, 24, 32, 48, 64, and 96 frames.

4. An optical scene list.

5. Compare the window burns of your key or ink numbers to those in the film list.

6. It compares the first video track from a previously exported list with the first video track of the changed sequence.

7. You need an audio timecode and reel number for each record.

Fundamentals of
Video Standards
and Hardware Primer

Adam Wilt

7

Lesson Files	Media > Lesson 07 Media
Media	Media > Lesson 07 Media > AJW's Filters
Time	This lesson takes approximately 50 minutes to complete.
Goals	Learn how video images are structured
	Learn the different types of analog and digital video
	Get a grasp on codecs and file formats
	Understand the basics of audio and timecode

Video Standards and Fundamentals

Armed with a thorough understanding of the different types of workflows, you have probably decided which workflow suits your projects best. The next step is to prepare your system for getting your work done, which will mean configuring and optimizing your system. We'll discuss how to do that in the third section of this book. Before you start in on those tasks, you'll save yourself time and hassle by first learning some concepts that you'll use throughout the rest of the book.

In this lesson, you'll learn the basics of video imaging and recording. You'll get an overview of the various formats, frame rates, and recording methods; and learn how video is compressed and stored in the digital domain. You'll also learn about audio for video and timecode. With this information you'll be well prepared to understand how to capture video and audio; what sorts of problems you're likely to run into and how to resolve them; and what combinations of formats and standards work together—and which ones do not.

You may find some of the topics very technical, perhaps more so than you want to deal with right now. If so, just skim them so that you'll know what to come back and reread when you find a need for that information.

Conversely, we've simplified many of the details and tried to focus on what's relevant to Final Cut Pro people; this lesson is a primer, not an encyclopedia. If any of this information whets your appetite for more, there are plenty of good books and Web sites covering video formats, technology, and engineering, some of which we'll mention in the lesson itself.

A foundation of knowledge built upon the basics will raise your editing to new heights.

Video Fundamentals

Before we can talk about tape formats, cabling and connectors, or capture settings, you have to understand the basics of the video signal. From our digital vantage point of 2005, a lot of video's technical details look downright nonsensical: what's with 59.94 Hz, 7.5 IRE setup, and dot-crawl? Yet they all resulted from careful design decisions made back in analog days, and most (if not all) make perfect sense once you know their background.

When you know how an image is structured, and how it's broken down for storage and transmission, you'll be able to choose the right kinds of connections for moving pictures around, and be able to diagnose arcane but common problems associated with interlacing and field order.

Frames, Scanning, and Sync

Video is a sequence of pictures; but the pictures themselves can be structured in a variety of ways. Fortunately, the need for transmitter and receiver to work together resulted in some fundamental principles that all modern video systems follow.

When you read this book, you start at the upper-left corner of a page, scan across a line of text, then return to the left edge to read the next line of text (assuming, of course, that this is not the Japanese or Hebrew version of this book). Reading a line at a time, you traverse the entire two-dimensional page, breaking each page down into lines of text.

Video works the same way, reading a single *scanline* across the image, then moving down to read another, and another, until an entire *frame* of video has been scanned. The basic video signal is an analog waveform (we'll get to digital later on), where zero voltage corresponds to black, and voltage increases in proportion to scene brightness.

In NTSC television, the brightness scale is calibrated in *IRE units*, with 100 divisions between zero voltage and the nominal white level (the level at which the display shows a full-brightness white image). In PAL, brightness is measured in millivolts, mV.

NOTE ▸ IRE units were standardized by the Institute of Radio Engineers, hence the designation. The IRE became the IEEE—Institute of Electrical and Electronics Engineers—and IRE units nowadays should be called IEEE units, but nobody ever does.

TIP ▸ FCP's internal Waveform monitor is calibrated in percent, from 0 percent to 100 percent nominal peak white. This is *not* the same as IRE units, as you'll see.

The structure of scanlines all stacked one atop another to form a complete frame is called a *raster*, hence the term *raster graphics* for images broken down into a regular pattern of scanlines, or *scanning raster* for the image structure displayed on the face of a CRT (cathode-ray tube).

Scanlines are separated by *horizontal sync pulses*, short negative voltage spikes inserted by the camera to tell the video display where one scanline ends and another is about to begin. The camera also generates a *vertical sync pulse* at the bottom of the image so that the display knows when to *retrace* to the top of the screen and start a new scan.

NOTE ▸ Vertical sync pulses have the same amplitude (height) as horizontal sync pulses, but are many times wider and have additional complications called *serrations* and *equalizing pulses*, which are interesting in their own right but beyond the scope of this lesson.

 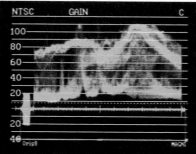

This waveform display shows scanlines complete with horizontal sync and colorburst.

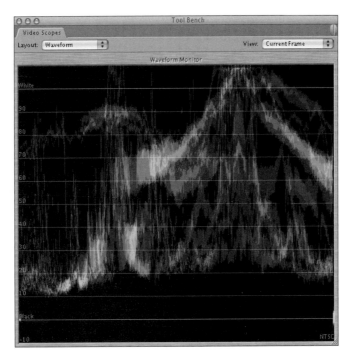

FCP's waveform display shows only picture, not sync or blanking.

Setup, Black, and Blanking

Early televisions were simple things: the video signal controlled the CRT's electron beam directly. You set the black level of the screen by fiddling with a "black level" or "picture" control; that control set the point at which the voltage of the signal just barely started to make the CRT's phosphors glow. If you misadjusted the picture control even slightly towards the "bright" side, you risked seeing a handful of diagonal lines running across your picture: the retrace of the electron beam as it completes one field and returns to the top of the screen to start the next one.

The NTSC standard fixed the problem by adding a *setup* or *pedestal* to the picture: a small voltage offset equal to 7.5 percent of the total brightness level. Setup raises the nominal *black level* a bit above the zero-voltage *blanking* level— the level at which the electron beam should be completely off, or blanked.

Setup gave you room for error; by the time you turned the brightness up enough to see the retrace lines, the blacks in your picture were milky gray.

Setup was a sensible solution in the early days of television, but modern TV sets blank the retrace completely, regardless of black level. Outside of North and Central America, setup is unknown, even in NTSC-using countries like Japan and South Korea. For most of the world, the black level is the same as the blanking level. But setup remains part of North American NTSC, and black is 7.5 IRE units higher than blanking, a detail that will return to haunt us in later lessons.

Fields and Frames

The more scanlines a frame has, the more vertical detail it shows. Of course, the more scanlines you have, the more time it takes to trace out the picture. Unfortunately, the phosphors in CRTs have a very short persistence: they don't remain bright for very long after the scanning electron beam passes by, and early television pioneers found that by the time they had enough scanlines to form a decent picture, they couldn't refresh the images quickly enough to prevent the displays from flickering abominably. Even though the frame rate was high enough to adequately represent motion, flicker made the pictures unwatchable.

The solution to the flicker problem was *interlace*: instead of progressively scanning the entire frame a line at a time, the way you'd read a page, the frame was divided into two *fields*, one comprised of all the even scanlines, the other of all the odd scanlines. Each field contains half the picture, so fields can be scanned (and displayed) twice as quickly as frames. Even though the total amount of information is the same as in progressive frame scanning, interlaced field scanning allows the CRT to be refreshed twice as quickly, so the flicker problem was overcome. The eye handily integrates the two interlaced fields into a full frame, and the net result is that you get enough scanlines to form a detailed picture while repainting the screen fast enough to minimize flicker.

Unfortunately, interlace introduces its own unique problems.

The first is simple terminological confusion: the same interlaced signal can be referred to by either its field rate or by its frame rate. NTSC television runs at 59.94 Hz, about 60 fields per second, or 29.97 Hz, about 30 frames per second. PAL runs at 50 Hz (field rate) or 25 Hz (frame rate).

It's not difficult to figure out what the numbers mean when you're dealing with NTSC and PAL, but once you start looking at HDTV, it's sometimes difficult to tell whether the field rate or frame rate is being used to describe a clip.

Second, the two separate fields don't really make up a proper frame, because they're not captured at the same time. Although each fills in the gaps of the other, the first field happens a field's time before the second. For static images, the two fields interlace smoothly, but if there's motion in the image, it shows up on still frames as "interlace combing" or tearing, a displacement of the moving objects in one field compared to the other.

NOTE ▶ The stills were extracted from the two short clips 60i.mov and 30p.mov in the media directory for this lesson. You might want to load them into a DV/DVCPRO NTSC sequence in FCP and see how they look in the Viewer and Canvas. To see what the clips *really* look like, set the Canvas to 100 percent, with the Show As Sq. Pixels setting off. (Both settings appear in the Zoom pop-up menu in the Viewer and Canvas, or in the View > Level menu.)

> **NOTE** ▶ FCP's Viewer and Canvas show you a true pixel-for-pixel representation only when Show As Sq. Pixels is turned off and the scale is set to 100 percent. You'll find that larger scales will seem to work with raw clips, but once you apply filters, the only way to see what you really have is to use these settings.
>
> Of course, if you can output the sequence to an NTSC monitor, you'll also see the difference in still frames there.

Because the two fields are really separate images, they have to be processed as such. That's why FCP has the Field Dominance setting in Sequence Settings: the setting tells FCP which field comes first in time. (If you get the setting wrong, rendered images show exaggerated combing artifacts when they're moving.)

Many filters and transitions work on a field basis for interleaved material, not a frame basis, to avoid combing artifacts. FCP also has to resize interlaced images using the two half-resolution fields separately instead of the entire full-resolution frame. This is one reason folks like progressive scanning when upconverting or downconverting or printing out to film: progressive images allow much crisper and smoother resizing with fewer artifacts.

> **NOTE** ▶ Interlaced images also have slightly less vertical resolution than progressive images, even on static pictures. Interlaced cameras apply slight vertical blurring during image capture to avoid *twitter* (frame-rate flicker) of fine details that only appear in one field or the other, and that, combined with various perceptual factors, means that the actual vertical resolution of interlaced images is about 0.7 × the expected resolution based on the line count.

Aspect Ratio

A picture's aspect ratio is the ratio of its width to its height. In TV terms, aspect ratio is most often expressed in integers: 4x3, or 16x9. Most standard-definition pictures worldwide are 4x3—4 units wide by 3 units tall—but the 16x9 widescreen format is increasingly popular, especially in Europe, and has been chosen as the aspect ratio for high-definition television. All current TV standards use one of these two ratios, though others have been used in the past.

4x3 can also be expressed as 12x9, for direct comparison with 16x9. 16x9 can be shot with a camera that captures 16x9 directly, or by adding an anamorphic lens to a 4x3 camera, which squeezes the wider image to fit in the narrower frame.

NOTE ▶ FCP normally displays standard-definition pictures as 4x3. If a clip or sequence has the anamorphic flag set, that picture will be shown as 16x9 within FCP. Depending on your video output, you may have to switch your picture monitor to 16x9 manually.

NOTE ▶ Most 16x9-capable cameras set the flag automatically when shooting in 16x9, and FCP reads that flag during FireWire capture. Footage shot with an anamorphic lens won't have the flag set, and capture though other capture cards may not sense the widescreen flag. In these cases, use a Capture Preset that sets the anamorphic flag explicitly.

NOTE ▶ You can change the state of the anamorphic setting for clips you've already captured by using Edit > Item Properties > Format, and for sequences with Sequence > Settings

In film, aspect ratio is normally given as a ratio to a picture height of 1: a 4x3 picture is 1.33:1, a 16x9 picture is 1.77:1. A full 8mm, Super8, 16mm, or 35mm frame is 1.33:1, but most "flat" (non-anamorphic) films are released in the USA as 1.85:1 (which is only 5 percent wider than 16x9, making 16x9 the favored format for digital filmmakers). "Scope" films (from "Cinemascope"), normally shot with an anamorphic lens, have an aspect ratio of 2.38:1.

TIP ▶ FCP handles both 4x3 and 16x9 material. FCP calls all standard-definition 16x9 material "anamorphic" because 16x9 images, viewed on a normal 4x3 monitor, are horizontally squished regardless of whether they were shot with a 16x9-native camera or with an anamorphic lens.

NOTE ▶ Anamorphic means "not (iso)morphic", or not equally scaled horizontally and vertically.

Widescreen pictures are often displayed on "narrowscreen" televisions by *letterboxing*, shrinking the image to fit and filling the space above and below with black bands. 4x3 images can be inserted into a 16x9 program by *pillarboxing*, adding black side panels on the edges of the 4x3 picture.

NOTE ▶ The odd terminology refers to British mailboxes, which are tall vertical pillars with thin horizontal slots for the mail.

Bandwidth, Resolution, and Line Counts

Bandwidth determines the resolution of an analog television signal, and *line count* is what measures the resolution. You'll see both terms used in equipment specifications, and in the never-ending arguments about which camera, VTR, or tape format is supposedly better than another.

Vertical Resolution

An NTSC television picture has about 483 *active lines*, scanlines carrying picture information. (There are 525 lines in an entire frame; the rest carry the vertical blanking and vertical sync. PAL has 576 active lines out of 625 total.) You might think, then, that the vertical resolution of an NTSC picture would be 483 lines, but interlace causes the effective resolution to be only 70 percent of the line count (the *Kell factor*), to about 338 lines.

NOTE ▶ In television, resolution is measured by individual TV lines—a black line beside a white line counts as two lines. In film, print, and most other media, resolution is measured in line pairs or cycles—a black line and a white line counts as only one line pair.

Horizontal Resolution

Horizontal resolution is measured over a width equal to the height of the picture, so you can compare horizontal and vertical resolution values on an equal basis. The formal measurement is thus TVl/ph—TV lines per picture height—although you'll often see it listed as "TV lines."

It turns out that each MHz of analog signal bandwidth results in about 80 TVl/ph. NTSC brightness signals have 4.2 MHz of bandwidth, or 336 TVl/ph. Thus an NTSC picture has essentially equal horizontal and vertical luma resolutions.

NTSC chroma's bandwidth of 0.5 to 1.5 MHz (depending on the exact color) yields an effective chroma resolution of only 40 to 120 TVl/ph. This low resolution doesn't bother us much because our eyes are so much less sensitive to fine detail in chroma than in luma.

Color Television

Monochrome television involves a single signal: brightness, or *luma*, usually given the symbol Y. (Although more properly it's Y', a gamma-corrected value.) Color TV requires three times the information: red, green, and blue (RGB). Unfortunately, color TV was supposed to be broadcast using the same spectrum as monochrome, using the same bandwidth, so having three times the information was a bit of a problem.

Engineers at RCA developed a truly brilliant solution. They realized that the frequency spectrum of a television signal had gaps in it largely unoccupied by picture content. They encoded color information in a sine-wave called a *subcarrier* and added it to the existing luma signal; the subcarrier's frequency fit within one of the empty gaps in monochrome's spectrum, so the luma information was largely unaffected by the new *chroma* information, and vice versa. The resulting signal remained compatible with existing monochrome receivers and fit in the same broadcast channels: they had managed to squeeze the quart of color information into the pint pot of existing monochrome broadcasting.

In this *composite color* system, the TV recovers color by comparing the amplitude and phase of the modulated subcarrier with an unmodulated reference signal. Differences in phase—the angle you can see on a vectorscope—determine the hue of the color; the amplitude—the distance of a color from the center of the vectorscope's display—indicates its saturation. The reference signal is transmitted on every scanline; it's the *colorburst* signal that you can see between the horizontal sync pulse and the left edge of the active picture.

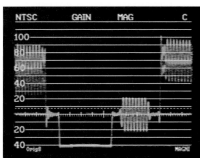

The picture monitor shows horizontal sync, blanking, and colorburst using its
pulse-cross function; the waveform shows the same information in the analog
signal itself.

Composite color has some side effects, of course. As we said, the luma and chroma signals are largely—but not completely—unaffected by each other. Certain spatial frequencies, often seen in herringbone jackets or other densely patterned clothing, can overlap the frequency used by the subcarrier and show up as *cross-color* artifacts, a shimmering moiré of false color floating on top of the affected image. Conversely, sharp color transitions along edges, as with brightly colored text or graphics, often show up as "dot crawl" or "chroma crawl," a *cross-luma* artifact appearing as series of colored dots marching up or across an otherwise straight edge.

In NTSC composite color, both the hue and the saturation are subject to distortion during recording and transmission, so NTSC monitors have adjustments for hue (make the faces green! No, make the faces purple!) and saturation. For this reason, NTSC—short for National Television Systems Committee—is often referred to as Never Twice the Same Color. PAL—Phase Alternating Line—adds additional signal alternations to automatically compensate for hue errors, so PAL sets have only saturation controls.

> **TIP** ▶ To fix distorted hue, use FCP's (one-way) Color Corrector (Video Filters > Color Correction > Color Corrector) or the Proc Amp's Phase control (Video Filters > Image Control > Proc Amp). To fix saturation, use the Sat control in the Color Corrector 3-way (Video Filters > Color Correction > Color Corrector 3-way) for real-time correction. You can also use the Sat control in the one-way Color Corrector, the Chroma control in the Proc Amp, or the Desaturate filter (Video Filters > Image Control > Desaturate), which lets you increase *or* decrease saturation.

Additionally, the carriage of color on a subcarrier limits the detail you can resolve in the color; sharp transitions in color show up as dot crawl instead of a crisp edge. NTSC and PAL limit chroma resolution to under a quarter of luma resolution. Fortunately, the human eye is much less sensitive to color details than brightness details; NTSC and PAL were designed with these limitations in mind.

Finally, adding color to the earlier monochrome standard caused interference with the sound signal when sound and picture were modulated for broadcast. To avoid interference, the picture frequencies—frame rate as well as color subcarrier—were slowed by one part in a thousand. The resulting broadcasts could still be played on existing monochrome receivers with no problem, but that one part in a thousand slowed the field rate from 60 Hz to 59.94 Hz, the frame rate dropped to 29.97 Hz, and dropframe timecode had to be used (when, later on, timecode was invented) to keep NTSC's times in sync with wall clocks, a very important consideration for broadcasters.

Color Recording

Broadcasting color is one thing. Recording it on tape, with all the instabilities and variability of electromechanical systems, is something else altogether. Many different approaches have been used, with differing benefits and side effects.

Direct Color

In the early days of color, the composite signal was recorded directly on tape, using 1-inch VTRs. Because the color is carried in the phase and amplitude of a high frequency signal (3.58 MHz in most NTSC systems, 4.43 MHz in PAL), any *timebase errors*—minor variations in playback speed that change the apparent phase of the color signal—result in ruined color. Playing back *direct color* recordings requires *timebase correction*, using memory buffers to smooth out mechanically-induced jitter. Timebase correctors (TBCs) for direct color playback were very expensive and were essentially specific to the format and type of machine being used.

Color-Under

Heterodyne or *color-under* recording developed as a way to record and play back color without the need for the expensive TBC. Inside the VTR, the chroma signal is "heterodyned down" to a much lower frequency and recorded "under" the luma signal. The magic of heterodyning is that when the playback signal is "heterodyned up" again, most of the timebase errors cancel themselves out, which reproduces usable color. Color-under is used in ¾-inch, VHS, Video8, S-VHS, and Hi8 formats, among others.

TBC-free color comes at a price: the chroma resolution of the color-under signal is reduced, and the precise timebase of the color subcarrier becomes muddled. The muddled subcarrier makes it impossible to separate the luma and chroma information as accurately as with direct color, so color-under recordings are harder to process in downstream equipment such as proc amps, TBCs, and frame synchronizers, and almost invariably suffer from diminution of high-frequency details.

Component

In the mid-1980s, Sony's Betacam and Panasonic's MII formats introduced *component* recording. In the mid-1980s, the Hawkeye/Recam/M, Betacam, and MII formats introduced component recording. A major problem with composite video is that once the luma and chroma are mixed together, it's pretty much impossible to recover the separate luma and chroma signals completely intact. Although this is irrelevant for final broadcast, since analog broadcasting uses composite color, it makes manipulation of the image in post production difficult, and dubbing composite color signals across multiple generations, even with TBCs, results in considerable quality loss.

Instead of subcarrier-modulating the signal, Betacam and MII record the luma component and two *color-difference* components separately, in different parts of the video track. Because the color signal is never modulated on a phase-critical subcarrier, it isn't subject to hue-distorting timebase errors or the resolution limitations imposed by subcarrier modulation.

Color-difference components fall under the general nomenclature of "YUV", although there are several variants—Y'UV, Y'/R-Y/B-Y, $Y'P_RP_B$, $Y'C_RC_B$—depending on the exact format or signal connection being used. There's nothing mysterious about YUV color; it's a simple transformation of RGB signals by matrix multiplication. YUV signals offer several advantages over RGB in the rough-and-tumble world of analog recording and transmission:

Gain imbalances between RGB signals show up as very noticeable color casts in the reproduced picture. The same degree of imbalance between YUV signals appears as a slight change in overall brightness or a change in saturation of some colors. To see what gain imbalances do to images, follow these steps:

1 Exit FCP if it's running.

2 Install AJW's filters from the DVD included with this book: Drag the folder AJW's Filters (Media > Lesson 07) into your Mac's Plugins folder (*Macintosh HD* > Library > Application Support > Final Cut Pro System Support > Plugins, where "Macintosh HD" is the name of your system disk).

If you're working on a shared system and don't have the permissions to drop the folder in the prescribed location, you can install it just for yourself in the Plugins folder in your home directory (*YourHomeDirectory* > Library > Preferences > Final Cut Pro User Data > Plugins). (FCP 1 through FCP 3 used different script locations; look in your User Manual for script installation instructions.)

If the filters don't appear when you run FCP, make sure the AJW's Filters folder and its contents are both readable and writable. Change the permissions as necessary, and the filters should show up inside FCP.

3 Start FCP and load the **DVStressTest3.tif** clip into the Viewer.

4 Put the clip into a 720 x 480–pixel Timeline and set the playhead so that the clip shows up in the Canvas. Double-click the clip in the Timeline to load it in the Viewer, then select the Viewer's Filters tab.

5 Apply the Effects > Video Filters > AJW's Filters > Channel Balance [ajw] filter to the clip.

6 Set the Green / Cb Gain slider to 70%, simulating an amplitude imbalance.

7 Change the Color Space setting from RGB to YCrCb (YUV) and back again while looking at the results in the Canvas.

8 Play with other Gain settings for the various channels and watch what happens in RGB mode and in YUV mode.

Timing differences between RGB signals appear as bright fringes of contrasting colors along the edges of objects, whereas in YUV the same amount of delay shows itself as laterally displaced colors with much milder edge effects. Follow these steps to see what timing differences do in RGB and YUV:

1   You already installed AJW's filters in the previous exercise, right?

2   Start FCP and load the **DVStressTest3.tif** clip.

3   Put the clip into a 720 x 480–pixel Timeline and set the playhead so that the clip shows up in the Canvas.

4   Double-click the clip in the Timeline to load it in the Viewer, then select the Viewer's Filters tab.

    If you're lazy like I am, FCP still has the clip loaded from the previous exercise. That'll do fine. Turn off or delete any filters already applied to the clip.

5   Apply the Effects > Video Filters > AJW's Filters > Channel Offset [ajw] filter to the clip.

6   Set the Green / Cb Horizontal slider to 10, simulating a timing difference.

7   Change the Color Space setting from RGB to YCrCb (YUV) and back again while looking at the results in the Canvas.

8   Play with other Horizontal settings for the various channels and watch what happens in RGB mode and in YUV mode.

Finally, as mentioned before, the human eye is less sensitive to color resolution than to brightness resolution. By transcoding color into YUV components, it's possible to reduce the bandwidth taken by the color components considerably without markedly affecting picture quality.

In digital recording and transmission, gain and timing differences are rendered moot, but the bandwidth reductions of chroma components is still quite valuable to eke out the most efficient storage on tape and disk. So most digital recorders employ YUV components with reduced-resolution chroma.

1   Look, if you haven't yet installed AJW's filters from the previous exercises, let's just admit that you're skimming the lesson and that you might as well skip this exercise, too!

2   Start FCP and load the DVStressTest3.tif clip.

    This synthetic test pattern has full resolution in all channels.

3   Put the clip into a 720 x 480–pixel Timeline and set the playhead so that the clip shows up in the Canvas. Double-click the clip in the Timeline to load it in the Viewer, then select the Viewer's Filters tab. If you have any filters applied to this clip, turn them off or delete them.

4   Apply the H. Chroma Blur [ajw] filter (Effects > Video Filters > AJW's Filters > H. Chroma Blur [ajw] filter) to the clip.

5   Set the Blur Amount slider to 2, and the Chroma Shift slider to 0.

    This simulates 4:2:2 sampling as used in Digital Betacam, D-5, and other high-quality, 601-specification video formats. (We'll define "601" later in the lesson.)

6   Turn the filter on and off while looking at the Canvas.

    Even with chroma blurred, the overall appearance of the clip is acceptable (thus bringing to mind the old phrase, "it's only television").

7   Set the Blur Amount slider to 4.

    This simulates 4:1:1 sampling (which we'll define later in the lesson), as used in NTSC DV25 and the DVCPRO formats. It's also close to the look of Betacam SP, although Beta SP's luma signal isn't as sharp.

8 Turn the filter on and off while looking at the Canvas.

Even 4:1:1 isn't too bad.

9 Turn the filter off or delete it from the clip's filter list.

10 Apply the Channel Blur [ajw] filter (Effects > Video Filters > AJW's Filters > H. Channel Blur [ajw] filter) to the clip.

11 Set Color Space to YCrCb (YUV), set the Green / CB slider to 2, and set the Blue / Cr slider to 2.

These settings roughly simulate 4:2:0 color sampling as used in PAL DV25, over-the-air DTV, and DVD MPEG-2 formats.

12 Turn the filter on and off while looking at the Canvas.

The high-end production market still has a need for keeping as much of the raw picture information as possible; the new HDCAM-SR format allows recording of full-bandwidth RGB signals. HDCAM-SR is discussed in Lesson 9.

Digital Video

Digital video started in the late 1980s as a means of improving recording quality in an analog world, so all the basic details of digital formats, at least for standard-definition television, descend directly from their analog forebears.

Digital composite recording digitized the existing analog composite waveform directly. The signal was sampled at four times the subcarrier frequency (*4fsc*), 14.32 MHz for NTSC signals. Digital composite was designed as a drop-in replacement for analog composite recorders and—even though they worked superbly for that purpose—they suffered because they recorded a composite signal in a world that was rapidly moving to component video for postproduction purposes. Except for certain niche uses, such as tape-based time-delay, you won't see many digital composite recorders these days.

Digital component recording followed the Betacam and MII model of recording a luma signal and two color-difference signals separately, keeping them pure for postproduction manipulation. Almost all standard-definition digital component recorders conform to some variant of the ITU-R BT.601 specification (formerly called the CCIR-601 specification, back when the International Telecommunication Union was still the International Consultative Committee for Radio—and Television).

Sampling

The "601 spec" calls for a sampling frequency of 13.5 MHz, yielding 720 luma samples per scanline. (There's an optional 18 MHz sampling rate in the spec, giving 960 samples per scanline, but very few recorders implemented it.) At 13.5 MHz, the limiting horizontal resolution is 540 TVl/ph (assuming a normal 4x3 picture aspect ratio), although in practice 500 TVl/ph is a better figure.

> **MORE INFO** ▶ There's always some low-pass filtering of the signal prior to recording to prevent aliasing artifacts. Charles Poynton's books *A Technical Introduction to Digital Video* and *Digital Video and HDTV Algorithms and Interfaces* are great references for this sort of detail.

> **NOTE** ▶ Both NTSC and PAL-compatible signals have scanlines taking about the same amount of time to display, so both formats are captured with 720 pixels per scanline in 601 digital video.

> **TIP** ▶ The active picture area in the NTSC standard spans only about 704 pixels in the 720-pixel 601 line. Some digital cameras respect the 704-pixel active area and record thin black bars on either side of the picture in the remaining pixels; others record an active picture across the entire line. If you shrink a picture down in FCP, you may need to crop the left and right edges slightly to hide the black bars.

That 720 samples or 500 TVl/ph figure is an upper limit for what 601 will resolve; it doesn't mean that anything recorded on a 601 format will show that resolution. A low-end DV camera or an off-air analog signal transcoded to 601 digital may yield considerably lower resolution, and a 35mm film transfer or an HD downconvert will have a hard limit of 720 samples but may appear sharper than the numbers allow; the perception of sharpness is more complex than a simple pixel count can capture.

> **MORE INFO** ▶ See www.adamwilt.com/TechDiffs/Sharpness.html for details (pun intended).

Pixel Aspect Ratio

The 601 spec, you'll notice, results in *nonsquare* pixels. Were the pixels square, a 4x3 720-pixel-wide picture would be 540 pixels (scanlines) tall, but "NTSC" 601 has 486 scanlines captured, whereas "PAL" 601 has 576. "NTSC" 601's pixels are slightly wider than they are tall; their *pixel aspect ratio* or *PAR* is 0.9. "PAL" pixels are slightly taller than they are wide, with a PAR of about 1.07. Keep in mind that PAR is measured as the ratio of height to width, whereas picture aspect ratio is width to height—yet another odd detail to trip up the unwary.

> **TIP** ▶ FCP avoids confusing PAR numbers, instead providing descriptive terms: "Square," "NTSC – CCIR 601 / DV," and so on. PAR is normally set up for you when you select a capture preset or a sequence preset.

Color Subsampling

The color-difference signals C_R and C_B are normally *subsampled* at half the rate of luma; the resulting ratio of luma to chroma samples is called *4:2:2*, apparently in a holdover from the 4fsc nomenclature.

There are variants to the 4:2:2 sampling structure. Some formats, like DVCPRO25, record 4:1:1 color—chroma samples at one-quarter the rate of luma. This may not sound like much, but it's still enough for about 135 TVl/ph chroma resolution—better than NTSC allows.

4:2:0 is used in PAL-compatible DV and DVCAM, and in MPEG-2 as seen in DVB (digital video broadcasting), DVD, and HDV. In 4:2:0, C_R is sampled at half the luma rate on one line, C_B on the next, and vertical filtering is used to reconstruct the image. 4:2:0 is problematic in interlaced video since the filtering has to happen on a field basis; unpleasant sawtooth-like artifacts are often seen on brightly-colored diagonals; and it's hard to perform color-oriented postproduction steps such as chroma-keying using 4:2:0—that's why "PAL" DVCPRO uses 4:1:1 even though other "PAL" DV25 formats use 4:2:0.

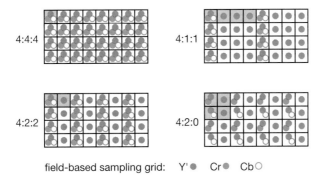

field-based sampling grid: Y'●   Cr●   Cb○

24p

Film is normally shown at 24 frames per second, which doesn't fit nicely into either the NTSC nor the PAL scheme of things, yet film is often shown on television, and there are now cameras shooting 24p (24 frames per second, progressively scanned) on tape.

NTSC transfers use a *3:2 pulldown* or *2:3 pulldown* process to convert 24 frames of film to 60 fields of video. The film is run at 23.98 fps, slowed one part in a thousand to match NTSC rates. The first film frame (the "A frame") is recorded to two fields of video. The second (B) frame is recorded to three fields. The third, or C, frame is recorded to two fields again, but since the B frame introduced an extra field, the C frame is recorded to the second field of one frame and the first of another. The D frame is again recorded to three fields, for a total of 10 fields or 5 full video frames for the four original film frames.

This four-frame *cadence* is repeated a total of six times per second, converting 24 frames of film to 60 fields (30 frames) of video.

Several standard-definition video cameras can perform the same pulldown, converting film-like 24 fps images into 60i video for recording on tape. However, this cadence splits the C frame across two different video frames, making clean extraction of the original 24 fps material difficult: two different video frames need to be decompressed to recover the C frame.

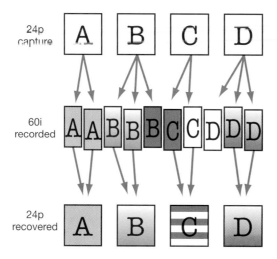

Panasonic developed an alternative cadence they call "24p Advanced" for the DVX100, DVX100A, and SDX900 cameras, syncopating the rhythm slightly for a *2:3:3:2 pulldown*. As you might guess from the name, the A and D frames are recorded for two fields and the B and C frames are recorded thrice. The resulting video is slightly less smooth than normal 24p when playing back as 60i video, but the C frame can be recovered from a single video frame, without having to decompress two different frames and steal a field from each. The Canon XL2 camera also offers a 2:3:3:2 pulldown in its 24p mode.

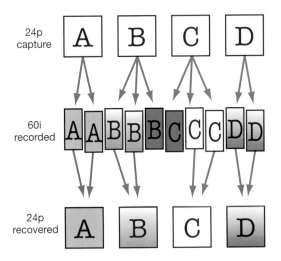

24p Advanced 2:3:3:2 Pulldown

You can capture 2:3:3:2 pulldown in FCP over FireWire with the pulldown removed in real time, resulting in 20 percent smaller files playing at a 23.98 fps rate. FCP can also remove advanced pulldown after the fact if such clips were captured at 29.97.

29.97 clips using 2:3 pulldown, whether shot in camera or transferred from film, can be converted to 23.98 clips using Cinema Tools.

TIP ▶ If you have captured 24p clips at 29.97, you can tell 2:3 clips from 2:3:3:2 clips by single-stepping through them in FCP while monitoring the FireWire output, or by setting the Viewer or Canvas to 100%, with the Show As Sq. Pixels setting turned off. If you see two interlaced frames in every five, the clip uses 2:3 pulldown. If you see only one, it uses 2:3:3:2 pulldown.

NOTE ▶ Two short 24p DV clips are available in the lesson directory: **24p.mov** and **24pa.mov**. You can experiment with them in FCP and in Cinema Tools.

MORE INFO ▶ For information on how 24p is recorded and how to deal with it in postproduction, go to www.adamwilt.com/24p/.

In the PAL-compatible world, film is normally sped up 4 percent to 25 fps, and transferred to tape frame-for-frame: a 1:1 pulldown. There is no fancy cadence to worry about, and every frame on tape matches a frame of film. Indeed, film shot for television in the PAL world has long been shot at 25 fps to begin with, so no speed changes (with accompanying pitch shifts in the audio) need to be accommodated.

PAL-format camcorders with "film-like" shooting modes likewise skip any attempt at recording 24p and simply record 25p.

Before the advent of 24p-capable NTSC-compatible camcorders, many digital filmmakers shot with PAL cameras—even in interlaced mode—to get the higher vertical resolution of the PAL frame and the easier transfer to film that the 1:1 pulldown factor provides. Even today, it's not always an easy choice to go with a 480-line 24p camera that transfers at normal speed instead of a 576-line 25p camera that requires a 4 percent speed change when printing out to film.

Standard-Definition Standards

Despite the variations, there are only two fundamental video standards you'll encounter in the standard-definition production universe, as outlined in the following sections.

525/59.94, a.k.a "NTSC"

Video in North America, Japan, and South Korea is based on the NTSC (National Television Standards Committee) broadcast standard. Although NTSC refers to a specific manner of encoding a composite video signal with subcarrier-modulated color, it's often used as shorthand for all the video formats that conform to NTSC's standards for timing, frequency, frame rate, and line count.

Frame Rate and Scanning

NTSC video has a frame rate of 30 Hz × 1000 ÷ 1001, normally abbreviated as 29.97 Hz. A 2:1 interlace is used, resulting in two fields per frame. The field rate is 60 Hz × 1000 ÷ 1001, or approximately 59.94 Hz. The line rate (frequency of horizontal scanning) is 15,750 Hz × 1000 ÷ 1001, or about 15.734 Hz.

> **NOTE** ▶ That annoying high-pitched whine that TV monitors make? That's the sound of the line rate, sitting right in the upper reaches of human hearing. The high-voltage amplifiers deflecting the electron beam in a CRT cause enough vibration for you to hear the whine.

Frame Size and Aspect Ratio

NTSC uses a 4x3 aspect ratio frame with 525 scanlines per frame. Of these, about 483 contain active picture content, and the rest are used for vertical blanking and sync.

When digitized to ITU-R BT.601 specifications, the active picture area is 704 pixels wide and 486 pixels tall. Some digital production tools use all 720 pixels per scanline for active picture content.

Signal Levels

Peak to peak signal: 1 volt, or 140 IRE units total.

100% white: 714 millivolts, or 100 IRE units.

Sync tip: –286 millivolts, or –40 IRE units.

In North America, NTSC composite black is at 54 millivolts, or 7.5 IRE. Outside North America, and in component digital and most component analog systems, black is at 0 millivolts, or 0 IRE.

Subcarrier Frequency

Color is subcarrier-modulated at 3.58 MHz in the composite signal.

Variations

Some parts of the world use NTSC timing and frame sizes but modulate color at the PAL subcarrier rate of 4.43 MHz. If an NTSC-4.43 tape is played back in NTSC-3.58 equipment, or vice versa, you'll see a monochrome picture.

NTSC-format DV records only 480 scanlines, not 486. When a DV frame is placed into 486-line raster, 4 blank lines are added to the top of the picture and 2 at the bottom.

24 fps material is normally carried in NTSC using a 2:3 pulldown, although the 2:3:3:2 pulldown is becoming more common for standard-definition digital cinematography. In all cases the 24p material is really shot (or transferred from film) at 23.98 fps and carried in a standard 29.97 fps signal.

30p captures 29.97 frames per second, breaking the frames into two fields for recording. (The "Frame Movie Mode" on some Canon and Panasonic camcorders is a form of 30p.)

There are also systems (like JVC's HDV cameras and Panasonic's DVCPRO-Progressive system) that shoot a full 480-line, 60 frame per second picture, but FCP doesn't currently support these systems.

625/50, a.k.a. "PAL"

PAL, or Phase Alternating Line, is a German-designed broadcast standard now used through most of the rest of world. PAL replaced several incompatible monochrome standards (such as the UK's 405-line broadcasts and France's 819-line television) and is now the basis for all standard-definition video that isn't NTSC-based.

Frame Rate and Scanning

PAL uses 25 frames per second with a 2:1 interlace, thus 50 fields per second. The line rate is 15,625 Hz.

Frame Size and Aspect Ratio

PAL's pictures have a 4x3 aspect ratio. There are 625 scanlines total, of which 576 are active. PAL, when digitized, also fits into a 720-pixel scanline.

> **NOTE** ▶ PAL has 20 percent fewer frames per second than NTSC, but each frame has 20 percent more scanlines. When digitized to 601 specifications, both standards require the same number of bits per second.

Signal Levels

Peak to peak signal: 1 volt. IRE units are not used in PAL measurement.

100% white: 700 millivolts.

Sync tip: −300 millivolts.

Subcarrier Frequency

Color is subcarrier-modulated at 4.43 MHz in the composite signal.

Variations

SECAM, Système Èlectronique Couleur Avec Memoire (sequential color with memory), is a transmission standard developed by the French, and used in France, Russia, and various countries in Europe and Africa where those two countries once held sway. SECAM is used for over-the-air transmission only; all the production equipment is PAL-based.

> **NOTE** ▶ Some wags state that SECAM stands for System Essentially Contrary to the American Method, but sadly there is no similar jocular derivation of the PAL acronym.

A fair bit of content in the PAL/SECAM world is now 16x9 widescreen material. A signal in the vertical interval triggers compatible TV sets to modify their scanning to show the program in its proper aspect ratio.

24 fps material is sped up 4 percent to 25 fps and transferred using, in effect, a 2:2 pulldown; film shot for television is often shot at 25 fps to begin with. Each frame of film transfers to two fields of video.

25p production cameras are becoming common for digital cinematography in the PAL world. 25p captures 25 full frames per second, breaking the frames into two fields for recording. (The "Frame Movie Mode" on some Canon and Panasonic camcorders is a form of 25p.)

High Definition

The BBC introduced high-definition television in 1936, with 405 total scanning lines (well, it was HDTV by the standards of the time). Modern HD started in the 1980s with a Japanese analog standard, 1125/59.94, with 1035 active scanlines, interlaced. Europe also developed an interlaced analog system, called Eureka, using 1250 scanlines total and running at 50 fields per second. Both systems used the 16x9 widescreen aspect ratio.

Both systems have been made obsolete by digital HD standards, and any program content you encounter from the earlier systems will have to be (and probably already has been) converted to one of the current standards, since analog HD capture cards for the Mac are nonexistent.

Digital HD falls into two camps: 1080-line standards and 720-line standards. The 1080-line standards evolved from the earlier 1035-line standards and run at 25, 29.97, and 30 frames per second interlaced, and 23.98, 24, and 25 frames per second progressive (although the recording is interlaced, the image capture is true progressive).

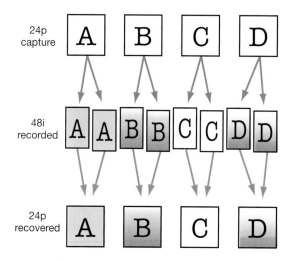

PsF (progressive segmented frame) recording of 1080p24 HD

You'll see the terminology *1080i* for the interlaced formats, and *1080p* for the progressives. FCP tags the HD formats with their image-update rate without respect to fields or frames: 1080i60 is 30 frames per second, interlaced (thus 60 fields per second); 1080p30 is 30 frames per second, progressive, no separate fields.

The 720-line formats, all progressive scan, started as a lower-bandwidth alternative to 1080i with roughly the same vertical resolution (no Kell factor degradation to account for). 720p normally runs at 60 frames per second, but there is a 30 fps variant, and 24 fps images are recorded on DVCPROHD equipment by performing a 3:2 pulldown, repeating each 24 fps frame either twice or three times in alternation to fill up all 60 frames on tape. 720p DVCPROHD even allows arbitrary frame rates between 1 and 60 fps to be shot; it flags each "new" frame with a special code to set it off from previous repeat frames in whatever pulldown sequence is required.

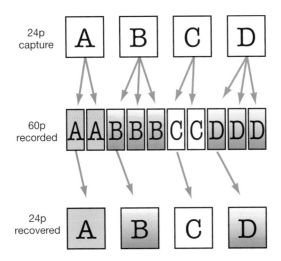

DVCPROHD recording of 720p24 as 720p60

As in the 1080-line formats, 720p can run at either integer frame rates or the NTSC-compatible rates 23.98, 29.97, and 59.94.

High-definition formats include the "integer NTSC" rates, especially 24 fps, for direct compatibility with film production. Film is normally produced for release at 24 frames per second, and having a true 24p mode, along with 30p and 60i, lets HD transfer to film with the exact same timebase. Filmstyle production often uses separate audio recording ("double system" audio), and having the exact same timing for film-originated and HD-originated material simplifies postproduction considerably.

However, the NTSC-derived television world still uses the fractional rates 23.98, 29.97, and 59.94, so that HD and SD material can share a common timebase (and so HD material can be played out using existing NTSC-oriented scheduling and automation systems). Film transferred to television in NTSC countries is slowed down one part in a thousand to match the fractional rates. (That's not so bad, really: in PAL countries it's sped up 4 percent to 25 fps.)

Almost all HD material is shot at PAL rates or fractional NTSC rates. Integer NTSC frame rates are sometimes used when HD material is to be used in a movie shot (and finished) on film but are rarely seen otherwise. Regardless, HD material is usually described by integer rates, so a 1080i60 clip may be shot at either 59.94 Hz or 60 Hz, and a 720p24 clip might be either 23.98 fps or 24 fps.

> **TIP** Final Cut Pro handles only NTSC-compatible and PAL-compatible frame rates for DVCPROHD over FireWire. True 24, 30, and 60 fps material can't be ingested using FireWire, though third-party uncompressed cards may allow it.

Sampling and Pixels

The HD formats themselves are specified using square pixels. A 1080-line HD image has 1920 pixels per scanline. A 720-line image has 1280 pixels per scanline.

"Full bandwidth" HD recording formats record all those luma samples, but normally subsample the C_R and C_B color-difference signals with the 4:2:2 ratio described earlier. (HDCAM-SR allows recording the original RGB signals in their full-resolution 4:4:4 glory: no color-space conversion, no subsampling. It's popular with the high-end film effects crowd.)

"Camcorder" HD formats usually subsample the luma signal as well as the chroma in order to get the data rate low enough to record on tape. As with subsampled chroma, the subsampled luma is interpolated back up to full resolution for conveyance over a serial digital interface.

> **MORE INFO** ▶ "High Definition Fundamentals" in "New Features in Final Cut Pro HD" has a lot of great information on HD formats, terminology, and the like. Get to it from inside FCP HD (4.5) by choosing Help > New Features. (FPC 5's documentation does not contain this information.)

Codecs and Compression

Uncompressed standard-definition video's data rate is 270 Megabits/second (about 34 Megabytes/second); 1080i60 HDTV runs at 1.2 Gigabits/second (150 Megabytes/second). That's a lot of bits, so many video formats—both on tape and inside your Mac—use compression to get the data rate down to something more manageable. A *codec* is the bit of software and/or hardware that manages this task; "codec" is short for COmpressor/DECompressor.

Of course, there are tape formats and capture cards to record and play back uncompressed video, too; we still refer to part of the system that records and retrieves the bits from disk as a codec, hiding our terminological imprecision with the dodgy excuse that in these cases, "codec" stands for COder/DECoder.

Even analog video, when recorded on a computer, requires a codec. First, the analog video is converted to digital using a bit of hardware called (not surprisingly) an analog-to-digital converter: ADC or A/D for short. Once in the digital domain, the codec handles putting the bits on disk (with or without further compression) and retrieving them for processing or output. On playback, digital is transformed into analog with a digital-to-analog converter: DAC or D/A.

Codecs and compression let us trade off quality against data rate. Roughly speaking, image quality increases with increasing data rate, but only roughly speaking. For example, the DV codec's data rate is 25 Megabits/second—about one-tenth the rate of uncompressed SDTV—yet its images are perfectly acceptable for most purposes. An MPEG-2 version of the same picture, played off DVD or over the air as digital television, might run one-quarter the data rate of DV, yet look as good. Although the MPEG-2 version might be four times more efficient in terms of compression, it's also much harder to produce, requiring far more processing time and often two passes through the codec.

Codecs achieve compression using three different methods:

Reducing the Data to Compress

By throwing away some of the image prior to compression, you reduce the overall data rate. For example, NTSC DV records only 480 out of the 486 lines the 601 spec calls for (on playback, the top four and bottom two lines are filled in with black), and only half of the 4:2:2 color samples are recorded, using 4:1:1 in NTSC and 4:2:0 in PAL. FCP's OfflineRT setting uses a Photo JPEG codec, throwing away over three-quarters of the picture, using only 320 samples horizontally and 240 vertically, compared to the 720 x 480 DV–NTSC picture.

You can also reduce the number of bits per pixel recorded. Most codecs record 8 bits per pixel (actually, 8 bits per luma or color sample), giving up to 256 gradations in brightness or color, although the 601-compatible codecs use a more constrained 219-step scale from 16 to 235 in luma. (The values outside that range accommodate "superwhite" and "superblack" excursions of the video signal.) Some allow 10, 12, or 16 bits per pixel for a smoother gradation, desirable when doing extreme color correction or high-caliber film work.

> NOTE ▸ Most digital videotape formats, including all digital camcorders (except Digital Betacam camcorders), record 8 bits per pixel, even if the camcorder is capable of outputting 10-bit signals on its SDI connector.

Spatial Compression

Most codecs that advertise compression get much of their efficiency from reducing spatial redundancy: most of the time, one pixel is not very different from its immediate neighbors.

Lossless codecs perform the compression with no loss of information: the decompressed picture is identical to the source picture. These codecs usually use a form of *run-length coding*, detecting runs of pixels with the same value and replacing them with a pixel value and a repeat count. Lossless compression is common on computers—it's used in the *zip* and *sit* file formats—but it's rarely used for video because it usually doesn't compress more than 2:1, yet it's computationally intensive. You will see it occasionally in workflows requiring lossless performance yet wanting some compression for data transmission and storage reasons, for example Apple's "Animation" andTheoryLLC's "Microcosm" codec.

Lossy codecs throw away information; the decompressed picture is not identical to the original, but ideally it's visually very close. Lossy codecs offer much higher compression ratios than lossless ones, anywhere from 4:1 to over 100:1 (albeit with more heavily degraded image). Such codecs often perform a *basis transformation*, a mathematical conversion from the spatial domain to a different domain in which the spatial redundancy can be more easily detected and removed.

> **NOTE ▶** You can think of basis transformations as doing to pixels what the RGB to YUV transform does to colors: they are just different ways of representing data to allow more convenient processing. Indeed, the RGB/YUV conversion is itself a basis transform.

The most common such conversion is the *Discrete Cosine Transform* (DCT) used in JPEG, MPEG, and DV formats, which converts pixels into frequency components. There are also codecs based on *wavelets*, including the codec used in the Immix VideoCube NLE of the early 1990s and the Cineform HD codec on the PC platform.

DCT-based codecs get their compression by throwing away frequency components in each DCT block—typically an 8 x 8 pixel area—that are close to zero. As more frequency components are discarded, more DCT artifacts appear in the decompressed image, the most common being "mosquito noise," spurious light and dark pixels "buzzing" around sharply-defined edges and transitions, such as sharp-edged text.

Wavelet-based codecs tend to result in softer images as compression is increased, perhaps with some "ripples" of faintly repeated detail dispersed across the picture. Although some people feel that wavelets give better images than DCTs do, wavelets are much harder to compute, and in real-time video work, processor time is precious.

Temporal Compression

So far, the techniques we've discussed all apply to single frames: each compressed frame stands on its own, with no reference to previous or following frames. This *intraframe* compression is ideal for editing since any frame can be easily retrieved.

Temporal compression exploits redundancies across time, since most frames are fairly similar to the ones just before and after. MPEG codecs take advantage of this by compressing *groups of pictures* (GOPs) together. Each GOP has one *I-frame* (intraframe-compressed) which stands on its own, and several *P-frames* (predicted) and *B-frames* (bidirectional) that encode only the differences between themselves and their neighbors.

> **MORE INFO ►** "Understanding GOPs and Frame Types", starting on page 140 of Compressor 2.x Help, or page 87 of Compressor 1.x Help (In Compressor, choose Help > Compressor Help), has an excellent discussion of GOP structure and the different frame types.

The B- and P-frames are only a fraction of the size of the I-frames, so *long-GOP* compression winds up being about three to five times more efficient than *I-frame-only*, or intraframe-only, compression for the same level of picture quality. MPEG-1, -2, and -4 all use long-GOP compression for DVD, digital television transmission, HDV, and Web video. (MPEG -2 and -4 also have intraframe-only modes.)

The drawback is that accessing any single frame may require decompressing some or all of an entire GOP. Although long-GOP compression is great for getting the most efficiency out of a bitstream, it's computationally expensive and makes random access and off-speed play modes very difficult. FCP 5 can use long-GOP media in the form of HDV clips, but working smoothly and efficiently with HDV requires a fast, powerful G5 for best results. (FCP also lets you capture HDV using the I-frame-only Apple Intermediate Codec, which requires less CPU power to decode on the fly, but takes up more space on disk.)

Wrappers and File Formats

It's possible to record a raw stream of compressed video data to disk, and iMovie does just that: it takes DV data coming across FireWire and stores it in DV stream files. Most programs, though, want to see a more structured file format, and that's where "wrappers" come in. Wrapper formats add *metadata*—data about data—to the raw video stream, making it easier for programs to manipulate video and audio information. Wrapper formats can carry information about audio sample rates, timecode, and similar information that makes it much easier for FCP to read the file correctly and keep its media synchronized. Wrappers can (and often do) contain multiple streams or tracks of information: a video track, two or more audio tracks, and a timecode track are common.

QuickTime, AVI, Windows Media, and Real are all wrapper formats.

It's important to distinguish between codecs and wrappers. A codec defines how the data is compressed, whereas a wrapper defines how the compressed data is packaged, as the name implies. You can have DV data in a QuickTime MOV file or in a Windows AVI file: it's the same video clip, only with different wrappers.

QuickTime

The most common wrapper format on the Mac, and the one used by FCP, is QuickTime. QuickTime is more than just a file format, it's an entire media-manipulation framework (witness QuickTime Player Pro, a very simple application that exposes some of what QuickTime can do, or the rich options in FCP's QuickTime Export dialog). QuickTime is cross-platform, having Apple implementations on Mac and on Windows, and some open-source support on Linux. Many of the codecs supported by QuickTime are also cross-platform, and the QuickTime architecture allows third parties to easily add new codecs.

QuickTime movies normally have the extension .mov. Although this isn't required on Macs, you should use it if you're going to be sharing files with PCs.

QuickTime allows for both *self-contained* and *reference* movies. A self-contained movie contains all the media it needs for playback: every frame of video, every sample of audio. A reference movie may contain some media but references other files on disk: for example, an FCP reference movie will contain any frames that FCP has to render at the time the movie is saved, but it will reference (point to) clips that don't require rendering in their original files as well as any pre-rendered render files.

AVI / Windows Media

PCs have their own native media architecture, known in its various developments and incarnations as Video for Windows, DirectShow, DirectX, and Windows Media. The common production file format normally has the extension .avi, standing for Audio Video Interleave.

QuickTime on the Mac (and, by extension, FCP) can usually open an AVI file as long as the underlying codec is compatible. DV files, for example, are usually readable. However, there are quite a few AVI codecs that don't have QuickTime equivalents, and there are some variants of the AVI file structure that may not work well with QuickTime.

TIP When you have problems with AVI files in FCP, ask the creator of the file to ensure that a compatible codec is being used, to write out a "Video for Windows" AVI file, and to keep file sizes under 2 Gigabytes.

FCP's QuickTime infrastructure can also export AVIs: choose File > Export > Using QuickTime Conversion, and select AVI from the Format list. Don't forget to choose a codec using the Options button.

Other Windows media file types are WMA (audio) and WMV (video). These typically contain highly compressed long-GOP media using Windows proprietary codecs, and are usually not usable in FCP.

Real Media

Real Media files, often with the extensions .ra and .rm, are files using Real's proprietary wrapper and codecs. Real files are encoded for final delivery using Real's proprietary player software and are not usable in FCP.

MXF and AAF

MXF, the Media Exchange Format, is an open, non-proprietary streaming file format used in some NLEs and video recorders. MXF files most often contain MPEG-2 media but may also wrap DV, DVCPROHD, and uncompressed video streams, among others. MXF files are not directly supported in FCP but may be in the future as the MXF format gains support across the industry. Currently, FCP 5 depends on Telestream's Flip4Mac MXF software to translate between MXF and QuickTime.

The Advanced Authoring Format, AAF, is "the mother of all wrapper formats" in that its aim is to wrap all aspects of a production—media, scripts, edit decision lists, camera metadata, color correction notes, and so on—in one big bundle. It may turn out to be a great cross-platform material exchange format, but its implementation is very complex. Currently FCP has some AAF interchange capability using import/export plug-ins from Automatic Duck, useful for moving projects between FCP and Avid, among other things.

Raw Stream Files

You may also encounter "unwrapped" media files, which may or may not be usable in FCP depending on their contents. The most common ones contain DV, MPEG-2, and uncompressed media.

DV and DIF files normally contain DV streams with both video and audio. They're usable in FCP, but the audio will require rendering.

M2V and MPG files are MPEG-2 elementary and program streams. These may or may nor be usable in FCP as source clips requiring rendering, and may or may not have usable audio embedded in them.

M2T files are MPEG-2 transport streams, as imported from HDV cameras over FireWire. These aren't usable in FCP, but may contain media accessible through demultiplexing with a third-party utility such as LumiereHD.

601 files contain uncompressed video and are normally openable in FCP.

You may also encounter *image sequences*, sequentially-numbered still images using PICT, TGA, TIFF, BMP, DPX, or similar files formats. These are generated by computer animation programs, film telecines, or film digital-intermediate processes, and consist of individual frames of a clip in numerical order. As long as FCP understands the basic file format, it can import the sequence.

> **MORE INFO ▶** For details on working with image sequences, see "Importing Numbered Image Sequences", Final Cut Pro Help, Volume 1, Section II, page 381.

Audio for Video

Ah, audio… always second fiddle when video is being discussed, yet sound is arguably more important than picture in the overall impact of a program. Fortunately, audio is fairly straightforward when compared to video's intricacies, at least from a technical standpoint, but there are a couple of details worth noting to avoid common pitfalls.

Single- and Double-System Recording

Sound recorded on videotape (or on film, for film cameras) is called *single-system* sound. It's convenient, since it's married to the image in perfect sync, and can be captured in sync at the same time as the picture.

Double-system sound is recorded separately, on DAT, minidisk, quarter-inch tape, or portable disk recorders. With double-system sound, a sync mark of some sort is needed to align sound to picture: a *clapstick* or *slate* is normally used, but anything that produces simultaneous visual and audible cues can be used. Sometimes a *timecode slate* is used; the camera shoots the image of the timecode being used on the sound recorder, and the timecodes are matched up in post.

Audio on Videotape

Audio is stored on videotape in a number of ways. *Linear* analog tracks are used in most analog videotape formats; the audio is laid down in its own track using a stationary head, just like reel-to-reel or cassette audio. Linear tracks can be overdubbed or recorded separately from the video track. The frequency response of a linear track is largely dependent on the "pull speed" of the tape format: how rapidly the tape moves past the head. By modern standards, linear audio tracks aren't especially high-fidelity.

AFM (Audio Frequency Modulation) tracks are analog audio tracks recorded by rotating heads in the same area of the tape as the video. Quality is usually very good, better than linear audio, but the audio cannot be recorded separately from the video.

PCM (Pulse Code Modulation) tracks are digital audio tracks recorded in their own segments of the video track by the video heads. PCM tracks are usually recordable separately from video and are of high quality.

Mono, Stereo, Multichannel

Audio is recorded to one or more *tracks*, each track containing a channel of sound. A single channel is *mono*, short for monophonic, but beyond that things get more complex.

Two tracks may contain two separate mono feeds, say, a shotgun mike and a lavaliere. The two channels are independent of each other, with their own separate levels and settings, and should be kept as separate channels within FCP: you would capture these unlinked (in FCP 5) or as "Ch 1 + Ch 2" (in earlier versions).

Alternately, two tracks might form a *stereo pair,* where the two tracks contain the left and right channel sounds of a single, stereophonic feed. These two channels should be panned left and right, respectively, and their levels should be ganged together so they fade up and down in sync. If you capture them linked (FCP 5) or as "Stereo" (earlier versions), FCP will perform the panning and ganging automatically.

> **TIP** Although you can convert a clip's audio from "Stereo" to "Ch 1 + Ch 2" and vice versa after the fact, life will be *much* easier if you select the proper format *before* capturing dozens of clips.

Sometimes a stereo pair arrives as a *mid+side* recording. MS recording is the audio equivalent of the RGB-to-YUV transform: the mid track contains the sum of the left and right channels, and the side track contains their differences. Unfortunately FCP can't handle mid+side stereo internally; you'll have to use a separate program to reformat the channels as left+right, or use an external processor to convert mid+side to left+right as you capture it. Fortunately mid+side recording is less common than left+right recording.

> **TIP** Mid+side played back as left+right will have one channel that sounds like a normal mono mix (the sum of left and right), and the other may sound weak, indistinct, and may have some sounds much louder while others are softer.
>
> In a pinch, if you do not need the stereo image, you can discard the side track and just use the mid track as a mono mix.

Multichannel audio is common on many modern videotape formats as well as tape- or disk-based digital audio recorders. With a multichannel recording, you really need to have the sound recorder's notes to determine how each track is being used and how to capture it.

Although FCP can capture up to 24 channels with the appropriate hardware, FireWire DV captures are limited to two channels at a time. If you need to capture more than two channels, you can either capture two channels at a time, making multiple passes through the media, or you can use an appropriate multichannel audio interface to capture the audio into FPC, bypassing FireWire.

Sample Rates

Digital audio may be sampled at various rates; the higher the rate, the better the high-frequency response will be, but the higher the data rate and storage requirements of the audio track will be. Sampling theory states that the highest frequency you can faithfully record and reproduce is half the sampling frequency (the Nyquist limit). In practice, the high-frequency response for audio sampled at a given rate will be slightly less than half the sample rate.

Human hearing is usually said to range from 20 Hz to 20 kHz, but NTSC broadcast audio doesn't extend past 15 kHz, nor does the response of many older people's ears (or younger people's ears, if they've listened to a lot of heavy metal with the volume turned up to 11). At a minimum you'd want audio sampling to occur at 30 kHz for NTSC transmission, or 40 kHz to cover the range of hearing. On the other hand, many film sound designers now prefer to record and mix at 96 kHz or 192 kHz, saying that the overtones otherwise lost have a perceptible impact on the audible frequencies.

You'll most commonly encounter sound recorded at 32 kHz, 44.1 kHz, and 48 kHz. 32 kHz is used by DV, DVCAM, and Digital8 camcorders in four-channel mode. (Some older DV camcorders can *only* record at 32 kHz.) 44.1 kHz is the sample rate used on CDs and other recorded media, and occasionally appears on DV tapes created on early DV NLEs. 48 kHz is the most common rate for professional audio and audio for video recording. Final Cut Pro happily handles these rates natively.

96 kHz and 192 kHz are available on some disk-based audio recorders. Capturing audio at this rate requires compatible third-party audio interfaces.

Rates below 32 kHz aren't normally seen in source media, but are often used for Internet or multimedia delivery. If you import such a clip into FCP, FCP can resample to a higher rate, but you won't have much in way of high frequencies, and the sound is likely to be dull and "muddy." (Of course, if you're looking for precisely that sort of sound—constrained by limited-bandwidth transmission media—then go for it.)

Bit Depth

Bit depth in sound, as in video, affects the smoothness, signal-to-noise ratio, and dynamic range of the captured signal. The standard bit depth for professional audio is 16 bits per channel, although some high-end equipment now records 24 or even 48 bits per channel. FPC 5 supports both 16-bit and 24-bit audio.

DV, in four-channel mode, records 32 kHz 12-bit audio using level-adaptive compression: the signal-to-noise ratio degrades slightly when the level is very high (when you can't hear the difference anyway), but retains the fineness and discrimination of 16-bit audio for soft sounds. Once inside the Mac, the DV codec's audio section converts it to 16 bits, so the 12-bitness of DV's four-channel mode is mostly a curiosity, not an operational issue.

Lower bit depths are often found, again, in media intended for Internet or multimedia delivery. If you use these media in FCP, they'll exhibit a higher noise floor: soft sounds will tend to be lost in a sort of hiss or hash of noise.

File Formats

Most production audio, if saved to disk, will be stored in AIFF or WAV (wave) files. AIFFs typically originate on Macs, WAVs on PCs, but both can contain 48 kHz 16-bit uncompressed audio, and both import perfectly well into FCP. AIFFs and WAVs also support sample rates as low as 8 kHz and bit depths of 8 bits per channel, and AIFFs may contain compressed audio using a variety of codecs, but these are not commonly found in production applications.

> **TIP** ▶ It doesn't hurt to look at an imported clip's properties when you import it to make sure the bit depth and sample rate are sufficient to give you high-quality audio.

Film audio is sometimes recorded using other formats, such as BWF (Broadcast Wave File: WAV with added timecode and metadata tracks). You may need to convert these files to AIFFs or WAVs using a third-party program before bringing them into FCP.

Compressed Audio

Most production audio is recorded uncompressed (at 1.5 Megabits/second for two channels of 16-bit, 48 kHz sound), but there are a few exceptions.

DV's 32 kHz 12-bit adaptive compression was described earlier; for all intents and purposes it can be treated as 32 kHz 16-bit uncompressed.

Audio recorded on minidisc uses Sony's ATRAC compression. It's a "perceptual codec" designed to throw away certain frequencies masked by louder sounds, so that the resulting playback is perceptually indistinguishable from the original sound. Whether it really *is* indistinguishable or not is a controversy best left unaddressed; regardless, people are using minidisc for location audio recording. Minidisc audio is decompressed for playback and captured as 16-bit uncompressed, so its compression is not something to worry about inside FCP.

MPEG-1, layer 2 audio is used in HDV cameras, compressing the audio 4:1 to 384 kbits/second. FCP 5 decompresses HDV audio during capture, and renders back to MPEG-1 Layer 2 when outputting to an HDV device.

MP3 (MPEG-1, layer 3) audio is used in iTunes, the iPod, and a variety of Internet and computer-related applications. Sometimes you'll get audio tracks (sound effects, second language tracks, and so on) as MP3 files; you can use iTunes or other third-party audio applications to decompress them to AIFFs for use in FCP. The quality of MP3s depends on their bitrate; 128 to 160 kbits/second gives quite usable audio, and lower bitrates give flatter and muddier sound.

Dolby E is a way to compress six channels of audio for studio transmission over a single AES/EBU two-channel connection. FCP can't handle Dolby E directly; you'll need a third-party product—typically a Dolby E decoder box—to convert the audio back into uncompressed form.

Dolby AC-3 is a low-bitrate format for delivering 5.1 audio (five channels plus a low-frequency subwoofer channel) on DVD or in digital television transmission. It's not intended for further production purposes; it's a delivery format only.

Locked and Unlocked DV Audio

FCP's capability to capture raw DV data across FireWire leads to an interesting audio synchronization issue.

DV cameras can record audio as "locked" or "unlocked." Locked audio, used in more professional equipment, uses an audio sample clock precisely tied to the video sample clock, so that audio and video sampling march in lockstep. Cameras recording unlocked audio, as the name implies, use an audio sample clock that is not precisely locked to the video clock. For example, audio that should be sampled at 48 kHz gets sampled slightly faster or slower: 48.009 kHz, or 47.998 kHz. The sample rate information stored with the DV data, however, still says 48 kHz; the DV specification allows only 32 kHz, 44.1 kHz, and 48 kHz *timebases*.

DV interleaves the audio and video on a frame basis, so when a tape is played back, the audio and video play in sync regardless of the audio clock used. And when iMovie imports a DV stream from tape, things likewise stay in sync.

When DV is stored in a QuickTime file, the audio is read out of each frame and resaved as a parallel track of AIFF-format audio. Each track of a QuickTime file has its own timebase determining the playback rate of the track.

With locked audio, the timebase stored in the DV data matches the sample rate of the audio, and the audio plays back at the proper rate, staying in sync with the picture. With unlocked audio, if the nominal and actual timebases differ, the audio will slowly drift out of sync with picture over the duration of the clip. For short captures, the drift is not noticeable, but captures over 4 or 5 minutes can show perceptible sync errors.

Final Cut Pro HD compensates for this automatically. When a DV clip is captured over FireWire, FCP counts the audio samples as it goes, so it can record the actual timebase in the resulting QuickTime file. (With previous versions, you had to turn on "auto sync compensation," but now FCP has this feature always turned on.)

Clips captured in FCP should always be in sync—as long as the clips are well-formed on tape. If a clip capture crosses a blank spot on the tape, or a scrambled frame, FCP can get confused and lose count, resulting in a bad audio timebase setting and resultant sync drift. If this happens, and you can't locate the bad frame on tape to avoid capturing across it, try recapturing again and/or break the clip into smaller clips and capture them individually.

By the same token, DV clips imported from other sources, such as programs saved to disk or tape with older versions of FCP or other NLEs, may show sync drift or slippage. In these cases, the sync drift may have been embedded in the program by the program writing the file; you may have to unlink audio and video and speed-change the audio to get it back in sync by trial and error.

> **MORE INFO ▶** The Final Cut Pro manual—also available in FCP by choosing Help > Final Cut Pro User Manual—is chock-full of really useful background information about audio. Have you looked at it recently?

Timecode

The only way to consistently log and capture a clip frame-accurately is to have some means of uniquely specifying each frame. *Timecode* serves this purpose: an address for each frame given in hours, minutes, seconds, and frames. Timecode values are shown in the format HH:MM:SS:FF and range from 00:00:00:00 to 23:59:59:FF, where FF is the highest frame number for that format: 23 for 24 fps media, 24 for PAL-rate video, and 29 for NTSC-rate video (all numbers are zero-based, so 30 frames are counted from 0 to 29). Negative timecodes aren't used.

TIP ▷ If you try to capture a clip too close to 00:00:00:00, the deck will want to back up into "yesterday's timecode." Once the deck (or the controller) thinks it has backed up before 00:00:00:00, it'll see its timecode as being around 24 hours, and it will try to rewind 24 hours further. That's why you should always set your first capture point at least as far into the tape as the pre-roll amount of the deck.

Timecode Formats

Timecode was originally added onto video formats not designed for it, so timecode had to "piggyback" on tape in a compatible way. *Longitudinal timecode* (LTC) masquerades as an audio signal (actually a 1-volt peak-to-peak square wave; not a very *nice* audio signal) and is recorded to tape like a linear audio track. (Some early VTR conversions used an existing audio track for LTC.) LTC readers and generators access this signal through a BNC connection (or, sometimes, an XLR), converting the square wave signal to and from a timecode number.

LTC can be read at normal play speeds easily enough, but fast or slow play can be problematic, and it's not readable at all unless the tape is moving. *Vertical interval timecode* (VITC) was invented to circumvent that problem; it's recorded as a series of light and dark pulses in the video signal just above the active picture, in the vertical blanking area. VITC requires readers and generators built into the video equipment itself, or offboard processors that are able to interpret the information from the video signal itself. VITC can be retrieved whenever a video image is displayed, even in pause mode, but it isn't accessible whenever the tape is unthreaded, as in fast-forward and rewind modes.

LTC and VITC readers and generators are common in older editing systems, but nowadays most editors get their timecode through a serial control port connection or over FireWire. Many professional analog VTRs record both VITC and LTC and read back VITC when the tape is threaded, falling back on LTC for high-speed shuttle modes.

The Society of Motion Picture and Television Engineers (SMPTE) and the European Broadcasting Union (EBU) have standardized the way LTC and VITC are recorded, as well as the interfaces used to retrieve them from tape, hence the terms "SMPTE timecode" and "SMPTE/EBU timecode."

Digital formats (and Video8 / Hi8) use their own digital implementations of timecode, which appear to the outside world as if they were LTC or VITC. Many digital decks are able to synthesize a SMPTE-standard LTC signal and insert regenerated VITC into their video outputs, so the exact format of the timecode on tape is of no importance except to the VTRs themselves. These timecodes aren't "SMPTE timecode" strictly speaking, but the distinction is irrelevant as far as operations are concerned.

> **NOTE** ▶ All digital VTRs record timecode, but not all analog ones do. Three-quarter inch, VHS, S-VHS, Video8, and Hi8 tapes especially may or may not have timecode on them. If you have the appropriate VTR, you may be able to write timecode onto such tapes, or you might want to dub the tapes onto a digital format for editing use.

Dropframe Timecode

PAL-rate video has a timebase of 25 Hz, and when 25 frames per second are counted, the running time shown by timecode exactly matches clock time. But in the NTSC world, counting 30 frames per second when the timebase is really 29.97 Hz results in a drift of over 3 seconds per hour, and timecode disagrees with clock time. That's not a big deal—unless you're running a TV station and need to keep schedules on track.

Dropframe timecode compensates for the drift by dropping certain timecode values, so that the timecode time catches up with clock time and stays roughly in sync. (Think of the dropped frame numbers like "leap frames" in reverse.) The formula is quite simple: timecode frame numbers 00 and 01 are dropped from the counting sequence at the start of every minute *not* divisible by 10. Thus the timecode sequence crossing the first minute boundary is as follows:

> 00:00:00;28
>
> 00:00:00;29
>
> 00:00:01;02
>
> 00:00:01;03

Those two dropped frame numbers are sufficient for timecode time to catch up to clock time.

To distinguish dropframe (DF) timecode from non-dropframe (NDF) time-code, the final colon is usually replaced with a semicolon.

Note that no actual video frames are dropped when using dropframe time-code. The timecode sequence drops numbers, but you're still getting all the frames you should. This is an important distinction sometimes lost on nervous commercial producers, who pay big rates to get their spots on the air and want to get every frame they're paying for.

PAL-rate shows and clips always use NDF timecode, of course. 24p material, even using a 23.98 Hz timebase, almost always uses NDF TC.

Film has its own versions of timecode, most notably edge codes and key numbers. See Appendix A in Cinema Tools Help for details.

> **MORE INFO** ▶ *Tube: The Invention of Television*, by David E. Fisher and Marshall Jon Fisher, is perhaps the most entertainingly readable narrative of how we've gotten into this mess.

Lesson Review

1. How are video images structured?

2. In analog composite video, what are luma and chroma and how are they carried?

3. How do Y/C video and component video handle luma and chroma signals differently?

4. What makes compression useful?

5. Give the pros and cons of lossy codecs.

6. Name two wrappers that can carry digital video.

7. How is audio for video usually carried?

8. What is the function of timecode?

9. What does drop-frame timecode do?

Answers

1. As a series of individual frames, which can be further subdivided into two fields.

2. Luma (brightness) information is represented as a voltage level. Chroma (color) is conveyed by a modulated subcarrier.

3. Y/C video separates the luma and chroma signals; component video carries the chroma as two separate color-difference signals.

4. Compression reduces the size of video data by exploiting aspects of the human eye and redundancies in the video information.

5. Lossy codecs provide more compression, but with reductions in image fidelity.

6. QuickTime and AVI.

7. It is carried in a variety of sample rates, bit depths, and track counts. Most professional audio is 48 kHz at 16 bits or greater.

8. It identifies each video frame with a unique number, allowing frame-accurate operations.

9. It drops certain timecode numbers to keep timecode time in sync with clock time in NTSC video.

8

Lesson 8
Hardware and Interfaces

Now that you've waded through the abstract fundamentals in the previous lesson, let's review the types of hardware you'll need to configure and set up your system. As mentioned in other lessons, Final Cut Pro is *scalable* and can support a range of workflows. So, it's important to learn about the characteristics of different components and how to hook it all up.

We'll start with a look inside your system to review the anatomy of a Mac and the hardware that powers Final Cut Pro.

We'll follow that with the types of video signals you'll encounter and their characteristics and qualities. We'll explore video cabling and connectors in detail. We'll also cover audio signals and cabling in enough detail to get you started, and we'll discuss timecode and control protocols and the interfaces they use.

Next we'll review common video and audio formats a FCP editor is likely to see. We'll look at the context in which the formats are used and ways to get contents into FCP with minimal losses.

In addition, we'll look at waveform monitors, vectorscopes, and rasterizers, mention video and audio monitors, and consider offboard processors that expand the capabilities and flexibility of an FCP suite.

Finally, we'll review the different methods and hardware used for getting video and audio into FCP. FireWire suffices for many purposes, but there are multiple plug-in cards and break-out boxes that can be used to connect almost any type of video and audio to an FCP system.

Computer Systems

Understanding your Mac's internal operations is not a prerequisite to working with Final Cut Pro, but it becomes increasingly necessary as you demand more from your system. The range of systems and workflows that FCP supports are discussed in detail in the first section of this book, which means in this lesson we can focus on the individual components and their role within the system.

As you assess the needs and demands of your workflow, it's vital to consider the complete system configuration. For instance, the processor and RAM in an eMac may meet the minimum requirements for DVCPRO HD, but the graphics card does not offer nearly the same performance of those installed in high-end pro systems.

Processor

Computers in the current Macintosh lineup include either a PowerPC G4 or PowerPC G5 processor. The G5 provides many advantages over its predecessor in terms of power and speed. Perhaps the most significant difference is that the G5 is built to support 64-bit computing. If the next generation of Final Cut Pro is written to take advantage of the G5 processor and the 64-bit capabilities of upcoming versions of Mac OS X, we may be on the cusp of a new era in hardware acceleration.

> **MORE INFO** ▶ Jon Stokes has published a comprehensive history of the PowerPC processor from 1993–2004 at http://arstechnica.com/articles/paedia/cpu/ppc-1.ars/1.

PowerPC G4

The G4 debuted in 1999 and is the current processor in the Mac mini, eMac, iBook G4, and PowerBook G4 computers. It is a 32-bit processor that features AltiVec technology, symmetric multiprocessing (SMP) support, and clock speeds that range between 1.2 GHz (12-inch iBook G4) and 1.67 GHz (17-inch PowerBook G4).

> **MORE INFO** ▶ The Freescale Web site features detailed specifications of their PowerPC processors, which are used under the name PowerPC G4 by Apple: www.freescale.com/webapp/sps/site/prod_summary.jsp?code=MPC7457&nodeId=018rH3bTdG8653.

PowerPC G5

The G5 first appeared in 2003 and is currently the processor used in iMac G5, Power Mac G5, and Xserve G5 computers. It is a native 64-bit processor that features SMP support and clock speeds, which range between 1.6 GHz (17-inch iMac G5) and 2.5 GHz (Power Mac G5).

> **MORE INFO** ▶ The IBM Web site includes information about their PowerPC processors, which Apple dubs the PowerPC G5: www-3.ibm.com/chips/techlib/techlib.nsf/techdocs/A1387A29AC1C2AF087256C5200611780.

RAM

Random Access Memory (RAM), or system memory, provides temporary storage for data the processor needs. RAM works to ensure that the data is available when the CPU needs it. In this way, it creates a bridge between the CPU and the much slower, but much larger, data storage provided by hard disks (hard disks are discussed in detail in the next lesson). Although the current dual 2.3 GHz and dual 2.7 GHz Power Mac G5 computers can hold up to 8 GB of RAM, 32-bit systems are only able to make use of 4 GB. The transition to 64-bit computing means that applications will, in theory, be able to access many times that amount. That said, the current cost of RAM makes the acquisition of large quantities impractical for all but the highest of high-end users.

Installing more RAM is one of the easiest ways to upgrade your Macintosh, letting you handle larger projects or keep Final Cut Pro, Motion, Live Type, and other production tools co-resident in memory. In most cases, RAM is categorized as a Customer Installable Part (CIP). This means that as long as you follow the specified procedures and do the installation correctly, you can install RAM yourself without voiding your warranty.

> **NOTE** ▶ On some portable computers, only one RAM slot is accessible. Check the documentation that came with your Macintosh for the status of your system.

If you decide to add more RAM to your computer, follow these general guidelines:

▶ Follow the installation instructions for your specific model at all times. This includes using any appropriate tools and making sure you under-stand Electrostatic Discharge (ESD) precautions.

▶ Since there are many different types of RAM and a multitude of vendors, check your System Profile or the documentation that came with your computer before making a purchase to make sure the new memory exactly matches the specifications required.

▶ Choose vendors that explicitly state that their RAM is Mac-compatible. RAM is such an important part of your computer that you want to make sure it meets the standards set by the rest of your system.

▶ Because your system has a limited number of RAM slots, plan your upgrades with an eye to the future. For instance, the four 512 MB cards that filled your 1.8 GHz Power Mac G5 may have made sense at one point, but now you will have to lose some memory before you can upgrade beyond 2 GB of RAM.

▶ After installing new RAM, run the extended system tests on the hardware test CD or DVD that came with your Mac. Current Macs are very sensitive to variations in the speed and timing of memory, and bad memory can manifest itself as random crashes, kernel panics, and other hard-to-predict behaviors. Although Apple's memory test routines aren't 100 percent per-fect, they are your primary tool for detecting memory that isn't quite up to snuff.

TIP ▶ RAM cards must currently be installed in equal sized pairs on all Power Mac G5 computers.

Graphics

The speed and power of the Graphic Processing Unit (GPU) in your computer has a direct impact on Mac OS X's capability to accelerate the rendering of complex images. The GPU is the display card's engine for texture mapping, compositing, shading, and other graphics-rendering tasks. Mac OS X currently uses a range of display technologies, such as OpenGL, Quartz, and Quartz Extreme, which take advantage of powerful GPUs. Motion similarly relies on the GPU for its operations. The promise of Core Image, Core Video, and other embedded technologies in Mac OS X is that they will further accelerate graph-ics performance in the Pro Apps when paired with a powerful GPU.

MORE INFO ▶ You can find additional information on the various graphics and media technologies in Mac OS X v10.4 (Tiger) at www.apple.com/macosx/overview/graphicsandmedia.html, and in John Siracusa's extensive review of the new Mac OS X at http://arstechnica.com/reviews/os/macosx-10.4.ars, specifically pages 13 through 16.

As with standard RAM, the amount of dedicated RAM installed on the display card determines the amount of data it can handle at any one time. Current Mac GPUs have anywhere from 64 MB to 256 MB of dedicated memory. Graphics acceleration technologies such as Quartz Extreme require graphics memory to run, and as time goes by, these technologies only increase their appetite for dedicated memory. Higher screen resolutions and dual displays also demand more memory. FCP workstations are well served by having the most GPU memory available; the performance of Motion is directly depend-ent on the amount of GPU memory available, and FCP will likely exploit the GPU's memory directly in future releases.

Dual-output cards let you drive two monitors simultaneously from a single GPU. (PowerBooks similarly let you extend the built-in display with an external monitor.) A dual-display system lets you spread your FCP workspace over more screen real estate, or lets you dedicate the second monitor to FCP's Digital Cinema Desktop Preview function.

You've probably already discovered that computer displays use a range of different connections. Common standards found on Macintosh computers include Video Graphics Array (VGA), Apple Display Connector (ADC), and Digital Visual Interface (DVI). DVI itself supports both digital-only connections (DVD-D) and digital or analog connections (DVI-I), depending on the pins in the DVI connector.

You can find inexpensive ($15 to $30) adapters to connect ADC cards to DVI- or VGA-equipped monitors, and DVI cards to VGA monitors. Connecting DVI cards to ADC monitors is also possible; ADC is essentially DVI with added power lines. However, a DVI-to-ADC adapter has to supply power to the monitor, so the integrated power supply boosts the costs of these adapters to around $100.

Which bus, or connection path, your graphics card uses is also important, because that will directly affect its capabilities and performance. A high-speed bus is important in a system that needs to process large, complex images.

AGP

Accelerated Graphics Port (AGP) is a newer, faster alternative to the Peripheral Component Interconnect (PCI) bus used for other plug-in cards in your Mac. AGP handles data more efficiently than standard PCI. It's designed expressly for interfacing to the GPU and works to reduce demands on both the CPU and RAM. AGP is the current standard for graphics in every Mac and is used by the fastest of the current generation of high-performance cards.

Device Drivers and Interconnections

Although AGP is designed specifically to increase graphics performance, several other technologies are employed within the current Mac lineup to connect devices. Some of the current standards include ATA, SATA, SCSI, PCI, PCI-X, FireWire, and USB. Exactly which of the standards your system uses depends on the specific model and revision. Details about the hardware configuration of your Mac can be accessed through System Profiler.

1   From the Apple menu, choose About This Mac.

2   Click the More Info button to launch System Profiler.

3   Select listed hardware components to see which standard they use.

FireWire is discussed in more detail in later sections of this lesson; hard drive technologies (ATA, SATA, and SCSI) are addressed in relation to storage in the next lesson.

> **MORE INFO** ▶ You can find technical details about particular Mac device drivers and bus technologies on the Apple Developer Connection (ADC) Web site at http://developer.apple.com/devicedrivers. You can find information about PCI and PCI-X technologies at www.pcisig.com.

When adding new devices to your computer, make sure that you review the manufacturer's documentation and follow guidelines carefully. For instance, PCI and PCI-X cards need to sit correctly in their slots and should be installed to maximize performance. This last point is particularly important because the PCI and PCI-X buses are a shared resource and can only operate at the speed of the slowest component you have installed. Improper installation may mean that the 33 MHz Ethernet card you salvaged from your last system could hamper the operation of your new super-fast PCI-X video card. Worse yet, you could permanently damage your system by installing a card in an incompatible slot.

> **MORE INFO** ▶ You can find information on installing PCI and PCI-X cards in the following Knowledge Base article: http://docs.info.apple. com/article.html?artnum=86790. You can also find information at corresponding ADC resources: http://developer.apple.com/documentation/ Hardware/Developer_Notes/Macintosh_CPUs-G5/PowerMacG5/ 4Expansion/chapter_5_section_3.html.

Video Interfaces

Connecting up video gear isn't difficult, but it's not entirely simple, either. You can choose among several kinds of video signals, and they vary in the quality they deliver. To keep things more interesting, different signal types often use the same kind of connector, so you can't just plug a cable into any physically compatible jack and expect things to work. Fortunately, you can master the complications with just a little effort.

Analog I/O

Analog video interfaces fall into three classes: component, Y/C, and composite. You'll find analog component on both standard-definition and HDTV equipment, though these days HD analog is usually reserved for monitoring purposes, not transfer into and out of FCP. Y/C and composite signals are only found on SDTV gear, or as SDTV outputs on HDTV gear.

Analog Video Interfaces at a Glance

Name(s)	Connectors	Quality	Comments
Component, YUV, YPrPb, Y/R-Y/B-Y	BNC x 3, RCA x 3, D-SUB (a.k.a. HDI-15; VGA connector, on some projectors)	Best; full bandwidth	Some component signals use RGB instead of VUV. SD and HD formats
Y/C, S-Video	4-pin Y/C, 7-pin Y/C	Very good; full luma bandwidth	SD only
Composite, VBS, "video"	BNC, RCA	Limited luma & chroma bandwidth; dot-crawl & false color artifacts	SD only

Analog Video Interfaces at a Glance

Name(s)	Connectors	Quality	Comments
RF, antenna	F-type coax	Poor to fair	Radio-frequency modulated, like an antenna or cable signal. Analog SD broadcast; digital SD and HD broadcast

Component Component connections provide the cleanest, highest-resolution signal possible, and you should use them whenever possible.

Three separate cables carry component video, one each for the luma signal and the two color-difference signals (although some interfaces, mostly on graphics equipment, monitors, and projectors, may offer an RGB component option). The normal nomenclature for this connection is YP_RP_B, though you'll sometimes see Y, R-Y, B-Y, or YUV labels. The sync signal is part of the Y signal in almost all cases.

Sync is normally carried on the Green channel in RGB, but sometimes you'll see a separate sync connection (which takes a combined vertical and horizontal sync) or separate horizontal and vertical syncs (mostly on computer graphics equipment).

Y/C Y/C, also called S-Video (and sometimes mistakenly called S-VHS), is the next best thing to component, and it preserves most of component's quality.

Two separate signals in one multicore cable provide Y/C connections. The luma is separate from the chroma, but the color-difference signals have been subcarrier-modulated into a composite color signal. Although this modulation reduces the quality of the color somewhat, having separate luma and chroma preserves all the resolution the luma signal is capable of and prevents the cross-luma and cross-color artifacts of a composite signal connection. Sync is carried in the Y signal.

Composite The lowest common denominator is composite: luma and chroma have been mixed together, just as in an analog television broadcast, and they suffer for it. Cross-color and cross-luma artifacts are likely to occur, and the resolution of both luma and chroma are compromised by the processing needed to extract them from a composite signal.

You'll find composite signals on almost every bit of video equipment. The connectors may be labeled video, comp., composite, or VBS, the latter standing for video, [color]burst, and sync.

There is a fourth analog connection: the *radio-frequency modulated signal* on the RF or ANT (antenna) connector. This carries a composite signal modulated on a carrier for transmission, and needs to be *demodulated* from whatever TV channel the signal is on to a *baseband* video signal, using the tuner in a VCR or a stand-alone demodulator. Unless you're working with live signals off-air or out of a cable or satellite box, you shouldn't ever have to deal with an RF signal as a video source.

Digital I/O

Digital connections fall into the general classifications of SDI, SDTI, and FireWire.

Digital Video Interfaces at a Glance

Name(s)	Connectors	Quality	Comments
SDI, Serial Digital Interface, 601	BNC	Uncompressed 4:2:2	Most common pro digital video connection
Dual-link SDI	BNC x 2	Uncompressed 4:4:4	4:4:4(:4) digital video (sometimes with alpha)
HD-SDI	BNC	HD 4:2:2	High definition video
Dual HD-SDI	BNC x 2	HD 4:4:4	HDCAM-SR, Viper Filmstream, etc.
SDTI	BNC	DV25 or DV50	DV data at 2x or 4x real-time using SDI as a transport
SDTI-CP	BNC	MPEG	MPEG-compressed using SDI as a transport
HD-SDTI	BNC	HDCAM/ DVCPROHD	Compressed HD using standard-definition SDI as a transport
FireWire, i.Link, IEEE-1394, FW400	4-pin or 6-pin FireWire	Depends on format	Used for DV, DVCAM, DVCPRO, DVCPRO50, DVCPROHD, uncompressed 4:2:2, and HDV data streams, depending on equipment
Parallel	D-shell connectors, ribbon cables	Uncompressed 4:2:2	Older connections on early SD digital VTRs

SDI The Serial Digital Interface is the most common digital video connection in production and postproduction. It's described in SMPTE standard 259M, and you'll often see that number used to specify the connection. Curiously enough, SMPTE 259M describes both the 10-bit 4:2:2 digital *component* connection we all know and love, and the 4fsc digital *composite* connection briefly used at the dawn of the digital age but now mostly extinct from the postproduction world.

Serial digital *component* video conforms to the ITU-R BT.601 specification, as discussed in Lesson 7. SDI can carry 8- or 10-bit 4:2:2 signals (8-bit signals have the two least significant bits filled with zeroes) and up to eight channels of digital audio embedded with the video, all at 270 Megabits/second.

> **NOTE** ▶ Not all equipment handles embedded audio. In some cases, you may need offboard embedders/disembedders to put audio into and to extract it from the SDI data stream.

Serial digital *composite* connections, as found on D-2 or D-3 VCRs, is not directly usable with FCP capture cards; you'd need to use an outboard composite-to-component *transcoder* (a box that translates between dissimilar signal types).

HD-SDI The high definition version of SDI runs at 1.485 Gigabits/second. Its SMPTE standard is 292M. HD-SDI is a digital component connection only, as there's no digital composite connection in HD.

Dual-Link SDI Both SD and HD SDI have dual-link flavors, for carrying more information than a single SDI link allows. Dual-link SDI is most often used with graphics systems and high-end capture equipment that support full 4:4:4 data transmission, both in RGB and YUV formats, and sometimes including an alpha channel as well. For example, dual-link HD-SDI is employed in the HDCAM-SR system for recording and transmitting 4:4:4 RGB HD for the digital filmmaking crowd.

SDTI The Serial Data Transmission Interface carries compressed video formatted using the SDI transport at 270 Megabits/second. It's commonly used to carry compressed DV25 data four times faster than real time, or DV50 data twice as fast as real time.

SDTI connections are common between similar bits of gear in a broadcast plant, but are rare in nonlinear editing. There aren't any capture cards for FCP that use SDTI connections.

SDTI-CP SDTI-Content Package is an SDTI variant used mostly with MPEG-2 data.

HD-SDTI Compressed HD video can be sent over an SDI connection at 270 Megabits/second. Both HDCAM and DVCPROHD formats have decks with HD-SDTI capability.

FireWire This multipurpose high-speed serial *bus* (an architecture allowing multiple points of connection, up to 63 in FireWire's case) is also called IEEE–1394 and i.Link. FireWire allows both *asynchronous* communications, data traffic sent on a random and unscheduled basis, and *isochronous* communications, where traffic is allocated a fixed and guaranteed amount of bandwidth. Isochronous communications may occupy up to 80 percent of a FireWire bus's bandwidth, with 20 percent reserved for asynchronous messages. Isochronous communications make FireWire suitable for transmission of video data, without dropping frames.

FireWire's most common implementation is 1394a, also known as FW400. It has a top speed of 400 Megabits/second (S400), but also allows 100 and 200 Megabit speeds (S100 and S200). A FireWire bus runs at the speed of the slowest device on it: if you plug an S100-only camera into an S400 port on a Mac, the FireWire runs at 100 Megabits/second. Indeed, most DV decks support only S100 speeds. (A few support S200.) A DV25 datastream, complete with audio and metadata, runs at about 28 Megabits/second, so the 80 Megabits/second of available isochronous bandwidth at S100 speeds is more than enough.

1394b, a.k.a. FW800, is a newer version of the standard that runs at up to 800 Megabits/second. At the time of writing, FW800 is implemented on G5 Macs, the 17-inch and 15-inch PowerBooks, and a variety of mass-storage devices (see Lesson 9), but all video devices—decks and capture systems—use FW400. FW800 is backwards-compatible with FW400; with the right adapter plug or cable (see the following section), you can plug FW400 devices into a FW800 bus.

Although FireWire is most often associated with DV25 camcorders and decks, it's not format-specific. FireWire carries DV25 (DV, DVCAM, DVCPRO), DV50 (DVCPRO50), and DV100 (DVCPROHD) datastreams with equal ease, and Final Cut Pro handles such streams natively. MPEG-2 is also transported across FireWire by HDV cameras, and uncompressed 601-format video travels over FireWire using interfaces from AJA Systems.

> **MORE INFO** ▶ See Lesson 9 for details about using multiple devices on the same FireWire bus.

Finally, some older digital VTRs and digital processing equipment used *parallel digital I/O*, which, prior to SDI, was the only way to move digital data in and out of the machine short of carrying a tape in your hands. If you can't find a VTR with SDI connections, you'll need to use a parallel-to-SDI converter like AJA's C10PS if you want to capture from that deck into FCP.

Cabling and Connectors

We've looked at interface formats; now it's time to look at the physical connections between devices. It would be convenient if every type of interface had a unique connector, but that's not the case: many interfaces share the same connector type or support multiple types of plugs and sockets. Here, then, is a listing of the common connectors and the formats that usually use them.

BNC These connectors are used for composite and component connections on professional equipment, and they are universally used for serial digital and SDTI signals. BNC connectors have a twist-lock sleeve to ensure a good connection that stays put.

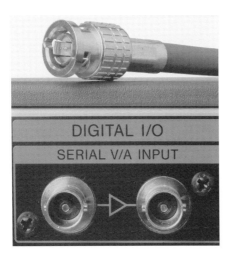

Many BNC connections on equipment are *loop-through*, meaning that the signal is not terminated in the equipment but is available on an output connector. If you don't *terminate* the connection by connecting up another bit of gear or by adding a 75Ω terminating resistor, the video may appear to be too bright and high contrast, may show ghosts (especially on long cable runs), or may fail to show up at all.

Some equipment with loop-through connections auto-terminates when you use only the input side of the connection. Some gear have slide switches beside the BNC connector to connect or disconnect an internal terminating resistor.

RCA You'll see RCAs used for composite and component hookups in consumer equipment (and some pro equipment where space is tight). You'll also see RCAs called phono connectors.

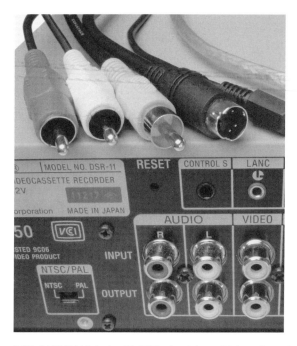

DSR-11 DVCAM deck with RCAs for right and left audio and composite video; 4-pin Y/C cable, 2.5mm LANC control cable, and 4-pin FireWire cable

RCA connections rarely loop-through; almost all terminate automatically.

It's tempting to use cheap audio cables for video when RCAs are involved. Although you can do so for short runs, you're better off using cables designed specifically for video; audio cables aren't designed for video's high frequencies and can cause ghosting, reduced color saturation, and an overall loss of sharpness.

4-Pin and 7-Pin Y/C cables use a 4-pin or (infrequently) a 7-pin connector.

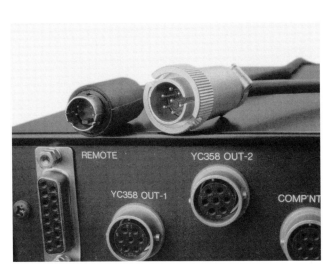

The 4-pin Y/C connector is used on most equipment with a Y/C connection. It's a bit on the flimsy side; the pins in the plug are somewhat fragile, so you need to exercise care when inserting and removing the connector. The friction of their contacts retains most 4-pin plugs, although there are some plugs with locking collars and sockets with the flanges to accept such locks.

One pair of conductors in the four-wire cable carries the luma signal and its ground; the other pair carries chroma and its ground.

The 7-pin connector with its locking collar is used on some JVC S-VHS decks and third-party equipment (like the I.DEN timebase corrector in the photo). It's a very solid and robust connector. Only four pins carry signal and ground; you don't use the other pins.

Y/C connections commonly found on S-VHS, Hi8, and DV equipment carry the chroma modulated at the frequency of the appropriate video standard: 3.58 MHz for NTSC, or 4.43 MHz for PAL. However, the 7-pin connector is also used on some color-under recorders (¾", Hi8, and S-VHS) to carry a "dub" signal, a raw Y/C signal in its internal, heterodyned form. These Y/C connections are not compatible with Y/C 3.58 and Y/C 4.43 connections—you'll get a monochrome image if you try to interconnect them. They're intended for use in dubbing between two decks of the same format, without heterodyning the color up and then down again. Some timebase correctors (TBCs) accept the color-under Y/C signal and perform the heterodyning internally.

> **TIP** ▶ You'll get better images from ¾" U-Matic tapes using hetero-dyned Y/C connectors than you will with a composite connection. You can use a transcoding TBC that accepts a Y/C 688 signal to convert the signal to Y/C 3.58 (or 4.43), or directly to component video. If you don't have access to such a TBC, the YCP-688 adapter from Y/C Plus (www.ycplus.com) converts Y/C 688 to Y/C 3.58 and back again.

Multiconductor Miniplugs Small camcorders use miniplugs where space is at a premium to carry both audio and video. A matching cable terminates in three RCAs (composite video and two channels of audio) and possibly even a 4-pin Y/C plug, allowing you to connect the camcorder to other equipment. The RCAs are usually color-coded with yellow being composite video, red being right channel audio, and white being left channel audio.

 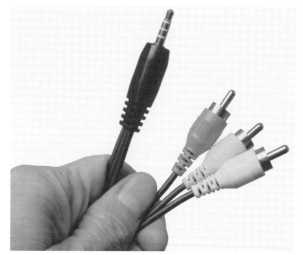

It's important to use the correct adapter cable for each camera; they vary in the number of contacts and the signals they carry. It's best to use the cable that came with the camera instead of substituting another that looks like it should fit; if you use the wrong cable, you may not get the signals you're expecting, and it's possible you could short-circuit the camera and damage it.

FireWire The FW400 port found on video equipment uses either a 6-pin plug or a smaller 4-pin plug. The 6-pin cable has two additional lines for power; the signal on the other four wires is the same. The FW800 port found on the G5 Mac uses a different connector still, but adapter cables bridge the gap handily when necessary.

With all FireWire connectors, be sure the cable is aligned properly with the socket before plugging it in. Despite keying in the shell to prevent plugging in the cable upside-down, many bold experimenters have found that it's easy enough to do so with a little bit of force. At best, things simply won't work; more commonly, the socket gets damaged, and if the cable carries power, you may get blown-out circuitry in the Mac or the VTR.

SCART Some equipment, mostly sold in the European market, has a dual-row multi-pin SCART connector. SCART carries composite, Y/C, or RGB component video, stereo audio, and status/control signals in various combinations. Breakout cables connecting SCART to standard connectors are available, but you'll need to know how your particular SCART connector is wired.

> **MORE INFO** ▸ See http://utopia.knoware.nl/users/eprebel/SoundAnd Vision/Engineering/SCART.html, or search the Web for "SCART pinout".

Older digital equipment used 25-pin D-shell connectors and ribbon cables for parallel digital I/O. (It's unlikely you'll encounter these in practice, but I mention them for completeness.)

Audio Interfaces

Compared to video, audio comes in a bewildering variety of signal types, levels, and connectors. With video, it's pretty clear how to connect things, and you'll see right away when you've made a mistake, but audio is more complex. Often, two bits of equipment won't have the same types of connectors, and seemingly simple connections may be plagued with hums, buzzes, noise, or distortion.

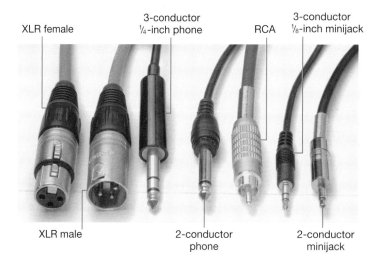

To the uninitiated, such problems appear random and their solutions arbitrary, but once you understand the different signal types and the connectors they use, you can patch together equipment with ease and troubleshoot audio problems with assurance.

Analog Audio

Analog audio comes in two flavors: line-level and mic-level. Line level is further subdivided into high-level, "professional" audio and low-level, "consumer" audio.

Analog Audio Interfaces at a Glance

Name(s)	Connectors	Comments
Line level (pro, +4dBm)	XLR, ¼" phone	Usually balanced, at least with XLRs
Line level (consumer, −10dBm)	RCA, ⅛" stereo miniplug	Usually unbalanced
Mic level	XLR, ¼" phone, ⅛" miniplug; specialty connectors used on some wireless mics	XLRs balanced, others unbalanced
Headphones	¼" phone or ⅛" miniplug	Variable level; can use as line-level outputs in a pinch, but headphone amplifier often adds noise

Line Level High-level pro audio has a nominal level of +4 dBm (+4 decibels compared to a standard reference of a signal dissipating 1 milliwatt across 600 ohms) and is usually carried on balanced cables with XLR connectors, although some systems use ¼-inch phone plugs.

> MORE INFO ▶ For a description of decibels, see www.sizes.com/units/decibel.htm or http://experts.about.com/q/1356/2442821.htm.

Balanced lines use three conductors: two conductors for the signal and one for a separate shield. The signal conductors are twisted together to reduce pickup of interference and noise and connect inside equipment in such a way that any noise common to both lines cancels itself out.

Two-conductor plugs carry unbalanced signals. Three-conductor plugs carry balanced signals (or two channels of unbalanced audio and a common ground, as with headphone plugs and stereo minijacks). ¼-inch phone plugs and ⅛-inch miniplugs come in both flavors: two conductors, called tip and sleeve, and three conductors called tip, ring, and sleeve. XLR connectors are solid and robust; they lock firmly in place and provide clean and noise-free connections. You'll find XLRs (also called Cannon connectors) on most pro audio and pro video equipment.

¼-inch phone plugs are more common on musical instruments, sound reinforcement gear, and audio mixers oriented towards musicians or where space is at a premium.

If a piece of gear has a "line" connector with an XLR or phone plug, it's almost always a high-level, +4 dBm connection, although sometimes it may be switchable to low-level.

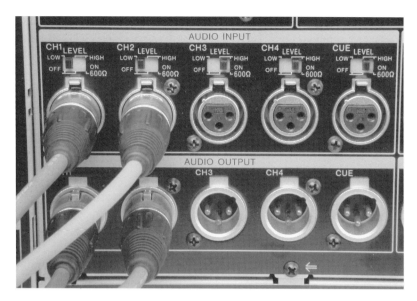

The XLR inputs on this Digital Betacam deck allow selection of high or low levels as well as 600-ohm termination for audio sources that need it.

Low-level audio has its nominal level at −10 dBm and normally travels on unbalanced, two-conductor cables with RCA plugs. RCA plugs and sockets may be color coded, with red for right channel audio and white (or black) for left channel audio.

Most consumer audio and video gear uses low-level audio connections.

Sometimes, mostly on compact consumer camcorders, audio will be bundled with video in a multi-pin miniplug connector as discussed earlier.

Mic Level Microphone audio has a nominal level of around −50 dBm, give or take a few decibels. Mic connections can appear as XLRs on professional gear, ¼-inch phone plugs on musical equipment, or ⅛-inch miniplugs on consumer gear. In the latter case, the connection is often for a stereo mic; the plug has three conductors instead of the two used for a monophonic mic. (You can get mono-to-stereo adapters to plug a mono mic into a stereo jack and get the same signal on both channels.)

Some inputs on professional camcorders and recorders let you switch an XLR input between mic level and line level.

Headphones You'll also encounter headphone outputs on phone plug and miniplug connections. These may be two-conductor, monophonic signals, but usually they're stereo with three conductors. Their nominal levels are variable, but are usually close to the –10 dBm line level; in a pinch, you can use a headphone output as a substitute for a low-level line output, but be warned that the quality of headphones outputs is usually much lower than the quality of line outputs.

Interfacing Analog Audio

If you have inputs and outputs of the same type, just connect them up, but if they differ, things get more complex.

You can sometimes connect low-level outputs to high-level inputs and vice versa by carefully adjusting input and output levels, but the basic 14 dB difference in the standards means that you're likely to run into problems. Low into high is the safer combination; if you turn the input gain control up, you can often get a sufficiently strong signal to work with, but you may well add more noise from the excessive amplification of the strong signal. Level-matching amplifiers, available from audio and video supply houses, can provide clean interfaces between consumer and professional levels.

Going the other way—high into low—is problematic because the high level of the incoming audio may exceed the capability of the low-level input circuits to follow the signal: you'll get clipping and distortion, even with the input gain turned way down. At the very least, you should use a *pad* or *attenuator*, a small inline adapter that cuts down the strong signal to an appropriate level for the low-level input. (Sometimes these are referred to as *baluns*, because they also adapt from the balanced line of the professional side to the unbalanced line of the consumer side, though many baluns simply convert between balanced and unbalanced without changing levels.)

Level-matching amplifiers are available for this task, too; often you'll find boxes that incorporate high-to-low and low-to-high matching amplifiers in the same package, side by side. Putting a line-level signal, whether low or high, into a mic input is almost certain to cause overloads and distortions. Again, there are pads and attenuators for this purpose, including some built into patch cables.

TIP Your local consumer electronics store often carries adapter cables designed to connect a stereo's line-level signal into a portable recorder's mic input. These cables normally have RCAs on the line-level side and miniplugs on the mic side. They're quite handy for feeding line-level signals into mic inputs when you have no better solution.

Some audio mixers have mic-level outputs for feeding portable recorders or cameras. You can boost these to line level using a mic-to-line amplifier, or the mixer itself may have a switch or menu selection to boost the outputs to line level. Plugging a mic-level output directly into a line-level input usually gives you a good approximation of silence; there isn't enough of a signal to even tempt you to run this connection without a proper adapter.

Digital Audio

Digital Audio Interfaces at a Glance

Name(s)	Connectors	Comments
AES/EBU, AES3	BNC (75 ohm), XLR (110 ohm)	2-channels per connector; Pro gear
S/PDIF	RCA (copper), TOSlink (optical)	Carries either AES/EBU 2-channel or Dolby AC3 5.1 audio; G5s, DVD players, home theater, etc.

Digital audio commonly moves around the studio as AES/EBU (Audio Engineering Society / European Broadcast Union) stereo pairs, two channels of 48 kHz audio combined into one signal. AES/EBU audio travels on 75-ohm unbalanced cables with BNC connectors, or 100-ohm balanced cables with XLR connectors. There are matching transformers or baluns available to convert between the two different signals.

AES/EBU audio may also be embedded in an SDI video signal. Many of the SDI capture cards for FCP support embedded audio; some don't even support separate audio. There are embedder/disembedder products available to break the audio out into its own signals, or to combine audio and video, depending on the needs of the equipment you're connecting together.

FireWire also carries digital audio, in combination with video or by itself using FireWire audio interfaces from MOTU, Roland/Edirol, TASCAM, MAudio, and others. These FireWire audio interfaces provide multiple channels (eight or more) of connectivity, terminating in analog and digital I/O ports. These are rapidly becoming the preferred way to handle multichannel audio on the Mac.

You may also encounter S/PDIF (Sony/Philips Digital Interface) audio connections on RCAs, miniplugs, or TOSlink optical connectors, like the ones on the back of the G5. S/PDIF carries stereo or 5.1 (five channel plus subwoofer) audio. Aside from DAT (Digital Audio Tape) recorders, it's mostly used for high-quality home theater sound.

As you might guess, there are converters to go between AES/EBU and S/PDIF interfaces, although they tend to be hard to find—try audio and musician supply houses.

Timecode and Control

In the early days of video editing, timecode signals and deck control were carried on separate connections. Timecode was conveyed on a BNC cable as an LTC signal, or was embedded in the video as VITC. Deck control was performed using manufacturer-specific interfaces, and there was a thriving market for translator boxes to make decks from Ampex, JVC, Panasonic, and Sony speak a common language.

Fortunately, those days are (mostly) gone. Modern decks interface using serial control protocols that carry commands, status, and timecode together. Final Cut Pro expects to talk to decks using either RS-422 or FireWire; if you can't find a deck to play back a tape that speaks one of those languages, or for which there is not a protocol converter, you'll probably be best off dubbing the tape to a more modern format on a VTR that allows modern control, or just use Capture Now to grab the video.

Control Interfaces at a Glance

Names	Connectors	Comments
RS-422, Sony serial, 9-pin	9-pin D-shell	Most common professional control interface
FireWire, A/VC	4- or 6-pin FireWire	DV, DVCAM, DVCPRO, and HDV equipment
LANC, Control-L	2.5mm miniplug, 5-pin miniDIN	Video8, Hi8, Betamax, ED-Beta, consumer DV gear

Control Interfaces at a Glance

Names	Connectors	Comments
Ampex RS-422, Ampex serial	9-pin D-shell	Ampex VTRs only; not compatible with Sony protocol
RS-232	9- or 25-pin D-shell	Industrial gear; manufacturer- and model-specific command protocols; usually not frame-accurate
VISCA	8-pin miniDIN	Sony industrial gear, Hi8 animation recorders
Control-M, Panasonic 5-pin	5-pin round connector	Panasonic VHS, SVHS
Control-S	Small miniplug	Some Sony gear; control only; no feedback
Parallel	Various, depending on manufacturer	Ancient VHS, ¾", and similar VTRs

RS-422

Most professional VTRs use a serial protocol commonly called RS-422 for timecode and control. (RS-422, strictly speaking, defines the electrical and signaling parameters of the serial link, not the protocol that runs on it, but that's an academic distinction for our purposes.) It's based on the serial protocol

Sony developed for its broadcast ¾-inch decks, although it's evolved over time and become the *lingua franca* of deck control. You'll also see it referred to as Sony protocol, 9-pin control, BVU-800 protocol, and BWV protocol, and many decks simply label it as Remote.

RS-422 ports on VTRs use a 9-pin D-shell connector. Macs no longer have serial ports built in, but many video capture cards incorporate them, and USB-to-serial adapters are available for Macs without such cards. The pinout used on VTR ports is unlike the pinout on 9-pin serial ports in the rest of the world, so you'll need to use a cable built specifically for the purpose of deck control. Most capture cards with RS-422 ports should have the appropriate cable bundled with them. For controlling VTRs with USB-to-serial adapters (most of which use the same round serial connector as older Macs), use cables from Addenda Electronics (www.addenda.com).

TIP ▶ Addenda Electronics carries cables and adapters for almost any serial-to-serial connection task. When in doubt, check their Web site for any oddball adapter you might require.

The RS-422 protocol includes frame-accurate deck control (on decks that support frame accuracy; not all do!) as well as full timecode capability. Depending on the deck, the timecode reported may be LTC, VITC, or digital timecode; it makes little difference as far as deck control goes. Over RS-422, a Betacam SP deck with SMPTE timecode, a Hi8 deck playing back Hi8 timecode, and a DVCAM deck playing back DV timecode all appear the same and afford the same frame-level addressability.

On appropriately equipped editing decks, RS-422 lets you insert video and audio separately and frame-accurately, so you can use such decks to insert-edit new scenes into existing programs using FCP's Edit To Tape capability.

NOTE ▶ You'll need to provide a common reference signal to the deck and the Mac for frame-accurate RS-422 control, as described in the "Sync and Blackburst Generators" section later in this lesson.

FireWire

FireWire carries control and timecode information along with video and audio. FCP comes equipped right out of the box to talk to decks using the FireWire port built into all current Macs.

Most DV, DVCAM, and HDV decks offer FireWire control, as do some DVCPRO, DVCPRO50, and DVPROHD decks. Basically, if a deck has FireWire for video and audio I/O, it offers FireWire control as well.

FireWire offers frame-accurate capturing, but FireWire-controlled decks aren't equipped to provide frame-accurate insert editing. You can use the assemble-edit capability of FCP's Edit to Tape and Print to Video functions, but not the insert-edit function of Edit to Tape.

Some decks offer both FireWire and RS-422 control. The RS-422 control usually has more capabilities than the FireWire control does; if your deck offers both, you may have better results with RS-422 than with FireWire, even if you're still capturing your video and audio over FireWire.

LANC

Some Sony VTRs, mostly in the consumer lineup, offer LANC control, also called Control-L. It's a serial protocol on a very small 2.5mm miniplug. (Older VTRs used a 5-pin plug.) With the RS-4/L adapter from Addenda Electronics or the LPort422 from Sweet Pea Communications (www.spcomms.com/lport), it's possible to control them using RS-422, letting you integrate such decks into a 422-controlled environment.

However, LANC is not frame-accurate, and the performance of decks controlled by LANC is somewhat hit or miss. You're better off finding a deck in the format in question (VHS, S-VHS, Video8, Hi8, and DV decks use LANC) that has RS-422 or FireWire (in the case of DV) than using the Addenda adapter. Of course, if you're using ED-Beta (Betamax's answer to S-VHS), you'll probably have to use the adapter, as ED-Beta and Betamax decks with RS-422 are mighty hard to find.

Other Interfaces

Aside from the three main control interfaces described earlier, you'll find a variety of other control schemes in use, usually on non-broadcast, non-DV decks, or on older equipment.

Ampex Serial Older Ampex VTRs used an incompatible RS-422 protocol. Solution: capture your tapes using a newer Ampex or Sony VTR.

RS-232 Some decks offer RS-232 serial control instead of RS-422. RS-232 decks typically use different (and more limited) command protocols than RS-422 has, so the simple answer—an RS-232 to RS-422 adapter—won't work with FCP.

FCP supports a limited number of RS-323-controlled decks directly with presets for the Sony S-VHS SVO-2100, Sony Betacam SP UVW-1400, and generic Panasonic and JVC 232 protocols; otherwise your best bet is to move the affected tape into a deck with RS-422 control.

VISCA A few Sony decks, mostly Hi8, use a serial protocol called VISCA (Video Systems Control Architecture), which FCP supports. VISCA, like LANC, isn't frame-accurate. FCP can use a VISCA deck (or a Sony VBox LANC-to-VISCA adapter), but you're more likely to get repeatable results using an RS-422-controllable deck in the appropriate format.

Control-M Also called Panasonic 5-pin, Control-M is used on some Panasonic decks. Sweet Pea's PanPort422 lets you talk RS-422 to these decks, with the same caveats as with LANC-controlled decks.

Control-S A control-only protocol used in some Sony equipment. You can send commands, but you can't get status or timecode back. Think of it like an infrared remote control using a wire.

Parallel Multi-pin parallel control ports were the state of the art prior to serial controllers. Don't even think about controlling such decks with FCP.

Caveats

No control system is perfect. The grapevine is full of reports of timecode slippage and inaccuracies with FireWire control, but RS-422 control isn't immune from such problems, either. Breaks in timecode, a gap between takes on tape, and improperly configured capture and deck-control settings inside FCP can play havoc with smooth machine control regardless of tape format or control type. Always test whatever setup you have for proper operation before committing yourself to frame-accurate operations, and capture with handles on your clips just to be on the safe side.

Analog Video Formats

Here's a listing of the analog formats you're likely to encounter in FCP work. We won't attempt to list all the analog formats ever made, or all those currently in use somewhere in the world; these are the ones likely to cross your path.

Analog Video Formats (SD) at a Glance

Names	Best FCP I/O	Best FCP Control	Comments
1-inch Type C	Composite through TBC	RS-422	Most common 1-inch format; obsolete
1-inch Type B	Composite through TBC	RS-422	Mostly European 1-inch format; obsolete
¾-inch U-matic & U-matic SP	Composite through TBC, Y/C through Y/C-688 converter, Y/C or component from Y/C-688-accepting TBC	RS-422	Still used for dailies and video workprints; best decks: BVU-900 series
Betacam, BetacamSP	Component YPrPb	RS-422	BVWs/CVWs best, then PVWs, then UVWs
VHS, S-VHS	Y/C, through TBC if no TBC in deck	RS-422	VHS looks better captured through Y/C from an S-VHS deck than via composite; Panasonic AG-7500 series is best, but hard to find
MII	Component YPrPb	RS-422	AU-650 best; AU-65 and later JVCs OK, too

Analog Video Formats (SD) at a Glance

Names	Best FCP I/O	Best FCP control	Comments
Video8, Hi8	Y/C, through TBC if no TBC in deck; FireWire from a Digital8 deck	FireWire	Video8 looks better captured via Y/C from a Hi8 deck than via composite from a Video8 device; EVO-9000 series is best; EVS-7000 also very good (but has only LANC control)
EIAJ Type 1, ½-inch reel-to-reel	Composite through TBC, if possible	Manual (no device control)	Obsolete; B&W and color variants; early ½-Inch does not conform to RS-170A specs and may require specialized TBC to recover signal
2-inch, Quadruplex, Quad	Composite through TBC	Manual (no device control)	Obsolete, though some systems still used for spot playback; best to dub to more FCP-friendly format
Betamax, ED-Beta	Y/C through TBC	LANC	Obsolete; best: SL-HF750/900/950/1000 (Betamax); EDV-9500 (ED-Beta)
Fisher-Price Pixelvision, PXL-2000	RF: use ANT input on VCR to decode to baseband, capture via Y/C or composite	Manual	Small cropped B&W images

1-Inch Type C

Type C is the most common 1-inch format, though Type B was popular in Europe. Type C defined high-quality video recording for a decade from the mid-1970s through the mid-1980s, until Betacam SP and MII formats brought the benefits of component recording to the world.

1-inch VTRs are no longer made, nor is 1-inch used for production, but much of the world's television history is stored on 1-inch tape. You may need to capture from 1-inch on occasion, but its doubtful you'll ever record back to it.

Primary Use 1-inch was most often used for studio recording. There were a few portable 1-inch machines, including the fabulous Ampex/Nagra portable, but the bulk and power requirements of 1-inch made it unsuited to field work.

Technical Details 1-inch uses reel-to-reel tape for direct color composite recording with 330 TVl/ph resolution. Reels of up to 3 hours are possible with reel extenders. Timebase correction is required for playback; TBCs are often designed for specific recorders, such as the Ampex Zeus. With TBC, this format is usable for up to 10 generations of dubbing. 1-inch tapes have two channels (sometimes three) of linear analog audio.

The most common machines are the Sony BVH series and the Ampex VPR series. Hitachi and others made Type C VTRs, too.

Best Interface to FCP Capture composite video through a good TBC. 1-inch is direct composite color; a good composite connection is as good as it gets. Late-model Sonys and Ampexes have RS-422 control.

¾-Inch and ¾-Inch SP (U-matic)

U-matic is a format you may have to capture from, but not output to unless you're involved in a ¾-inch-based postproduction workflow. Its manufacturers have officially discontinued ¾-inch, but it will likely live on for many years due to its widespread acceptance.

¾-inch pictures tend to suffer from multigeneration recording, with timebase errors, color smearing, and noise being common problems.

Primary Use ¾-inch was used for ENG (Electronic News Gathering), professional/industrial video before BetaSP and DV came along, and studio production and postproduction. It's still used for offline dubs in film telecine and video postproduction. ¾-inch portapaks (portable VTRs separate from the camera) were commonly used for field production, but ¾-inch was never a camcorder format.

Technical Details U-matic uses ¾-inch wide cassette tape for color-under recording at 688 kHz. Three-quarter-inch resolution is about 280 TVl/ph; 340 TVL/ph for ¾-inch SP (Superior Performance). Maximum cassette length is 60 minutes. ¾-inch plays back without TBC, but timebase correction vastly improves the picture. With TBC, it's usable for two to three generations. SP decks can play non-SP tapes, but most early non-SP decks can't play SP successfully.

U-matic has two tracks of linear audio, although one channel is sometimes used for timecode. On lower-end VTRs, only channel 2 audio is dubbable after the tape has been recorded.

Sony machines dominate: you can find the VO-5000 series of industrial level machines (parallel control, no timecode) in every corner of the planet. The broadcast lineup, especially the BVU-800 and BVU-900 (SP) series machines (both with serial control and timecode), were common in broadcast and postproduction up until Betacam came out.

Panasonic and JVC also made U-matic VTRs but never achieved the ubiquity or the reliability of the Sony machines.

Best Interface to FCP U-matics provide composite video, unless you use a TBC with a U-matic dub (Y/C 688) connector to output Y/C or component, or use the YCPlus YCP-688 adapter to convert the dub signal to Y/C 3.58. Timebase correction helps. Late-model Sony VTRs have RS-422 control and timecode; a BVU-900 series machine is likely your best bet.

Betacam and Betacam SP

Betacam SP has been the de facto standard high-end analog format for nearly 20 years. Beta started off with the broadcast-grade BVW series, then spawned the professional-level PVWs and the industrial UVWs. Generally speaking, BVWs give superior audio and video performance to PVWs, and PVWs are better than UVWs. Beta SP has become the VHS of the professional world—it's everywhere—so it will be with us for many years to come, despite the fact that Sony has stopped building Betacam VTRs.

Primary Use Betacam was introduced as a portable ENG camcorder format, but quickly became the standard format for EFP (electronic field production) and postproduction due to its high performance, convenience, and low cost (comparatively speaking). It superceded 1-inch in studio work and ¾-inch in field production. Only with the coming of Digital Betacam did Beta SP relinquish the high-end laurels, and the DV formats are now displacing it in the rest of its applications, but it is still very common.

Technical Details Betacam uses a ½-inch cassette tape originally based on Betamax. Beta uses analog component recording with a resolution of 300 TVl/ph for Betacam, and 340 TVL/ph for Beta SP. Small cassettes hold up to 20 minutes; large cassettes hold 90 minutes. Timebase correction is built-in on studio decks, as the color signals are time-compressed 2:1 for storage on tape and require a framestore for playback. (Some field recorders and camcorder backs only play back a monochrome signal unless a separate adapter is used.) Beta SP can go 10 generations.

Betacam has two channels of linear audio; Beta SP adds two channels of AFM audio. Only the linear audio is dubbable after the fact.

BVW SP decks have all four channels of audio; most PVW- and UVW-series VTRs provide access to only the two AFM channels, though there are after-market kits to add linear audio to these decks.

Betacam uses metal oxide tape, SP uses metal tape. SP decks play non-SP tapes, but the reverse is not true.

Sony invented the format and built most of the decks, but licensed the design to Ampex for a while. (Ampex Betacams are virtual clones of the Sonys but have different audio circuitry and a CVW model designation.)

Best Interface to FCP Beta decks have analog component (YP_RP_B) video and RS-422 control. You can also play back Betacam and Beta SP over SDI using Sony's high-end Digital Betacam and IMX decks.

VHS and S-VHS
The ubiquitous VHS format will be with us until the end of time.

VHS is very sensitive to contrasty signals and saturated colors. It often helps when outputting to VHS to do the following: use the Y/C connection on an S-VHS deck, avoid "superwhite" levels (whites above 100 percent) in the video, and keep color saturations low, especially in the reds.

Primary Use JVC developed VHS as a home video format, but it migrated into the professional world and S-VHS was even used for a short time by some broadcasters. Camcorders are available but bulky. S-VHS-C uses a 20-minute compact cassette, but it requires a cassette adapter for playback in standard decks and is somewhat more prone to playback errors and instability as a result.

VHS is still a very common distribution format, though DVD is starting to erode its dominance.

Technical Details VHS uses ½-inch cassette tapes for color-under recording at 629 kHz. VHS offers 230 TVl/ph resolution, S-VHS has about 400 TVl/ph, but image stability, color, and noise are poor. The VHS formats seem especially poor at reproducing *accurate* color. 160-minute maximum tape time at SP speed, but LP and EP speeds allow more time on tape at the expense of picture quality. S-VHS decks play VHS tapes, but most VHS decks cannot play S-VHS tapes.

VHS has one or two channels of linear audio and may have two channels of "Hi Fi" (AFM) audio. It rarely has timecode except on high-end professional S-VHS machines.

Professional S-VHS decks with RS-422 were (and are) made by JVC and Panasonic and even, grudgingly, by Sony. Consumer decks are made by every conceivable manufacturer in the electronics universe.

With integral TBCs and digital noise reduction circuits, top-end S-VHS machines make a very acceptable first-generation picture, but multigeneration performance is poor—three generations at most.

Best Interface to FCP Use a professional S-VHS deck with RS-422, built-in TBC, and Y/C connections. A consumer deck with Y/C (but without RS-422 and possibly requiring an external TBC) is second best. VHS can be captured via composite if necessary, but even VHS looks better when captured via Y/C.

Video8 and Hi8

8mm systems originated as consumer camcorder formats to reduce the bulk of VHS and Betamax camcorders. They succeeded in that respect, though they brought their own characteristic problems. Video8 and Hi8 tapes are especially subject to wear and tear, and dropouts are a big problem. Try to capture material cleanly on the first pass. It may be worth rewinding and recapturing the same material into a separate clip; dropouts frequently occur in different places on different passes, so you may be able to use the frames in one clip to replace frames in the second.

Primary Use 8mm was a home-video camcorder format, later expanded with some home VCRs and portable "Video Walkman" decks, with and without LCD screens. With some reluctance from Sony, Hi8 was pushed into professional applications due to its small cassettes, long run times, and affordable gear. DV's arrival killed the professional applications of Hi8, but it remains current in low-end consumer camcorders.

Technical Details Both formats use 8mm tape in small cassettes for color-under recording at 734 kHz; resolution is 240 TVl/ph for Video8 and 400 TVl/ph for Hi8. The 8s have better color accuracy than the VHS formats, generally speaking, but somewhat more timebase instability, and are very prone to dropouts. Tapes record 120 minutes at SP speeds, twice that at LP speeds with a noticeable drop in picture quality. Video8 plays back in Hi8 decks, but not vice versa.

Audio is recorded as mono or stereo AFM sound, not dubbable separately but of very high quality. Some decks and camcorders added two channels of dubbable PCM digital audio: 32 kHz sampling, 8-bit nonlinear recording that sounds surprisingly good.

Pro Hi8 gear has timecode, as does some consumer gear.

Sony is the primary supplier of Video8 and Hi8 equipment, though Kodak, Kyocera, Toshiba, Hitachi, and others made some gear.

Best Interface to FCP Video8 and Hi8 play back best in an EVO-9000-series VCR with timebase correction, noise reduction, and RS-422 control, using Y/C outputs. An EV-S-Series home VCR with TBC (but with LANC control, not RS-422) is the next best choice for analog capture.

Digital8 camcorders and Video Walkman decks play back Video8 and Hi8 tapes as DV data over FireWire, but without timecode.

Other Formats

You may occasionally encounter tapes in the following formats.

½-Inch EIAJ Type 1 ½-inch was a reel-to-reel monochrome and color format before the days of ¾-inch. Capture via composite, preferably with the help of a good TBC. Type 1 decks have no machine control to speak of other than mechanical switches.

2-Inch Quadruplex Quad is the granddaddy of them all. Quad decks started the videotape revolution, but are almost entirely extinct these days. Quad uses composite video and has no usable machine control as far as FCP is concerned.

Betamax, ED-Beta Betamax was Sony's ill-fated competitor to VHS, and ED-Beta attempted to counter S-VHS with almost no success outside of school sports recording, medical imaging, and other niche uses. ED-Beta decks have Y/C connections and are controlled via LANC.

MII MII was Panasonic's response to Betacam, and successor to the original component format, Panasonic's and RCA's Recam. MII is comparable to Beta SP in quality and has RS-422 control, but chroma levels may need tweaking as MII color component levels are slightly different than Beta SP's.

Fisher-Price Pixelvision A cult favorite among video artists, Pixelvision recorded a grainy, pixellated monochrome image on cassette audiotape. Capture via composite, and don't expect much: a Pixelvision picture occupies only a small portion of the screen and won't win any awards for quality.

Digital Video Formats

Except as mentioned, all these formats record digital component video and uncompressed audio at 48 kHz, 16 bits per channel. Transfer to and from FCP is as uncompressed video and audio over SDI, sometimes with audio as separate AES/EBU connections.

Digital Video Formats (SD) at a Glance

Names	Best FCP I/O	Best FCP Control	Comments
BetacamSX	SDI	RS-422	Rare outside of news
D-1	SDI; parallel-to-SDI	RS-422	Obsolete
D-5	SDI	RS-422	Current favorite SD mastering format; 10-bit

Digital Video Formats (SD) at a Glance

Names	Best FCP I/O	Best FCP Control	Comments
Digital8	FireWire	FireWire	DV25 on 8mm tapes
DV, DVCAM, "miniDV"	SDI or FireWire	RS-422 or FireWire	RS-422 allows Edit-to-Tape
DVCPRO, DVCPRO25, D-7	SDI or FireWire	RS-422 or FireWire	RS-422 allows Edit-to-Tape
DVCPRO50	SDI or FireWire	RS-422 or FireWire	RS-422 allows Edit-to-Tape
Digital-S, D-9	SDI	RS-422	JVC's ½-inch DV50
Digital Betacam, DigiBeta	SDI	RS-422	Top-end SD camcorder format; 10-bit
IMX, D-10	SDI	RS-422	MPEG-2 at 30, 40, 50 Mbit/sec
P2	SDI, FireWire	RS-422, FireWire	Panasonic's "professional plug-in"; carries DVCPRO and DVCPRO50 data
XDCAM	SDI or FireWire (DVCAM only)	RS-422, FireWire (DVCAM only)	Records either IMX or DVCAM on optical disks

Digital Video Formats (SD) at a Glance

Names	Best FCP I/O	Best FCP Control	Comments
D-2 and D-3	SDI via AJA C10PS; analog composite	RS-422	Obsolete digital composite VTRs; SDI on VTR, if available, is serial digital *composite*, not component!
DCT	SDI	RS-422	Obsolete Ampex studio format
DVD	Software transcoding	N/A	
MicroMV	Y/C	LANC	MPEG-2 on tiny tapes

Betacam SX

Beta SX is an oddball format, with the bulk and cost of Betacam SP but with a picture quality arguably lower than DV. Some news organizations swear by it, but aside from that niche it hasn't seen much success.

Primary Use Beta SX was designed as a drop-in digital replacement for Betacam SP (most of the equipment looks and works just like Beta SP gear) in ENG, and that's how it's used.

Technical Details SX uses $\frac{1}{2}$-inch cassette tape, recording 8-bit video with 4:2:2 sampling and GOP-2 MPEG-2 compression at 19 Megabits/second (roughly 6:1 compression). Large cassettes hold up to 194 minutes; small cassettes hold 62 minutes.

Beta SX has four channels of 48 kHz audio.

Sony is the sole supplier.

Best Interface to FCP SX provides SDI transfer with RS-422 control.

D-1

D-1 was the first cassette-based digital component format. It's no longer used for production, but you may see archived material on D-1.

Primary Use D-1 was used for uncompressed digital studio production and high-end graphics. It was never a camcorder format; the cassettes were too bulky.

Technical Details D-1 records 4:2:2 10-bit uncompressed video on ¾-inch tape cassette. It had four channels of 48 kHz audio.

Best Interface to FCP D-1 decks may need a parallel to serial adapter like the AJA C10PS. SDI transfer with RS-422 control is the way to go.

D-5

D-5 is the current high-end standard for uncompressed SDTV recording.

Primary Use D-5 offers top-quality uncompressed digital recordings for studio production, graphics, and mastering. It's a studio format only; there aren't any portapaks or camcorders.

Technical Details D-5 uses ½-inch tape cassette for 4:2:2 10-bit component uncompressed recording with four channels of 48 kHz audio.

Panasonic is the sole supplier.

Best Interface to FCP SDI transfer with RS-422 control.

Digital8

Digital8 uses DV25 recording on Hi8 cassettes. Digital8 machines are a great way to capture Video8 and Hi8 tapes, which the Digital8 player turns into a DV datastream.

Primary Use   Digital8 is the digital replacement for Video8 and Hi8. There are no studio decks; camcorders and Video Walkman VTRs only.

Technical Details   Digital8 uses the same tape cassettes as Hi8. It records 4:1:1 (NTSC) or 4:2:0 (PAL), 8-bit video with DV compression at 25 Megabits/ second (5:1 compression). A two-hour Hi8 cassette holds 60 minutes of Digital8 material.

Digital8 has two channels of 48 kHz audio or four channels of 32 kHz audio.

Sony is the primary supplier.

Best Interface to FCP   Use FireWire to transfer the DV datastream, with FireWire control.

DV25: DV and DVCAM

DV25 is the Betacam SP of the digital age.

DVCAM differs from DV in that its tape speed is 33 percent faster, and its audio is always locked (see Lesson 7). Its picture quality is identical to DV's.

DV is sometimes called miniDV by those who mistake a cassette size for a tape format.

DV LP speed is highly problematic: dropouts, mosaic patterns, or an outright refusal to play are common. The tape speed is simply too slow for mass-manufactured equipment tolerances. "Friends don't let friends use LP speed."

Primary Use   DV and DVCAM are used for everything from home video to ENG, EFP, and digital filmmaking.

Technical Details DV and DVCAM use a tape cassette with 6.35mm metal evaporate (ME) tape. They record 4:1:1 (NTSC) or 4:2:0 (PAL) sampling, 8-bit video with DV compression at 25 Megabits/second (5:1 compression). The miniDV cassette holds one hour at DV SP speeds, 40 minutes at DVCAM speed, or 90 minutes at DV LP speeds. (There is also a thinner tape stock providing 80 minutes at DV SP speeds.) In all cases, image quality is the same; the difference is in resistance to dropouts and in tape interchangeability. The standard (a.k.a. large) cassette holds 4.5 hours at DV SP speeds or 3 hours at DVCAM speeds.

DV and DVCAM have two channels of 48 kHz audio or four channels of 32 kHz audio.

DVCAM decks play back DV tapes at SP speeds. Most Sony DV decks play back DVCAM, but most decks from other manufacturers do not.

DVCAM is Sony's creation, and Sony is the sole supplier (except for a couple of pro camcorders from the likes of Ikegami and Hitachi using Sony transports). DV equipment is available from multiple vendors.

DV disk recorders are available from Focus Enhancements, Promax, Laird Telemedia, Sony, and others. They all provide FireWire video I/O, and most can also attach as FireWire disk drives, providing access to captured clips as DV streams, QuickTime movies, or AVI files.

Primary Usage DV25 is used for everything from home video to ENG, EFP, and digital filmmaking.

Best Interface to FCP DV was made for FireWire transfer of its compressed datastream. Some DVCAM decks also offer SDI transfer of uncompressed video, which some find superior if they're working in an uncompressed project.

Both FireWire and RS-422 control are available, depending on the VTR. RS-422 is generally considered to give better, faster, and more repeatable control.

DV25: DVCPRO

DVCPRO, a.k.a. D-7, is Panasonic's professional version of DV25. DVCPRO is more dropout resistant than DV and DVCAM, and may be a better archival choice due to its wider data tracks and MP tape formulation, but is a less universally accepted format than DV and DVCAM. DVCPRO is more widely used in news and broadcasting, however.

Primary Use DVCPRO is used for ENG, EFP, and digital filmmaking.

Technical Details DVCPRO uses a 6.35mm tape cassette with metal particle (MP) tape. It records 4:1:1 (even in PAL), 8-bit video with DV compression at 25 Megabits/second (5:1 compression). The small cassette (larger than DV's mini cassette) holds 1 hour. The large cassette holds 3 hours.

DVCPRO supports two channels of 48 kHz audio only, plus a linear analog cue channel for use when shuttling the tape at high speed.

DVCPRO decks can play back DV and DVCAM. (Mini cassettes require an adapter.) Picture quality is identical to other DV25 formats, but the datastream is slightly different, so a direct FireWire dub between DV/DVCAM and DVCPRO is not possible unless the deck translates the data on the fly (a feature of the AJ-D455 VTR).

Panasonic is the primary supplier of DVCPRO equipment.

Best Interface to FCP As with other DV25 formats, FireWire transfer of the compressed datastream gives first-generation results on the few decks that offer it. (Most DVCPRO VTRs do not have FireWire.) SDI transfer of uncompressed video, which some find superior if they're working in an uncompressed project, is available on many VTRs.

Either FireWire or RS-422 control may be available, depending on the VTR. RS-422 is generally considered to give better, faster, and more repeatable control.

DV50: DVCPRO50 and D-9

Panasonic and JVC ganged up two DV codecs to make the DV50 formats. Panasonic's DVCPRO50 is growing in popularity, while JVC's D-9 has been fairly limited in its appeal and availability.

Primary Use DV50 is used for high-end EFP, studio mastering, and digital filmmaking. DV50 is a low-cost alternative to Digital Betacam in the high-end market.

Camcorders are available in both formats.

Technical Details DVCPRO50 uses DVCPRO cassettes; D-9 (a.k.a. Digital-S) uses metal tape in VHS cassette shells. Both record 4:2:2, 8-bit video with DV compression at 50 megabits/second (3.3:1 compression), with four channels of 48 kHz audio. Panasonic makes DVCPRO50 gear with some second-sourcing, mostly for camcorders. JVC is the sole supplier for D-9.

DVCPRO50 decks play back DVCPRO, and some play DV and DVCAM as well. Some D-9 decks can play back VHS and S-VHS over SDI.

Best Interface to FCP DV50 provides SDI transfer with RS-422 control, or FireWire transfer of the compressed DV50 datastream with RS-422 or FireWire control (for DVCPRO50 only). FCP handles DV50 natively. FireWire capture is preferred for 24p material; FCP can extract 24p advanced footage on the fly during capture.

Digital Betacam

DigiBeta is a very high-quality format using mild compression. Aside from D-5, it's the only 10-bit recording format available, and it's much more common than D-5 due to lower costs and its small tape size, which allows it to be used as a camcorder format.

Primary Use DigiBeta is common in high-end EFP, digital filmmaking, and studio mastering. Both studio decks and camcorders are available.

Technical Details DigiBeta uses ½-inch Betacam-based tape cassette with metal tape for 4:2:2, 10-bit recording with roughly 2.5:1 DCT compression.

It has four channels (plus an analog cue channel) of 48 kHz, 20-bit audio.

Sony is the sole supplier. The DVW-A500 VTR can play back analog Betacam and BetaSP tapes and output them as SDI datastreams.

Best Interface to FCP DigiBeta decks offer SDI transfer of uncompressed video with RS-422 control.

IMX

IMX is Sony's second foray into MPEG-2 recording (after BetaSX), and it marks a shift in emphasis from the VTR being a video device to the VTR being part of a data-oriented studio. IMX equipment is priced between DVCAM and Digital Betacam (closer to the latter than the former) so it hasn't yet taken the market by storm, but expect to see it grow over the coming years.

Primary Use IMX is found in broadcast and studio applications: ENG, EFP, and studio mastering. IMX is still fairly new, and it hasn't settled into a well-defined niche yet.

Technical Details IMX uses 1/2-inch tape in Betacam-type cassettes with 4:2:2 sampling and 8-bit I-frame-only MPEG-2 recording at 30, 40, or 50 Megabits/second.

IMX supports eight (!) channels of 16-bit audio or four of 24-bit audio, both at 48 kHz.

IMX decks can play back Betacam, Betacam SP, Betacam SX, and Digital Betacam tapes. They also provide 2x transfer of the MPEG-2 datastream via SDTI-CP, and some offer an Ethernet interface for FTP (file transfer protocol) access of video clips in MXF wrappers.

So far, IMX is a Sony exclusive. IMX decks have the MSW moniker.

Best Interface to FCP IMX offers SDI transfer of uncompressed video with RS-422 control. FCP 5 can also use IMX files natively, using Telestream's Flip4Mac MXF Import Component to read files via a network connection to the IMX-format eVtr.

P2

P2 (Professional Plugin) is Panasonic's foray into solid-state recording. P2 is still too new to have made much of an impact, but its influence will grow in years to come, especially as the memory chips get cheaper.

Primary Use P2 is use in ENG and other applications where the speed and robustness of solid-state recording outweighs the considerable cost of the memory chips. Once memory prices decline, who knows where P2 will wind up?

Technical Details P2 uses SD memory cards, ganged four each on PC card adapters. P2 records DV25, DV50, or DV100 data in MXF wrappers (see Lesson 7). P2 camcorders have slots for two to five adapters and some allow recording in round-robin fashion: you can swap cards while recording is in progress.

Best Interface to FCP Right now, FireWire transfers or SDI transfers appear to be the main options for capturing P2 clips, although P2 card readers for Mac may be in the offing.

XDCAM

XDCAM is Sony's blue-laser disc format. It provides a new, non-tape-based medium for DVCAM and IMX datastreams. Like P2, it'll be interesting to see how it evolves.

Primary Use XDCAM should fit wherever DVCAM and IMX equipment is used.

Technical Details XDCAM uses DVCAM and IMX recording on 12cm blue-violet laser optical discs. Video and audio parameters are the same as with DVCAM and IMX recording.

Sony is, so far, the sole supplier.

Best Interface to FCP XDCAM provides SDI transfer of uncompressed video with RS-422 control, or FireWire transfer of compressed DVCAM data. FCP 5 can also use IMX files natively using Telestream's Flip4Mac MXF Import Component to read XDCAM files over a network from Ethernet-equipped XDCAM decks.

Other Formats

The following are a few of the other digital video formats.

D-2, D-3 D-2 and D-3 are digital *composite* recorders. They have SDI, but not SDI you can use unless you have a digital-composite-to-digital-component transcoder. Alternately, you can capture the analog composite signals.

DCT DCT was Ampex's short-lived studio postproduction format, using digital component video compressed about 2:1 in large cassettes. Capture it via SDI.

DVD Third-party utilities such as MPEG Streamclip (www.alfanet.it/squareD-5/mpegstreamclip.html) or DVDxDV (www.DVDxDV.com/) let you extract MPEG-2 video from DVDs and transcode it to more tractable editing formats like DV25, but mind the rights and permissions of the copyright holders on commercial DVDs.

J-Series VTRs Not a format per se, Sony's J-series line of videotape players is designed to provide a low-cost playback mechanism for any professional ½-inch Sony SDTV format: Betacam, Beta SP, Beta SX, Digital Betacam, and IMX; even HDCAM in the top-end models.

MicroMV Sony's consumer MPEG-2 long-GOP format uses FireWire to transfer video to Sony's consumer editing software, but to nowhere else. A Y/C transfer is your best bet with FCP.

High Definition Formats

So far, we've been discussing standard-definition formats, but HD is coming on strong. Here are the HD formats you're likely to encounter.

Digital Video Formats (HD) at a Glance

Names	Best FCP I/O	Best FCP Control	Comments
D-5 HD	HD-SDI	RS-422	Current favorite HD mastering format
DVCPROHD, D-12	SDI, FireWire	SDI, FireWire	
HDCAM, D-11	HD-SDI	RS-422	
HDCAM-SR	Dual-link HD-SDI	RS-422	
HDV	FireWire	FireWire	Supported in FCP 5's; until then use HDVxDV or Lumière HD to capture and transcode for earlier versions
D-VHS	FireWire	FireWire	Use HDVxDV or Lumière HD to capture and transcode
D-6, Voodoo	SDI	RS-422	True uncompressed HD
HDD-1000, HDVS	Transfer to modern HD format	N/A	Obsolete 1035-line HD reel-to-reel

D-5 HD

D-5 HD is the industry standard top-quality HD recorder, at least so far.

Primary Use D-5 HD is used for high-quality studio recording and mastering. It's not a portable format.

Technical Details D-5 HD uses ½-inch tape cassette, the same as D-5, for 4:2:2, 8-bit recording with roughly 4:1 DCT compression, or 10-bit with 5:1 compression. It handles all HDTV formats, whether 720-line or 1080-line.

The format has eight channels of 24-bit audio or four of 20-bit audio, all at 48 kHz.

Panasonic is the sole manufacturer.

Best Interface to FCP D-5 HD offers HD-SDI with RS-422 control.

DVCPROHD

DVCPROHD is Panasonic's DV100 HD format, with both camcorders and studio decks. 720-line and 1080-line variants are available. The HDC-27 Varicam camcorder shoots 720p24 using a 2:3 pulldown, as well as any speed from 1 fps to 60 fps with varying pulldowns.

Primary Use DVCPROHD is used for HDTV production and digital filmmaking.

Technical Details DVCPROHD uses 6.35mm tape cassette, the same as DVCPRO. It supports all HD formats, depending on the recorder; subsampling the image spatially and then recording it as 4:2:2, 8-bit video with 6.7:1 DV compression.

DVCPROHD subsamples 1920 × 1080/60 to 1280 × 1080; 1920 × 1080/50 is subsampled to 1440 × 1080; 1280 × 720/60 is subsampled to 960 × 720.

DVCPROHD has eight channels of 16-bit 48 kHz audio.

Most DVCPROHD decks play back DVCPRO50, DVCPRO, DV, and DVCAM tapes, upconverting them on the fly.

Best Interface to FCP DVCPROHD supports FireWire transfer of compressed DV data, or HD-SDI transfer of uncompressed video, with RS-422 or FireWire control. FCP can extract the Varicam's pulldown automatically when FireWire transfer is used.

HDCAM

HDCAM was the first practical portable digital HD format. Camcorders shoot 1080-line video. The 24p-capable HDW-F900 CineAlta is the most common camera used for HD digital filmmaking.

Primary Use HDCAM is used for HDTV production and digital filmmaking.

Technical Details HDCAM uses ½-inch metal tape in a Betacam shell. Cameras shoot 1080i/60, 1080i/50, 1080p/25, 1080p/30, and (in the HDW-F900) 1080p/24. HDCAM subsamples the 8-bit video as 3:1:1 (1440 × 1080 luma, 480 × 1080 chroma) and records it with 4.4:1 DCT compression.

HDCAM has four channels of 20-bit 48 kHz audio.

Sony is the sole supplier.

Best Interface to FCP HDCAM provides HD-SDI with RS-422 control.

HDCAM-SR

HDCAM-SR is Sony's new high-quality format based on HDCAM. It's still too new and expensive for widespread adoption, but offers both high-quality 4:2:2 YC_RC_B recording and 4:4:4 RGB recording.

Primary Use SR is designed for top-quality HD recording and mastering, especially where full-color resolution must be preserved for postproduction purposes. (Hint: George Lucas bought a bunch of these decks.)

Technical Details SR uses ½-inch metal tape in a Betacam shell and provides lossless MPEG-4 recording of the 4:2:2 8-bit signal in 1080- or 720-line formats with 2.7:1 compression, 4:4:4, 10-bit RGB recording using 4.2:1 compression is available with add-on boards.

HDCAM-SR has 12 channels of 24-bit 48 kHz audio.

Sony is the sole supplier.

Best Interface to FCP SR offers HD-SDI for the 4:2:2 video, or dual-link HD-SDI for the 4:4:4 RGB option using a capture card and codec for this format.

HDV

HDV is HD at DV prices. It's still very new, but it may mushroom in popularity once more equipment becomes available.

Primary Use HDV is a camcorder format intended to jump-start customer demand for HDTV sets and services, but like DV before it, it may wind up taking over a wide swath of the low-end HDTV production marketplace.

Technical Details HDV provides HD recording on miniDV cassettes. It uses 4:2:0 sampling for both 720p and 1080i formats; recording 8-bit video with long-GOP MPEG-2 compression at 19 Megabits/second for 720p and 25 Megabits/second for 1080i.

Current HDV cameras from JVC record 720/30p as well as 480p/60, both in 16×9, as well as 480/60i, 4×3 DV. A PAL-country version records 576p/50. The current Sony models record 1080/50i or 1080/60i, as well as 480/50i or 480/60i in DV or DVCAM. Future cameras from multiple vendors may offer 1080/50i, 1080/60i, 1080/24p, 720/60p, and 720/24p, among others.

HDV records two channels of 48k, 16-bit audio with 4:1 MPEG-1 Layer 2 compression.

Best Interface to FCP FCP 5 supports HDV capture and playback over FireWire, using either HDV-native editing or the Apple Intermediate Codec for timeline rendering. Earlier versions of FCP work with HDV using third-party add-ons like HDVxDV or LumièreHD to capture HDV and transcode it to DVCPROHD or other formats compatible with FCP 4.

Other Formats

The following are a few of the other high-definition formats, both digital and analog.

D-VHS A data-recording "bit bucket" format created by JVC to record off-air DTV signals. It's also used for low-cost HD program distribution; its recording format and FireWire interface are comparable to HDVs, utilizing MPEG-2 transport streams at up to 28 Megabits/second. Best interface is via FireWire using a D-VHS-compatible tool such as Lumière HD.

D-6 A 4:2:2 uncompressed digital format with a whopping 1.5 Gigabit/second data rate and dinner-tray-sized cassettes to match. It's both expensive and rare. HD-SDI is the way to get video out of the decks, using RS-422 control.

HDD-1000 Now-obsolete uncompressed digital reel-to-reel tape format characterized by impressive tape speeds and staggering per-minute costs. Ask for a transfer to a more FCP-friendly format.

HiVision, W-VHS, Eureka Analog HDTV recording formats of various sorts, usually recording 1035-line video (the predecessor to the current 1080-line standards). Eureka was Europe's short-lived 1250-line, 50Hz interlaced format. Ask for a transfer to a more FCP-friendly format.

Analog Video Formats (HD) at a Glance

Names	Best FCP I/O	Best FCP Control	Comments
HiVision	Transfer to digital HD format	N/A	Analog 1035-line HD; obsolete
Eureka	Standards-convert to modern HD format	N/A	Short-lived 1250/50 European standard; obsolete
W-VHS	SDI via AJA HD10A or similar converter	Manual	Affordable; low-bandwidth 1035/1080i format on VHS-sized cassettes

Analog Audio Formats

Analog audio is rapidly going the way of analog video, only more so. The digital revolution hit audio before it hit video, and the transition is further along. Still, you may need to deal with analog audio; here are the basics of the formats you're most likely to encounter.

Reel-to-Reel

¼-inch reel-to-reel is frequently used for film location audio, typically on a Nagra recorder (the standard film sound recorder, built by Nagra/Kudelski in Switzerland). Nagra audio typically runs at 7.5 inches per second (ips) or 15 ips, and it has an embedded Pilotone track, a sync reference signal at a nominal 60 Hz. Nagra playback is synced using a resolver to read the Pilot one signal and slave the Nagra's motors to 60 Hz, either using AC line frequency, a high-precision crystal oscillator, or a 60 Hz reference signal put out by the equipment the Nagra is syncing to.

There are other ¼-inch recorders for film sound, such as Stellavox and Uher machines, but they are less common. Each brand of recorder typically had its own way of recording a sync signal; check with the source of the tape if you're not sure how (or if) you should resolve a sync reference.

Other ¼-inch tapes may simply be *wild sound*, without a sync reference.

Nagra audio is usually full-track: the mono or stereo recording occupies the full width of the tape; when you reach the end of a reel, you rewind it for playback, just like video. Other tapes may be full-track with one or more channels, but half-track tapes are also common, where you turn the reel over once it's completed and record in the other direction. If you play back a half-track tape on a full-track recorder, you'll hear "backwards audio" from the other direction mixed with the forwards audio you expect to hear.

Multi-track audiotape is more common as a studio production format than as a field-recording format. Like multiple audio tracks on the FCP Timeline, multi-track keeps multiple channels in sync and allows for overdubbing one track while listening to another. Some multi-track tapes have a sync reference, and some even have LTC (most commonly used with a chase lock synchronizer, which listens to the timecode signal from a VTR and slaves the audio recorder to it, "chasing" the timecode), but again it's highly dependent on the recorder you use and the workflow you use with it.

Audio connections can be RCAs, phone plugs, XLRs, or even "banana plugs" on some Nagras—separate, fat plugs for signal and ground.

Compact Cassette

Cassettes are sometimes used for location audio, mostly as wild sound. Fidelity is lower than with reel-to-reel, but the convenience and portability of cassette audio was worth the losses in sound quality.

You make cassette connections usually via RCAs, though some professional studio decks have XLRs as well.

Notes

Analog audio recorders are typically calibrated for one kind of tape: oxide, ferrichrome, metal, and so on. Some have selection switches to set the bias current and equalization for the tape type. Bias current is only used while recording; EQ needs to be properly set for both recording and playback, or frequency response will suffer.

Analog frequently employs noise reduction schemes, especially on cassette. Dolby B, Dolby C, and dbx are the most common approaches; you should label tapes with the noise reduction used so that you can use the corresponding playback setting. Using the wrong setting may result in more audible noise, frequency distortions, reduced dynamic range, and "pumping" or "breathing" artifacts from uncompensated compression.

Resolving sync on analog tapes usually means locking the recorder to line frequency during capture so that the sound doesn't drift with respect to picture. You can use a common start mark, such as a filmmaker's clapper, to align picture and sound in sync by manually aligning the sound of the clapper with the frame in which it closes.

Digital Audio Formats

It's common to record separate sound on digital devices these days. Unlike analog audio, digital audio is self-clocking: digital audio by its nature contains synchronizing information, so that playback happens at the same precise speed as recording. Maintaining a common start mark between picture and sound remains an issue; unless the digital format includes timecode, you need a clapper or other start reference to match picture to sound.

DAT

Digital Audio Tape records 44.1 or 48 kHz, 16-bit uncompressed stereo audio on a 4mm tape cassette. Interface is via analog RCAs or XLRs, or by digital S/PDIF connections. DAT gives very clean audio assuming the microphones and preamps are of high quality.

Pro DAT machines may include a timecode track so that you can marry field recordings to picture in a double-system recording setup without the need for a clapper or other common start mark.

MiniDisc

Sony's MiniDisc format records 44.1 kHz 16-bit stereo using Sony's proprietary ATRAC codec. Each new track is individually addressable, recordable, and erasable, and the recorders are small, lightweight, and fairly sturdy, so MiniDisc has found favor as a location audio recorder, often in situations where you would otherwise use a wireless microphone. A MiniDisc recorder is simply stuck in an actor's pocket or gaffer-taped to his body, and a wired mic is attached to it.

Portable consumer MiniDisc recorder outputs tend to be analog stereo mini-plugs only, as you'd use with headphones. Professional MiniDisc recorders and home units (not portables) add S/PDIF, RCAs, and/or XLRs for input and output, allowing more connection flexibility. Some even include USB for direct connection to computers.

Flash Memory and Hard Disk Recorders

Small recorders using flash memory or hard drives are also filling the need for cheap, portable, rugged location recorders. They run the gamut from cheap consumer devices recording MP3 audio only, with nothing more than stereo miniplug outputs, up to high-end consumer and professional devices recording MP3, WAV, or BWF formats and offering a full complement of analog and digital I/O connections.

Most of these machines include a USB connection for quick transfers to and from a computer. Some even have FireWire. You can mount these devices on the Mac desktop as drives, and drag files to and from them.

Multi-Track Disk Recorders

Film audio is increasingly turning to multi-track hard disk recorders, allowing you to record multiple microphones or submixes on their own tracks simultaneously. Like their lower-end cousins, they offer the choice of compressed or uncompressed formats, and most include USB or FireWire (or both) connectivity to move the recorded audio to a computer for further production.

Measurement Tools

Measurement tools give you an objective handle on the technical parameters of your picture and sound and help ensure that you're getting consistent, high-quality results.

Waveform Monitors

The Waveform monitor (WFM) shows you a graph of the video signal, plotting the amplitude (voltage) of the signal vertically and time horizontally. The WFM lets you see exactly what the black level of your picture is; whether the whites in your images exceed 100 percent and whether the combined luma and chroma exceed broadcast-safe levels. The WFM come in handy when trying to color-correct two scenes: it unambiguously shows you any difference in levels.

An external WFM shows you what's happening with the video signal outside the active picture area, something that FCP's built-in WFM cannot do. You can use the WFM to view the sync pulses, blanking intervals, and colorburst of your equipment, letting you diagnose problems with equipment or with tapes of uncertain quality.

Most importantly, the external WFM serves as a quality-control element, ensuring that what you see inside FCP is actually making it onto the tape without level changes or other impairments. An external WFM lets you monitor signals at any point in your equipment chain; the FCP WFM only shows you what the digital video inside FCP looks like.

In its most common usage, the width of the display shows the duration of a single scanline, so the "picture" on the WFM is literally a voltage graph of the video image. The WFM thus shows you information on the brightness of your picture, just as a picture monitor does, but the WFM does it in a calibrated and measurable way.

With a composite video signal, the WFM literally plots the voltage of the signal against time. Filters let you see the entire signal complete with the color sub-carrier signal, show just the luma signal, or show just the color subcarrier by itself. (FCP's built-in WFM shows just luma by default; you can superimpose the color information by choosing Saturation from the WFM's pop-up menu.)

Component and digital WFMs have modes to show you their raw signals, but they also synthesize the same view you'd get with a composite WFM, because that view is so useful in monitoring the overall status of the signal.

Vectorscopes

A vectorscope is a specialized display showing you only the color information in your signal. The vectorscope's main value comes in color correction: just as the WFM instantly shows you mismatches in levels, the vectorscope shows you an unbiased view of the colors in a scene. As you switch between two shots, or wipe between them, the vectorscope reveals color differences that may be too subtle to see by eye—and it certainly gives you a good idea of how to adjust the controls in the 3-way color corrector to get the scenes to match.

The vectorscope also aids in system setup: SMPTE or EBU color bars, displayed on the vectorscope, should display dots in the calibrated target regions; if they do not, you can adjust the saturation and color controls in the offending piece of equipment until they do line up. (Vectorscopes are also useful in calibrating color signals inside cameras, TBCs, and the like, but those details will have to wait for the Peachpit book *Optimizing the Insides of Your Cameras and Studio Equipment.*)

The center of the vectorscope is where grays reside: any signal in the center indicates an area of the picture with no color, whether white, black, or any shade of gray in-between. As you move away from the center, color saturation increases; as you move around the face of the display, you vary the hue. In essence, the face of the vectorscope is a color wheel against which the colors in your video are plotted.

Rasterizers

Rasterizers, or signal monitors, are computerized tools performing the same functions as stand-alone WFMs and vectorscopes, but displaying their results on video or computer monitors. Simple ones, like the Magni MM-400 shown, do little more than replicate the functions of the stand-alone scopes. More complex ones include audio metering, signal quality logging, gamut warnings when a signal exceeds defined limits, and picture-in-picture displays so you can see picture, audio levels, and measurements on the same screen.

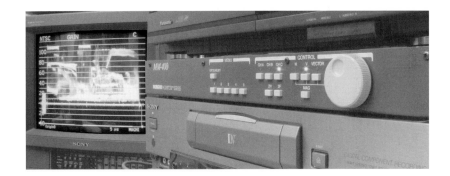

FCP's Video Scopes

FCP has its own measurement tools built in in the Video Scopes window. In addition to a WFM and vectorscope, FCP includes a histogram and an RGB parade display. The histogram shows the distribution of brightness values through the image; the parade is essentially a WFM for each of the red, green, and blue channels of information, showing you when you're in danger of clipping a color component even when the WFM is well within limits.

These are valuable and useful tools, but they have three limitations:

▶ The internal scopes show you only what's happening inside FCP. They can't tell you anything about the video signals elsewhere in your studio.

▶ FCP's scopes don't show you every line of video; they sample every sixteenth line for performance purposes. That means they can miss fine details less than 16 scanlines tall. Small specular highlights, for example, are easily missed, so you might think you have a picture that's broadcast legal when in fact some parts of it exceed 100 percent brightness.

▶ FCP's scopes update only when you pause playback. They don't give a running commentary on video as it's playing.

It's worth having access to at least an external WFM if you're planning on finishing programs in FCP, just to catch things the internal scopes miss.

Picture Monitors

A good picture monitor is an invaluable final check for image quality. Computer screens don't render colors and brightness quite the way a picture monitor does, nor do they show the image cropping that a monitor's overscan does. (Televisions overscan the image, cropping about 10 percent off the edges of the picture, to ensure that innocent civilians are never exposed to the horror of an image smaller than the bezel of their TV screen.)

The standard reference for video monitoring and color correction is a CRT monitor using a SMPTE Type C phosphor. Most good professional and broadcast monitor lines have Type C phosphors; the spec sheet for the monitor should mention it if it's used. The Type C phosphor has a calibrated color gamut and response, so—assuming the monitor itself is properly calibrated and white-balanced—the monitor will reproduce a picture the same way as any other Type C phosphor-equipped monitor will. Consumer televisions don't have standardized phosphors; most make a picture stronger in blue than they should. (Because blue phosphors are bright, and consumers tend to buy the brighter of two sets they see, manufacturers "cheat" towards blue for a competitive advantage.)

A good monitor has high resolution (600 TVl/ph or more for an SDTV monitor), an underscan button so you can see all the edges of the picture, and a blue-only switch so you can easily calibrate the monitor to color bars.

LCD monitors are usually disparaged for precise work; in the past their color gamuts and white points have been too inaccurate for critical monitoring. LCDs have improved markedly in recent years, but they still tend to have difficulties displaying the entire tonal scale without some brightness or color distortions.

Monitor Speakers

As with picture monitoring, accurate sound monitoring is essential for doing good work. Good monitor speakers have a flat and neutral response; the inexpensive speakers sold for computer use typically have peaks and valleys in their frequency response that distort or "color" the sound, possibly hiding sonic defects or masking problems with intelligibility.

You can press good headphones into service, especially where the venue doesn't lend itself to critical listening (hotel rooms, trade show floors, and so on), but most sound mixers prefer a good set of near-field monitor speakers in a controlled listening environment to headphones when the location allows for it.

It doesn't hurt to have "bad speakers" available, too. You need to ensure that your final mix works even when the thunderous bass and soaring treble accents get lost during playback on cheap speakers. Some editors keep an old, beat-up TV monitor with a tinny, 3-inch oval speaker handy, just to ensure that their pristine programs are watchable and intelligible even under less-than-ideal circumstances. Others use the cheapest computer speakers available. Both approaches work well.

Offboard Processors

FCP's internal filters and tools are capable of a lot, but it's useful to have external processors to fix, route, and condition signals before you capture them. They add capability and flexibility when working outside of FCP, too.

Proc Amps

Proc amps, short for processing amplifiers, are used to correct brightness and color problems in video images. They typically have four controls: DC Level or Pedestal to adjust the black level of the image; Gain or Contrast to adjust the overall strength of the video signal; Color or Saturation to tweak color strength; and Hue or Phase to correct problems in hue. (Make the faces less green! No, make the faces less purple!)

Fixing the image *before* it comes into FCP means that you'll have full latitude to tweak it as needed during editing; if you capture a distorted image, you'll use up that latitude simply fixing what's broken, and you may have irreparably lost details (typically in highlights or shadows) that could have been saved prior to capture.

Proc amps also regenerate clean sync pulses and colorburst (if the signal is composite or Y/C) to ensure clean captures, which is very useful if the original signal has been degraded due to multiple generations of dubbing.

Some also allow adjusting Y/C delay: in color-under formats, chroma can drift sideways compared to luma, and it drops down a scanline with every generation of VHS or Video8 dubbing.

Proc amps may also offer noise-reduction options and image sharpening options. These can be useful at times, but must be used with care to avoid degrading the image more than improving it.

TBCs

Timebase correctors compensate for the horizontal jitter and timebase instability that analog formats suffer from. TBCs are by nature built into all digital VTRs, and many analog ones (Betacam especially), but are often absent in consumer and industrial ¾", VHS, and Video8 decks. If you work with analog formats and your playback decks don't have TBCs built in, a separate, stand-alone TBC can be a lifesaver.

Most TBCs offer at least the basic proc amp controls, so you can use them to correct and clean up images as well as stabilize them. Many provide transcoding capabilities: they can capture from one signal format, such as composite, and output composite, Y/C, and component simultaneously.

Audio Mixers

Most editors keep a small audio mixing board beside their FCP systems. The Mac's output, as well as the output of CD players, VTRs, and other sound sources is routed through the mixer, which provides a convenient, centralized volume control for all these devices. A mixer also comes in handy for performing voice-overs, dubbing between VTRs, and performing various other sound-adjusting tasks. The mixer's outputs are fed to the monitor speakers, headphones, and even back into the Mac's audio input as required.

Sync and Blackburst Generators Video equipment needs to be synchronized to work together; anyone putting together a multichannel video studio or A/B roll linear editing suite has to provide house sync to all VTRs to ensure they run in lockstep. But even in a single VTR FCP system, you may need to provide a reference signal to the VTR to ensure proper operation; Betacam decks especially seem to misbehave unless they're provided a stable sync signal on their reference inputs.

Generally speaking, you'll need reference run to your deck *and* to your Mac if you're using RS-422 control, even for decks that work fine without reference. RS-422 protocol works best when its commands are sent coincident with the start of each field, and the only way to assure this is for both Mac and deck to be running in sync. You usually won't see frame-accurate captures and edits to tape if you're missing a common reference signal.

Some capture cards provide a reference signal output; others need reference input.

Reference is a composite signal, containing video (commonly just black), color-burst, and sync, hence the term VBS: video, burst, and sync. Because the signal has a black picture and colorburst, you'll often see sync generators called black-burst generators. You'll also see the term *genlock* used for blackburst reference.

Even HD VTRs accept an SDTV composite reference signal, although some also have inputs for HD *tri-level sync*, which requires its own generator.

No consumer decks or camcorders have reference inputs, nor do many DV and DVCAM decks. But as you move up the price scale, more decks have reference connectors, and many of them need reference to work properly. Decks that need reference, but aren't getting it, exhibit a variety of symptoms: black bars rolling through the picture, vertical jumps or rolls in the picture, and erratic capture and recording performance among them.

Sync, blackburst, or reference generators are small boxes that do nothing in life other than put out stable, clean, black video, for the purpose of synchronizing and stabilizing devices that need it.

Some FCP capture cards generate their own sync signals to feed to a VTR while others have a genlock input to receive the same signal being fed to the VCR by an external sync generator.

TIP ▶ If you don't have a reference generator in your DV-oriented shop and you rent a Betacam or other high-end deck for a job, you can use a DV camera with the lens capped as your reference source. There's nothing magical about reference: any stable source of black video will work.

Distribution Amps

You may need to send a video or audio signal to multiple places at once: video and audio to a rack of VHS machines for dubbing, or blackburst to all the VTRs in your shop, for instance. Distribution amps (DAs) simply amplify and replicate one signal across multiple outputs, allowing you to feed all those devices from one source.

Patch Panels and Routing Switchers

If you wire up your equipment in one configuration and never change it, you won't need patch panels or routing switchers. But most of us change things around from time to time, varying which VTR is captured from or which video source is displayed on a monitor. Patch panels and routing switchers let you repatch or reroute signals easily, without having to crawl behind racks or desks and fiddle with the back panels of the gear.

Patch panels are passive devices with no active electronics. An array of jacks presents the inputs and outputs of the equipment wired to it, and you make connections between two jacks with a patch cord. Some jacks are self-normaling: When no cord is plugged in, the jack on top is connected internally to the jack below it, so that the panel with all cords removed is connected in a "normal" configuration.

Switchers are active devices that amplify and route signals electronically. They connect sources to destinations at the push of a button. Most of them also serve as DAs; one input can be sent to multiple outputs.

Both devices come in a variety of formats—audio, analog video, digital video—and connection types: BNCs, RCAs, even FireWire.

Purists may prefer the unadulterated signal path of the patch panel, whereas others prefer the convenience and flexibility of switchers.

Capturing Video and Audio

Finally: how do you get video and audio into and out of FCP?

DV over FireWire

If you have a Mac running FCP HD, and a DV-format deck with FireWire, you're all set: FCP supports all flavors of DV (DV, DVCAM, DVCPRO, DVCPRO50, and DVCPROHD) captured and played back over FireWire. Plug a FireWire cable between deck and Mac, select the appropriate capture preset in FCP, and (if necessary) set the deck up for FireWire transfer, and you're good to go. (See your deck's manual; DVCPRO machines may require menu manipulation to "talk FireWire.")

The DV datastream is copied across FireWire in its native form, without decompression. What you get on disk is the same as what was written to tape (unless you choose to capture to OfflineRT format; FCP can transcode DV25 to OfflineRT, a Photo-JPEG format, which saves you eight times the space).

FCP can extract 24p Advanced pulldown (2:3:3:2) material on the fly when you use FireWire transfer, resulting in 23.98 Hz clips ready to use in a 23.98 timeline.

FireWire DV Converters

Many vendors offer converters/transcoders that plug into FireWire, converting from DV25 on the FireWire side of the box to standard-definition analog composite, Y/C, component, or SDI on the other side. These boxes let you capture all manner of video formats into FCP, as long as you don't mind using DV25 as your editing format. Sony built the first such converters, but they've been discontinued (and supported NTSC only).

The Canopus ADVC100 is a typical example. It offers composite and Y/C video I/O as well as locked stereo audio on RCAs. It's switchable between NTSC and PAL formats and even lets you add and remove 7.5 IRE setup in the analog domain.

As you move up the spectrum, DV converters add component and SDI connections, XLR analog audio, AES/EBU digital audio, and even built-in timebase correction and proc amp controls for massaging incoming analog signals. Canopus, Datavideo, Laird Telemedia, Miglia, Miranda, Promax, Sweet Pea Communications, and others build them.

NOTE ► Apple made changes in the FireWire on the 2004 G5s that may be incompatible with the FireWire implementations in some early-model DV cameras and DV converters. If a camera or converter doesn't work with a new G5, try it on an older Mac, and try a different DV device on the G5, before assuming something is wrong with the FireWire port on either the Mac or the DV device.

TIP ► Many DV camcorders and decks can transcode between analog inputs and FireWire outputs on the fly, although you may have to dig through the machine's menus to enable this feature. You can use such decks as analog-to-DV converters if you don't wish to buy a separate converter box.

FireWire Uncompressed Converters

AJA Video Systems builds several converters under the Io label that interface standard-definition analog and/or digital video, audio, genlock, and RS-422 control to Macs over FireWire, using an uncompressed video codec co-developed with Apple.

FireWire's 320 Megabit/second isochronous bandwidth has plenty of room for uncompressed video's 270 Megabits/second as well as eight channels of audio, timecode, genlock, and RS-422 control, so these boxes let you capture any format of SD, uncompressed, without having to open up your Mac and use up a precious PCI slot for a capture card.

HDV Over FireWire

Final Cut Pro 5 supports HDV capture and playback over FireWire in both a native HDV mode and a transcoding mode.

In native mode, operations are the same as with DV: you can log clips by time-code and batch capture them or use "Capture Now." After editing your show, you can print to video, recording the timeline to HDV tape.

In transcoding mode, the HDV datastream is copied across FireWire in its native form and transcoded on the fly to the Apple Intermediate Codec, a low-loss, I-frame-only codec designed to optimize responsiveness on the HD timeline while preserving quality.

When you choose the intermediate codec for captures, however, FCP 5 offers only a simple tape-naming dialog instead of the Log and Capture window; you capture the tape in a single pass, and FCP breaks the tape into scene-based clips as it captures. Future versions of FCP may offer a more smoothly-integrated Intermediate Codec workflow.

After editing, FCP renders the timeline back to HDV's highly compressed MPEG-2 before sending it back out to FireWire when you print to video.

The choice of workflow is yours: using the Intermediate Codec is a bit less convenient, but provides better multi-generation performance if you bounce clips between FCP and Motion, Shake, Combustion, or After Effects. Using the HDV-native workflow offers a more seamless editing experience (FCP's native HDV implementation is superb and responsive) and its rendering quality is very good.

Of course, you can also capture via FireWire using either codec, and edit HDV material into a DVCPROHD or uncompressed HD timeline.

PCI Cards

PCI cards plug into the internal expansion bus of your Mac and provide ana-log and/or digital I/O, RS-422 control, and genlock as required. Most provide capture to uncompressed codecs as well as one or more compressed formats (a DV format or a Photo-JPEG format, usually). Some provide hardware acceleration of simple effects and some filters.

PCI cards vary in their bus speeds (33, 66, 100, or 133 MHz) and PCI-X compatibility. PCI-X, used in the newest G5s, gives the best performance.

Most PCI cards have more I/O options than the back-panel slot allows. They usually ship with hydra-headed adapter cables running from the high-density connector(s) on the card to a handful of BNCs, XLRs, RCAs, Y/C jacks, and the like. These cables are certainly sufficient to wire up the system, but they're not especially convenient if you need to rewire things.

An extra-cost option to deal with the connector problem is the break-out box (BOB), a tabletop or rack-mounted box with all the necessary connections. BOBs make rewiring the system a lot easier; they're like the back panel of a VTR with all the jacks neatly lined up and labeled. Each card has its own BOB (or selection of BOBs) along with the necessary card-to-BOB cable; BOBs aren't interchangeable between different brands or models of cards.

Here's a list of recent PCI card offerings, in alphabetical order by vendor. It's fairly correct as of press time, but ask your supplier or go on the Web for current information. Prices and features vary considerably and change from time to time as hardware gets modified and software gets updated.

AJA Video Systems AJA (www.aja.com) offers two PCI cards in addition to the Io series of FireWire interfaces: Kona LS and Kona 2.

Kona LS supports 10-bit SDI, as well as component, composite, and S-Video I/O with 12-bit A/D. It handles DV25 and DV50 playback as well as playback and capture of both uncompressed and JPEG-compressed video, and it supports 3:2 pulldown removal and insertion for 24p material.

Kona 2 supports 10-bit SDI, HD-SDI, and dual-link HD-SDI for 10- or 12-bit 4:4:4 HD, It also provides SD-to-HD upconversion, HD-to-SD downconversion, analog component outputs, and DVCPROHD hardware acceleration. Kona 2 includes a hardware-based "Qrez" 4:1 compressed codec in addition to uncompressed capture, and hardware acceleration of DVCPROHD timelines, allowing more real-time effects than would otherwise be the case.

Both Konas have BOBs available for easier connectivity.

Kona cards allow the video outputs to be used as desktop extensions outside of FCP, so you can (for example) work in Photoshop or After Effects and see the results directly on a video monitor.

Aurora Video Systems Aurora's IgniterX cards (www.auroravideosys.com) start off with SD capture and playback of composite and Y/C SD video, along with unbalanced audio. Upgrades or options allow for component, SDI, AES/EBU audio, LTC I/O, genlock, RS-422, and 24 fps support (2:3 pulldown removal and insertion).

Igniters work with uncompressed video, or use MPEG-A codecs for compressed video.

Aurora's newer Pipe series starts off with Pipe: a composite and Y/C I/O card with 8-bit capture and playback, unbalanced audio, and genlock. PipeSDI is a digital-only card: 10-bit SDI and AES/EBU, plus RS-422 control. PipePRO adds 10-bit analog outputs (composite, Y/C, component, and audio) to 10-bit digital I/O, and PipeHD provides 10-bit HD-SDI I/O with downconverted analog monitoring.

Pipe cards capture and play back uncompressed only.

Blackmagic Design DeckLink cards from Blackmagic Design (www.black-magic-design.com) range from analog component-only (DeckLink SP) or 10-bit digital-only (Decklink) cards, to digital cards with analog monitoring (DeckLink Pro) or analog and digital I/O both (DeckLink Extreme).

For HD work, there's the 10-bit DeckLink HD with SDI in either SD or HD; the DeckLink HD Plus, adding genlock and separate AES audio I/O; and the 12-bit DeckLink HD Pro, which adds 14-bit analog monitoring and dual-link HD-SDI capability.

All the DeckLinks support several real-time filters and transitions, including cross dissolve, proc amp, and the 3-way color corrector. They provide a video desktop function like the AJAs do, play out DV files directly (without real-time effects), provide RS-422 control, and supply SDI sync: no genlock required.

DeckLinks have 8- and 10-bit uncompressed codecs.

Digital Voodoo The SD line from Digital Voodoo (www.digitalvoodoo.net) includes the FCP HD-compatible SD|Flex, with 10-bit processing and the full complement of analog (composite, Y/C, and component) and digital I/Os.

Flex includes video desktop capability and real-time acceleration of the 3-way color corrector, dissolves, and several other filters.

The SD-Edit is an SDI output-only card (not every editing system needs ingest capabilities, especially with the shared-storage options discussed in Lesson 9), whereas the 64RT has SDI input and output.

Digital Voodoo's HD cards start with the HD|Fury with HD-SDI I/O, real-time downconversion to SD, and eight channels of AES audio. The HD|Vengeance adds dual HD outputs and dual-link capability.

Digital Voodoo also has two output-only HD cards. The HD|Iridium outputs HD only (no SD downconversion) in single- or dual-link formats, while the HD|IridiumXP adds the real-time downconverter.

The Digital Voodoo cards work with uncompressed as well as Photo-JPEG codecs. They work in either RGB or YUV modes with hardware colorspace conversion. They also include nifty features like onboard keyers for superimposing graphics on live video, or outputting a key signal—but FCP doesn't support these added capabilities.

Matrox The RTMac from Matrox (www.matrox.com) is a unique card built around a hardware DV25 codec. Analog composite and Y/C video and unbalanced audio I/O are converted to DV25 and edited like any other DV source; it's like having a DV converter box on a card instead of dangling off of FireWire. The RTMac also accelerates a variety of dissolves, wipes, and motion effects in hardware, and it provides a VGA-compatible second monitor output, too, so you can connect another computer monitor and extend your desktop. RTMac comes with its own BOB.

The RTMac supports FCP 3 and FCP 4 through 4.1, but FCP HD is not supported and development of the Matrox drivers has been discontinued.

RTMacs capture to and play back DV25 video.

Pinnacle Systems CinéWave from Pinnacle Systems (www.pinnaclesys.com) is a hardware-accelerated video engine of considerable flexibility. Depending on the break-out box(es) you get, you can deal with analog video and audio in all its varieties (Pro Analog), 10-bit SDI with embedded audio (Pro Digital), SDI I/O with separate AES/EBU audio and analog monitoring (Pro Digital Plus), full analog and digital I/O (Pro Digital and Analog), and HD-SDI with embedded audio (Pro HD Digital). These BOBs can be mixed and matched at any time.

CinéWave lets you play out DV25, DV50, uncompressed, Photo-JPEG, LiveType, and RGBA clips in the same Timeline without rendering. It offers simultaneous SD and HD outputs, upconverting or downconverting as required. You can capture HD to the DVCPROHD codec. Real-time 2:3 pulldown removal and insertion are provided for 24p material.

CinéWave has both 8- and 16-bit uncompressed codecs as well as its own CinéOffline compressed codec, DVCPROHD capture capability, and support for playback of multiple codecs.

> **MORE INFO** ▶ Have a look at *Video Basics and Equipment*, Volume 1, Chapter 2 of Final Cut Pro Help. The FCP team did a great job on the book that ships free with every copy of the program.

Lesson Review

1. Why do you need so much computer power when editing video?
2. What are the three most common analog video interfaces, and how do they compare?
3. What are the three most common digital video connections?
4. How are they different?
5. At what levels is analog audio carried?
6. What gear do you need to convert between different analog audio levels?
7. What connections carry digital audio?
8. List three essential measurement tools in video editing.
9. Name some ancillary equipment that would ease interfacing tasks and round out a studio's capabilities.
10. Can FCP use FireWire directly to capture and play back video and audio?

Answers

1. Video makes heavy demands on the CPU, RAM, and graphics card.

2. Component, Y/C, and composite. Of the three, component video is the highest quality; composite is the lowest.

3. SDI, SDTI, and FireWire.

4. SDI carries uncompressed video, SDTI carries compressed video, and FireWire carries either one, depending on the application.

5. At high line levels, low line levels, and mic levels.

6. An amplifier or attenuator.

7. FireWire, RCAs, BNCs, XLRs, and optical links.

8. Waveform monitors, vectorscopes, and accurate picture monitors.

9. Audio mixers, DAs, TBCs, proc amps, patch panels, and switchers.

10. Yes it can, as well as a large selection of third-party interfaces.

9

Lesson 9
Storage Overview

You've mastered video concepts and standards, know what formats are available, and understand the best way to hook up a VTR to your Mac so you can capture some video and audio.

Now, where do you put all that data?

The short answer is: hard drives. Lots of hard drives.

The long answer is what this lesson is all about. Hard drives, sure, but how many, what kinds, and how do you hook them up? Video data rates can run from 300 KB/second (OfflineRT) to over 150 MB/second (uncompressed 10-bit 1080i29.97), a spread of 500:1. What works for OfflineRT probably won't handle full-up HD, and heavy-duty drive arrays for HD are overkill for OfflineRT. Picking the right storage for the task involves knowing how drives work, how to rate their performance, and how to connect and combine them to provide the needed speed and space.

Hard Drive Basics

While you can just buy hard disks and plug them in, you'll have better luck with them if you understand how they work and how they're connected. The spec sheets don't tell the whole story; hard drives vary in performance depending on how full they are, and the ways in which they're connected and format-ted affect how well they can supply a steady stream of video data. Fortunately, the details aren't that difficult to grasp, and once you know the basics you'll be able to read between the lines of the manufacturer's data sheets and pick the best drives for your needs.

Hard drives are fairly simple electromechanical devices. One or more *platters*, metal or glass disks coated with magnetic material, are mounted on a hub and spun at about 100 revolutions per second. Magnetic read/write heads scan across the surface of the platters to read existing data or record it anew.

Each platter may be coated on one or both surfaces (top and bottom alike). Each coated surface has its own head, and the heads are attached to arms, suspending them just above the magnetic layer. The arms in turn are connected to a com-mon mechanism that either rotates or slides back and forth, to move the heads between the outermost parts of the platters and the innermost sections closest to the hub.

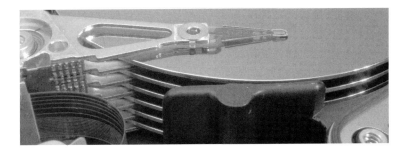

Each surface is divided into a bunch of concentric circles, or *tracks*, within which data may be recorded. All the tracks addressable with the arm assembly in one place form a *cylinder*.

Within tracks, data are stored in *sectors*, the smallest addressable chunk of storage from the disk drive's standpoint. Each sector may hold something like 512 or 1024 bytes. Each track contains sector markers so the drive can find the sector it needs. (The drive actually reads and writes an entire sector at a time; it has no way to individually address "bit 3 of byte 12 of sector 14," for example. That's a complication handled by the drive's controller.)

The smallest chunk of data the Mac OS sees is the *block*, a collection of one or more sectors. (In the PC world, a block is usually called a *cluster*.) Lumping several sectors together into blocks makes for more efficient disk access. If your sectors are 512 bytes, and your blocks contain 8 sectors or 4 kilobytes, you can read a 1 MB file by asking the disk for a block 256 times. Asking the disk for a sector would require 2,048 separate calls; the Mac would spend all its time asking for data instead of digesting it. It's more efficient to make a few large requests instead of many smaller ones.

There's a trade-off in block sizing: make the blocks too small, and your I/O subsystem spends all its time handling piffling little requests; make them too big and you waste space on the disk. The smallest amount you can allocate for a file is one entire block, and the file's space grows in block-long increments. Small, slow disks, like floppies (remember them?) usually have block sizes of a single sector, whereas huge, fast arrays like Xserve RAIDs may use blocks of 4 MB for video I/O. Desktop drives are somewhere in-between, of course; 4 KB blocks are typical.

NOTE ▶ For single disks you initialize with OS X's Disk Utility, you don't need to worry about block sizes: Disk Utility picks sensible sizes for you. If you set up RAIDs or SANs, the RAID or SAN administration software may very well ask you for a block size, and that's why we're wasting your time with this stuff in the first place.

Starting with an empty disk, the heads write data into each track within a cylinder in turn until the entire cylinder is full. Then the arms step to the next cylinder, and the heads write new data into it, and the cycle repeats, cylinder by cylinder, until the disk is full. Disks normally write from the outermost cylinders inwards, the same way a phonograph record starts playing from the outside inwards. Of course, once you've written a bunch of files and then deleted some, the progress is a bit less predictable; we'll cover that in a bit.

Raw Performance Factors

Drives are rated by their rotational speed. Slow laptop drives spin at 4200 RPM (revolutions per minute); faster laptop drives and some desktop drives run at 5400 RPM. Most desktop drives these days turn at 7200 RPM; expensive, high-performance drives may run at 10,000, 12,000, or even 15,000 RPM.

All else being equal, data transfer speeds scale with rotational speeds, but you pay the price in dollars, power consumption, heat generation, and reduced longevity. Faster drives, in addition to sucking more power and generating more heat, tend to run noisier, too, an important consideration if you're filling up a quiet editing suite with the things.

The outermost cylinders of current drives have roughly twice the diameter of the innermost cylinders, thus they have twice the linear storage space (the circumference being $2\pi r$, of course). (See? High-school geometry *was* good for something.) Because the platters rotate at a fixed speed, the outermost cylinder passes beneath the heads twice as quickly as the innermost cylinder. Bits are recorded on the platters at a fixed density (number of bits per inch of travel, if you will), so bits on the outermost cylinders get read and written about twice as fast as on the innermost cylinders. As you fill a drive up with data, the read/write speed decreases from its maximum when the drive is empty to only half that when the drive is full. The general rule of thumb is that you'll have 80 percent of the drive's performance when it's two-thirds full, but that performance drops off rapidly thereafter.

When a cylinder has been read or written to, the arm assembly moves the heads to the next cylinder. This process takes a long time by disk drive standards: the assembly has to move, to lock onto an embedded servo track (the "lane markings" that divide one track from its neighbors), and then wait for the desired data sector to come flying past the heads. Thus, whenever the heads *seek* to a new cylinder, there's an interruption in the data flow.

All else being equal, a drive with a shorter seek time will provide smoother data flow with fewer interruptions than comparable drives with longer seek times. It may seem brief enough to you and me, but to an impatient computer, hungry for data, the delay could mean the difference between smooth playback and a dropped frame.

It's not so bad when a file is recorded sequentially from cylinder to cylinder and all the data are contiguous. But as you use a drive, writing and then deleting files at random, the free space on the drive starts looking like Swiss cheese: little holes here and there. This *fragmentation* means that files start getting spread out in discontiguous chunks, and the drive spends more time seeking and less time reading and writing.

All else being equal, a drive with low fragmentation will record and play back data faster and more smoothly than a heavily fragmented drive. (Note that OS X performs defragmentation automatically as you read and write to a drive. Also note that if you erase a media drive between projects, you automatically defragment it. Running separate defragmentation utilities under OS X is usually not useful because of these factors.)

To help smooth and speed the flow of precious data, modern drives use memory *buffers*, serving the same purpose as cache memory on processors. While writing, data can flow into the cache even as the heads are busily seeking to new cylinders; on playback, clever algorithms can fill the buffer with data not yet requested that *might* be needed, minimizing the time the computer spends waiting on balky mechanical systems.

All else being equal, larger buffers result in smoother performance with fewer delays and higher sustained data transfer rates. 2 MB buffers are common on commodity drives at this time, and higher-performance drives typically carry 8 or 16 MB buffers—but these figures are constantly changing, and a year from now they may be entirely different.

You'll notice I keep saying, "all else being equal." The sad truth is, unless you control for all other variables, these performance factors give only a vague indication of actual performance. Although faster is generally better, less fragmented is better, and larger buffers are better, the actual performance of a drive is conditioned by all of these factors in combination. But you can't predict performance based on these raw numbers alone.

For example, this year's 4200 RPM drives are faster than the 5400 RPM drives from a couple of years ago: bit density has increased, and the data-buffering algorithms have improved, so data flows to and from the disk much faster.

Two seemingly identical drives from different manufacturers—both current-model, 7200 RPM, 250 GB drives with 8 MB buffers—may show radically different performance in real-world tests, because their designers took different approaches to buffering and caching the data.

What really counts are a drive's *sustained read* and *sustained write* figures. These are measurements of the actual data throughput over a reasonably long period of time. And at that, consider that sustained rates are usually measured on outer cylinders of a reasonably unfragmented drive. Performance on the inner cylinders of a highly-fragmented disk is likely to be a disappointing fraction of the quoted specification.

> **NOTE** ▶ *Burst* or *peak* throughput figures are sometimes provided in a drive's specifications; these measure how quickly the drive and its electronics can supply a chunk of data in best-case conditions, not cases where heads need to seek across cylinders, buffers need filling, and the like. Video and audio capture and playback rely on sustained data rates, not peak rates.

Ready to despair? Don't worry, there are several things you can do, both before and after getting your drives, to predict and verify performance:

▶ Read the drive's specifications for the rated sustained read and write speeds. Remember, these numbers are best-case sustained numbers; derate them to 80 percent if you expect to fill the drives to the two-thirds point, or 50 percent if you plan to fill them with captured video (unless the specs say the numbers were obtained with two-thirds full or completely full drives). Also compare seek times, buffer sizes, and rotation rates to get an overall feel for how one drive compares to another.

▶ Several Web sites measure real-world performance, so you don't have to extrapolate manufacturers' numbers to actual results. Robert Morgan's "Bare Feats" (www.barefeats.com) is probably the best. Robert tests drives, drive arrays, graphics cards, FireWire ports, and the like, and is even so kind as to run FCP rendering tests on different Macs every so often.

Various "tweaker" Web sites, like ExtremeTech.com and TomsHardware.com, are great places to find drive performance tests as well as all manner of inside-the-box technologies—though these sites tend to be rather geeky and somewhat more PC-oriented than is *entirely* necessary.

▶ Can't find real-world information on drives you already have? You can run your own tests using the SpeedTools Utilities from Intech Software (www.speedtools.com) or the command-line tool DiskTester from Lloyd Chambers ($20 shareware, via email at disktester@llc4.com. Put "DiskTester" in the subject line of your email).

▶ Run tests with FCP itself: try capturing to and playing back from the drives in question, and see how well they work. If your capture card supports multiple data rates, you can ratchet the rates up and down to find the drives' breaking points. For playback, try setting up multiple picture-in-picture effects to multiply the number of streams being played in real time. Don't forget to test with Timelines containing fast cuts and multiple clips; such Timelines have the same stress-inducing effect as fragmented clips do. Playing or scrubbing a Timeline backwards is an especially good test, since the drives have to supply all the frames out of sequence.

> **TIP** If you find Bare Feats useful, help Rob out with a PayPal or snail-mail donation, using the link provided for that purpose. Rob provides the Mac community with an invaluable service, and he should be encouraged.

Oh, one more thing: The way a drive is interfaced to your Mac is another important factor. Both the native interface on the drive itself (that is, ATA or SCSI), as well as how it's connected to your FCP system (directly, in a FireWire case, across a network, or through a Fibre Channel switch) affect the actual performance you'll see. We'll cover interfaces and connections a bit later.

Disks, Partitions, and Volumes

The disk as we've described it is of no use to your Mac until one or more *volumes* have been created on it. A disk is a *physical* device, that is, something you can drop on your foot. A volume is a *logical* device, one visible to your computer as a usable place to store data, but it may not have a direct correspondence to a single physical device.

You create volumes when you initialize or format a disk (in Disk Utility, this happens when you erase a disk). OS X creates the necessary data structures, such as the catalog listing all the files and folders on the volume, and the bitmap, which tells the Mac which blocks are used by existing files and which are free to use for new ones.

Disks can be *partitioned* into two or more volumes. Each volume is a separate logical entity; each mounts on the desktop as a separate drive. There are nearly as many arguments about partitioning as there are Mac users; I'll just mention a couple of pro-partitioning points you may want to consider.

Partitioning for Data Segregation

Although you usually want to keep media on dedicated drives, there are perfectly legitimate reasons to partition disks into separate "system" and "media" drives.

If you're doing field production with PowerBooks, for example, you have only one internal drive; it's fast enough for DV capture and playback, and a lot more convenient than external FireWire drives. Partitioning the internal disk lets you store project media on its own drive, so when you're finished with it, you can simply erase it instead of having to ferret out captured clips, render files, and the like from your Final Cut Pro Documents folder on your system drive.

Erasing the media partition eliminates any fragmentation that might have occurred during the project, too. Deleting project folders from a system disk does nothing to clean up fragmentation issues.

Note however that the separate partition is a *logical* drive, not a *physical* drive—it still shares its mechanism with any other volumes on the same disk. If your Mac needs to fetch a file from the system volume in the middle of a capture, the same heads writing the captured data have to run off to the system partition in search of the required file, possibly causing dropped frames. There are still good reasons to store your media files on a *physically* separate disk, even when it seems inconvenient!

Partitioning for Performance

You may have disks that perform adequately on the outer cylinders for the data rates you need to support, but aren't quite good enough on the inner cylinders for video purposes. You can partition the disks into media volumes on the higher-performance outer part of the disk, and either store less critical files on the inner part or simply leave it unused. With careful configuring, you can sometimes wind up with more storage at a lower cost than if you bought drives sufficient to sustain capture all the way to the inner tracks.

> **MORE INFO** ▶ Bare Feats describes one such case, using cheap, large SATA drives in place of faster, smaller, more expensive SCSI drives: www.barefeats.com/hard35.html.

Drive Formats

When you initialize a volume, Disk Utility asks you for a volume format. You normally have at least two choices, including "Mac OS Extended" and "Mac OS Extended (Journaled)." These are the correct choices for best performance. (Mac OS Extended is also known as HFS+.)

The two formats are identical except for journaling. Journaling is a high-reliability scheme in which Mac OS keeps a separate *journal* of all changes made to the file system as they're happening, even before the volume's catalog and bitmap get updated. The journal lets the drive survive power outages and system crashes with a better chance of avoiding data corruption.

If you're on the edge of acceptable performance, you may get better results with the non-journaled format, but the differences are small: Journaling slows things down by only a few percent, not usually enough to notice amongst all the other factors affecting data transfer. Nonetheless, some capture device vendors suggest turning journaling off.

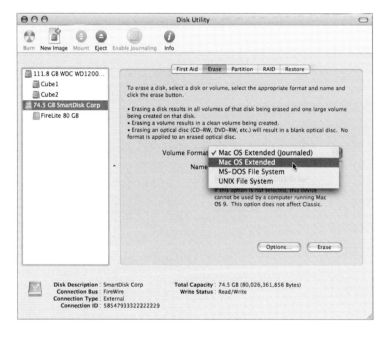

Other options you'll see will be MS-DOS File System and Unix File System. The MS-DOS option is useful for FireWire and other removable drives to be shared with PCs, but it's not efficient enough for media capture and playback. (Although you *may* be able to capture or play back low-bit rate formats like DV.) Likewise, the Unix choice isn't suitable for video capture.

> **TIP** ▶ If you're configuring a RAID, SAN, or certain third-party external drives, you may be given other options. Check the product's documentation for the proper format to use. Xsan, for example, needs to be set up as ACFS, *not* Mac OS Extended!

There's another gotcha to watch out for: FCP sets its default scratch disk to ~/Documents/Final Cut Pro Documents, where ~ is a user's home directory. Normally, that works fine, at least for DV capture. However, if a hapless user is so bold as to turn on File Vault, things won't work so well. File Vault converts the user's home directory and everything it contains into an encrypted disk image: every byte of data read or written therein has to go through encryption and decryption.

There are two simple fixes to this problem: turn off File Vault, or move FCP's scratch disk outside the user's home directory

Drive Interfaces

So far, we've discussed drive performance factors at a low level and disk configuration at a high level, without looking at how drives connect up to the Mac in the first place. The interfaces between drives and computers put limits on performance, and the technology behind the interface sometimes has greater impact than the raw interface speed might suggest. Even the fastest drive, if connected through a CPU-intensive interface like USB 2.0, won't reach its maximum potential, and you're more likely to see dropped frames, stuttering playback, and the like. Likewise, using FireWire both for disks and DV cameras may be simple, but it's not always the interface that yields the best performance.

ATA

ATA (Advanced Technology Attachment) disk drives are used in G3s, G4s, Xserve G4s, and Xserve RAIDs. They're commonly available and very affordable. They're also called IDE (Integrated Drive Electronics) or PATA (Parallel ATA) disks.

The moniker "ATA" covers a staggering variety of interfaces, running from a pokey 3.3 MB/second up to 100 MB/second. In Mac parlance, the interface speed in MB/second usually follows the ATA name, such as "ATA/33" or "Ultra ATA/100." Faster, of course, is better—as long as the Mac supports the faster interface. Connecting an ATA/100 drive to an ATA/33 controller means the drive's communications run at a maximum of 33 MB/second. The Mac's operating instructions list the interface speed, or check the specifications online at www.info.apple.com/support/applespec.html.

> **MORE INFO** ▸ If you're missing the manual for any recent Mac, you can find it online at www.info.apple.com/support/manuals.html.

Until recently, ATA drives were limited to a maximum size of around 137 GB. An extension to the ATA spec, Large Block Addressing, broke through that barrier, but most ATA Macs are limited to seeing the first 128 GB: only the G4 Mirrored Drive Door and G4 Xserve computers can use larger ATA disks on their built-in controllers.

ATA drives have been the commodity drive of the past decade and are available in all sizes and interfaces, from 2.5-inch laptop drives through 3.5-inch and the now rare 5.25-inch desktop drives. Laptop drives (as of spring 2005) top out at 80 GB capacity and 5400 RPM, with 4200 RPM drives being the most common. Desktop drives get as big as 250 GB and commonly run at 5400 or 7200 RPM. Transfer rates vary considerably, but common desktop drives will sustain 35 to 40 MB/second and peak at 60 MB/second.

An ATA interface uses a 40-pin connector with a 40- or 80-conductor, 2-inch-wide ribbon cable. (An ATA interface faster than 33 MB/second uses an 80-conductor cable with added ground wires, but the same 40-pin connector as with slower versions.) Two drives can be connected to their controller on a single cable.

ATA drives have four-pin power connectors and configuration jumpers. Check your Mac's manual and drive manual for the correct setting of the jumpers: drives can be set for master, slave, or cable select modes; recent Macs usually want cable select, but depending on the Mac and the cable used, a different setting may be required.

Separate ATA interface cards can be had, but they're not especially useful for Macs: there's not normally enough room inside the box to install more drives than the Mac's built-in controllers support, and an 18-inch cable length limit and the hard-to-route ribbon cables restrict ATA drives to be internally mounted. You can add ATA drives outside the box using FireWire or SCSI cases that use ATA for the drive connection, though.

If you're intent on adding more internal ATA drives than your Mac supports, Promax (www.promax.com) offers ATA cards and mounting bracket kits. Bear in mind that G4 towers don't always have the best internal airflow, and over-heating is a possibility.

SATA

Serial ATA interfaces are used in G5s, G5 Xserves, and increasing numbers of third-party drive enclosures. SATA is widely seen as the successor to parallel ATA, and SATA's higher interface speeds have led some vendors to include their highest-performance drive mechanisms in their SATA product lines.

SATA replaces the bulky 40-pin parallel ATA connector and cable with a svelte seven-pin connector and thin (1/4-inch) cable, doubles the cable length to 1 meter, and eliminates those pesky configuration jumpers: SATA cables are point-to-point, connecting a single drive to its controller.

Current SATA interfaces run at 150 MB/second, with future designs expected to run at two and four times that rate.

Advancements in the control protocol are coming, too: "command queuing" allows more efficient stacking of pending commands, so the drive and computer spend more time exchanging data and less time waiting on each other. As of summer 2004, tagged command queuing and native command queuing drives and controllers are just becoming available, but they promise, on average, a 30 percent improvement in performance over nonqueued interfaces.

Serial ATA drives, though relatively new, are already as affordable as parallel ATA drives of comparable speeds and capacities. Standard desktop drives hold from 120 GB to 250 GB or more, and typically run at 7200 RPM.

Many early SATA drives are really parallel ATA/100 drives with parallel-to-serial "bridge chips," but native SATA drives are starting to appear. (In practice, it's not a big deal; few current drives can deliver data fast enough to saturate ATA/100 interfaces to begin with.)

Some vendors sell high-performance "enterprise class" drives, optimized for speed. Western Digital's Raptor series has 36 GB and 72 GB drives, both running at 10,000 RPM and sustaining a whopping 72 MB/second transfer rate.

Drives like this give you the performance normally reserved for the "premium" SCSI and Fibre Channel interfaces at commodity prices. Note, however, that you've traded capacity for speed: you can capture video pretty darned quickly, but not much of it. Aside from the lower capacity, you'll also want to make sure these drives are well cooled; fast-spinning disks tend to run hot.

Separate SATA interface cards are available, as are mounting kits (not Apple approved!) to stick several more drives into Apple's G5 chassis. Promax, WiebeTech, and Swift Data sell the kits complete with cards; Sonnet, Acard, FirmTek, and others sell the cards alone. Netcell's RAID XL cards include hardware-based RAID 3 mode, and several vendors, including Promax, build SATA RAIDs based on it.

SATA cables can be run outside the chassis to separate drive enclosures, but SATA wasn't initially designed for this sort of use. Early adopters sometimes came to grief due to insufficient cable shielding, the somewhat fragile SATA connector, and unreliable firmware on first-generation SATA controllers when the drives were used in a RAID. These issues are being addressed over time, and external SATA storage systems from reputable vendors like Promax are becoming robust and reliable. Conservative system builders still prefer SCSI for external arrays; only time will tell if the newer SATA arrays develop an equally good reputation.

You can also find SATA-to-ATA "bridge kits" for converting parallel ATA drives to SATA interfaces. Apple does not support the use of such boards with its internal SATA controllers, but third-party SATA card suppliers may have different attitudes. Although you may be tempted to use existing ATA drives this way, you're probably just as well off sticking them into FireWire enclosures, SCSI-connected RAIDs and JBODs, or keeping them on-hand as spares for parallel ATA Macs. (RAIDs and JBODS are defined in the "Storage Architectures"section later in this chapter.)

SCSI

The Small Computer Systems Interface was *the* hard disk interface in Macs until ATA was adopted in the late '90s. It's currently used for high-performance interconnects, mostly to and within separate drive enclosures and hardware RAID systems. There's still a lot of SCSI equipment of all types in the Mac world, both drives inside the box and devices outside the box. SCSI is a systems-level interface, and connects tape drives, scanners, removable media drives, and the like, in addition to plain-old hard disks.

SCSI is a high-level, high-performance interface, allowing devices to go off and handle data requests without making the host computer sit around and wait for the results, so the computer can get more work done while waiting for the data to arrive.

Of course, this performance comes at a cost: SCSI interfaces are more complex and expensive than ATA or SATA interfaces. SCSI drives these days tend to be aimed at higher-performance markets instead of commodity desktop applications, so the drives themselves are often higher-performing devices with prices to match, typically costing between 2 and 10 times as much as ATA or SATA drives of comparable sizes.

SCSI has been around since the early '80s and has undergone considerable evolution. There are "narrow" and "wide" flavors (8- and 16-bit wide data paths); normal, "fast," "ultra," and "ultra2" speeds (5, 10, 20, and 40 MHz signaling, with 80 MHz transmission using double-clocking in ultra3 and later versions), and three different signal types on the wires: single-ended, high-voltage differential (HVD), and low-voltage differential (LVD).

These can be combined in various permutations to yield such mouthfuls as "fast wide SCSI," "wide ultra2 SCSI," and the like. In the latest SCSI generations, a total-throughput nomenclature has been adopted, hence "Ultra/160 LVD" for an interface with 160 MB/second data rate using LVD signaling.

The earliest SCSI buses allowed a grand total of 8 devices to be connected; more recent versions support 16 devices in a daisy-chain configuration. (In both cases, one of those devices must be the host computer.) Each SCSI device on a bus needs to be assigned a unique ID number. On bare drives, you'll find jumpers for this purpose; on SCSI enclosures, there's usually a set of switches or pushbuttons you can use to change the ID.

Both ends of the SCSI chain need to be *terminated* for the bus to operate properly. Some devices have internal terminations; some have jumpers or resistor packs to be installed or removed; some require the use of external terminators, which usually plug into the last open connector in the chain. (External SCSI devices that do not automatically terminate the bus internally typically have two connectors, and the terminator plugs into one of these.) To add to the complication, some terminators are passive, and some are powered. Hey, SCSI has been around for over two decades and has seen a lot of changes—you get that.

If you have two devices with the same ID on the same bus or if you get the bus termination wrong, utter confusion results, usually in the mind of the poor user. SCSI setups are very sensitive to misconfiguration; if the system misbehaves, suspect cabling, ID, and termination issues.

As long as the signal types match up, you can often interconnect different types of SCSI devices with adapter plugs and cables: SCSI is carried on 25-pin D-shell connectors, 50-pin and 68-pin dual-row headers, 68-pin flat connectors in two different sizes, and even 80-pin connectors. The bus will run at the speed of the slowest device connected and powered up.

However, interconnecting single-ended, HVD, and LVD devices will not work: you'll blow up the interface circuitry and let out all the magic smoke. There are "multimode" LVD interfaces that will work with single-ended SCSI, but they'll only work at single-ended interface speeds.

> **NOTE ▶** Electronic devices are widely assumed to work because of "magic smoke" contained inside integrated circuits. The proof of this concept is found in the fact that when incompatible devices are hooked up or improper voltages are applied, chips often emit a burning smell and all the magic smoke comes out, after which the devices cease to function.

SCSI hardware is supposed to have different identifying icons depending on the signaling interface used:

Icons for single-ended (SE), HVD (DIFF), LVD, and multimode LVD/SE SCSI, respectively; image courtesy Information Technology Industry Council

When in doubt, assume incompatible signal types on SCSI devices until you can check spec sheets or instruction manuals.

Older Macs with 25-pin D-shell SCSI ports usually support the original 5 MB/second SCSI interface. Current Mac SCSI cards speak Ultra/160 LVD (with an interface speed of 160 MB/second) or Ultra/320 LVD (320 MB/second).

SCSI's most common use these days is connecting external drive enclosures to Macs. Many RAIDs connect this way, taking advantage of SCSI's high speed and long cable lengths. SCSI cables can run a minimum of 1.5 meters for single-ended interfaces, and up to 12 meters for LVD interfaces. (HVD can run to 25 meters, but HVD interfaces aren't being made any longer.)

The drives inside SCSI enclosures may use SCSI; in such cases (pun intended) the SCSI interface may simply chain from drive to drive, with the case providing little more than power supplies, ID setting wheels, and mounting rails. Higher-end enclosures with active electronics often use SCSI externally but may use a lower-cost interface like ATA internally. Medéa's VideoRAID series started this trend, and several other vendors have picked up on it.

> **MORE INFO ▶** All you ever wanted to know about SCSI, including a comprehensive list of the various flavors available, is at www.pcguide.com/ref/hdd/if/scsi/.

Fibre Channel

Fibre Channel is a very high performance bus interconnection, with prices to match. Fibre Channel is used as the interface to Xserve RAID systems, and is the connection of choice in building Storage Area Networks (SANs).

Fibre Channel uses serial communications at 1, 2, or 4 Gb/second, for throughputs of 100, 200, and 400 MB/second. 2 Gb FC is the most common at present; both Apple's dual-channel FC PCI card and the Xserve RAID run their ports at 2 Gb/second. You can run Fibre Channel over copper cables with up to 30 meters between devices, and over fiber optics for up to 50 kilometers. This means you can move noisy storage systems out of the edit suite and into soundproofed machine rooms.

Fibre Channel allows up to 126 devices on a bus. In its simplest form, FC is used for a point-to-point connection, as between a G5 and an Xserve RAID. If you want to add more devices, you need to configure them in a *loop* using the FC-AL (arbitrated loop) protocol, or a *fabric* architecture using Fibre Channel switches. We'll discuss this more in the section on SANs.

Point-to-point connections work with Xserve RAID because the entire RAID (make that each half of it: Xserve RAID is really two sets of drives, each with its own FC interface) is only one FC device. Like the Medéa boxes, Xserve RAID uses low-cost ATA drives internally with a dedicated RAID controller, and appears to the outside world as one Fibre Channel device.

Fibre Channel controllers, called Host Bus Adapters (HBAs), tend to be fairly expensive (Apple's own dual 2Gbit FCHBA, at $499, is one of the *cheaper* ones), and building comparable circuitry directly on a drive is similarly pricey, so Fiber Channel-native drives tend to be reserved for the highest-performance, least price-critical segments of the marketplace. FC drives can cost anywhere from 3 to 10 times as much as ATA drives of the same capacity (if not speed). Capacities tend to be small and data rates high; sizes run from 18 to 300 GB with speeds of 10,000 and 15,000 RPM and sustained transfer rates of up to 94 MB/second on the outer tracks, 62 on the inner tracks. (At these speeds and prices, it's common to see rates specified as ranges: buyers of such drives want to know all the gritty details.)

Although native Fibre Channel disk arrays are available, Fibre Channel is commonly used in the Mac world for high-speed connections to dedicated RAIDs comprised of ATA or SATA drives.

Fibre Channel is hot-pluggable, meaning you can connect and disconnect Fibre Channel devices with the system power on. (Be sure to dismount any drives mounted on your desktop before pulling out their cables, of course!) With a point-to-point connection that's no big deal: you either have the device connected, or not. With FC-AL, hot-plugging a device triggers the Loop Initialization Protocol (LIP) event, while hot-plugging a fabric generates a Registered State Change Notification (RSCN) sequence. Both the LIP and RSCN are mechanisms whereby all the devices on the channel reset themselves to the presence or absence of the device triggering the event, and both events interrupt any data transmissions in progress: you *will* drop frames if this happens. We'll discuss RSCNs more in the section on SANs.

Fibre Channel cables are delicate: at the data rates they run, even slight deformations of the conductors may cause spurious errors, intermittent faults, or complete failure. Coiling a cable too tightly, pulling it around a sharp corner, or simply stepping on it are enough to damage it beyond repair. The damage need not be visible to be real. If your Fibre Channel system isn't delivering the throughput you expect, try swapping out the cables for known good ones.

FireWire

FireWire is commonly used to connect Macs to DV devices or external disk drives—often both at the same time, when editing with PowerBooks—as well as a variety of other devices like DVD burners and iSight cameras.

FireWire, a.k.a. IEEE-1394 and i.Link, is a high-speed serial bus used for connection to storage devices as well as media devices. Macs connect to DV, DVCAM, DVCPRO, DVCPRO 50, DVCPRO HD, and HDV video recorders (see the previous lesson) using FireWire's *isochronous* mode, and hook up to disk drives using FireWire's *asynchronous* mode. Both modes can be active at the same time: bandwidth not reserved for isochronous traffic is available to any asynchronous communications that want it, and even then, 20 percent of the channels' bandwidth is reserved for asynch traffic.

FireWire is a bus architecture supporting up to 63 devices. The FireWire ports found on G3s, G4s, iBooks, and PowerBooks are 1394a or FW400 ports, capable of running at speeds of 100, 200, or 400 Mb/second (S100, S200, and S400 speeds). At S400, the maximum data rate is 50 MB/second, though 40 MB/second is a more realistic sustained number. G5s, high-end PowerBooks, and third-party PCI cards (and CardBus cards for PowerBooks with PC Card slots) offer FW800 (1394b) with an S800 data rate: about 80 MB/second sustained.

Like the other buses described, FireWire runs at the speed of the slowest device plugged in. DV and DVCAM devices typically support only S100 speed, cutting bus throughput to about 8 MB/second, just barely adequate for DV work. DVCPRO decks are switchable between S100 and S200 speeds, and higher-bit rate decks support faster speeds. Observe that all the FireWire ports on a Mac are on the same bus—even the FW400 and FW800 ports on the G5s—so plugging a Handycam into your Mac will drag your FW800 drive down to one-eighth of its normal bus speed. Many people wishing to use DV decks and FireWire drives at the same time purchase a PCI card providing a separate FireWire bus, so that devices can be segregated by speed.

FireWire drives are frequently used for low-bit rate editing, as with DV25. You can use them with higher bit rates, but this tends to be problematic; although

FireWire is reasonably efficient, it adds another protocol layer between computer and disk, so communications are slower than with an internal disk.

FireWire is hot-pluggable, but note that doing so interrupts all data transfer on the bus for over a second as the devices on the bus vote on who gets to drive the bus. If you plug in or unplug a FireWire device while capturing to a FireWire drive (or moving DV data to or from a DV device), you *will* drop frames.

FireWire cables may run up to 4.5 meters. There are special, equalized cables that allow for longer runs, from Markertek and Focus Enhancements, among others.

FireWire is not a native drive interface; FireWire drives are ATA or SATA drives with a "FireWire bridge" interface attached. Most current bridges work perfectly well, but earlier ones can cause problems. First-generation FireWire bridges may not accommodate drives larger than 137 GB (just like older ATA interfaces in Macs); some perform poorly in terms of overall data transfer (the Oxford 900 chipset is often implicated, although your author has a 900-based FireWire enclosure that's never dropped a frame); and some may need updating or replacing to work with recent firmware revisions in the G5's FireWire interface.

Additionally, the first releases of OS X 10.3 changed the sequencing and usage of certain FireWire disk commands, leading to data loss with some FireWire bridges. Fingers were pointed at Oxford 911 chipsets, but the problem appears to have been more widespread. Most Oxford-using drive enclosure manufacturers offered Oxford firmware updaters on their Web sites, and by OS X 10.3.3 (if not 10.3.2) the problem seemed to have been corrected in OS X's FireWire control.

Although the drive-eating problem existed, the workaround appeared to be ensuring that all FireWire drives were dismounted before shutting down the Mac, and then not plugging them in until the Mac had booted up. Many Mac users have latched onto these workarounds as permanent safety measures even though the problem seems to have been cured.

Some video devices don't work well with FireWire drives. Some combinations of DV devices and FireWire drives simply refuse to play together at all. Single-chip Canon camcorders are frequently implicated, but plenty of folks use those same camcorders with FireWire drives without problems. Similarly, iSights are often accused of corrupting FireWire disk data transfers (your author has never had a FireWire disk corrupted by his iSight, but your author may simply be unusually lucky), and making Aurora Igniter PCI cards refuse to work. In general, it's best to unplug devices you don't need to have on the bus when you're not using them. If you find that a camera or deck doesn't cooperate with your FireWire drive, try a different brand of FireWire drive or a different DV device.

Six-pin FW400 and FW800 connectors include power and return lines, so that devices can draw power from the bus. Be careful when plugging cables in: even though the connectors are polarized to prevent it, you can insert the plugs upside down if you're enthusiastic enough. Crossing the power and data lines this way is enough to let all the magic smoke out of your Mac or your FireWire drive, or both.

USB

The Universal Serial Bus is in many ways the successor to the older Apple Desktop Bus: a serial bus for the connections of various accessories, like mice, keyboards, and even storage devices. USB drives, like FireWire drives, aren't USB-native, but use bridges between ATA or SATA drives and the USB connection running back to the Mac.

USB 1.0 and 1.1, the original versions, top out at 12 Mb/second, for a piddling 1.5 MB/second transfer speed. Hi-Speed USB 2.0 runs at a more respectable 480 Mb/second, giving it 20 percent more bandwidth than FW400, at least in theory. (I have to mention the "Hi-Speed" part because there are USB 2.0 devices out there that run at pokey old USB 1.1 speeds.)

In practice, USB suffers from being a CPU-driven protocol; the controlling computer has to be much more involved in data transfers over USB than over

FireWire. Thus, sustained transfer rates tend to be slightly lower on Hi-Speed USB 2.0 than on FW400. And that's in the best case, when a fast computer is being used and isn't doing anything else; if the Mac is busy doing other things (like rendering a real-time effect and displaying the output in the Canvas), performance falls off even more.

Hi-Speed USB suffers just like other multiple-speed buses do: plug in one 12 Mb device, and the entire bus slows down to 12 Mb. Fortunately, each USB 2.0 port on the G5 has its own internal hub, so you can segregate 12 Mb and 480 Mb devices from each other just by plugging them into different ports.

USB is fine for offline data backups and for moving projects from system to system, but it's simply not efficient enough to be the interface of choice for media drives. Although some brave souls have made Hi-Speed USB 2.0 drives work for DV editing without seeing *too* many dropped frames, it's just not robust enough for video work, especially not when FireWire is available.

When a drive provides both FireWire and USB, use the FireWire connection.

Storage Architectures

Disks and interfaces are all well and good, but when you're pushing uncompressed HD around, a single disk just isn't going to do it for you. Fortunately, you can arrange disks to provide both greater capacity and higher speeds. We'll review these storage architectures here, starting with an introduction to some useful concepts and buzzwords. We'll look at organizing disks into RAIDs for better performance, then discuss shared storage using NAS and SAN setups.

Concepts and Buzzwords

Storage, like video, has its own set of cryptic acronyms, buzzwords, and concepts. We'll define enough of them so that you can decode spec sheets and marketing documents like a pro.

Ports, NICs, and HBAs

A port is a communication connection, whether Ethernet (networking), Fibre Channel, FireWire, USB, or the like.

A NIC, or network interface card, is a plug-in PCI or PC Card board with one or more networking ports on it.

An HBA, short for Host Bus Adapter, is a Fibre Channel port on a plug-in card.

Hubs and Switches

You connect multiple Ethernet, Fiber Channel, or FireWire devices to each other using hubs or switches.

Hubs are "dumb" party-line devices: any communication that comes in on one port gets replicated on all other ports. All hubs do is provide multiple points of connection; they don't direct or partition data flow at all. Every device hooked up to a hub sees all the data traffic going between any two devices. If 10 devices are hooked up, and 5 are talking to the other 5, each talker winds up with about 20 percent of the available bandwidth, because all the conversations are sharing the same "virtual wire."

By contrast, switches are "smart" devices that work more like a telephone switchboard or a video routing switcher. Switches learn what devices are connected to which ports, and direct data traffic so that it flows only between the devices concerned by it, and other devices don't see it. Switches allow faster communication because devices see only the traffic intended for them. If 10 devices are hooked up, and 5 are talking to the other 5, each talker winds up with about 100 percent of the available bandwidth because each conversation has its own "virtual circuit" through the switch, and all connections are said to run at "full wireline speed."

Hubs are cheaper than switches, but don't provide nearly the same level of performance. Switches also do a much better job of partitioning: if one device on a switch starts misbehaving, the switch can isolate its traffic from the network, whereas a hub simply rebroadcasts it, potentially bringing all connected devices to their knees.

RAID

RAID is short for Redundant Arrays of Inexpensive Disks—although not all RAIDs are redundant, nor are the disks always inexpensive! RAIDs gang multiple disks together to improve reliability, speed, or both. We'll discuss RAIDs in detail shortly.

JBOD

JBOD (Just a Bunch Of Disks) is used to describe storage enclosures that hold, well, just a bunch of disks. In a "true" JBOD, the disks aren't ganged together in a RAID configuration, although the controller may *span* them, essentially turning them into one large virtual disk by using them sequentially. JBOD is often used to describe any box of disks that has a "dumb" controller, like a Fiber Channel hub connecting FC disks to the outside world, even if the box is part of a RAID.

SBOD

A "Switched Bunch of Disks" is a JBOD with a smart, switching controller. It's used to differentiate high-end enclosures with integrated Fibre Channel switches from JBODs with mere hubs. SBODs are the latest twist in high-performance disk arrays and are only now starting to filter out of the labs and into the marketplace.

DAS

Any disk or RAID connected directly to your Mac is Direct Access Storage, or DAS. DAS gives you the fastest, lowest-latency performance, all else being equal, because it's yours—all yours. Your Mac owns the storage entirely and need not contend with other users for its use, and DAS has the lowest communications overhead between the Mac and its data. The file system runs on your Mac, and it has direct access to the blocks of data on the drives.

NAS

Network Access Storage, or NAS, is shared storage using networked file sharing. At its simplest, you're using NAS when you mount another Mac's shared drives on your desktop over the network. There are also dedicated NAS boxes stuffed full of high-speed drives whose sole purpose is to provide shared storage across a network, but you access them just like any other networked Mac. Your Mac makes file-level requests over the network; the server Mac or NAS box translates those requests to block-level requests in its own file system and provides the requested data.

SAN

Storage Area Networks connect multiple clients and shared storage using a high-speed connection, usually Fibre Channel. SANs provide fast access to shared storage: a special file system driver runs on your Mac providing block-level access to the drives, while at the same time handling the potential conflicts from other clients accessing the same files or volumes.

RAIDs

RAIDs are collections of disks ganged together to form a single *logical unit* (LUN) so as to provide higher reliability, higher speed, or both, than a single drive would provide.

Both software and hardware RAIDing is possible; OS X has simple software RAID capabilities built in. A hardware RAID controller gives better performance than software RAIDing does because it doesn't burden the computer with RAID housekeeping. But software RAIDing is better than no RAIDing at all. Sometimes software and hardware RAIDing are used together, as we'll see.

RAIDs employ three strategies in various combinations to work their magic, as outlined in the following sections.

Striping

You can improve speed by *striping* data across two or more drives. Information is broken into small chunks and read and written to all the drives, each drive storing one chunk and sharing the overall load. For example, if you have two drives striped, all the even bytes of data might be written to one drive and all the odd bytes to the other. The performance you see is close to the performance of a single drive multiplied by the number of drives in the stripe set.

Striping improves performance but does nothing for redundancy: if any drive in a stripe set fails, you've lost all the data on all the drives. Striping is good for data you can easily replace, like logged and captured media files and render scratch areas, but it's not so good for hard-to-replace stuff like your system, your project, and—most importantly—your invoice files.

Spatial efficiency with striping is the same as with single drives: 100 percent. Since no data are replicated, every bit counts: a stripe set made from two 250 GB drives has 500 GB available for data storage.

Mac OS X has built-in support for striping; you can set it up using Disk Utility.

Mirroring

You can protect data with *mirroring*, a real-time backup strategy usually using two drives. All incoming data is written to both drives in parallel, so if one fails, the other one has a complete copy of all the data.

Mirroring does nothing at all for write performance (it may even slow writes down, especially with software mirroring), but with certain controllers it can improve read performance since reads can be shared by the two drives.

Mirroring *is* redundancy: there's a full backup copy of all the data written. If a drive fails, you can proceed, using the remaining drive, and *rebuild* the mirrored drive after replacing the failed hardware. Of course, if your remaining drive fails before you've rebuilt the mirror, you will lose your data.

Mirroring's spatial efficiency is 50 percent. Mirroring one 250 GB drive with another 250 GB drive means you have the space for only 250 GB of data, since each bit is written twice, once on each drive.

Mac OS X has built-in support for mirroring; you can set it up using Disk Utility.

Striping with Parity

RAIDs using parity split the difference between the pure performance orientation of striping and the conservative data protection of mirroring. Instead of duplicating none of the data or all of it, they record extra *parity bits* for every bit of data coming in. The parity bits can be used to reconstruct data in cases of drive failure.

A simple case of parity recording involves adding a parity drive to a two-drive stripe set. Parity data are written such that the sum of all the bits recorded in parallel across the three drives always equals an odd number:

Drive 0	+ Drive 1	+ Parity	= Sum
0	0	1	1
0	1	0	1
1	0	0	1
1	1	1	1

("Hang on!", you say, "1+1+1=3, not 1!" Right you are, but for parity purposes, all we care about is that least-significant bit, the one that says even or odd. In case you're wondering, it's called *modulo 2* addition, in which you ignore any part of the number greater than one.)

Let's assume drive 1 fails, and its data are lost. We can recover its data just by looking up its value in the *truth table* just shown, which gives every permissible combination of bits on Drive 0, Drive 1, and the parity drive. (And at that, the Sum column is superfluous; it's only there to show how the math works.)

As it turns out, truth table lookups are *very* fast to implement in hardware, so no "real math" needs to be done at all once the truth table is designed. Incoming data are passed through the truth table to generate parity, and the same table is used in the event of drive failure to re-create the lost data, regardless of which drive failed: it works equally well to replace the data from Drive 0, Drive 1, or the parity drive.

As long as only one drive at a time fails, you won't lose any data. And in the example given, you get twice the performance of a single drive, since this parity setup is basically a two-drive stripe set with an added parity drive.

This sort of scheme can be extended across more than three drives, and often is. Parity storage can be kept on a single drive, as in RAID 3, or distributed among the data drives in RAID 5.

Performance is almost as good as in a striped set without the parity drive, though writes can take a bit longer.

Redundancy in the case of single-drive failure is assured, and spatial efficiency is equal to (# drives without parity) ÷ (# drives with parity). In the example in the preceding section, three 250 GB drives yield 500 GB of usable space, with 250 GB taken up by parity data, for 67 percent spatial efficiency.

RAID Levels

These approaches are combined in various ways characterized as RAID levels, which are simple numerical identifiers. We'll cover the most common ones here. Single-digit RAID levels form the basic building blocks of RAID architectures. Two-digit levels combine two RAID levels at once, with the first digit describing the "lower level" RAIDing, and the second the "higher level" RAIDing. Well, *most* vendors do it that way, but RAID terminology is one of those things that different vendors interpret in different ways. When in doubt, ask the vendor for details.

> **MORE INFO ▶** Probably the best summary of every possible RAID level is at www.pcguide.com/ref/hdd/perf/raid/.

RAID 0 Pure striping, as described in the "Striping" section. RAID 0 is a good choice for storing media files when you're on the cheap. Spatial efficiency and performance are high, and you can even use OS X as your RAID controller. But there's no protection for your data: lose a drive, and you've lost the entire RAID.

RAID 1 Mirroring, as described in the "Mirroring" section. Not recommended for media files because RAID 1 doesn't improve performance over a single drive.

RAID 3 Parity striping at the byte level, using a dedicated parity drive. RAID 3 adds data protection to RAID 0 and is a great choice for storing large, sequentially-accessed files, like audio and video. With parity localized to a single drive, performance stays high even with a single drive failure, but the parity drive can be a bottleneck when lots of random writing is occurring, so for general-purposes RAID 5 is usually better.

RAID 5 Block-level striping with parity distributed among the different drives on a block-by-block basis. Distributing parity across the drives tends to improve random write performance compared to RAID 3, but RAID 3 usually performs better for sequential reads, especially when a drive has failed.

RAID 0+1 Also called RAID 01, but 0+1 avoids the confusion of 01's leading zero. RAID 0+1 uses striping first, then mirroring. Two sets of disks are made into stripe sets, and then one set is used to mirror the other. RAID 0+1 is for those who need RAID 0 performance levels with fault tolerance and can afford to double the number of drives used to obtain that robustness. Note that a single drive failure knocks the entire mirror set offline, and the whole darned thing needs to be rebuilt when the drive is replaced.

RAID 10 Mirroring first, then striping. Like RAID 0+1, but may perform a bit better when a drive has failed, and tends to rebuild more quickly, since failure of a single drive requires the rebuilding of only that one drive.

RAID 30 Multiple RAID 3s are striped together. RAID 30 gives better performance than the same number of drives in a single RAID 3 set, but depending on how the drives are divided up (many small RAID 3s, or fewer but bigger RAID 3s?) performance can be difficult to predict, and RAID 30s tend to be expensive for the performance and space they yield.

RAID 50 Multiple RAID 5s are striped together. Like RAID 30, good performance and reliability but with attendant complexity and cost.

RAIDs for Video and Audio Generally speaking, RAIDs 0, 3, and 5 give you the best bang for the buck when it comes to media storage.

RAID 0 is the winner when sheer performance is required and when you need to maximize storage space. When you're working at high data rates, as with uncompressed HD, RAID 0 may be the way to go to keep array costs within reason and eke out as much online storage as possible. Just keep your source tapes around in case the array should suffer a failure.

RAIDs 3 and 5 sacrifice some performance for reliability; maybe you won't stream as many channels of real-time video, but you may sleep better at night knowing a single drive failure won't wipe out your media. RAIDs 3 and 5 are often preferred when you have lots of important media online, especially in a shared-storage environment, and loss of the array would entail huge inconveniences.

With many array controllers, RAID 3 is preferred over RAID 5 for media storage. Apple's Xserve RAID, on the other hand, is better optimized for RAID 5, and that's the preferred format even for media storage.

RAID Level Comparison

RAID Level	Storage Efficiency	Read Performance	Write Performance	Data Redundancy
0	Highest	Very high	Highest	No
1	Low	High	Medium	Yes
3	High to very high	Medium	Medium	Yes
5	High to very high	High	High	Yes
0+1	Low	High	High	Yes
10	Low	High	High	Yes
30	High to very high	High	High	Yes
50	High to very high	Highest	Highest	Yes

If performance is paramount, and cost is no object, RAIDs 30 and 50 are worth considering. On the Xserve RAID, RAID 0 gives the best write performance, and RAID 50 excels at reads and does nearly as well on writes. Because you usually need to play back more streams simultaneously than you write, RAID 50 is the way to go if you must maximize performance—you might choose RAID 50 when setting up a multiuser Xsan system, for example.

How do you decide which RAID level to implement? Read the recommendations in following lessons, of course, but also consult with vendors of the arrays you're considering and talk with other FCP users and systems integrators who've set up similar systems. RAID controllers vary from vendor to vendor, performance "sweet spots" differ between systems, and your requirements will vary depending on media type, number of users, and workflow patterns.

Combining capture cards, RAID controllers, and disk drives is a complex task with multiple independent variables; there is no "right" answer that works in every case. But, of course, that's why you get paid the big, big money to put FCP systems together!

Network Attached Storage

Network Attached Storage—shared drives you can see on the network and mount on the desktop—has long been used for simple file transfers between systems, but the combination of low-bit rate media and fast networking have led to the occasional use of NAS for video editing in shared-media environments.

Fast Ethernet, a.k.a. 100BaseT, runs at 100 Mb/second, allowing roughly 7 to 8 MB/second of data transfer in the best case. Gigabit Ethernet, now standard on G5s and the larger PowerBooks, runs 10 times as fast, with practical transfer rates between 30 and 60 MB/ second. With DV25 requiring only 3.6 MB/second, even Fast Ethernet should allow a stream or two of playback across the network.

In practice, this works—up to a point. Ethernet has the speed, but it doesn't have guaranteed *latency*: if a packet of data is dropped, it gets retransmitted later, and there's nothing in the way Ethernet works (well, not under the TCP/IP protocol at the root of Mac networking) to prevent packets from being lost. Indeed, TCP/IP works like a party line: anyone wanting to speak just shouts out. If two devices try to talk at the same time, they both shut up, and try again some random time later. As a result, there's no way to guarantee *quality of service*. (There are network protocols that guarantee QoS, but they aren't currently applicable to networked file sharing.)

Although Ethernet speeds are consistent in the long term, short-term latencies can be extremely variable. What's more, the variable time it takes to ship a frame's worth of data over Ethernet is added to the time it takes the server computer to fetch it from whatever local storage it's using. Ethernet is also optimized for small bursts of data, not large chunks of video; it takes nearly 80 separate transmissions (packets) to send a single DV25 frame, making Ethernet a fairly inefficient transport mechanism. These give NAS the longest and most variable latencies of any storage architecture we consider.

What this means to the FCP editor is that networked media drives *will* drop frames. Not very frequently perhaps, if the network and storage are well designed, but you'll see dropped frames sooner or later.

NAS requires the use of switches, not hubs, on the Ethernet network. Unless you're simply hooking one Mac up to another Mac, the file server needs to use

Gigabit Ethernet to avoid being overloaded by multiple clients. Some NAS "appliances," like EditShare or HUGE Systems' SanStream, have Gigabit switches built in: simply connect your client Macs to the server with GigE cabling and you're done.

NAS is useful in shared-storage applications when cost or mechanics preclude the use of a SAN, but the workflows used in NAS environments must allow the occasional dropped frame. If you're seriously considering NAS, take note of the following:

- FCP works happily right out of the box with DV25 or lower-bit rate media over 100BaseT or Gigabit Ethernet. Higher-bit rate media, like DV50, starts dropping frames whenever a dual-stream effect, such as a dissolve, is played back.

- Enabling "jumbo frames" on Gigabit Ethernet improves performance. Your NIC, switch, and server must all support jumbo frames for this to work. OS X 10.2.4 and later supports jumbo frames, but you'll need to add a separate NIC since Mac motherboard Ethernet lacks jumbo support.

- Plan to capture from tape and play out to tape from the server itself, avoiding network bottlenecks when real-time performance is mandatory. Otherwise, consider capturing to and playing out from local drives on the FCP Mac: move media to the server after capture, and render your finished Timeline to the local disk as a self-contained QuickTime movie for playout purposes.

Storage Area Networks

SANs give you direct-access speed to a pool of shared-access storage, enabling collaborative production workflows with the ease and speed of local storage. Such capabilities don't come cheaply, of course: SANs can be expensive and complex to set up. With the exception of the MicroNet SANcube, discussed shortly, each client Mac needs a Fibre Channel HBA and SAN software installed; the combination costs $1,500 or more (as of Summer 2004). You'll also need a Fibre Channel switch, enough Fibre Channel-equipped RAIDs to meet your bandwidth and capacity needs, and possibly a *metadata controller*. A what? Read on.

SAN Concepts

When you read a file from direct-access storage, the Mac's file system driver translates your file-level request ("open file 'project.fcp' and give me the first 2 KB of its data") into block-level commands ("mark 'project.fcp' as opened for read, and retrieve its first four blocks—124, 125, 132, and 137—from disk").

When you read the same file from network-attached storage, your Mac sends the file-level commands over the network to the server, and the server translates them into block-level accesses, handling all the overhead of file sharing so that multiple clients don't conflict with each other.

In a SAN, your Mac's SAN file system provides the same block-level access to files as with direct-attached storage, but it must simultaneously tell every other machine on the SAN what it's up to, since every SAN participant has the same block-level access to the storage. Communicating this file system *metadata* (literally, "data about data") expeditiously, keeping all the SAN participants' views of the volume's catalog and bitmap in sync, and avoiding file system corruption make SANs much more complex than the other file systems discussed so far.

Adding to the fun is the fact that metadata communication requires lots of tiny packets of information sent at seemingly random intervals, whereas block-level data transfer involves the sequential and orderly flow of very large packets of information. An infrastructure that supports one may not be the best for the other, and vice versa: Ethernet makes a lot of sense for metadata transfer; Fibre Channel is better optimized for large blocks.

SANS typically use one of two approaches for dealing with this complexity. The differences affect both the underlying architecture of the SAN and how you can use it, as well.

Volume-Level Locking Some SANs offer *volume-level locking*. These SANS let multiple computers read from a volume, but only one at a time can write to it. Since reading doesn't change the file system's low-level metadata aside from "who has this file open for read", many computers can read from the same volume simultaneously without fear of file system corruption.

Metadata management tasks regarding which disk blocks hold valid data, how big files are and where their data blocks reside, and where files are listed in the volume's catalog, is relegated to the one computer with write access. When you write a file, the catalog and bitmap changes can be shared in a leisurely fashion once all the data have been committed to disk. When a file is deleted, the catalog is updated, and then the underlying data structures like the bitmap are adjusted to free up the disk space. The writing computer needs merely to publish its metadata changes to the other SAN participants; there's never the problem of keeping two metadata-changers closely synchronized.

Such SANs typically share what metadata they need to via the same communications fabric they use for block-level data transfer, such as Fibre Channel or FireWire. They are simple to set up and administrate, with user-level tools for mounting SAN volumes for read-only or read/write access.

Volume-locking SAN systems are available from CharisMac (FibreShare), CommandSoft (FibreJet), Rorke Data (ImageSAN), and Studio Network Solutions (SANmp), among others.

It's also worth mentioning one of the first SANs available for Macs: MicroNet's SANcube. The SANcube provided volume-locked shared storage for up to four Mac OS 9 participants, using FireWire 400 for its fabric via a built-in switch. This made it extremely inexpensive. Sadly, the OS X drivers for SANcube don't support shared storage, so it's more notable for its innovative approach than for its current level of functionality.

File-Level Locking SANs like Apple's Xsan offer *file-level locking* and therefore have to tackle the metadata problem head-on. File-locking SANS let multiple computers read and write to the same volume simultaneously, so multiple computers can change the catalog and bitmap.

File-level locking, while providing increased file-sharing flexibility, requires a more sophisticated approach to metadata. File-locking SANs typically segregate file system metadata from user data, both in storage and transport.

Metadata controllers—dedicated servers such as Xserves—store and manage metadata. The SAN participants connect to the metadata controller (MDC) using Fast Ethernet or Gigabit Ethernet, sharing file system data through the MDC. The MDC fields file system requests and translates them into block-level instructions that the participants use to access data directly from the shared storage over a high-speed Fibre Channel fabric. In Xsan, the MDC also stores its metadata on the SAN through its own Fibre Channel link.

In essence, the MDC serves as a centralized file server as far as arbitrating access to the storage is concerned, while each computer still performs its own direct access to the storage itself. This division of labor provides each SAN participant with a synchronized and consistent view of the shared storage, without the bottleneck caused by moving user data though a single, centralized file server.

Of course, this level of sophistication has its own cost: you now have two networks to deal with, an Ethernet network for metadata, and a Fibre Channel network for user data. We'll discuss these issues in a bit.

Which SAN approach is right for your system? Volume-locking SANs offer easier setup and administration, but your workflows must allow for having only one Mac writing to a volume at a time. File-locking SANs offer greater working flexibility, but at a considerable cost in setup and administrative complexity.

Volume-locking SAN vendors say their systems are faster due to the simplicity of metadata exchange allowed by volume locking. File-locking SAN vendors claim *their* architecture is faster because the metadata is segregated on its own network. In reality, the relative speed differences of the two designs, all else being equal, will pale in significance compared to the operational and administrative differences the two designs impose.

In short, there's no easy answer here. You simply have to design your storage architecture based on current and future needs and pick the system that works best for you. SANs are evolving rapidly and their use in collaborative video production is just starting to become widespread, so your best resource will be other FCP users and system integrators with early-adopter experience. When in doubt, learn from the experiences of others.

Volume Structures SANs offer considerable flexibility through *storage virtualization*—the capability to create logical storage volumes atop varying physical devices. SANs like Xsan give you a lot of freedom in structuring your volumes though several levels of logical organization between the physical disks and the mounted volumes. You can optimize a volume for storing high-bit rate sequentially accessed video files or low-bit rate latency-critical audio files; for ultimate speed or ultimate redundancy; or any other combination of performance parameters you desire.

The lowest-level organizer in Xsan (we'll use Xsan as our example henceforth; once you understand Xsan's components, you'll be well prepared to look at other SANs) is the RAID, or *LUN* (logical unit). You set up RAIDs (assuming you're using Xserve RAIDs) using RAID Admin as you would for direct-attach uses.

Then, using Xsan Admin, you assign the LUNs to one or more *storage pools*. Data written to a storage pool is striped across all the contained RAIDs using RAID 0 techniques. So, a storage pool is essentially a "RAID of RAIDs," adding a zero to whatever the underlying RAID setup is: if your RAIDs are RAID 5, your storage pool performs like RAID 50.

Since storage pools use RAID 0 techniques, each RAID in the pool should be structured the same way, with the same speed and capacity.

Finally, you create volumes containing one or more storage pools. (You can even add storage pools to existing volumes.) Xsan volumes treat storage pools the same way as JBODs treat disks: as available space without any special organization, so storage pools don't need to be the same size or speed.

Indeed, you can build volumes with different storage pools, each optimized f or different media types, and define where data will be stored using *affinities*. Affinities associate folders with storage pools, effectively providing "soft partitions" within volumes. For example, you can define affinities for Capture Scratch and Render Files folders and a fast, high-performance storage pool within an FCP volume, and set up affinities for Audio Capture Scratch and Audio Render Files pointing to a low-latency storage pool in the same volume. When you then point FCP towards the FCP volume as its scratch disk, its various captures and renders will automatically wind up using the appropriate storage pools within the volume.

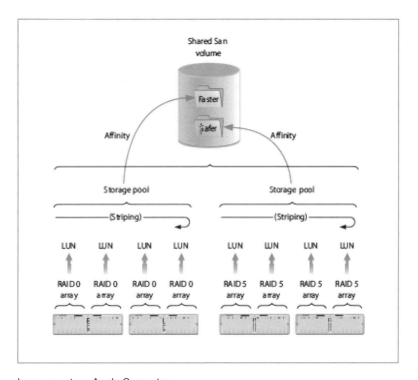

Image courtesy Apple Computer

Fabric Design All SANs require a properly designed storage fabric—the high-speed data networking between the participating computers and the shared storage. Each SAN vendor has its own recommendations for approved components and architectures, and it's worth spending some time with the installation manuals and the information on the vendor's Web site before making your shopping list. Xsan has been qualified with various switches from Brocade, Emulex, and Qlogic; check the current list at www.apple.com/xsan/compatibility.html.

In general, SAN Fibre Channel fabrics require fabric-capable switches, not hubs. The switches should be capable of isolating RSCNs (Registered State Change Notifications, as discussed previously) to the port they occur on, to avoid disrupting traffic throughout the rest of the SAN. (Qlogic calls this capability I/O Stream Guard.) The switches should also be fully *nonblocking*, so that traffic between any two ports on the switch can travel at full speed regardless of the traffic in the rest of the switch.

Even though Fibre Channel switch prices are declining rapidly, don't be surprised if the switch winds up being the single most expensive hardware component in your system. As the central point through which all your high-bandwidth data flows, its performance is critical to SAN operations. No amount of clever RAID design and high-speed disks can break through a bottleneck imposed by an insufficiently muscular switch.

If your SAN requires a separate MDC, it's best to give it its own dedicated Ethernet network, too. Although it's possible to run the metadata traffic on the house network, you'll hurt your SAN's performance with all the network slowdowns and traffic jams possible on a general-purpose net. You can install a second NIC in each Mac for the metadata network, leaving the built-in network interface connected to the house network for file sharing, downloading software updates, and surfing the iTunes Music Store. An inexpensive way to get optimal performance is to invest in a dedicated, high-performance Ethernet switch and high-quality Cat 6 cables.

System Administration When you set up shared storage for multiple users, you become not only a storage and fabric guru, but a network administrator, too.

The topic of network administration is worth a whole book in itself, but we can at least touch on some of the issues you'll face.

Xsan Admin provides volume-level access control through masking and mapping—allowing certain users to see some volumes, and not others. You can also restrict certain users to mounting specified volumes as read-only.

If you want to administer file and folder permissions on a user and group level, bear in mind that OS X determines permissions based on user and group ID numbers, not human-readable user and group names. Unless all the Macs sharing a SAN are centrally administered (using OS X Server's Open Directory, for example) it's possible for user and group IDs to differ from Mac to Mac, even if the human-readable names are the same. When the IDs differ, a user logging into one Mac may not see the same SAN resources he saw when using a different Mac—or even worse, he may see the resources, but be unable to open the project and media files he used on that other machine. Keeping the IDs consistent across all the connected Macs avoids this problem. You don't have to use Open Directory to administer users and groups, but it makes things a lot simpler; editing each Mac's NetInfo database by hand is not for the faint of heart.

Xsan Admin lets you specify *quotas* for users and groups. Quotas limit the amount of storage a user or group can consume—that way you won't have one user filling up the entire SAN at the expense of everyone else.

If your MDC fails, the SAN becomes unusable until it's replaced (the SAN itself should survive the outage; MDCs maintain journal files on the SAN to allow state recovery following such a failure). Xsan lets you specify *failover* MDCs, so that if (or when) the primary MDC fails, a backup MDC takes over with minimal disruption in SAN service. Any connected Mac G4 800 MHz or faster with 512MB RAM per volume can serve as a backup MDC, even an FCP system. But many SANs are set up with a dedicated backup MDC such as a second Xserve so that all connected workstations can continue to do the jobs they normally do.

We'll cover these issues in more detail in later lessons.

Performance and Capacity

Finally, the questions we've all been waiting for: How much storage do I need, and how fast does it need to be? There are, generally speaking, three answers to these questions: the minimalist, the realistic, and the extravagant.

The minimalist answers are easy to obtain (but, as you'll see, they're only a starting point). Simply put, your storage must be capable of playing back all the real-time streams you need simultaneously, and it must be big enough to hold all the media you need for a production.

For example, if you intend to capture and play back one stream of DV25 media (rendering any effects and transitions), you'll need a storage system capable of supplying at least 3.6 MB/second. If you are producing a 15-minute show rendered out as a self-contained movie and have a 3:1 shooting ratio (3 minutes captured for every minute in the finished piece), you'll need 1 hour of DV25 storage: about 13 GB.

If instead you need to play back three real-time streams of DV50 material without rendering, you'll want to provide storage with 3 times DV50's data rate of 7.2 MB/second, or 21.6 MB/second.

You can use the tables at the end of this lesson to deduce the requirements for many of FCP's media types; for any not listed, render a 1-minute Timeline using the appropriate codec, frame rate, and frame size to derive the necessary numbers: measure the resulting file size and multiply by 60 for the storage needed for an hour; divide by 60 to get the required data rate per second.

For third-party codecs, try downloading the software codec from the vendor's Web site and running the same test.

> **NOTE** ▶ DV and uncompressed codecs do not vary in their bit rates or storage requirements depending on scene content, but many other codecs—including Photo-JPEG and Motion JPEG—do. Such codecs can vary in their data rates by a factor of five based on scene complexity. To be on the safe side, render your tests using FCP's noise generator (in the pop-up menu, lower-right corner of the Viewer), or try capturing typical footage through your capture card and saving it using your test codec.

The calculations get a bit more complicated with shared storage like Xsan systems, since you have to consider multiple workstations accessing the storage at the same time, perhaps using media with different bit rates—one fellow wanting six streams of DV25 while another expects two of DVCPROHD 24p. Even so, it's easy enough to calculate the answers for each workstation alone and then add them together to get the total requirement.

Simple enough, isn't it? Unfortunately, the minimalist answer rarely suffices. FCP accesses data in a "bursty" manner, not a continuously smooth-flowing stream, and storage subsystems that just barely meet sustained transfer requirements can't keep up if they have to seek rapidly and frequently from one clip to another. A drive that plays back a single clip on the Timeline for hours at a time may cause dropped frames when presented with a Timeline comprised of rapid-fire cuts.

By the same token, "just enough" storage is rarely enough. Even that 3:1 15-minute show will have intermediate renders, alternate versions of portions of the Timeline, and associated graphic files, sound effects, Soundtrack loops, Live Type titles, and Motion compositions, pushing its storage requirements beyond those suggested by the simplistic minimalist calculation.

The realistic answer is that you need to provide a margin of performance and capacity above the minimalist requirements. How much margin is open to interpretation; it's accepted practice to set the requirement for DV25 drive performance at twice the minimalist bit rate, but it's unclear if you need a full 2x margin for uncompressed HD production.

Nonetheless, the general consensus appears to be that providing twice the required sustained bandwidth gives you enough margin for safety, regardless of the media type you're using. Following this rule, calculate the minimalist answer as described earlier in this section, multiply by two, and provision bandwidth accordingly.

For capacity calculations, a similar judgment can be made, although it's more subject to variation depending on your FCP workflow patterns. Some editors work very abstemiously; others produce render files, alternate versions, temporary graphics, and sound mixes with wild abandon. For the former, providing twice the minimalist capacity may be more than enough; the latter may take five or more times the calculated storage.

Realistically, plan using the factor of two, and adjust as necessary based on expectations and experience.

Finally, of course, there's the extravagant answer. In the words of an old MTV motto, "Too much is never enough." Practically speaking, there's more than a grain of truth in this answer; whatever storage you plan for today will come to seem too small and too limiting down the road. Parkinson's Law applies to bandwidth and storage just as to time: whatever you provide today will be filled tomorrow—or if not tomorrow, the day after.

Data Rates and Storage Requirements for Common Media Types

We rendered out 1-minute tests from FCP itself using the specified settings to derive these tables. Each clip had two channels of 16-bit 48 kHz audio in addition to the video track.

Captures in the corresponding formats should be very close to these numbers, but may differ slightly due to different QuickTime packaging strategies used on captures compared to renders.

Audio

Format	MB/ second	MB/ minute	GB/ 10 minutes	GB/ 30 minutes	GB/ hour
2 channels 16-bit 48 kHz	0.183	11	0.11	0.33	0.66

SD Formats

Format	MB/ second	MB/ minute	GB/ 10 minutes	GB/ 30 minutes	GB/ hour
DV25 24p	2.93	176	1.76	5.28	10.6
DV25	3.62	217	2.17	6.51	13
DV50 24p	5.68	341	3.41	10.2	20.5
DV50	7.05	423	4.23	12.7	25.4
Uncompressed 8-bit SD 24p	16.20	972	9.72	29.2	58.3
Uncompressed 8-bit SD	19.67	1,180	11.8	35.4	70.8
Uncompressed 10-bit SD 24p	21.00	1,260	12.6	37.8	75.6
Uncompressed 10-bit SD	26.17	1,570	15.7	47.1	94.2

Notes:

▶ For SD formats, there's no difference between NTSC and PAL-format data rates; NTSC has 20 percent more frames per second, but PAL's frames are 20 percent larger. The differences cancel out.

▶ DV25 is used in DV, DVCPRO, and DVCAM; DV50 is used in DVCPRO 50, and DV100 is used in DVCPRO HD.

▶ All NTSC-derived rates are shown as integral rates, that is, 29.97 is shown as 30 and 23.98 is shown as 24. There is only a 0.1 percent difference between true NTSC storage requirements and integer frame rate requirements.

HD 720 Formats

Format	MB/ second	MB/ minute	GB/ 10 minutes	GB/ 30 minutes	GB/ hour
DV100 720p24	5.68	341	3.41	10.2	20.5
DV100 720p60	13.92	835	8.35	25.1	50.1
Uncompressed 8-bit 720p24	41.33	2,480	24.8	74.4	149
Uncompressed 8-bit 720p60	103.17	6,190	61.9	186	371
Uncompressed 10-bit 720p24	55.67	3,340	33.4	100	200
Uncompressed 10-bit 720p60	139.17	8,350	83.5	251	501

Notes:

▶ All formats are listed by frame rate, not field rate; "1080i30" in the table is what FCP calls "1080i60."

▶ Uncompressed rates shown for reference. Verify using the uncompressed 720p codec supplied with your 720p capture card.

▶ 720p30 HDV captured to the Apple Intermediate Codec is likely to have maximum data rates between DV100 720p24 and DV100 720p60.

▶ All NTSC-derived rates are shown as integral rates. For instance, 29.97 is shown as 30 and 23.98 is shown as 24. There is only a 0.1 percent difference between true NTSC storage requirements and integer frame rate requirements.

HD 1080 Formats

Format	MB/second	MB/minute	GB/10 minutes	GB/30 minutes	GB/hour
DV100 1080p24	11.17	670	6.70	20.1	40.2
DV100 1080i30	13.92	835	8.35	25.1	50.1
Uncompressed 8-bit 1080p24	92.83	5,570	55.7	167	334
Uncompressed 8-bit 1080i25	19.67	1,180	11.8	35.4	70.8
Uncompressed 8-bit 1080i30	116.00	6,960	69.6	209	418
Uncompressed 10-bit 1080p24	123.67	7,420	74.2	223	445
Uncompressed 10-bit 1080i25	128.83	7,730	77.3	232	464
Uncompressed 10-bit 1080i30	154.67	9,280	92.8	278	557

Notes:

► All formats are listed by frame rate, not field rate; "1080i30" in the table is what FCP calls "1080i60."

► DV100 is used in DVCPRO HD.

► DV100 has the same data rates for 1080i25 and 1080i30, but FCP does not currently support DVCPRO HD 1080i25.

► 1080i30 has the same data rate as 1080p30, and 1080i25 has the same as 1080p25.

► 1080i30 HDV captured to the Apple Intermediate Codec is likely to have maximum data rates comparable to DV100 1080i30.

▶ Uncompressed rates shown for reference. Verify using the uncompressed 1080 codec supplied with your 1080 capture card.

▶ All NTSC-derived rates are shown as integral rates, that is, 29.97 is shown as 30 and 23.98 is shown as 24. There is only a 0.1 percent difference between true NTSC storage requirements and integer frame rate requirements.

Offline Formats

Format	MB/ second	MB/ minute	GB/ 10 minutes	GB/ 30 minutes	GB/ hour
OfflineRT NTSC 24p	0.99	59.3	0.593	1.78	3.56
OfflineRT NTSC	1.19	71.4	0.714	2.14	4.28
OfflineRT NTSC (simple)	0.31	18.4	0.184	0.552	1.1
OfflineRT PAL	1.02	61.3	0.613	1.84	3.68
OfflineRT HD 24	1.07	64.1	0.641	1.92	3.85
OfflineRT HD 25	1.11	66.3	0.663	1.99	3.98
OfflineRT HD 30	1.29	77.4	0.774	2.32	4.64
MJPEG-A NTSC	2.15	129	1.29	3.87	7.74
MJPEG-A NTSC (simple)	0.42	25.2	0.252	0.756	1.51

Notes:

▶ OfflineRT uses the Photo-JPEC codec. All OfflineRT figures were derived using the default settings in FCP's supplied sequence presets.

▶ The MJPEG values were obtained by changing the Photo-JPEG codec to the Motion JPEG A codec in the default sequence presets, but leaving all other parameters the same.

▶ The "(simple)" values were obtained by rendering FCP's built-in color bars, and they are provided for reference with the corresponding "busy" values, obtained by rendering FCP's internally generated randomized color noise. Photo-JPEG shows almost a 4:1 variation in data rate depending on scene content, whereas Motion JPEG A shows a 5:1 variation. Real-world clips will fall somewhere between these extremes, but the "busy" values should be used for planning purposes.

Lesson Review

1. Name four factors that determine disk drive performance.

2. What are RAIDS and what do they do?

3. List a few RAID levels used for video editing.

4. What are the three main storage architectures?

5. Do SANs allow volume-level or file-level locking?

6. What determines the minimal performance you need in your storage?

7. What does storage capacity depend on?

Answers

1. Rotation rates, latencies, buffer sizes, and connection interfaces.

2. RAIDs are disk arrays used to improve performance and provide redundancy.

3. RAID levels 0, 3, and 5 are good for video, and Apple's Xserve RAID is optimized for RAID 5.

4. Direct-access storage, network attached storage, and storage area networks.

5. SANs allow either one, depending on the SAN architecture.

6. The number of simultaneous real-time streams you need to record or play, and the bit rates of those streams.

7. The amount of footage to be captured, as well as render files, intermediate or temporary rendered timelines, graphics, and audio files.

Configuring Final Cut Pro and Managing Your System

Jonathan Eric Tyrrell | Charles Roberts

10

Configuring Mac OS X

Mac OS X is an integral part of your Final Cut Pro system. Although FCP is designed to take advantage of specific technologies embedded in the operating system, such as Quartz Extreme, Core Audio, and symmetric multiprocessing (SMP), in a broader sense Mac OS X defines your virtual environment. With that in mind, in this lesson you'll learn about strategies to streamline Mac OS X, various optimization tools, and some power user tips to further support your workflow. If you prefer a shortcut to setting up your preferences for FCP, you can skip to the end of this chapter and read the "System Preferences Checklist" section.

Improving Final Cut Pro Performance

Final Cut Pro and Mac OS X work together straight out of the box, so you may not have felt the need to modify your system preferences yet. But there are several adjustments you can make to the operating system to improve the performance of FCP. Most of the steps are fairly straightforward, but are sometimes overlooked. In general, with each preference setting, you should deactivate any automatic processes and limit tasks that don't contribute to your specific workflow.

System preferences present a varying range of options, and in this lesson we address only those that are immediately relevant to optimizing FCP. Refer to Mac Help (Cmd-? in the Finder) for more information on additional settings. Use the list at the end of the lesson as a quick reference guide.

> **NOTE** ▶ Depending on how Mac OS X has been configured for your system, you're likely to need an administrator password to access and modify some of the system preferences covered in this lesson. (Different kinds of user accounts are addressed specifically in a later section.)

Disable Energy Saver Controls

The Mac OS X Energy Saver preference affects the way your computer consumes power. It does this by monitoring certain activities and putting components to sleep when they're not in use. There's usually some latency involved in waking up a system. When you're working with Final Cut Pro and want to get the best performance from your system, you need to change the Energy Saver settings.

1   Open System Preferences by clicking its icon in the Dock, opening it from the Finder menu, or by accessing it directly in the Applications folder.

2   Click the Energy Saver icon.

NOTE ▶ If you're using a portable Mac, you may need to click the Show Details button to reveal the sleep control settings.

3   Drag the first slider to the Never setting.

NOTE ▶ The second slider controls when to set the monitor to sleep. This operation doesn't usually affect the performance of FCP, but you should check the documentation of your third-party devices—some PCI expansion cards and older USB devices can cause the computer to stop responding if the screen goes to sleep. If you use an affected device, you should check for software updates to see if the issue is resolved and disable this option if it hasn't.

4   Ensure that the Put the Hard Disk(s) To Sleep When Possible check box is deselected.

5   Click the Options tab.

6   Select the Restart Automatically After a Power Failure check box.

7   From the Processor Performance pop-up menu, choose Highest to maximize your system performance at all times.

NOTE ▶ The Processor Performance option varies from computer to computer, but in general it provides a method to reduce power consumption and heat generation. The technology behind this is called dynamic frequency switching (DFS) or dynamic power stepping (DPS). When activated, it will lower the speed and voltage requirements of some components at times when there is less demand on the system.

Set Desktop & Screen Saver Preferences

Rotating Desktop images and animated screen savers demonstrate the elegance of the Quartz Extreme engine. They also make demands on the CPU that can detract from important tasks such as rendering. To maximize the performance of FCP on your system, you should make sure that all such effects are turned off.

1   In the System Preferences window, click the Desktop & Screen Saver icon.

2   Deselect the Change Picture check box if it is active.

    NOTE ▶ Once the parent feature is disabled, the dependent configuration settings become inaccessible.

3   Click the Screen Saver tab.

4   Drag the Start Screen Saver slider to Never to prevent the screen saver from ever activating.

Deactivate Sharing Services

Mac OS X offers a range of network services, including AFP (Apple File Sharing Protocol), FTP (File Transfer Protocol) access, personal Web sharing, Windows sharing, printer sharing, and now, with Mac OS X 10.4, Xgrid. It also supports various administration tools—such as Remote Login, Apple Remote Desktop (ARD), and Remote Apple Events, a personal firewall—and the ability to share a computer's Internet connection. Be aware that most of these features involve hidden applications, which run continuously *in the background* of your system. Though the Unix foundation of Mac OS X supports true multitasking and can perform different tasks simultaneously, you should refrain from running a Web server, Internet sharing, or similar service. This will help reduce any overhead and ultimately get the best possible performance from Final Cut Pro. If you have a specific reason to use one of the services, make sure you have deactivated it again before you launch FCP.

> **NOTE** ▶ Xgrid was developed by Apple's Advanced Computation Group. It creates the ability to distribute tasks across groups or clusters of computers, operating on a similar principle to Apple Qmaster, which shares rendering jobs between systems. For more information on Xgrid, go to www.apple.com/macosx/features/xgrid.

1   In the System Preferences window, click the Sharing icon.

2   Deselect any active check boxes under the Services tab.

3   Click the Firewall tab, and confirm that you don't have a firewall enabled.

NOTE ▶ Although a firewall is something you should definitely use if your system is connected to the Internet and it doesn't have a lot of overhead, a router with a built-in firewall to keep your internal network protected is preferable. A number of companies, including Belkin, Asante, Linksys, and Netgear, produce inexpensive routers.

4   Click the Internet tab, and make sure that you're not offering to share your Internet connection with any other computers.

5   Once you're satisfied that you're not running any unnecessary processes, click the Close button to apply any changes and exit system preferences.

You'll learn how to view processes in "Mac OS X Administration" later in this lesson.

Establish Security Settings

If data security is important to you—perhaps you edit in the field on a PowerBook G4—then there are several ways to keep your files safe with Mac OS X. Later in this lesson, you'll learn about user accounts and file permissions, both of which offer control over access to your system at a fundamental level. Additional measures, such as requiring password login, can be activated using the security system preferences. Though password prompts create additional steps, they don't affect the performance of Final Cut Pro. However, there are other features, especially FileVault, you shouldn't use in conjunction with FCP.

FileVault provides Advanced Encryption Standard (AES) 128-bit encryption for your Home folder. We recommend that you don't use FileVault with FCP, because media files tend to be too large to encrypt and decrypt on the fly. Working this way will tax your CPU unnecessarily and may result in dropped frames during capture or playback. If all of your scratch disks are located on separate drives (or at top-level if you're restricted to using one hard drive), you may not experience a problem, because FileVault does not affect files outside the Home directory. To ensure maximum performance while you're editing, make sure FileVault is not protecting your system.

MORE INFO ▶ For additional information on FCP and FileVault, see http://docs.info.apple.com/article.html?artnum=93454.

1   Re-open the System Preferences window, click the Security icon.

2   Check the Security window to see whether FileVault has been enabled. Turn it off on your FCP editing station.

NOTE ▶ To start and stop FileVault, you must have space on your hard drive that's at least equal to the size of your Home folder. Also, make sure you don't force your computer to shut down during the encryption process—you could lose or corrupt data. For more information, see www.apple.com/macosx/features/filevault.

3   Make sure the automatic Log Out After check box is not selected so that it doesn't interrupt file encoding in Batch Monitor.

4   Make sure the Use Secure Virtual Memory check box is inactive.

NOTE ▶ Activating secure virtual memory should not affect performance in FCP unless your system is already overtaxed. Unless you need it, there's no advantage to be gained from having it switched on.

Customizing Your Mac OS X System

You need to modify some additional system preferences in order to fully optimize your system design and workflow. In this section, you'll learn about adjustments that are geared towards configuring Mac OS X to work with specific hardware, including dual displays and digital receivers. You'll also modify features that affect your working methods, such as the Dock, Exposé, Dashboard, and Spotlight.

> **NOTE** ▶ Though we don't address them in this lesson, you should be aware that some applications, including Adobe Version Cue, Telestream Flip4Mac, and Apple Qmaster install additional preferences, which are listed under the Other category in the System Preferences window.

Set Up Displays

As previously noted in the Lesson 8, Macintosh computers support a wide variety of display solutions. Whether you are using one, two, or three displays, or cutting on the largest Cinema Display or a PowerBook G4, you can customize Final Cut Pro to make the best use of the available screen real estate. Before you start arranging windows in FCP, you first need to set up and configure displays in system preferences.

1   In the System Preferences window, click the Displays icon.

> **NOTE** ▶ If you have additional displays connected to your computer, you may need to click the Detect Displays button before your system will recognize it. If everything is connected properly, a corresponding preferences window should appear.

> **TIP** ▶ To collect multiple preference windows together on the same screen, click the Gather Windows button.

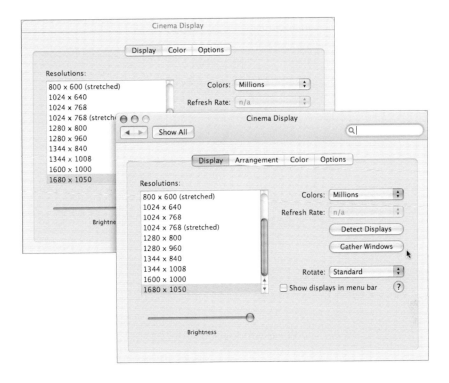

2   Select one of the options listed under Resolutions.

Computer displays usually support a range of resolutions; the supported settings will vary among models. Which one you choose depends on the nature of your workflow and the resolution you find most comfortable and effective.

TIP ▶ If you are testing window arrangements in FCP and different display resolutions, you may need to relaunch the application to access some of the presets. This is due to the system check Final Cut Pro performs as it loads to determine the configuration of your system. Some options, such as Dual Screen arrangements and Multiple Edits are only available with specific setups.

TIP ▶ If you select a resolution that is not supported by your display, your screen might go blank, and you will be unable to readjust the settings. A Safe Boot should fix the problem in Mac OS X 10.4—hold down the Power button to shut down the computer and hold down the Shift key after the startup tone. Solutions for Mac OS X 10.3.9 or earlier are available on the Apple Web site: http://docs.info.apple.com/article.html?artnum=106564.

3 Confirm that the Colors pop-up menu is set to Millions to ensure that your video displays at the appropriate bit-depth.

4 The Refresh Rate option is not available for LCD displays, but if you are working with CRT, choose 85Hz for optimum performance in Final Cut Pro.

MORE INFO ▶ For more information of displays and Final Cut Pro, see the Apple support documents at http://docs.info.apple.com/article.html?artnum=58640 and http://docs.info.apple.com/article.html?artnum=25117.

NOTE ▶ To maintain brightness settings at a fixed level, PowerBook G4 users may want to turn off the automatic brightness control by deselecting the Automatically Adjust Brightness As Ambient Light Changes check box.

5 Click the Arrangement tab if you are working with multiple displays; if you're working with one display, skip ahead to step 8.

NOTE ▶ The Arrangement tab is only visible if multiple displays are connected to the system.

6 Drag the blue screen icons to define the relationship between your displays.

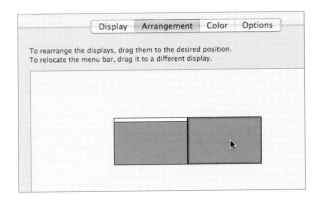

MORE INFO ▶ You can use the Arrangement pane to configure more than two displays; see the "Setting Up Multiple Displays as an Extended Desktop" topic in Mac Help.

7 Drag the menu bar icon to set your primary display.

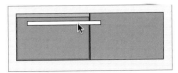

8 Make sure the Mirror Displays check box is not selected.

Don't mirror displays while working with FCP, because this is likely to overtax your system and result in dropped frames. If you need to mirror your display, use a DVI splitter or similar device.

9 Click the Color tab.

10 Confirm that the model selected in the Display Profile list matches your display.

The precise representation of color varies from display to display, so it is important that you choose the correct setting. You can further adjust Apple displays using the Display Calibrator Assistant (click the Calibrate button), but Final Cut Pro does not use ColorSync to calibrate or compensate colors. For this reason, leave gamma settings at the 1.8 Standard Gamma setting.

TIP ▶ Due to differences in the way that colors are represented, never rely on a computer display for online workflows. As suggested in other lessons, you should use a properly calibrated external monitor to ensure that color is rendered accurately.

NOTE ▶ You can use the controls under the Options tab, which is only available if you're using an Apple Cinema Display, to modify the behavior of buttons on the display.

Control System Sound

Mac OS X and Final Cut Pro also support an extensive range of audio hardware. (Refer to Lesson 8 for more information on specific interfaces.) After you have connected your device to your system, you need to configure Mac OS X to use it.

NOTE ▶ FCP is a Carbon application, and it uses the standard sound output preferences. Cocoa applications such as Soundtrack Pro are controlled via the Audio Midi Setup application.

1   In the System Preferences window, click the Sound icon.

2 If you like to work with alerts and sound effects enabled, choose your preferred alert sound from the list of available noises. If you prefer to turn alerts off, skip ahead to step 4.

In order to hear the sounds, you need to raise both the Alert Volume and the Output Volume.

3 Choose Internal Speakers from the Play Alerts and Sound Effects pop-up menu.

It's typical to route the alerts and effects to the internal speakers to prevent them from playing through your main monitors.

4 Drag the Alert Volume slider to set a level for alerts and sound effects.

Dragging the slider all the way to the left turns off alerts.

NOTE ▶ Whether you activate Play User Interface Sound Effects and Play Feedback When Volume Keys Is Changed is largely up to individual preference—neither will affect the performance of FCP. As with alerts sounds, you want to be careful not to play them through your main sound system.

5 Click the Output tab.

6 From the list of available devices, select the output device you want to use.

NOTE ▶ Power Mac G5 computers include a Digital Out port, which utilizes the S/PDIF format, sometimes called Toslink, to transfer digital audio directly to a range of devices, including digital receivers that support 5.1 audio. Once you select the Digital Out port, the volume slider is disabled at the maximum level setting, and you will need to control system volume using the output device. For more information on using the Digital Out port, refer to the Apple Web site: http://docs.info.apple.com/article.html?artnum=86438 and http://docs.info.apple.com/article.html?artnum=86415.

7   Drag the Balance slider to the center.

8   Drag the Output Volume slider to set the overall level of your audio output. It's usually a good idea to choose a high setting and use your external monitors to control the levels.

When working with audio, keep the output volume at a consistent level and make adjustments within Final Cut Pro rather than raising the level for quiet sounds and lowering it for loud sounds. This is the only way you can effectively judge the average loudness of your mix. Play a section of a project that represents the average volume to help you make the appropriate adjustments. Once your levels are set correctly, any changes to the master setting should be infrequent.

9   Click the Input tab.

If you use the FCP Voice Over tool, you'll need to connect an audio input device to your system.

10   From the list of available devices, select an appropriate input device.

11   Use the Input level to monitor the sound, and use the Input volume slider to adjust the level appropriately.

Manage Dashboard & Exposé

Exposé is intended to help you streamline your working methods and support multitasking operations. For example, if you have multiple windows open in FCP, and you've misplaced the Viewer, simply press the Exposé shortcut for Application Windows (F10 by default) and all the open windows in current application *tile* across the screen.

Dashboard is one of the new features introduced in Mac OS X 10.4. It creates an additional environment for you to run *widgets*—small accessory applications, built around common Web standards, such as HTML, CSS, and JavaScript, which usually perform very specific functions. When you click to make Dashboard appear, you have immediate access to your installed widgets. Once you have performed the required task, Dashboard disappears and you continue with what you were originally doing.

The default Exposé shortcuts—F9, F10, and F11—will most likely be familiar to you as the keys used in Final Cut Pro for Insert, Overwrite, and Replace. In Mac OS X 10.4, Dashboard also overrides F12—the FCP shortcut for Superimpose Clip. Without modifying Exposé and Dashboard, when you press one of the shortcuts, the Mac OS X user interface functions will override the FCP commands. Press F9 and you will display all open windows; F10 will show open windows in the current application; F11 will reveal the Desktop; and F12 opens Dashboard. If you rely on the keyboard to do your editing, you need to decide whether you want to modify these shortcut keys.

Though it's easy to remap the keyboard in Final Cut Pro, adjusting well-established habits can require a little patience and perseverance. The alternative is to customize Exposé and Dashboard, which is equally easy to do, but be aware that you're making a system-wide modification and you could inadvertently create conflicts with other applications.

1   In the System Preferences window, click the Dashboard & Exposé icon.

2   Press and hold Option while you choose a new keystroke from the All Windows, Application Windows, and Desktop pop-up menus.

You can replace F9, F10, and F11 with any combination of the standard modifier keys (Cmd, Option, Ctrl, and Shift). Option-F9, Option-F10, and

Option-F11 are popular choices amongst FCP users because they don't currently conflict with default commands in Final Cut Pro.

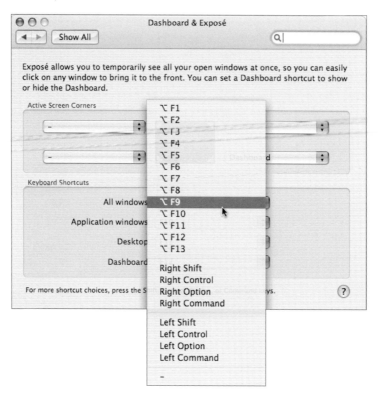

3   Press and hold Cmd-Option while you choose a new keystroke from the Dashboard pop-up menu.

Modifying Dashboard is a little more complicated because Final Cut Pro already uses F12 (Superimpose Clip), Cmd-F12 (External Video: All Frames), Ctrl-F12 (Play: Rate 6), Option-F12 (Refresh A/V Devices), and Shift-F12 (Show Current on External Video). The combination of Cmd-Option-F12 doesn't interfere with any of the default Final Cut Pro short-cuts. If that doesn't work for you, another alternative would be to deactivate the keyboard shortcut (by selecting dash [-] from the menu).

Then you would need to open Dashboard by clicking the Dock icon or by setting an Active Screen Corner.

TIP ▶ If you choose to set an Active Screen Corner, the bottom right does not conflict with default FCP window arrangements.

TIP ▶ You deactivate individual shortcuts by selecting the dash option at the bottom of each menu.

MORE INFO ▶ For more information, consult the Keyboard Shortcuts topic in Mac OS X Help.

Multitasking with Exposé

One way to utilize Exposé when you're working in Final Cut Pro is to quickly drag and drop files into your projects from the Finder.

1   Copy one of the media folders (Lesson 11 Media, for example) from the other lessons onto your Desktop.

2   Create a new project in FCP.

3   Press your Desktop Exposé shortcut (F11 by default) to hide all open windows and reveal the Desktop.

4   Click and hold the media folder.

5   Still holding the mouse button down, press the Desktop Exposé shortcut again, and the FCP windows should move back into position.

6   Drag the media folder to the Browser to create a new bin.

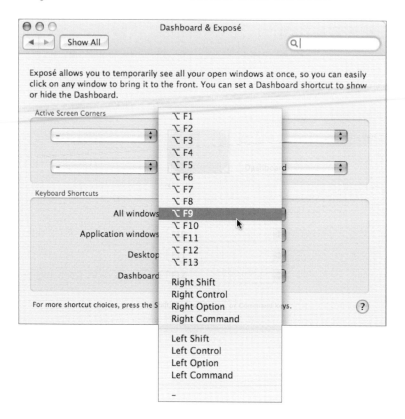

Widgets for FCP Users

There are currently over a thousand widgets available, and new applications appear daily. The Apple Web site features a comprehensive resource to help users find and download widgets (www.apple.com/downloads/dashboard).

Amongst the many widgets, there are some that you might find useful when you're working with FCP, optimizing your system, and tracking system performance.

▶ Hardware Monitor Widget Edition

Registered users of the shareware application, Hardware Monitor (www.bresink.com/osx/HardwareMonitor.html), can use this companion widget to quickly access Mac OS X sensor readouts and monitor the status of system hardware.

www.apple.com/downloads/dashboard/status/hardwaremonitorwidgetedition
.html

▶ Final Cut Pro Forum Search

Search the German language Final Cut Pro forum, www.finalcutpro.de.

www.apple.com/downloads/dashboard/blogs_forums/
finalcutproforumsearch.html

▶ Los Angeles FCP User Group Searcher

Quickly perform a Google search of the popular LAFCPUG Web site.

www.apple.com/downloads/dashboard/blogs_forums/
losangelesfcpusergroupsearcher.html

▶ Sysstat

Monitor current system activity, including CPU and memory usage, network statistics, uptime, and the top three processes.

www.apple.com/downloads/dashboard/status/sysstat.html

(System activity is discussed in more detail later in this lesson.)

▶ Transmit

Transfer files over a network connection with drag-and-drop simplicity.

www.apple.com/downloads/dashboard/networking_security/
transmitftpwidget.html

▶ Version Tracker

Keep track the latest Mac OS X software updates.

www.apple.com/downloads/dashboard/news/versiontrackerwidget.html

MORE INFO ▸ Consult the Dashboard topic in Mac Help for information on how to download, install, and create widgets. You can find more information on removing widgets on the Apple Web site: http://docs.info. apple.com/article.html?artnum=301629.

Search with Spotlight

The first time you log into Mac OS X 10.4, Spotlight immediately begins indexing all the files on your computer. Two stores are created during this process: one for metadata (descriptive information about your files) and the other for selected file content. Whenever you create or modify a file, the new information is added to the index. Spotlight can be very useful to FCP users; it will allow you to create Smart Folders to collect the most recently updated project files together, or instantly search through the Final Cut Pro manuals.

Instant Search Results

1   Click the Spotlight icon in the menu bar, or press Cmd-spacebar.

2   Type a search query into Spotlight's text field.

A list of results appears the moment you start typing. As you enter more text, the results become more refined.

3   Click an item from the list to open it.

TIP ▸ You can also use the up and down arrow keys to navigate the results list. Press Enter to open an item.

Prioritizing Results and Privacy Settings

You can customize Spotlight to prioritize results and restrict access to certain areas.

> **MORE INFO ▶** Details on which areas Spotlight searches by default are documented in an Apple Knowledge Base article: http://docs.info.apple. com/article.html?artnum=301533.

1 In the System Preferences window, click the Spotlight icon.

2 Deselect categories you do not want to search.

3 Drag the remaining categories to define the order of your search results.

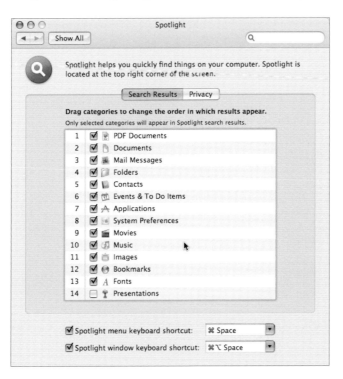

NOTE ▶ The default Spotlight shortcuts conflict with the default Input Menu commands and some of the commands within Motion. Refer to the Keyboard Shortcuts topic in Mac Help for more information.

4 Click the Privacy tab.

5 Click the Add (+) button.

6 Select the areas of the computer you would like to shield from Spotlight, and click Choose.

If you select partitions, the entire partition will become invisible to Spotlight and will no longer be indexed.

TIP ▶ If you connect a drive to your system and need to override Spotlight, you can also use the Privacy feature to interrupt active indexing. Any areas that are not part of the index cannot be searched with Spotlight.

TIP ▶ You can use this same technique of choosing items in the Privacy tab to force Spotlight to re-index your hard drive. After you have made an item private, Spotlight will have to re-create its record if you choose to reintroduce it.

Creating Custom Metadata

You can add keywords to files and folders as special Spotlight comments that you can then use in your searches.

1 Create a new project in Final Cut Pro.

2 Save the project to your hard disk.

3 Select the new project file in the Finder.

4 Choose File > Get Info (Cmd-I).

5 Add the keyword *myComment* to the Spotlight Comments text field.

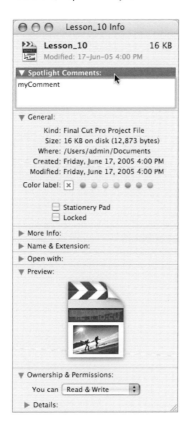

6 Close the Info window and use Spotlight to search for your keywords. The file or folder you modified should appear in the results.

Creating Smart Folders

Spotlight searches can also be saved as Smart Folders, which will dynamically update to include relevant files as they appear in the index.

1 In the Finder, choose File > New Smart Folder.

2 Leave the default search criteria, Kind, in the first pop-up menu.

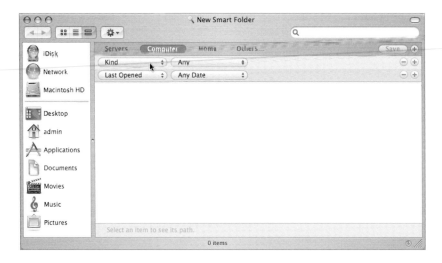

3 Choose Others from the second column pop-up menu to further limit your search.

4   Choose Final Cut Pro Project File from the third pop-up menu.

A list of all the FCP projects on your system appears in the window.

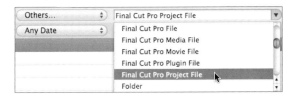

5   Choose Other from the first pop-up menu in the second row.

6   Scroll down the list and select Spotlight Comment.

> **TIP**   You can also type *Spotlight* into the Search field.

7   Click OK and choose Is from the second pop-menu.

8   Type *myComment* in the text field. Your project is automatically added to the folder.

9   Click Save.

10   Name your new Smart Folder and save it to your hard disk.

11   Create and save another new project in Final Cut Pro.

12   Open the Info window and add *myComment* to the Spotlight comments.

13   Close the comments window and open your Smart Folder on the Desktop.

   Both FCP files should be listed.

Indexing Final Cut Pro Help Files

The Final Cut Pro user's manual and Help documents are stored as PDF files inside the FCP package. In most cases, Spotlight is able to search the content of PDF documents, but in their default location the FCP Help files are inaccessible.

If you want to use Spotlight to search through these documents, you need to copy them to a different location.

One way to access the Help documents is to individually select the manuals from the FCP Help menu and save each file into area of your hard drive included in the Spotlight index.

> **MORE INFO** ▸ See the Apple Web site for specific instructions: http://docs.info.apple.com/article.html?artnum=301571.

Or you can access all of the documents in the Final Cut Pro package.

1   Open the Applications folder and Ctrl-click the Final Cut Pro application.

2   Choose Show Package Contents from the contextual menu.

A new window opens to reveal the Contents folder inside the FCP package.

3   Navigate the Finder to locate the Final Cut Pro Help folder—for English localizations, it's located in Contents/Resources/English.lproj.

You'll need to change the path for non-English installations—to access the French localization, for example, you'll need to use the hierarchy Contents/Resources/French.lproj.

4   Choose Edit > Copy Final Cut Pro Help.

5   Open your Documents folder and choose Edit > Paste Item.

The Final Cut Pro Help folder copies into Documents.

6   In the menu bar, click the Spotlight icon or press Cmd-spacebar to open a new Spotlight search.

7   Enter the search term *Multicamera Editing*.

8   Click to open New Features.pdf.

The document opens and highlights the first instance of the search term.

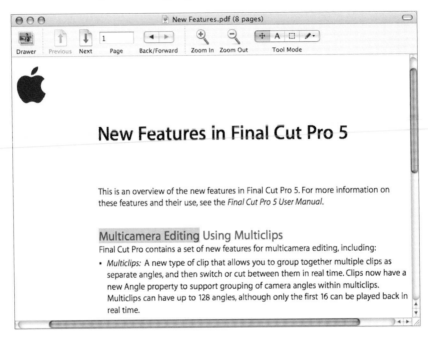

Hide the Dock

To maximize your screen real estate, you may want to hide the Dock. You can also position it on different sides of the display to accommodate different working methods.

> **TIP** If you want more than the standard three positions: Left, Bottom, and Right, a third-party application like Marcel Bresink's TinkerTool (www.bresink.com/osx/TinkerTool.html) will allow you to choose further options.

Some users shy away from the Dock, and use third-party alternatives instead, such as DragThing (www.dragthing.com), LaunchBar (www.obdev.at/products/launchbar), and Drop Drawers (www.sigsoftware.com/dropdrawers).

Mac OS X Administration

Once you have configured Mac OS X to create the optimum environment for
Final Cut Pro, the next step is to equip yourself with some tools and techniques
to help you maintain the peak performance of your system. In this part of the
lesson, you'll learn how to work with user accounts, manage software updates,
control permissions, perform routine maintenance tasks, and administrate
processes to keep Mac OS X optimized for FCP.

Understanding User Accounts

Mac OS X is a true multiuser environment built around an established Unix
file system and permissions model. To understand what this means, it's important to recognize that there's a difference between Mac *users*—people who use
Macintosh computers—and Mac OS X *accounts*—symbolic profiles that are a
core feature of every Unix system.

Mac users work with their computers every day to perform a wide range of
tasks—from email and Web surfing, video and sound production, to enterprise server management and advanced high-performance computing—but
for each task the core system remains fundamentally the same. Each of these
users will log in to their Macs using a specific type of Mac OS X account,
which will define their relationship and access to the system and files.

Defining Mac OS X Accounts

There are several types of built-in Unix accounts. Most of them work unobtru-
sively behind the scenes to support the system. There are three accounts that
are usually associated with human users, which you can work with to control
user operations and manage access to different files.

▶   Normal (Non-admin)—Users of normal accounts are able to work with
     applications, modify personal preferences, and perform general day-to-day
     tasks. They do not have access to administration tools and are not permit-
     ted to make changes to the system configuration. Normal users own indi-
     vidual Home directories, which they alone have access to, and which
     contains all their files and preferences.

Mac OS X identifies three levels of normal user, Standard, Managed, and Simplified, which are defined by varying levels of access to applications and system controls.

▶ Administrator (Admin)—The first account created by Mac OS X Setup Assistant is an administrator user. Administrators are able to create and define other user accounts; configure system-wide settings; access administration utilities such as NetInfo Manager; and install applications or resources that can be accessed by every user on a system.

▶ System Administrator (Superuser or root)—The System Administrator is a unique account that has access to every configuration setting, preference, and file, including all the hidden system files. The System Administrator account is disabled in Mac OS X by default to help protect the system. You can activate it with NetInfo Manager or the command line, but use it judiciously, to perform only specialized administrative tasks.

TIP ▶ One way to protect the overall integrity of your system is to also restrict the time you use a general admin account. By logging in as a standard user, you'll be prevented from making system-level changes.

MORE INFO ▶ By default, Mac OS X installs five standard Unix system accounts: daemon, nobody, root, unknown, and www. Refer to the Apple Developer Web site for further explanation: http://developer.apple.com/internet/security/securityintro.html.

Account Management

Normal users can access the Accounts pane of system preferences only to modify their own account information, whereas admin users are able to change options for every user and can create or delete accounts. Standard account preferences include Password, Picture, and Parental Controls. If you're modifying the account you're using, you can also manage Login Items through this preference pane.

NOTE ▶ The Parental Controls pane is new to Mac OS X 10.4. It replaces and extends the previous Limitations feature in earlier versions.

Login Options

Administrators can access Login Options to specify a default account or define the appearance of the login screen. You can increase security by requiring each user to enter a user name and password to control use of the system, and if you need to track activity, you will be able to isolate events to individual accounts. You can also use Login Options to activate Fast User Switching.

Fast User Switching enhances multiuser support because it allows two or more individual accounts to be active on a single system at the same time. For your optimized Final Cut Pro station, it's best not to enable this feature to prevent active processes in other accounts from affecting the performance of FCP.

> **MORE INFO** ► Refer to Mac Help for further information on how to create accounts, manage multiple users, enable root access, and specific login options.

Working with Permissions

Unix systems use a model that is based on the concept of *permissions* to control access to individual files. Every single file and folder in Mac OS X has an associated set of permissions. They are used to define which users can open, modify, and save files.

Understanding Permissions

In Unix systems, there are three different kinds of permissions:

► Read (r) permission is required to open and read the contents of a file or directory.

► Write (w) permission is required to modify and save changes to a file or directory.

► Execute (x) permission is required to launch an application or search a directory.

You can apply different sets of permissions to each file to control access separately for three distinct Unix entities:

▸ *Owner* refers to the user who created the file. Any file a user creates should list the user as the owner.

▸ *Group* provides an efficient means of administrating similar user accounts and assigning shared permission profiles.

▸ *Others* represents a catch-all category that encompasses any user who is not the owner or a member of a recognized group.

> **MORE INFO** ▸ Refer to the Apple Developer documentation for further information on Unix file systems and permission models: http://developer. apple.com/documentation/MacOSX/Conceptual/BPFileSystem/index.html.

In total, there are nine separate permissions for each file: read, write, and execute for owner, group, and other. They are traditionally represented as *triplets* in the command-line environment. You can view the permissions of any file in a directory by using the ls command.

1 Launch Terminal (/Applications/Utilities/).

2 Type the command ls at the command prompt and press Return. The list command generates a list of files in the current directory.

> **NOTE** ▸ The default location for all Terminal sessions is the user's Home directory. If you need to return to the Home directory at any time, type the command cd and press Return. If you use the change directory command and do not specify a directory, you automatically navigate to your current Home directory.

3 Type ls –a, and press Return to list all the files, in a directory, including those whose names begin with a period (.) and are normally hidden in the Finder.

4   Type the command ls –l, and press Return to generate a long-form list.
With this command, you are able to view more information about the files
in a directory, including owner, group, and permissions.

drwx——— 4 FCPeditor staff 136 Jun 17 01:14 Desktop

drwx——— 4 FCPeditor staff 136 Jun 17 00:53 Documents

drwx——— 20 FCPeditor staff 680 Jun 19 10:14 Library

drwx——— 3 FCPeditor staff 102 Jun 17 00:49 Movies

drwx——— 3 FCPeditor staff 102 Jun 17 00:49 Music

drwx——— 4 FCPeditor staff 136 Jun 17 00:49 Pictures

drwxr-xr-x 4 FCPeditor staff 136 Jun 17 00:49 Public

drwxr-xr-x 5 FCPeditor staff 170 Jun 17 00:49 Sites

The first character in a long file listing represents the type of item. A
hyphen (-) represents a standard file, a d indicates a directory (folder),
and an l identifies a symbolic link, or alias. The next nine characters represent the file permissions. The r, w, and x abbreviations represent read,
write, and execute, respectively, and are grouped together to indicate
which permissions are granted to the owner, group, and others.

NOTE ▶ Mac OS X 10.4 includes support for Access Control Lists (ACL),
which expand the way permissions work beyond standard Unix configurations. An ACL offers a more flexible solution to working with permissions. For example, ACL allows for individual files to have more than one
owner and for each owner to be assigned unique permissions. Refer to
John Siracusa's extensive review of Mac OS X 10.4 for further information
on how Access Control Lists work: www.arstechnica.com/reviews/os/
macosx-10.4.ars/8.

Changing Permissions Using the Finder

There may be occasions when you want to change file permissions. For example, you might want to allow non-admin users to share FCP plug-ins or LiveType effects. You may also need to modify permissions on Final Cut Project files you receive as email attachments. Mac OS X follows general Unix principles and allows users to modify permissions of any file or folder in the Finder by using the Info window.

1   In the Finder, choose Go > Go To Folder (Shift-Cmd-G).

2   Type */Library/Application Support/* and click Go.

3   Select the LiveType folder and choose File > Get Info (Cmd-I).

4   Click the Ownership & Permissions disclosure triangle to reveal the You Can pop-menu, and click the Details triangle to view the complete permissions profile.

5   Click the Lock icon to activate the Owner pop-up menu.

6   Choose your admin account from the Owner pop-up menu.

> **TIP** ▶ The Finder may not reflect changes immediately. Log out and log back in to see modifications in effect.

7   Choose Read And Write from the Others pop-up menu.

8   Click the Apply To Enclosed Items button to modify the permissions of the LiveType folder and subdirectories.

9   Close the Info window.

Changing Permissions Using the Terminal

You can also change permissions directly in the Terminal.

1   In the Finder, choose Go > Go To Folder (Shift-Cmd-G).

2   Type */Library/Application Support/* and click Go.

3   Open a new session in the Terminal.

4   Type sudo chmod -RP 766. This command will override your usual permissions and allow you to make changes to a system-owned directory. The chmod, or change mode command, allows you to set new permissions, and the RP option sets a recursive action to change subdirectories while ignoring symbolic links. 766 represents the new permissions numerically.

Decimal Number	Permission	English Translation
0	---	No permissions
1	--x	Execute only
2	-w-	Write only
3	-wx	Write and execute
4	r--	Read only
5	r-x	Read and execute
6	rw-	Read and write
7	rwx	Read, write, and execute

NOTE ▶ The sudo command lets you act as though you are a superuser. Use it with extreme caution.

5 Drag the LiveType folder into the Terminal.

The directory path appears after your command.

6 Press Return and enter an admin Password.

7 Type ls -l and drag the LiveType folder into the Terminal. All the directories should have rwxrw-rw- permissions.

drwxrw-rw- 15 root admin 510 May 11 10:53 Effects

drwxrw-rw- 14 root admin 476 May 26 11:24 Images

drwxrw-rw- 3 root admin 102 May 6 2003 LiveFonts

drwxrw-rw- 2 root admin 68 May 6 2003 LiveType Data

drwxrw-rw- 4 root admin 136 May 26 11:24 Movies

drwxrw-rw- 9 root admin 306 May 6 2003 Objects

drwxrw-rw- 10 root admin 340 Apr 18 2004 Templates

drwxrw-rw- 11 root admin 374 May 6 2003 Textures

8 Type exit and press Return to end the session. Every user should now be able to share LiveType Effects and other media using the top-level LiveType directory.

Repairing Permissions Using Disk Utility

Occasionally, permissions may be set inappropriately, creating inconsistencies in your system. Most of the time this will occur when an installer has made modifications to the system; you should not need to *repair* permissions frequently. If you find that you need to fix permissions regularly, you should review your practices to see if you can isolate the root cause of the problem.

> **MORE INFO** ▶ Some prefer the use of the terms *restoring*, or *resetting*, permissions. Refer to John Gruber's article on Software Update procedures at www.daringfireball.net/2004/12/software_update.

1   Launch the Disk Utility application (/Applications/Utilities).

2   Select a Mac OS X volume.

    If the Permissions buttons are dimmed, you have selected a volume that has no Mac OS X system installed. You can repair permissions while booted to the Mac OS X system partition, unlike with Disk Repair, which you cannot use when you are booted to the partition in question.

3   Click the Repair Disk Permissions button.

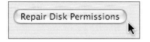

Permissions repair doesn't alter critical directory information; it just resets the Apple-installed files and folders permissions to what they should be for the system to operate at peak efficiency. So, don't worry about Repair Disk Permissions upsetting your personal files' permissions because it affects only Apple-installed files and folders.

> **MORE INFO** ▶ For more information on this subject, consult Apple's Troubleshooting Permissions Knowledge Base document: http://docs.info.apple.com/article.html?artnum=106712.

Repairing Permissions Using the Terminal

You can also run the repair permissions process directly from the command line.

1   Launch the Terminal (and log in as an admin user if necessary).

2   At the prompt, enter the command diskutil repairPermissions / and press Return.

3   When the process is complete, type exit to log out.

Manage Software Updates

There are many reasons to update your software, including access to new features, compatibility requirements, bug fixes, and security patches. If you're working with a range of hardware and software solutions, there's a lot to keep track of. To maintain your station most effectively, you need to develop strategies around updates to preserve performance and protect the overall integrity of your system.

Before you install anything new, spend some time researching a particular update. Things to consider include features of the update—confirm that it will address your needs; specific system requirements—check that the update is intended for your system; and compatibility issues—make sure the new software, especially any third-party solutions, supports your system. You should also ask yourself why you're installing the software—is it to enhance general performance, for security, or to fix a problem with your current software? If you're in the middle of a project, do you need the update to be able to continue? Do you have time to troubleshoot any problems that may arise? Have there been any reports of issues regarding an update? You need to be well informed to properly weigh the benefits and costs before you make a decision.

> TIP   Although there are valid reasons why you might need to update your system in the middle of a project, especially if an update should resolve an issue, it's generally a good idea to plan major updates when there's nothing critical on your system.

Once you have decided to install new software, the next step is to make a complete backup of the system and all your important files.

> **NOTE** ▸ You can create a disk image to back up your files using Mac OS X Disk Utility application.

Applying Updates

The Software Update feature in Mac OS X helps you manage updates by reporting new or revised software and providing descriptions about its purpose. By default, Software Update regularly performs an automatic check for new and updated Apple-distributed software via your computer's Internet connection. This is great for keeping you informed of the latest releases, but to be in complete control of your system, you should deactivate automatic checks in your system preferences and perform updates manually.

> **TIP** ▸ It's common practice amongst some Mac users to repair permissions before installing new software. In terms of software installation, unless you require atypical permission settings, repairing permissions shouldn't create problems.

1   In the System Preferences window, click the Software Update icon.

> **TIP** ▸ You can also use the Software Update shortcut in the Apple menu; you no longer need to navigate through system preferences.

2   Click the Check Now button.

If new software is available, a separate Software Update window opens to display a list of the software it has found.

3 Use the check boxes to select which updates you would like to download.

> **TIP**▶ You can instruct Software Update to disregard certain updates by choosing Update > Ignore Update or by pressing Delete on the keyboard. If you need to reinstate updates, select Software Update > Reset Ignored Updates.

4 Choose Update > Download Only to download the selected updates to the Packages directory in your top-level Library folder. When you want to install the update, double-click the package and follow the online instructions.

You could click the Install Now button to download and install the software automatically, but the download option is useful if you want to apply updates strategically, archive installer packages, or use tools such as Apple Remote Desktop to distribute updates to other computers.

> **NOTE** ▶ Sometimes the most recent update does not appear in the Software Update window—usually because you need to download and install another, incremental component before others become available. So, performing a further check after you have completed an update is usually a good idea.

Tracking Updates

If you disable the automatic update feature by unchecking the Check For Updates check box, you can keep track of the very latest announcements several ways. One of the most convenient methods is through RSS. You can subscribe to RSS feeds using Safari 2.0, which is included with Mac OS X 10.4 RSS, or by using dedicated news aggregators like NetNewsWire (www.ranchero.com/netnewswire), NewsFire (www.newsfirerss.com), or NewsMac (www.thinkmac.co.uk/newsmac).

An increasing number of sites use RSS, including Apple, which provides two feeds to keep you notified of the latest system and video software:

▶   Mac OS X—http://docs.info.apple.com/rss/macosx.rss

▶   Video—www.apple.com/main/rss/downloads/video.rss

> **MORE INFO** ▶ Refer to the Apple Web site for more information on Safari and RSS: www.apple.com/macosx/features/safari.

Perform Maintenance Tasks

Unix systems are designed to be as robust and as self-sufficient as possible. Alongside security and management features, Unix also utilizes a series of maintenance tasks. These tasks, commonly referred to as cron jobs, are scheduled to run automatically at regular intervals. Technically, cron is a term used to create any previously scheduled task, but in this context, it tends to mean specific procedures, such as rotating system log files and rebuilding system databases.

If your Mac is awake in the early hours of the morning, typically a time when other activity is at a minimum, Mac OS X will perform three differently scheduled processes: daily, weekly, and monthly. If you shut down your computer nightly, you might want to run these tasks manually to keep your system functioning at full capacity.

A number of applications will help you run maintenance tasks, including MacJanitor (http://personalpages.tds.net/~brian_hill/macjanitor.html), Cocktail (www.macosxcocktail.com), and TinkerTool (www.bresink.de/osx/TinkerTool.html).

> **NOTE ▶** Make sure that you download only software that is compatible with your version of Mac OS X.

You can also run each script from the command line in Terminal.

1   Open a new session in Terminal.

2   Type the command sudo periodic daily, press Return, and enter an administrator password when prompted.

3   Once the process is complete, enter the command sudo periodic weekly and press Return.

> **NOTE ▶** Wait for Terminal to ask for the next command. Terminal may take a few minutes for each process, especially if the process has never been run before.

4   Type sudo periodic monthly and press Return to run the final command.

5   Type exit to complete the process.

> **MORE INFO ▶** For more information on maintenance tasks in Mac OS X, see Apple's Knowledge Base article: http://docs.info.apple.com/article.html?artnum=107388.

Monitor System Activity

Mac OS X v10.3 and 10.4 include an application called Activity Monitor, which replaces Process Viewer from earlier versions. With Activity Monitor, you can observe and manage every process that is currently running on your computer, from the essential kernal_task to the less vital iCalAlarmScheduler. By tracking processes, you can see if your system is working exactly as you intend and that nothing is reducing the performance of Final Cut Pro.

1   Open Activity Monitor (/Applications/Utilities).

Activity Monitor provides a range of different information about your system, including the Unix process ID (PID), name, and associated user for every active process, as well as details about the resources each process is currently using.

2   Click the % CPU column heading to sort the list according to which process is making the most demands on the main processor.

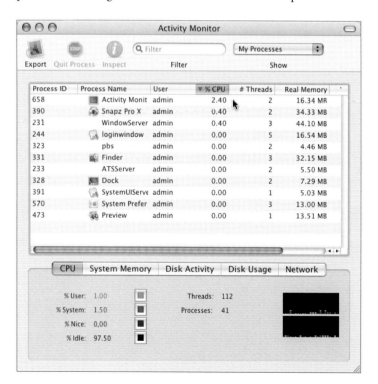

You can click the other headings, search for specific processes, or choose different options from the Show pop-up menu to further sort the processes on your system.

3   Select any process, and click the Inspect icon to see information about that specific process.

    TIP ▶ You can also double-click a process to view the same information.

You can use the Activity Monitor to cancel a specific process that you do not recognize or that you think may be unnecessary.

1   Select a process in the Activity Monitor window.

2   Click the Quit Process icon.

    NOTE ▶ Be careful—quitting some processes may immediately log you out of the system!

3   Read the text in the alert box and choose an appropriate response.

MORE INFO ▶ To further help you identify different processes, Gordon Davisson has compiled a list of some of the most common in Mac OS X: www.westwind.com/reference/OS-X/background-processes.html.

System Preferences Checklist

You'll need to configure Mac OS X whenever you set up a new Final Cut Pro station, to achieve optimum performance. Once you understand how different Mac OS X features affect FCP, it becomes a matter of running through a standard checklist of the various options:

▶ Energy Saver—Set the sleep setting for computer, monitor, and hard disks to Never. Select the option to restart automatically after power failure. Set the processor performance to Highest.

▶ Desktop & Screen Saver—Deactivate the Change Picture and Start Screen Saver options.

▶ Sharing—Turn off All Services, Firewall, and Internet Sharing.

▶ Security—Turn off FileVault and Use Secure Virtual Memory. Make it optional to require a password to wake the computer.

▶ Displays—Use optimal or native resolution for your display, millions of colors, and select a refresh rate of 85 Hz, if applicable, to your display. Disable Automatically Adjust Brightness for PowerBook G4 systems. Do not select Mirror Displays.

▶ Sound—Play alerts and sound effects through internal speakers. Make the output volume high.

▶ Dashboard & Exposé—Modify keyboard shortcuts to avoid conflicts with FCP.

▶ Dock—Select the option to automatically show and hide the Dock.

▶ Software Update—Check for updates manually.

Lesson Review

1. To optimize FCP performance, when should Energy Saver put the computer to sleep?

2. Should you activate FileVault if you want to maximize performance in Final Cut Pro?

3. Does mirroring displays affect the performance of Final Cut Pro?

4. Why might FCP users need to modify the default Exposé and Dashboard keyboard shortcuts?

5. How do you prevent Spotlight from indexing certain areas of your system?

6. What are Smart Folders?

7. Why do you need to copy the Final Cut Pro manuals for Spotlight to index them?

8. What are the three Mac OS X user accounts usually associated with human users called?

9. What are the three standard Unix file permissions that can be given to users?

10. What is the function of the sudo command?

11. What is a PID?

Answers

1. To optimize FCP performance, Energy Saver should never put the computer to sleep automatically.

2. You should not activate FileVault if you want to maximize performance of your system.

3. It is not recommended you mirror displays through System Preferences when you're working with Final Cut Pro, because it will draw too much power from the graphics card. If you need to mirror a display, you should use an external splitter.

4. FCP users may need to modify the Exposé and Dashboard shortcuts because they conflict with default FCP commands.

5. You can prevent Spotlight from indexing specific areas of your system by adding directories to the list under the Privacy tab in the Spotlight preferences pane.

6. Smart Folders are saved Spotlight searches that update dynamically to create a virtual organization system.

7. By default, the manuals are stored inside the Final Cut Pro package, which is not indexed by Spotlight. If you copy the files out of the package to an area that is part of the index, you can perform Spotlight searches of the manuals.

8. The three user accounts typically associated with human users are normal, administrator, and superuser (root).

9. Standard Unix file permissions are read, write, and execute.

10. When you're working at the command line, the `sudo` command lets you work temporarily as superuser (root).

11. Every process in a Unix system is assigned a unique PID, or process ID.

11

Lesson Files Lessons > Lesson 11 Project.fcp

Media Media > Lesson 11-12 Media

Time This lesson takes approximately 90 minutes to complete.

Goals Customize your installation of Final Cut Pro

Understand the various support options available to registered users of FCP

Use various tools to identify and locate all the files associated with Final Cut Pro

Set up Final Cut Pro and optimize your settings to maximize performance

Set preferences and use other techniques to streamline your work

Configuring Final Cut Pro

Once you've set up your hardware and streamlined Mac OS X, the next step is to install, test, and optimize Final Cut Pro. There are many ways to customize the software to better support a particular workflow. Generally, these options are not tied to individual projects, but relate to the overall performance of FCP and behavior of certain tools or functions. Occasionally, you may change some of the settings during a project to facilitate different tasks. In this lesson, you'll learn how to configure Final Cut Pro, test performance, and optimize your setup.

Installing Final Cut Pro

Final Cut Pro ships on multiple discs. But on Mac OS X 10.4 systems, once you've started installing the software, all you need to do is insert discs when prompted. The first disc in the FCP box provides all the files required to install Final Cut Pro 5, LiveType 2, Cinema Tools 3, and Compressor 2. Subsequent discs contain the standard LiveType media elements, including LiveFonts, templates, objects, and textures.

> **NOTE** ▶ The initial disc also includes PDF documentation for all of the FCP applications and an Extras folder that contains LiveType extras, EDL access, head leaders for Cinema Tools, and the DVX-100 Audio Sync tool.

> **NOTE** ▶ If you're installing FCP as part of Final Cut Studio, the process is essentially the same, but you will also have discs for DVD Studio Pro 4, Motion 2, Soundtrack Pro, and various media assets. Users upgrading from Final Cut Pro 4 should note that Soundtrack has been replaced with a new application called Soundtrack Pro, which is only available as a stand-alone application or as part of Final Cut Studio.

Working Through the FCP Installation

Before you install Final Cut Pro, use Software Update as described in the previous lesson so both Mac OS X and QuickTime are completely up-to-date. As with system updates, you should also make sure that you have a current backup of your important data—catastrophes may be uncommon, but if something should go awry, you'll be better able to recover.

> **NOTE** ▶ Final Cut Pro 5 requires Mac OS X 10.3.9 or Mac OS X 10.4 (or later).

The Final Cut Pro installer functions a little differently depending on which version of Mac OS X. New features streamline and consolidate the process on Mac OS X 10.4 systems to make FCP a one-click install. Variations in the way the installer behaves will be noted in the following exercise, but if you require separate instructions for Mac OS X 10.3.9, these are included in your Final Cut Pro documentation.

Custom Installation

If you don't need the complete Final Cut Pro package or require the optional media files—perhaps you're using a PowerBook G4 and don't need to maximize the space on your hard drive—you can easily customize your installation to meet the needs of your workflow.

1   Insert the Final Cut Pro 5 installation disc.

   TIP ▸ Although you can install each Final Cut Studio application one at a time using the independent installers on the individual discs, your serial number probably won't work unless you start with the main installation disc.

2   Double-click the Install Final Cut Pro 5 icon to launch the installer application.

Install Final Cut Pro 5

3   Click Continue to perform a system check.

   This is used to confirm whether your system meets the Final Cut Pro 5 minimum requirements—the installer will only work on supported systems.

This package contains a program that determines if the software can be installed. Are you sure you want to continue?

If you're not sure about the source of this package, click Cancel to prevent it from running the program and installing the software.

Cancel   Continue

> **NOTE** ▸ If you are installing Final Cut Studio, you may find that you can install some applications and not others. For example, some systems may not be able to offer the graphics performance required by Motion 2. In this situation, you should still be able to install the other applications.

4   After you have read the onscreen welcome information, click Continue.

5   If you accept the terms of the Software Licensing Agreement, click Continue and then Agree to continue with the installation.

6   Select the startup disk and click Continue.

> **NOTE** ▸ You need to select your startup disk at this stage even if you ultimately intend to install different components on separate drives.

7   Enter your registration information in the Licensing dialog.

Type the serial number exactly as it is printed on the label. If you're upgrading FCP, the installer will search your system for an earlier serial number. If it doesn't find one, you'll need to enter it manually to continue.

> **NOTE** ▸ If your computer is not connected to the Internet, you'll need to register Final Cut Pro later. You can register products online manually (https://register.apple.com) or mail the registration card included in your FCP box.

8   In the Custom Install window, choose only the applications that you need
for your workflow—for example, if you don't work with film matchback,
you're not required to install Cinema Tools.

NOTE ▶ If you're installing FCP on a Mac OS X 10.3 system, you need to
click Custom Install before you can select individual components.

An item that is checked but dimmed is a required component that *must* be
installed. An item that is dimmed and unchecked cannot be installed
because your system does not meet the minimum system requirements.

TIP ▶ Position the mouse pointer over any unchecked items to reveal
the requirements that are not met.

9   Click the LiveType disclosure triangle to reveal additional items.

NOTE ▶ On Mac OS X 10.3 systems, you need to configure and install
media files in a separate operation.

10   If you want to change where the LiveType media files are stored, click the
LiveType Media folder icon and select a new location to store the files on
your hard drive.

> **TIP** ▶ FCP media files can be stored anywhere on your local system and on external drives. Installing the files on SAN volumes is *not* recommended however—performance will suffer because the files and packets are too small to be managed efficiently. In a multiuser environment, you need to make sure that everyone who requires access to the files has the appropriate permissions. Refer to the section on permissions in the previous lesson for further information.

11 Click Install or Upgrade to begin the installation.

> **NOTE** ▶ It is normal to see the Upgrade button, even if you are installing FCP for the first time. In this context, the Upgrade button appears because the installer has identified at least one file it has in common with the target system.

The installer opens a dialog with a list of all the discs required for the installation.

12 Click Continue Installation.

13 Enter an admin username and password to authenticate the installer, and click OK.

You can track the installation process by watching the progress bar. The installer will prompt you to insert additional discs as they are required until the installation is complete.

> **NOTE** ▶ If you're installing FCP on a system running Mac OS X 10.4, you do not need to click anything outside the installer application. With earlier versions of Mac OS X, you will need to install LiveType media files separately.

> **NOTE** ▶ QuickTime no longer needs to be registered separately. It is now registered automatically as part of the Final Cut Pro 5 or Final Cut Pro Studio installation process.

14 Click Close after the installation is complete.

NOTE ▶ If you have a volume license for Final Cut Pro or Final Cut Studio, disk images can save you time with multiple installations. If you mount the individual images, the installation will progress without the need for you to insert the individual optical discs.

Updating Final Cut Pro

You can download FCP updates through Mac OS X Software Update (as described in the previous lesson). It's generally recommended that you keep your applications current because new versions may have improved feature sets, performance enhancements, and increased stability. On a high-end system, it's important to make sure your third-party software and hardware support the update before you apply it.

NOTE ▶ Occasionally, you'll encounter an update for Pro Application Support, which is used to unify features, functionality, and interface components among Apple's professional applications.

Final Cut Pro Support

There's a vast array of resources to support FCP users from Apple as well as the wider community. You can reference a number of useful tools directly within the application. From the Help menu in Final Cut Pro, you can access the onscreen user's manual, Final Cut Pro Web sites, and a directory of Apple Certified Training Centers. On the Apple Web site, you will find links to educational information, discussion boards, external Web sites, regional user groups, third-party products, and a list of Apple Certified Pro Users around the world.

> **TIP ▶** In the previous lesson, you learned how to create copies of the FCP user's manual so it could be indexed by Spotlight. If you open the manual via the Final Cut Pro Help menu, you will open the original files inside the FCP package.

AppleCare provides three primary tiers of official support for Final Cut Pro: Knowledge Base (KB) articles, telephone support, and a service called Professional Video Support.

AppleCare Knowledge Base

KB articles are freely available in the Support section of Apple's Web site. If you want to access the site through FCP, make sure you're connected to the Internet, then choose Help > Final Cut Pro Support to open the home page of Apple's FCP Support site in your default Web browser.

> **NOTE ▶** If your editing system is not connected to the Internet, meaning you cannot access the site through FCP, you can use any Web browser to manually navigate to the same site: www.apple.com/support/finalcutpro.

From the Support home page, you can select direct links to different KB articles, PDF documents, downloads, discussion boards, training facilities, external resources, and information on professional assistance.

AppleCare Telephone Support

Registered users in the United States, Canada, Europe, and Japan are automatically eligible for 90 days of complimentary telephone support from the day they purchased Final Cut Pro. This 90-day service is only intended to provide assistance with fundamental tasks for novice users, such as basic installation, launch, and recovery of FCP.

NOTE ▶ Standard AppleCare coverage varies from region to region. Users in other territories should check their product documentation for details and contact information.

Apple hardware is also covered by AppleCare support. Standard coverage includes the same complimentary 90-day telephone support and also a 1-year limited warranty on parts and services. Purchase of an AppleCare Protection Plan will extend coverage to three years.

AppleCare Professional Video Support

Professional Video Support is a premium package designed for professionals working with high-end systems and any of the Final Cut Studio applications. Subscribers are guaranteed expert email and telephone support 12 hours a day, 7 days a week for 1 year. Services cover Apple hardware integration in addition to software troubleshooting.

Contacting AppleCare

If you telephone AppleCare, be ready to provide them with the following information:

▶   Final Cut Pro Support ID (not to be confused with your serial number), which is included in the information that came with FCP

▶   The specific model of your computer

▶   The version of Mac OS X currently installed on your system

▶   How much RAM is installed in your system

TIP ▶ You can locate more detailed information about your computer and software using Apple System Profiler. (Go to Applications/Utilities/ System Profiler or click the More Info button in the About This Mac window.)

▶ The specific version of Final Cut Pro on your system (In FCP, choose Final Cut Pro > About Final Cut Pro)

▶ The amount of memory assigned to FCP (In FCP, choose Final Cut Pro > System Settings and click the Memory & Cache tab)

▶ The make and model of any third-party hardware components installed in your system

▶ The name and version of any third-party plug-ins or other software you're using in conjunction with FCP

MORE INFO ▶ See the Apple Service and Support Guide document that came with FCP for further details on AppleCare support.

Support Profile

Another way to gather the information AppleCare requires about your system is to create a support profile. A support profile is an archived collection of text files that provide an exhaustive profile of your system configuration. AppleCare Support may ask you to create a support profile and email it to them to help with troubleshooting your system.

1 In Final Cut Pro, choose Help > Create Support Profile.

2 Choose a location to store the new profile.

3 Click Save.

4 In the Finder, navigate to your new profile.

5 Double-click to open the archive file.

6 Open the ProfileData folder, and use a text editor to view the individual files.

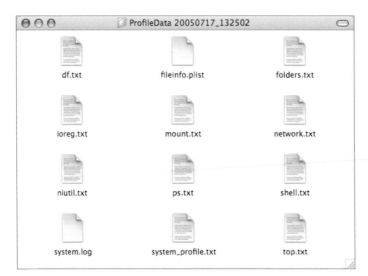

TIP ▶ Support profiles are a great way to compare system configurations, identify issues, and diagnose problems. Rather than examine each file line by line, use an application like TextWrangler (www.barebones.com /products/textwrangler) to automatically compare the differences between documents.

Priming Final Cut Pro

Unlike some turnkey solutions, Final Cut Pro provides a flexible software environment and is able to support a wide variety of hardware solutions and accommodate a diverse range of tasks. In order to create the optimum conditions for your specific workflow, you need to set up FCP to take the best advantage of your system's resources. In this section of the lesson, you'll learn how to set scratch disks, manage the way memory is allocated, adjust real-time performance, and configure audio outputs.

Assigning Scratch Disks

Scratch disk is a generic term used to identify space on a hard drive for temporary, rather than permanent, data storage. When you're working with Final Cut Pro, media files, caches, and the Autosave Vault are all considered transient—you work with them on individual projects and then clear space ready for the next. You can create a scratch disk on a separate physical drive, a partition, or a combination of both. Usually, when you're setting up a high-end system, you should use different locations to optimize performance. All you need to do is tell FCP exactly where to put your files.

Setting the Primary Scratch Disk

You can't actually run Final Cut Pro without a designated scratch disk—you're prompted to choose the default location when you launch the application for the very first time. Once you set your scratch disks, that information is stored in your FCP preference files. Whenever you trash the preference files everything will be reset to the initial settings the next time you launch FCP.

> **TIP** ▶ To prevent problems during capture, use distinctive names for your drives—use dissimilar combinations such as Alpha and Beta, Artoo and Threepio, or Murch and Schoonmaker rather than Media and Media 1. Unless you're working with Xsan and shared storage, you should be able to change the names of your partitions or disks without reformatting. You can also assign names in Disk Utility when you initially set up your drives. Refer to Apple's Web site for further details: http://docs.info.apple.com/article.html?artnum=36726.

1   In the Finder, choose Go > Go to Folder (Cmd-Shift-G).

2   Enter the path */Users/*(username)*/Library/Preferences/* and click the Go button.

3   Drag the Final Cut Pro User Data folder to the Desktop.

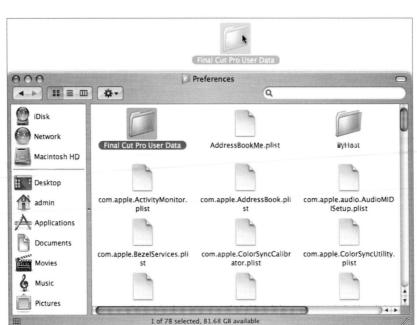

If you've already been working with FCP on your system and want to pre-serve your setup, switch to a separate user account or take other steps to back up your Final Cut Pro preferences. The next time you launch FCP, it will be as though you are doing so for the first time. Quit Final Cut Pro and drag the folder back into your Preferences folder once you've completed the exercises.

NOTE ▶ You could use an application like FCP Rescue 5 (www.apple. com/downloads/macosx/video/fcprescue.html) to first back up and then trash your existing preferences.

4   Launch FCP.

5   Choose the format you work with from the Setup For pop-up menu to assign default project settings.

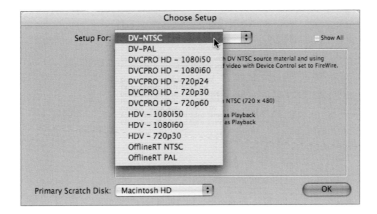

6   Click OK.

By default, FCP 5 creates the primary scratch disk directory in the User Documents folder.

NOTE ▸ If your deck is not connected, and you see the External A/V window, click Continue.

7   Open your Scratch Disk folder in the Finder.

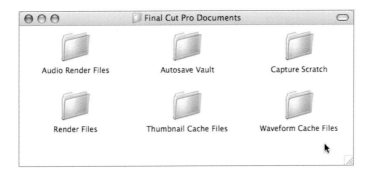

Inside you should see a Final Cut Pro Documents folder, and inside that several more subdirectories. This is how FCP separates and structures your files.

Resetting Scratch Disks

Unless you're working on a system with a single local hard drive, you'll need to change the default location of your scratch disks to specific media directories. Occasionally, you might also encounter a Missing Disk alert, which means at least one of your scratch disks is offline and needs to be reconnected or reset. The process of setting scratch disks in both cases is identical.

> **NOTE** ▸ Select an area on your media drives, or designate an area on your startup disk if no other drives are available. If you are working with a SAN solution, do not create the scratch disk at the root level of your network drive. Refer to the Xsan lesson in this book for further details

This exercise involves deleting your Scratch Disk folder, after which you will not be able to retrieve its contents.

1   Choose Final Cut Pro > Quit (Cmd-Q).

2   Drag your Scratch Disk folder to the Trash and choose Finder > Empty Trash.

3   Launch FCP again. The Missing Disks window will open to alert you to the lost scratch disk.

4   Click the Reset Scratch Disks button.

5   Click the Set button next to the missing disk.

6   Create a new folder to use as your scratch disk, and click Choose.

7   Click OK to confirm your selection.

8   Click Continue to open FCP.

Assigning Separate Media Scratch Disks

Unless you're working with low-resolution media, or editing on a PowerBook G4, when you're creating and optimizing a high-end system the optimal place to store media is on a fast, dedicated hard drive. (Refer to Lesson 9 and Lesson 15 to review the different options for storage and Xsan implementation, respectively.) You can set up to 12 separate scratch disks for your media files at once, and separate video from audio and captured files from rendered files. FCP always uses the disk with the most space first and moves onto the next one only when the original is full.

1   In FCP, choose Final Cut Pro > System Settings (Shift-Q).

2   Click the first unassigned Set button under the Scratch Disks tab.

3   Create a new folder and click Choose.

4   Select the check boxes under Video Render and Audio Render for the new scratch disk.

5   Click to deselect the Video Render and Audio Render check boxes under the previous scratch disk.

> **NOTE ▶** One disk must always be active, so you need to activate the second scratch disk before you disable the first.

TIP ▶ With local drives, you can set scratch disks based on performance. Slower, smaller drives might be sufficiently powerful for audio files, which means your faster, larger drives can focus on video files. Individual drives have two basic operations—read and write—and with some configurations, you can optimize performance by using separate drives for capturing and rendering media. When you are rendering, the computer must read captured media and write the render files. If you divide these tasks between drives, you reduce seek time and improve data flow.

6   Enter a value appropriate for your hard drives in the Minimum Allowable Free Space On Scratch Disks field.

   NOTE ▶ Performance decreases when disks are more than two-thirds full.

7   Click OK to save your changes and close the System Settings window.

Managing Waveforms and Thumbnails

By using cache folders, FCP doesn't need to redraw waveforms and create thumbnails. Without the Waveform Cache, FCP would constantly need to analyze audio files and create a new picture of the sound. Similarly, without the Thumbnail Cache, FCP would access video files and create preview images all the time. Storing and reusing the images files in this way is much more efficient because FCP is relieved from the task of re-creating a waveform or thumbnail whenever they are required.

As with media files, your Waveform and Thumbnail Caches need a home. Storing the data on a fast media drive may mean that your system can access them quicker, but it also means that your dedicated drive is no longer focused on its primary task, which may slow performance. In a later lesson on Xsan integration, you will learn that you *should not* store your cache folders on Xsan volumes. Storing the cache files on a local drive, including your startup disk, will not trouble most systems, but because the cache files are not project specific, nor is there need to back up the data, you *should not* store them in your projects directory.

1   In the System Settings window (Shift-Q), click the Set button for the Waveform Cache.

2   Select an area to create your cache and click Choose.

3   Click the Set button for the Thumbnail Cache.

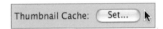

4   Select an area to create the cache and click Choose.

5   Click OK to save your changes.

In the event that either your Waveform or Thumbnail Cache becomes corrupt, simply delete the individual directories in the Finder. The next time you launch Final Cut Pro, the cache folders will be re-created.

NOTE ▸ Because FCP uses the Waveform and Thumbnail Caches to keep track of data, their sudden absence can cause unpredictable behavior. You should always quit the application before you delete them.

The way data is stored in the two cache folders is quite different. There are only two files in the Thumbnail Cache: a Cache file and Data file, which contain the current information about *all* open projects and sequences. In the Waveform Cache, each clip acquires a unique file, and the cache folder may contain many hundreds of files, including some from projects that are no longer current.

One way to improve all-around performance is to reduce the number of thumbnails and waveforms you're working with.

1 Open the **Lesson 11 Project.fcp** file.

2 In the Browser, double-click the *RT Video Performance* sequence.

3 Choose Sequence > Settings (Cmd-0) and click the Timeline Options tab.

4 Choose Name from the Thumbnail Display pop-up menu to remove thumbnails from your clips in the Timeline and maximize performance.

▶ Name Plus Thumbnail is the standard setting used to display a single thumbnail image at the head of each clip.

▶ The Filmstrip setting transforms the appearance of each clip into thumbnails. The number of thumbnails is determined by the current zoom setting. At maximum zoom, you'll be able inspect each frame in the Timeline, but the extra processing required to create and manage thumbnails for every frame will reduce performance.

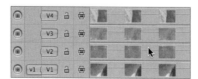

5 Click OK to apply your change to the open sequence.

6 Open the RT Audio Performance Sequence.

7 Choose Show Audio Waveforms from the Timeline Display pop-up to toggle waveform display on and off.

Remember to turn off waveforms to maximize performance.

TIP ▶ You can also activate filmstrip display by using the Timeline Display pop-up. However, when you use this method to select Show Video Filmstrips in the Timeline window, you'll revert to default Name Plus Thumbnail setting.

8 Click the Timeline Track Height (Shift-T) buttons to view the waveform at different sizes.

9 Use the zoom controls to enlarge details of the waveform.

NOTE ▶ You can create new default settings that will be applied to all new sequences under the Timeline Options tab in User Preferences (Option-Q).

Create the Autosave Vault Folder

The Autosave feature of Final Cut Pro provides a level of protection for your project files. By default, once you've saved and named a project, FCP will automatically save a copy of the project at predefined intervals. What this means is that should something untoward happen to your project file, and it is rendered unusable, you have the option of *reverting* to a version in the Autosave Vault.

Each file in the Autosave Vault is an exact copy of your project, with a change to the filename, which is appended with a timestamp to indicate the moment the backup was created. By naming files sequentially in this way, FCP can store multiple versions of your project and give you the option of recovering different stages in your edit.

> NOTE ▶ Despite all its benefits and functionality, you should use the Autosave Vault to augment your manual backup routine rather than replace it.

Setting up your Autosave Vault is a two-step process: specifying the location and setting the interval between each save and the number of iterations to be kept.

1   Choose Final Cut Pro > System Settings (Shift-Q).

2   On the Scratch Disks tab, click the Autosave Vault Set button.

3   Navigate to an appropriate location on your system to create the Autosave Vault directory, and click the Choose button.

> NOTE ▶ As with the cache folders, the Autosave Vault *should not* be stored on a SAN volume.

4   Click OK to save your changes and close the System Settings window.

5   Choose Final Cut Pro > User Preferences (Option-Q).

6   Make sure the Autosave check box is selected.

7   Enter a value in the Save A Copy Every field to specify how often your project should be saved to the Autosave Vault.

The default value of 30 minutes is usually appropriate; it provides enough time for the project to have changed significantly. You'll notice a brief interruption every time your project is saved. Increase the space between saves if this feels invasive.

8   Enter a value in the Keep At Most field.

This value determines how many copies of an individual project will be archived at any one time in the Autosave Vault—the maximum is 99.

Once the limit has been reached, FCP simply moves the oldest project to the Trash to create room for new files.

9   Enter a value in the Maximum Of text field to specify how many individual projects you want keep backups for at any one time.

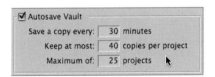

How many you'll find useful depends on your workflow. The default value of 25 may be too high for single-user systems, but may not be enough if the system is shared between several editors.

As the Autosave Vault fills up, FCP will manage the space by removing the oldest projects to make way for new ones.

10 Click OK to save your changes and close the User Preferences window.

TIP▶   Even with Autosave enabled, you should continue to manually save your project at regular intervals.

Now that you have created the Autosave Vault, you need to be able to retrieve your projects. In Lesson 12, you'll learn how to use the Restore feature to select and open archived projects.

Managing Memory Resources

One way to maximize performance in FCP is to limit the use of virtual memory by Mac OS X. The first step is to make sure that you have enough RAM installed in your system to support your workflow. Then you can use memory management features in Final Cut Pro to allocate memory, as it is required.

Memory and Cache Settings

Memory resources are configured using the Memory & Cache tab of the System Settings window. When you change the settings, you should choose values based on the needs of your workflow and customize settings for specific tasks—every time you assign more RAM to one feature, you'll reduce the amount allocated to other areas.

1   In the System Settings (Shift-Q) window, click the Memory & Cache tab.

2   Drag the Application slider under Memory Usage to set the percentage of available RAM Final Cut Pro should use.

How much RAM is available to FCP is determined by the amount Mac OS X and other applications are using. The minimum amount is 125 MB. If the amount of available RAM dips below that threshold, you will be unable to select the Application slider. Reduce the number of active applications or install more RAM to increase the amount you can assign.

NOTE ▶ If you have more than 4 GB of RAM installed in your system, you might wonder why you cannot assign more RAM to FCP. The current version is not able to address as much as that yet. However, you should experience increased performance when you're engaged in round-trip workflows where you have additional applications open at the same time as FCP; they will be able to make use of the additional RAM.

3   Drag the Still Cache control to set how much of the available RAM should be allocated to real-time playback of still images.

    The more RAM you make available to the cache, the more still frames your system will be able to play in real-time. This means that you can adjust the way FCP manages still image performance based on your work-flow, increasing real-time playback for some projects and reducing for others to make more memory available for other tasks.

4   Enter a value in the Disk field under Thumbnail Cache to set the maxi-mum size of the cache. Increase the size if you like to work with large icons in the Browser, or if your project contains lots of clips and you want to display thumbnails.

5   Type a value in the RAM field to set the amount of RAM you want to allocate to thumbnail images. Increase the amount if you scrub through thumbnails a lot and need to improve performance.

6   Click OK to save your changes and close the System Settings window.

Levels of Undo

Final Cut Pro can support up to 99 levels of undo; the default is 10. The ability to undo actions is definitely useful—it's great to experiment and try things out—but working with a lot of levels can quickly become unwieldy. Final Cut Pro also needs to store each change you make to your project in case you want to step back; too many levels of undo will begin to affect system performance.

Zero levels of undo would make the least demands on your system, but it's likely to interfere with your ability to work effectively. To optimize performance, limit the number of undo levels to something practical—a setting that you actually use regularly—and integrate other tools, such as Revert and Restore, or techniques, such as incremental saves. At a certain point, creating new versions of your sequences becomes more efficient than testing ideas and undoing a multiple series of steps. The Autosave Vault and the Revert feature—both of which are covered in the next lesson—can also help you recover earlier versions of your project.

Recent Clips

The List Recent Clips preference controls the number of clips that appear in the Viewer's Recent Clips pop-up menu. The default value is 10 clips, and the maximum is 20. As with levels of undo, the way you work should guide your choice. FCP stores information in order to track each clip, so for optimum performance, you need to find a balance between what's practical and the allocation of system resources.

The only way to reset the Recent Clips pop-up without quitting FCP is to use the List Recent Clips setting in the User Preferences window.

1   Click the disclosure triangle next to the Video Clips bin in **Lesson 11 Project.fcp.**

2   Open the DV-NTSC bin and double-click one of the clips to open it in the Viewer.

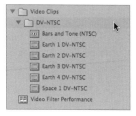

3   Double-click another clip to open it in the Viewer and then repeat to open two more clips.

4 Click the Recent Clips pop-up menu, which is already populated with your first two clips.

5 Choose one of the clips to load it back into the Viewer.

6 Load more clips into the Viewer to further populate the list until you have at least five entries.

7 Choose Final Cut Pro > User Preferences.

8 Enter a value of *1* in the List Recent Clips field.

9 Click OK to apply your change and close the User Preferences window.

10 Click the Recent Clips pop-up menu to confirm that it has been reset.

11 Open User Preferences and assign a new value to the List Recent Clips setting.

Establishing Real-Time Performance Levels

Though real-time performance is ultimately determined by your system configuration, the filters you're working with, and the amount of memory currently assigned to Final Cut Pro, a number of tools and strategies can help you make the most of your existing hardware.

Optimizing RT Video Performance

The technology that drives real-time performance in Final Cut Pro is called RT Extreme; it's intended to remove the need to render effects while you edit. There are a range of RT Extreme settings that modify the way FCP will handle video performance. Exactly how you should set up your system depends very much on your hardware and the needs of your particular workflow. If your system is fast enough, you'll be able to play several streams of high-resolution video, or apply a series of high-quality filters, effects, titles, and transitions without affecting your ability to play back your video in real-time. On smaller systems, such as a PowerBook G4, you'll be able to make use of the different quality settings to preview complex edits and effects. You need to understand the different options, and you should test real-time performance to develop a complete profile of the full capabilities of your system.

In the following exercise, you'll configure FCP to display the highest-quality video. Once you've established the extent of your system's capabilities, you can begin to modify each setting to increase real-time performance.

> **MORE INFO** ▶ Not all codecs support playback by RT Extreme. Refer to the Supported RT Extreme Playback Codecs section of the FCP user's manual for additional details.

1   Choose Final Cut Pro > System Settings (Shift-Q), and click the Playback Control tab.

2   Choose Safe from the RT pop-up menu.

The Safe setting guarantees that video will only play at the quality and frame rate you set. If FCP cannot play the video at this setting, you will either have to render or change modes. With the Unlimited setting, you'll increase real-time performance, but FCP may reduce quality and drop frames to play back your video.

3   Choose the High option from the Video Quality pop-up menu.

The differences between the four quality settings are based on discarded pixels and compression algorithms. High quality images are full frame, full resolution; use them if you need to view the best image. Medium and Low quality offer *quarter frame resolution*—they display only every second pixel and scan line. The difference between Low and Medium is based on different decompression techniques; Low is faster, but Medium looks better. The Dynamic setting is new to Final Cut Pro 5; it enables the application to adjust playback quality between High, Medium, and Low as required to sustain real-time performance.

NOTE ▶ Some codecs may only support High and Low settings.

4   Choose the Full option from the Frame Rate pop-up menu.

Use the Full option to play your sequences at the setting you have assigned. The Half and Quarter settings give you the option to reduce the frame rate by half and a quarter, respectively, to increase real-time performance. The Dynamic setting allows FCP to shift between each of the settings to maintain real-time performance as required.

5   Choose Accurate from the Gamma Correction pop-up menu, if it is active.

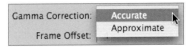

The Gamma Correction menu is only available if your graphics card does not support gamma correction and the CPU handles the work. The Accurate setting will yield the best picture, but it requires more processing and may reduce real-time performance. Use the Approximate option to increase real-time performance, and use Accurate if you need to see the best picture.

6   Click OK to save your changes and close the System Settings window.

> **NOTE ▸** You can also access many of the playback control settings by using the RT pop-up menu in the Timeline window.

> **MORE INFO ▸** See the "Settings and Options in the RT Pop-Up Menu and Playback Control Tab" section of the FCP user's manual for further details on the playback control settings and how they relate to particular workflows.

7   Choose Final Cut Pro > User Preferences (Option-Q).

8   Make sure that the Limit Real-Time Video To check box is not selected.

In some situations, you may want to manage real-time performance by restricting the data rate of video streams—perhaps you're working in a SAN environment or using a PowerBook G4 with a slower hard drive. You can assign a value to place a cap on the data rate using the Limit Real-Time Video option. For the purposes of this exercise, it's important not to impose any limits in order to understand the full capabilities of your system.

9   Confirm that the Report Dropped Frames During Playback check box is selected.

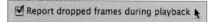

10 Click OK to save your changes and close the User Preferences window.

11 Close any active projects and open **Lesson 11 Project.fcp**.

12 In the Browser, double-click the *RT Video Performance* sequence.

The sequence contains nine overlapping tracks of DV-NTSC video. The first six tracks are visible; the last three are not.

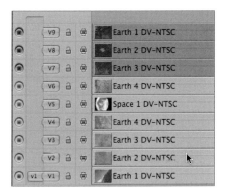

13 Choose View > Loop Playback (Ctrl-L) to toggle on loop playback.

14 Press the spacebar to play the sequence.

If you see a red render bar above your sequence, your system cannot play and scale the six simultaneous streams of DV in real-time. Turn off the visibility of the tracks until the render bar turns dark gray.

TIP ▶ Position the pointer over a colored area of the render bar to see information about the real-time or render status of that section.

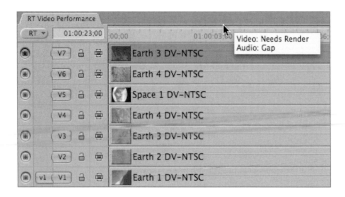

If your system can play the tracks without dropping frames, let the sequence play for a minute or more until you are satisfied that your system can play the video for a sustained period. Turn on the visibility of other tracks in the sequence until you see the red render bar.

Once you've established how many real-time video tracks your system can support at the highest quality settings, you can repeat the test using different configurations to create a complete profile of your system's real-time performance.

Testing Video Filters

The performance of real-time effects is based on your hardware configuration, including CPU speed, RAM, third-party video acceleration, and external playback. It also depends on the video format you're working with, your current RT settings, and which filters you're using. Some video filters require more processing power than others. RT Extreme can also be used to increase real-time performance when you're working with filters to reduce the amount of

rendering you need to do. When you do need to render, there are some steps
that limit the time you spend rendering.

1   Close any open sequences in the **Lesson 11 Project**.

2   Make sure that all of your RT options are set to display the highest quality
settings. (Refer to the previous exercise if you're unsure about which
options to modify.)

3   Choose Final Cut Pro > User Preferences (Option-Q), and click the
Render Control tab.

4   Ensure that the Filters, Frame Blending For Speed, and Motion Blur check
boxes are all selected.

Turning off these options will lower processor-intensive operations through
reductions in the quality of the image, which increases real-time performance. If you deselect Filters, FCP will ignore all filters in your sequences. You
can also prevent FCP from synthesizing in-between frames on speed adjustments by deselecting Frame Blending For Speed. Deselect the Motion Blur
check box to stop FCP from creating motion blur in your video.

NOTE ▶ Unless you're doing an offline edit and require quick renders, set
both the Frame Rate and Resolution pop-up menus to 100% to maximize
quality. Lowering the frame rate or resolution of your render files will
reduce render times but lower the quality of your images.

5   Click OK to close the User Preferences window.

6   In the Browser, double-click the *Video Filter Performance* sequence.

7   Select the clip in the Timeline.

8   Choose Effects > Video Filters > Blur > Gaussian Blur.

If you scroll through various submenus, you'll see that some filters are displayed with a bold typeface, but others are not. Only bold filters will play in real-time at the current settings and configuration.

9   Check that Loop Playback is selected, and press the spacebar to play your sequence.

10   If your sequence plays without dropping frames, repeat steps 7 through 9 until you see the dropped frames warning.

Once you've established how many Gaussian Blur filters you can apply to a clip and still play back a high-quality image in real time, you can duplicate the test with different RT settings and other filters to fully understand how your system performs.

NOTE ▶ When you do need to render, you can use Final Cut Pro's Auto Render feature (located under the General tab in the System Preferences window) to make the most efficient use of your time. With the Auto Render options turned on, your computer will render sequences while you're away from your computer.

Hardware Accelerators

As an alternative to the software-based RT Extreme engine, you can also improve real-time performance by using third-party hardware accelerators.

(Refer to the PCI cards section of the hardware and interfaces lesson for details on individual cards.)

1 Choose Final Cut Pro > System Settings (Shift-Q), and click the Effect Handling tab.

2 Review the list of available codecs and assign a device to the relevant formats using the individual pop-up menus.

NOTE ▸ The list of codecs will vary depending on your specific card.

3 Click OK to save your changes.

Optimizing RT Audio Performance

The Real-time Audio Mixing preference enables you to set the maximum number of individual tracks you can mix in real-time—given the necessary hardware support. Once that limit has been exceeded, you'll need to render your audio before you can play it. By working with this setting judiciously, you'll be able to control the way audio is handled in FCP and reduce or increase performance as your workflow requires.

> **MORE INFO** ▶ See the "Real-Time Audio and Video Options" section of the Final Cut Pro user's manual for specific information about differences between the Audio Playback Quality settings.

As with video performance, simply adding tracks to the Real-time Audio Mixing preference doesn't override the fundamental fact that real-time performance is determined by your hardware and the complexity of your work. Before you embark on a project, you should run some performance tests to fully appreciate how your system performs.

1   In FCP, choose Final Cut Pro > User Preferences (Option-Q).

2   Enter a value of *32* in the Real-time Audio Mixing field.

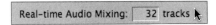

> **NOTE** ▶ The Audio Playback Quality pop-up menu is used to control the way files of different sample rates are converted to match your sequence settings. If all of your audio files conform, audio playback quality should not be an issue. If there is a mismatch, converting the files will use extra processing power and reduce performance in other areas. The Audio Playback Quality setting determines how much work will be required. Refer to the "Mixing Sample Rates" and "Using Real-Time Sample Rate Conversion" sections in the Final Cut Pro user's manual for more information.

3   Ensure that the Report Dropped Frames During Playback check box is selected.

4   Click OK to close the User Preferences window.

5   Choose View > Loop Playback (Ctrl-L).

6   Open **Lesson 11 Project.fcp**.

7 In the Browser, double-click the *RT Audio Performance* sequence.

The sequence contains NTSC bars and tone and 32 tracks of 48 kHz 16-bit audio.

8 Press the spacebar to play the sequence.

If you see the dropped frames warning, your current system configuration does not support real-time playback of this many high-quality audio tracks. Delete a track from the sequence, or click the visibility control to make the track inaudible, and repeat step 8.

If the sequence plays successfully without dropping frames, you know that your system supports at least 32 tracks of high-quality, real-time audio. Insert more audio tracks and add clips from the Audio Clips bin.

Adjust the Real-time Audio Mixing setting in User Preferences and play to test the sequence until you see the dropped frames warning.

As with video performance, once you've determined how many real-time audio tracks your system can support at the High setting, you should repeat the test at different Audio Playback Quality options to develop a profile of your system performance.

Testing Audio Filters

As you begin to apply filters and transitions, real-time performance will be affected by the additional demands they place on your system. You'll see the red audio render bar and hear a series of beeps when FCP needs to render your audio. The Beep When Playing Unrendered Audio check box in the Playback Control tab of System Settings toggles the beeps on and off.

> **TIP** Render video effects and audio filters, or use the Mixdown command, to further optimize real-time performance.

Like video filters, different audio filters require varying amounts of processing power, and they'll affect your system's real-time performance when you work with them. In terms of CPU usage and your system configuration, individual filters can sometimes occupy the equivalent of several real-time tracks.

1   Close any open sequences.

2   Choose Final Cut Pro > User Preferences (Option-Q).

3   Enter a value of *2* in the Real-Time Audio Mixing field. This is the lowest value you can assign.

4   Choose High from the Audio Playback Quality pop-up menu.

5   Click OK to save your changes.

6   In the Browser, double-click the *Audio Filter Performance* sequence.

The sequence contains a DV-NTSC video clip with mono audio

7   Select the clip, and choose Effects > Audio Filters > Apple > AUBandpass
to apply the filter.

The render bar over the clip should turn red to indicate that the audio
needs to be rendered before it can be played.

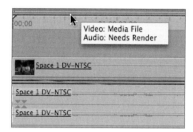

8   Choose Final Cut Pro > User Preferences (Option-Q).

9   Increase the Real-Time Audio Mixing value to 3, and click OK.

10 Repeat steps 8 and 9 until the render bar changes to dark gray and you can
play the clip.

The exact number of real-time tracks the filter requires varies from system to
system. Remove the filter and repeat the test with other individual filters to see
the demands that they will place on your system and how they will affect real-
time performance.

> **NOTE** ▶ If FCP is performing high quality conversions on your audio
> clips, it will also increase the demands on your system and reduce RT
> performance. Use a low quality setting or standardize your files using
> QuickTime Conversion.

Audio Outputs

Depending on your hardware configuration, you may need to customize FCP's Audio Output settings to match your setup and workflow. If you have the appropriate hardware, FCP can output up to 24 discrete tracks of audio. Once you have connected your output device, you assign outputs in either User Preferences (to create universal settings) or Sequence Settings (to define outputs for individual sequences).

> **NOTE ▶** Your audio device must support Core Audio or have a compatible Core Audio driver.

1   Make sure your audio device is connected to your system. (Refer to the hardware and interfaces lesson for information on audio standards, and review Lesson 10 for details on how to set up audio equipment in Mac OS X.)

2   Choose Final Cut Pro > User Preferences (Option-Q), and click the Audio Outputs tab.

3   Click the Duplicate button to create a new preset.

4   Choose the required number of audio channels from the Output pop-up menu.

5   Use the Grouping controls to create discrete or stereo outputs for each pair.

6   Choose a value from the Downmix pop-up menu appropriate to your
workflow.

> **MORE INFO** ▸ Refer to the "Downmixing Multiple Audio Channels to a
> Stereo Mix" section in the FCP user's manual for further details.

7   Assign this new preset a name in the Name field before clicking OK to
create the preset..

8   Confirm that your new preset is selected under the Audio Outputs tab.

9   Click OK to apply your changes and close the window.

Working Efficiently with Final Cut Pro

Among the many ways to work with FCP, there isn't really any one way that's
intrinsically superior to any others—most are a matter of habit and what feels
comfortable to you. You need to know what your options are though; you may
find some features will help you be more efficient or enable you to handle the
application more fluidly. If you can learn to use these features and incorporate
them into your workflow, you'll find you can optimize your process and use
your time more effectively.

Configuring Functional Settings

Many of the tools in Final Cut Pro can be modified and adapted to better meet
your needs. As you experiment and test different settings, you'll discover new
techniques that will enhance your use of the application.

Handling Media

Under the General tab in the System Preferences window are options to help you synchronize independent media sources and determine when you should be alerted about dropped frames.

▶ When you're working with professional equipment that requires a separate audio interface with video genlock input, or audio that needs to be synchronized with video, you need to make sure that the Sync Audio Capture To Video Source If Present check box is selected.

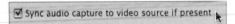

▶ To ensure the integrity of your video files at all times, select the Report Dropped Frames During Playback, Report ETT/PTV On Dropped Frames, and Abort Capture On Dropped Frames check boxes. With these options selected, FCP will issue an alert when frames are dropped while you're capturing or during general editing; and when you're performing the Edit to Tape function or printing to video.

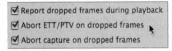

Modifying Editing Tools

A number of settings under the Editing tab in the User Preferences window allow you to alter the default behavior of some of FCP's editing tools.

▶ When your project involves working with still images or creating freeze frames, it's useful to be able to set the default duration. The Still/Freeze Duration setting is especially important if you're importing an animated image sequence and want to be able to import several files at once with a set duration. Once they're imported, you can edit them into your sequence without further need to adjust their duration.

In FCP, *duration* refers to the interval between In and Out points. You can modify the duration of individual clips once they have been imported.

1   Open the User Preferences (Option-Q) window and click the Editing tab.

2   Enter a value of 5 seconds (00:00:05:00) in the Still/Freeze Duration field.

3   In the **Lesson 11 Project.fcp** file, choose File > Import > Folder.

4   Locate the Still Images folder in the Lesson 11 Media directory and click Choose.

5   Double-click the Still Images bin to open a separate bin window.

6   Double-click **Shuttle 001.jpg** to open it in the Viewer.

The image will appear to be squashed because FCP does not yet recognize it is *anamorphic*.

7   Scroll to locate the Anamorphic column in the Browser and click to insert
     a checkmark next to **Shuttle 001.jpg**.

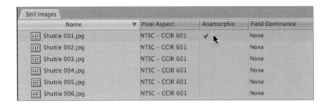

The image should now be displayed correctly in the Viewer.

TIP ▶ You can also select anamorphic display in the Item Properties
window.

Also notice that the default duration is set to 5 seconds, but that this can
be modified by changing the in and out points.

8   Change the name of the bin to Still Images Long.

9   Open the User Preferences window (Option-Q) and click the Editing tab.

10   Change the Still/Freeze Duration value to 1 frame (00:00:00:01) and click
     OK to apply your change.

11 Re-import the Still Images folder and double-click the new Shuttle 001.jpg image to open it in the Viewer.

Note that it has a set duration of 1 frame.

12 Insert checkmarks in the Anamorphic column of the Browser for all of the image files in the new Still Images bin.

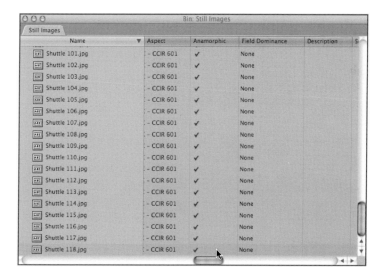

You have to do this manually because QuickTime media files do not currently support embedded anamorphic metadata flags.

13 Hold down the Option key and choose File > New Sequence (Option-Cmd-N).

14 Choose DV NTSC 48 kHz Anamorphic from the pop-up menu and click OK to create the new sequence.

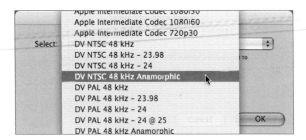

15 Rename the sequence *Stills* and double-click to open it in the Timeline window.

16 Select all the images in the new Still Images bin and drag them into the sequence.

17 Press the spacebar to play.

▶ Because each image has a set duration of 1 frame, the sequence should appear to play like standard video.

▶ If you encounter unrendered frames, you can increase the size of the Still Cache (refer to the earlier section in this lesson for specific instructions) or render the sequence before you can watch all of it.

▶ When you use the Play Around Current control, the number of frames FCP plays before and after the playhead is determined by the Preview Pre-roll and Preview Post-roll settings, respectively. Increase the number of frames to extend the number of frames FCP will play whenever you use this feature.

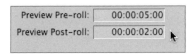

▶ When your workflow involves film matchback or the online will take place in a tape-to-tape suite, the Dupe Detection controls are especially useful. Assign a value to the Handles field to identify frames that may be lost during the negative cut, and enter a Threshold value to require a specified number of duplicate frames be detected before you receive a warning. There are six colors used to indicate individual sets of duplicated frames: red, green, blue, white, black, and purple. If there are more than six instances, the colors are reused.

MORE INFO ▶ See the "Options for Displaying Duplicate Frames" section of the Final Cut Pro user's manual for specific details.

▶ Customize the way tools behave in the Trim Edit window. When you work with dynamic trimming, enabled edit points automatically follow the position of the playhead. The Trim With Sequence Audio option allows you to hear all of the audio tracks in the sequences while you work with the J, K, and L keys. Choose Trim With Edit Selection Audio (Mute Others) to mute everything but the selected audio tracks in a sequence. Enter a new value in the Multi-Frame Trim Size field to change the default length of the multiframe trims you create with the Trim Back and Trim Forward buttons.

▶   By default, whenever you click the visibility buttons in the Timeline, FCP will issue an alert if the change affects render files. Prevent FCP from automatically losing render files whenever you hide tracks by selecting the Warn If Visibility Change Deletes Render File check box.

▶   Modify the way that FCP records keyframes by choosing different options from the Record Audio Keyframes pop-up menu to increase or reduce the number of keyframes the application creates as you adjust the controls.

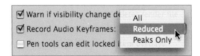

Customizing Default Options

Although Final Cut Pro can adapt to accommodate a wide range of workflows, editors often develop habits or ways of working that suit their needs. If every time you create a new project you find yourself modifying the same settings and preferences, you should modify the default options to better suit your workflow.

Modifying the Interface

▶   Not every column in the Browser will be relevant to your workflow, and different information can be more significant at different points in your project. Ctrl-click the headings to show and hide columns until you have access to the information you require.

As with other elements in FCP you can save customized column layouts. By default, FCP includes standard column and logging layouts. You can also create your own to meet special needs.

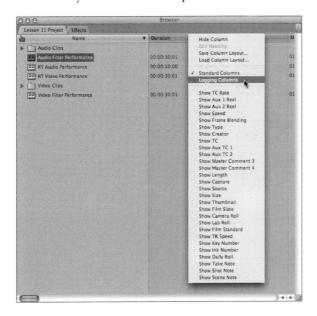

TIP ▶ You can drag individual columns or use the hide and show feature to rearrange the Browser.

▶ New to Final Cut Pro 5 is the ability to modify the text size displayed in the Browser. Open User Preferences (Option-Q) and use the Browser Text Size pop-up menu under the General tab, or Ctrl-click in the Browser and choose a size from the Text Size submenu.

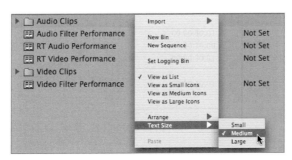

▶ Use labels to color-code items in the Browser. Ctrl-click clips, sequences, or bins, and choose colors from the Label submenu.

Change the meaning of individual labels by using the Labels tab in the User Preferences window.

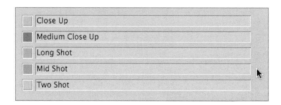

▶ The Timeline Options tab is accessible through the User Preferences window. Use it to change the starting timecode of your sequences, define the default number of tracks in a sequence, and change the way tracks are displayed. This is only for new sequences. Don't forget the sequence settings also.

▶ A lot of editors like to work with keyboard shortcuts. If you find the default commands awkward or are more familiar with a different layout, Final Cut Pro provides tools to remap keys and create your own custom layouts, which you can then share amongst users and systems. To manage shortcuts, choose Tools > Keyboard Layout > Customize (Option-H).

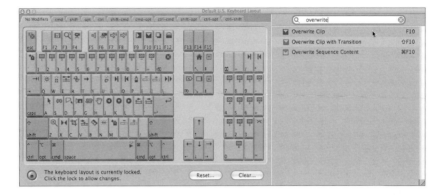

▶ Each window in FCP contains a button bar, to which you can add buttons to create easier access to commonly used functions. Final Cut Pro 5 includes default button layouts for Audio Editing, Media Logging, and Multiclip (choose Tools > Button Bars). You can easily add buttons using the Button List window (Tools > Button List)—simply search for the action you require and drag the button to the button bar you find most convenient.

Streamlining FCP Operations

▶ Final Cut Pro 5 includes a new feature that allows you to designate which directories FCP should search when you're reconnecting media files, which is especially useful when you're working with large SAN volumes. Open the System Settings (Shift-Q) window and click the Search Folders tab to specify which areas Final Cut Pro is to search.

▶ If your workflow involves sharing still images, video, or audio clips with other applications, you can increase the efficiency of your workflow by defining the default external applications you use to modify files. Select the External Editors tab in the System Settings window to choose your preferred solution.

NOTE ▶ Final Cut Pro also includes increased integration with other applications in the Final Cut Studio suite to increase efficiencies in round-trip workflows.

▶ By default, FCP will return to the last open project whenever it is launched. This can be inconvenient if you're working on different large projects, and it takes the application a while for everything to load, or if you're working on a shared system and you have to close someone else's project before you can get to work. Deselect the Open Last Project On Application Launch check box under the General tab of the User Preferences to disable this feature.

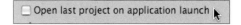

Uninstalling Final Cut Pro

Final Cut Pro 5 doesn't include an automatic uninstall feature, and as with previous versions, you need to delete files manually to completely remove the application from your system.

Identifying Files

The first step is to locate the thousands of files associated with FCP on your system. For the most part, all you need to do is identify the parent directory and remove that from your system rather than delete them one by one. There are a couple of ways to locate the files. The first method requires the FCP installer application, the second the Terminal.

Using the Installer

1   Insert your FCP installer disc.

2   Double-click the Install Final Cut Pro 5 icon to launch the installer application.

3   Click Continue to give the application permission to check your system.

4   After the Installer launches, choose File > Show Files (Cmd-I).

5   Click the disclosure triangle next to Final Cut Pro to see all of the files included with the installer, along with their default locations.

6   Drag to select the list.

7   Choose Edit > Copy (Cmd-C).

8   Open a text editor and paste the list into a new document.

Using the Terminal

1   In the Finder, choose Go > Go To Folder (Shift-Cmd-G).

2   Enter the location */Library/Receipts/FinalCutPro.pkg/Contents.*

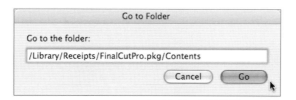

3   Click Go to open the Contents folder.

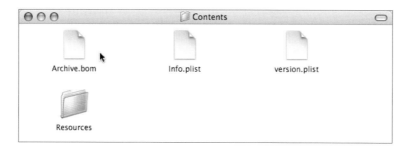

4   Launch the Terminal application (Applications/Utilities).

5   Enter the command lsbom –s.

    The command lsbom lists each of the files inside the bill-of-materials file.

    TIP ► If you do not have permissions to read the file, you can also use
    the command sudo lsbom –s to temporarily give yourself root access. You
    will need an administrator password, and you should take the standard
    precautions associated with the superuser account.

    NOTE ► You can display just the directories by using the command lsbom
    –d. Enter the command man lsbom in the Terminal to access further infor-
    mation about the lsbom command.

6   Type a space and drag the Archive.bom file from the Finder window to the Terminal window.

7   Press Return to view the list.

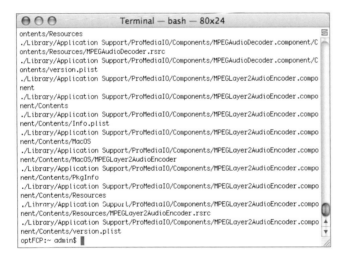

8   Drag to select the list in the Terminal window and choose Edit > Copy (Cmd-C).

9   Open a text editor and paste the list into a new document.

Deleting Files

Before you delete any files, remember that it's a permanent and destructive action. Make sure you're removing only the files you intend to. If you use any of the other Pro applications, be aware that some files are shared between applications.

Use Go To Folder in the Finder to locate the parent directories. Rather than delete each file one by one, analyze your list of files to identify the parent directories, and drag those to the Trash. For example, the Final Cut Pro application (Final Cut Pro.app in the Terminal) and Final Cut Pro Additional Easy Setups directory (Final Cut Pro Additional Easy Setups.localized in the Terminal) both contain many other files.

> **TIP** ▶ You can also use the Unix rm command in the Terminal to permanently delete files. Enter the command man rm to read more about the remove command.

> **MORE INFO** ▶ A list of directories to delete to uninstall Final Cut Pro HD is available on the Apple Web site: http://docs.info.apple.com /article.html?artnum=93811.

Lesson Review

1. Which software should you update before you install Final Cut Pro?

2. What are the names of the three additional applications that come with Final Cut Pro 5?

3. What can you use a support profile for?

4. What does Final Cut Pro use scratch disks for?

5. Should the Final Cut Pro cache files be stored on an Xsan volume?

6. How do you specify a limit on real-time bandwidth?

7. What effect does the new Dynamic setting have on video quality?

8. Why do some audio filters affect real-time performance more than others?

9. What are the default Final Cut Pro 5 button layouts used for?

10. Why is the Handles option useful when you're working with dupe for film matchback?

Answers

1. You should update Mac OS X and QuickTime before you install Final Cut Pro.

2. Cinema Tools 2, LiveType 2, and Compressor 2.

3. To collect the information required by AppleCare or to use as a comprehensive inventory of different systems to compare setups.

4. Final Cut Pro scratch disks are used to store temporary data, such as media files, caches, and the Autosave Vault.

5. Cache files should *never* be stored on an Xsan volume—they are too small for the software to handle efficiently.

6. You can Limit Real-Time Video To a specified data rate in the User Prefrences window under the General tab.

7. To sustain real-time performance, the Dynamic option enables FCP to adjust video playback quality between High, Medium, and Low settings as required.

8. Different audio filters make varying demands on the CPU. Some processor-intensive filters use multiple tracks of real-time bandwidth.

9. The default FCP 5 button layouts are used for audio editing, media logging, and working with multiclips.

10. Handles are used to identify frames that may be lost during the negative cut.

12

Managing Final Cut Pro

Final Cut Pro utilizes a range of different files to support various operations and preserve individual user settings. For day-to-day use, individual projects, specific interchange standards, and media files represent the most visible examples. Preference files, caches, and custom user settings perform functions behind the scenes to support your use of the application and make your workflow more efficient.

In this lesson, you'll learn about directory structures, file locations, and administrative controls. You'll also gain experience with different backup strategies and media management techniques. Developing these skills will help you better organize your projects, and by working with files at both a project and user level, you'll advance your abilities with Final Cut Pro.

Administrating Project Files, Preferences, and User Data

Organizing your workspace is fundamentally important. Effective file management not only enables you to use FCP more efficiently, but because you know what your assets are and where to locate them, it also fosters greater creativity.

Establishing a New Project

Although there may be as many ways to structure and organize an FCP project as there are people working with the application, you can follow some general guidelines to make things easier and more efficient. Generally speaking, you need to keep each project self-contained and separate media assets from other files. Most importantly, your system needs to make sense to everyone who uses it—the best way to do that is to keep it simple.

> **NOTE ▶** Maintaining a defined structure in which you keep individual projects separate will not only help while you are working, as you will learn later in this lesson, it will also make archiving your project easier.

Manual Administration

Manually organizing your files is a matter of creating a centralized, or master, directory on your system and collecting files there. If you spend some time creating a defined set of directories at the beginning of each project, you'll effectively streamline file management tasks.

1   In the Finder, choose File > New Folder (Shift-Cmd-N) to create a new directory on a local drive; this will be where you collect and store all of your Final Cut projects.

The most suitable location for the folder is determined by the requirements of your workflow. Typically, this will be somewhere on your startup disk or a different physical drive you don't use for media storage. If you are the only user who needs to access the project, place it within your

Home directory. However, if more than one user will be working on the project, you can make the folder either at root level or within the Shared folder of the User directory. If you choose to create the folder at the root level, you may need to follow the steps in the lesson on configuring Mac OS X to change the directory's permissions so that other users have *read* and *write* access.

NOTE ▸ The Shared folder in your User directory already has the appropriate permissions assigned by default. Later in this lesson, you'll learn how to use it to share customized user settings with different users.

2   Change the name of the new folder to *FCP Projects*—or something equally appropriate.

3   Create and name a second folder, *Lesson 12*, inside your new FCP Projects folder for this project.

4   Within the Lesson 12 folder, create another subfolder named *Lesson 12 Projects*.

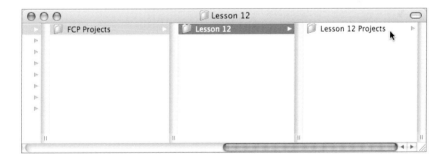

In a real-world situation, each project folder should include separate, appropriately labeled folders for *everything* that relates to a specific project, including non-timecode media (stills, graphics, sound effects, music), schedules, budget information, scripts, correspondence, and miscellaneous notes. If you maintain this strategy, every time you need something you'll know exactly where to find it. Stray files won't float around your system, and your projects will be much easier to archive.

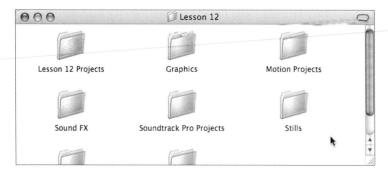

NOTE ▶ You'll notice later in the lesson that FCP actually uses a similar directory structure to organize media files.

TIP ▶ You can further organize project folders by using color labels to identify the most current and highest priority projects. Add project folders to the Finder window's sidebar or to the Dock for easy access.

TIP ▶ You could create a workflow in Automator to perform many of these actions to create new project directories in the Finder.

5   Open FCP, and choose File > Close Project to close any open projects.

6   Choose Final Cut Pro > System Settings (Shift-Q).

7   Under the Scratch Disks tab, confirm that your media directory is correctly selected, and click OK.

> **NOTE ▸** If you need to make any changes to the scratch disk settings, refer to the "Priming Final Cut Pro" section of the previous lesson.

8   Under Final Cut Pro > User Preferences, make sure the Audio Outputs tab is set to the Default Stereo Preset.

9   Choose Final Cut Pro > Easy Setup.

10 Choose the DV-NTSC preset from the Setup For pop-up menu.

11 Click the Setup button to confirm your selection.

12 If everything is correct, choose File > New Project to create a new project.

13 Choose File > Save Project As and name your project Lesson *12 New Project.fcp*.

14 Navigate to your Lesson 12 Projects subfolder and click Save to create your project.

Define a simple and easy-to-remember naming convention for your project files. It's much easier to retrace your steps if everything is clearly and accurately labeled. Implement sequential naming strategies or include the editors' initials in projects when you're working in a team.

> **NOTE ▸** You need to save your project immediately to preserve your settings and allow Autosave to function. Establish a convention early and stick to it. It is common to use the name of the project and the date it was created, which is the model used in the Autosave Vault. Your files do have a timestamp, so you may like to use other descriptive elements. Whatever you decide, keep it simple!

Virtual Organization

If you're used to sorting clips in the Browser in a variety of ways, Spotlight in Mac OS X 10.4 creates similar opportunities for you to organize project files.

One method is to apply a folder action to your project directory and use Spotlight Comments to tag any files you save there. If the files are ever moved or misplaced, you can use a Spotlight search or create a Smart Folder to locate them.

1   Open the Automator application (/Applications/Automator).

2   In the Library column, select the Spotlight icon.

3   In the Action column, double-click the Add Spotlight Comments To Finder Items option.

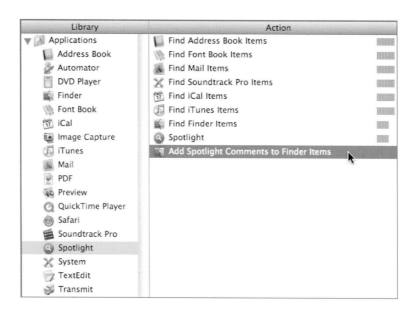

4   Enter *L12Asset* in the action text field, and check the Append To Existing
    Comments check box.

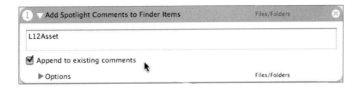

> **NOTE** ▶ It's important when creating a Spotlight Search to use a unique
> and appropriate identifier—something that's specific enough to help
> Spotlight locate only the files you need.

5   Choose File > Save As Plug-in (Option-Cmd-S).

6   Name the action *Lesson 12 Spotlight Comment*.

7   Choose Folder Actions from the Plug-in For pop-up menu.

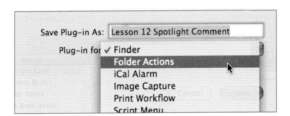

8   Choose Other from the Attached To Folder pop-up menu.

9   Select the Lesson 12 Projects folder you created in the last exercise and
    click Open.

10 Select the Enable Folder Actions check box and click Save to apply the action to the folder.

NOTE ▶ You can apply, disable, or edit folder actions at any time. Simply Cntrl-click the folder you want to modify in the Finder and choose the appropriate option from the contextual menu.

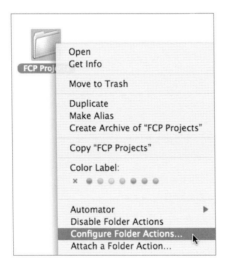

11 Create a new project in Final Cut Pro (File > New Project).

12 Choose File > Save Project.

13 Name your project *Lesson 12 Action Test.fcp*, and save the file in the Lesson 12 Projects folder.

14 Open the Lesson 12 Projects folder in the Finder and select the Lesson 12 Action Test file.

15 Choose File > Get Info (Cmd-I), and your custom tag appears in the file's Spotlight Comments text field.

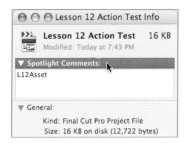

> **TIP** To add the custom Spotlight Comment to files you've already created, simply drag the files out of the Lesson 12 Projects folder temporarily. When you drag them back in again, the comment is added. You could create a stand-alone workflow in Automator to apply the comment to existing files.

You can now use the Spotlight Comment in conjunction with other search criteria and metadata to create customized Smart Folders. For example, you could search by Spotlight Comment and Date Modified to maintain a list of your most current project files. (Refer to Lesson 10 for details on how to work with Smart Folders.)

Protecting and Archiving Projects

Project files embody every aspect of your work in Final Cut Pro. They represent all the time you've invested and the creative decisions you've made. Preserving the integrity of your project files should be one of your priorities—make it part of your daily workflow. Think of project files as precious objects, and be proactive about protecting them. Creating regular, incremental backups of current projects will dramatically reduce your losses in the event of something like a hard drive failure, which could otherwise be catastrophic. Returning to an old project is also quite common, especially with the advent of DVD and other digital distribution technologies. A well-organized archive will be invaluable if you should need to reestablish a project.

Safeguarding your files requires creating backups and secure, permanent archives. There are a number of ways to do this, including using optical media, secondary or portable hard drives, and remote storage. Whichever option you choose, you should make sure that it is a *failover* system with built-in *redundancy*.

The first way to protect your project is to make sure you save it at regular intervals. Whenever you create a new project file, you should immediately save it into your designated project folder. Even though Autosave will begin to function after the first save, you should continue with manual saves and create incremental versions to preserve different stages of your project as it progresses.

The next step in preserving your data is to use co-location, which means you store files in more than one place so that you're not relying on a single device. It could simply mean that you burn your projects to CD or DVD at the end of each session, or you copy files onto a removable drive to take away with you at the end of the day. If you make two copies, you can leave one in a safe or security box at your facility and take the other home with you. A more sophisticated method would be to upload your files to a server in an enterprise class datacenter. Such facilities usually include secure data backup, power regulation, and fire suppression as part of their service.

Deciding which strategy is right for you will depend on your particular circumstances and what you can afford to invest in a backup solution. Ultimately, you may use a combination of strategies—saving to an offsite server and a removable drive, for instance.

Once you have a plan in place, you need to follow through and be consistent in your implementation. If you've organized your project, Mac OS X has tools that can streamline the process of creating and securing your daily archive.

Locking Files

Locking project files will prevent accidental modification or deletion of work you want to preserve. Having locked a file, you'll be unable to make any changes or move it to a different directory, including the Trash.

1   In the Info window, click to select the Locked check box. A lock appears in the file's icon.

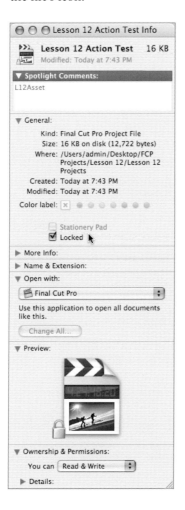

MORE INFO ▸ Locked files in Mac OS X will override Unix file permissions—even if you have write access, you will not be able to modify the file. To unlock a file, you need to deselect the check box in the Info window. Refer to the Apple Knowledge Base article, "Unable to move, unlock, modify, or copy an item in Mac OS X" for additional details: http://docs. info.apple.com/article.html?artnum=106237.

2   Close the Info window.

Back Up to Optical Disc

You can store several hundred megabytes (MB) of data using current CD technology, and several gigabytes (GB) with DVD. The latest version of the Apple SuperDrive supports dual-layer DVD+R discs, which have a capacity of 8.5 GB. With the advent of new high-capacity optical discs, you'll be able to store many times that amount of information on a single disc.

MORE INFO ▸ For further details on new DVD technologies, see http://en.wikipedia.org/wiki/Blue_ray and www.blu-ray.com.

Burn Folders are a new feature in Mac OS X 10.4—they help streamline the process of creating archives on CD or DVD.

1   In the Finder, choose File > New Burn Folder.

NOTE ▸ Project files are relatively small, and it might seem unnecessary to use a new disc every time you back up your work—though you might think of the discs as an additional level of redundancy in your system. If you want to fill each disc, you need to use Disk Utility or third-party applications such as Toast (www.roxio.com/en/products/toast) to burn multisession discs. See "Recording On a CD-R Disc More Than Once" in Disk Utility Help for further information.

2   Name the new folder *Lesson 12 Burn*.

3   Drag the files you want to back up to the new Lesson 12 Burn folder.

Notice the alias arrow appears as you drag the files to the folder. This happens because rather than move or copy files into the Burn Folder, what you add are aliases, which point to the original files on your hard drive. When you burn a disc, the Finder simply copies the files and leaves the originals untouched.

When you've added all the files you want to backup to the folder and are ready to burn a disc, simply Control-click the Burn Folder, or select it in the Finder and choose File > Burn Disk.

NOTE ▸ You should always examine the contents of your discs to test the integrity of the burn, especially if you eventually plan to remove the files from your hard drive.

Backup to Remote Storage

The general principle of remote storage is that you back up your files to a secondary hard drive, which resides at a separate geographic location. There are many solutions you can work with, ranging from portable hard drives (including iPods) that you carry with you, to dedicated datacenters that you access via the Internet.

If you have a .Mac account (www.mac.com), you already have secure online storage on Apple's servers. Uploading files to your iDisk is just like copying files between local disks or partitions. Mac OS X 10.4 introduced a new iDisk Sync feature, which can be configured to make the transfer process completely seamless.

NOTE ► In Mac OS X 10.3, you need to manually mount your iDisk before you can upload files. For Mac OS X 10.2 or earlier versions, you need to download the iDisk Utility (www.mac.com/1/idiskutility_download.html) application or use an FTP client application such as Panic's Transmit. (See Lesson 15 for more information on file transfer solutions.)

1   Open System Preferences, and click the .Mac icon.

2   If you've already established a .Mac account, your information should already be entered in the .Mac Member Name and Password fields under the Account tab.

NOTE ► To continue with the exercise, you need a .Mac account. Click the Learn More button to access the .Mac Web site (www.mac.com) and sign up for a free 60-day trial.

3   Click the iDisk tab, and click the Start button if you haven't enabled iDisk syncing yet.

When you enable syncing, a special iDisk partition is created on your computer.

4   Choose the Synchronize Manually option to control exactly when files are transferred.

NOTE ▶ Your iDisk partition will mount on your Desktop.

5   Close the System Preferences window.

6   In the Finder, choose File > New Window (Cmd-N).

7   In the Sidebar of the Finder window, click the iDisk icon to view its contents.

8   Select the Documents folder and choose File > New Folder (Shift-Cmd-N).

9   Name the new directory *FCP Projects*.

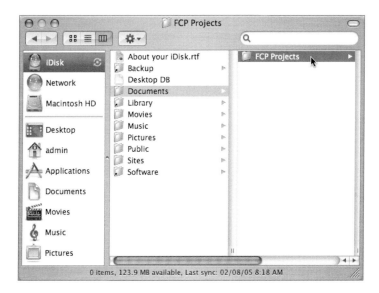

10 Select the files you want to back up, and drag your files to your new FCP Projects folder.

TIP ▶ You might choose to create an archive of your files, since it's more convenient to transfer a single file to your iDisk. Although an archive is not necessary in this process, it will serve as a protective envelope around your files. See the section on zipping and stuffing files in Lesson 15.

11 Click the Sync icon next to the iDisk icon, and your computer will synchronize the contents of your local iDisk folder with the folder on Apple's servers.

NOTE ▶ Other hosting solutions and large storage email accounts will function adequately as an alternative to .Mac. Refer to Lesson 15 for further information on transferring project files.

NOTE ▶ A number of applications, including Backup (www.mac.com/1/iTour/tour_backup.html), Retrospect (www.dantz.com/en/products/mac_personal/index.dtml), and RsyncX (http://archive.macosxlabs.org/rsyncx/rsyncx.html), can be configured to perform automatic backups.

Recovering Projects

The Revert and Restore features in Final Cut Pro provide additional means to recover project files that effectively complement your manual backup routine. Both options can be accessed directly within FCP and can help you manage your work.

Revert

The option to revert projects is especially useful if you want to quickly undo a series of steps and return the project to the state it was in the last time you performed a manual save. If you're mindful of when you save your project, you can use Revert to confidently experiment and explore different tangents in your work. If you use Revert as an alternative to multiple undo actions, you need to be aware that it is a *destructive* step—there's no equivalent to redo, and all of your changes will be lost.

> **NOTE ►** You can also save test versions of your file to facilitate experimentation. Working with incremental files enables you to preserve each deviation and maintain a record of your process.

1   Open the Lesson **12 Project.fcp file.**

2   Choose File > Save Project As.

3   Name your project *Lesson 12 Working.fcp*, and save it into your project directory.

4   Select one the video clips in the *Revert* sequence.

5   Choose Effects > Video Filters > Image Control > Desaturate.

6   Choose Effects > Image Control > Tint and use the filter controls to choose a color.

7   Choose File > Revert Project.

8   Click OK in the warning dialog box to acknowledge that your changes will be lost and your project will be returned to the state it was in the last time you saved it.

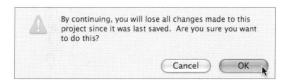

Restore

The Restore feature utilizes files stored in the Autosave Vault to recover projects. How often a file is placed in the vault and how many iterations are kept in the archive is determined by your Autosave preference settings. (Refer to Lesson 11 for instructions on how to properly set your Autosave Vault.)

1   Choose Final Cut Pro > User Preferences (Option-Q).

2   Ensure that the Autosave Vault check box is active, and change the Save A Copy Every setting to 1 minute.

> **NOTE ▶** In a real-world situation, creating a backup of your project every minute is highly impractical. You should choose a setting that enables you to have made significant changes to your project.

3   Click OK to save your changes and close the User Preferences window.

4   Double-click the *Restore* sequence in the Browser.

5   Apply filters to individual clips for approximately 3 minutes, until Autosave has had at least 3 opportunities to archive your project.

> **NOTE ▶** If you've been working with the project for longer than 3 minutes, you may see additional versions stored in the archive.

6   Choose Fle > Restore Project.

7   Click the From pop-up menu and scroll down to select the third option.

8   Click Restore.

NOTE ▸ You will most likely have different timestamps.

9   In the warning dialog box, click OK to acknowledge that unsaved changes
will be lost.

NOTE ▸ Even though you have selected the earliest version of the file, all
the other versions remain accessible through the Restore function.

10   Choose File > Save Project (Cmd-S) to update the file.

NOTE ▸ The Restore function in FCP 5 replaces the open project file.
In earlier versions it opened the archived project and required that you
re-name the project immediately.

You should never save a file into the Autosave Vault. This is not only
important in terms of organization, but the Autosave Vault also operates
a first-in/first-out policy with files, and you may find items you've saved
in there unexpectedly moved to the Trash.

11   Open User Preferences and reset the frequency of automatic saves.

Sharing
With Final Cut Pro, you can share a wide range of resources, including media,
clip information, third-party plug-ins, entire projects, and individual user
settings. This kind of functionality means that FCP can support a variety of
workflows and enable *round-trip* migration between users, applications, and
platforms.

Media

Final Cut Pro works with storage area network (SAN) solutions and is compatible with administration tools such as Apple's Xsan. FCP respects Mac OS X file permissions, enabling multiple stations to access the same media files simultaneously. (Refer to Lesson 7 for more information.)

Clips

Final Cut Pro 5 includes increased support for sharing clips between other applications. You can now *send* clips directly to Soundtrack Pro, Motion, or Shake.

When you share media files, you're sharing the raw material of your project. When you share clips, you're sharing information about how you're using your files. It is this data that you can share between the other Pro applications, and any changes you make in those applications will be immediately reflected in Final Cut Pro. FCP continues to support files created in other applications such as Maya, After Effects, and Photoshop.

> **NOTE ▸** If you exchange files between other applications, make sure you keep settings, such as pixel aspect ratio and color space, consistent or that the application is able to perform adequate conversions to properly support round-trip workflow.

Third-Party Plug-ins

FCP also continues to support third-party plug-ins (including After Effects plug-ins). Compatibility can be an issue, and you need to make sure you're using the appropriate plug-ins for your version of FCP. If you're working with third-party plug-ins, and the license permits, you can also transport them between different Final Cut Pro installations.

Projects

Sharing projects between Final Cut Pro users is remarkably easy. When you're moving projects between different systems using identical versions of FCP, you only need to reconnect media before you're ready to work. (See Lesson 5 for more information on reconnecting media files.) If you're transferring projects between different versions of Final Cut Pro, you do need to be a little careful. Although you are able to open a project created in FCP 4 in FCP 5, advances in the technology driving the application mean that project files are not immediately compatible with earlier versions, and a FCP 5 project will not open directly in FCP 4.

On the occasions you need to transport a FCP5 project to an earlier version, you'll need to use one of the interchange formats such as XML or EDL. (Refer to Lesson 5 for specific details on how to work with these formats.) XML interchange was introduced in FCP 4.1 and is the recommended solution if your systems are able to support it. For earlier versions, you'll need to generate an EDL to open your project in the earlier version.

> **NOTE ▶** Not all video formats will be supported in earlier versions of Final Cut Pro.

User Settings

With Final Cut Pro 5, it's possible to share custom user settings, including button bars, keyboard layouts, hardware settings, and window arrangements. You can manually copy settings files to other systems or set up a shared directory to make them available to other users on your network.

1   Drag the Final Cut Pro windows to create a custom layout.

2   Choose Window > Arrange > Save Window Layout.

3 Click the disclosure triangle to expand the window, and navigate to the Shared directory (/Users/Shared/).

4 Click the New Folder button, and name the new directory *Window Layouts*.

5 Create a name for your layout and click Save.

> **NOTE** ▶ Individual window layouts can be saved in the user's Window Layouts folder. If you are transferring layouts manually, this is the directory to which you should copy files in other user accounts.

6 Open System Preferences, and click the Sharing icon.

7 Select the Personal File Sharing check box.

> **NOTE** ▶ Typically, you would use a dedicated file server computer rather than an FCP workstation to share files. (Refer to Lesson 10 for more information on Sharing services.)

Any users who connect to your system will now be able to access the shared Window Layouts directory and load the layout into Final Cut Pro.

> **TIP** In FCP 5, you can also load different user settings, hardware profiles, and plug-ins using a network server. Refer to the Final Cut Pro user's manual and the Late-Breaking News About Final Cut Pro 5 documents for more information about this feature.

Streamlining Project Configuration

If your particular worflow involves repetitive tasks , you might consider using Mac OS X to streamline certain jobs.

Creating Stationery

A stationery file is the Mac OS X equivalent of a template; once you've activated a file's stationery setting, you'll create a copy of the file every time you attempt to open it. Rather than set up each file you make from scratch, you can use stationery to create a default template.

1   Choose Final Cut Pro > Easy Setup (Ctrl-Q).

2   Choose DV-NTSC from the Setup For pop-up menu, and click Setup.

3   Choose File > New Project (Shift-Cmd-N) to create a new project.

4   Choose File > Save Project (Cmd-S), name your project Lesson *12 Template*, and save it into your Lesson 12 Projects directory.

5   Click the Generator pop-up menu and choose Text > Text.

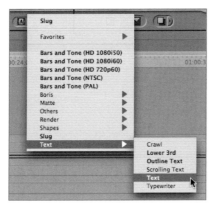

6   In the Viewer, click the Controls tab and change the Text to *My Template Project*.

7   Drag the new title into the Browser and change the clip name to *Title*.

8   Choose File > Save Project.

9   Choose File > Close Project.

10 Select your Lesson 12 Template file in the Finder and choose File > Get Info (Cmd-I).

11 Click the disclosure triangle next to General to reveal file details.

12 Select the Stationery Pad check box. The image inside the file's icon disappears.

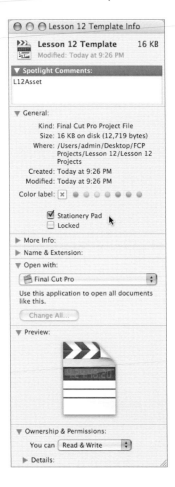

13 Close the Info window.

14 Double-click the Lesson 12 Template file to create copy of the file. The copy that opens in FCP includes the Title clip you created and settings you assigned.

Lesson 12 Template copy

15 Choose File > Save Project As immediately, and rename the project.

Automating Tasks

As you learned earlier in this lesson, in Mac OS X 10.4, Automator can now be used to manage repetitive and time-consuming jobs. At this time, Final Cut Pro is not an AppleScript-able application, but there are a number of tasks, such as resizing and renaming image files, you can perform outside of FCP to streamline your workflow. Converting the frame size of multiple image files is the kind of process that's perfectly suited for Automator. Before you import images into FCP, you need to make sure that the dimensions and pixel aspect ratio are compatible with your sequence settings. There are actions in Automator that perform both of these operations; you just need to create a workflow around them.

1 Launch Automator (/Applications/Automator).

2 In the Library column, click the Finder icon.

3 In the Action column, double-click the Get Folder Contents icon to begin your workflow.

Click the Repeat For Each Subfolder Found check box, if you want to include subdirectories whenever you execute the workflow.

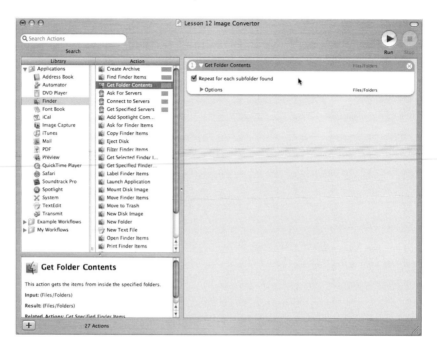

4   Double-click to apply the Copy Finder Items action, and choose Other from the To pop-up menu.

5   Navigate to your Lesson 12 Project directory and click the New Folder button.

6   Name your new folder *Converted Stills* and click Create.

7   Click Open to select your new folder.

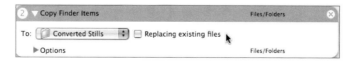

8 Double-click the Rename Finder Items action.

9 Choose Make Sequential from the first pop-up menu; this allows you to rename the files and apply a sequential number sequence.

10 Click the New Name radio button and enter the name *Lesson 12 Stills*.

11 Choose After Name from the Place Number pop-up menu and enter *1* as the starting number.

12 Choose Space from the Separated By pop-up menu.

13 Select the Make All Numbers check box, and enter the value *2*.

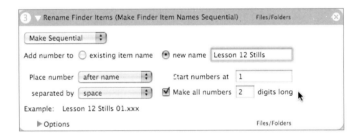

14 In the Library column, click the Preview icon and double-click to apply the Pad Images action.

15 Enter a Width value of *720* and Height value of *540*.

16 Click to activate the Scale Image Before Padding check box; you should be careful when resizing images that you don't lose quality by enlarging your picture too much.

17 Double-click the Crop Images action.

18 Choose To Dimensions from the first pop-up menu and Scale To Height from the Scale Before Crop pop-up menu; this will squash or stretch the image before it is cropped.

19 Enter a Width value of *720* and Height value of *480* to allow for nonsquare DV-NTSC pixels.

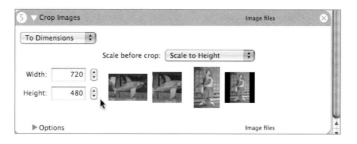

20 Choose File > Save As Plug-in.

21 Name your plug-in *Lesson 12 Image Converter*, and choose Finder from the Plug-in For pop-up menu.

22 Click Save to create your plug-in.

23 In the Finder, open the Lesson 12 Media directory.

24 Cntrl-click the Raw Stills folder and choose Automator > Lesson 12 Image Converter from the contextual menu to activate the workflow.

Feedback on the workflow is provided in the menu bar.

> **MORE INFO** ▶ You can download prebuilt Automator workflows on the Apple Web site: www.apple.com/downloads/macosx/automator.

Managing Media Files

In Final Cut Pro, media is defined as video, audio, still images, and motion graphics. Some of your media will have timecode that connects it to external sources; other media will have been created on a computer; or in the case of stock footage, music, and sound effects libraries, the media will come from non-timecode-based sources. You need to develop a system to keep track of your files and effectively manage each resource. FCP contains a number of tools to help you manage media assets, and you need to develop routines to preserve others.

Captured Media

Captured media files are automatically stored in the Scratch Disk directory or directories you defined in the System Settings window. The most appropriate place to store your media is determined by your system configuration and the specific requirements of your workflow. (Refer to Lesson 3 for suggestions on how to organize your media files.)

For the most part, you can manage captured media within FCP, and there's very little need to work with the files in the Finder. However, if you do need to locate the media file for a particular clip, you can always Cntrl-click a clip in FCP and choose Reveal In Finder from the contextual menu.

FCP places captured files into a defined directory structure in which each project is assigned a separate subfolder within the Capture Scratch directory.

Rendered Media

FCP also stores render files in designated directories that you assign in System Settings. As with captured media, the exact location of your rendered media is determined by your workflow.

The Constant Frames subfolder inside the Render Files directory is new to Final Cut Pro 5. Its purpose is to improve performance by providing a designated storage area for still image and generator render files.

Another new feature in Final Cut Pro 5 is the ability to control the render quality of motion effects. In earlier versions of FCP, there is only one standard setting, which is now identified as the Fastest option. In Final Cut Pro 5, you can also select Normal and Best settings to increase the quality of your render files.

Every time you render a clip, Final Cut Pro generates a new media. Over time, the number of render clips can build up and will need to be purged. You can manually delete the files in the Finder, as you can with captured media, but it's often more convenient to use the Render Manager in FCP.

1   Open the *Lesson 12 Project.fcp* file.

2   In the Browser, double-click the *Render Manager* sequence.

The sequence contains nine tracks of DV video that should need rendering.

▶   If you do not see the red render bar above the clip, make sure you have Safe RT and the highest quality settings selected.

▶   If you still do not see the render bar once you've changed the RT settings, add a non-bold video filter to one of the clips in the sequence.

NOTE ▶ If you don't want to wait for the entire sequence to render, you can trim the clips or hide tracks to reduce the amount of work your system has to undertake to create the file.

3   Choose Sequence > Render > Both (Cmd-R). The sequence should render, and the red bar should disappear.

4   Choose Tools > Render Manager to open the Render Manager window, and use the disclosure triangles to locate the render files for Lesson 12 Project.

5   Click to insert a checkmark in the Remove column adjacent to the Lesson 12 Projects folder, and click OK.

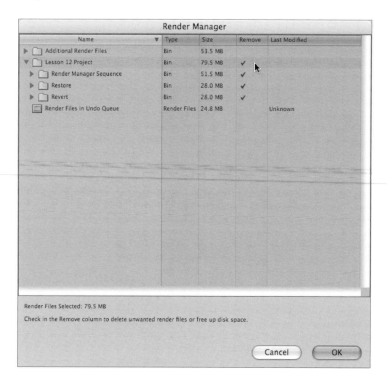

6   Click Yes in the Alert window to confirm that you understand your undo queue will also be deleted.

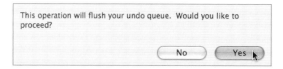

FCP will immediately delete your render files, and you should again see the red render bar above your clip in the Timeline.

Archiving Media

It's rare to want to back up media that already exists on tape or other time-code-based format, but most workflows usually involve media from other sources such as sound effects, music, and stock footage, or files that have been created on the computer, such as motion graphics. You need to develop a system to organize such media and take steps to ensure that they're archived along with your project files.

Non-timecode media will not be deleted when you perform Make Offline operations in the Media Manager, but you need to exercise caution when you use the Make Offline command in the Browser because your files will be deleted from your system. This may be an inconvenience if you need to capture media again, but it could create a bigger problem if you delete the only version of a file you generated on the computer.

To avoid the problem of deleting important media, gather all non-timebased files and include every item in your backups and permanent project archives. Also make sure you keep track of changes to the file, and use incremental saves to preserve different versions.

With stock footage, sound effects, and music, it's vital that you keep comprehensive records of the sources and other descriptive information about the media, especially if you need clearance on some of the files.

> **NOTE ▶** Before you install Soundtrack Pro on your system, make a backup of the original Soundtrack loops since some of the loops have been changed and others renamed as part of the update.

Working with Media Manager

The Media Manager in Final Cut Pro provides a powerful and versatile alternative to working in the Finder when you want to move, copy, and delete timecode-based media files. Non-timecode media is not affected by Media Manager operations and still needs to be organized manually. (Refer to Lesson 5 for specific instruction on using the Media Manager.)

Whenever you complete a project, you can easily drag the folder to the Trash. If you want to be certain that you've removed every file, it's much easier to use the Media Manger or to Ctrl-click clips in the Browser and choose Make Offline from the contextual menu.

Reestablish a Project

When you retrieve a project from your archive—you need to copy the project and the associated media onto your system. Once you open your project, if you need to recapture media, you simply select the Batch Capture option, and Final Cut Pro will ask you to supply the appropriate sources.

Lesson Review

1. Which feature in Mac OS X 10.4 can you use to add custom metadata to files?
2. If you need to share a project between different user accounts on the same system, what kind of permissions should the project folder have?
3. Which application new to Mac OS X 10.4 do you use to create custom actions to batch process repetitive tasks?
4. Which Mac OS X Finder setting overrides standard Unix permissions?
5. What is the essential quality of a robust backup system?
6. Which method of file recovery makes use of the Autosave Vault?
7. What is the first thing you should do when you have recovered a project from the Autosave Vault?
8. Which interchange format can you use to open a Final Cut Pro 5 file in Final Cut Pro 4.1?
9. What kind of user settings can you share across a network?
10. What is the fundamental difference between captured media and rendered media files?

Answers

1. Spotlight Comments.

2. The shared directory needs to grant read access to the group or individual users who need to work with the project files. If you want collaborators to be able to save changes to the file in the shared directory, they will also need to have write permissions.

3. Automator.

4. File locking will override Unix permissions.

5. You should only rely on a backup system that has redundancy built in.

6. The Restore option enables you to open projects that have been archived in the Autosave Vault.

7. Immediately save the file once you have restored it.

8. You can export either an EDL or XML file to import a FCP 5 project into FCP 4.1. XML interchange was introduced in version 4.1—it is the recommended format.

9. You can share button bars, window arrangements, hardware setups, plug-ins, and keyboard layouts across a network.

10. The fundamental difference between captured media and render files is that captured media is transferred onto your system from an external source, whereas rendered media is generated on your computer.

Integrating Your System

Matthew Geller

13

Lesson 13
Implementing Stand-Alone Uncompressed Systems

Now that your FCP system is optimized for work with DV and other native compressed formats, your thoughts may turn to transforming the system into a no-compromises, uncompressed editing system.

Uncompressed editing allows you to bring in and push out each frame of video as purely as possible, without the image artifacts and color loss that come with compressed formats. Compositing of multiple tracks, effects, and text can all be done without worrying about how compression might affect these multiple layers.

The process is quite simple, although it might get a bit expensive. Fortunately, the prices for the hardware for the transformation have plummeted in the last few years.

You'll need two new devices to handle uncompressed frames: a capture device that retrieves the frames from, and lays them back to, the tape deck, and a storage array that has the horsepower to read and write the appropriate data rates for the formats you want to work with. You might need a few more devices, depending on which capture and storage device you settle on.

Capture devices and storage options are explained in great detail in Lesson 8. Our assumption is that you've read these parts of the book, since we'll refer back to them from time to time.

Roll up your sleeves, blow the dust off that machine, and let's get going.

The Implementation Process

Our process will consist of seven steps:

1. Plan, select, and acquire the necessary components.

2. Install hardware inside and outside the computer.

3. Install/update storage drivers and software (if necessary).

4. Create RAID sets or volumes.

5. Install FCP (if necessary).

6. Install capture device drivers.

7. Configure FCP to use the new storage and capture hardware.

We'll follow this somewhat formal method, since our choices of hardware are profoundly rich and diversified.

Let's start with a simple planning exercise, to guide you in selecting the hardware. We won't advocate one option over another, but hopefully you'll find the information helpful in making your selection.

Next, we'll power down the machine and install the appropriate internal devices. These most often come in the form of PCI cards installed in the PCI or PCI-X slots in your Mac. We'll then attach the storage device to the Mac as well.

After that, we'll install any drivers or software needed to drive your storage. In some cases, your chosen storage system won't need any additional drivers or software, so you'll be able to skip this step.

Then we'll use Disk Utility to set up the storage hardware to make the HFS+ (Hierarchical File System, the Mac OS file system) volumes that will store your uncompressed frames.

If the system is brand-spankin'-new, you'll then install FCP as outlined in Lesson 10 of this book.

Penultimately, we'll install the necessary device or deck control drivers for the capture scenario you've selected.

And finally, we'll configure FCP to recognize and work with the new hardware.

Planning Your System

As with any major undertaking involving the purchase of new equipment, and the temporary downtime of your current setup, proper planning will ensure that you get the right equipment for your needs, both currently and down the line.

Before reading on, ask yourself two basic questions:

► *Which video formats will I be working with on a regular basis, and which formats might I begin to use in the near future?*

Eventually, we're all going to be doing HD production—the question is, when? Moving to HD uncompressed equipment is the most expensive option in this lesson, no doubt. But since the equipment usually handles SD formats as well, should you take the plunge now to invest in this higher-capacity equipment?

Once you wrestle with this one, you'll have a general idea of how to shop for a capture device. The device you want will be able to capture (and play back) the highest level of video format that you've come up with.

► *How much uncompressed storage capacity, in minutes, do I need for my workflow?*

To calculate this number, think of the scale of your average project. Are most of your projects 30-second spots or 2-hour documentaries? As you work, do you usually capture lots of material, or just enough to get the project done?

For many folks in post-production, a rule of thumb is to take the length of a finished piece and multiply it by 5. The result gives enough room for the material that you'll end up not using, as well as render files.

Next, multiply this "average scale" value by the number of projects you might have on your system concurrently, and this will yield the total amount of storage, in minutes, that you'll need.

Next, by using the tables in the "Data Rates and Storage Requirements for Common Media Types" section of Lesson 9, multiply your minutes times the megabytes per minute rate of the highest level of video standard that you'll be using. Divide this value by 1,000. This will yield roughly the size, in gigabytes, of an appropriate storage device for your system. Be sure to allow lots of wiggle room for unexpected storage needs.

To summarize, you get your final value of size in gigabytes by using this formula:

	the length (in minutes) of an average project
×	a multiplier that accommodates your scrap and scratch (5 is good)
×	the number of possible concurrent projects
×	the MB/minute rate of the highest level of video from Lesson 9
÷	1,000
=	the size, in gigabytes, of an appropriate storage device.

Using the answers to these two questions, you can begin to look for capture and storage devices tailored for your workflow.

Selecting the Right Capture Device

There is a blessing/curse paradigm going on in the capture device market for FCP right now. The blessing is that device prices have never been cheaper. The curse is that devices have never been more plentiful, and as a result, choosing one is quite tricky. For example, there are 22 individual products, offered by four separate manufacturers, that provide SD-SDI input to FCP. Because of the glut, you benefit: the competition and the apparent movement to commoditize these devices has brought about a dramatic drop in price.

The following table has a comprehensive list of capture devices compatible with FCP, at press time. It lists each device's capability to *capture* the four major uncompressed formats of professional video ingestion in the industry today:

▶   Analog component signals from Sony Betacam SP and similar decks

▶   Standard-Definition Serial Digital Interface (SD-SDI) signals from Sony Digital Betacam and similar decks

▶   High-Definition Serial Digital Interface (HD-SDI) signals from Sony HDCAM, Panasonic DVCPROHD and D5 HD, and similar decks

▶   Dual-link (two cable) HD-SDI signals from Sony HDCAM SR and similar decks

To start the selection process, create a list of devices that capture the format you are most likely to use now or in the future. Of course, there are many differences between the individual devices, specifically what kind of formats the devices can output as opposed to input. But the best way to whittle down the choices is to start with a device that will handle the input. After that, you can compare prices and extra features until you come upon a device to call your own. Web sites are provided for your research journey.

Capture Devices in a Nutshell

Product	Analog Component	SD-SDI	HD-SDI	Dual-Link HD-SDI
AJA (www.aja.com)				
Io	X	X		
Io LA	X			
Io LD		X		
Kona LS	X	X		
Kona 2		X	X	X

Capture Devices in a Nutshell

Product	Analog Component	SD-SDI	HD-SDI	Dual-Link HD-SDI
Aurora Video Systems (www.auroravideosys.com)				
IgniterX Pro	X			
IgniterX SDI		X		
IgniterX Studio	X	X		
PipeSDI / Pro		X		
PipeStudio	X	X		
PipeHD		X	X	
Blackmagic (www.decklink.com)				
Decklink SP	X			
Decklink 2 / Pro		X		
Decklink with Multibridge SD	X	X		
Decklink Extreme	X	X		
Decklink HD / HD Plus		X	X	
Decklink HD Pro		X	X	X
Decklink HD Pro with Multibridge	X	X	X	X
Multibridge with PCI Express	X	X	X	X
Digital Voodoo (www.digitalvoodoo.net)				
SD Edit		X		
SD Flex	X	X		
SD Spark	X	X		

Once you have settled on a smaller group of devices, you can consider very important issues such as the following:

▶ *Audio input*: It's a given that any device capable of analog component video capture in the capture devices table also has standard balanced and unbalanced analog input channels for audio capture, but devices vary as to how many channels. As for digital audio, devices vary greatly with the format they use to capture audio and in how many channels they can input and output. For example, many devices simply capture digital audio embedded in the SD or HD-SDI signal path. But what if you have an older digital deck that doesn't support embedded audio? Buying hardware that supports more than two input channels is a good investment in case you receive source tapes that have more than two channels recorded. Check the specs on each manufacturer's Web site to make sure your device captures the audio formats you use.

▶ *Genlock*: Most analog decks require a reference/blackburst/genlock (terms are interchangeable) signal, and most capture devices need to receive that same reference signal to synchronize to the deck. Fortunately, every device listed in our table capable of analog component video capture also has a genlock input. All you need is a genlock generator to feed the input. Companies such as VideoTek (www.videotek.com) and Horita (www.horita.com) make popular models.

▶ *Analog video monitoring*: Many devices in our table, regardless of their input capability, can output through analog component cables. This lets you monitor your edit without a deck present, through a relatively low-cost analog component-input monitor. The devices that don't output this way need a more expensive, SDI-enabled monitor or a pricey digital-to-analog converter box in order to view the output.

▶ *Audio monitoring*: Many devices listed in the table also let you monitor the FCP output through a host of digital or analog audio ports. This lets you listen to your edit, without a deck present, on inexpensive digital or analog audio monitors. Again, some devices don't, so check your options, especially if you rent high-end decks for your projects and don't have them around every day.

▶ *Deck control*: Digital Voodoo and Aurora Igniter products need an external USB configuration using the ubiquitous Keyspan USB Twin Serial Adaptor (www.keyspan.com) and a special DIN-8-to-DB-9 cable to hook up to (most commonly) the RS-422 control port on the back of your deck. However, all devices from AJA, Blackmagic, and the Aurora Pipe products come with built-in deck control. With these devices, you need a straight DB-9-to-DB-9 cable to control the deck.

▶ *Versatility*: Most devices listed in the table have PCI cards that either have direct video and audio ports on the back of the card, or connect to a cable snake or break-out box (BOB) for easy configuration. Alternatively, AJA's Io products actually communicate to FCP through the FireWire interface, which is excellent for moving these devices to whichever machine needs them, but also calls for a separate PCI FireWire host bus adaptor (HBA) if you intend to use an Io product while simultaneously having your DV deck hooked up to the system.

Selecting the Right Storage System

If you thought there was a lot to choose from with capture devices, just wait until you see the diversity of the direct-attached storage solutions for FCP. We say "direct-attached" since we are dealing with storage that will be directly attached to this system only.

If reliability were the only factor in choosing storage, the old adage of "you get what you pay for" would apply. But speed, capacity, power consumption, noise level, and redundancy, not to mention cost, will also drive your decision.

In this section, a more generalized set of categories needs to be established. We'll start with these categories to make your selection process easier.

Here are the major categories of direct-attached storage available for FCP at press time:

Do-It-Yourself Striped Arrays

This category offers the most primitive solution to your storage problem, and it's definitely more suited for the technically savvy. Do-it-yourself (DIY) arrays involve buying individual SCSI, Fibre Channel, or SATA hard disk drives, installing them in an empty enclosure or "cage," connecting them to the computer via a like-flavored PCI Host Bus Adaptor (HBA) card, and using software to stripe them together.

The benefit is cost: DIY arrays are the cheapest solution since you buy individual components.

The downsides are plentiful. No software RAID tool for the Mac can do high-performance redundant RAID levels, only 0 or 1, so these arrays offer no redundancy at the speeds necessary for uncompressed work. Further, as was discussed in Lesson 9 these arrays' data rates drop significantly as the array fills up. Finally, technical expertise required to configure the drives within the enclosure and hook up cables between drives makes them improbable solutions for the left-brain-impaired members of the community.

The following manufacturers produce DIY SCSI and Fibre external array solutions:

▶   Archion (www.archion.com)

▶   PC Pitstop (www.pc-pitstop.com)

▶   SCSI4ME (www.scsi4me.com)

SATA arrays are being praised in the independent geek-editor community because they offer very low cost and very high data rates and storage capacities, despite the limitations mentioned earlier. SATA HBAs with four or eight external ports, made by folks such as Sonnet Technology (www.sonnettech.com), are just now emerging in the market. These HBAs allow you to create DIY SATA arrays without cables dangling out of an empty PCI slot in the back of your Mac. With this simple advance, SATA arrays will be perfect for locally created render files for Xsan systems. See Lesson 15 for more information.

The following manufacturers produce DIY SATA external array solutions:

▶   Firmtek (www.firmtek.com)

▶   Granite Digital (www.granitedigital.com)

▶   MacGurus (www.macgurus.com)

SATA arrays can also be built by cramming more SATA drives into the G5 box itself, enabling high-speed arrays within the G5. Be warned, however, that these systems interfere with the G5's cooling systems and definitely void the G5's warranty.

The following manufacturers produce DIY internal SATA array solutions:

▶   Wiebetech G5Jam (www.wiebetech.com)

▶   TransIntl SwiftData200 (www.transintl.com)

Prebuilt Striped Enclosures

This category is identical to the one just mentioned, except that the enclosures or cages are prebuilt. You just hook them up, with an appropriate HBA, to the Mac, and stripe them with software.

These units cost more, since the installation and cabling has already been done for you, but they're still a little cheaper than the bridge enclosures mentioned next. You can purchase prebuilt stripe enclosures from the following manufacturers:

- ▶ The DR Group DRaid (www.thedrgroup.com)
- ▶ Granite Digital
- ▶ Promax SATAMAX (www.promax.com)
- ▶ Rorke Data Systems (www.rorke.com)
- ▶ StorCase (www.storcase.com)

Built-In Hardware RAID Controlled Bridge Enclosures

This category is by far the most crowded and incorporates the most popular storage systems for Final Cut Pro. The word "bridge" refers to the fact that the interface on the outside of the enclosure is different from the interface of the disk drives. Bridging circuitry converts the language of the host bus into the language of the drives. Even better, this circuitry almost always incorporates a hardware-based redundant RAID scheme on the installed drives, adding high-speed redundancy to their appeal. Finally, because the internal intelligent circuitry, called a controller, is present, these units appear as a single device to the Mac, which makes the formatting process simple and quick. The appropriate HBA is still needed within the Mac to talk to the unit's controller, however.

Three primary bridges used in these types of systems are SCSI-to-ATA/SATA, Fibre-to-ATA/SATA, and FireWire-to-ATA/SATA, where the term before the hyphen is the controller's protocol, and the term after the hyphen is the drive type.

In the relatively new Fibre-to-ATA/SATA category, Apple's Xserve RAID stands out as an attractive option, since it offers sustained data rates necessary for uncompressed 10-bit HD production, even when the drives are configured in RAID 5. You achieve these rates when you bring the two controllers on the Xserve RAID together in RAID 0 using software, which is called RAID 5+0. But many other manufacturers have created systems that compete with the

Xserve RAID and provide more *availability* (fail-proofing) with failover controllers and the capability to RAID more disks together in one array. A Fibre Channel HBA is necessary to connect these devices to your Mac.

SCSI-to-ATA/SATA has been around for some time, and you have many choices. Storage capacity and data speed determine which device meets your needs. Inventiveness also plays a part with these units. For example, Huge System's arrays have a "turbo" feature that places the drives in the array at RAID 3, which is good for redundancy but bad for performance. To counter the performance hit, it limits storage to only the outer sectors of the drives, effectively shutting out the parts of the drives that deliver subpar performance.

The following manufacturers produce Fibre-to-ATA/SATA and SCSI-to-ATA/SATA units:

▶ Apple's Xserve RAID (www.apple.com/xserve/raid)

▶ ADTX (www.adtx.com/us)

▶ Archion

▶ Atto Technology (www.attotech.com)

▶ Digistor (www.digistor.com.au)

▶ Huge Systems (www.hugesystems.com)

▶ JMR (www.jmr.com)

▶ Medéa (www.medea.com)

▶ Raid, Inc. (www.raidinc.com)

▶ Rorke Data Systems

▶ StorCase

FireWire-to-ATA units—commonly known as basic FireWire drives—are nothing new. But recent advances in controller hardware have made it possible to place multiple (usually two to five) ATA or SATA hard drives inside of a box, and create simple hardware-based RAID 0 or 5 arrays within them. A FireWire bridge allows these arrays to be connected to a simple FireWire bus (usually

FW800). In these devices, performance usually drops substantially as the drives fill up, but precautions have been taken for this situation. With G-Tech's G-RAID, for example, the second drive of its two-drive array starts writing data at the center of the platter, as opposed to the outside. Having the two drives write data at opposite sides of their platters evens out the performance as the drives reach full capacity.

Further, almost any FireWire-to-ATA device needs a dedicated FireWire HBA PCI card installed in your machine. The data rates of these HBAs far outperform the built-in FireWire ports of your Mac (especially the G5). FireWire HBAs are also necessary to keep the built-in FireWire ports available for DV decks or products such as AJA's Io.

Although FireWire-to-ATA devices deliver performance for only basic uncompressed SD workflows (less than 80 MB/s sustained), they provide usable storage at appropriate data rates and low prices. This makes them perfect for creating render volumes for systems that are attached to Xsan.

The following manufacturers produce FireWire-to-ATA/SATA units:

▶ Archion

▶ G-Tech (www.g-technology.com)

▶ LaCie (www.lacie.com)

▶ Wiebetech

The Final Comparison: Cost vs. Storage and Speed

With all of the preceding guidelines, finding a device that will meet your needs now and in the future may still be a challenge.

Using the storage capacity size in gigabytes that you calculated earlier, you can draw up a short list of devices that have this capacity. Using the data rate needed for your most ambitious video format, you can further narrow the list with devices in your capacity range that handle sustained data rates comfortably above what you need. Lastly, cost comparisons will hopefully yield a smaller field of devices.

Selecting a Host Bus Adaptor (HBA) Card

Make sure to choose an appropriate PCI-based HBA for the storage system you have selected. The choices are relatively easy.

If you're going Fibre, the best choice is Apple's Fibre HBA card. It beats other manufacturer's two-port card prices by as much as $2,000.

SATA HBAs are relatively new, and at press time offer up to eight external ports. There are also internal multi-port HBAs, but they involve stringing cables from the inside of the Mac to the outside, usually through an open PCI slot, which is not recommended. Two-port external SATA HBAs for two-drive RAIDs provide excellent storage and speeds for SD production. A four-port HBA hosting four drives yields enough bandwidth for 720p HD work. Eight port HBAs, driving eight drives, can provide bandwidth for just about any uncompressed format, as long as you're willing to put up with the RAID not being redundant.

The following manufacturers produce SATA HBAs:

▶   Firmtek (www.firmtek.com)

▶   HighPoint (www.highpoint-tech.com)

▶   NetCell (www.netcell.com)

▶   Sonnet Technologies (www.sonnettech.com)

If you're hooking up to a SCSI host, ATTO's UL4S or UL4D cards are about the only ones with reliable, regularly updated drivers. The S model has a single host bus; the D has a dual host bus. Your storage device choice will determine which one you need.

As mentioned earlier, you need a dedicated, separate FireWire HBA to guarantee the lower-speed transfer rates of FireWire-to-ATA/SATA units. Many manufacturers make FireWire HBAs, among them LaCie and Sonnet.

RAID Software

If you chose either of the striped array configurations mentioned earlier, you will need to create a RAID with software. Apple's Disk Utility provides a quick and easy way to create RAID 0 arrays from multiple devices, and since it comes free with your OS, the price is right. However, there are positive rumblings in the industry about SoftRaid (www.softraid.com), as it provides greater flexibility with creating RAID 0 arrays and offers slightly better performance optimizations for video work to boot.

Installing Hardware

At this point, you've selected your capture and storage devices, and are ready to hook them up to your Mac. Let's start with internal installations first, and then hook up the external gear.

Internal Installations

You may have already deduced that you are going to need to install at least one (HBA), and usually two (HBA and capture card), PCI devices in your machine.

The process is as simple as opening up the G5 (or G4) and installing the cards in one or two available PCI slots. But which slots? Ah, there's the dilemma.

In a G4 or in some lower-end G5s, you really have no limitation as to the location of the cards, since these machines contain ordinary shared-bus PCI slots running at 33 MHz. Sadly, a lot of the high-speed performance of modern capture cards and HBAs are lost on these types of slots, and that is why these Macs are becoming outdated for uncompressed production.

In the high-end dual-processor G5s (early production 1.8 and 2 GHz duals, and current 2 and 2.5 GHz duals), however, consider the super-fast PCI-X 133 MHz slot 4 versus the bus-sharing PCI-X 100 MHz slots 2 and 3.

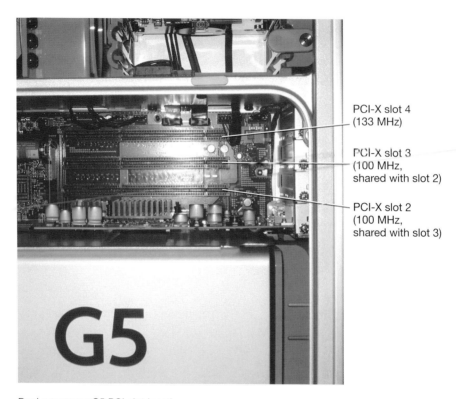

PCI-X slot 4
(133 MHz)

PCI-X slot 3
(100 MHz,
shared with slot 2)

PCI-X slot 2
(100 MHz,
shared with slot 3)

Dual-processor G5 PCI slot locations

The golden rule for installation on these machines is to place whichever card, capture or HBA, has the highest speed into slot 4. This is because the isolated bus on slot 4 will slow down to the speed of that card, and that card only.

Then place the slower card(s) into either slots 2 or 3. But don't put a card in either of these slots that is slower than the other one, as the shared bus for slots 2 and 3 will slow down to accommodate the slower of the two cards and remain at that speed.

What if you're lucky enough to get two cards that run at 133 MHz? In that case, the common procedure is to place the capture card in slot 4 and the HBA in slot 2 or 3, again making sure that there are no cards going into remaining slots that would slow down the HBA's performance.

In G5s with super-duper, two-slot-hogging graphics cards (ATI Radeon 9800 XT or nVidia GeForce 6800), slot 2 won't be available anyway. This causes some issues when configuring an uncompressed system using SATA drives, or for Xsan. See Lesson 15 for more information.

Hooking Up Storage to the HBA

Close your Mac; we're all done with the internal wrangling. With one to three cards placed in the appropriate slots, it's time to connect your storage to your HBA.

FireWire Connection

FireWire HBAs are a cinch: simply connect the FireWire-to-ATA/SATA device to your FireWire HBA with a FireWire cable (preferably FW800). Cable lengths of no more than 3 meters (10 feet) are recommended.

SATA Connection

As mentioned previously, SATA HBAs currently offer up to eight external ports. If you had room to install two HBAs, you can now connect up to 16 drives that will be striped together. In any case, make sure to use high-quality, externally shielded SATA cables to hook up your drives to the HBA.

Fibre Connection

With Fibre devices, you have a choice in cable substrates and connectors. If using the recommended Apple Fibre HBA, you'll need SFP connectors on that end of your cables. Most Fibre-to-ATA/SATA units have SFP connectors on the other side as well, but check to make sure, as adaptors from one type of connector to another are quite expensive.

The 2.9 meter (9 feet) copper cables that come with the Apple Fibre HBA can usually connect the HBA to the storage. But in case you wish to place your somewhat noisy Fibre storage unit far from your editing system, optical cables will do the trick. You can run optical cables up to 10 kilometers. You'll need to purchase SFP transceivers for each end of each optical cable to convert the electrical signals to optical ones and back. See Lesson 15 for more details on optical Fibre cable connectivity.

SCSI Connection

The ATTO UL4 series of cards use 68-pin LVD connectors, but there are differences between the single- and dual-channel models. The UL4S uses one high-density 68-pin (HD68) connector. However, in order to fit two connectors on the back of the card, the UL4D uses very high-density cable interconnect 68-pin (VHDCI) connectors. Most striped SCSI enclosures, and almost all SCSI-to-ATA/SATA storage devices, have HD68 connectors on them, so you'll need the appropriate cable (no more than 12.5 meters, or 37 feet long), to connect your unit to the HBA. SCSI is a bit of an antiquated protocol, and it needs to be terminated. Make sure to attach an HD68 terminator to any unused connector on the SCSI chain to finish the install.

> **TIP** ▶ Don't try to cut corners on the quality of any of the connections we just mentioned, especially with SCSI cables and terminators. Fibre and SCSI are expensive, but spending serious coin on the cables will yield a more reliable direct-attached storage system.

Installing the Keyspan USB Twin Serial Adaptor (If Necessary)

If you have installed a capture device that doesn't have built-in device control, take the time now to install the Keyspan adaptor into an available USB port on the back of your Mac. While you're back there, connect the DIN8 connector of your DIN8-to-DB9 control cable to port 1 on the Keyspan device.

NOTE ▶ The numbers of the twin ports on the device are somewhat hard to discern, since they are printed in faint white on top of white transparent plastic. Make sure you have a flashlight back there.

Powering Up the Storage and Computer

Now that you have an attached storage system, it's a good practice to always power up the storage before powering up the Mac, in that order. You'll probably encounter one or more warnings that look like this when the machine starts up.

Don't panic. That's the OS's way of telling you that there are new devices available to be initialized as storage volumes, but they aren't initialized yet. Click the Ignore button on these windows for the time being, so that you can make sure you have the appropriate drivers and software to configure your storage system.

For FireWire-to-ATA/SATA RAIDs, these volumes are usually preformatted and will simply pop up on the Desktop, ready for use. In that case, you can skip all the way down to the "Installing FCP" section of this lesson. However, if you also get the warning when the machine fires up, proceed directly to the "Creating Volumes from Single-Host RAIDs" section later in this lesson.

Installing/Updating Storage Drivers and Software

A few more software installations are necessary, in some cases, before you proceed to volume creation. Perform these steps only if you have the applicable scenarios.

ATTO Card Driver Updates

This section is necessary only if you've installed an ATTO SCSI HBA in your G5. This card will need an updated driver, and perhaps a firmware upgrade as well, all of which you can download from www.attotech.com/software. After a briefly annoying free registration game, you'll be able to navigate to the latest drivers and firmware for your card. After you download them, double-click the installer packages and restart the machine for each one.

SATA HBA Drivers

In some cases, you'll need to install drivers for your SATA HBA, which either came with your card or can be found on the manufacturer's Web site. A restart will be required after you install the drivers.

Cooking an Xserve RAID

If you've decided to use an Apple Xserve RAID for your storage, the good news is that it's probably configured straight out of the box for video usage. Any size Xserve RAID (for 4, 7, or 14 drives) has its drives preconfigured as a RAID 5, which then either need to be initialized as a single volume (with the 4- or 7-drive configuration) or striped together to further increase performance (with the 14-drive configuration).

If the RAID is in fact *just* out of its box, it will need to be plugged in (using both cords), turned on (with the power button in the back), and "cooked." It must be left running for up to 36 hours (really) for a sector-by-sector drive verification process. When all of the blue lights on the front of the box turn off, you can power off the unit by holding down its power button for a few seconds. You can then move on to the following steps.

Other Xserve RAID Preparations

The Xserve RAID controller firmware might need an upgrade, so use the RAID Admin program (usually located in /Applications/Server/) that came with your Xserve RAID to connect to it via an Ethernet cable, find out its firmware version, and update it if need be.

Installation of SoftRAID (If Necessary)

The popular SoftRAID software, mentioned previously, will give you slightly better performance than Disk Utility for a software-striped array, or to stripe together the two controllers of an Xserve RAID. If you have chosen to use SoftRAID, install the software at this point. We won't cover the use of this app in this lesson, so consult the documentation that came with the software to RAID your devices together.

Volume Creation

Now it's time to initialize your storage system and turn it into a usable volume. You have two options. If you're initializing a striped array of separate drives, or aggregating the two controllers (called logical unit numbers or LUNs) of an Xserve RAID, use the first method that follows, "Creating RAID Sets." However, if you're simply mounting a device that will appear as a single device to the OS, such as a bridge array or a single controller of an Xserve RAID, use the second method, "Creating Volumes from Single-Host RAIDs."

Creating RAID Sets

Creating RAID sets with Apple's Disk Utility is a breeze. The hard part—installing the appropriate hardware and drivers—is behind you. When you launch Disk Utility, you should see the devices, which means that the OS recognizes them. Then, you simply need to do a little dragging and dropping to create the RAID volume.

We'll use this technique to create a volume from two scenarios: RAIDing together a series of devices to create a striped RAID 0, or RAIDing together a few host RAIDs, such as the two 7-drive LUNs of an Xserve RAID, to create a RAID X-0 configuration.

1   Launch Disk Utility, found in /Applications/Utilities.

Observe the device and volumes that show up in the left column of the interface.

2   Click any one of the devices that you intend to place into the RAID.

NOTE ▶ If you are putting together a FireWire-based RAID, or are using disks that already have formatted volumes, remember two things: first, any data on that volume is about to be destroyed, and second, you need to click the device name, not the volume name, in order to get to step 3. The device name is the weird one; it starts with its size in gigabytes and usually includes the manufacturer's name and the model number of the mechanism.

3   In the upper right of the Disk Utility window, click the RAID tab.

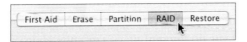

4   Drag the device that you selected in step 1 into the Disk window in the lower-right portion of the interface.

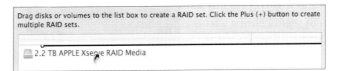

5   Drag each additional device that you want to use in the RAID set into the
    window as well.

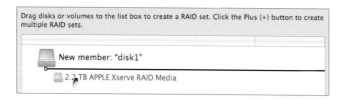

NOTE ▸ It doesn't really matter in what order you drag each device into
the Disk window, since the OS will figure out how to send data to each
device. But if you're cautious, drag the devices, one by one, in the order
that they appear in the list at left, from top to bottom.

Now let's set up the particulars for the set.

6   Set the RAID Type to "Striped RAID Set."

7   In Volume Format, choose Mac OS Extended. Do not choose Mac OS
    Extended (Journaled), or any of the other settings.

8   Keep the RAID Scheme set to Stripe, since that's what you want.

TIP ▸ Avoid journaling media storage, since it slightly reduces the volume's performance.

The RAID Set Estimated Size number tells you the projected size of the
volume once it's created.

9   Click Create.

You'll be prompted to confirm this decision.

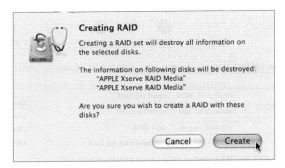

10   Click Create.

In a moment, you should see the RAID volume appear on your Desktop.

11   Quit Disk Utility.

Creating Volumes from Single-Host RAIDs

In the case of storage devices with internal RAID controllers, these units will present only one device to the OS, through the host adaptor that they are attached to. For example, popular SCSI-to-ATA/SATA and Fibre-to-ATA/SATA units have internal RAID controllers, and as a result, will show up as a single device only through either the SCSI or Fibre Channel HBA card installed in your Mac.

These drives are also easy to configure. Again, using Apple's Disk Utility, let's format this single-unit device into a Mac OS Extended volume.

1   Launch Disk Utility, found in /Applications/Utilities.

Observe the new device(s) that show up in the left column of the interface.

2   Click the device that bears the name of your single host.

NOTE ▶ Different hosts have different names. In most cases, the device you are looking for will be the only one that doesn't have a volume name nested underneath it.

3   In the upper right of the Disk Utility window, click the Erase tab.

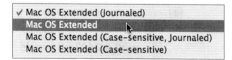

4   From the Volume Format pop-up menu, choose Mac OS Extended. Do *not* choose Mac OS Extended (Journaled).

TIP Avoid journaling media storage, since it slightly reduces the volume's performance.

5   Name your volume in the Name box.

Common names are WHERE_MY_MEDIA_GOES or GIANT_VOLUME.

6   Deselect the "Install Mac OS 9 Disk Driver" check box, since you don't need that.

7   Click Erase.

You'll be asked if you really want to proceed.

8   Click Erase.

In a moment, you should see the volume appear on your Desktop.

9   Quit Disk Utility.

Testing Read and Write Speeds

Right now is a good time to test the throughput, or read and write speeds of your newly created volume. What's critical here is to make sure that your volume will handle the speeds for the highest data rate of video you intend to work with. AJA and Blackmagic supply excellent drive speed test programs with their driver software, but there are other third-party programs such as Intech Software's Speed Tools (www.speedtools.com) and Lloyd Chambers' DiskTester (www.llc4.com/software/disktester/), which runs only in the Terminal but is quite versatile.

Installing FCP (If Necessary)

If you are upgrading your current FCP system for an uncompressed workflow, you can obviously skip this step.

However, if you are creating the system from scratch, now is the time to install FCP, after the hardware has been installed, the storage drivers are in place, and the storage volumes are created.

Note well that we haven't yet installed the drivers for the capture device. This must take place *after* FCP installation, since all the necessary folders and preference files must be in place before we install the capture drivers.

For a detailed explanation of installing FCP for the first time on a system, as well as the tweaking of Mac OS X for use of FCP, see Lesson 10 and 11.

Installing Capture Device Drivers

This process is also a breeze. All the device manufacturers offer their latest drivers in a downloadable form on their Web sites. Our only advice here is to *always* use the latest driver from a manufacturer's Web site, as opposed to the driver on the CD that came shipped with the device. Manufacturers are fastidious in supporting their devices, and the drivers that shipped with your device may already be outdated.

Unless you enjoy living on the edge, don't download a "beta" version of a driver that the company may be offering to the public on a trial basis. Instead, look for the formal release—the one without the ominous "b" in its version number. Check the major discussion lists to see how people are faring with a new release in drivers. Most importantly, *never* change or install new drivers in the midst of an important project.

Every manufacturer's driver auto-installs when you double-click the application package that mounts after you download the driver.

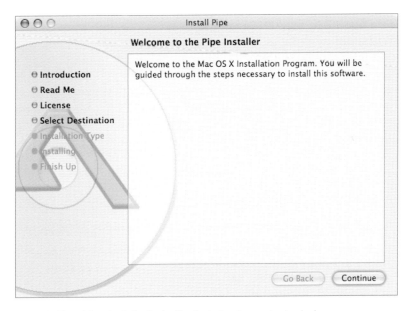

Aurora's Pipe driver installer looks like just about everybody else's.

Although we can't show them all to you, rest assured that it's as simple as installing FCP software. Check with online FAQs and help pages if you have trouble during the download process.

Installing Keyspan Serial Drivers

If you installed the Keyspan twin serial adaptor, you'll want to install the drivers at this point and then test to see if the device is being recognized. Follow these steps:

1   Download the latest Keyspan driver from Keyspan's Web site (www.keyspan.com).

2   Double-click the installer and follow the installer prompts to install the driver.

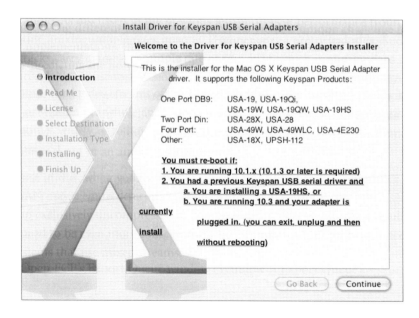

3   After installation is complete, restart your computer.

4   When the computer restarts, launch your System Preferences and click the Network pane.

A window appears announcing the detection of some new ports. This is a good sign.

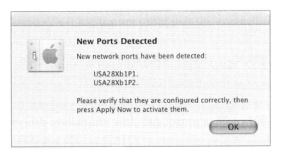

5   Click OK.

6   From the Show pop-up menu in the Network preference pane, choose Network Port Configurations.

7   Uncheck your new ports in the list: USA28Xb1P1 and USA28Xb1P2.

This won't affect your use of this adaptor to control decks, but it will tell Mac OS X that you aren't interested in trying to network with these ports.

8   Click Apply Now.

9   Quit System Preferences.

Configuring FCP for Your New Hardware

The final step involves configuring FCP to recognize your new storage and capture hardware. The main concerns here are to make sure FCP recognizes the new volume that you created in the previous section, assuring that you will be able to control the tape deck with new deck control settings, and having access to the "easy setups" that every card manufacturer creates for its particular capture device.

Configuring Storage Settings

This procedure is simple, and it is executed exactly the same way as mentioned in the section on scratch disk assignments in Lesson 12, except that now you will select your newly created, super-fast volume as the target for your capture and render files. Brush up on that section in order to accomplish this task.

Configuring Device Control

Configuring device control is dependent on whether your device has built-in control or relies on the services of the Keyspan adaptor. Most built-in device control settings will be automatically configured into easy setups. But for those with the Keyspan device, follow these simple steps to create a device control setting for your system.

1   Launch FCP.

2   Choose Final Cut Pro HD > Audio/Video Settings.

3   Click the Device Control Presets tab.

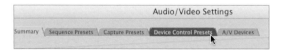

4   Click the Duplicate button.

We'll actually duplicate whatever setting is current to create our Keyspan control preset.

5   In the Name field, type *Keyspan Deck Control*.

6   In the Description field, type *I will always use this setting when I wish to use my little Keyspan Device to control my deck.*

7   From the Protocol pop-up menu, choose the appropriate device control protocol for your deck.

In most cases, this will be Sony RS-422, as most decks, Sony or not, can emulate this protocol.

8   From the Port pop-up menu, you should be able to choose the Keyspan Port 1, USA28Xb1P1.1.

NOTE ▶ If you don't see the Keyspan ports in this menu, two things might be true: You didn't install the Keyspan device drivers, or the device isn't plugged in.

9   From the Frame Rate pop-up menu, choose the appropriate frame rate for the work you'll be doing. For you North American Standard Definition types, keep the rate at its default 29.97.

Your settings should look like this:

10 Click OK.

11 Duplicate this setting, if necessary, for any other protocols or frame rates you'll be using with your system. Make sure to save them with appropriate titles to differentiate them.

12 Back in the Audio/Video Settings window, click OK.

13 Quit FCP.

Selecting Easy Setups

Every capture device manufacturer creates easy setups for each video format that your specific device captures. All you need do before working with a specific audio and video port, video format, frame size, and bit depth is to select its corresponding easy setup from the Final Cut Pro pull-down menu. Other devices, such as Aurora's Pipe and the Blackmagic Decklink cards, will have additional preference panes located inside your System Preferences in order to control which input or output ports are active.

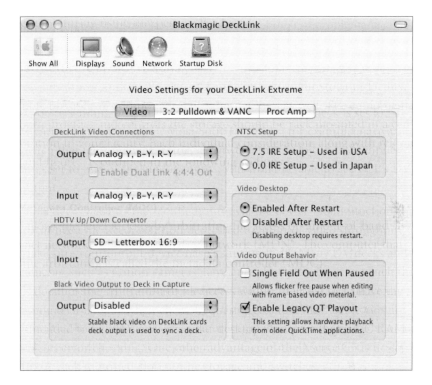

Blackmagic Decklink settings are configured within a pane inside the System Preferences.

Some manufacturers, such as Digital Voodoo and AJA, offer stand-alone applications that control the device's features.

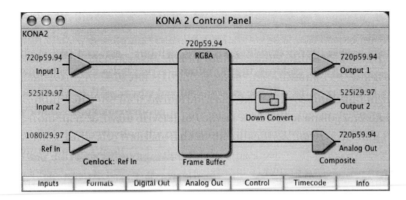

AJA's Kona 2 settings are configured with a stand-alone application.

Be sure to consult the user guide that came with your device to learn about all of the unique features.

Getting Additional Help

There you have it: an FCP uncompressed system, planned, configured, installed, and tweaked. If you ever have problems while putting together the system, you'll probably be able to find answers online at the various techno-geek forums on 2-pop (www.2-pop.com) or Creative Cow (www.creativecow.net), or your local user group. Lastly, there's no shame in hiring a professional consultant (http://consultants.apple.com) or Apple Pro Video Value Added Reseller (www.apple.com/finalcutpro/proresellers.html) to help you with all or some of the implementation process.

Lesson Review

1. What are two main questions to ask yourself before implementing an uncompressed workflow?

2. When choosing a capture card, what is the first factor to consider?

3. What three factors should you consider when choosing storage?

4. In an uncompressed system, how should you select an HBA?

5. When installing PCI cards in the Mac, what must you be careful not to do?

6. Name two utilities you can use to create volumes.

7. How can you get the latest driver for a capture device?

Answers

1. Which video formats will I be working with now and in the near future? How much uncompressed storage capacity, in terms of minutes, do I need for my workflow?

2. Input formats.

3. Capacity, data rates, and cost.

4. The HBA must match either your striped array or bridge array device.

5. Install the cards in such a way that their performance will decrease with bus slowdowns.

6. Disk Utility and SoftRAID.

7. Download it from the manufacturer's Web site.

14

Integrating FCP Systems into Networks

A typical post-production facility is an amalgam of various creative people, processes, media formats, computer systems, and software. So it's important that your Mac running Final Cut Pro interfaces properly with the rest of this digital world.

This lesson focuses on a bit of theory on Macintosh file formats, to be sure you have enough background knowledge of why files behave the way they do when they travel from one computer to another, to a server on a network, out over the Internet, and back again.

Then we'll explore the steps involved in connecting to servers that use file systems other than what you are used to. Finally, we'll lay down some essential procedures to make sure your files remain intact as they venture out from your computer onto the Internet.

Understanding Mac OS X File Formats

In order to preserve the integrity of your digital files when they leave the cozy cocoon of your Mac, let's first define a few terms so that we're all on the same page.

A *file* is simply a repository for data. It has a beginning and an end, and it also has a name. Files reside on your hard drive. When you want to use a file, you open it and do something with its data.

In most operating systems, a filename *extension* (such as .jpg for JPEG and .doc for Microsoft Word documents) gives clues as to the file's contents. If for some reason the filename extension is omitted or erased, the operating system has no idea what the file is, or how to open it.

Mac files have traditionally had more to them than the typical computer file, in two ways.

First, Mac files never needed filename extensions, because the Mac's disk file system, called the Hierarchical File System (HFS), stored metadata (or data about data) for each file on the hard drive, remembering what kind of file it was, which application made it, what icon to use for it, and so on. Mac OS X, with its adoption of HFS, continues to do this.

Second, Mac files sometimes have two separate repositories, called *forks*, for data in a single file, though this is getting rarer. The *data fork* contains good old-fashioned data, just like a non-Mac file. The *resource fork*, however, contains resources that the file uses to interact with the user, such as special text, icons, pictures, sounds, and the like.

The issue for the typical Mac file is how it travels and eventually resides on a file system other than HFS. Since most other file systems don't have a metadata layer like HFS, Mac files without filename extensions appear as poor little orphan files when you copy them over to these file systems. Further, if provisions aren't made for the precious resource fork of a Mac file, it gets stripped out of the file entirely when traveling to other file systems, leaving its data fork brother all alone.

Fortunately for us, FCP project files contain only data, and no resource fork at all. In version 5, for the first time FCP saves out an automatic filename extension (.fcp), but it hides this extension, much like its other Pro application cousins do.

A Word on Other File Types and Filename Extensions

The Finder recognizes a QuickTime file if it simply has a .mov extension appended to its name. Therefore, it's extremely important to append a .mov extension to *any* QuickTime file you export from FCP, especially if the file is destined for a machine or server other than a Mac.

When must you do this? Oddly enough, when you use File > Export > QuickTime Movie. The Using QuickTime Conversion option automatically adds a .mov extension to your filename.

Thankfully, most of the Apple Pro Applications automatically append filename extensions to their project files. Cinema Tools is the sole exception. Here are the extensions for other applications:

▶ .dspproj—DVD Studio Pro
▶ .ipr—LiveType
▶ .loop—Soundtrack
▶ .stmp, .stap—Soundtrack Pro
▶ .motn—Motion
▶ .shk—Shake

Using File Servers

Now that you have a thorough understanding of filename structure, you can safely connect to just about any server in your facility and pass FCP files with ease. But how to connect and mount them? The steps differ depending on whether your facility's server(s) are Mac- or Windows-based. We'll go over the simple steps involved when using each kind of file server.

OS X (and OS 9) Servers

OS X servers use a special file protocol to transfer files called Apple File Protocol, or AFP. This protocol preserves file metadata during the trip. The servers themselves usually have their storage volumes formatted as HFS, so file metadata resides there as well. This is why transferring Mac files from a Mac to a Mac server and back is seamless.

Here are the steps to connect to a Mac server.

1   From any Finder window, click the Network icon.

A list of available domains on your network appears.

2   Click the Local domain.

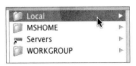

This is usually where Mac servers appear.

3   Click the Mac server in the list.

4   Click Connect.

To see the available shares for
server "MAC_OS_X_SERVER", click
Connect.

A dialog box appears, asking you to authenticate your username and password on the server.

5   Type your credentials in order to log in.

Note that even though AFP requires authentication of some form, many administrators allow you to log in to the server as a "guest." Contact your server administrator for more information.

After you authenticate, a window with a list of available share points will appear. Share points are volumes, or folders on volumes, that the administrator has made available to you based on your access to the server.

6 Double-click the share point you wish to mount.

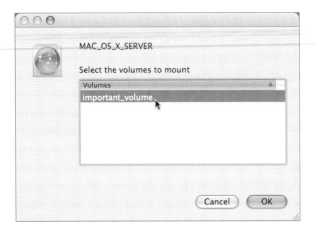

Your server share point should show on the Desktop as an icon, and it also appears as an icon in any Finder window.

7 Use your server.

Windows Servers

Windows servers, with the limitations mentioned previously, allow much simpler file transfer and file storage.

Files are transferred using two protocols, Server Message Block (SMB) or the newer Common Internet File System (CIFS). Windows servers may also have the capability to talk to Macs using good old AFP, although implemented by an older and more primitive version than on Mac servers. They store files using the Windows NT File System (NTFS).

Versatile machines that they are, Macs connect to Windows servers using either AFP or Apple's implementation of the open-source program Samba.

Before sending a file over to the Windows server, don't forget about the issue of resource forks in some Mac files. OS X's file manager, in conjunction with Samba (a built-in open-source application that allows UNIX systems to connect to SMB networks), strips out the resource fork, if present, and saves this data in a completely separate file on the server. It places a percent sign (%) in front of its filename, which in Windows makes the file hidden to anyone looking in the folder. So if you copy a Mac file called photo.psd to a Windows server, the original data fork gets saved in a file called photo.psd, and the resource fork is stripped out and saved in a file in the same folder called %photo.psd.

Then, when coming back, this separate file is read and reassembled into a complete Mac file after it copies to the Mac. Nifty, huh?

There are more elegant, but pricey, solutions to connecting to Windows servers from the Mac. Thursby Software's popular DAVE and ADmitMac programs offer a more sophisticated solution to forked files than Samba. Their protocol places resource fork information directly behind the raw data of a file, with a "wall" between the two. This allows you to have a single file on the Windows server. PC users see only the data fork, but Thursby's products also see the resource information behind the wall and use it to reassemble the Mac file when it copies back over. Go to www.thursby.com for more info.

To connect to a server using good ol' Samba, do the following:

1   In the Finder, choose Go > Connect to Server.

2   Type in either the domain or IP address of the Windows server using one the following nomenclatures:

smb://domain_or_ip_goes_here/thisfolder

cifs://domain_or_ip_goes_here/thisfolder

3   Click Connect.

4   You are then prompted to authenticate your domain, username, and password to the server.

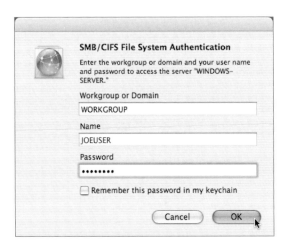

After you authenticate, a window with a list of available share points will appear. Share points are either volumes, or folders on volumes, that the administrator has made available to you based on your access to the server.

5   Choose the share point you wish to mount from the pull-down menu and click OK.

The share point icon pops up on the Desktop and also appears as an icon in any Finder window.

6   Use your server.

Permissions Issues with Servers

Sometimes you may not have access to folders you should be entitled to. Or perhaps you find you can't rewrite a file you've copied to your Desktop from a server.

These issues arise from permissions settings set incorrectly on the server, or from a misunderstanding of correct permissions settings that were created, usually for good reason.

If you connect to servers as a guest, permissions on files are usually ignored when copying to and from a server. That way, all users can read and write to accessible folders on the server. However, if you use authentication to get into your server, your administrator might have set up specific permissions to protect your assets or those of other users.

Consult your administrator to resolve these issues.

Sending Files over the Internet

From time to time, you might need to send Final Cut Pro project files, and perhaps some XML content files, over the Internet to another FCP user.

Remote facilities are often used to create offline edits of a project, for example. When the cut is complete, the project file is emailed to another facility to complete the project.

If you find yourself using the Internet to send these kinds of files, the facility that receives your file probably did not do our exercise to force the Finder to recognize .fcp file extensions. What now?

One approach is to preserve the HFS metadata for Mac files by encoding them into a compressed wrapper. That way, every aspect of the file, including its metadata type, is preserved during the encode.

Zipping and Stuffing

To preserve the file system metadata of files such as FCP project files, or even small QuickTime movies, your best bet is to encode them into a compressed file using OS X's built-in pkzip feature or a third-party utility such as Allume's StuffIt.

Think of this process as placing your files in a weatherproof Pelican case, readying them for the arduous journey through the perilous Internet. This way, your offering can be unencoded on the other end, with your files' icons, file system metadata, and actual content intact. The following sections show examples of each method.

Zipping a Single File

1   In the Finder, Ctrl-click your FCP or other file and choose Create Archive of [filename] from the shortcut menu.

In a moment, a zipped archive of the file, with an extension of .zip, will appear.

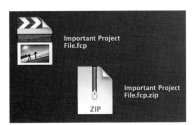

Zipping Multiple Files

Use this method to create a .zip archive of a group of files you want to send through the Internet.

1   In the Finder, place all of your files into a newly created folder.

2   Ctrl-click the folder and choose Create Archive of [folder name] from the shortcut menu.

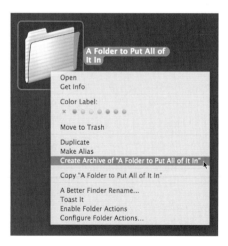

In a moment, you'll see your archive of the folder, with a .zip file extension, ready for sending.

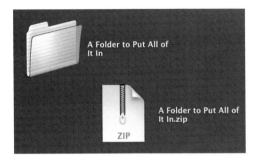

Using Allume's StuffIt

Allume offers several file encoding products, including the all-encompassing StuffIt Deluxe. But their no-frills offering, StuffIt Standard, comes preinstalled on OS X, and you can get updates to this free version from Allume's Web site (www.stuffit.com).

You can use StuffIt in lieu of OS X's built-in .zip file maker, in case your recipient requests it. The process is the same, except you'll drag the file or folder onto the DropStuff application in order to make the file.

1   Drag your FCP or other file onto Allume's DropStuff application.

You might encounter a registration request for the program. You can either register the application or click Not Yet.

The StuffIt file, with an extension of .sitx, will appear, with a little cardboard box icon to boot.

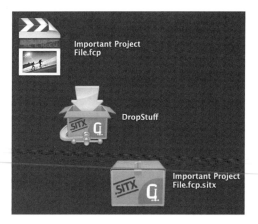

Attaching Encoded Files to an Email

Now that you have the file or files encoded inside of an archive wrapper, you can simply place the file in an email as you usually do, by dragging and dropping.

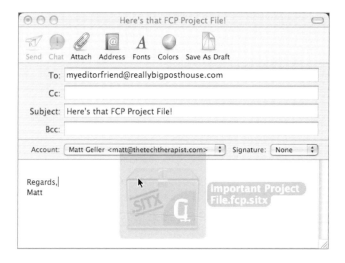

Placing Files on an FTP Site

Your files can also be uploaded safely to an FTP site, using an FTP client such as Transmit (www.panic.com).

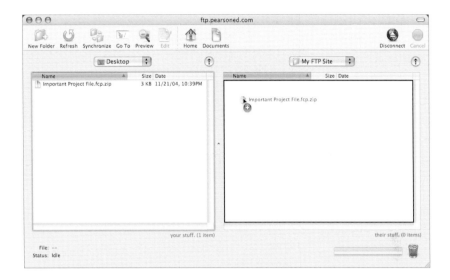

Unencoding on the Other End

When the user receives the email or downloads the FTP file you have sent, all she needs to do is double-click the archive. OS X's built-in unzipper or Allume's StuffIt Expander will decode the archive and deliver the file, with its metadata intact.

Working with Files from Proprietary Systems

QuickTime files are an almost universal exchange system when transporting media from the Final Cut Studio to other applications on different platforms, such as Adobe After Effects and Boris Red running on Mac or Windows boxes. However, you might also have to deal with files from systems that have proprietary file formats, such as Avid Media Composer Adrenaline and Meridien or Autodesk Media and Entertainment Flint and Flame. The following sections offer solutions and tips to prepare media files going to or from these systems.

Avid Adrenaline and Meridien Systems

Projects exported as OMF compositions from Avid systems can be converted to Final Cut Pro project files (and vice-versa) using a nifty set of applications from Automatic Duck, Inc. (www.automaticduck.com). Namely, the Pro Import FCP module allows FCP to import OMF compositions exported from Avids, and the Pro Export module allows FCP project files to be exported into Avid-compatible OMF compositions.

Often, Avid editors offer up a QuickTime file of a particular clip from an Avid project, or perhaps a final version of an edit. They often use the Same As Source setting from their QuickTime export, which yields a file that's unreadable by a non-Avid-based Mac system. This is because Avid uses proprietary codecs for their exported QuickTime files, which fortunately they offer for free on the Web. Even if you don't think you'll ever need these codecs, the following steps will prepare you in case the need arises:

1   Point a browser to
     www.avid.com/content/3555/Avid%20Meridien%20Codecs%20Mac%20OSX.sit

     After this downloads to your Desktop, you will find in a folder (named Avid Meridien Codecs Mac OSX Folder) two QuickTime codec components named AvidAVDJCodec.component and AvidAVUICodec.component

2   Drag these items to your hard drive's /Library/QuickTime folder, where they will live with their other component brethren.

3   Restart your machine.

Now, you'll be able to use QuickTime files exported from an Avid project on your system.

Autodesk Media and Entertainment Stone Systems

Products, such as Flint and Flame, use their own proprietary Stone system for storing media files. To turn these into usable QuickTime files, you can use Xstoner (www.xstoner.com). This is a combination of software: a server that resides on the Flint or Flame, and a client that resides on the Mac. The software allows networked Mac systems to browse the contents of the Stone file system and transfer image sequences into appropriate QuickTime files for use in FCP.

Importing Image Sequences into FCP

Sometimes, you may receive an image sequence from a Autodesk Media and Entertainment system, which is simply a folder full of single images that when played back one after the other, yield the moving image. Although FCP has no specific way to import image sequences as clips, you can perform the following steps to bring them into QuickTime Player, and then export a QuickTime movie, which can be used in FCP:

1 Launch the QuickTime Player.

2 Choose File > Open Image Sequence.

3 Navigate inside the image sequence folder, highlight the first image in the sequence, and click Open.

4 Select the Frame Rate needed for the sequence and click OK.

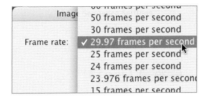

The sequence will open into a QuickTime window.

5 Choose File > Export to export the sequence into a QuickTime file.

6 Make sure Movie To QuickTime Movie is selected in the Export pop-up menu.

7 Click the Options button to change the codec used for the export, if necessary.

8 Name the file to export and click Save.

9 Quit QuickTime Player.

Now the file is ready for importing into FCP.

Lesson Review

1. What are some differences in the ways Windows and Mac file formats store information about file types?

2. Some Mac files may have two forks to hold file content. What are they?

3. Final Cut Pro 5 saves its project files with what filename extension?

4. Name a smart precaution to take when sending files over the Internet.

5. What do programs like Automatic Duck and Xstoner do?

Answers

1. File systems like Windows store information about file type directly in the name of the file, using filename extensions. Macintosh file formats use a database within their file system to store information about file type.

2. Data and resource forks.

3. .fcp

4. Files destined for Internet travel should be encoded in a wrapper using OS X's .zip file function or Allume's StuffIt.

5. They allow FCP systems to interact with proprietary systems from Avid and Autodesk Media and Entertainment.

15

Lesson Files　　None

Media　　None

Time　　This lesson takes approximately 3 hours to complete.

Goals　　Learn what Xsan is and how it can help your facility

Understand the importance of extensive planning before implementing a SAN

Acquire a specific list of equipment needed for the SAN

Implement a SAN, complete with directory services for the clients

Optimize an Xsan Installation for use with Final Cut Pro

Xsan Implementation

Apple's Xsan Shared Storage System solves an industry-wide problem: how to share large digital media files among many users, allowing simultaneous access to any particular file, while providing data security and integrity. And you get breathtaking performance to boot!

At this point, you may have decided to implement an Xsan system at your facility, or you're weighing the complexity and costs involved. In either case, this chapter provides an overview of the necessary planning, a detailed implementation section that yields an actual six-seat Xsan system, and instructions on how to set up FCP for real-world production work with Xsan.

Xsan software allows tremendous flexibility in the way its components are implemented and configured, and this chapter is by no means intended to be a standard by which to set up Xsan systems. Instead, it's a digest of some complex concepts and techniques, and it offers insight into Xsan's functionality. As you will see, there is an intimate association among the operation of Xsan, OS X Server, and Fibre Channel and Ethernet networking. Knowing all these concepts is essential to successfully implementing Xsan systems. It is highly recommended that you use an integrator with Xsan Medallion status to help integrate your Xsan system.

Before you read the information and try the exercises in this chapter, make sure that you understand the terminology and concepts in Lesson 9, especially the information on RAIDs, RAID levels, SAN concepts, and Xsan itself.

Planning the SAN

Before you spring for all of the equipment needed to bring an Xsan system to life, you need to pull out a pencil and a calculator and make some plans for the implementation of a system.

The Importance of Planning

Planning the SAN ensures

▶   The proper blend of security and performance for your SAN

▶   The reduction of the points of failure of the SAN

▶   A path for growth

With the flexibility and convenience of shared storage comes the necessity for proper security and performance guarantees. In small facilities, full access to every file for every client on the SAN may be acceptable, but other facilities may wish to keep certain projects secret and available to only a select group of editors. Files on the SAN may require different levels of redundancy, depending on their importance. Performance must meet the day-to-day needs of the facility in order to replace its current direct-attached systems. These all require planning infrastructure of both the physical components of the SAN and the actual creation of storage areas and folders on the SAN volume(s).

Most of us are unfortunately aware of the consequences of having important direct-attached storage go down and the headaches of not having network file servers available. With SANs, these worries are combined. Fortunately, there are redundancy provisions for almost every part of Xsan, so if a hardware or software component fails, a similar component can pick up the ball and keep the SAN online. Proper planning of the infrastructure, and buying the right equipment to implement it, can minimize your SAN's chances of failing.

Most importantly, proper planning lets you smoothly upgrade and enlarge the SAN when your needs outpace the SAN's current capabilities. One of Xsan's most outstanding features is that you can add storage or clients to it with almost no downtime. Having an eye to the future while planning makes sure that the proper infrastructure and equipment is there to accommodate perhaps sudden and drastic increases in storage availability or client need.

Bandwidth Considerations

We'll start our planning with the most important of all considerations: bandwidth. For the SAN to work properly, it must provide enough throughput so all clients can hum away, reading from and writing to the SAN simultaneously.

There are two essential bandwidth considerations when planning your SAN:

▶   Bandwidth need—A calculated maximum bandwidth that all clients could conceivably pull from the SAN if operated simultaneously

▶   Bandwidth availability—The calculated maximum amount of throughput your SAN will provide

We want our bandwidth availability to be higher (by a certain margin of comfort) than our bandwidth need.

In our calculations, we'll start with bandwidth need first, since its result will dictate the equipment necessary to create the larger bandwidth availability.

Calculating Bandwidth Need

Bandwidth need is based on the following:

▶   The number of clients you will have on the SAN

▶   The highest level of video, film, or audio formats your facility uses

▶   The maximum number of real-time streams you need to work on recurring projects

To calculate bandwidth need, you simply multiply these three considerations together. This yields a value, in megabytes per second (MB/s), that will determine the theoretical maximum need at any given moment of your SAN.

Using the tables in the "Data Rates and Storage Requirements for Common Media Types" section of in Lesson 9, you can easily calculate your SAN's bandwidth need.

Two examples will illustrate the calculation:

A 10-seat SAN for a news facility works entirely with package editing using the DV25 format. Each editor uses primarily an A/B roll technique, and therefore needs up to three streams of real-time availability, since cross-dissolves and titles could occur simultaneously in a given sequence. So this SAN's bandwidth need is: 10 clients × 3 streams × 3.65 MB/s per second, which yields 109.5 MB/s.

A three-seat boutique post facility SAN uses SD most days, but is flirting with doing high-end 720p 24-frame based work in 10-bit uncompressed as well. We'll give them a luxurious three streams of real time in this format, provided that they have the top-of-the-line G5s to do it. So the bandwidth need is: 3 clients × 3 streams × 55.67 MB/s = 501.03 MB/s.

A Word on Mixed-Stream Environments

In the previous calculations, we didn't mix compressed and uncompressed workflows in a single SAN, although you might have mixed workflows in your facility. Using different kinds of video streams yields a unique challenge for SAN implementations: the storage controller has a much harder time accurately predicting the needs of a client requesting data from the storage.

Uncompressed video streams offer great predictability, since every frame being read or written is a whole and complete frame. Compressed streams vary, sometimes widely, as to how much data is transacted per frame, since they are compressed.

Because of this, when you're using mixed streams, the overall performance of the SAN may seem to deteriorate, as compared to its performance when serving up exclusively uncompressed or compressed streams of data. As a result, you need to be even more conservative when estimating the bandwidth need in systems that use mixed streams.

Calculating Bandwidth Availability

Bandwidth availability is based on the following:

▶ The number of LUNs you have

▶ The number of physical disks per LUN

▶ The RAID level of these LUNs

▶ How the LUNs are gathered into storage pools

▶ The nature and redundancy of your Fibre network

As a general rule of thumb, when using Apple Xserve RAIDs as your storage, and assuming LUNs that are formatted with seven drives in a RAID 5 configuration (as they are when you open the box), you can conservatively plan bandwidth availability with this formula: 80 to 100 MB/s per port, or 160 to 200 MB/s per Xserve RAID.

This formula will generally aggregate upwards. This means that four Xserve RAIDs, with eight seven-drive LUNs, combined into a single storage pool, are currently yielding a total bandwidth availability of 640 to 800 MB/s. You may also consider having multiple volumes, each with their own specific bandwidth availability, which allow you to shuttle availability around to creatives and projects that need it most.

The efficiency of your storage will also increase if you can use a single LUN to create an initial storage pool that is specifically designated for the metadata information of the SAN, and then use your remaining LUNs to create a second storage pool exclusively for regular data. The downside with this plan is that you usually end up allocating a tremendous amount of space for a relatively small amount of metadata, but using this method will increase the efficiency of the SAN.

Lastly, how your SAN nodes and controller ports are connected to the Fibre Channel switch is critical for accurately calculating bandwidth availability, since the very nature of the switch topology can affect this number. The general rule of thumb here is that any particular client port should have the least amount of cable "jumps" to the storage ports for greatest efficiency. More on Fibre switches in a moment.

Storage Considerations

Right after bandwidth considerations come storage size needs. You increase storage by adding hard drives in a LUN, adding LUNs in a storage pool, or adding storage pools to a volume.

In many cases, bandwidth considerations alone will dictate the size of your volume(s) for Xsan, but if you need more storage than your results deliver, there is no harm in increasing your storage, provided that each of your volumes stays within the current 16 TB limit.

Provisioning for future storage increases is also an important consideration, and it is quite easy to implement, provided your infrastructure can handle it.

An Example of Instantaneous Storage Increase

Let's say your calculations yielded a SAN that has four LUNs consisting of seven drives each in RAID 5, and you chose to implement this with two fully configured Xserve RAIDs. If you needed additional storage in the future, you could simply add two additional Xserve RAIDs to the volume by adding their four LUNs to a new storage pool and adding this pool to the pre-existing volume. This would instantaneously double the size of the volume.

Volume Size Limitation

The current size limitation for an Xsan volume is PB (petabyte, which equals one million gigabytes), so you probably won't exceed that for quite a while. Larger volumes require metadata controllers using the fastest Xserves, loaded with RAM, which you'll learn about in a moment.

Xsan can handle as many as eight volumes per SAN, so another choice for increasing storage capacity is to add another volume to the SAN, making sure that it consisted of the right combination of LUNs, LUN populations, and RAID levels that satisfied our bandwidth requirements calculated in the previous section.

RAID Levels for Video Work with Xsan

For video work, there is little argument to going with any RAID level other than 5 when using Xserve RAIDs, since the built-in RAID 5 optimization makes their performance very close to RAID 0. Xserve RAIDs out of the box come preconfigured for RAID 5. You can find more information on this in the RAID Admin documentation or Lesson 13.

If you have the luxury to implement a metadata-only storage pool in your volume, then a two-drive RAID 1 LUN should be created, in order to have a complete clone of the metadata on both drives, in case one fails.

How these RAIDs are cobbled together is an art—"LUNscaping." Consult the *Xsan Quick Reference Guide* (Peachpit Press) for more information on how RAID sets are combined together to create efficient and versatile volumes.

Workflow Considerations

Besides the fundamental changes to aesthetic paradigms that come with shared storage environments, there are several practical workflow considerations to note as you move your facility into a SAN.

Switching from Auto-Login Local Directories to a Centralized Directory

Yes, it's true. You've read about it, and maybe went into denial, but you have to wrap your mind around it now: Xsan systems need a centralized directory in order to work seamlessly, mainly because of the way Xsan grants file access in real time to requesting users. Each user must have a unique identity on the SAN, so that no one gets confused about who is asking for access and who has access at any given moment. Xsan uses the numerical user ID (UID) and group ID (GID) of each user in order to determine their identity.

As you will see later in this lesson, whenever a Mac is born into the world, it starts its life with a UID of 501, a GID of 501, and administrator access to the files of the hard drive. So if two or more admin users on separate Macs tried to get access to the same file on the SAN at the same time, whether reading or writing, major confusion would break out as to which user had access. (Will the *real* 501 please stand up?) File corruption or even storage failure could result if two users tried to write to the same block of storage at the same time. Scary!

To completely eradicate this issue, we implement a centralized directory—ideally Open Directory in OS X Server—that will grant unique user IDs for every user who intends to use the SAN, and have those users log in to their client machines.

Centralizing the directory with Open Directory (once it's established) makes the creation and management of your SAN user base quite simple.

Lastly, since FCP and other creative applications sometimes look for absolute path structures to write some of their preference, cache, and log files, home folders will remain on the local hard drive, even though we will use a server to log in to our accounts.

Migrating Former Stand-Alone Editing Bays to Xsan Clients

As the previous concept sinks in, it might occur to you that there are pre-existing editing systems that you may wish to turn into Xsan clients. These machines are a little bit trickier to implement into Xsan than new machines, since important data exists in the main user account (and perhaps other user accounts, if the computer is shared with other creatives).

Because all users of Xsan will be created in the centralized directory of OS X Server's Open Directory, user data will need to be carefully transferred from the old NetInfo-based local user folder to the new LDAP-based local user folder. Then, proper ownership commands will need to be performed on these files so that they live happily in their new home. Can you say chown three times fast? If not, go hire an ACSA.

There may also be pre-existing media files on the direct-attached storage that would do much better on your SAN once it's in place. Never fear with this: shared files can simply be copied, at blissfully fast speeds, from this storage to the SAN once it's running. However, if currently direct-attached Xserve RAIDs are destined for Xsan usage, all of their data must be backed up prior to the conversion, as Xsan's file system is completely different from HFS+.

Provisioning Ingest/Layback Stations

A delightful consideration when implementing a SAN is the equipment that *won't* be needed when storage is being shared among users and computers.

Our SAN will still require video files to be ingested off of and laid back to tape or other sources, but for the first time, not every editing bay needs to have the proper decks, monitors, calibration equipment, and high-end capture cards in order to do so. A particular client or group of clients can have this expensive equipment, while other bays can be set up for offline editing, or editing with proper monitoring using inexpensive hardware.

Infrastructure Considerations

Xsan requires the addition of a Fibre Channel infrastructure to your facility, and quite possibly an additional set of Ethernet lines as well. The equipment that both provides and controls the storage should be rack mounted in a central location in your facility. Each individual consideration, along with relevant facts and figures, is outlined in the following sections.

The Metadata Controller (MDC)

Xsan allows file-level locking by arbitrating file access on an out-of-band Ethernet network, called the metadata network (MDN). The computer that does the arbitrating is called the metadata controller (MDC).

MDCs do all of the arbitration of file access within their RAM, to have the least amount of latency when clients request access to a file. Xserve G5s are recommended to be MDCs over regular desktop G5s since their ECC RAM has built-in error checking. One other advantage of the Xserve G5 is its capability to be rack mounted close to the storage and switches.

The MDC needs an initial pool of 512 MB of RAM, plus an additional 512 MB of RAM for each volume it will handle. MDCs handling volumes over 16 TB need as much RAM as you can afford to put in the Xserve.

Standby MDCs

You need at least one MDC in an Xsan system, but having two is better for redundancy. The standby MDC sits at the ready in case the primary MDC fails, and takes over the duties of the MDC in as little as half a second. If you choose not to implement a standby MDC, you may assign a current client to standby MDC status. However, in the rare case that a client acting as standby MDC actually takes over, that client's and the overall SAN's performance will substantially decrease if you try to do anything else with the client, especially edit in Final Cut. This is why having a proper standby MDC is critical, especially in large implementations.

Choosing the Right Fibre Channel Switch

Fibre Channel switches are the very heart of a SAN, and here you get what you pay for.

Switches can be divided into two main categories: *arbitrated loop* and *fabric*. Arbitrated loop switches manage traffic by routing exclusive conversations between two individual ports on the switch, whereas fabric switches allow simultaneous conversations between every port. Further, fabric switches also allow greater flexibility when creating inter-switch links (ISLs) between multiple switches. ISLs extend the fabric nature of the Fibre network by cascading data (think two-way waterfall) between switches, offering an easy way to expand the number of ports available for clients and storage, and also providing redundancy in conversation routing, which helps to reduce any point of failure in the switches themselves.

As you can imagine from these descriptions, fabric switches carry far larger price tags for all the extra features and flexibility! In some Xsan implementations, these extra features are critical to ensure the proper availability and bandwidth of the Fibre network.

Of the switch manufacturers that Apple currently certifies, three of the four make fabric switches for Xsan. Cisco (www.cisco.com) MDS 9000 series and Brocade (www.brocade.com) are considered industry paradigms and have price points to boot. Qlogic (www.qlogic.com) switches are priced more competitively and offer one particular model (SANbox 5200) that has an attractive feature: more ports on the unit can be opened when needed by purchasing an unlocking code from the manufacturer.

This leaves us with Emulex (www.emulex.com), whose Apple-approved models are exclusively arbitrated loop (355 and 375). These models have In-Speed technology, which allows them to have simultaneous conversation functionality similar to fabric switches. They are the least expensive Apple-approved switches.

Fabric switches provide the greatest efficiency and flexibility when creating SANs for post-production work, and they will be most likely specified for Xsan systems. Although Emulex arbitrated loop switches are excellent price points for database and graphic arts implementations, they are not recommended for video-based SANs.

Lastly, since the number of ports on the switch is critical in choosing a particular model, each manufacturer offers switches with varying numbers of ports. You'll need to select a switch, or a set of linked switches, that provide the correct number of ports for both your current needs and your future plans. For every Xserve RAID on our SAN, you need two ports; for every client, you need two ports; and for each MDC, one port. Further, you will need extra ports if you want to create ISLs between switches, and most importantly, if you want to add storage or clients to the SAN in the future.

Ethernet Switches for the MDN

You will need an additional Ethernet switch to handle the metadata network. Gigabit Ethernet switches are recommended, especially since almost all nodes have Gigabit Ethernet ports these days, but 100BaseT switches will suffice as well. The switch doesn't need to be managed, although it is possible to provision a zone on an existing managed switch that is large enough to carry the traffic for every node and isolate the traffic to just the nodes on the SAN.

Ethernet NICs and Fibre HBAs

For implementations where access to a pre-existing directory, network servers, or the Internet is necessary, each client node will need an additional Ethernet network interface card (NIC). Xserve G5s acting as MDCs won't require Ethernet NICs since they have two built-in Ethernet ports. In some cases, you might run out of slots on PowerMac G5s for an Ethernet NIC. Read more in the implementation section about how to circumvent this issue.

Apple's Fibre Channel host bus adaptors (HBAs) are the most sensible choice for HBA cards, since they often cost half or a third the price of typical cards on the market. One card is necessary for every node (MDC or client) on the SAN.

When buying either Ethernet NICs or Fibre HBAs, be sure to get the fastest speed available. Apple currently offers 133 MHz PCI-X versions of both these cards.

Cabling and Run-Length Issues

SANs pose a new challenge to the physical logistics of your facility: since the storage is centralized, where do you put it? Most facilities opt to place the storage in their core, which is a room filled with rack-mounted computers, drive arrays, decks, and other equipment that geeks drool over. Since servers and switches (both Fibre and Ethernet) are also usually rack mounted, the connections between these components and the storage RAIDs are done with relatively short cables.

However, the actual editing bay client nodes, sometimes located hundreds of feet away from the core, need extra-long runs of cabling in order to connect to the main SAN components. Further, and even more importantly, Xsan implementations that have the centralized directory, Internet, or other services on an outer network need two Ethernet cable runs from each client node. In some cases, this means that a new Ethernet infrastructure needs to be created apart from a pre-existing one.

In general, CAT 6 or 5e Ethernet cabling for both the metadata network or the outer network can have relatively long runs, up to 329 feet (100 meters). If these runs are too short to connect to the core, repeater mechanisms can be inserted within the cable runs to refresh the signal strength, or convert the Ethernet signal to an optical Fibre signal and back, and boost their total length.

Lastly, the Fibre Channel infrastructure is almost always a new addition to the facility. Thankfully, Fibre Channel cables can consist of either short-run copper substrate, with a maximum recommended length of 10 feet (3 meters), or super-long-run optical substrate, with a maximum recommended length of 10 kilometers. Note that Fibre Channel optical cables are expensive and require equally expensive electrical-to-optical transceivers on each end. The following table illustrates your choices for optical Fibre Channel cabling.

Optical Fibre Cabling Options

Cable Width	Maximum Run Length	Transceiver Needed
9 microns	10 km	Longwave
50 microns	500 m	Shortwave
62.5 microns	300 m	Shortwave

Optical Transceivers

Apple-recommended transceivers for optical cable are made by Finisar, JDS, and Pico Lite. You can find a full list of model numbers on the Xserve RAID technical specifications page: www.apple.com/xserve/raid/specs.html. What's important in implementing transceivers is that you stay consistent with manufacturer and model on both sides of the optical cable.

Power Considerations

With Xsan systems, the elements that usually stack together in a rack in the core of your facility, the Xserve(s), Xserve RAID(s) and switches, must all be connected to robust, reliable, filtered, and most importantly uninterrupted power. With their redundant power supplies, disk drives, and fans, these components draw huge amounts of power, so make sure that your core is wired properly, and that you provide a UPS that will allow the core system to run for at least a half hour in the event of a power failure, so that the system can be shut down formally.

Typical Topologies

The following figures show typical topologies for production environments. Again, these are guides, intended to provide a summary of the previously discussed information as you plan and acquire your equipment for integration.

The Three-Seat Boutique

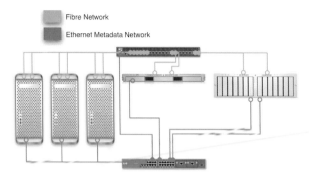

In this example, we have three clients accessing a total of 3.9 TB of storage. The SANs bandwidth availability with one fully populated Xserve RAID is 160 to 200 MB/s. This SAN is isolated: the system is not connected to an outer network, which is perfect for implementations where the content being edited is highly confidential. Because of this, and because the SAN is relatively small, the Xserve is both MDC and directory server. For convenience, Ethernet cabling runs from both controllers of the Xserve RAID and the Fibre switch, in case they need to be administered.

The Six-Seat Episodic Team

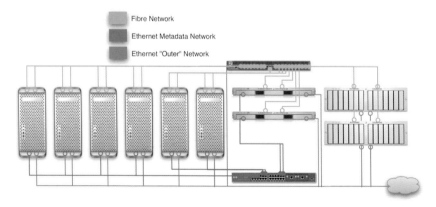

In this larger implementation, we have six clients accessing a total of 7.9 TB of storage. The SANs bandwidth availability with two fully populated Xserve

RAIDs is 320 to 400 MB/s. This SAN is connected to an outer network. Notice that all trivial Ethernet components are now routed to this outer network, and only the nodes of the SAN are on the metadata network. Further, we have a standby MDC available to take over MDC duties in case the primary MDC fails. For directory services, we have three choices:

▶ The primary MDC is the open directory master of the SAN, with the standby MDC as a replica.

▶ The standby MDC is the open directory master of the SAN, with the primary MDC as the replica.

▶ The directory has been moved to the outer network, thereby allowing the Xserves here to just be MDCs.

The 10-Seat Post Facility

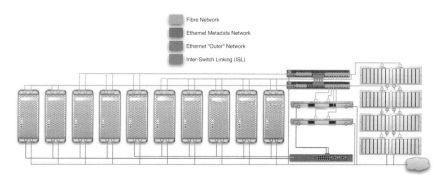

In this implementation, 10 clients share 15.99 TB of storage. This SAN's bandwidth availability with four fully populated Xserve RAIDs is a whopping 640 to 800 MB/s. Because of the number of Fibre cables in this topology (32 total), an additional switch has been implemented. Data cascades effortlessly between the two switches because a high-bandwidth inter-switch link (ISL) has been made with six user ports on each switch. Think of it as a data river that flows bidirectionally between each switch. A primary and standby MDC are mandatory with such a large implementation, and to keep their roles simple and efficient, the directory is implemented on the outer network.

Installing the SAN

Now that we've gone over the fine points of planning the SAN, and you have made purchase decisions relevant to the bandwidth and capacity needs of the SAN, it's time to hook up the spigots and get the thing running.

> **NOTE ▶** Before you go barreling into these steps, make sure you realize that your Xserve RAIDs need to be "cooked" (powered up for the first 36 hours of its life for a format and verification process) in order to work optimally when added to the SAN. So, if your Xserve RAID is brand new, take it out of its box, hook up both power cords to the Xserve RAID and to the wall, power it up from the button in the rear, and leave it alone—for a day or so. When all the blue lights turn off, hold down the power button for a moment until the unit shuts down. Then you can begin.

Installing the Fibre Channel and Ethernet Cards

First, with all equipment powered down, we will install the necessary internal hardware for our SAN.

1   Install Fibre Channel host bus adapter (HBA) cards into each Mac (G4, G5, or Xserve) that is being connected to the SAN directly.

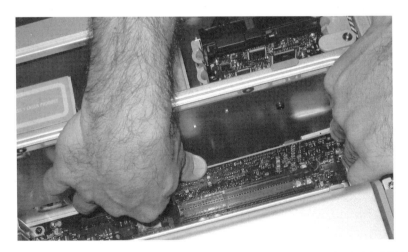

Installing the Fibre HBA into a G5 PowerMac, in this case, into slot 4 (133 MHz PCI-X)

Installing the Fibre HBA into an Xserve G5

NOTE ▶ Fibre Channel cards are most often installed into PCI-X slot 2 or 3 of G5s (the slots that are closer to the bottom of the computer), reserving the upper PCI-X 133-MHz slot 4 (and its isolated PCI-X bus) for fast cards such as capture cards. However, if a particular machine will not need capture hardware, install the Fibre Channel HBA into slot 4. Alternately, if your G5 has a fast capture card in slot 4, and has a nVidia GeForce 6800 or ATI Radeon 9800 graphics card, your choice of where to put the Fibre card will be limited to PCI slot 3, due to the extra thickness of these graphics cards. There are no limitations to where you install the Fibre Channel controller card on a PowerMac G4 or either G4 or G5 Xserve.

PCI-X slot 4
(133 MHz)

PCI-X slot 3
(100 MHz,
shared with slot 2)

PCI-X slot 2
(100 MHz,
shared with slot 3)

Dual-processor G5 PCI slot locations

The next step is necessary if you intend to have the Macs in your SAN access your facility's network or the Internet.

2   Install Ethernet network interface cards (NICs) into each Mac (G4 or G5) that needs to connect to the facility's network.

> **NOTE** ▶ Wow, it's getting crowded back there. If you have a capture card installed in PCI slot 4 and a Fibre card in slot 2 or 3, your choice is simple: install the NIC in the last remaining slot. However, if you have one of the double-wide graphics cards mentioned in the last note, a Fibre card in PCI slot 3, and a capture card in PCI slot 4, you have run out of slots! Unless you intend to use Airport as your outer network (which has its own security issues), Apple is currently recommending not using a capture card in a G5 that sports a double-wide graphics card that will also be on an Xsan. Alternately, you can now spring for the newer single-slot ATI X800 card that is able to drive 30-inch monitors. In this case, the bandwidth-hungry Fibre card should be reinstalled in PCI slot 4 and the Ethernet NIC in PCI slot 3. Xserve G5s come with two built-in Ethernet ports, so you won't need a NIC for these machines.

Connecting the Fibre Channel Network

Get your thumb and forefinger ready—it's time to make the connections necessary for the Fibre Channel network to function.

1   If you are using optical cables for your Fibre infrastructure, make sure to attach the optical transceivers, mentioned earlier, to each end of your optical Fibre cables.

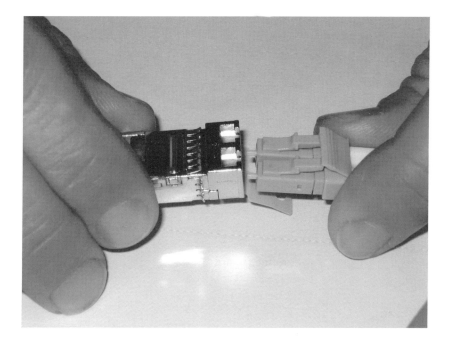

NOTE ▶ When using optical Fibre cable, take great care not to bend, kink, tread on, or otherwise mistreat the cables, because they are very susceptible to failure if any part of the Fibre substrate is damaged. Optical cables should be laid into conduit, rather than pulled through. Faulty optical cables are also very hard to troubleshoot, apart from simply changing them out to see if the problem goes away. Needless to say, it's best to have more cable than necessary in order to do this.

2 Connect either copper or optical Fibre cables to both ports of each Fibre Channel controller card on each Mac, including your server, that is being connected to the SAN.

Connecting a copper Fibre cable to a G5 PowerMac Fibre HBA

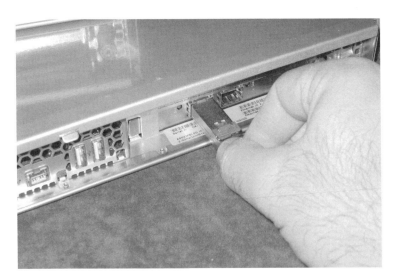

Connecting a copper Fibre cable to an Xserve G5 Fibre HBA

NOTE ▶ Although not mandatory, hooking up two cables to each Fibre Channel HBA allows the multipathing function of the Xsan software to function. If one port fails, the other port will take over for communication. Having two cables will also increase the data bandwidth capability of each computer, which is critical when implementing Xsan for post-production use. However, MDCs read and write such small amounts of data to the SAN that one cable is sufficient for hooking the MDC to the switch.

3   Connect either copper or optical Fibre cables to both controller ports of each Xserve RAID that is being connected to the SAN.

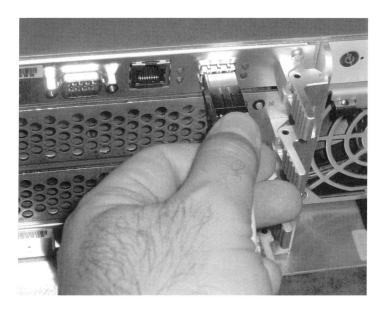

NOTE ▶ In this exercise, you'll configure two Xserve RAIDs, but your implementation may use more or fewer. Just make sure you have enough ports on your Fibre switch for everyone.

4   Connect all the other ends of the cables to the Fibre Channel switch.

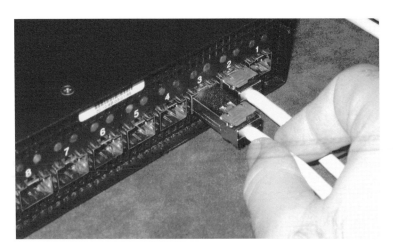

NOTE ▶ If you truly want to geek out on the connections to the Fibre switch, the customary protocol is to hook up connections for the Xserve RAIDs to the last available and active ports on the switch. The MDC (and standby MDC) nodes get hooked up to the first available ports. The client nodes get hooked up to the ports right in the middle.

We won't cover zoning of Fibre switches, or whether switches auto-sense if connectors are optical or copper. Most recommended switches do not have preset zones, and they automatically sense what kind of cable is plugged into what port, which makes them easy to use. However, many switches require specialized firmware for use with Xsan. To that end, be sure to consult the manuals and support sites of your switch for more information.

Connecting the Private Metadata Network

We will now hook up the Ethernet network that will handle the metadata. Some installations that are not concerned about connecting the machines on the SAN to the facility's network will create their private network out of the built-in Ethernet ports on the Macs. However, if you need to have your SAN machines also on the facility network, and have installed Ethernet NICs in each G4 or G5 that will be on the SAN, you will then create your metadata network with either the NIC or the built-in port, with the remaining port used to access the outer network. Just make sure to be consistent across all nodes, as to which interface you will use. For Xserve G5s, we will use the en0 (lower) port to configure the metadata network. Later on, you can assign the settings for the facility network to the built-in port on G4s and G5s, and the en1 (upper) port on Xserves.

1   Connect CAT 5e (or better yet, CAT 6) Ethernet cables to the appropriate Ethernet port (built-in Ethernet port on G4s and G5s and first-generation G4 Xserves, and the lower port labeled 1 on Xserve G5s) for each Mac on the SAN.

Connecting a CAT 5e cable to the built-in Ethernet port on a G5 PowerMac

Connecting a CAT 5e cable to port 1 (lower) of a Xserve G5

2   Connect the other end of each cable to your Gigabit (1000BaseT) or 100BaseT Ethernet switch.

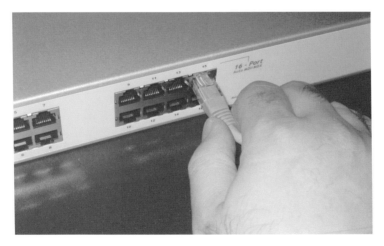

Connecting a CAT 5e cable to the GigE switch

Implementing Directory Services, Part 1

It's now time to create the directory server that will be responsible for creating and managing the users and groups on the SAN.

If you already have a directory set up at your facility, whether it is being served up by Mac OS X Server's Open Directory or Microsoft Windows' Active Directory, you may want to bind your controller and client nodes on your SAN to that pre-existing directory, using the outer Ethernet network. If so, you can skip this section.

However, on installs of six or fewer client nodes, it is permissible for an Xserve running OS X Server to also act as the controller node for the SAN. For larger installs, you will want OS X Server running on a separate Xserve, and a separate G5 or Xserve acting as the controller node. Think of the difference between a small restaurant and a huge banquet facility: the former can get away with one chef, whereas the latter definitely needs a main chef and a sous-chef.

We will assume you have purchased an Xserve that will serve up directory services for the SAN while simultaneously acting as its primary MDC, and that you have an install of six or fewer client nodes. Therefore, we will proceed as follows:

1   Configure the Xserve.

2   Update the Xserve's OS X Server to the latest version (if needed).

3   Create an Open Directory Master on the Xserve.

4   Set up the users and groups of our SAN.

5   Install Xsan software.

6   Configure the Xserve as the primary metadata controller (MDC).

This section covers the first three of these steps. We will cover the remaining three steps later.

We hope you found the previous sections blissful and mindless, because that state of mind will now end. As we said before, this part will be easier with an Xsan Medallion and/or ACSA-certified integrator at your side or in your head, whichever is more convenient.

What We Won't Cover

Regardless of the size of your SAN, the configuration of OS X Server is the same. Because of space constraints, here is what we will *not* cover in this section:

► Installing a fresh copy of OS X Server on an Xserve

► Updating an Xserve's OS X Server software from 10.X.X to 10.3.X or 10.4.X

► Installing, updating, or configuring OS X Server on a G5, rather than an Xserve

► Implementing OS X Server on the outer network of the SAN

For more information about these scenarios, you can go to the following online resources:

► www.apple.com/server/documentation—Apple's excellent online documentation page

► consultants.apple.com—Apple's online search tool to find ACTC and ACSA consultants in your area

► www.afp548.com—An online forum specifically oriented toward OS X Server implementation

► www.macosxhints.com—An online forum focused on OS X in general, but with excellent threads on OS X Server as well

There are also excellent Web resources for Xsan implementation:

► www.xsanity.com—A Web site specifically dedicated to the foibles of Xsan implementation

► www.creativecow.net—Their Apple Xsan forum is a frequent hub of new ideas and solution

> NOTE ► The installation process described in the following sections is solely for implementing directory services for use with Xsan. OS X Server has many services to offer your facility, such as Web and mail services, firewall protection, and the like. In the following steps, we will only be implementing directory services for an isolated SAN system.

Configuring a Client Node to Act as a Temporary Remote Admin

1   Power up the Ethernet switch for the metadata network.

2   Power up the Xserve.

> **NOTE** ▶ Most Xserves are headless, meaning they have no graphics cards installed to drive a monitor. As a result, most are configured and adminis- tered remotely. If you already have a PowerMac or PowerBook that has the OS X Server Administration Tools installed on it, you can connect this machine to the Ethernet switch to perform this part of the process, and skip steps 3 and 4.

3   Power up another Mac on the network that will serve as a client node.

    We will use this Mac to configure the Xserve remotely.

4   Log in to this Mac on an admin account.

5   Install OS X Administration Tools on this client node.

> **MORE INFO** ▶ The OS X Administration Tools are a free download from www.apple.com/support/downloads. Make sure to download any update to the tools to make sure they are the latest.

6   Install Apple Remote Desktop on this client node.

> **MORE INFO** ▶ Apple Remote Desktop (ARD) is an indispensable part of remote control and configuration of any network. It also costs money. For more information, see www.apple.com/remotedesktop.

Configuring the Xserve Remotely

Now that we've installed the OS X Server Administration Tools software on our client, we can connect to and configure our Xserve.

1   Continuing on the client node, launch the Server Assistant application, located in /Applications/Server/.

2   Select "Set up a remote server" and click Continue.

You will be presented with a list of servers, and hopefully, through the magic of Bonjour, you will see the Xserve, with the default name of local-host waiting to be configured.

3   Double-click in the Password column for the Xserve and type in the first eight characters of the Xserve's serial number, then press Return.

TIP ▸ You can find the serial number of an Xserve on a label in the back, along the bottom panel, under the PCI slots. You will probably have to remove your connected Fibre cable to see the number. You can also find the serial number on a side of the box that the server came in. If you are using a G5 desktop as your server, remove the side panel, and you will see the serial number at the bottom part of the inside frame.

4   Click Continue to authenticate the server.

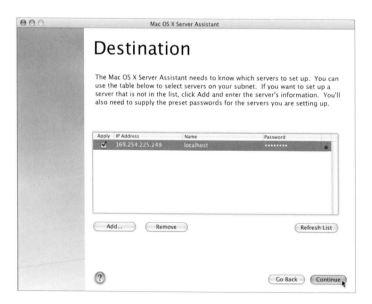

You will then be passed to the main configuration screens. You will be asked for the language to configure the server in, the keyboard configuration, and finally the serial number for OS X Server.

You will then be prompted to create an admin account on the server, which you will then use to log into it remotely from now on. Choose this admin username and password wisely.

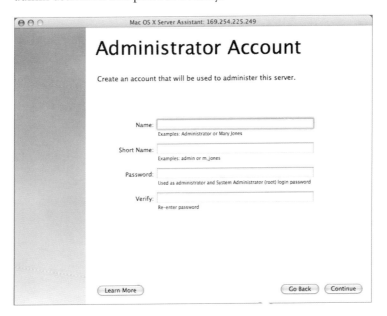

The next screen will ask for the server's name to replace the default name localhost. In our case, we'll use a short, sweet name for our server: mdc.

5   Enter *mdc.local* in the first two fields of this screen, but only *mdc* in the last, then click Continue.

Our server's name from now on will be mdc.local. You will now be at the
Network Interfaces screen.

6   Turn off all interfaces except for the Built-in Ethernet port's TCP/IP, then
click Continue.

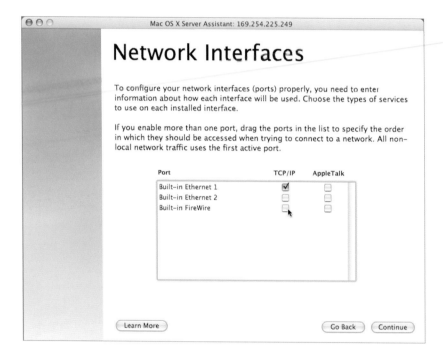

You are now presented with the TCP/IP Connection screen.

In order for our metadata network to have as little chatter as possible, we
will configure static IP addresses for each machine. We'll start with the
Xserve and work our way out from there. The following table has suggestions for private address ranges for the isolated network. In our steps, we'll
use the ten-dot range.

Private Network Address Ranges

Private Address Range	Associated Subnet Mask	Comments
10.0.0.0 – 10.255.255.255	255.0.0.0	10/8
172.16.0.0 – 172.31.255.255	255.240.0.0	172.16/12
192.168.0.0 – 192.168.255.255	255.255.0.0	192.168/16

7   In the TCP/IP Connection window, choose Manually from the Configure pull-down menu.

8   Type *10.1.0.1* in the IP Address box, *255.0.0.0* in the Subnet Mask box, and finally *10.1.0.1* in the Router box, then click Continue.

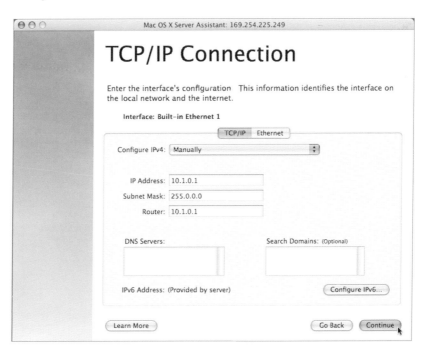

NOTE ▶ Notice that we have placed the same address in both the IP Address and Router boxes. The metadata network actually has no router, since its information is not being routed to or from a larger network. The reason for the fake router address is for the routing tables of the server, just in case a client machine asks for data not on the metadata network. The server, when queried, will simply drop this request.

If you invested in a managed Ethernet switch, the switch itself will have an IP address. In this case, you can assign the router setting for step 8 to the address of your managed switch.

9 In the Directory Usage screen, leave the "Set directory usage to" pull-down menu as Standalone Server, then click Continue.

NOTE ▶ Most seasoned OS X Server administrators would tell you that you should really create an Open Directory Master once the server is configured and properly running. They would be right, so we'll be promoting this server to an Open Directory Master after we have it up and running.

The Assistant then asks if we'd like to employ other services.

10 In the Services screen, click the last check box—Apple Remote Desktop Client—then click Continue.

We will need ARD on in order to further configure or update the OS of the server using Apple Remote Desktop.

11 Select the appropriate time zone from the Time Zone screen, then click Continue.

12 In the next screen, Network Time, deselect the "Use a network time server" button, and click Continue.

Since we are not connected to the Internet on this metadata network, trying to ping an external time server will just add chatter.

13 Finally, review all of your settings and click Apply.

After a few minutes of configuration time, you will be presented with a box stating that the server needs to be restarted.

14 Click Continue Now to restart the Xserve, or just wait until it restarts itself.

15 Quit the Server Assistant.

Hopefully, you have a frothy beverage to enjoy at this point, because you are 87.3 percent done configuring your Xserve. Mazel Tov!

Setting the Client Node's Static IP Address

As you'll recall, we configured our Xserve with a static IP address. In order to talk to it again, we'll have to configure our client node with complementary IP information.

1 Still on the client node, choose System Preferences from the blue Apple menu, and go to the Network pane.

2 From the Location pull-down menu, choose New Location.

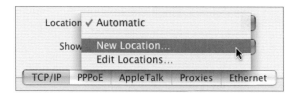

3 Name the new location *Metadata Network* and click OK.

4 From the Show pull-down menu, choose Network Port Configurations.

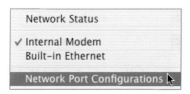

5 Turn off all ports except for Built-in Ethernet.

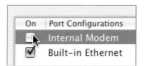

6 From the Show pull-down menu, choose Built-in Ethernet.

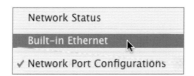

You will be looking at the TCP/IP Settings for this machine.

7 From the Configure IPv4 pull-down menu, choose Manually.

8 Type *10.1.0.100* in the IP Address box, *255.0.0.0* in the Subnet Mask box, and *10.1.0.1* in the Router box.

NOTE ▶ Again, if you are using a managed Ethernet switch on your metadata network, place the IP address of the switch in the Router box for step 8.

This will be the address for this client node.

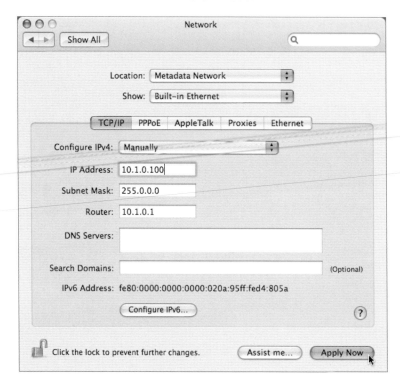

9   Click Apply Now and close the System Preferences window.

Updating the Xserve to the Latest Version of OS X Server

If you have the luxury of having the latest OS X Server install discs, you can skip this step. If not, you'll need to update your server software to the latest version. This is true even if your Xserve is not acting as an MDC. Since our metadata network does not currently connect to the Internet, you will do a little old-fashioned sneaker-net transfer of the update packages to the network.

1   From your facility's network, download the latest Mac OS X Server Combined Update from www.apple.com/support/downloads.

2   If you are running an older Xserve G5, download the Xserve G5 Firmware Update 5.1.7f1, also available from the URL in step 1.

3   Transfer these packages to a FireWire drive.

4   Plug the FireWire drive into front FireWire port of the Xserve.

5   On the client node, launch Apple Remote Desktop.

6   In the Remote Desktop Setup screen, enter an admin username and password identical to the admin account for the server, then click Done.

Both your MDC server and your local client pop up in ARD's scanner list, which shows up by default.

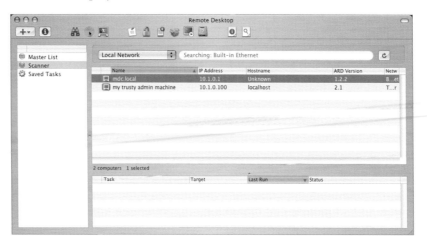

In some cases, the ARD client we turned on when we configured the Xserve will be an older version. Follow these steps to update the client software on the Xserve to the latest version.

1   Select the MDC server in the list.

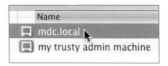

2   Choose Manage > Upgrade Client Software.

You will be prompted to add this computer to the Master List.

3   Enter *mdc.local* in the DNS name box, and the username and password of the admin account for the server in the appropriate boxes, then click Add.

4   In the Upgrade Client Software screen, click Upgrade.

It will take a little while to install and start up the new ARD client software on the server. A status window will pop up to inform you of the progress of the upgrade.

5   When the upgrade is complete, close the Status window.

Now that we have the right version of the ARD client software running on the server, it's time to install the packages from the FireWire drive.

1   Back in the main window of ARD, click your MDC server, then click the Control icon in the toolbar.

A login screen appears.

2   Enter the admin account username and password, and click the Log In icon.

3   Now that you are in, install each package from the FireWire drive.

    NOTE ▶ If you perform the Xserve G5 firmware update, you will be required to shut down the Xserve and hold down the power button when starting it up again to reprogram the firmware. Read the About document that comes with the firmware update for more information.

4   When all your packages have been installed, quit Apple Remote Desktop.

Creating the Open Directory

In the next steps, we will set up the server to serve a directory using Open Directory. This will allow us to create a listing of users and groups that will be universally accessible throughout the network. We'll use the Server Admin application to do this.

1   From our trusty client node, launch Server Admin, which you'll find in /Applications/Server/.

When the program launches, you will be prompted to add a server to administer.

2   Enter *mdc.local* in the Address box, and the username and password of the admin user in the next two boxes, and click Connect.

Information about the server loads into the window.

3   From the list of services at left, click the Open Directory service.

4   Click the Settings tab.

5   Change the Role from Standalone Server to Open Directory Master.

You'll then be prompted to enter information about the directory.

6   The directory admin username and password should be different from your "regular" server admin username and password for security reasons, but it's your choice. The dialog box suggests a username of "diradmin." Fill in the rest as shown in the following image.

7 Click Save.

Setting Up Users and Groups Using Workgroup Manager

Now that the directory is created, we'll run Workgroup Manager and populate the directory with some users and groups. The users and groups we'll create will be fake, just for fun, but feel free to substitute your actual users and groups instead. We do this now, because once we set up and configure the client nodes, and bind them to the directory, the users of the SAN will already have been set up in the directory: all your users will have to do is log in to the machine on which they'll be working.

1 With Server Admin still open, click the handy Workgroup Manager button in the upper-left corner of the interface.

Workgroup Manager automatically launches.

MORE INFO ▶ Since Server Admin and Workgroup Manager are used so often with one another, they have hot link buttons to the other program in the upper-left corner of their interfaces.

2 At the Workgroup Manager Connect screen, type *mdc.local* in the Address box, and the directory administrator username and password in the next two boxes, and click Connect.

Once we're connected, the main Workgroup Manager appears. From here, we'll first add some groups.

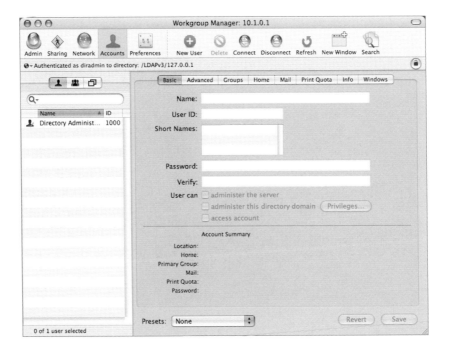

1   In the upper left of the window, click the Groups tab.

2 Click the New Group button in the toolbar.

A new group, Untitled 1, with the GID of 1025, appears in the list at the left.

3 In the Name box, type *Creatives*.

The short name creatives automatically gets created as you type.

4 Click Save.

5 Use steps 2 through 4 to create two more groups: *Editors*, with a GID of 1026, and *Graphics*, with a GID of 1027.

When you're done, your three groups should look like this:

🧑‍🤝‍🧑 Creatives	1025
🧑‍🤝‍🧑 Editors	1026
🧑‍🤝‍🧑 Graphics	1027

Next we'll create some users for our directory.

1 Click back on the User tab in the upper left.

2 Click the New User button in the toolbar.

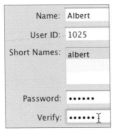

A new user, with the name of Untitled 1 and the UID of 1025, appears in the list in the left.

We will now modify the name of this user.

3 At the right, in the Name box, type *Albert*, then press Tab twice.

Albert's short name is, rightfully, albert.

4 In the Password and Verify boxes, enter Albert's password.

For fun and ease, just enter *albert* for the password.

Name:	Albert
User ID:	1025
Short Names:	albert
Password:	••••••
Verify:	••••••

5   In the upper area of the window, click the Groups tab.

6   Click the plus (+) button at right to assign some groups to Albert.

A drawer appears, with your newly created groups in a draggable list.

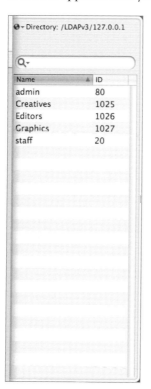

7 Drag the Creatives group to the Primary Group ID box (which currently states 20) in the main window.

Albert's primary group ID changes to 1025, that of the Creatives group.

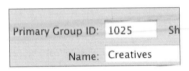

8 Drag the Editors group to the Other Groups box.

9 Also drag the staff group to the Other Groups box.

We make Albert a member of staff since staff is a system-level group.

10 In the upper right of the window, click the Home tab.

We will now establish that the user's home directory will mount locally where they log in from, which is necessary for FCP to run correctly.

11 Click the plus (+) button to add a home directory path.

A dialog appears for you to place in the path information.

12 In the Home box, type *Users/albert* and click OK.

13 Click Save.

The user info is saved into the directory.

14 Use steps 3 through 7 to create another user, *Bonnie*, making her password the same as her short name. When assigning groups to Bonnie, make her Primary Group ID Creatives, and her three other groups: Editors, Graphics and staff. Then, instead of steps 11 through 13, substitute the following steps.

15 After you click Bonnie's Home tab, you'll see a /Users home directory path already specified for her. Click the little disc icon in the list that has /Users listed next to it, which will highlight it.

16 Click Save.

Bonnie's info is saved into the directory.

NOTE ▶ After creating the first user in a directory, as you did with Albert, Workgroup Manager assumes you wish to have all additional users' home directories along the same path. This is why it was not necessary to manually put in the path for Bonnie's home directory.

17 Use the same steps to create a final user, *Charles*, whose password is the same as his short name. Charles' Primary Group ID should once again be Creatives, but let's make Charles exclusively a graphics guy: only place Graphics and staff in his Other Groups box. Finally, make sure to click the Home tab and make sure his home directory is also /Users.

To review, we have all three folks in our Creatives and staff groups, but Albert is exclusively an editor; Charles is exclusively a graphics guy; and the multi-talented Bonnie is a member of both. This is just one of many group schemes you can use to divide your users into manageable chunks.

You could also group folks by title or even the job number of their current project. You can see that adding, modifying, and deleting users and groups through the Workgroup Manager is very powerful.

18 Quit Workgroup Manager.

Congratulations are in order again, because we have now finished setting up the first, and most difficult, part of our Directory Server. Now, let's get the SAN actually up and running.

Installing Xsan Software

It's time to get the software installed on each machine on the SAN. We'll first get our other client nodes booted and configured on our metadata network, so we can do as much of this as remotely as possible.

Setting the Additional Client Nodes' Static IP Addresses

NOTE ▶ Every additional client node must have an admin account, and you should log into this admin account as you configure the machines in the next two subsections.

1   Start up each additional client node, and log in as an admin user.

2   For each additional client node, follow steps 1 through 9 in the "Setting the Client Node's Static IP Address" section, but modify step 8 slightly by entering *10.1.0.101* for the next node's IP address, then *10.1.0.102*, and so on.

3   For ease of implementation, it helps to place each machine's IP address on a sticky note on the edge of its screen.

Installing Xsan Software via ARD

Now we will install the Xsan software on all of our machines that will be on the SAN, which includes all of our client nodes and our Xserve.

1   Get back onto our trusty Admin client node, and pop the Xsan Software Install CD into the optical drive.

2   When you see the CD mount on the Desktop, double-click the CD icon to open it.

3   Find the Install Xsan.mpkg application and drag it to the Desktop.

4   Eject the CD.

5   Launch Apple Remote Desktop.

Now that you've added all the other client nodes onto the metadata network, you'll see their IP addresses in the main Remote Desktop window. Now we will upgrade the ARD client software on all these machines, in one step, like we did with our Xserve earlier.

1   Select all the client Nodes in the current scanner list.

2   Choose Manage > Upgrade Client Software.

    You will be prompted to add each computer to the Master List.

3 Enter the username and password of the admin account for that particular
client in the appropriate boxes, then click Add.

4 Repeat step 3 for each client node.

5 In the Upgrade Client Software screen, click Upgrade.

6 When the upgrade is complete, close the Status window.

From here, you can install the Xsan software on all your machines, and the
Xserve, in one step, from one location.

1 Select all the client nodes (except the one that you are currently on) and
your MDC server in the list.

2 Choose Manage > Install Packages.

3 Drag the Install_Xsan.mpkg icon from the Desktop to the Install Packages window.

4 Click the "Restart target computers after installation" check box.

5 Click Install.

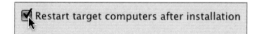

The Xsan software will automatically copy over to, and install itself on, each of your selected computers. They will also all restart when finished.

6 When the task is complete, close the Status window.

NOTE ▶ You may not want to install the Xsan Admin application (the program that administers the SAN, similar in design to Server Admin) on any machine belonging to anyone you wouldn't want trying to administer the SAN. But perform the install using the preceding method anyway. If you don't, some system resources that aid the MDC in first discovering the clients may not be installed. You can always manually delete the Xsan Admin application, located in /Applications/Server, from the client machine once the software has been installed and the machine has restarted.

Further, we are assuming that every client node has OS X 10.3.8 installed on it. If it doesn't, use ARD to update each client node to 10.3.8, then install the Xsan software.

7   Quit Apple Remote Desktop.

8   Finally, install the Xsan software on the Mac you are using to do all of this centralized work. (It's right there on the Desktop.) It needs Xsan as well!

9   When the installer finishes, restart the machine.

Implementing Directory Services, Part 2
Now that we have all the software installed, it's time to get the client nodes bound to the directory that we set up earlier.

Binding the Client Nodes to the Directory Server
We will configure the Directory Access application—found in each client node's /Applications/Utilities folder—to look for directory information from our Xserve. This way, end users will be able to log in from a client node and be able to have proper access to different directories on the SAN volume(s). More importantly, each end user and group will have unique user and groups IDs, which will make the MDC very happy.

1   After our Admin client node has restarted from its Xsan software install, launch Apple Remote Desktop on it.

2 Select the first additional client node on the list, and click the Control icon in the toolbar.

3 In this client node's Control window, launch the Directory Access application, found in the /Applications/Utilities folder.

4 Observe the lock icon in the lower left. If it's locked, click it and authenticate with the admin username and password for that client node.

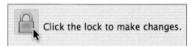

5 In the middle of the window, click the LDAPv3 listing, then click Configure.

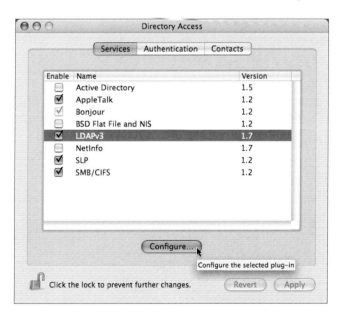

6 Click the blue disclosure triangle next to Show Options.

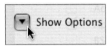

7 Click New to create a new configuration.

8 Type mdc.local in the Server Name or IP Address box.

9 De-select the Use For Contacts check box, and click Continue.

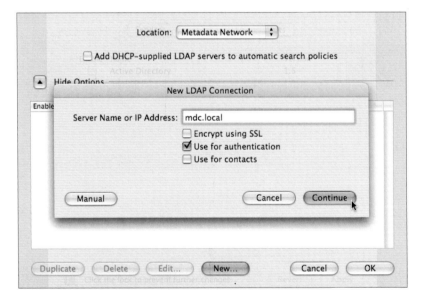

10 Click OK to leave this sub-window.

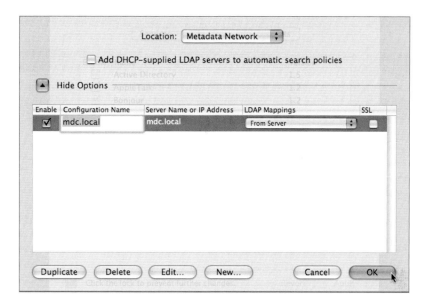

11 Click OK to complete the binding.

12 Quit Directory Access.

13 Close the Remote Desktop control window for this node.

14 Repeat steps 2 through 13 for each additional client node.

Now let's remember to bind our Admin client to the directory as well.

1 Leave Remote Access running, and launch Directory Access on the Admin client.

2 For this final client, follow steps 3 through 12 in the preceding exercise.

Finally, we will shut down all the machines, before we fire up everything in sequence and get ready to configure the SAN.

1   Back in Remote Desktop, select all machines, including your MDC server, on the Remote Access list (except your Admin client), and choose Manage > Shut Down, then click the Shut Down button.

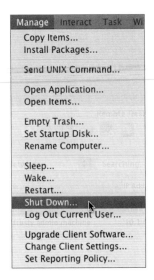

Watch in glee as all the machines shut down.

2   Quit Remote Desktop on the Admin client.

3   Shut down the Admin client.

Setting Up and Configuring the SAN with Xsan Admin

These final steps will allow us to get our storage and our nodes together and create a SAN. Let's go.

Firing the Whole Thing Up

It's time to power everything up, in sequence, in order to use Xsan Admin to create and configure our SAN.

1   Power up, in order, the

   ▶   Ethernet switch (if not already on)

   ▶   Fibre switch (these take up to two minutes to power up)

   ▶   Xserve RAID (wait until all status lights in the front of the unit are on)

   ▶   Xserve (and wait until it's fully up, then...)

   ▶   Clients

   NOTE ▶   Wait a minute! We haven't talked about setting up or configuring our Xserve RAID! In our exercise, we will make four assumptions:

   ▶   All Xserve RAIDs, no matter how many drives they have in them, come from the factory preconfigured as RAID Level 5. Because the Xserve RAID is optimized for RAID 5 usage, you might not see much better performance if you reformat it to RAID Level 0. So, our suggestion is to leave it as is.

   ▶   You've read the little note about "cooking" your RAID. If not, go back near the beginning of the "Installing the SAN" section and read it.

   ▶   Your RAID is either fresh from Apple or has had its firmware updated to the latest and greatest version. If not, use RAID Admin to upgrade the firmware of your RAID. See Apple's support Web site for more info on this.

   ▶   You are configuring two Xserve RAIDs, but you can configure as many as you like, up to 256 5.6 TB Xserve RAIDs per volume! You'll just be labeling and throwing more LUNs into your storage pool. More on that later.

Authenticating and Serializing Nodes

The pieces of the puzzle will come together in this next step, where we use the powerful and simple Xsan Admin app to create and mount the SAN.

1 Once again from the trusty Admin client, launch the Xsan Admin application, located in /Applications/Server.

Upon launching, the program will ask for an address to log into. We will give it the address of the machine we want to be the metadata controller, which is our server.

2 In the Address box, enter *mdc.local*, then authenticate with the name and password of the server's admin account, and click Connect.

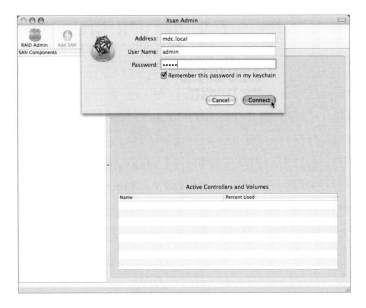

3 Click the Setup tab.

Hopefully, you'll see as many entries as you have nodes in your SAN in the list that appears: your MDC server, plus the IP addresses of all of your clients.

We're now going to validate all our nodes with serial numbers, so make sure to have them handy. Remember, you'll need a unique serial number for each node, including the metadata controller.

1 Double-click the entry for your MDC server.

A window drops down, prompting you for information.

2 From the Role pop-up menu, choose Controller.

The Failover Priority should automatically be set to High, and Built-In Ethernet should appear under the last pop-up menu.

3 Enter the serial number.

Enter on of your serial numbers, and if you with, fill the Registered To and Organization fields with appropriate information.

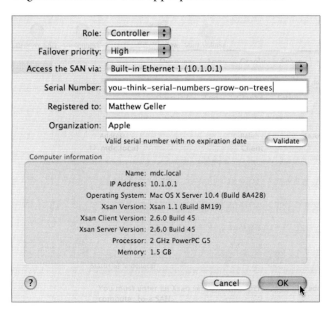

We are setting our server to be the MDC (and only MDC) of this SAN. Further, the first MDC will always get a high failover priority, because we will want this node to be the MDC first. Later, if you add more MDCs, you'll set their priorities in the order you would want them to take over the SAN in case one fails. Lastly, with the selection of the built-in Ethernet of the server, we have officially dubbed our Ethernet network the metadata network.

4 Click OK.

Your MDC server should have a green light next to it, reflecting its new status as an MDC.

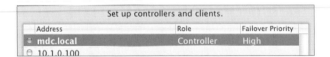

5 Double-click your first client node.

You will be presented with an authentication for this address.

6 Type in the administrator's user name and password for this machine and click Authenticate.

In a moment, the listing will show an orange dot next to it, meaning that a successful authentication has happened across the network.

7 Double-click this client node again.

You are prompted for a serial number.

8   Type in a new serial number for this node, and click OK.

Since this node is a client, we needn't change anything once the password is in place. We should return to the list with this node shining green as well.

9   Repeat steps 5 through 8 for the rest of your client nodes.

When you are finished, all nodes should have green lights shining.

10 In the SAN Name box, type a name for your SAN.

This isn't the volume name; just a nice name for the SAN in general.

11 In the lower-right corner of the interface, click Save.

You will see the SAN name reflected in the SAN Components list at left.

Assembling and Starting the Volume

This part is really fun: here you get to get to create a huge storage volume by dragging and dropping icons!

1   In the upper area of the interface, click the LUNs tab.

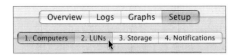

You'll see four (or more or less, depending on the number of Xserve RAIDs you have on hand) LUNs with yellow dots in this list. These LUNs are ready for use, but are not labeled as Apple Cluster File System (ACFS) LUNs for our volume, so we'll do that now.

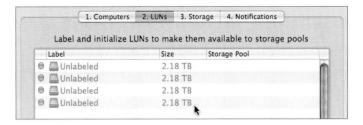

NOTE ▶   For factory-fresh Xserve RAIDs, you'll see two LUNS per Xserve RAID on your Fibre switch. If you see fewer than two, check connections on the switch or on the back of each RAID.

2   Double-click the first LUN.

A window drops down and asks for a label name.

3   Type *LUN1* into the box and click OK.

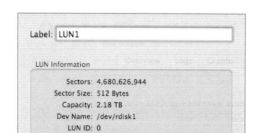

4   Repeat steps 2 and 3 for each additional LUN, incrementing the number at the end of the name each time (*LUN2, LUN3, LUN4*).

5   When finished, click Save.

The labels are applied to the LUNs, which now gleam green.

NOTE ► Once LUNs are labeled for Xsan's ACFS, they are no longer available for good old HFS+ formatting. In order to get them unlabeled, I'm afraid you'll have to venture into the command-line interface and use the cvlabel command, which will be necessary if you ever intend to use these LUNs for HFS+ again. More info on this in the Xsan Admin Guide.

6   In the upper area of the interface, click the Storage tab.

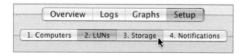

Here is our volume playground.

7   Click the Volume icon.

A window drops down to ask for a volume name.

8   Type in the name for your volume, and click OK.

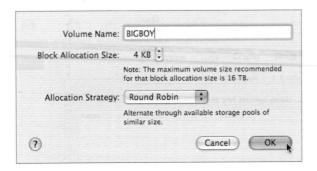

An icon for your volume appears in the Storage window.

You just entered the name of the disc that the nodes will see mounted on the Desktop. We will leave the other settings (Block Allocation Size and Allocation Strategy) unchanged because they are set up perfectly for general purpose video file usage. You can read more about them in the Xsan Admin Guide.

9   Click the Storage Pool icon.

A window drops down to ask for information about this storage pool.

10   Type *POOL1* in the storage pool Name box.

11   Click "Any data" for the "Use for" setting.

NOTE ▶ We have the option of creating our initial storage pool exclusively for metadata and process journal information only. This is to increase performance on nonmetadata storage pools by isolating the relatively small and articulate metadata to its own pool. One day you might do this. Today, this storage pool will contain both the aforementioned data and regular ordinary data, happily commingling.

12 Leave the Stripe Breadth at 256 blocks and click OK.

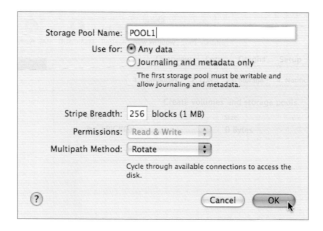

NOTE ▶ Apple says that a Stripe Breadth of 256 blocks yields the best general use performance on fully populated (14-drive) Xserve RAIDs.

Also, someone somewhere on our SAN will want read and write permissions, so we'll keep that setting at its default.

Finally, the Multipath Method is set to Rotate to switch to a second Fibre cable if the first one fails.

A Storage Pool icon appears, indented inside your volume.

13 Click the Available LUNs button.

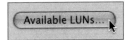

A drawer reveals your ready-to-drag, labeled LUNs.

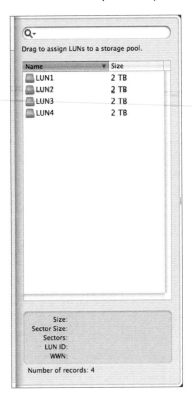

14 Grab them and drag them to your pool.

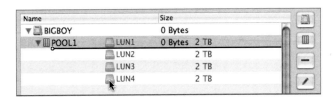

Your volume is now built. Look how big that thing is!

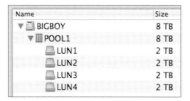

15 Click the Close Drawer button.

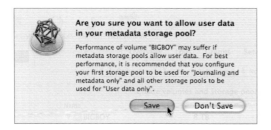

You are prompted with a warning about mixing metadata and user data in the same Storage Pool. As mentioned earlier, you should avoid this for best performance, but for our exercise, it'll suffice.

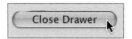

16 Click Save.

The volume creation process takes just a moment.

17 In the upper left of the interface, click the disclosure triangle next to your SAN name.

Your volume pops up nested below it.

18 Select the volume name.

19 Click the Start Volume button.

Again, another pause as the volume gets ready to be mounted. After a while, you'll see a green light next to the volume name at left.

Mounting the Volume on the Nodes

Notice now that when clicked on the volume, our button names have changed. Now the interface changes its context to the settings of our volume. This is how we will mount the volume on the nodes.

1 Click the Clients tab.

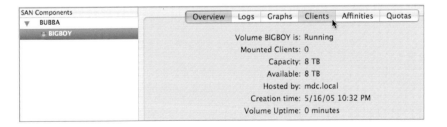

A list of your authenticated and serialized nodes appears.

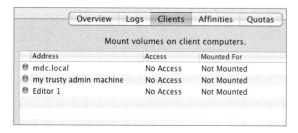

Now don't go crazy here. Although we can mount the drives on all clients simultaneously, let's mount one node at a time.

2   Select one of your client nodes (the one you are currently working on is ideal) from the list.

3   Click the Mount Read & Write button.

After a short pause, you'll see a thing of beauty on your Desktop: a SAN volume to call your very own.

4   Repeat steps 2 and 3 for all the additional nodes, including your server!

5   Have fun running around the room(s), watching the volume pop up on everyone's Desktops.

This is required.

NOTE ▶ Okay, a bit of seriousness here is necessary. If any of your nodes have gone to sleep during this process, it's best to wake them up before you try to mount the volume.

Implementing Directory Services, Part 3

At this point, you've probably picked this book back up after putting it down hours ago and playing extensively with your volume, establishing crazy speed tests and discovering all kinds of interesting phenomena that happen with file-level locking cluster file systems. So, if you can, put your lab coat away, and let's get down to the big reason why we created a directory in the first place, and that is to create specific areas on the SAN where different users or groups have access and read/write permissions. The exercises here are designed more for stimulating creative solutions for your storage challenges than dictating how they should look, but feel free to steal any part that works for you.

Creating Root-Level Directories

Next, we'll look at Xsan Admin's capability to create root-level (and only root-level) folders on the volume, and then we'll assign specific permission to those folders. If our workflow is simple, and we need general areas where one group can get into and others can't, Xsan Admin will do the trick for us.

> **NOTE** ▶ We can always set permissions to volume folders deeper than root level by simply creating them in the Finder, getting information about the folder, and setting permission settings there. Even though all the computers on our SAN are bound by a centralized directory, meaning that our directory's users and groups appear in everyone's lists, we'll probably want to make these folders when logged into the server via ARD, or by using OS X Server Workgroup Manager. You can learn more about setting detailed file and folder permissions in the OS X Server Admin Guide.

1 Back in Xsan Admin, click your volume and then click the Affinities tab.

> **NOTE** ▶ You must have the volume mounted on the MDC for the Affinities and Quotas tabs to work in Xsan.

2   In the upper-right area, click the plus (+) button to create a root-level folder.

A window drops down to ask for a name and affinity for the folder.

3   Type *Editors Work* in the Name box.

4   From the Storage Pool Affinity pop-up menu, choose POOL1.

5   Click OK.

A folder appears nested inside the volume.

NOTE ▶ Affinities are an excellent feature of Xsan that we're not able to leverage here, since we have only one measly storage pool. Essentially, we could direct all data placed in this folder to a specific storage pool in our volume, allowing us to save the data to a faster or more secure storage pool. Neat, huh? Read more about it in the Xsan Admin Guide.

Now let's set specific permissions for this folder.

1   Click the Editors Work folder.

2   In the lower-right area, where the permissions data is, click the plus (+) button.

Another drawer appears with a list of all our directory's users.

3   Drag the drawer out a little more to see the UIDs for everyone in our crowded list.

NOTE ▶ Sorry for the clutter, but this list is a proper server list, which includes process users. These users are not people, but actual system processes that have usernames.

4   Click the Groups button of this drawer.

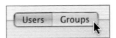

Now we see all the groups in our directory, plus all the server groups, with their corresponding GIDs.

5   Find the Editors group and drag it to the Group box in the lower portion of the interface window.

6   For extra security, change the Other settings to No Access.

No one but the Editors group will even be able to get into the folder, let alone read or write to it!

7   Using your knowledge of this interface, create another root-level folder called *Graphics Work*, and assign Read & Write permissions to the Graphics group. Lock this folder to all others, just like you did with the first folder.

8   Finally, create a *Creative Drop Box* folder, and assign Read & Write permissions to the Creatives group, but Write Only access to Others. This way, anyone can drop something in this folder for use by the Creatives.

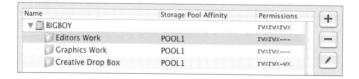

9   Click Save to save all this work.

10   Quit Xsan Admin.

To review: we have the Editors Work folder that will be available only to the Editors group; the Graphics Work folder, available only to the Graphics folks; and the Creative Drop Box, which all Creatives have access to, and anyone else can drop stuff for the Creatives in. Now let's have a look at how our directory works.

Logging in as Directory Users

What we'll do now is log out of a machine (any client node on the SAN will do), and log in as one of our users, to see the effect of these root-level folders we've created.

1   Choose Log out (Username) from the Apple menu or press Cmd-Shift-Q on the client node to log out.

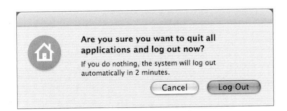

2   Press Return to confirm.

When the login window appears, you will now see an Other icon.

3   Click the Other icon.

4   Authenticate as Charles (username charles, password charles).

5   Open the volume and look at the permissions of the folders.

Looks like Charles, who is a graphics guy, can get into the Graphics and Creative folders, but not into the Editors'.

6 Log out and authenticate as Albert this time.

7 Open the volume and take a look.

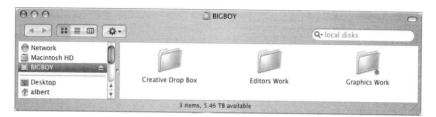

Albert, being a cutter, can't get into the Graphics folder. This may be a problem, but hopefully you know how to fix it. Let's move on.

8 Log out and authenticate as Bonnie.

Bonnie, talented cat that she is, has access to all the folders, since she is a member of both the Editors and Graphics groups, and also is a creative.

9 Log out and authenticate as the administrator on that machine.

10 Open up the volume.

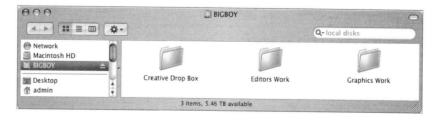

What? We gave access to everyone only with the Creative Drop Box, but even then it was only write access. Why can the client's admin get into all these folders?

The answer is simple. The admin of this machine bears the same UID as the admin for the server, 501, so Xsan sees them as the same user.

As we said earlier, every new OS X Mac, when it first starts up, gives the first user admin access and a UID of 501, just like it did with our server. Do you see the chaos we would have if we didn't have a proper directory? Do you also see why that, on a SAN, you can't give out admin privileges willy-nilly anymore?

So, as a rule, we need to add a strong password for the admin user for each of our nodes on the SAN, and create regular non-admin users for those who will use the SAN day-to-day. Some facilities will elect to create an "install admin" user that will have admin privileges in order to install applications, plug-ins, and the like. These specialized admin users should be created locally in System Preferences > Accounts, making sure they have a UID other than 501, so that they are never confused with the 501 admin of either the server or client node.

Optimizing FCP on Xsan Systems

Now that we've implemented a fully working SAN, there a few more tweaks to be done for each client node to ensure maximum throughput and minimal hassle when using FCP.

Keeping Login Computers Consistent

Centralized directories give most facilities the unique convenience of being able to log into any computer on the network as a particular user and having that user's data, preferences, Desktop pattern, and Desktop clutter come up on that computer. This phenomenon is called having network home folders. But as you read in our steps earlier, we explicitly created local home folders for our users, in order to satisfy FCP's sometimes quirky write requests.

Because our home folders will be created locally, creatives should log in to the same machines every time, in order to preserve their user experiences.

Since the directory is centralized, there is no harm in logging into someone else's computer with your user, but once you do, a new home folder is created on that machine, with brand-new subfolders, new preference files, and so on. So, if a creative ever does this and wonders where their Dock items are, you can explain what happened.

What Files Go Where?

A plethora of files are created in the course of an FCP project. Having read this far into the book, you'll no doubt have specific ideas about where these files should go. Slight adjustments have to be made when using Xsan in your workflow.

Project and Cache Files

Clearly, project files, waveform and thumbnail caches, and Autosave Vault files should be saved locally. Project files that will be shared for collaborative work can be copied to an appropriate Xsan volume folder once they have been created.

Capture Scratch and Stock Video

Setting Capture Scratch folders on Xsan volumes is absolutely encouraged. Even though you may want to set every client's Capture Scratch folder to the same folder on the volume, you should set up *unique capture scratch folders per user*. This allows more-structured organization of captured media.

Stock video files should also be located on the Xsan volume. Read further for ideas of affinity assignments for stock video files.

Stock Music and Sound Effects

Since the bandwidth requirements for music and sound effects are so low, and since a typical facility has so many of these files, their storage could be relegated to a regular file server, or a separate Xsan volume. This allows you to keep the performance-robbing hits for these files off of your video volume. You may also store the sound files on the Xsan volume, provided that they are copied locally before they are actually used within a project.

Render Files

We may want to immediately assign a certain folder of the SAN as our main Final Cut Pro scratch disk, render folders and all, as we have learned to do in other areas of this book. But alas, we might be disappointed with the Xsan's performance if we do so.

To understand why, remember the last time you did a long render. It took much longer to render that file than it took to play it back when you were done, right? Final Cut Pro's rendering engine simply opens up a QuickTime file, writes frames to that file as fast as it can render them, and then eventually closes the file when it's done. Sometimes, with very powerful machines and the rendering of still images, the QuickTime file can be created in less time than its playback speed. But in most cases, render times take much, much longer.

With Xsan, as this QuickTime render file remains open, little tiny hits on the Fibre network, especially from several users at once, will interfere with anyone else's ability to stream real-time clips.

One way to solve the issue is to create a separate LUN or LUNs, on a separate Xserve RAID controller, which can be assigned to a separate Storage Pool and Volume, dedicated to rendering. Because render files aren't as important as captured clips (they can always be remade), you could create RAID 0 LUNs to benefit from a small increase in performance.

An alternative, robust long-term solution for this issue is to create small direct-attached render arrays for your client machines.

Direct-Attached Render Arrays for Use with Xsan

Since some of you may be using high-bandwidth clips, this may require having small, high-speed direct-attached storage on your local machine for the very purpose of creating and playing back render files. The key point to remember is that render file storage almost never needs high-speed write capability, just reads. If that doesn't make sense, remember the scenario we just explored: render files almost always get created at much slower than real-time speeds, but then need to be played back in real time.

See Lesson 9 for more information on creating inexpensive small-sized high-speed storage for your systems.

Creating Affinities for Different Kinds of Media Files

As we explored in the planning section, you may want to create separate volumes, or specific storage pools within volumes, that have RAID levels other than 5 for specific kinds of media files.

For example, stock footage used in day-to-day projects almost never needs any kind of redundancy protection, since they can always be reloaded from tape, CD, or DVD back onto the SAN. They just need to be available at high speed. Therefore, storing them in a root-level folder with an affinity assignment to a RAID 0 storage pool is ideal.

Alternately, outputs of picture-lock edits, client approvals, or any other finished QuickTime file might get saved out to a folder that has an affinity to a RAID 1 storage pool. This ensures that these files can be accessed even when the primary storage goes down.

The Dreaded Umask

Because the Xsan volume is essentially a gigantic UNIX volume, it is governed by UNIX permissions rules. Therefore, the permissions of any file that is created on it, or copied to it, is determined by the umask, or user permissions mask, of the user creating or copying them.

The default umask setting for an OS X user is 022, and this number is used to offset the normal permission setting of a new folder or file, which is 666. That's not the sign of the devil, mind you; that's a simple numerical explanation that the user, his or her group, and the rest of the world can all read and write to the file.

If we subtract each number of the set 022 from its 666 counterpart, we get 644, which means that the user can read and write to the file, but the users' group and the rest of the world can only read from it.

This causes a problem with collaboration, especially when a group cannot place files inside of a folder that was created by one of its members, or if they can't save over a single collaborative FCP project that gets the incremental edits of a group of people.

How to fix it? There are several solutions.

One is to permanently reset the umask to 002, which would make all folders and files created by any Xsan user readable and writable by their groups. You can write a simple shell script and send it out to all your users to make the change permanent. Nifty shareware programs such as Marcel Bresink's TinkerTool (www.bresink.com/osx/TinkerTool.html) will do it in a nice GUI.

Another solution is to create an AppleScript droplet, or regularly running the application (chron script) that changes group permissions on all new files and folders on the Xsan volume on a regular basis.

In either case, knowledge is half the battle with this slightly annoying side-effect of collaborative storage.

Assigning Quotas to Ensure Adequate Space for Everyone

Xsan's Quotas feature is ideal for creating invisible fences inside of the volume, so that no particular user or group can hog more than their share of the storage.

In collaborative post-production environments, this will be essential to make sure that every person and project gets adequate space.

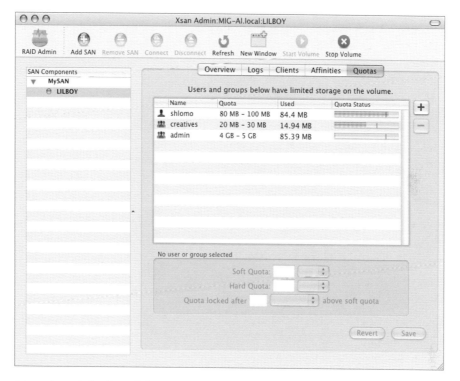

A sample quota implementation

The implementation of quotas is simple, and it is done directly in the Xsan Admin application. Users and groups can have "soft" quotas assigned that they must adhere to. Administrators can be notified by Xsan Admin via email or pager if any user or group exceeds their soft quota. After a certain time, these soft quotas turn to "hard" quotas, disabling any further writes until the particular user or group cleans up their act and gets their total space usage below their soft quota again. Users encountering this in the Finder get a −1425 write error to inform them of their inability to write to the SAN.

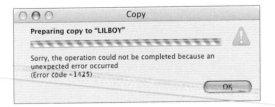

New to Xsan 1.1 is the Xsan User Quotas application, which allows your users to see where they stand on usage. Learn more about quota assignment in the Xsan Admin Users Guide.

Using the Bandwidth Limiter Inside Final Cut Pro

New in FCP 5 is the Limit Real-time Video To checkbox, which is in User Preferences. You can use it in conjunction with Xsan to limit bandwidth "hogging" from any individual client machine, by simply restricting the amount of real-time video to a certain MB/s value. If your current sequence needs more than the specified limit, the render bar turns red. Rendering at this point reduces the need to one stream. This feature is excellent for large implementations where a reasonable limit imposed on every machine yields greater performance for all. Use it by calculating the maximum number of streams needed multiplied by the data rate for that stream to arrive at the limit amount, which is placed in the User Preferences for that machine.

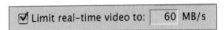

Lesson Review

1. What areas of technical knowledge do you need in order to perform Xsan integration?

2. Why is a centralized Xsan directory critical?

3. Why should metadata networks be as isolated as possible?

4. What is the first thing to consider when determining the type and amount of storage hardware to get?

5. Give three options for where Final Cut Pro render files can be created on an Xsan system.

6. Once Xsan is up and running, should you use the original 501 user on the client nodes?

Answers

1. You need extensive knowledge of Fibre Channel networking, Ethernet networking, OS X Server, and Xsan software itself.

2. So that all Xsan users have unique user ID numbers, file and folder permissions can be set easily, and the SAN can be easily expanded.

3. To ensure low latency with file access arbitration.

4. Bandwidth, specifically bandwidth need and availability.

5. a) Directly on the main SAN volume, within folders that have affinities to specific storage pools. b) On a separate SAN volume dedicated to render files. c) On small, fast, direct-attached storage for each client node.

6. No. You should create an install admin user with admin privileges, with a UID other than 501, for users who need to authenticate to install software on their machines. The original 501 user should be used for administrator access to each client machine.

Troubleshooting
Final Cut Pro

Charles Roberts

16

Introduction to Troubleshooting

In previous sections, we've discussed how to design your optimal workflow, chose the appropriate hardware, configure and maintain your system optimally, and integrate your system effectively into your production environment.

Knowing how to troubleshoot is an important part of maintaining a secure, reliable video editing workstation. As stable as FCP is, one can never predict where difficulties will be encountered in individual workflows, so you have to learn how to do the detective work.

This section takes a look at the most common errors and mistakes encountered by Final Cut Pro editors, and shows how to troubleshoot these problems when you encounter them. This lesson explains the basic methodology of troubleshooting. Lessons 17 and 18 are quick-reference guides to help you quickly resolve the most common issues users tend to encounter.

In this lesson, we'll start by reviewing the standard process of eliminating the obvious to isolate the cause of unexpected behavior.

Primary Troubleshooting Questions

Good troubleshooting relies upon on a reductive approach—isolating the source of the problem by eliminating its possible causes. This is done step-by-step, working from the most likely to the least likely cause.

Like any good detective, your first job is to ensure that you actually have a problem by eliminating any outside or unrelated factors that might have influenced your computer at the time the unexpected behavior occurred.

Before you begin methodical troubleshooting, there are three primary questions to ask: did it work before, did you check the documentation, and can you repeat the problem?

"Did It Work Before?" or "What Has Changed?"

Perhaps the most important question to ask is whether the issue existed in the past or if this is a new issue.

If, for example, you are using a new feature you've never used before, that's a likely source of error. The fastest way to correct it is to check the user's manual to make sure that you are using the feature properly.

If you are using a feature that you have used in the past, then you have a frame of reference. Ask yourself if anything has changed since using the feature last. In particular, have you added, changed, or removed any software or hardware?

If everything seems to be completely in order, perhaps something less obvious has changed. There are many circumstances to consider in any workflow. You might be working with higher- or lower-resolution media (DV as opposed to HD, for example). Perhaps previously you were working on very short projects with minimal hard drive requirements, but now you are working with hour-long sequences and larger amounts of media. Perhaps you have never worked with Photoshop multi-layer images before. There are always differences between any two given projects, and careful consideration of those differences will often clarify where the new problem developed.

NOTE ▶ It's a common-sense rule that you should try to avoid upgrading critical software or hardware while in the midst of a project. Innocent-looking software updates that appear a week before you deliver a big project can upset your entire system. It's safest to wait until you are between projects to upgrade any hardware or software in your system.

Similarly, avoid any unrelated software installations. If you must install other software, then keep good records, so that at a glance you can see the correlation between installs and problems. For instance, your list may show that you installed a new anti-virus utility last week, and now FCP will not autosave. It's important to keep good records in any situation where more than one person is an administrator on a single station.

"Did You Check the Documentation?"

The Final Cut Pro user's manual contains a wealth of documentation that thoroughly cover how the application works. Nobody likes to read software manuals, but doing so will make it far easier to use FCP effectively, avoid known issues, and adapt your workflow early in the game when you encounter unexpected problems.

Final Cut Pro Help provides quick access to FCP documentation, including the user's manual, late breaking news, and new features.

Other great resources are the Apple Final Cut Pro Support page (www.apple.com/support/finalcutpro/) and Apple's Weekly Knowledge Base changes email list (www.lists.apple.com/mailman/listinfo/weekly-kbase-changes). Both resources make it easy to stay up to date on the latest technical information about your products.

Checking any or all of these resources for reports of identical error messages or symptoms is often the fastest way to your solution.

"Can You Reproduce the Problem?"

In the rare event that you uncover inexplicable behavior that's not described in the manual or online support documents, your next step is to make sure that the behavior you're encountering is consistent and repeatable.

As you attempt to repeat the behavior, write down each step you take. Try not to add variables to the process as you test the behavior, because it's important to demonstrate repeatability when determining the causes of your problem.

It's an unfortunate reality that some issues occur intermittently, and so are hard to reproduce. This can certainly be frustrating, and can indicate that what appears to be a small issue is larger in scope. But the repeatability rules still apply, and you need to be able to demonstrate what elements were in play when you encountered the behavior.

Document Your Investigation

This is the other side of documentation: the documentation that you keep as you troubleshoot. In order to keep yourself and any other troubleshooter on a logical path to solving problems, you have to document your investigation.

When troubleshooting, it's easy to become confused and repeat irrelevant steps or miss an important factor that would have been obvious had you been looking at it on paper rather than simply trying everything you can think of. If anyone else is working with you, your notes help to eliminate redundant troubleshooting.

Narrow the Search

Once you've ruled out obvious external factors, checked the documentation, confirmed that you do in fact have a repeatable problem, and written down the steps to re-create the problem, it's time to narrow the search. There are, again, three questions you can ask yourself to help focus your troubleshooting.

"Is It Hardware- or Software-Related?"

What you're really asking here is, "Which is more likely: a hardware problem or a software problem?" The right answer will rule out half the universe of possible causes, so it's worth spending a moment to ask yourself this question.

If you just installed new software, and now your camera is not being recognized, it is most likely that the software you installed is causing the issue. Similarly, if a problem occurs only when you are working with one specific drive, common sense dictates that you should check that drive first.

Common sense should be your guide here, because symptoms alone will probably not be enough to tell you whether the cause of the problem is hardware- or software-related. For instance, faulty RAM can cause behaviors that resemble those caused by software problems, since the OS and running applications are loaded into RAM.

In these situations, you may need to rule out both software- and hardware-related causes, but it's still worth asking yourself which is more likely, and starting there. Look for other clues: in this example, if the same quirky behavior is observed in every application you run, that would make the RAM more suspect.

"Is It Mac OS- or Final Cut Pro–Related?"

If you're fairly sure that the problem is software-related, you can go a step further to determine whether the problem occurs at the system level or is specific to Final Cut Pro.

Error messages can give you insight here—is the alert a system or FCP alert? That might seem like a minor distinction, but it will point you in the right direction.

If your camera is not being recognized by Final Cut Pro, can you see the camera in the Apple System Profiler or in iMovie? If you can, then the problem is likely to be Final Cut Pro–related.

As with the hardware versus software discrimination, these issues aren't always clear-cut, but spending a moment to determine whether it's more likely that the problem lies with your system or your software can save you time during your sleuthing.

Is It a Problem of Performance, Quality, or an Error Message?

Another useful way to categorize the problem you're encountering is to determine if it's a quality problem (audio out of sync, dropped frames), a performance problem (throughput speed, playback speed, render speed), or an error message (nothing looks wrong, but you get an error when you try to perform an action).

Each of these three classes of problems implies a certain set of solutions. Categorizing your problem this way will help ensure that you try the likeliest fixes first.

In Lesson 17, we'll look at the most common quality problems and their solutions. In Lesson 18, we'll tackle the most commonly-encountered performance problems and error messages.

Eliminating the Obvious: Quick Fixes

Most issues can be resolved with very little hand wringing.

When encountering unexpected behavior, there are a couple of very quick tests you can perform to isolate and rule out the more common problems that users encounter.

Now that you've considered whether your problem is more likely to be software- or hardware-related, and FCP- or Mac OS–related, the next step is to eliminate the obvious with an appropriate quick fix. Often these quick fixes will clear up the problem entirely.

Restart the Application

It's almost too obvious to state, but if indications are pointing to a software problem, the first thing to do is always to restart Final Cut Pro. Simple, quick, and never a bad idea.

Shut Down and Restart the System

The next quick fix is to try shutting everything down, including the computer (use Apple menu > Shut Down) and any connected peripherals, camcorder, or deck. Then start up your computer, followed by your peripherals. Then launch Final Cut Pro.

This allows your machine to reset itself completely. The more complicated the hardware and software in your edit bay is, the more likely that a malfunction can occur. Completely resetting your system brings it back to square one, and often can fix the problem.

Note that in many cases, a full shutdown is required, rather than choosing Restart from the Apple menu.

Create and Log In as a New Admin User

This quick fix involves creating a new admin user to see if the issue is isolated to the user you're currently logged in as.

Although you could go into your home library and remove your preferences to eliminate preferences as the cause of a problem, it's easier to simply log out of your current user and log into a clean user specifically created for the purpose of troubleshooting. When you log in as a new user and run FCP, you can check the same project, media, and hardware using a fresh set of preferences. Don't forget that you will need to move a copy of the project you're testing to the /Users/Shared folder in order to access it using the new user account.

This is the fastest way to rule out several issues at once. Because FCP preferences are stored in the user's folder, problems specifically caused by corrupt or incorrectly set preferences will in all likelihood not exist for other users on the same system. Any special software that exists only in your home folder can be ruled out as well.

If you still see the same behavior, you can safely bet that preferences are not the issue, and you'll have to broaden the scope of your investigation. If on the other hand the problem disappears, then you know that the issue is related to something within your user login. Although that might be preferences, it could also be anything else installed there, such as applications (plug ins, presets, and so on) that you installed only in your user folder, conflicting applications that your user automatically starts at login, and anything else that your user employs that is not shared by other users.

> **NOTE** ▶ Startup applications are only listed in the Accounts system preference in the Startup Items pane. In some instances, that Startup Items pane may be the only way you would know that an application was running in the background.

After using a new user for testing issues, delete the new user. You should create a brand-new user the next time you need a fresh account for troubleshooting.

> **MORE INFO** ▶ FCP Rescue is a good third-party tool developed specifically for manipulating FCP preferences files (http://fcprescue. andersholck.com/).

Remove FireWire, USB, and Other Devices

External devices have the potential for creating conflicts, whether from special drivers required by the device, or simply because the device or device software is not compatible with other devices. This extends to devices you wouldn't normally think of, such as FireWire and USB hubs. Sometimes PCI cards or RAM, and even hard drives, can cause conflicts for one reason or another.

This obviously shouldn't keep you from investing in the products you need to get your job done, but keep the potential device conflicts in mind when you're troubleshooting. One useful quick fix is to remove all devices you are not troubleshooting.

For instance, when troubleshooting an Edit to Tape issue, you only need the deck or camcorder, your project, and the project media (hopefully located on your internal hard drive) to isolate the issue. After you've solved your problem, you can reconnect the other devices you need.

Eliminating Environmental Factors

There are a few more possible causes to consider before you start looking at well-documented issues and troubleshooting steps discussed in Lessons 17 and 18. These are less-than-obvious factors that you have to train yourself to look for as you continue building your system.

The environment in which your edit bay is located has an important impact on how well your system works. Computers don't respond well to extremes of temperature, voltage, or other factors that are more common than you might think in our technologically advanced civilization.

Temperature

Although you see a sleek metal case on the outside, your Macintosh's processors and hard drives are generating heat inside, which it distributes and ejects with internal fans. But if the room it's blowing into isn't much cooler, then you can expect heat to become an issue. Ideally, working room temperatures should not exceed 75 degrees F.

Also, look around your room for less obvious heat influences. Is the Macintosh positioned near a window where it receives full sun? Is it positioned near an air conditioning vent, making it subject to rapid changes in temperature?

Another drawback of positioning your computer near air ducts is that the Mac's air intake will pull in a higher-than-normal amount of dust. Not only does dust build-up increase the temperature of your Macintosh, it also can generate static electricity.

Cables and Wiring

Also consider what might be referred to as the *physical plant*, or the hardware interfaces of your editing station. This means any sort of connectors for hard drives or decks, PCI card input/outputs, or even the UPS power supply for your edit bay. Any hardware going into or coming away from the case of your Macintosh is an interface with the outside world, and will probably receive some physical abuse during its normal operating lifetime. Damaged cables and connectors are a leading cause of unexpected crashes, erroneous Timecode break messages, and Log and Capture failure.

Make sure your cables are easily accessible and in good shape. If you need to plug and unplug them on a regular basis, you might want to invest in cables that are better quality than those that come packaged with many third-party devices. Consider adding a FireWire hub or extender to your Macintosh to avoid repeatedly plugging cables directly into the Mac. In addition, extenders will boost the signal carried by the FireWire cable and may make performance more consistent.

Power Supply

When troubleshooting a system, make sure your power supply is conditioned and there is enough overhead in the circuit to safely run everything you have plugged in to the wall.

The public power distribution system is notorious for inconsistent delivery. In most homes and facilities, the rated 110 volts of AC can fluctuate anywhere from 90 to 120 volts. Computers are sensitive to changes in voltage and can crash or hang when power supply voltage fluctuates.

The only way to achieve a consistent current is through a power conditioner. Most moderately priced uninterruptible power supplies (UPS) contain a power conditioner, meaning that your Mac receives constant voltage from the UPS's internal battery rather than fluctuating voltage directly from the wall outlet. The battery itself is constantly charged from the wall outlet. Professional post-production facilities may have much more resilient power conditioners built into their circuit breakers.

Most UPS units also have a limit to the number of amps they can provide from the battery. In general, the more amps a UPS battery can provide, the more devices you can plug into its battery backup and conditioner, and the more it costs. Not sure? Add up the number of amps on the devices you have plugged in, and then measure it against the specifications on your UPS (and the amps that your circuit breaker provides). Most devices will have the number of amps they draw listed somewhere on the device.

Practical Search Methodologies

Once you've eliminated the obvious and the environmental and tried your quick fixes, there are two methods that can help you isolate the cause of the problem quickly. Both use the process of elimination to reduce the variables. They are the *one-step reductive* and *split-half search*.

One-Step Reductive

In the one-step reductive method, you remove all variables of the system one at a time. If the first component you test doesn't eliminate the problem, then you move on to the next logical cause. This method works best when you have a lot of clues to the source of the problem and a strong hunch, based on experience, observed behavior and perhaps help from a colleague.

Let's say that FCP can't capture video at all, but operates fine otherwise. You eliminate the quick fixes and move on. Having asked the right questions from the first section of this lesson, you realize that Norton Antivirus was installed earlier in the week. Quickly, you go online to the Apple Knowledge Base Web site and a couple of the other popular FCP Web forums and do a search that confirms that Norton Antivirus causes conflicts with FCP capturing.

At this point, armed with such a specific lead, you can make a direct attempt to correct the problem. You uninstall Norton Antivirus, restart the computer, return to FCP, and attempt the capture again. Voila, the problem is solved.

This is a great situation for using the one-step reductive method, because you have so much confirmation and corroboration that matches your situation. If you keep up with the Knowledge Base and the online Web communities (and perform regular maintenance on your system), most issues you encounter can be solved this quickly.

Split-Half Search

In cases where you have little specific information about an issue, turn to the split-half search. Perhaps the issue is as-yet undocumented by Apple. Perhaps it is so intermittent that you have yet to develop any clues about the source. Perhaps there are so many variables that eliminating them one by one just isn't an option.

Using the split-half search method, you test and eliminate whole groups of components at a time.

Imagine for a moment that you have six USB devices and a FireWire scanner on your station, one of which is causing an intermittent issue with your third-party capture card.

Finding the problem device is difficult because of the intermittent nature of the problem. And imagine if the problem is actually caused by the simultaneous use of *two* or more of the devices, so that it only occurs when they are both present.

Clearly, you wouldn't be able to discern the problem by disconnecting the devices one at a time. But you could disconnect them all and then reattach three of them simultaneously (let's say starting with the oldest, the most reliable, or the ones which use Apple's native drivers) and then proceed with your work. If the problem doesn't occur, then you know the problem is not with the first three devices.

You write this all down, disconnect the first three devices, and reconnect the last four. If the problem reoccurs at this point, you have now narrowed the issue down to one or more of these four devices. Now you can perform another split-half search of these four USB devices.

Troubleshooting Remotely

Sometimes you can't be at the workstation you're troubleshooting. Or you may be getting phone assistance yourself from an Apple Professional Video Support technician. In these situations, there are several tools you can use to smooth the process of long distance troubleshooting.

The first is to document your troubleshooting carefully. If you are helping another user with his or her machine, keep your questioning to objective and tangible observation. Help the user on the other end reduce the elements in his or her workstation logically until you get to the root of the problem. Use the System Profile to get an exact portrait of the hardware and software on the machine in question.

If you are a network administrator and need to regularly assist users at a distance, you might consider investing in Apple's Remote Desktop software. In addition to being able to actually see the behavior the user is experiencing, you can access his or her remote system directly.

Support Profile

Like the System Profile, the Support Profile generates a series of system reports containing nearly everything that could possibly be of use to support technicians trying to replicate the issue you are experiencing.

1   Launch FCP and choose Help > Create Support Profile.

2   In the Save pane, select to the Desktop and click Save. After a brief delay, a file is created on the Desktop.

3   Navigate to the Desktop and double-click the file with the .tgz suffix. The file will automatically uncompress and generate a folder full of diagnostic records that FCP has culled from your system.

When you create a Support Profile, FCP goes under the hood of your system and makes a copy of nearly everything that could be of use to a troubleshooting detective, from crash logs and your FCP preferences to various measures of system status and performance.

This information will help you particularly during remote troubleshooting. One nice feature of the Support Profiles is that it generates the profile automatically as a small compressed file (averaging about 200K) that you can attach to an email.

Lesson Review

1.   What are the three primary questions to ask before you begin methodically troubleshooting an issue?

2.   Why is it essential to document your steps as you troubleshoot?

3.   Once you have ruled out obvious external factors, name three questions you can ask yourself to help narrow your troubleshooting search.

4.   There are a number of quick fixes you can use to eliminate the obvious before you embark on methodical troubleshooting. Name three.

5. Name two environmental factors that can cause issues with your Final Cut Pro system.

6. Describe the one-step reductive search method.

Answers

1. Did it work before, did you check the documentation, and can you repeat the problem?

2. In order to have a record to refer to, and to keep yourself and any other troubleshooter on a logical path to solving the problem,

3. Is it hardware-related or software-related, is it Mac OS X–related or FCP-related, and is it a problem of quality, performance, or an error message?

4. Restart the application, shut down and restart the system, and disconnect all FireWire, USB, and other devices.

5. Temperature, and faulty cables or wires.

6. Remove each variables of the system one at a time. If the first component you test doesn't eliminate the problem, then move on to the next logical cause.

17

Lesson Files	None
Media	None
Time	This lesson takes approximately 120 minutes to complete.
Goals	Explain the causes of dropped frames with FCP
	Explain the causes of out-of-sync video and audio
	Identify the symptoms and causes of display issues such as interlace artifacting, field tearing, and field dominance
	List the causes and solutions of common luminance and digital video color space problems (such as clipping and clamping)
	Explain the causes of common still image import problems and how to avoid them

Operational Troubleshooting: Video and Audio Issues

This lesson discusses the most common audio and video-related issues editors may encounter when using Final Cut Pro, and how to resolve them. These issues include

▶ Dropped frames (page 724)

▶ Out-of-sync audio and video (page 744)

▶ Audio distortion and playback problems (page 754)

▶ Field tearing and field dominance problems (jagged edges, jerking motion, and so on; page 767)

▶ Luminance and color-space problems (page 776)

▶ Still image issues (page 788)

You can read this lesson straight through to learn how to solve these problems, or you can use it as a troubleshooting guide when you experience issues.

If you're experiencing a problem and have already eliminated the quick fixes described in Lesson 16, you need to do more methodical troubleshooting. Although the following chapters are not comprehensive, they can speed up your sleuthing of some of the most common issues you may encounter.

To make it easy to find a solution to your problem, consult the tables at the beginning of each section. Look for the symptom that most closely resembles what you're experiencing, then refer to the page listed with the possible solutions for that symptom.

Solving Dropped Frame Problems

The dropped frames warning message may be the most misunderstood error message in Final Cut Pro. Understanding the causes and likely solutions can make all the difference in solving the issue quickly.

Dropped frames occur when, during either capture or playback, FCP and your Macintosh can't process and deliver the number or size of frames of video per second required by the video standard you are using. FCP expects to display or write a new frame of video at certain time intervals. If the frame does not arrive on time because it was delayed elsewhere within your system, FCP will *drop* (skip) that frame. Capture or playback either continues with the frame missing or stops with a warning message, depending on your preference settings.

The first question to ask when troubleshooting dropped frames is whether the issue occurs consistently in particular situations, or intermittently—and whether dropped frames occur during capture or playback.

Dropped Frames at a Glance

Type of Problem	Symptom	Possible Cause	Solution
Intermittent dropped frames during capture or playback	#1: Problem occurs despite correct FCP settings	Hardware does not meet the requirements for your video format	Check hardware system requirements; page 727
	#2: Problem occurs despite a fast disk drive and ample storage	Incorrect (or incorrectly configured) software driver for the storage solution	Check software driver and configure it correctly; page 729
	#3: Problem occurs after an OS upgrade	Incorrect Mac OS X setup	Configure your Mac operating system correctly; page 730
	#4: Problem occurs on some clips that display an orange bar	Incorrect use of Unlimited RT feature	Configure your Unlimited RT settings correctly; page 731
Consistent dropped frames during capture or playback	#1: Problem occurs when a camera or deck is connected to a FireWire drive on the same bus	Congested FireWire bus	Add an additional FireWire bus to your system; page 732

Dropped Frames at a Glance

Type of Problem	Symptom	Possible Cause	Solution
	#2: Problem occurs with a new FireWire drive	New drive isn't fast enough or large enough for your video format	Ensure adequate storage capacity and drive speed; page 734
Consistent dropped frames only during capture	#1: Problem occurs at capture even though you can play back the same content from the scratch disk	Wrong storage solution for the job	Use the right storage solution for the job; page 735
	#2: Problem occurs after you've captured and deleted lots of footage	Storage drive incorrectly configured or formatted	Configure and format your storage drive correctly; page 736
Consistent dropped frames only during playback	#1: Problem occurs only with one particular clip	Long frame, or duplicated frame, in a clip	Delete long frames; page 738

Dropped Frames at a Glance

Type of Problem	Symptom	Possible Cause	Solution
	#2: Dropped frames or picture stuck on a single frame	Scroll bars in Canvas or Viewer window are interfering with playback	Get rid of scroll bars; page 740
	#3: Issue occurs at specific clip or location in the sequence	Corrupted clip or media; too many tracks of audio	Re-render media; delete and recapture or replace the clip or media; force an audio mixdown; page 742

Intermittent Dropped Frames During Capture or Playback

Symptom #1: Intermittent Dropped Frames Despite Correct FCP Settings

"I intermittently get dropped frames warnings on capture or playback and I know my FCP settings are appropriate for the video and audio I am working with."

Background

Your system may have insufficient processor speed or memory, inappropriate hardware, such as the wrong graphics card, or not enough memory assigned to processing tasks.

Your Mac and its peripheral hardware must meet the minimum requirements for running FCP and ideally should exceed them. Lesson 8 describes the system components that are critical to good performance. The more you ask of FCP, the more it taxes your hardware resources. Remember that some capabilities in FCP, such as working with DVCPRO HD, and some resolution settings in the Digital Cinema Desktop Display become available only when you have the appropriate hardware resources to support them.

Solution

If you encounter dropped frames, whether in capture or output of video, first look at your Macintosh's hardware to see if you're starving FCP of resources. Use the specifications listed in Lessons 7 and 8, along with Apple's current recommendations (www.apple.com/finalcutstudio/finalcutpro/specs.html), as a guideline.

Make sure that your Mac, its hardware, and the decks or cameras you use to capture and output are suitable for the type of video you're working with. In particular, check

▶ Computer processor speed

▶ Graphics card speed

▶ Amount of RAM

▶ Amount of storage (must meet the scratch disk performance requirements for your video format)

> **NOTE** ▶ In some cases, FCP will alert you to a hardware deficiency. For instance, if you try to run 1080i DVCPRO HD content on a Power Mac G4 with dual 800 MHz processors, a unique dropped frames warning will specifically point out that your machine doesn't meet the minimum specifications for that format. However, you won't receive a specific message from the application when a lack of RAM or an anemic graphics card is the cause of the dropped frames.

Symptom #2: Intermittent Dropped Frames Despite Fast Disk Drives and Ample Storage

"My UW-SCSI card should be fast enough, and my drives are striped in a RAID, but I'm still getting dropped frames on capture or playback."

Background

Even the most capacious, well-ordered storage system won't perform well if the software that drives it isn't working right. Although some storage solutions are completely plug and play—such as internal SATA drives and FireWire drives—others, such as SCSI and Fibre Channel drives, require add-on hardware cards. In most cases, these cards require accompanying software drivers in order to work correctly. Because Apple may not be writing these drivers, third-party manufacturers don't always optimize them in lockstep with new versions of the Mac OS and other Apple releases. It isn't uncommon for a new version of the Mac OS to break or disable third-party drivers, which can disable third-party controller cards and make drives inaccessible.

Solution

Check online Web forums that specialize in FCP, such as Creative COW (www.creativecow.net) and 2-Pop (www.2-pop.com), to see if the software driver for your card is mentioned. Media creators use these forums to report problems with software updates—let them test the waters for you.

Then, contact the manufacturer of your controller card or storage device to find out if a newer version of the driver is available.

> **NOTE ▶** Remember, if an issue is not preventing you from completing your project, it's best to finish your project before updating any software, including device drivers.

Symptom #3: Intermittent Dropped Frames After an OS Upgrade

"I just upgraded (or reinstalled) my operating system and I keep getting dropped frames intermittently; everything worked perfectly before the upgrade."

"I get dropped frames warnings, but only when the Canvas and Viewer are on my older, second computer monitor."

Background

Since your OS preferences settings return to the default when you install a new operating system, some of those settings may not be optimal for FCP. In fact, they may be telling your computer to do things that slow down Final Cut Pro, such as decrypt data or display at a low resolution. The preference settings may even be telling your computer to operate at a slower speed to save power. Configuring your OS properly for FCP can solve dropped frame problems and others as well.

Solution

Here are some key OS preferences to check if you're getting dropped frames (for more detail on proper system preferences, see Lesson 10):

▶ Display—If this goes below 75 Hz on CRT monitors, it can cause FCP to have problems displaying on the computer screen what goes out to FireWire or other video output. Set the computer screen to millions of colors so that FCP can translate video properly, avoiding bottlenecks.

▶ Energy Saver—On PowerBooks and G5s, make sure Energy Saver is turned off. Using the Lowest or Automatic setting can slow down your processor speed. Other settings in Energy Saver, such as computer, display, and hard disk sleep, should be set to Never (or off).

▶ Desktop & Screen Saver—Turn off the option to change the Desktop picture, and set the screen saver activation to Never.

▶ FileVault—In general, turn off FileVault since the de-encrypting of data can slow down FCP. Also, make sure FCP projects are not linked to any media files within the encrypted Home folder, otherwise you're guaranteed to get dropped frames.

▶ Exposé—Keyboard strokes should be reassigned so they don't interfere with the FCP function key shortcuts (see Lesson 10).

In addition to setting your preferences correctly for FCP, make sure you keep network activity to a minimum when performing processor-intensive tasks like capture and playback. It's fine to be connected to a network, but in critical editing sessions be sure to disable all unnecessary sharing services (using the Sharing pane in System Preferences).

Symptom #4: Intermittent Dropped Frames on Clips with an Orange Bar

"I keep getting dropped frames warnings on certain clips, which incidentally have an orange bar I've never seen before. Some clips with the orange line don't drop frames though."

Background

If you've chosen the Unlimited RT option in the Timeline's RT pop-up menu, FCP ignores its own estimated limit of how much video can be safely played back without dropping frames. Video that normally would have a red line (indicating it needs to be rendered) may instead have an orange render line, indicating that FCP will attempt to render the frames as it plays back.

Solution

When you first choose Unlimited RT, Playback Video Quality is set to Dynamic by default, meaning that video quality will be scaled up or down to maintain the Playback Frame Rate. If the Playback Frame Rate is not as important to you as the video quality, you can set the Playback Frame Rate to Dynamic and set the Playback Video Quality to High. However, this may result in FCP skipping frames to maintain the frame rate.

If you're bothered only by the reports of dropped frames during playback, not by the dropped frames themselves, you can keep using Unlimited RT and just turn off the reports. To do so, look on the General tab of the User Preferences and deselect Report Dropped Frames During Playback. But don't forget to turn it back on when you are finished with Unlimited RT, so that you don't accidentally drop frames without your knowledge and explicit permission.

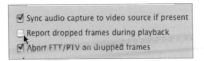

Consistent Dropped Frames During Capture or Playback

Symptom #1: Dropped Frames When a Camera or Deck Is Connected to a FireWire Drive on the Same Bus

"I'm capturing DV from my camera onto my FireWire drive using my PowerBook, and I'm constantly dropping frames."

Background

This problem involves using a FireWire daisy chain, which is tempting but not recommended. If you have a camera or deck connected to a FireWire drive on the same FireWire bus, you're setting yourself up for dropped frames or device-related communication issues.

Although FireWire 400 has a theoretical speed of 400 megabits, or 50 MB/s, not all devices can communicate over FireWire that quickly. DV decks and cameras, in particular, work at much slower data rates, usually at a standard 100 megabits, or 12.5 MB/s. Thus, your FireWire drive, which normally can deliver a data rate of 16 MB/s (because it is a single physical drive), might be able to deliver only 5 or 6 MB/s when placed behind a DV deck on the FireWire bus.

Dropped frames due to a congested FireWire bus are rarely a consistent problem, but they become more likely if other factors are present. Say you are working with a Mac that has 512 MB of RAM, a relatively fragmented drive, and a deck on the same FireWire bus. Any one of these factors alone might not cause an immediate dropped frames warning, but the three together are quite likely to cause problems.

Solution

If you're working with video formats other than DV, don't use a FireWire drive for capture or playback of your project. If you're working with DV, keep the camcorder and FireWire drive connected to different FireWire buses. Although your Mac may have up to three FireWire ports, there is only one FireWire bus.

> **NOTE ▶** If you have a newer PowerBook or desktop PowerMac with both a FireWire 400 port and a FireWire 800 port, you may still get dropped frames due to FireWire bottlenecks, because the two different standards share the same FireWire bus on the motherboard.

The way to add an additional FireWire bus to your system depends on the type of system you have:

▶ If you have a PowerBook, you can use a PCMCIA FireWire Cardbus card. Having the scratch disk FireWire drive connected to a completely different bus from the DV deck eliminates the possibility of data-stream bottlenecks. (iBooks don't have a PCMCIA Cardbus slot.)

▶ If you have a PowerMac, consider adding a PCI FireWire expansion card. Although you can locate the deck or camera on one port and other FireWire devices on another, both FireWire ports share the same bus, so you can still get bottlenecks. A FireWire expansion card provides a completely separate FireWire bus.

Symptom #2: Dropped Frames with a New FireWire Drive

"I'm getting dropped frames warnings with a new drive I recently purchased."

Background

The key to trouble-free FireWire drive use is to remember that a FireWire drive is just a normal ATA drive attached to a FireWire cable. You have to treat the FireWire drive just like any other drive you might employ in FCP, with regard to standards, throughput, maintenance, and upkeep.

Solution

Make sure that the FireWire drive is fast and large enough to support the video format you are working with. For instance, many editors working with FireWire DV may want to use FireWire drives for storage. The DV format isn't particularly demanding, but you must set the minimum drive specifications at 7,200 RPM.

Also, make sure the *bridge*—the device that converts data on the drive into a data stream that can travel to the Macintosh and back—is of recent vintage, such as the Oxford 911 (FireWire 400) and 922 (FireWire 800) chipsets. Some of the earliest FireWire bridge chipsets offered irregular throughput that didn't utilize the full potential of the FireWire 400 50 MB/s data rate.

If you are working with a more demanding format, such as uncompressed 8-bit or HD footage, you may get slower throughput. Theoretically, FireWire 800 has enough throughput to handle both of these formats, but if the drive isn't fast enough to handle the data rate, it doesn't matter how fast data can travel through the cable. The drive is usually the slowest link in any media storage chain. Consult Lessons 8 and 9 for information on data rates and storage solutions.

Consistent Dropped Frames Only During Capture

Symptom #1: Dropped Frames Even Though You Can Play Back the Same Content from the Scratch Disk

"I get dropped frames warnings very shortly into every single capture, although I can usually play back the same type of video content that is already on the scratch disk."

"I get a dropped frames warning every time I try to capture or play back anything at all."

Background

If you're getting dropped frames consistently, even though you're sure your Mac and other hardware meets the requirements of the format you're working with, you may have an inadequate storage solution.

Four factors of your storage solution are critical to capture and playback: bus speed, drive speed, *overhead* (extra bandwidth needed for the file system and other activities) and free (unfragmented) space. Other factors, such as the formatting of your drive, partitioning scheme, and RAID level can also affect the performance of your system. Since capture is a more intensive process than playback, you may find that you drop frames during capture, but not during playback.

Higher-data-rate formats, such as uncompressed standard and high definition video, will generally require RAIDs that are striped together using software or a proprietary hardware card. If a RAID isn't configured correctly, you can expect trouble.

There are some features that, although ideal for convenience, may impact performance. For example, Xserve RAID uses a feature called RAID Now, allowing a RAID volume to become available as it is being built. Another fantastic feature is the ability to restore the contents of a RAID 5 disk while maintaining availability of the RAID set. In none of these circumstances do you want to capture high-bit-rate video while these processes are in progress.

Other factors, such as background processes on your computer can also affect storage performance. When you first install Mac OS X 10.4, or when you add a new storage volume, Spotlight performs a thorough indexing of your mounted volumes. This activity can take many hours depending on the size of the volume. While the indexing takes place, you can expect some degradation in your hard disk performance.

Solution

Make sure that your storage system's bus speed, drive speed, and overhead are adequate for the technical requirements of the type of video you want to edit. Lesson 7 covers the specific requirements of the various video formats.

Symptom #2: Consistent Dropped Frames After Capturing and Deleting Lots of Footage

"I've been capturing lots of footage and deleting it. Lately I get a dropped frames warning every time I try to capture anything at all."

Background

Even when formatted correctly, disk performance declines when data on the hard drive becomes fragmented. The problem occurs because data is located on different parts of the drive rather than contiguous blocks.

If your storage system is set up and formatted correctly and is not fragmented, but you are still experiencing consistent dropped frames, your storage system may not be in good working order.

Solution

▶ Make sure your drives are fast enough.

▶ Not all drives perform equally. For example, you can significantly increase the performance of your Xserve RAID by using 400 GB drive modules, rather than 250 GB drive modules.

▶ Drives that provide acceptable performance internally may not perform at their optimal level in an inexpensive FireWire enclosure. Consider both the drive manufacturer specifications as well as the control and interface specifications when purchasing external drive storage.

▶ Make sure you have ample disk drive space and that drives are not too fragmented.

The Mac OS X startup volume should have a minimum of 250 MB, and preferably 375 MB, of free disk space available. You may need more free disk space to install a system update. Keep as much disk space available as possible.

Equally important is the free space available on your storage disks.

If you have a dedicated hard drive (or at least a dedicated scratch disk partition), erase your hard disk prior to your capture session. If you are working with existing media and have room on another partition, you can use Disk Utility to create an image of your media partition, then erase and restore your media partition using your backup. (You can learn more about using restore images from Disk Utility Help.)

You can also use Disk Utility to verify and repair data and permissions on your disk, identify the S.M.A.R.T. (operational) status of your hard disk, as well as identify the format and partition structure of your disk.

To defragment your hard disk, you can use a third-party disk utility (choose Apple menu > Mac OS X Software). Remember to back up your data before you defragment your disk.

Consistent Dropped Frames Only During Playback

Symptom #1: Dropped Frames with One Particular Clip

"I am getting dropped frames warnings when trying to capture one particular clip in a logging bin filled with offline clips. All other clips capture fine. There is no timecode break on the tape."

Background

One other cause of consistent dropped frames during is the *long frame*, which causes dropped frames warnings even though no frames are actually dropped. Unlike with a clip that has true dropped frames, there is nothing technically wrong with a clip containing a long frame. A long frame is simply a video frame that lasts longer than a frame is supposed to, according to the format of video you are using.

For instance, say you were using the DV NTSC codec, which should have exactly 29.97 frames per second, but FCP captured a frame with the frame length of 3 normal frames. Such a frame length may sound odd, but keep in mind that there is no limit to the configuration of digital video. There could be a frame rate of 15, 24, 29.97, or any other rate the system requires. Thus, if you end up with a long frame, FCP will use it. However, you will see that some of the frames appear to be missing, giving the appearance of a lag or still image on some of the frames.

Obviously, long frames aren't something you want when you capture video, but they do occur in rare instances. If you've enabled the option on the General tab called Abort Capture On Dropped Frames, long frames (or other dropped frame incidents) that do occur will be aborted with a dropped frames warning message. Otherwise, FCP will capture long frames when they occur—and the clips in which they are captured will generate the same long frames each time you try to capture them with the same In and Out points.

Solution

Since legitimate long frame problems caused by a QuickTime fluke are almost always the first frame of the capture, you can avoid such problems by using these techniques:

▶ Always capture your clips with a minimum of 1-second handles. (Handles are the extra footage beyond the In and Out points of the logged clip.) If you include a handle at the beginning of a clip, any long frames that occur will be located in the handle, and not in the part of the clip you want to edit into a sequence.

▶ When you do get a long frame, try repositioning the capture In point you are using for the clip to another frame of video on the tape. In most cases, this clears up the problem and allows capture of the same material without the long frame.

If you aren't sure whether a clip has a long frame, you can manually test the clip with a command in the Tools menu.

1   Select the clip in question in the project tab.

2   Choose Tools > Long Frames > Mark.

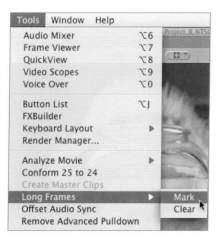

If there are long frames in a clip, FCP will identify the long frame with a marker labeled *Long Frame*, followed by the number in order of occurrence. You can remove the marker by using the normal marker-removing method or by choosing Tools > Long Frames > Clear.

If there is more than one long frame in the clip, or if the long frame occurs anywhere other than the very beginning of the clip, adjust the In and Out points and attempt a recapture.

Symptom #2: Picture Is Stuck on a Single Frame

"My hardware and settings are all appropriate, and I'm getting a signal out to my FireWire DV deck, but when I attempt playback, the picture is stuck on a single frame."

Background

FCP is extremely flexible and allows you to design and save the layout of your onscreen workspace according to your own private whims. But certain window choices make it difficult for FCP to deliver video and audio reliably and at the highest quality—and it's very easy to make mistakes in this area. So, if you encounter odd playback issues, check that window position/scale or incompatible windows aren't causing the interference.

One of the most important rules to know about FCP is that it can't output video or audio at the appropriate frame rate when there are scroll bars in the Viewer or Canvas. Scroll bars will appear any time the Viewer or Canvas is zoomed in, making it impossible to fit the entire video frame in the window. If your Viewer or Canvas tabs have scroll bars in the frame, FCP *will* drop frames

on playback. Video output to FireWire DV or capture cards will freeze on
a frame as the playhead happily moves along the Timeline. The Viewer or
Canvas will play back at a severely reduced frame rate, depending on how far
the window is zoomed into the frame. Worse still, this sort of frame-dropping
doesn't register as a dropped frame in playback, so you just end up with weird
choppy output.

Solution

To avoid this situation, always look out for scroll bars in the Canvas or the
Video tab of the Viewer. If you see them, press Shift-Z, the keyboard shortcut
to Fit to Window. Fit to Window, a command found in the Viewer Video tab
and the Canvas scale pop-up menu, always scales the contents of any FCP
window such that the entire contents are visible and scroll bars aren't present.

If you are zooming in and out for effects work, get used to using Zoom
In (Cmd-+) and Shift-Z, rather than Zoom Out (Cmd--), since Fit to

Window will always return the window's content to its optimal size in the window frame.

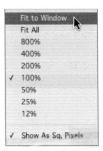

> **NOTE** ▶ You can inadvertently end up with scroll bars by loading a Window Layout preset, either from the FCP native set or one that you have created and saved in your custom settings. Although these presets rearrange the windows to the layout you choose, they don't perform a Fit to Window. If your windows weren't already set for Fit to Window before recalling the window layout, chances are you will immediately end up with scroll bars.

Symptom #3: Dropped Frames at a Specific Clip or Location in a Sequence

"I know that all my settings are correct for what I'm trying to do, but I consistently get dropped frames warnings during certain sections of my sequences."

"If I play back my sequence with the playhead in the Timeline window, it plays back fine, but Edit to Tape and Print to Video always drops frames."

Background

You can probably think of a dozen ways to make a particular clip more interesting. Using all of those ideas may require more than your computer can handle in real time.

You can easily step back in time by first loading clips into the Viewer and then deselecting effects in the Filters tab. Move back to the Timeline and play back your sequence again.

Forcing a Render All (Option-R) is also a good way to render material that your computer would otherwise try to play back in real time.

It is also possible for clips, media files, and even render files to become corrupted for unknown reasons. It happens rarely, but when it does, your sequence will not function properly when the offending file is being processed.

In theory, any workstation that runs FCP can deliver at least eight tracks of audio in a sequence without extra hardware support, as long as there are no audio filters applied to the tracks. No matter what you have in those tracks, FCP should be able to mix them all down into the number of tracks your current audio output device can handle.

Unfortunately, that theory doesn't always hold true in the real world. If you have a less-than-optimal situation (such as a lack of RAM or slow processors), in which FCP can't deliver as many tracks as it should, you can end up dropping frames.

Several factors can contribute to this type of less-than-optimal situation. A storage drive that is filled beyond 85 percent of capacity could be a risk factor. Another might be an overfilled and fragmented drive that prevents FCP from simultaneously accessing several different media files to mix down several audio tracks. Likewise, if the audio clips in your audio tracks are very short, and the sequence is composed of very fast cuts, your drives may not be able to jump back and forth quickly enough. FCP believes that it can mix the tracks so it doesn't give you a red render line, but you get a dropped frames report during playback.

Solution

To rule out a corrupted render file, you can use the Render Manager to delete render files you think may be corrupt and then re-render the sequence.

If you suspect a corrupt clip or media file, open the clip into the Viewer from the Timeline and play back the clip. If your findings are inconclusive, with your Viewer active, choose Export As QuickTime Movie. Then re-import your clip into your sequence. You can also go back to the original source media if all other troubleshooting fails.

In order to check whether your dropped frames are related to audio mixdown troubles, look at the number of clips and the number of audio tracks in the part of the sequence where the dropped frames warning occurred—and consider what you're asking FCP and your scratch disk drives to deliver. A lot of short, fast cuts spread over several different tracks might explain the dropped frames report.

Fortunately, this situation is easy to fix. All you have to do is force an audio mixdown of the affected area of the sequence, as follows:

1   Set an In and Out point in the sequence.

2   Choose Sequence > Render Only > Mixdown.

When you perform an audio mixdown, FCP generates an audio render file for the range of frames you specify. When the sequence is played back, FCP doesn't have to access and mix five different audio files together simultaneously in real time; it just reads the single, mixed-down render file, and your dropped frames report disappears.

> **NOTE** ▶ It's usually a good idea to perform an audio mixdown for a sequence prior to performing an Edit to Tape or Print to Video operation, especially on sequences over an hour long, where the interruption of output due to a dropped frames warning at minute 90 means you have to output the whole thing to tape again!

Solving Audio and Video Sync Issues

Another issue that FCP users sometimes encounter is audio and video going out of sync during playback. There are several different causes, from mistakes in your settings to the very nature of DV and QuickTime. Determining whether the problem you encounter is *progressively* or *consistently* out-of-sync will give you your main clues as to why this is occurring and what you can do to address it. First let's look at what *progressive* and *consistent* mean in terms of audio and video sync.

Out-of-Sync Audio and Video Problems at a Glance

Type of Problem	Symptom	Possible Cause	Solution
Audio and video progressively out of sync	#1: Clips go rapidly out of sync and exhibit audio artifacts	Incorrect capture or sequence settings	Correct your capture or sequence settings; page 746
	#2: Correct capture settings, but clips go slightly out of sync after several minutes, and a red or green line appears in the Timeline above the clip	Nonstandard sample rate in recording device	Convert your audio sample rate; page 746
Audio and video consistently out of sync	#1: Monitor playback is consistently out of sync with output device	Bus latency (the pathway to the output device is delaying the signal)	Adjust latency between your monitor and output device; page 748
	#2: Video and audio sent to separate devices are consistently out of sync with each other	Bus latency (the pathway to the output device is delaying the signal)	Adjust latency between your output devices; page 750
	#3: Audio consistently out of sync when using a Panasonic AG-DVX100 camera	Missing DVX-100 Audio Sync tool plug-in	Install the DVX-100 Audio Sync tool in the plug-ins folder; page 751

Audio and Video Progressively Out of Sync

Symptom #1: Clips Go Rapidly Out of Sync and Exhibit Audio Artifacts

"My clips go rapidly out of sync in the Viewer or sequence, in addition to hearing the beeping sound saying FCP wants to render the audio. I may also hear some crunching artifacting noises."

Background

Using the correct sample rates in your capture settings is critical for avoiding out-of-sync audio. FCP and QuickTime use the number of samples per second to determine the timing of audio in playback. If an audio clip is identified as having been sampled 48,000 times per second (48 kHz), FCP plays it back at 48,000 samples per second. If the initial identification of the sample rate is wrong, FCP will be busy performing a sample rate conversion so that the file's playback rate matches your sequence sample rate.

Solution

The only way to guarantee that you don't encounter this problem is to make sure that your capture settings match the sample rate of the tape. With DV tape, this will be a default sample rate of either 48K or 32K, depending on how the camera was set. On DV cameras, these two rates are identified as 16-bit and 12-bit, respectively. Unless you have a DV tape that was recorded in 32K, you should always use 48K sample rates.

Symptom #2: Capture Settings Are Correct, But Clips Go Slightly Out of Sync After Several Minutes, and a Red or Green Line Appears in the Timeline Above the Clip

"My settings are right, but my video and audio still go slightly out of sync after playing back for several minutes."

"I know my settings are correct, but sometimes when I put my 48K clips in a 48K sequence, I still get a 'resample on-the-fly' green or 'render' red line on the audio clip in the sequence."

Background

One of the biggest problems with DV audio as a format is that sample rates aren't always standard. Some professional DV cameras and decks offer what is called *locked audio*, whereas the majority of prosumer DV cameras use a non-standard *unlocked* audio sampling method.

With locked audio, the audio digitizer is extremely precise, and an audio sample rate of 32 kHz or 48 kHz will have exactly that number of samples per second. Audio sync is virtually guaranteed, because the ratio between the number of samples and number of video frames over a specific (short) time period are always the same. For instance, with locked 48 kHz audio, there are always exactly 8,008 audio samples for every five frames of NTSC 29.97 video (1,601.6 samples per frame).

Theoretically, all 48 kHz and 32 kHz recording devices use locked audio. Unfortunately, many aren't that precise. Some cameras are worse than others, and the irregularity of these devices can be very frustrating. Prior to Final Cut Pro 4, FCP included a Sync Adjust Movie feature that calculated these variations so that audio always stayed in sync.

With FCP 4 and later versions, sample rate calculation happens under the hood at the end of each capture. Every clip you capture is analyzed, and if the sample rate is off, FCP makes a slight adjustment to the clip's sample rate setting so that it plays correctly. That's why sometimes you put a 48 kHz clip in a 48 kHz sequence and you get a red or green line in the clip telling you that it isn't matched to the sequence. FCP may have detected it as being a 48,048 Hz clip rather than standard 48 kHz and recalculated it accordingly. Whenever FCP has to resample clips on-the-fly in a sequence, you will get that red or green line.

With unlocked audio, one of the most common non-standard sample rates you will encounter is 44.1 KHzkH. Because the number of frames required to find a common denominator between 44,100 KHz and video's frame rates is so large, the sample rate's relationship with time (and frame rate) usually fluctuates. Your track may start out on time and end on time, but during the course of playback, it may speed up or slow down to fudge the numbers and bring it into sync.

Solution

If you must use audio CD tracks with a native sample rate of 44.1 kHz, make sure you convert the sample rate of the track you are importing prior to editing the clip into the sequence. (For more information on sound file imports, see Lesson 13.)

Another reason you might end up with 44.1K clips is if you used the onboard mic or mic input of a Macintosh to record voice-overs in the Voice Over tool. As of this writing, the Macintosh uses a 16-bit 44.1 kHz sample engine for its onboard mike input, so unless you upgrade to another audio digitizing tool or use a DV camera, your Voice Over tool recordings will be in 44.1 kHz. Upgrading your recording device and doing voice-overs at 48 kHz doesn't have to be expensive. There are several decent USB audio adapters on the market, and you can use a DV camera or deck to do voice-over recordings.

Audio and Video Consistently Out of Sync

If the out-of-sync behavior you are experiencing stays the same from the beginning of the clip throughout playback, it's called *consistently* out of sync. Rather than gradually drifting over time, when clips are consistently out of sync the initial relationship between video and audio is *offset* by a certain time frame. The offset amount remains constant throughout the clip.

The origins of consistently out-of-sync clips are completely different from those of progressively out-of-sync clips. Whereas progressively out-of-sync clips are usually the result of sample rate confusion, consistent out-of-sync behavior is almost always the result of *latency* caused by an unequal divergence between the audio and video streams or signals themselves.

Symptom #1: Monitor Playback Is Consistently Out of Sync with Output Device

"My Canvas or Viewer and FireWire DV deck video monitor are out of sync by about four frames. It isn't causing inaccuracies, but it makes me dizzy to watch one stagger behind the other when I play back my sequence."

Background

The most common cause of lack of audio sync is *bus latency.* This refers to the fact that the pathways to your various output devices from FCP are very different. Each may require more or less processing, or they may simply delay the signal because the data pathway itself is slow.

For instance, if you're sending both video and audio out to your FireWire DV deck to your production monitor, the audio and video on your production monitor are in perfect sync, because they are traveling through the same bus and are experiencing the same latency delay. If during the same playback, you glance back and forth between the Viewer or Canvas window and your FireWire DV output, however, the FireWire output lags slightly behind the Viewer or Canvas. This is the latency between the desktop monitor and output device.

Solution

There is no complete cure for bus latency, but there is a salve for its symptoms. The trick is to equal out the latency of your devices by inserting a short delay in the desktop playback of the Viewer and Canvas.

1   Choose Final Cut Pro > System Settings.

2   Look on the Playback Control tab. Find the Frame Offset field.

    The default setting is 4 frames.

Adding a frame offset will introduce a delay in playback of the Viewer and Canvas window to compensate for necessary offsets in matching the playback to the chosen output device. The default value for this field is 4 frames, since that is generically the correct offset for any FireWire device you are trying to match.

Symptom #2: Video and Audio Sent to Separate Devices Are Consistently Out of Sync with Each Other

"My video and audio are consistently out of sync. I am monitoring audio from my Mac speakers and video from my DV camera or other similar split audio/video output."

Background

Matching up the FCP windows to your video output isn't the only latency issue you might encounter. With FCP, you can send video and audio out to different output devices. Say you want to send video to an uncompressed capture card while sending audio to a USB audio breakout box. This is guaranteed to cause a glaring audio/video sync offset, probably by quite a few frames. A common occurrence of this problem is when editors use their Macintosh's headphone jack or USB speaker system along with their FireWire DV output device to monitor video.

Solution

Correcting this sort of latency is a little more complicated. First, you have to determine whether or not the devices in question can even have their latency corrected. Generally, the cheaper the device, the less likely it is to have latency offset control. If neither of your devices has latency control, you won't be able to address the issue and will have to send your audio to the same output device as the video. If you need to use a separate output device for higher output quality, you may have to buy equipment that has the ability to correct latency.

Since latency is a consistent problem that is associated with particular electronic pathways in your audio and video devices, setting the latency is something you really only have to do once. Measuring latency is quite challenging, since you can't measure it when parked on a frame.

The simplest, least expensive way to approach latency offsetting is to shoot footage of a film clapboard slate repeatedly being closed, then capture and then repeatedly loop playback of the footage. Watch the slate being closed and listen for the spike of the audio waveform. Keep adjusting the offset in your audio output controller, and you will eventually get the offset to within a frame. If you require absolute precision in setting these offsets, you may need to consult a professional VAR or servicing agent, since getting the accuracy down to a small fraction of a second is usually beyond the ability of the human eye to detect.

> **TIP** You can measure the recurrent latency between two different output devices by making a single recording using both of them. If you play a countdown clip with a "2-pop" or a slate from the Timeline out to your different video and audio outputs, but patch these different outputs to a single deck, the latency will be recorded to tape. Examine the number of frames that the sync is off, and you have the exact latency!
>
> As an example, if you were using FireWire DV for your video output, but using a USB audio converter for audio, you could patch video out of the DV deck and audio from the USB device to any old VHS deck. Quality in the recording doesn't matter; you are simply looking for latency here.

Symptom #3: Audio Consistently Out of Sync When Using a Panasonic AG-DVX100 Camera

"My audio is consistently a few frames off at both head and tail of clip. I shot with the Panasonic AG-DVX100 camera in."

Background

Tapes shot in the Panasonic AG-DVX100 24P DV camera require a special plug-in to adjust for the way it handles audio and video sync when recording. The plug-in ensures that there is accurate audio and video sync after capture by adding a slight frame offset to any clips you apply it to.

Solution

Install the plug-in from the FCP installer CD (DV Camera Tuner Scripts > Extras). To do that, first you need to install the DVX100 Audio Sync tool.

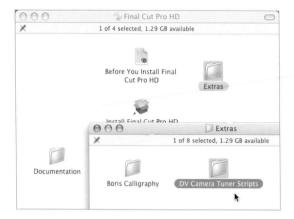

1   Shut down FCP, and then look on your FCP HD installer CD for the Extras folder. Double-click it to open the folder.

2   Find the DVX100 Audio Sync tool and move it to the Library > Applications Support > Final Cut Pro System Support > Plugins folder.

    You might have to authenticate this copy with an admin password since this destination folder is set to read-only.

3   Open FCP again. Open a clip into the Viewer (or select it in the Browser).

    Normally, you should only select clips that were captured from tapes recorded in the DVX100 camera, but for the purposes of this exercise you just want to see what the plug-in does.

4   Choose Tools > Offset Audio Sync.

When installed, the DVX100 Audio Sync tool creates a new menu item that gives the ability to offset audio playback for select clips. When you choose the Offset Audio Sync command, a dialog appears.

Specify how far the audio should be offset. For clips captured from DVX100-recorded tape, this should remain at the default 2-frame offset. For other cameras, you may need to use a different setting. For up-to-date details, consult the Knowledge Base on the Apple Web site.

When you apply the command, the clips are permanently offset by the frame number you chose for accurate sync with the video.

5   Click Cancel to keep from applying the offset to the clips you selected (unless they are actually clips recorded by a DVX100 camera that require the offset).

Don't be concerned that this offset will affect anything else in your project. The Frame Offset command must be applied directly to the clips. It doesn't affect media files themselves and only affects the clips you apply it to. If you import the clip's media file into another project (or the same project), the newly imported clip would not carry the offset and you would need to reapply it. But if you drag and drop the offset clip from one project to another, the new master clip *will* carry the offset.

Don't confuse this special frame offset tool with the Frame Offset in the Playback Control tab of the System Settings dialog, discussed earlier in the section on bus latency. That frame offset was a method of getting the FCP internal Viewer and Canvas to match up with various video output devices.

NOTE ▶ Don't use this offset to correct bus latency between output devices, as described in the previous section. Since this offset actually affects the playback relationship of the audio and video media, using it to address bus latency would make the output from your devices sound in sync, but would throw them out of actual sync rather than correct the latency. Bus latency should always be corrected by controlling the output device that has the latency, not by adjusting the elements you are editing.

Solving Audio Distortion Problems

As you're editing, it's important to listen for audio problems, because FCP can't "hear" bad audio the way your ears can. It might tell you when the audio clips or causes a certain level of distortion, but it can't tell you that your mixes aren't perfect, or that there was noise in your original recordings.

If you hear problems, such as audio artifacts (clicking, beeping, stuttering, scratching), unexpectedly high audio levels, or a lack of filtering effects during playback, investigate what might be causing these problems. For help in this investigation, consult the following table, which will point you toward the possible cause of your problem and the section you can read to find out how to fix it.

Audio Distortion Problems at a Glance

Type of Problem	Symptom	Possible Cause	Solution
Audio artifacts occur during playback	#1: Clicks, beeps, or stuttering during playback in Viewer or sequence	Capture settings don't match actual sample rate for content being captured	Correct your capture settings; page 756
	#2: Artifacts occur during playback in a sequence; green line visible above clip in Timeline	Sequence settings don't match capture settings for all clips edited into the Timeline	Match sample rates of sequence clips; page 757

Audio Distortion Problems at a Glance

Type of Problem	Symptom	Possible Cause	Solution
	#3: Imported audio clips click and stutter during playback	Audio clips are compressed as MP3 or MP4	Convert audio clips to an uncompressed format, page 759
	#4: Imported MP3 and MP4 files click and stutter, iTunes Music Store downloads won't import	File formats not supported by FCP	Use supported file formats; page 760
High audio levels during playback	#1: Loud playback despite setting optimal levels when shooting	Clips were captured as non-stereo and waveform interference is boosting total audio level	Relink mono channels as stereo; page 761
Playback unaffected by audio filters	#1: Changes to filter settings seem to have no effect on output	Clips were captured as non-stereo, so filters apply to one channel only	Apply filters to both channels; page 764
Audio sounds tinny during playback	#1: Audio playback sounds thin and tinny	Audio digitized using low sample rate or bit depth	Resample the original audio files; page 765

Audio Artifacts Occur During Playback

Symptom #1: Artifacts During Playback in Viewer or Sequence

"I have captured a lot of clips, but when I play them back in a Viewer or a sequence, I hear clicking, beeping, stuttering, or scratching. There are also some audio/video sync issues."

Background

If you're hearing clicking, beeping, stuttering, or scratching sounds during playback, and you're sure that the problem isn't bad source audio or a defective cable or connector, then incorrect FCP settings are probably your culprit.

When you're capturing content, if your audio capture settings aren't exactly the same as the content you're attempting to capture, you're setting yourself up for trouble. You're likely to end up with audio artifacts that FCP will be unaware of, thus unable to alert you that anything is wrong.

Using incorrect capture settings is a common mistake among new FireWire DV editors. Many DV cameras, by default, are set for 12-bit audio, which corresponds to 32 kHz audio in FCP. Since there is no capture preset for 32 kHz in the Audio/Video settings, new users usually assume that 48 kHz (16-bit in cameras) is the correct setting. Telling FCP that 32 kHz can be captured similarly to 48 kHz audio can result in clicking, stuttering, beeping, and scratching, and the audio may go out of sync with your video.

Solution

If you've captured content with incorrect settings, the only way to correct the problem is to recapture the clips with an audio capture preset that correctly reflects the audio sample rate of the tape content.

Let's say you've mistakenly captured 32 kHz audio with a 48 kHz capture setting. Since it's a bad idea to mix sample rates in a sequence, you'll want to export the 32 kHz audio and convert it to 48 kHz to match the other 48 kHz content you will be using. (See the section on sound file imports in Lesson 13.)

Symptom #2: Artifacts Occur During Playback in a Sequence, and a Green Line Is Visible Above the Clips in the Timeline

"I have captured a lot of clips, but when I play them back in a sequence, I hear clicking, beeping, stuttering, or scratching. When I play them back in a Viewer they sound fine. There is a green line on the clips in the sequence."

Background

Just as your capture settings must match the actual sample rate for the content you are capturing from tape, your sequence settings must match the capture settings for the clips you edit in. Although the results of a mismatch won't be as extreme as with incorrectly captured clips, you still need to address it for optimal performance and quality.

FCP can detect clips with different sample rates than those of the sequence and resample them on the fly as you play back the sequence, putting a green line above each clip in the Timeline. However, this resampling has a number of detrimental effects on FCP performance. First, resampling audio on-the-fly steals processor power, giving you less RT functionality and risking the occurrence of dropped frames. Although resampling won't directly cause dropped frames, stealing too much processing power at a weak moment could yield them in other areas of the application.

Second, resampling on the fly can also yield audio artifacts. When FCP resamples mismatched sample rates in a sequence, it uses your choice of quality settings (Low, Medium, or High, specified in your User Preferences) to do so. The default setting of Low can create particularly noticeable clicks and crackles. Medium quality uses more processor power, but still generates background noise. High quality does a much better job of converting mismatched sample rates (much like exporting and converting the sample rate manually). In most cases, though, setting the pop-up menu to High will yield a red render line, requiring a render for playback.

> **NOTE ▶** The preferences for audio quality settings affects only clips that are out of tolerance with the sequence sample rate. This means that audio clips that are identical to the sample rate of the sequence are not affected by any changes in the quality preference.

Solution

The best way to deal with this problem is to avoid resampling in the sequence altogether. That is, edit clips into a sequence only when they share the same sample rate as the sequence.

If your clips don't match the sample rate of the sequence, export the audio portion and convert the sample rate. (See the sound file import section of Lesson 13 for the method of converting sample rates.)

If you must use mismatched sample rates in a sequence, you can perform either a render or an audio mixdown (Sequence > Render Only > Mixdown).

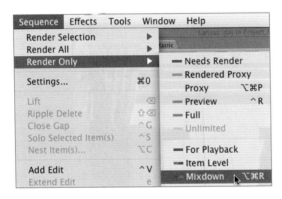

However, if you'd rather edit than render every time you change an edit, do it the right way and avoid mismatching sample rates.

> **TIP**▶ The Audio Playback Quality pop-up is irrelevant for Edit to Tape and Print to Video operations, because FCP always uses High quality or audio playback under those operations. Even so, you should always perform a quick audio mixdown before engaging in Print to Tape and Edit to Tape operations to avoid unexpected dropped frame interruptions during output.

Symptom #3: Imported Audio Clips Stutter and Click

"My imported audio clips seem to click and stutter and sometimes cause FCP to drop frames."

Background

Like still image imports, sound files must formatted and treated correctly. Using compressed formats, file types not acceptable to FCP, and inconsistent sample rates and bit depths can cause audio problems.

Like video, digital audio uses codecs. These codecs can use compression schemes to lower the data rate of the audio stream, making for easier Web delivery when perfect audio reproduction isn't a necessity but easy distribution is. There are many different audio codecs; some are geared more towards voice reproduction and others for the full frequency range of music. Most audio compression schemes use some method of temporal compression, or compression that discards data based on changes in the audio stream over time, rather than compressing every individual sample equally.

Solution

Any audio you import into FCP should be uncompressed audio if possible. If you have an audio clip that consistently clicks and sputters, you probably need to export the offending audio clip, change the format to AIFF and set the Compressor to Uncompressed.

1   Select the clip in question in the Viewer or sequence.

2   Choose File > Export > Using QuickTime Conversion.

The export will convert the compressed audio to uncompressed, and at the same time let you convert the sample rate, which is also probably incorrect for your sequence.

3   Choose AIFF from the Format pop-up menu.

4   Click the Options button to enter the Sound Settings dialog.

5   Set the Format to Linear PCM, Channels to Stereo, and the Sample Rate to 48 kHz.

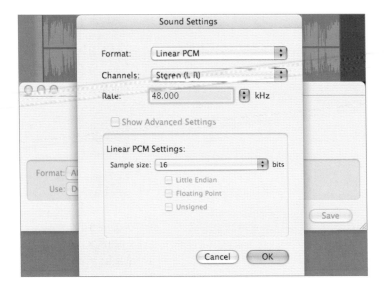

After clicking through and saving the converted audio file to your media drive, import it to FCP and use it in the place of the original. Be aware that this will not improve the quality of the audio file, which was already compromised in the original compression, but it should eliminate any clicking or potential dropped frames warnings.

Symptom #4: MP3, MP4, and iTunes Music Store Downloads Click on Playback or Will Not Import

"My imported MP3 and MP4 files click and stutter irregularly in the sequence and I can't import my iTunes Music Store downloads."

Background

MP3 and MP4 files are not supported in FCP. Files that use MP3 and MP4 encoding will skip on playback as the FCP QuickTime engine fights to perform the MPEG decoding and keep in sync with the video in the sequence. Converting such files to AIFF by export will often not solve the situation, as it will leave blank drop-outs in the audio track.

Another important new audio type is the special MP4 AAC file format that the iTunes Music Store utilizes. When you download files from the ITMS, they become available in your iTunes music library for playback. Unfortunately, this AAC format is protected under digital rights management lock and key. So although you can open such files in QuickTime Pro and iTunes, you cannot export and convert them to a usable format, nor can you import them directly into FCP.

Solution

There are free utilities on the Web that do a decent job converting MP3 and MP4 files, or you can burn the track to an audio CD and then use iTunes or QuickTime Pro to import and convert the track to a true 48K AIFF file.

High Audio Levels During Playback

Symptom #1: Loud Playback Despite Setting Optimal Levels When Shooting

"I carefully set my levels in-camera to an optimal level when shooting, but when I play back in a sequence, the levels are much louder, and in some places actually clip."

Background

Unexpectedly high audio levels during playback are usually due to the tracks having been recorded as individual mono tracks rather than as stereo-linked tracks. Since the FCP default value for Audio Format (Log and Capture > Clip Settings) is dual mono—in other words, two individual mono tracks—it's easy to unintentionally record stereo audio as paired mono tracks that aren't stereo-linked. And one of the unfortunate effects of doing so is that your audio levels can get boosted by waveform interference between the two tracks.

Audio is composed of waves. When two sound or audio waveforms are matched, they can interfere with each other. If the waves are *out of phase*, meaning that the peak of one track's waves occur at the same time as the trough of the other, you get *phase cancellation*, and the total level of sound for both tracks decreases significantly. Phase cancellation is rare for audio captured into FCP, because the audio is captured into FCP with the same timing it had when recorded. Phase cancellation is more of an issue when recording audio in the field or when working specifically with analog audio cables.

When the waveforms are *in phase*, the force of each wave is combined together to arrive at a new, higher audio level. If your two audio tracks are very similar, your audio levels might unexpectedly boost by +3 db or more. If your recorded audio had very high levels already, you might experience clipping that wasn't in your original recording.

Stereo-linked tracks make an adjustment for this type of situation, assuming that the two tracks are a mixdown of a single sound environment and will definitely have in-phase interference between the tracks. But there's no such adjustment for dual mono audio; the two audio tracks are assumed to be different enough not to experience in-phase interference.

So, when you are capturing sources such as DV through FireWire, in which the audio tracks were recorded in stereo in the camera, its very important to maintain the stereo relationship through the capture and into the clips with which you'll be editing.

Solution

If you have already captured clips and accidentally brought your stereo clips in as dual mono, you can manually "stereo-ize" any two mono clips together, provided the two clips are in a sequence and in adjacent tracks (for example, tracks 1 and 2 or tracks 3 and 4). The process is simple and entails the following steps:

1   Select a clip in a sequence with a video and two audio clips.

2   Press Option-L or choose Modify > Stereo Pair.

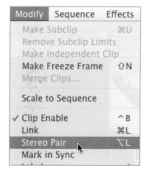

When you do this, the stereo triangles appear, identifying that this clip is now a stereo clip.

3   Double-click to load it into the Viewer.

The clip loads into the Viewer window, but rather than having separate tabs for the two audio channels, there is one stereo tab. The Filters tab has a single Stereo filters bar, rather than an individual bar for each of the two audio clips.

4   Choose Modify > Link to return the clip to its previous video and audio linked selection status.

TIP ▶ If you find that you need to raise the levels of your clip more than 12 dB, you can nest the items and have an additional 12 dB available for gain adjustment within the nest's audio tab in the viewer.

Playback Unaffected by Audio Filters

Symptom #1: Changes to Filter Settings Seem to Have No Effect on Output

"I applied an Equalizer, Reverb, or other audio filter to my audio clip, but no matter what I do to the filters settings it appears to have no effect on output."

Background

When FCP uses its default audio capture setting (two individual mono tracks) to capture a pair of audio tracks, it captures both audio tracks and includes them in the clip, but it doesn't link them as stereo. Although the audio clips are linked with regard to selection status (that is, if you select one audio clip, the other audio clip and video clip will be selected), each audio clip is handled separately for levels and panning. Loading such a clip into the Viewer, you will find that each mono audio track has its own audio tab, which contains discrete level and pan controls.

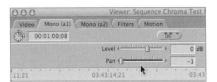

If you choose Stereo before capturing a clip, however, the clips are linked for selection status, level control, and panning. When a clip's audio tracks are linked in a stereo relationship, there are special triangular markers connecting the two. When such a clip is loaded into a Viewer, both audio channels are loaded into a single stereo tab that shows both audio tracks' waveforms, along with a single pan and level slider that affects both stereo-linked clips. Level adjustments will affect the clips exactly the same, whereas panning affects the clips inversely, sending the two tracks to opposite channels. Panning in the center means that the two stereo tracks are right down the middle, lacking stereo separation.

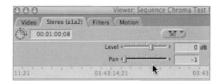

Because stereo-linked clips are treated equally, other actions also affect both tracks equally. For instance, when you apply a filter to one clip in a stereo clip, FCP understands that the filter should be applied to both clips. On the other hand, with a clip captured as dual mono, a filter must be separately applied to both clips, and the filters' controls must be addressed individually.

Many new users aren't aware that FCP is capturing their clips as nonstereo audio by default. When they later apply a filter to the clip, it is applied only to a single channel of the audio. When they make adjustments to the filter applied to one clip, the clip without the filter doesn't change, giving them the sense that nothing is changing in the overall audio clip; in fact, it is—but only in one channel!

Solution

To hear the effects of a filter on a pair of tracks inadvertently captured as mono, rather than stereo, you can either apply the filter to both tracks individually or, better yet, relink the tracks in a stereo relationship.

Audio Sounds Tinny During Playback

Symptom #1: Digital Audio File Sounds Tinny or Thin

"I imported an audio file, but it sounds very tinny and thin when I play it back in FCP."

Background

Digital audio is created by *sampling* analog audio. The digitizer, be it your DV camera, a DAT recorder, or an audio PCI card, analyzes the level and frequency of the analog audio it has been fed. It looks at each wave and generates binary values to describe them. The number of times per second the audio is measured is referred to as its sample rate. The number of binary values it uses to describe each sample is the bit depth. The more frequently the audio is sampled, the higher the quality and the higher the subsequent data rate. Similarly, the higher the bit depth of the sample is, the more accurately the data describes the audio wave.

The minimum sample rate to deliver professional quality audio is usually considered 48 kHz; the minimum bit depth for two-channel stereo audio is 16-bit. As technology improves, 24-bit, 96 kHz digitized audio will become more widely available. We've come a long way from simple audiocassettes, but we still have a long way to go.

> **NOTE** ▶ The sample rate of 44.1 kHz is quite close in quality to 48 kHz and shares its native bit depth of 16-bit. It is the sample rate of the audio CD standard, and quite good for most serious audio applications.

When your audio is digitized with a low sample rate and bit-depth setting, the resulting audio can sound vastly different from the original. Low sample rates throw out important high-frequency information as they digitize. Low bit-depth settings will reduce the dynamic range of the source audio, and can produce digital artifacts in the new file. You will often end up with a tinny-sounding file similar to a "telephone voice" when sample rates and bit depths are set too low.

Solution

Resample the audio. Although you can resample your audio using QuickTime Pro to bring it up to the higher quality sample rate and bit depth of 16-bit and 48K, you will need to start again with the original audio source, since digital audio that has passed through such low-quality sampling no longer has the original frequencies. Once you sample audio, you can only throw bits away, you can't restore them.

Solving Field Tearing Problems

Field Dominance and Tearing Problems at a Glance

Type of Problem	Symptom	Possible Cause	Solution
	#1: Jagged edges on exported video frame, horizontal flicker, or fuzzy scrolling	Time aliasing	Use a true video monitor or fix edges in Photoshop; page 768
	#2: Video jerks or has erratic output when parked on a frame	Interlacing when using an external monitor	No solution; this is normal behavior; page 769
	#3: Horizontal flicker on text and other high-contrast screen objects	Interlacing when using text graphics	Select the right graphic elements, reposition clips, or apply a blur; page 770
	#4: Scrolling text is sometimes fuzzy	Text and horizontal scan rate interfere with each other	Vary your scan rate; page 772
	#5: Playback jerks in frames with motion	Incorrect field dominance setting	Make sure you have the correct setting; page 774

Symptom #1: Jagged Edges on Exported Video Frame, Horizontal Flicker, or Fuzzy Scrolling Text

"I exported a still frame out of FCP to work with in Photoshop. The frame has very jagged edges on some parts of the frame but not others."

"I see horizontal flicker and edge crawling on and scrolling text looks fuzzy"

Background

When interlaced video fields are scanned a fraction of a second apart (1/59.94 of a second in NTSC and 1/50 of a second in PAL), the fields can contain different information. This is called *time-aliasing*. By contrast, a single frame of film records motion "evenly" during the 1/24 of a second of exposure.

You won't see time-aliasing during normal playback of interlaced video as the two fields are "blended" together. But when you look at an individual interlaced field, any motion in the field appears to have *field tearing*, or jagged edges, where there are differences between the two fields. (If you don't see this tearing in NTSC or PAL video, it's because there is no motion in the frame.)

One issue this causes for some editors is that field tearing shows up in exported stills. You might not see the field tearing in the Viewer or the Canvas, because FCP displays both fields simultaneously. But you will certainly see the tearing once the still is in Photoshop.

Solution

First, try using a true video monitor to detect problems. Find a frame that contains the content you want but without movement. This is much easier when viewing interlaced formats on a true video monitor. This will allow you to see individual fields, as they would appear as still images.

If you can't get a frame with reduced movement, use Photoshop's Video filter to remove interlacing. It allows you to choose which of the two fields you want to retain and then replaces the other field with it, generating a clean still image. You can also choose to interpolate them, making one frame by averaging both fields, but this may result in unacceptable softening and blurring of the original.

Symptom #2: Video Jerks or Has Erratic Output When Parked on a Frame

"Why is my video output jerking when the playhead is parked on a frame?"

"The video output is erratic when the playhead is parked on a frame."

Background

FCP shows both fields simultaneously in the Viewer and Canvas when the playhead is parked on a frame and set to a scale of 50% or higher. If you are editing footage using an external monitor, be prepared to see video frames jump back and forth when the playhead is not moving in the Timeline. This also may occur when creating a freeze frame. as portions of the video frame appear unsteady.

With interlaced video, FCP displays both fields of a single frame, even when the playhead is parked. Your video output device cannot simultaneously display both fields from this output like the computer monitor can; rather, FCP is rapidly sending one field then replacing it with the next, just as if it were playing frames normally. Thus on a parked frame, you will see both fields flickering back and forth.

The computer monitor is a non-interlaced display, and thus doesn't alternate fields when showing both fields. This isn't apparent when the Canvas or Viewer Scale pop-up menu is below 100%, but change the percentage to 100% or more and you will see the actual interlace field tearing.

Solution

In these instances, there is not necessarily a fix when you notice erratic output on a video device when parked on a frame. You are simply viewing a single, interlaced frame and you will not see this jerky output while playing at normal speed.

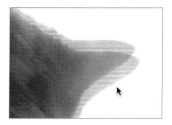

Symptom #3: Horizontal Flicker on Text and Other High-Contrast Screen Objects

"My text is blinking and flickering, and ants seem to be crawling around the edges."

Background

Two problems often encountered when using text graphics are horizontal flicker and edge crawling. Although they look a little different, they are both the result of the same interlacing phenomenon.

Text and other graphic elements are composed entirely of high contrast lines that are either straight or curved. Interlace scanning uses many horizontal lines that alternately disappear every 1/50 or 1/59.94 of a second. When a graphic element's horizontal and diagonal lines interact with the horizontal interlaced scan lines, you get flicker in horizontal lines and edge crawl in diagonal ones.

With edge flicker, the top horizontal scanned line of a letter or graphic appears to blink rapidly. This is caused by the top line being in one field, but not in the adjacent field. The line only appears 29.97 or 25 times per second rather than 59.94 or 50, producing the flicker as it flashes on and off.

Edge crawl occurs on sharp diagonal lines because of the way these lines are created using horizontal scanning. Horizontal lines are easy to display because only two scan lines are required to display a horizontal line in both fields without flicker. But anything other than a perfectly horizontal line, such as a vertical or diagonal line, is created using a stack of very short horizontal lines. Since interlacing diagonal lines requires that each line describe a new width, the interlace flicker from the horizontal line manifests as a distinct crawling illusion along the edge of text and other graphics.

The way a diagonal line is built using horizontal rasterized scan lines.

Solution

If you want to avoid this situation, use graphic elements with horizontal lines that are a minimum of two pixels wide. Use bold sans serif fonts rather than serif fonts with thin design elements. Using larger graphics is also helpful. Although this will not eliminate the problem of interlace artifacting, the casual viewer will likely not notice any remaining artifacts.

If you are still concerned with the amount of interlace artifacting, there are two ways to minimize, if not completely eliminate, interlace flicker and edge crawl. The first is to nudge the clip in question either up or down in an attempt to align the lines contained in the graphic with the scanning lines drawing the screen. In many cases, just nudging the clip twice up or down eliminates half the flicker.

1   Select the graphics clip in the sequence.

2   From the Canvas pop-up menu, choose Image+Wireframe.

3   Use Option-up arrow to move the clip up.

As you do this, monitor the results in a broadcast monitor until you see the best positioning, taking into account screen composition and interlace flicker.

There's one other method that's a little more flexible for screen composition because it lets you leave the text element anywhere you want in the frame. Apply a small amount of Blur, like .5 or less, to the graphics clip using a Gaussian Blur video filter. The Gaussian Blur filter effectively spreads the edge of the text over several different scan lines so that an edge of the image is always present in each field, rather than flickering on and off. Be aware that this method sacrifices some sharpness.

TIP ▶ Although the standard FCP Gaussian Blur filters apply a blur for you, you can salvage a lot of detail in the clip without losing the sharpness by using a third-party blur filter (such as the AJW filters included on this book's DVD-ROM) that offers blurring in a specific dimension. If you apply a blur value only in the vertical dimension, you can spread the edge of the text across more scan lines where they are causing interlace trouble without also blurring the horizontal dimension that *isn't* causing trouble.

Lowering the contrast between the graphic and the background can also ease the problems of flicker and edge crawl, if you have the freedom to choose your text colors and backgrounds. The more extreme the contrast, and the more saturated the color, the more likely you will notice flicker and edge crawl. Lowering contrast doesn't eliminate it; it just hides the fact that it is occurring.

Symptom #4: Scrolling Text Is Sometimes Fuzzy

"My scrolling text seems to ripple between fuzzy and sharp. Blurring doesn't help. It doesn't occur when parked on a frame."

Background

You may have noticed that sometimes credit rolls look terrible. You may have also noticed that adding blur does nothing to help the situation. Text may appear to warp or curve and flicker as it makes its way up the screen. Unfortunately you are seeing even more results of the perils of interlacing fields. Credit rolls, unless carefully constructed, suffer from a phenomenon referred to as *beating*.

Beating is a broad term that refers to two or more waves, such as sound waves, interacting with each other, which saps a little energy from each. This happens often in sound production. Playing two very similar notes together at high volumes can cause sound levels in a room to go up and down very quickly, creating a "beating" sound. The loss of energy produces an *oscillating*, or repeating, rhythmic pattern of interference between the original waves.

This also occurs in scrolling titles when one wave—the text as it moves up the screen—interferes with another wave—the horizontal line scanning as it travels down the screen in the other direction. As the scanning beam draws the text going in the opposite direction, it misdraws the text and makes it appear to pulse. As with flicker, this cannot be observed in the Canvas or Viewer, because the computer screen doesn't perform time-aliased interlacing.

Unfortunately, adding Blur won't help with this problem the way it could solve the previous interlace problem. And if you need a text scroll, nothing else is likely to suffice. Actually, resolving this problem is quite easy.

Solution

There's a mathematical approach to determining the speeds that will and won't result in beating. Take the field rate of the format you use, 50 for PAL and 59.94 for NTSC, which for simplification we will round off to 60. If a text element travels up the screen at a rate of 50 (PAL) or 60 (NTSC) scan lines per second, the text will look terrible. If however you double this rate to 120 (NTSC) or 100 (PAL) lines per second, the scan beam actually redraws the text object's fields correctly without artifacting. Triple it, and the artifacting returns; quadruple it, and artifacting disappears. Beating only occurs on odd multiples of the scan rate.

As a final note, it's important to always watch your text scrolls on a true interlaced monitor. This is true even if you are working with a non-interlaced format such as offline film editing or one of the progressive scan HD formats. Although non-interlaced HD formats will not natively suffer from beating, down-conversions of that HD or film content to standard definition, such as is necessary for films distributed on DVD/VHS or simulcasting both HD and SD versions of a program in broadcast, will suffer from it.

Symptom #5: Playback Jerks in Frames with Motion

"Video playback (not parked on a frame) seems to jerk when there is motion in the frame, but is normal when there is no motion."

Background

The key to treating this symptom is understanding *field dominance*, which takes the interlacing concept a step further. In analog systems, there are two fields in every frame, and they are played in the order of first field, second field. But digital codecs do not have to follow this law. In fact, in most cases, professional digital video codecs do not. They fields are ordered according to *field dominance*, or field order.

In field dominance, the dominant field in a frame of video is scanned first, followed by the remaining field. In most modern video codecs, like the DV and Apple's Uncompressed codecs, the lower field is dominant, making the field order second field, first field, second field, and so on. Some applications refer to field dominance as first–second or odd–even field dominance.

Although in normal playback you don't see any difference between upper or lower field dominant material, you *will* see a difference if the field dominance for a clip is set incorrectly. Remember that field interlacing is time-aliased, meaning that the visual information in one field is actually recorded slightly later than the previously scanned field. If the dominance for a clip is set incorrectly, this time-aliasing between the fields is reversed. When this reversing happens, video will appear to stutter.

You're not likely to run into field dominance issues when using built-in presets. Incorrect field dominance settings mostly occur when interacting with video generated by other applications, proprietary codecs, and complex rendering systems.

Solution

Many 3D and compositing applications allow you to *field render*, or render QuickTime movies using fully interlaced frame rate (59.94 or 50 fields per second as opposed to 29.97 or 25 frames per second). This is important for animation, because it allows much smoother motion and other effects.

Animation applications like Motion accomplish field rendering by treating each field as an individual frame. This allows motion animation between video fields rather than between frames, yielding very smooth animation. This feature can be turned off to preserve CPU bandwidth, so check Motion project settings to make sure this feature is enabled.

When the animation is rendered back out, Motion uses the field ordering specified in the project settings. This is critical, because you are creating a complete integrated, interlaced movie file. If you use the wrong field order, the fields will not play back correctly, causing the video to appear to stutter during playback.

Which field dominance is correct? Generally, standard definition formats such as DV and DVCPRO use lower (field 1) dominance, while high definition formats such as HDV and DVCPRO HD use upper (field 2) dominance. Animation-based formats such as Motion JPEG, as well as all progressive formats (obviously), use no field dominance.

If you are still unsure, consult the documentation that comes with the capture card or other device you use to digitize or transcode video into FCP.

You might think that you can manually reverse the field dominance in the Final Cut Pro Item Properties for the incorrectly rendered clip. But it's not an option because once you insert a manually reversed clip into a sequence, it would require rendering, meaning you lose quality. A sequence (which uses a specific codec) can only support clips with a single field dominance.

Although there are a few third-party effects filters out there that will "reverse the fields" for you, using them is a last resort; rendering these filters will recompress the clip, and you'll lose quality. It's best to render the file out again with the rendering application, using the correct field dominance.

Solving Luminance and Color Space Problems

Luminance and the range of possible color values for video frames are two areas of digital video that confuse everyone at some point or other. In addition to keeping track of the analog standards, there are several digital standards that are easy to confuse. Also, the world of HDTV is upon us, and it too has its own specifications for how to handle luminance and color.

The relatively common issues associated with luminance and color when working in FCP mostly have to do with mismatches between luminance ranges and how it is handled when FCP works with the three primary color spaces used in digital video production.

Luminance and Color Space Problems at a Glance

Type of Problem	Symptom	Possible Cause	Solution
Clipping	#1: Areas of flat and gray footage	High luminance levels	Avoid luminance levels above 100 IRE and use color correction in FCP; page 777
	#2: Black isn't a true black	Black level is too high	Set true black levels to 0 IRE; page 779
Luma and chroma clamping	#1: Footage dims	Illegal chroma levels	Keep luminance level below 100 IRE in sequences requiring RGB rendering; page 781

Solution

There are two ways to deal with the problem of clipping. First, avoid illegal values when shooting video. Although the DV format can record up to 110 IRE, that's 10 points above legal. You can use the zebra stripes in your camera to identify luminance values above 100 IRE so that anything you shoot is guaranteed to be within the broadcast-legal range from the moment you tape it.

Another method is to use color correction in FCP. Since you can shoot into the extended 110 IRE range that your camera is capable of recording, this gives you more *exposure latitude*, or a greater range of exposure values. Although you are recording detail that is above legal, you can use color correction tools in FCP to pull that illegal luminance back down into range. As long as you do not clip your whites, you can easily pull down values up to 109 IRE back down into a legal range.

Symptom #2: Black Isn't a True Black

"My blacks aren't black; can I have true blacks in video?"

"I've been color correcting black to a 7.5 IRE setup, but my blacks just get washed out."

Background

The bottom end of the luminance scale is known as *black level*. Just like 110 IRE is the absolute brightest white value that can be recorded before clipping, 0 IRE is the darkest black that can be recorded. Clipping black levels is usually referred to as "crushing the blacks." When you crush the blacks, you create areas of the frame with no detail. Although true black, like you see in film, isn't really possible (because of the difference between the way film celluloid and video tubes make light), you can get decent blacks in video that resemble the look of film properly transferred to video.

DV's 0 IRE value is actually illegal in the NTSC world (with the exception of Japan).

For PAL and Japanese NTSC users, 0 IRE is correct. But if you use NTSC and you're not in Japan, the true nominal black level is set at 7.5 IRE. This is a vestige of the analog video broadcast system. The range of IRE levels between 0 and 7.5 created problems in the luminance and refresh of a frame, and so the legal bottom level for blacks was established at 7.5. The range between 0 and 7.5 was called the setup and made off-limits to broadcast-legal signals.

Of course, now that we are in a mostly digital world, that black level interference in the analog video signal is not a problem. In fact, it only becomes an issue when a piece of video is broadcast. Video cameras and all but the most expensive professional digital video decks ignore it completely.

Solution

Like extending the exposure into the illegal luminance range of 110 IRE, NTSC users should consider allowing black levels to dip below 7.5 IRE when shooting footage. When generating footage with a DV camera, you want to set true black levels all the way down to 0 IRE. And while your footage is in post-production, you want to continue to use 0 IRE as your black level, correcting true blacks by extending them down to 0 IRE.

The right time to add setup, or adjust IRE, is when you're encoding video in the NTSC analog format, which displays black at 7.5 IRE.

Most DV decks do not add setup at the analog outputs. If you need to provide analog tape dubbed from a digital video source, and you know that you need to add setup to it, your system may require the addition of a Proc Amp Time Base Corrector or some other analog adjustment device, as well as the addition of a true analog Waveform monitor to measure the setup signal accurately.

Luma and Chroma Clamping

Symptom #1: Footage Dims

"My footage dims as I go into a transition and returns to normal after I leave the transition."

Background

Although FCP is a digital video editor, meaning that it uses RGB values to calculate luminance and chroma values, it adopts a YUV workspace so that you are always working with true broadcast values. (Professional editors work with YUV source material and need to deliver YUV products.) You can run into problems if some element in your project does not use YUV to process video colors.

Luma and chroma clamping appear as a slight darkening in bright areas of a video frame after rendering. When present, you can normally see it in transitions and areas where part of a clip is rendered and the other is not. Also, a sequence might look completely normal when in playback, but when playback is stopped, luminance levels appear to jump a few IRE levels.

Under most circumstances, the appearance in the Viewer or Canvas will not appear to change, because the phenomenon has to do with the translation of luminance values between RGB and YUV color spaces, which occurs only in true video output rather than in the computer monitor preview. Computer monitor playback always shows RGB levels directly from the FCP digital video engine and does not display in YUV. This is why definitive color correction should always be done on a calibrated production monitor rather than the Canvas or Viewer.

Although FCP edits in a YUV space, it doesn't always have to render new video frames within that YUV space. When you render video, you have a choice between rendering using YUV 8-bit (the norm for DV), YUV-10 bit (a much larger color space still based on YUV-legal limits only available when editing an uncompressed 10-bit sequence), and RGB, which you can choose in the Video Processing tab in Sequence Settings. If you use either of the YUV rendering modes, your YUV material is rendered using calculations that do not jeopardize the YUV luminance and chroma limits. It's "YUV in equals YUV out."

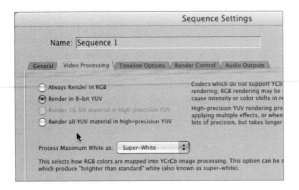

But if you choose the RGB option, FCP scales the smaller YUV luma and chroma range up to the larger RGB space to perform its luma and chroma calculations. This translates as stretching the YUV range of 16 to 235 up to a 0 to 255 range. This can be necessary, for instance, if you are using After Effects–type plug-ins in FCP, which only process color in the RGB color space. In order to make sure that your sequence's rendered clips all use the same consistent color space, when you use RGB-native plug-ins, you must always use RGB-only rendering as applied from the Sequence Settings Video Processing tab.

Luma clamping is caused by the potential clipping of broadcast-illegal values when scaling from YUV to RGB. RGB values, which extend from 0 to 255, include luminance values that are broadcast-illegal. (To give you a frame of reference for digital-to-broadcast values, the international CCIR 601 digital video standard set the YUV legal luminance values in the RGB realm at 16 to 235. So 16 in the RGB scale equals 0 IRE on the YUV scale, and 235 equals 100.)

FCP normally maps any digital values it receives (whether RGB or YUV) to its own independent scale of 0 to 100 percent. For YUV values, this gives an easy translation of one to one, 0 being absolute black and 100 being absolute white, both for YUV and for the FCP independent luma percentage value.

But if you want to render YUV material using RGB calculations, FCP has to map YUV's 16 to 235 set of values to the full RGB scale, which exceeds in definition YUV's possible luminance values.

It becomes necessary to scale 16 to 235 YUV up to the full range of RGB's 0 to 255 scale in as near as possible to a one-to-one relationship. Although that's technically impossible, FCP does a pretty great approximation. It's likely that if you render YUV material using RGB rendering for such purposes as using After Effects filtration, you will not notice the difference.

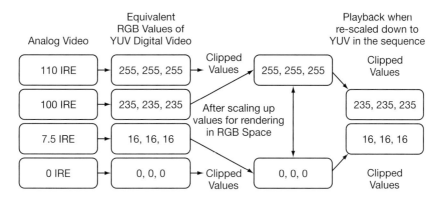

Where you will see a difference is in the situation that causes luma clamping. YUV, particularly from DV source material, is actually capable of "greater than white" values. We call these values Superwhites. Although such values are broadcast-illegal, DV still records visual detail up to 109 IRE (110 IRE corresponding to complete white).

> **TIP** The ability to record detail above the legal broadcast level is a valuable asset to "run and gun" videographers, because it assures that even if you overexpose your footage a couple of stops, you have a buffer from clipping that would normally occur at 100 IRE. Color correction can be used in post-production to pull the illegal values back down and rescue the overexposed, though not clipped detail. DV is not alone in this regard; most professional formats will also record detail far above the legal levels.

Having illegal levels in FCP and then using RGB rendering can lead you into the trap that causes luma clamping. When FCP scales YUV's values up to

RGB's, it maps based on the legal values of 16 to 235. (16 is scaled down to 0 and 235 is scaled up to 255.) The YUV illegal Superwhite values from 101 to 109 cannot be scaled above 255 (RGB's limit) and thus are clipped. Afterwards, when the values are scaled back down to YUV for playback, the range of luminance values above 100 IRE have been lost through the clipping, generating lower values than were present prior to the clipped scaling.

Thus, when a clip with Superwhite values is played back in the sequence and part of it has been rendered in RGB, you see its luminance jump a little where the Superwhite values were clipped. It's subtle, but when the clipping is within the same clip, such as in a transition, it's quite noticeable.

Solution

The only way to avoid luma clamping is to make sure that no footage used in a sequence where RGB rendering is required has luminance values that exceed 100 IRE. As long as none of your clips exceed 100 IRE, FCP will always scale luminance without clipping. Although the RGB color space may introduce very slight, nearly undetectable, differences in the extremes of color values, the luminance will be accurate both going to and coming from RGB.

Symptom #2: Graphics Are Brighter Than Highlights

"When I import still graphics they seem brighter than the highlights in my video footage."

Background

Now that you're familiar with the White or Superwhite values in YUV DV (see previous section), let's look at one other circumstance in which you might have luminance level issues. It's possible to run into problems if you are using Photoshop stills, QuickTime movies using RGB-based codecs (such as Animation), or the Text Generators in the FCP Effects tab, which all process color in the RGB color space. Using them can create problems if the luminance of the graphics and text does not match the smaller range of the YUV video you're editing.

Solution

To solve this problem, you must choose the correct settings so that FCP will make non-YUV footage match the range of your edited footage. To do that, use the White/Super-White pop-up menu in the sequence settings window. Use Superwhite if any of the video footage in the frame (other than your titles) exceeds 100 IRE in the Waveform Monitor. Use White if all your video levels are safely below 100 IRE and legal.

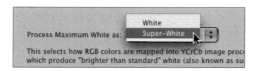

Changing this setting will not affect your YUV DV footage; it will only adjust the luminance level of the imported footage when it is rendered. When you view the footage in the Video Scopes on the Toolbench and change the pop-up menu back and forth, you will see the luminance levels scale up and back as the graphic's luminance is adjusted to match your target YUV range.

Color Space Differences

Symptom #1: Banding and Striping in a Video Frame

"Why is there banding or striping across my gradients in a rendered video frame?"

Background

RGB has a much larger color space than YUV. RGB, using 8-bit color depth, can generate over 16 million different colors between white and black, just at or beyond the level at which human eyes can differentiate color difference.

RGB is great because it is standard across most digital video systems. As software and hardware become more powerful, greater bit depths are likely to become available. 10-bit color will increase the possible color values into the trillions.

If 8-bit is so great, who needs 10-bit or higher? The answer lies in color definition. Computer systems are great, but they can only do the best with the information you give them. If you shoot a sunset horizon that goes from middle gray to orange at nearly 100 IRE, your eyes, and perhaps a 16-bit RGB system, will see an infinite gradation between the two values. But even though an 8-bit system can see millions and millions of color variations, it isn't infinite. So when the computer generates RGB values for the gradient, it has to round off colors that it can't match. When it does this, you see banding, or boundary stripes across the frame where there are no RGB values in the color space to define it.

Solution

This is where greater bit depth comes to the rescue. A 10-bit system generates more color variations, making the banding a lot less likely to occur. With 16-bit color depths, you would be hard-pressed to come up with gradients that band other than specialized test-patterns. In general, in all but the worst cameras, you will see very little of the banding just described, because the camera's circuitry actually handles a lot of the color rounding and error correction before the frame is recorded onto tape. A DV camera, using the 8-bit DV codec, generally will record beautiful levels of saturation and chromatic detail.

Where you have to be careful and choose your codec carefully is in the post-production phase. When you bring footage into the system, you have to make sure that the great gradients and minute detail you shot stay in the footage when you render it, so that beautiful sunset vista shots don't end up looking like the wrong sort of rainbows. If you see banding after rendering footage that did not have banding before you added effects, you may need to move up to a higher bit-depth codec. This may be more expensive and involve adding uncompressed hardware, but it's likely worth the added expense when you have to have the cleanest gradients possible.

Greater color range also provides more "headroom" when translating between color spaces. Converting from 8-bit RGB to 10-bit YUV results in better color accuracy than when converting to 8-bit YUV.

Symptom #2: Output Differs from Onscreen View

"Why does the video output look different from what I see in the Canvas and Viewer?"

Background

YUV NTSC and PAL have much smaller color spaces than RGB. Although they can certainly be composed of the same 8-, 10- and 16-bit bit depths, implying more possible chroma variations, they are limited to the possible color variations of color broadcast television standards, which were locked into place over 40 years ago. Although television sets have improved in the past four decades, the color standards have never changed to ensure backward compatibility for broadcast color to all televisions.

YUV is considered a lowest common denominator in video, because, even with relatively inexpensive cameras, you can acquire color and luma detail that will not be seen once the footage is lowered to the broadcast standard, for instance when viewed on a home television set. Ideally, you want to get the best quality footage with the highest range possible so that when the footage is tailored for broadcast, it maintains as much quality as possible.

Solution

When editing in FCP, you have to use not only the computer's monitors for the Viewer and Canvas, but also true video monitors from your video output source. The big difference between the two is that the FCP Viewer and Canvas use the RGB color space to display on the computer screen, while your analog video output uses the much more limited YUV range.

Unless you will be restricting your video to computer monitors, its imperative that you view your video on a properly calibrated video monitor. This is also true for the Digital Cinema Desktop Preview feature that sends the video output to a second (or even the primary) computer monitor, since that monitor shows you the RGB scale.

One unique option for users of uncompressed output devices like capture cards and media converters is referred to as a video desktop preview. Some devices will let you use a YUV-type production monitor as an extra computer monitor. The feature lets you drag application windows like the Viewer or Canvas, or even Photoshop images and the like into a broadcast color space to see what they will look like before being sent out the real video output. This can be very convenient if you are developing content in applications that have no native video output. Check with your device documentation to see if your output device offers this tool.

Solving Still Image Issues

FCP can take in an unusually large number of file formats, such as Photoshop files, meaning that you can generate footage from nearly any source and integrate it into your project. The trick is performing such imports correctly, using suitable source material. What follows are a few of the most common issues users encounter when importing the range of file formats FCP supports.

Still Image Issues at a Glance

Type of Problem	Symptom	Possible Cause	Solution
Image sizing and scaling issues	#1: Fuzzy and pixelated images	Images have been scaled above 100 percent	Use a graphics program to resize your graphics; page 790
	#2: Project opens slowly and is unresponsive	High-resolution images used in project	Restrict image resolution; page 791

Still Image Issues at a Glance

Type of Problem	Symptom	Possible Cause	Solution
Scaling and interlace arti-facting	#1: Footage flickers or ripples	Graphics with thin lines	Enlarge image or apply a blur; page 792
Photoshop image problems	#1: Loss of some Photoshop-applied effects	Photoshop features are incompatible with FCP	Flatten effects or avoid specific Photoshop fea-tures; page 793
	#2: Disappearing texture and drop shadows	Use of vector-based images	Rasterize Photoshop images; page 793
	#3: Stretched images	Mismatch of pixel shapes	Use Photoshop to "squeeze" the images; page 796
	#4: Movie loses transparency	Missing or reversed alpha channel	Reverse the alpha channel; page 799
	#5: Graphics lose sharp edges	Alpha channel is incorrectly assigned	Switch the alpha channel; page 801

Image Sizing and Scaling Issues

Symptom #1: Fuzzy and Pixelated Images

"When I scale a still image above 100% in the Motion tab, it becomes pixelated or fuzzy."

Background

In print media, you can vary the resolution of an image (measured in dots per inch, or dpi) to get more or less sharpness. A video frame on the other hand has no variation in resolution. No matter how big your video monitor is, its native resolution is 72 dpi. When you bring a 72 dpi image into FCP, it has a "one to one" relationship with what you will see on the resulting video output to the deck. It will appear at its highest, non-interpolated quality when it is scaled to 100% in the Motion tab. This is why we say it is native at 72 dpi.

> **NOTE** ▶ The only exception to this maxim is the PC platform's use of 96 dpi for PC computer monitor resolution. Mac's have always matched the standard 72 dpi resolution of broadcast video. This should only concern you if you are generating video destined for the Web that needs to look identical on both PCs and Macs.

You can use higher resolution images in FCP HD, which supports nearly unlimited pixel frame sizes. Using higher resolutions in graphics lets you keyframe Ken Burns–style pan-and-scan animations and gives you more flexibility when tweaking the size of the image for better screen composition.

Scaling images above 100% in the Motion tab of the Viewer may result in *pixelation*—a form of artifacting that appears as fuzzy or blocky loss of detail—which is the result of FCP trying to make up pixels that did not exist in the original.

Solution

Although small adjustments may not result in noticeable quality loss, you should use a dedicated graphics application to resize your graphics.

Symptom #2: Project Opens Slowly and Is Unresponsive

"My project containing a lot of high-resolution scanned images takes 10 or more minutes to open."

Background

There is a drawback to using high-resolution images in a FCP project; the higher the resolution in the image, the more processing required to make it available to the project. This can result in very slow project launches and frequent "preparing video for display" delay alerts.

Solution

In general, restrict the resolution of your images to the maximum that is useful to avoid performance hits.

If you need to use a resolution higher than 72 dpi, one tool you may find useful is Scan Guide Junior, which is included in the Extras folder on this book's DVD. The tool performs a simple calculation to help you determine the correct dpi for an image. For example, an 8" x 10" image at 72 dpi will look pixelated when doubled in size. However, if the original image had a resolution of 144 dpi, doubling the size of the image would result in no discernable loss of quality.

Scaling and Interlace Artifacting

Symptom #1: Footage Flickers or Ripples

"When I scale clips below 100%, the footage seems to flicker or ripple."

Interlace artifacting is not limited to freeze frame effects and still images. It is also a common occurrence with pan-and-scan animation of high-resolution images. When you create graphics with lines as thin as a single interlaced line, this can cause flicker or twitter when the frame is sent out to an interlaced format like standard definition video. Although the image may look completely steady on the computer monitor, it will twitter and flicker on a real video monitor. For that reason alone, it's important to monitor video out to a real video monitor.

This phenomenon is common with animated pan-and-scan stills, because typically the image you start with is scaled down from a higher resolution. The result is that some lines in the image become smaller than you anticipated and reach the single-scan line limit that yields interlace flicker.

Solution

If you are getting this flicker, but for design reasons you cannot enlarge the image itself, apply a slight blur to the image using either the Gaussian Blur or Flicker filters. Although you lose some of the detail, you will also lose the distracting flicker. Keyframing the Gaussian Blur to increase the amount of blur as the image shrinks and begins to flicker will give you a more inconspicuous blur.

Photoshop Image Problems

Symptom #1: Loss of Some Photoshop-Applied Effects
"I was told that my Photoshop image can be directly imported and used in Final Cut Pro. How come my layer effects such as stroke and drop shadow are missing from my imported image?"

Background
FCP has great integration with Adobe Photoshop, but there are limitations. Files created in any version of Photoshop can be imported, but only Photoshop 3.0 features (such as opacity, composite modes, layer order, and layer name) are supported for import.

Solution
You must flatten layer effects and other unsupported features prior to importing them into Final Cut Pro. Flattening effects is not the same as using the Flatten Image command, which combines all layers of a Photoshop file into a single layer. If you flatten only the effects, Final Cut Pro will still continue to recognize the individual layers and layer names when importing.

Symptom #2: Disappearing Textures and Drop Shadows
"My imported Photoshop text images lose their textures and drop shadows."

Background
FCP doesn't recognize vector-based imagery. This includes Photoshop textures and drop shadows. Vector graphics are differentiated from bitmap or raster graphics in that vector graphics use straight or curved lines to display an image. Raster graphics use a certain number of dots, or pixels, to display

an image. Although you won't see much apparent difference in the computer interface between the two, they use radically different ways of calculating and displaying imagery.

Vector graphics can use simpler ways to describe geometric shapes and color values than rastered graphics, although this isn't always in your best interest. For instance, a 50 pixel by 50 pixel square requires only four 50 pixel lines, or vectors, to describe, since that is the number of lines required to describe a square. A raster on the other hand would have to display 250 individual pixels to describe the same square. Simple shapes require little information to build in vector-based systems, which is why they are very popular with animation graphics destined for distribution on the Internet. Many applications, such as Photoshop, that do not produce moving images also make heavy use of vector graphics, since they're used for accuracy rather than small file size.

Raster graphics are more the standard for video, however, because video tends to contain far more complex shapes than vector graphics could realistically address. Although the square mentioned in the preceding paragraph is easily described by vectors, a human face contains a nearly unlimited number of individual geometric shapes. A decent vector-based image of your face might contain several thousand different shapes inside that 50-pixel square image. The raster however is always limited to displaying the same 250 pixels for the square. If the resolution of the raster is high enough (remember that it is always 72 dpi for video), you get a high-quality image of a face using the same 250 pixels, versus the thousands of different vectors necessary for a comparable quality vector-based image.

Solution

Since video uses raster images rather than vector images, any vector-based effects in your Photoshop images will disappear when imported into FCP. But you can still access them; you simply have to rasterize the Photoshop image prior to moving it into FCP. Although Photoshop contains a Rasterize command, it does not completely rasterize all the effects you probably want to carry over.

In order to bring everything over on import, you have to convert the individual layers to a bitmap prior to saving them in Photoshop. The easiest method of accomplishing this is to merge each individual layer with a new, empty layer. When layers are merged in Photoshop, all vector effects are converted into individual pixels, which can be displayed correctly in FCP.

To keep your original multiple layers from merging into one composite single layer, create an empty layer for each layer that contains effects, and then click the Eye icons to make only a single effects layer and a single empty layer visible. Finally, choose Merge Visible. Repeat this for all layers until you have true rasterized layers for each effects layer. Similarly, you could create the empty layer underneath the vector-based layer, then choose Merge Down, which will merge the current layer with the layer directly below it.

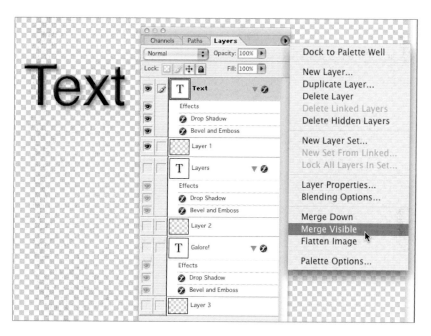

Remember that once you rasterize and save the file, you can't make changes to the text or vector imagery. Just make sure you save a production copy of your images prior to rasterizing so that you can make changes if necessary.

Symptom #3: Stretched Images

"Imported graphics files appear stretched from the original appearance when they were created in Photoshop."

Background

Individual pixels are the basic building blocks of an image. When packed tightly together, a group of colored pixels appears to merge into an image. In this regard, digital images are no different from their relatives in the print world; both print and digital images use dpi, or dots per inch, as a measure of resolution.

That's where *pixel aspect ratio* comes in, which is the relative width of a pixel to its height. A square pixel has a pixel aspect ratio of 1:1. DV uses narrow nonsquare pixels, with a pixel aspect ratio of approximately 0.9:1, while HDV 1080i uses slightly wider pixels closer to 1.3:1.

The pixel aspect ratio (PAR) is not all that difficult to calculate if you know the total number of lines contained in the video format, and the aspect ratio of the format.

Formula for 4:3 D1 or DV NTSC	Formula for 4:3 D1 or DV PAL
PAR = 486 × 4 ÷ 3 = 648 (square pixel resolution) ÷ 720 (nonsquare pixel resolution) = 0.9:1.	PAR = 576 × 4 ÷ 3 = 768 (square pixel resolution) ÷ 720 = 1.067:1

Early digital video codecs used a square pixel shape to create images. But with the introduction of modern, more efficient codecs, the nonsquare pixel came into prominence. Today, nearly all video codecs used in studio video production use nonsquare pixels. Square pixels are still used when the video output is destined for computer screen or broadcast output. The codec you use determines whether the pixels are square or not.

An image's pixel aspect ratio isn't much of an issue when working with elements generated either by capture or one of the FCP generators, because FCP natively adapts to whichever codec you are using. In the digital realm, a pixel is a pixel. Square or nonsquare makes no difference to the computer. But pixel aspect ratio does become an issue when you create graphics files in a square pixel application, such as Photoshop, for use in FCP when the video you are mixing it with uses a nonsquare pixel video codec.

> **NOTE ▶** Photoshop CS actually has a nonsquare pixel option, though for simplification, this lesson will assume the user is working with an earlier version. The technique used to adapt square pixel images to a nonsquare shape will work equally well with Photoshop CS, if the user opts not to work natively with a nonsquare pixel shape there.

Solution

Dealing with such a mismatch of pixel shapes is simple with a little foresight. If you start your project in the broadcast format dimensions, when you bring your graphic into your sequence, the image will be handled properly. If you don't want your graphic quite that big or have already created it, you simply squeeze or stretch the image (depending on the codec you are using in FCP) the same degree that the FCP nonsquare codecs will adjust the image when you import the file.

To apply this difference in Photoshop, create your graphics normally, then as a last step, use the Image Size command to vertically squeeze the image.

1   Choose Image > Image Size and deselect Constrain Proportions.

2   Choose Percent from the pop-up menus, then set Height to 90% for
NTSC, or set the Width to 93.75% for PAL.

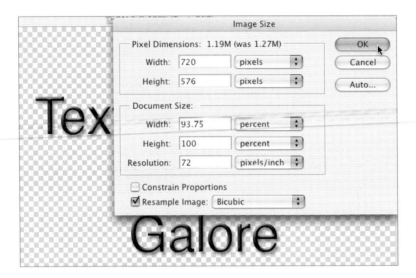

3   Save the file, and then import it to FCP.

When inserted into a DV or D1 sequence, the squeezed image's pixels are
interpreted as nonsquare rectangles and are stretched on output exactly
the same amount that they were squeezed in Photoshop.

NOTE ▶ This treatment is not necessary for single-layer flattened still
images. These images are not imported as sequences and are therefore
recognized by FCP as the square pixel images that they are. FCP can
correctly interpret square pixel images because they are not yet part of
a sequence when you use them. If your imported image is not brought
in as a sequence, it will automatically have the correct aspect ratio.

Why use images that must be squeezed instead? Flattened images have no
transparency and cannot have more than a single layer, which is much
more useful than having to perform a quick squeeze on a multilayer image
with alpha channels.

Symptom #4: Transparency of a Movie Disappears

"I imported a rendered movie that has an alpha channel, but the transparency disappeared or is backwards."

Background

If you have used Photoshop to generate titles for FCP sequences, you have probably already encountered the capability of FCP to automatically interpret *alpha channels*, which are an extra color channel that can be included with files that use certain codecs. Not all codecs support alpha channels (the DV codec for instance does not), but many do. This allows you to create text graphics in applications like Photoshop and superimpose them over video clips.

You can also include alpha channels with video clips rendered out of video compositing applications such as Adobe After Effects or Apple Shake. In most cases, this is as seamless an operation as is importing Photoshop files. You tell the rendering application to include any transparent areas as an alpha channel, and then FCP detects it on import.

> **TIP** To include an alpha channel when rendering a file out of a compositing application, you usually need to do a couple of things. First, make sure you are rendering using a codec that supports alpha channels, such as animation. When you choose the codec, make sure that you select Millions of Colors + for the color space (the + means an alpha channel is present) and that you select RGB and Alpha for the export.
>
> Different applications will have different toolsets for this operation, but it must be set for them all. Remember that if there are no transparent areas in the frame, you won't see any transparency in the import, though an alpha channel that you include could be used later for transparency manipulation after the render.

Alpha channels aren't always handled in a standard manner by all applications. The alpha channel uses levels of brightness to determine how transparent a pixel is in an image, similar to the way the other color channel works. When a pixel in the red channel is very bright (or more accurately, has a higher value), it is very red; when a pixel in the alpha channel has a high value, it is very transparent. Given the values of all the color channels for a pixel, you know its brightness, chroma, and, with an alpha channel, its transparency.

This can break down, however, when different applications use opposing values for transparency. Most application use white for the color that indicates transparency in the pixel, but a few use the opposite black. When this is the case, FCP might misinterpret the value of the alpha channel for the pixels in the image, either reversing the transparency or ignoring it altogether.

Solution

If you import a file and the subsequent clip's transparency is reversed or missing, you can try a couple of things. First, test to see if the alpha channel is simply reversed. To do so, select the clip and choose Modify > Reverse Alpha. Reverse Alpha is actually a setting for each individual clip, so you are toggling it on when you choose it. If Reverse Alpha does not do the trick, be sure to toggle it off before moving to the next symptom and solution.

Symptom #5: Loss of Sharp Edges on Graphics

"My imported graphics or movie files have edge artifacting rather than sharp, clean edges."

Background

There are three ways in which alpha channels are implemented in FCP. The first, None/Ignore is very obvious; if there is no alpha channel, or if you want to disregard one, this would be appropriate. The remaining two methods are more direct. Alpha channels can be either *straight* or *premultiplied* with either black or white pixels.

With a straight alpha channel, the alpha retains its distinct value as a channel, giving a transparency value for each pixel. This yields a very clean, well-defined edge to the transparent and opaque parts of the image. However, this can sometimes lead to problems when subtle levels of transparency are necessary, as with lens flares, special shading, and other gradient transparencies. Often, the entire image with alpha channel is premultiplied with either black or white pixels. Premultiplied alpha channels are generally more accurate, and they are the standard for images coming from Photoshop and other applications.

The problem occurs if FCP misinterprets the alpha channel.

If it mistakes (or is assigned) a straight alpha when it should have revealed a black or white premultiplied one, you would likely experience a ringing, artifacted fringe around the edges of the transparency.

Solution

If you see this in your image, choose Modify > Alpha Channel and switch from whatever FCP has interpreted to the other type, such as Straight to Black or White.

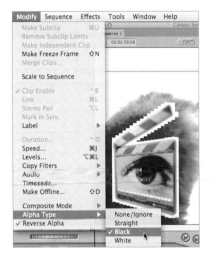 

Note that alpha channels can be premultiplied with either black or white pixels, and that the alpha interpretation, like the Reverse Alpha setting, must be assigned for each clip; changing the master's alpha interpretation alone won't change any other affiliate or copy in your project.

Lesson Review

1. Since most digital video codecs use non-square pixels, unlike Photoshop and other still-image applications, how do you get your images to appear correctly in your sequences?

2. How do you access Photoshop texture and drop-shadow effects in FCP?

3. There are numerous causes of dropped frames in FCP. Name three.

4. If your video output looks different from what you see in the Canvas and Viewer, how do you solve that problem?

5. What's the primary cause of audio distortion in a sequence?

6. What should you do if a clip isn't stereo linked?

7. What are two sorts of out-of-sync audio? What causes each?

8. What can you do to avoid problems with audio if you're using Panasonic's AG-DVX100 camera?

9. Can FireWire drives share a chain?

10. If you don't correctly set HDV and DV on FCP and the camera or deck, what symptom will you see?

Answers

1. Perform a reverse-squeeze operation to correct images.

2. Rasterize the layers containing the effects.

3. FCP is unable to keep up with the frame rate of your video standard (such as NTSC, PAL, HD); hardware issues; software malfunction or incompatibility; FCP settings misconfiguration; or pushing Unlimited RT and audio mixdown too far for your Mac's capabilities.

   A duplicated frame is a type of innocuous dropped frame that occurs as an anomaly. You can disregard it in most situations.

4. Use both a computer monitor and a true video monitor to view your work.

5. Improper settings at the capture, editing, or output stages of editing.

6. Apply audio filters individually to both mono audio clips linked to the video so that you don't hear one channel without filtration.

7. Progressive and consistent. Progressively out-of-sync audio can be caused by botched settings, video recordings with nonstandard sample rates, or having captured over blank videotape and timecode breaks. Consistently out-of-sync audio is usually a result of latency caused by routing audio and video through different devices that process the signals at different speeds.

8. Tapes recorded in Panasonic's AG-DVX100 camera require that you install a special tool found in the Extras folder of the installer CD. Note: This isn't a problem with AG-DVX100A cameras.

9. No. FireWire drives can share a FireWire bus with a DV deck or camera, but should never share a chain.

10. If they aren't set correctly, you'll get "No Communication" errors.

18

Operational Troubleshooting: File, Format, or Device Errors

In Lesson 17, we looked at the common causes of video and audio display or playback errors. This chapter discusses another category of issues: those involving missing or offline files, connectivity problems, and system or device errors. We'll look at:

▶ Missing scratch disk or offline file problems (page 806)

▶ Missing audio or video output (page 815)

▶ FireWire connectivity problems (page 830)

▶ 24P capture and pulldown issues (page 840)

▶ System lockups and error alerts (page 844)

Like the previous lesson, this lesson is designed as a series of shortcuts— a way to help you identify and solve common issues quickly. It is not intended to replace the troubleshooting methodology described in Lesson 16, and you should refer to that lesson if the suggested solutions here do not solve your problem.

Solving Missing Scratch Disk or Offline File Problems

To operate properly, Final Cut Pro relies on links between project files and media on the scratch disk volumes. Because of the nature of DV media files and the need for high-bandwidth access, it's often recommended that media and project files be stored on different volumes.

When these volumes are disconnected or renamed, or the files are moved, renamed, or duplicated, it is possible for the links to become broken, resulting in one of two errors: a missing scratch disk volume or offline clips. Fortunately, in Final Cut Pro the process of relocating your scratch disk volumes and relinking your project and media files is straightforward.

Scratch Disk and Offline File Problems at a Glance

Type of Problem	Symptom	Possible Cause	Solution
Missing scratch disk	#1: A dialog at launch says your scratch disk is missing	The missing disks are not present or not powered on	Remount scratch disk, page 807
		You are no longer using the disk in question	Reset scratch disk, page 807
Offline files at launch	#1: Project's clips are offline and unavailable	Project has a missing scratch disk	Reconnect offline clips, page 809

Scratch Disk and Offline File Problems at a Glance

Type of Problem	Symptom	Possible Cause	Solution
	#2: Offline clips are inaccessible through the Reconnect Media dialog	Changed some media file names or captured clips into a project you can't access	Force-link clips to media, page 812
Problems importing audio files from CDs	#1: Audio files drop frames and go offline after relaunching FCP	Referencing the audio files from the CD in the CD-ROM drive	Copy audio files to hard drive before importing them into FCP, page 813

Missing Scratch Disk

Symptom #1: A Dialog at Launch Says Your Scratch Disk Is Missing

"I just launched my project, and I got a Missing Disks dialog stating that it can't find my scratch disk volume."

Background

If you use external drives for scratch disk volumes, at some point you will probably start up FCP without having connected or powered on your external drives.

When you launch FCP 4 and later, the application checks to see if the assigned scratch disk volume is present and mounted. If it is, FCP starts up normally. If it is not, you encounter a Missing Disks dialog.

Solution

The three options offered in the Missing Disks dialog—Quit, Check Again, and Reset Scratch Disks—are tailored to the most likely reasons your scratch disk volume might disappear.

▸   **Quit.** If your currently assigned scratch disk volume is not available at all (for example, you forgot to bring it with you), you probably don't want to start up your project until you have the drive, because it's likely storing your current media. FCP allows you to Quit the application before making any further changes and then retrieve and connect the missing drive. Restart FCP, and the project will launch up and link normally. This procedure will keep you from accidentally unlinking all your clips.

> **NOTE** ▸ If you open your project with the scratch disk volume missing, an Offline Files dialog appears, identifying the offline clips. If you were then to click OK in that dialog and save, your project would be saved in an offline state, because it is impossible to relink the files when the scratch disk is missing.

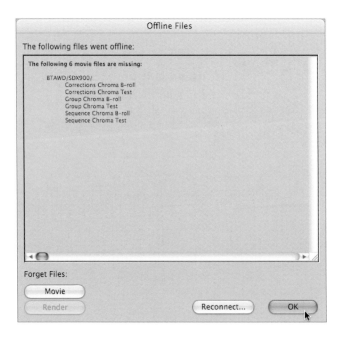

▶ **Check Again.** If the drive is present but not powered up or dismounted (for example, you dragged it to the Trash), FCP will stay in a holding position until you mount the scratch disk volume. Power up the disk and wait for it to appear on the Desktop, or use Disk Utility to mount the disk manually. Then click the Check Again button in the Missing Disks dialog. When FCP finds the missing volume, the Check Again button turns into the Continue button. Click Continue, and the project will start up normally.

▶ **Reset Scratch Disks.** If FCP is looking for a scratch disk assignment that has been removed (for example, from a previous project), you'll need to reassign a new scratch disk. Click Reset Scratch Disks. The Scratch Disk preferences will appear, where you can safely assign the scratch disk to whatever disks are available to the system at that moment. Click Continue to start work on the project.

NOTE ▶ The Missing Disks dialog appears only when the assigned scratch disk volume is missing. If your clips are located on other volumes that are present, those clips won't be knocked offline.

Offline Files at Launch

Symptom #1: Project's Clips Are Offline and Unavailable

"I launched a project with my scratch disk missing and accidentally saved it. Now that the scratch disk is available again, how do I relink?"

Background

FCP uses both project files (metadata) and QuickTime movies (media) to make video editing possible. Although the two are normally linked from the moment they are introduced by capture or import into the project, that linkage is as temporary as you want it to be. As we saw in the first section of this book, you can make project clips offline from within FCP itself. And of course, launching a project with missing scratch disk volumes will make the media unavailable to the project and render its clips offline.

Solution

In most cases, when your clips go offline, you just need to reconnect them. Doing so is easy. You can attempt to reconnect all clips and sequences, or you can selectively reconnect them one at a time.

If you just want to make sure you get everything, there's no reason to select clips individually (with the exception of files whose names have changed and that need to be relinked manually); just click the project tab, press Cmd-A to Select All, and then choose File > Reconnect Media.

In the following Reconnect Files dialog, you can tell FCP not to relink render files and clips that are already online, meaning that you will only be relinking the offline clips. If you don't want to reconnect all offline clips, you can manually select the clips you do want to reconnect and then return to this box.

NOTE ▶ You don't have to reconnect both master clips and their affiliate clips in sequences. FCP's clips have a robust master-and-affiliate relationship. When a master clip in a project tab is relinked, all its affiliates are as well, including any clips edited into sequences.

After you've identified the type of clips you want to bring online, click OK, and FCP will begin exhaustively searching for file names that match the last known media file linked to the clip. If such a file exists on your drives, FCP will find it. Once FCP locates the file, quickly take a look at the directory path to make sure that FCP has found the file you want it to find. If you have a duplicate of the clip, or if you have media files with the same names in other folders, FCP might find these first. Without checking the file you relink to, later on you might accidentally throw your clip offline again because you relinked to an irrelevant file.

Before you click OK, make sure that Reconnect All Files in Relative Path is checked. If it is, FCP will look for any files in the same directory path that can be relinked to any other clips in your project before moving on to the next item to relink. If you keep your scratch disk volumes orderly and distinct, as discussed in Lesson 6, reconnecting usually takes only a few clicks, even for the most complicated projects.

Symptom #2: Offline Clips Are Inaccessible Through the Reconnect Media Dialog

"I've changed some media file names in my scratch disk folder, and now the clips are offline, but the Reconnect Media dialog won't let me select the file I want to connect the clip to."

"I have offline clips in my project, and I just realized that they were captured yesterday by a colleague into another project I don't have access to. Can I force-link my offline clips to his media files?"

Background

The time may come when you have to go against the grain and make FCP do something it doesn't want to do. Although FCP sees the initial linkage of clip and media, that relationship is completely flexible. You can not relink clips with media that were originally captured or imported together, but also force-link clips to media files that are completely unrelated.

Solution

Follow the method of reconnecting media files described in the preceding section. When FCP reaches the Choose a File dialog, uncheck the Matched Name Only checkbox to gain the ability to select any file you want.

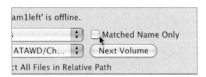

You can use the Show pop-up menu to screen the files that show up in the window to Video, Audio, or Still Image, or simply to show All Files in a given directory.

The only thing you have to remember when force-reconnecting files is that if you are force-connecting clips that already exist in a sequence, you have to maintain a relation between clip duration and the media file you are force-reconnecting it to. In fact, FCP will warn you with a conflict dialog box stating the properties of the clip that don't match those of the original. If a clip is longer in duration than the media file you are force-connecting it to, the clip will be trimmed automatically to match the media limits of the clip it is now linked to. The reverse isn't true, however, and short clips won't be extended on relink; they will only have the extra frames added to their handles. Master clips in the project tab simply conform to the new media-file durations, with no In or Out points.

Problems Importing Audio Files from CDs

Symptom #1: Audio Files Drop Frames and Go Offline After Relaunching FCP

"I import tracks from my audio CD into FCP, but they go offline the next time I restart my project."

"I imported tracks from an audio CD into FCP, but I get dropped-frames warnings every time I play the clip."

"I hear crackling and popping from my imported audio CD tracks."

Background

FCP can easily use audio tracks taken from audio CDs, but if you don't perform the import correctly, you may end up with offline clips or dropped-frames warnings each time you try to access the clips. This occurs because FCP, unlike other nonlinear editors, does not duplicate media when it imports a file.

When you import a file into an FCP project, it creates a clip linked to the media file you imported, rather than generating yet another media file in your scratch disk. This is a very good idea, particularly for importing elements like graphics files and video files rendered out of other applications, such as Apple Motion or Adobe After Effects. It's digital, and it's already on your disk; why duplicate it?

The problem is that some users forget this when importing audio CD tracks. If you insert an audio CD and then choose File > Import > File and select a track from the CD, you are linking the imported clip directly to the CD itself. This creates three separate and distinct problems.

First, the clip in your project will be online only as long as that audio CD is still in the CD tray. If you shut your project down, remove the CD from your Mac, and restart the project, the CD the clip was linked to will have disappeared, forcing the clip offline. FCP will not tell you why the clip is offline, because as far as FCP is concerned, the CD was a legitimate source location. Only you know that it was not a permanent drive.

Second, each time you attempt to play the clip linked to the CD (assuming that the CD is still in the tray and the clip is not offline!), your Mac will have to play the actual CD itself to retrieve the data the clip is linked to. Anyone who has booted a Mac up from an installer CD will tell you that optical disks, like CDs and DVDs, are very slow. FCP will not be able to keep up with the frame rate while trying to read the optical disk and will generate dropped frames alerts.

Finally, if you get this far, you are very likely to end up with crackling or out-of-sync audio. As discussed in the previous lesson on FCP performance troubleshooting, mixing sample rates in an FCP sequence is a pretty bad idea. Audio CD tracks carry a uniform sample rate of 44.1 kHz, which is nonstandard and not acceptable for use with video. Although FCP has the means to resample nonstandard audio on the fly, the results are usually less than acceptable. Resampling at Low Quality in the Audio Playback Quality pop-up menu of the User Preferences dialog can yield crackling or popping artifacting unless you render the material out in an audio mixdown.

There is no reason to end up in this situation. When you want to import an audio CD track, use the Export Queue window included in FCP:

1   Pop the CD into the CD tray.

2   Open FCP's Export Queue window (Window > Export Queue).

3   Drag the file(s) from the CD into the Export Queue window.

4   Click the Batch folder, and click the Settings button at the bottom of the window.

5   Click the Destinations button to set the destination for the converted files. This will most likely be your Capture Scratch folder.

6   Choose AIFF from the Format pop-up menu.

7   Click the Options button, and choose your desired sample rate and bit depth. This will most likely be 48 kHz and 16 bit.

8   Click OK to close the conversion window.

9   Click the Export button in the bottom-left corner of the Export Queue window.

10   Your newly converted files are now local to your hard drive and can be imported into FCP.

The bonus is that you can import and connect the entire contents of the CD in one conversion step by dragging the entire disk into the Export Queue window.

Solving Problems of Missing Audio or Video Output

An output device is any device you use to convert FCP's data stream to some format of video, such as DV, SDI, analog composite, or component. Any time you send video to a monitor other than the computer monitors connected to the graphics card of your Macintosh, you are sending to an output device.

A few common factors prevent video or audio from being sent out to your target output device. These factors range from device-specific settings on the output device to FCP's internal controls and toggles for A/V output.

To find the solution to your missing-audio or -video problem, first determine whether both types of output are missing or just one, and whether the output is partially missing or completely absent. Then consult the "Missing Audio and Video Problems at a Glance" table, and find the symptom description most similar to what you're experiencing. The table will point you toward the possible cause of your problem and the section you can read to find out how to fix it.

Missing Audio and Video Problems at a Glance

Type of Problem	Symptom	Possible Cause	Solution
Missing or impaired A/V output	#1: No video or audio output	Incorrect window settings	Double check and correct settings
		Communication error	Restart your Mac
		Log and Capture or Edit to Tape window is open	Close these windows, page 817
	#2: Missing output on FireWire deck or camera	DV device disconnected, off, or not set to receive DV stream	Correct your FireWire device settings, page 818
	#3: Output sent through PCI capture card is missing or impaired	Malfunctioning or incorrect software driver or hardware settings (incorrect media input selected on deck or monitor)	Correct your PCI hardware settings and software driver, page 819

Missing or Impaired A/V Output

Symptom #1: No Video or Audio Output

"My hardware and settings are appropriate, but I get no video or audio output at all."

Background

If you lose video or audio output while editing, FCP's windows are a good place to check before you start tearing apart your whole system, as a few easy-to-fix problems may be relevant.

Solution

Check the following windows and window settings:

▶   External Video and Video Playback settings in the View menu.

▶   Set External Video to All Frames.

▶   Video Playback should indicate an active connection (checked in bold). If None is selected, Final Cut Pro has lost the connection with your camcorder or deck.

▶   If your camcorder fell asleep or was not connected, choose Refresh A/V Devices; then choose the correct settings.

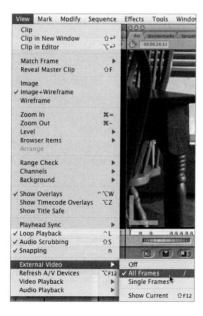

▶ On rare occasions a communication error may occur, such as when you switch to a different camcorder or deck, or when you change your output to a different broadcast standard (for example, from DV NTSC to DV PAL; some DV decks are capable of operating under both standards). If this happens, you may need to save your project and restart your Mac so that FCP can recognize the new device or standard.

▶ FireWire DV editors sometimes disable output of video and audio accidentally by leaving the Log and Capture window open after completion of capture. When you are editing with External Video set properly, FCP delivers video and audio output to your chosen device. But FCP's FireWire input and output can operate in only one direction at a time. (This may not be true for all capture devices; check your documentation.)

▶ Check to see whether you have left the Log and Capture or Edit to Tape window open during your session, as FCP can't output video from the Canvas or Viewer with Log and Capture open. Pressing Cmd-8 will bring the Log and Capture window to the front, whether it is open or not.

Symptom #2: Missing Output on FireWire Deck or Camera
"FCP View External is set to All Frames, and my DV device shows up in my Video Output settings, but I am getting nothing on my deck or camera."

Background
FCP communicates with DV decks and cameras through a single, bidirectional FireWire cable. Just sending output through the cable, however, isn't sufficient to make sure that the deck or camera can receive the output. The deck or camera must be set up correctly to receive the DV stream, and FCP must be set up correctly to send it.

Solution
Check the following settings on your output devices, and correct them as needed:

▶ Make sure the Log and Capture and Edit to Tape windows aren't open. FireWire can't move video in and out of FCP simultaneously. If either Log and Capture or Edit to Tape is open, the deck or camera will be automatically set for DV Out, and it won't be able to receive video output from FCP.

▶ If you're sending output to a camera, make sure it is set on VTR or Play mode. If the camera is in Camera mode (ready to record footage from the camera section), it can't receive and negotiate a DV stream from the FireWire port.

▶ Remove any tape from your deck or a camera if you aren't capturing or printing or editing to tape. Playback of tape in DV decks and cameras (even when the deck is paused) overrides input of the DV stream.

▶ If you're sending output to a DV deck, make sure the deck is set to pay attention to the DV input. Most Sony DV decks, for example, have a switch that tells the deck to toggle between the analog and DV inputs. If it's set to one of the analog inputs, you won't be able to see FCP's DV output.

▶ Some decks need further configuration via the device menu functions or might need the Record button depressed to monitor video throughput.

▶ Make sure your output device hasn't shut itself off. Many DV decks and cameras, such as Canon cameras, have auto shut-off modes, in which the device turns off if it's not accessed within a given period. Because for many devices, A/V output from FCP through a FireWire cable doesn't constitute accessing, your A/V output might disappear in the midst of an edit session. If your A/V output simply disappears during an edit session, and you wake up the deck or camera and still have no output, you may need to refresh the device by using the View External option, described in the next section.

Symptom #3: Output Sent Through PCI Capture Card Is Missing or Impaired

"FCP View External is set to All Frames, and my capture card shows up in my Video Output settings, but I am getting nothing or a garbage signal out of the video outputs."

Background

PCI capture cards are the second-most-common output devices for FCP, after DV decks and cameras—and they work in conjunction with several elements that you need to check if you encounter output problems.

PCI capture cards use their own proprietary hardware circuits (and instructions from their software drivers) to convert a variety of analog and digital formats. These cards also translate data in the other direction, converting FCP's sequence into the output type that the card uses.

Because capture cards are all third-party products, they generally require software drivers—one of the first elements you need to check if something goes wrong. Older cards that interface with professional decks use serial deck control, giving you a second element to examine.

Solution

Check and correct the elements of your system one at a time, as needed, in the following order:

▶ If this is the first time you have used the card, verify that you have the card installed in the correct slot. For example, your card may work in either a PCI or PCI-X slot but may perform best in the PCI-X slot. If you have multiple PCI cards, you may need to place the cards in specific locations for best performance. Checking with the vendors of your cards is the best place to start.

▶ Shut down your Macintosh and any decks connected to your card to correct any confusion in the software driver. Start the computer back up, and test the issue. If the video output doesn't reappear, you may need to uninstall and reinstall the device's drivers, and check for new drivers from the manufacturer of the device.

▶ Check the settings of your capture card and deck, as well as those of any necessary serial controller or adapter. Make sure your deck or monitor is set to the proper video input.

▶ Consult your deck and output device documentation to see whether you need reference video to record to your deck. Some decks are very dependent on reference video signals to function properly.

Some analog component decks require a reference signal to stabilize the analog video signal before recording. Lack of a video reference signal can result in noise, horizontal and vertical sync rolling, timecode inaccuracy in capture, and error messages on the video deck. Usually, a composite video signal from the same source as the component video feed can be used as a reference. If such a signal isn't available, you can add a *blackburst* and *genlock* device to the signal chain to provide "house sync" for reference. House-sync reference is often critical for Edit to Tape operations involving Insert edits.

Missing or Impaired Video Output

Symptom #1: Input and Output Hardware Are OK, But Video Output Is Still Missing

"I have no video output on my target output device."

"View External Video is set to All Frames, but I still have no video output on my target output device."

Background

If your video output has disappeared, and you have determined that nothing is wrong with your input and output hardware and cabling, first choose View > Refresh A/V Devices. Then make sure you have chosen the correct External Video and Video Playback settings.

▶ If this is the first time you are using this feature, make sure that FCP supports this feature with your external device. For example, FCP 5 does not support external HDV video or audio monitoring.

Solution

If no video was available when you launched FCP, check whether the toggle that enables and disables video output in the View > External Video contextual menu is set to Off. Set it to All Frames to toggle video output back on.

If the toggle enabling video output is set to All Frames, yet you still have no video output, you need to verify that FCP can see your device. Go to the View > Video Playback contextual menu, which should show all available video outputs. The first option, None, disables video output. If you have a FireWire deck or camera of NTSC, PAL, or any flavor of DVCPRO25 or 50, all these options will be available. (If you don't have a DVCPRO50 deck, selecting will likely result in output failure.)

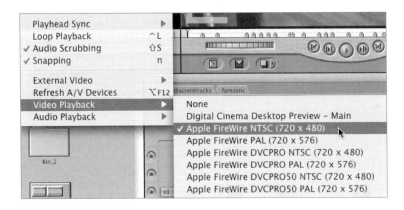

If you have selected a device for output but it has disappeared during the course of the edit session, the word [Missing] will appear before the name, informing you that it is trying to use a device that is unavailable. If the deck was turned off, turn it back on, wait for a second or so for the Macintosh to detect it, and then choose View > Refresh A/V Devices. Finally, return to the Video Playback contextual menu, and confirm that the deck is present and selected.

Symptom #2: Output Problems While Using Digital Cinema Desktop Preview

"I'm using a Digital Cinema Desktop Preview and getting a lot of visual artifacts."

Background

A new feature that DVCPROHD users will find particularly useful is the Digital Cinema Desktop Preview option. This feature is actually an adaptation of what was called the Desktop 2 option in FCP 2, long before HD functionality had appeared. Digital Cinema Display Preview lets you use a second computer monitor connected to your AGP graphics card function as your video output device for any video edited in the Canvas or Viewer.

Although this new option is useful, the settings can be confusing—and certain choices can cause you to end up with artifacts on your display.

Of the four settings available for Digital Cinema Desktop Preview on a second desktop monitor, the best for reducing artifacts is Normal. Normal indicates that the video resolution of the clip or sequence will fit into the normal resolution of the desktop display without stretching to fit it. If you were previewing a 720 x 480 NTSC DV sequence to a second desktop display that had a resolution of 1280 x 854, the DV sequence would be much smaller than the full screen, appearing very tiny. If the second desktop's resolution were set to 800 x 600, the DV sequence would take up a much larger area of the frame. The Normal setting scales the video frame only if the sequence frame is larger than the current resolution of the monitor you are using for preview. Minimizing the chance of scaling is a good idea, because scaling generates visual artifacts; what you see isn't what you get.

The other available settings involve more scaling or other undesirable effects. For example, Full Screen stretches or squeezes the video frame so that at least one dimension of the frame matches the resolution of the preview monitor—often causing nasty artifacts, especially with DV. Raw means that no scaling or pixel-aspect-ratio adjustments are ever made—which is useful for analyzing undoctored pixels in a given frame but generally causes anamorphically incorrect frame sizes that don't come close to matching your screen resolution.

Solution

In general, you'll get the best results if, before setting the second monitor as the Digital Cinema Desktop Display, you use the Display system preference to set the monitor's resolution as close as you can to the resolution of the format you'll be working with (such as 1280 x 854 for DVCPROHD 720P footage and 800 x 600 for DV NTSC or PAL). Then choose the Normal setting. Following that process, your footage will closely match the full size of the second monitor without scaling.

Partially or Entirely Missing Audio Output

Symptom #1: Audio Is Missing or Coming Out of Incorrect Output Device

"I've got video *coming out of the right output device, but there is no audio."*

"Audio is coming out of the wrong output device."

"Audio is coming out of the Macintosh."

Background

FCP can output audio to a different output device than the video. This can be a great option if you are using a professional audio interface for your project. You might be sending the video signal to a FireWire DV device or capture card, for example, but sending all eight tracks of audio out discretely to an eight-track ADAT setup or other multichannel recording system.

Having this ability means you have to be more careful with your settings than you previously were to prevent unintentional separation of your audio and video.

Solution

Choose Sequence > Sequence Settings, and verify your audio settings in the General tab. For example, make sure the sample rate and bit depth are appropriate for your device. It's also important to check the number of outputs selected in the Audio Outputs tab.

In general, there are two ways to match your audio output to your video output: the manual method and the automatic method.

▶ With the manual method, you use the audio and video playback options in the View menu to match audio to video explicitly. For example, choose View > Audio Playback > FireWire DV to route the audio from a DV sequence to match a setting of View > Video Playback > Apple FireWire NTSC (or PAL or DVCPRO) for video.

▶ With the automatic method, you first select the proper output for video and then choose View > Audio Playback > Audio Follows Video. That setting will always override the current Audio Playback setting and automatically route it to wherever the video output is being sent.

Another setting to check if your audio and video still aren't matching up is the Sound system preference. If you want your audio to be routed through your Macintosh's onboard audio resources (built-in audio or third-party PCI or USB audio devices) rather than being sent to a specific output device, like a DV deck, you may need to choose the device in the Sound system preference as well as FCP.

Symptom #2: FCP Won't Output More Than Two Channels of Audio at a Time

"I have an output device that handles more than two channels of audio at a time, but my FCP tracks mix down to only two of the output device's tracks."

Background

Although FCP always had the ability to work with up to 99 tracks of audio in a sequence, you were limited to 2 channels of audio output and capture at a time, due to limitations in the QuickTime architecture. FCP can now handle up to eight channels, depending on the device you are using.

If you have an audio interface that supports more than two channels of audio output at a time, you can create audio presets that route your sequence audio tracks directly out to specific channels of the audio output device. In general, this requires a device that has CoreAudio driver support, enabling both Quick-Time and FCP to recognize it as a legitimate output device.

If you don't explicitly create multichannel audio presets, however, FCP will use its default Audio Output preset for standard two-channel stereo—potentially creating confusion for you if you don't know about this default.

Solution

To enable FCP's multichannel audio output capability, you need to create an audio preset for the number of channels your output device supports, as follows:

1   Choose Final Cut Pro > User Preferences > Audio Outputs tab.

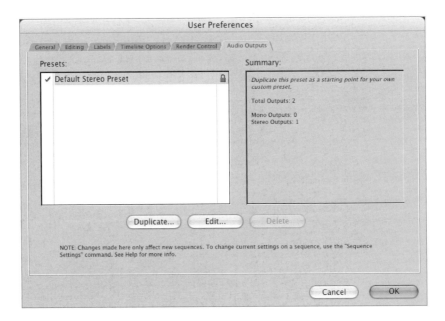

2   Click the Duplicate button to get to the Audio Outputs Preset Editor.

The Audio Outputs Preset Editor is a template used to create new presets for use with your multichannel output device.

3   After typing a name and description for the preset, click the Outputs
    pop-up menu to select the number of outputs your device has.

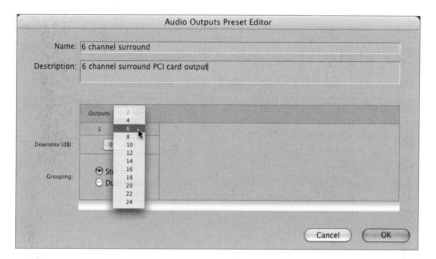

When you do so, you will get several pairs of potential tracks—for example,
six outputs yields three pairs. Each output pair contains a Stereo or Dual
Mono switch and a pop-up control for adding downmix (dB) level reduction. The choice between dual mono or stereo grouping depends on the
type of work you are doing.

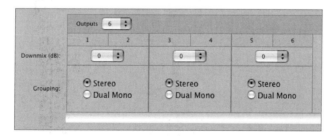

Downmix level control can be important, particularly when you send similar or identical mono audio tracks through two grouped channels. Because of the way that audio waves interact, this can lead to a situation in which the audio channels either double the level of audio by being grouped together or cancel each other out if they are thrown slightly out of phase.

In general, stereo audio equipment will eliminate such wave interference, but that isn't guaranteed. If your audio levels boost or diminish unexpectedly after you create a new preset, you may need to try subtracting or adding downmix levels.

4   Click OK to create the preset and then OK to leave User Preferences.

Next, you need to choose the output device to which FCP should apply the multichannel audio preset.

5   Choose Final Cut Pro > Audio/Video Settings.

6   In the subsequent dialog, click the A/V Devices tab, choose the output device you want to monitor with, and click OK.

7   With the sequence active in the Timeline window, choose Sequence > Sequence Settings.

8   On the Audio Outputs tab, click the Presets pop-up menu, and choose the multichannel preset you created in steps 1–4.

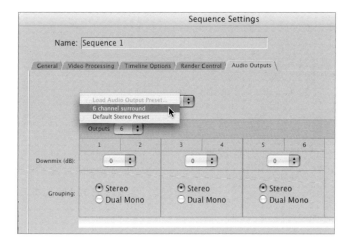

9 Finally, Ctrl-click each audio track in the sequence (right around the
Autoselect track toggle), and route it to a dedicated audio output track
in the contextual menu.

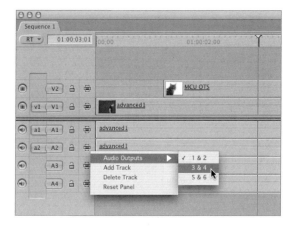

Note that if you chose Stereo grouping in the preset, Ctrl-clicking the
track gives you the option of choosing a pair, whereas with Dual Mono,
you can route any track to any output channel.

Solving FireWire Connectivity Problems

FireWire is a great form of connectivity. It's fast, convenient, painless, and inexpensive. One cable is all it takes to get data from one device to another, with few or no special settings to maintain. But as with all connectivity standards, you can run into problems with it. Here are some troubleshooting tips.

FireWire Connectivity Problems at a Glance

Type of Problem	Symptom	Possible Cause	Solution
Nonmounting FireWire drive	#1: Disconnected FireWire drive doesn't mount	Drive was improperly disconnected	Remount your improperly disconnected drive, page 832
	#2: FireWire drive doesn't mount despite correct connection	Bad cable or damaged port	Improve your FireWire connections, page 833
Dropped frames with daisy-chained FireWire drives	#1: Dropped frames during playback and recording to daisy-chained FireWire drives	FireWire drives and DV deck are sharing the same bus	Separate FireWire drives and video devices to separate buses, page 834
Lack of communication with FireWire deck or camera	#1: Insert editing is unavailable with current device	Unsupported device or machine control protocol	Use compatible deck or switch device control protocols, page 836

FireWire Connectivity Problems at a Glance

Type of Problem	Symptom	Possible Cause	Solution
	#2: Log and Capture reports no communication with connected device	Camera or deck not set to DV or HDV (depending on the type of video format you are working with)	Correct your FireWire device settings, page 837
	#3: Can't communicate with connected AJ-HD1200A deck	Incorrect menu settings for this deck	Make sure your settings are correct, page 837
Capture interruptions and failures over FireWire	#1: "Unable to Lock Deck Servo" message during capture attempt	In point for capture is too close to first frame of video on tape or preroll setting is too short	Make sure your device can reach needed playback speed, page 838
	#2: Interrupted captures and spotty performance when using RAID-0 volumes of FireWire 400 or 800 drives	Conflicts and bottlenecks on shared FireWire bus	Optimize your system for HD through FireWire, page 839

Nonmounting FireWire Drive

Symptom #1: Disconnected FireWire Drive Doesn't Mount

"I accidentally disconnected my FireWire drive or knocked its cable loose while the drive was mounted. Now the Mac OS tells me the disk is unreadable or it doesn't mount on the Desktop."

Background

As stated earlier, FireWire drives are just like any other drives in your system. When you want to remove a FireWire drive from the Macintosh, you have to inform the Mac that you are doing so, just as you do with any other type of drive. This may be news to those who are migrating from a PC environment and are used to yanking drives off the system at will. With the Macintosh, you have to dismount any drive that you want to remove. Doing so is easy; just drag the FireWire drive to the Trash, or Ctrl-click the drive and choose Eject *name of the drive*.

Solution

If a drive becomes disconnected improperly, you may see a brief dialog informing you that a FireWire device isn't responding or has been removed improperly. Whenever this happens, stop immediately, shut down your Macintosh, and power down any drives. When your entire system has been shut down, remove and reseat any FireWire cables; then restart your system.

In most cases, your FireWire drives will reappear promptly; Mac OS Extended formatting is pretty resilient. But if the drive doesn't show up, you quite probably have incurred severe directory damage to the drive. Open System Profiler (in the Utilities folder) to check that the FireWire drive is actually present and recognized by your Macintosh. If it is not, the drive may have suffered physical damage—a subject to be discussed subsequently. If the device shows up, however, you can attempt to repair the drive's directory structure.

If you are lucky, the drive will also appear in the left sidebar of the window when you open Disk Utility, Mac OS X's formatting and disk-repair utility. Depending on how badly the disk was damaged, you may or may not see the formatted partition grayed out underneath the drive. If you see the drive at all, select it and click Repair Disk in the bottom-right corner of the window.

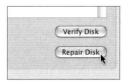

Again, if you are lucky, Disk Utility may be able to fix and remount the volume. In many cases, if Disk Utility can actually see the disk, it can perform the repair. Unfortunately, sometimes the first data that gets corrupted is the drive's initialized information. When the drive's data is unreadable, Disk Utility won't be able to repair the drive's directories.

If the drive did not appear in Disk Utility, try using a third-party disk utility like Alsoft's Disk Warrior (www.alsoft.com/diskwarrior) to ferret out the real data from corrupted volumes and bring volumes back from the dead. The important thing is to purchase Disk Warrior or an application like it before a problem like this occurs that so you aren't stuck with a dead drive at 11 on a Friday night for a Saturday tape delivery.

Symptom #2: FireWire Drive Doesn't Mount Despite Correct Connection

"My FireWire drive doesn't appear on the Desktop, though it's powered up and appears to be connected correctly."

Background

FireWire's 6-pin connector carries an active electrical circuit called *bus-power*. Bus-power can deliver electricity to some low-demand devices like 2.5-inch mini-FireWire drives, iPods, and the like so that you don't have to use an external power supply for the device.

The problem is that with cheaper cables and FireWire bridges, there is the risk of having this hot pin short out and fry your drive—and potentially even your Macintosh's FireWire ports.

Solution

If the drive doesn't show up in System Profiler, you need to shut your computer down again, disconnect the drive from the Macintosh, and examine the cables and the drive's FireWire port.

Also, remember that the FireWire 400 standard limits cable lengths to 14 feet. Although you're unlikely to find FireWire 400 cables longer than that, they do exist. If you notice an inordinately long FireWire cable, particularly in environments with a lot of heavy-duty electrical devices like speakers and production monitors, think about switching the cable out with more reasonable lengths, or invest in a FireWire cable extender to boost signal integrity and strength.

Dropped Frames with Daisy-Chained FireWire Drives

Symptom #1: Dropped Frames During Playback and Recording to Daisy-chained FireWire Drives

"I'm getting dropped-frames alerts while using my FireWire drive and a FireWire deck. I've used both on other systems that worked fine. I have the FireWire deck connected to the FireWire drive, which is connected to the Macintosh."

Background

A FireWire chain consists of multiple FireWire devices strung together in a straight cable path directly to the computer. Thus, the Macintosh FireWire port is plugged into a FireWire device, which is connected to another FireWire device, which is connected to another FireWire device, and so on until you reach the last device. In general, FireWire DV cameras and decks always occupy the end of a FireWire chain, because they don't have a second port to loop through to another device.

The difference between a FireWire *port* and a FireWire *bus* is an important distinction. A *bus* is a primary interface with the motherboard of the computer. We say that your Macintosh has an ATA bus and a FireWire bus because these buses are direct interfaces with the motherboard. A port, on the other hand, is a connector that allows you to interface with a bus. A motherboard has a bus (typically, one FireWire bus per Macintosh), and a bus can have one, two, or even three ports. Thus, your Macintosh might have two ports on the single FireWire bus, whereas your PowerBook might have only one port on the one FireWire bus.

When two devices are connected to a single bus, they can interfere with each other's data interchange with the motherboard, slowing all operations.

Solution

For extremely high-demand uses, such as high-data-rate uncompressed and HD video, make sure that you don't share a FireWire bus between both a deck and a drive. Doing so is almost guaranteed to cause bottlenecks and dropped frames. When using the AJA I/O Standard Definition Uncompressed capture device, for example, you absolutely must add a second FireWire bus to your Macintosh, typically by adding an inexpensive PCI FireWire expansion card.

If you're not running uncompressed or HD video, you might expect to be able to get away with sharing a single FireWire bus between a DV deck or camera and a FireWire drive. But this is still far from optimal since even the most advanced FireWire deck interfaces are built to deliver data at a dramatically slower speed than hard-drive bridges and generally provide only about one-quarter of the top possible FireWire 400 throughput (about 12.5 MB per second, as opposed to a potential 50 MB per second).

The only way to guarantee that bottlenecks and data collisions in the FireWire bus won't cause dropped frames and other issues is to move either the FireWire drive or DV deck or camera to another FireWire bus. This is easier and cheaper than you would imagine. A PCI FireWire 400 or 800 expansion card can be found for around $30 and will solve the question completely. For PowerBook users, a similar solution can be found with PC Card or Cardbus FireWire adapters. Alas, iBooks have no such Cardbus slot and will be more limited in this regard.

Lack of Communication with FireWire Deck or Camera

Symptom #1: Insert Editing Is Unavailable with Current Device

"In the Edit to Tape window, I can perform Assemble edits but not Insert edits."

Background

FireWire DV support Insert edits and can perform Assemble edits only with the Edit to Tape functions. The difference between Insert and Assemble edits is that Assemble edits overwrite all tracks on the tape as content is recorded. Although you have to give FCP an In point on the tape to start recording from, it simply records all video and audio tracks from that In point on the tape, recording over anything that was already on the tape.

An Insert edit, on the other hand, allows the user to edit any of the content in your project onto select tracks of the recording device. For example, you might want to record only video on the tape and leave the previously recorded audio tracks intact. Because of the accuracy required when recording individual tracks to tape, serial device control is required for Insert editing in Edit to Tape.

Solution

Although serial device control is mostly limited to expensive professional decks, certain higher-end DV decks have RS-422 and other serial interfaces. If your DV deck has such a serial interface, and you use it as your device control, you may very well have access to Insert editing via your DV deck. To do so, you will need to address your Device Control preset in Audio/Video Settings, changing its protocol from FireWire to your choice of serial interface.

Symptom #2: Log and Capture Reports No Communication with Connected Device

"I have my DV deck or camera connected to the Macintosh, but Log and Capture reports no communication. I also get no audio or video output from the Canvas and Viewer."

Background

Although all DV cameras have different menus and setup procedures, they all have two main modes: Camera and VTR. Camera mode, obviously, is for shooting and recording video through the lens. VTR (Video Tape Recorder) mode is for playback—and, with some cameras, recording—of video using the available video and audio inputs. But with only one exception, FCP can't access a DV camera unless it is in VTR mode.

Solution

If your Macintosh is hooked up to a DV camera, and the camera isn't recognized, make sure you don't have the camera set to Camera mode.

If you are using an HDV camcorder or deck, make sure you are in the correct setting. A camcorder set to DV will not be recognized as an HDV camcorder.

There is one exception. If you are using the camera as the microphone input in the Voice Over tool, you must set the camera to Camera mode. Then set the Source pop-up menu in the Voice Over tool to DV Audio to make the incoming audio stream available.

Symptom #3: Can't Communicate with AJ-HD1200A Deck

"I connected to the 1200A deck, and set up my FCP Capture and Sequence presets, but I can't get a signal to or from the deck."

Background

With DVCPRO HD and HDV, high-resolution HD content can be captured directly through a FireWire cable. This is revolutionary, because previously, capturing HD content required a PCI capture card and a very fast drive solution. With the implementation of these two products, HD content can be captured with the simplicity and flexibility of standard-definition DV FireWire capture. And because the HD content is digitally compressed during shooting, the throughput and storage requirements are quite minimal by comparison— not much higher than the minimums for FireWire DV capture.

Although FireWire capture of HD content is seamless and simple, you have to get it set up properly, or it won't deliver the results you are looking for. The AJ-HD1200A's menu settings are very specific, and if you don't get them exactly correct for your footage, you may get garbled video or no video at all.

Solution

Make sure that you read the deck's documentation thoroughly and get all the settings just right.

Because the 1200A deck is capable of performing HD and SD standards conversions internally, you have to set it for the desired output format.

Capture Interruptions and Failures over FireWire

Symptom #1: "Unable to Lock Deck Servo" Message During Capture Attempt

"I keep trying to capture a clip, but I constantly get an 'Unable to Lock Deck Servo' message."

Background

The safest way to edit video is always to use timecode for capture. If you capture by logging with timecode, you can easily recapture your clips and sequences from tape if anything ever happens to your scratch disk volumes. But by its very nature, timecode places a particular demand on your deck or camera with regard to playback speed.

All decks and cameras that use timecode need the tape's playback speed to be exact, so they use precision motors called *servo* motors. When the motors turning the deck transport reach the precise speed required for accurate time-code, they *lock the deck servo*, guaranteeing that the speed will remain constant until the capture is complete and the deck stops.

To ensure that the deck has enough time to get the tape running at the right speed before a capture starts, FCP uses a *preroll* setting, defined in the Device Control preset of your Audio/Video Settings. When a capture is initiated, the deck rolls back the number of seconds and frames specified in the preroll setting and starts playing. By the time it gets to the first frame you want to capture, the deck is up to speed, and the servo is locked.

You can get the "Unable to Lock Deck Servo" message if you set an In point for capture that is too close to the first frame of video on the tape. For example, if your preroll setting was for 3 seconds, and you set an In point for capture at the timecode value 00:00:00:02, FCP could not back the tape up 3 seconds to include 3 seconds of preroll and would likely generate a servo alert.

Solution

Always mark your In points after the first frame that could be captured, given your current Device Control preset preroll setting. If your preroll setting is 3 seconds, you can't set an In point on any frame earlier than 00:00:03:01. Always shoot at least 10 seconds of footage (referred to as *head*) on your tapes before you begin recording actual useable footage.

The only other way you can encounter this message is if your camera or deck really does need more preroll time than you are giving it in the preroll setting. Some prosumer DV decks and cameras take a little longer to get up to speed and lock the servo. This is easy to correct. You simply need to create a new Device Control preset with a longer preroll setting.

Symptom #2: Interrupted Captures and Spotty Performance When Using RAID-0 Volumes of FireWire 400 or 800 Drives

"I built a four-drive RAID-0 of matched FireWire 400 or 800 drives. It should be fast enough as far as data rates are concerned. Why am I still getting interrupted captures and spotty performance?"

Background

If you're using FireWire 400 and 800 drives, you're likely to run into conflicts and bottlenecks on the FireWire bus. As mentioned earlier, sharing a bus between a FireWire drive and FireWire deck or camera isn't always reliable, and with higher-resolution formats like DVCPRO HD, even more headroom is necessary.

Solution

As with the AJA I/O uncompressed converter, when capturing DVCPRO HD through FireWire, the AJ HD1200A needs to be the only item on the FireWire bus. Adding a FireWire 400 or 800 PCI card will separate the FireWire buses and give you greater throughput. Data streaming through FireWire from the deck won't collide or interfere with data streaming from the processor to the FireWire scratch disk.

You can also choose to switch to non-FireWire drives, such as internal SATA drives, or a high-speed RAID, such as an Apple Xserve Raid.

Solving 24P DV Capture and Pulldown Issues

Many editors are now entering the exciting world of 24P production, whether in DV, HD, or film postproduction. (We use the term 24P for both true 24 and 23.976 frame-per-second video, although you'll learn about the variations between them later in this section.)

FCP, as well as many third-party capture devices, has the ability to detect and read the 24P advanced pulldown flag. When you capture 24P advanced clips by using the dedicated DV NTSC 48 kHz Advanced (2:3:3:2) Pulldown Removal, FCP automatically removes the tagged frames. FCP regards the subsequent clips as true 23.98 fps clips without any trips into Cinema Tools for reverse telecine.

When editing 24P footage in FCP, there are a few places where you might run into problems.

24P DV Capture and Pulldown Problems at a Glance

Type of Problem	Symptom	Possible Cause	Solution
Render errors	#1: Red render lines in 24P sequences	You edited clips in sequences with the wrong editing time-base, or you didn't remove the pulldown	Use the right timebase and remove pulldown, page 841
Pulldown errors	#1: FCP can't find pulldown information	Your deck or camera doesn't read non-drop frame timecode	When capturing 24P, use a camera that reads non-drop frame time-code, page 842
	#2: Trouble removing pull-down after cap-turing footage	You didn't change capture preset before capture	Use FCP's Remove Advanced pulldown feature, page 843

Render Errors

Symptom #1: Red Render Lines in 24P Sequences

"I keep getting red render lines in my 24P sequences. Which frame rate is correct?"

Background

The generic term 24P, when used with DV, DVCPRO, and certain HD formats, is actually something of a misnomer. 24P footage recorded on DV-NTSC is always 23.98 fps recorded with a pulldown at 29.97 fps. Even 23.98 fps is something of a misnomer, because it is a contraction of 23.976 fps. Because 23.976 is a mouthful, editors commonly refer to it as "twenty-three nine eight." This should not confuse you too much, but it is rather important to understand. Some formats, such as Panasonic's DVCPRO HD, can use variable frame rates from 23.98, 24, 30, and 60.

Because DV NTSC runs at 29.97 fps rather than an even 30 fps, it is known as a *noninteger frame rate*. It is difficult to perform a pulldown of the solid integer film rate of 24 fps into 29.97 evenly. The standard cadence of 2:3:2:3 doesn't quite fit. Because we are working with digital video frames, it's relatively easy for the technology to slow the frame rate of the recorded video slightly to make an even ratio similar to the ratio between 24 and 30. Thus, to match NTSC's true rate of 29.97, a rate of 23.976 is used.

Capture settings must match the footage on the tape; then the sequence settings must match the captured clips' settings. 24P footage from DV cameras always uses a 23.98 fps frame rate pulled down into 29.97 (rather than 24 fps pulled down into any variation of NTSC). Because it is pulled down into NTSC 29.97 fps, you can either capture it normally and remove the pulldown manually or have FCP or a third-party capture device remove the pulldown automatically.

Solution

After capture and removal of the pulldown, you can edit the clips only in a 23.98 sequence. If you attempt to edit the media in sequences with other editing timebases, you will see a red render line. Likewise, if you do *not* remove the pulldown, either manually or automatically, you will get a red render line unless you insert the clip in a 29.97 sequence.

Pulldown Errors

Symptom #1: FCP Can't Find Pulldown Information

"I keep capturing my 24P clips, but FCP says it can't find any pulldown information to remove the extra fields."

Background

24P systems use a pulldown pattern to insert and remove extra fields to match NTSC frame rates. Therefore, it is imperative that no frame numbers are skipped in a video clip. For all original 24P video frames to match up with a contiguous timecode number, all timecode numbers must be present, before and after pulldown removal. You can't use a timecode system that skips numbers.

Drop frame timecode uses a system of skipping timecode numbers to keep the timecode clock synced up with the real-world clock (see Lesson 1 and 2 for an elaborate examination of the differences between the various timecode formats). Thus, 24P formats always use a non-drop frame timecode format. When shooting, this is not much of an issue, because 24P cameras will automatically enforce a non-drop frame timecode in 24P footage.

Solution

When capturing 24P, however, you must use a deck or camera that can actually read non-drop frame timecode. If you are using the camera you shot with, such as the Panasonic AG-DVX100A camera, or if you are using an HD, DVCPRO, DVCAM, or otherwise professional deck, this is probably not an issue. But if you use a cheaper DV deck to capture your 24P DV footage, you could end up in trouble. Not all decks or cameras can do this, because non-drop frame timecode is not an issue for most NTSC production. If you aren't sure, check your device's documentation before relying on it to capture and remove pulldown from 24P footage.

Also remember that standard pulldown (2:3:2:3) is different from advanced pulldown (2:3:3:2). FCP cannot automatically remove standard pulldown (added in telecine as opposed to being added in the camera). If you are having problems removing a pulldown, capture it normally as a 29.97 fps clip. Then step through the frames one at a time, noting the patterns of judder frames.

Symptom #2: Trouble Removing Pulldown After Capturing Footage

"I forgot to change my Capture preset before capturing 24P footage. How do I remove the pulldown after footage is captured?"

Background

24P footage recorded with the advanced pulldown cadence must have the pull-down removed so that the footage can be edited in a 23.98 fps sequence. There are two ways to remove that pulldown: automatically or manually. You can remove the pulldown automatically by choosing the DV NTSC 48K Advanced Pulldown Removal Capture Preset before capturing. When the capture is complete, FCP goes through each clip and sets the frame rate to 23.98; the job is done.

Solution

If you forget to set the capture preset to remove the pulldown at capture, or if you are working with imported 24P files, you can remove the pulldown after capture by selecting the clip and then choosing Tools > Remove Advanced Pulldown. FCP will remove the pulldown with the same results.

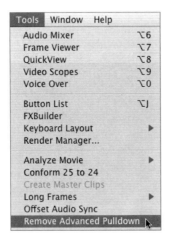

Solving Application-Level Errors and System Failures

The more you work with Final Cut Pro, the better you get at distinguishing between error alerts generated by the system and those generated by the application. In this section, we'll look first at application-level errors, including out-of-memory errors and unexpected quits, and then we'll look briefly at several types of system-level hangs or crashes.

For more information, refer to Lesson 10 to review how to set up your system preferences to get optimal performance from FCP. For a comprehensive list of the possible system-level error alerts, consult a book dedicated to the Mac OS.

System Lockups and Failures at a Glance

Type of Problem	Symptom	Possible Cause	Solution
Error alert	#1: General error alert while FCP is running	Impossible task or corrupt file	Perform error-minimization steps, page 847
	#2: Out-of-memory error appears while FCP is running	Corruption in one or more of the following: a sequence, a clip in a sequence, or a sequence or render file	Disable corrupted sequences and sequence elements, page 849
Unexpected quit	#1: FCP crashes when a specific project or sequence tries to load	Corrupted project or media file	Fix the crash-prone project or sequence, page 850

System Lockups and Failures at a Glance

Type of Problem	Symptom	Possible Cause	Solution
	#2: FCP crashes randomly	Corrupted preferences files or other files, insufficient or faulty RAM, introduction of faulty hardware or software	Perform general maintenance and evaluation steps, page 851
System hang or kernel panic	#1: Complete system lockup: frozen pointer onscreen	Damaged file directories, hardware incompatibilities, or processor problems	Perform lockup-recovery steps, page 853
	#2: System hang: prolonged spinning beach ball	Processor-intensive activity or delays in communicating with external device	Restart and reset devices, perform hang-recovery steps, page 854
	#3: Kernel panic: Mac OS interface replaced by message advising restart of Mac	Faulty RAM or hardware, problematic device drivers or other software	Perform system troubleshooting steps, page 855

Error Alert

Symptom #1: General Error Alert While FCP Is Running

"I get a general error message when I use Print to Video."

Background

A Final Cut Pro general error alert appears when the system, hardware, user, or media asks FCP to do something that the application's code can't perform. It's called *general* because FCP's code doesn't have a specific error alert identifying the situation.

A general error is the type of problem that does not cause the application to quit or the system to lock up. You still have time to save your work and, ideally, address the problem without having to restart the computer or even relaunch the application.

For example, the error described in the quote could have several causes, including a loose FireWire cable connecting the computer to the camcorder, or two applications simultaneously attempting to claim a FireWire camera or deck as the video output device. In both cases, the problem could be fixed without having to restart the Mac.

Solution

When you encounter a general error, first click through the alert and save your work. Next, eliminate user error: review your work and make sure you are asking Final Cut Pro to perform a task it is capable of doing at that stage of the project.

If the error recurs, reset your preferences, and restart the application and project. Then return to where you were before the general error occurred, and see whether the error recurs.

If it the error does recur, determine whether the problem is a clip, a sequence, a render file, or the original media. To do so, look around to see what is going on in the system. Does the error occur when the playhead encounters a specific clip? Does it occur only in the Viewer or the Sequence, or only when encountering the same clip in both? Can the clip in question be viewed in the Viewer but not in the sequence? Has the clip been rendered?

You can eliminate media files as the culprits by taking all your sequence clips offline and then reconnecting and testing them, one by one.

1   Select the sequence or project clips causing the problem (or all of them, if you aren't sure).

2   Choose Modify > Make Offline.

3   Choose the Leave Files on Disk radio button.

4   Choose File > Reconnect Media, make sure that Reconnect Files in Relative Path is disabled, and reconnect the first clip.

5   Return to the project where you encountered the problem, and see whether the clip you reconnected produces the behavior you are troubleshooting. If so, make it offline again and move to the next clip. If not, leave it online and move to the next clip.

The idea here is that you leave any problem-causing clips offline and leave any benign clips online. When you are finished, you will be able to recapture clips with one keyboard shortcut and checkbox. It should be obvious after a short while if a corrupt file is the root of the problem. If all clips in a sequence produce the same problematic behavior, it's doubtful that they are all corrupt—in cases of media file corruption, it is rare to find more than one corrupt file.

> **TIP** ▶ You can double and even triple the speed of this isolation troubleshooting by using a slight variation of the split half search. You will remember from Lesson 16 that the split half search technique lets you hone in on a single problem file by testing half the files at a time. If you test the first half and find no problems, you can assume that the problem is in the second half.
>
> To apply that method to this situation, select two or three clips to reconnect at a time; then test each one. Reconnecting clips is the slow part; testing usually takes only a second.

Symptom #2: Out-of-memory Error Appears While FCP Is Running

"While playing a sequence, I get a red out-of-memory error in the Canvas."

Background

Out-of-memory errors are widely misunderstood to mean not having enough memory installed to run FCP. That's possible if you've got less than 512 MB of RAM installed. But if you encounter this error on a system with 1 GB of RAM or more, the problem lies elsewhere.

This error message actually means that FCP has run out of memory *for the operation it is trying to complete*. It's not a common error message, and usually indicates corruption in a sequence, a clip in a sequence, or a render file.

Solution

If you get an out-of-memory error message, perform these steps:

1   Open the sequence.

    If you can open a sequence and the error does not appear, the sequence itself is probably not corrupt. Next, you want to see whether render files are the problem.

2   Select all the clips in the sequence, and copy and paste them into a new, fresh sequence.

    Render files are locked to the sequence in which they were generated. Copying the clips to a new sequence leaves the original sequence's render files intact while letting you test the sequence contents divorced from the render files. If the problem remains, a corrupt media file might be the culprit.

3   Copy and paste a few clips at a time from the original sequence into the new sequence until you encounter the problem.

When you find the clip that's causing the problem, take a closer look. Does it use third-party filters? Does taking the clip offline eliminate the problem? Is there anything else unique about it, such as being a still image file or a video clip generated by another application?

Unexpected Quit

Symptom #1: FCP Crashes When a Specific Project or Sequence Tries to Load

"My system seems to be working fine for all but one sequence. When I try to load that one sequence, FCP crashes."

Background

Many things can cause unexpected quits. The unexpected quit is actually not an application alert, like the general and out-of-memory errors; it is a system-level error alert that tells you an application has experienced a fatal error. This means FCP has encountered a problem so severe that it can't continue running.

Although it is quite rare, you can encounter an unexpected quit if your project contains corrupt sequences, clips, or render files. If you can launch FCP, but when you load a particular project the application crashes, suspect that the project may contain a corrupt item. Similarly, if you can launch your project, but the application crashes when you try to load a particular sequence, that sequence may be corrupt.

Solution

The only way to determine your project contains corrupt files is to make the media related to the project or sequence offline. If you are unable to launch the project at all, force the media offline by disconnecting or by leaving your scratch disk volumes dismounted. When the media is offline, attempt to open the project.

If the project still doesn't open, it may have been irreparably corrupted, and the media is likely not the culprit. If you arrive at this conclusion, it's wise to go into your backups and the Autosave Vault, and find the most recent version that doesn't exhibit the corruption. Duplicate that backed-up file, and begin working again. It's not a good idea to invest a great deal of work in a project that you know is corrupted.

If, on the other hand, the project or sequence does open, your next job is to reconnect the media one file at a time, retesting the project each time, until you find the file that is causing the problem. (Use the steps described in "Symptom #1: General Error Alert While FCP is Running," earlier in this section.) Don't forget to save regularly, because when you find the corrupt file, FCP is likely to crash again, and you'll have to link the nonproblematic clips all over again.

Symptom #2: FCP Crashes Randomly

"I get unexpected quits randomly. They don't seem to be related to any particular project or media I am working with."

Background

If unexpected quits are a chronic problem, incorrect system setup or inadequate system maintenance are the most likely causes. The first thing to do is to evaluate your system and perform thorough maintenance.

Solution

▶ Perform routine maintenance.

Repairing permissions and refreshing preferences are two of the most common cures for the quits. Perform routine maintenance every week and manually trash and reset your preferences every couple of months.

▶ Make sure the amount of RAM meets specifications.

Insufficient installed RAM can cause unexpected quits and other errors. Final Cut Pro's minimum amount of required RAM is insufficient if you plan to run many applications in the background.

▶ Use the Autosave Vault.

If it's been a while since you manually backed up, you might need to go into Project Restore when you open FCP. Next, perform a quick Preferences reset, restart FCP, and get back to work.

▶ Test with the new Final Cut Pro preferences.

If the unexpected quits return, you'll have to go a little deeper. Moving your FCP preferences (located in your user library in /Library/Preferences/ Final Cut Pro User Data) to the Desktop and running FCP will let you determine whether the cause is related to something specific to your real user. Running a copy of your current project with new preferences allows you to isolate whether the problem is with something in your user folder or the project itself.

▶ Check third-party software and hardware.

Has any software or hardware changed in your system recently? Remove all FireWire and USB devices, and run FCP again. If the problem disappears, consider switching out any FireWire or USB cables, because an $8 cable could be at the root of the problem.

Beyond FireWire devices, other factors can cause quits, including conflicting video and audio output devices and drivers, permissions problems on non-Apple-installed files, and directory-level disk errors.

▶ Check the FCP crash log.

You can use the Console utility to view logs (historical records) of application and system activity. This includes log files that may contain information about why or how an application crashed. The system.log file contains general information about system-level activity.

You can also use Console to navigate to the CrashReporter folder in the user's Library/Logs folder to locate the Final Cut Pro.crash.log file.

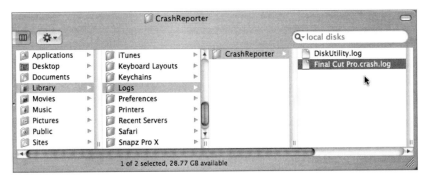

Although the content of those log listings can seem a little opaque to the average user, the information is gold to Apple Pro Video Support technicians who might be assisting you in troubleshooting.

▶ Test for bad RAM chips.

Faulty RAM is a common cause of unexpected quits in the Mac OS. Particularly if you are running aftermarket RAM chips, you may have introduced a problem into your system. Problems resulting from faulty RAM chips are notoriously intermittent, and just because RAM has worked fine for six months doesn't mean that it can't send your system into a tailspin tomorrow morning.

Checking for bad RAM is an intensive and invasive task. But if no other troubleshooting steps uncover a problem, it's a logical step. Test for faulty RAM by switching it out, stick by stick, running with only one stick at a time (or two, in the case of G5s that require interleaved RAM) until you encounter the quits or other-aberrant behavior. Although the Apple Hardware Test CD that comes with your Macintosh has a utility for testing RAM, it may not catch intermittent errors.

Purchase RAM only from reputable dealers—namely, ones that offer lifetime return and cross-ship guarantees.

System Hang or Kernel Panic

Symptom #1: Complete System Lockup, Frozen Pointer Onscreen
"My mouse pointer is frozen and I can't move anything on my screen."

Background

System hangs and kernel panics are more serious forms of crashing. In a *system hang,* the operating system locks up and is no longer interacting with the outside world. In a *kernel panic,* the system generates an error message notifying the user to restart the computer. We'll look at system hangs first.

There are two kinds of system hangs: a *complete lockup* and what is affectionately called a *beach ball.*

A complete lockup is characterized by a frozen mouse pointer on the computer screen. Although the computer is still powered up and you see the Desktop, it doesn't respond to any interaction from the user.

Solution

When your mouse pointer freezes, restart your computer. It is safest to choose Apple Menu > Shut Down, wait 10 seconds, and then press the power button to restart.

A complete lockup often results from damaged file directories, which means that you may also need to perform disk repairs, using Apple Disk Utility or a third-party utility. If the system hang occurred while you were running FCP, you should refresh your preferences files as well, because it's possible that they were damaged when the crash occurred.

A complete lockup can also be the result of hardware failure or incompatibility. If you are experiencing complete lockups, even after correcting directory-level problems, first eliminate hardware add-ons such as RAM, PCI cards, and USB and FireWire devices.

In extreme recurrent situations, complete lockups may indicate processor problems. Check to be sure that ventilation and room temperature are adequate, as overheating can have an impact on processor performance.

Symptom #2: System Hang, Prolonged Spinning Beach Ball

Background

When any application runs into a delay, the mouse pointer converts into a spinning color wheel, or "beach ball." When the delay is over, FCP gets right back to work where it left off. Not all appearances of the beach ball indicate a system hang; in fact, most beach balls last only a few seconds.

Solution

Because the beach ball indicates that FCP is still functioning, you should always give the hang a reasonable amount of time before resorting to force-quitting and restarting. For example, projects with very long sequences or large numbers of clips and media can take minutes rather than seconds to open. Likewise, loading a high-resolution still image into a project that is already open can cause a prolonged beach ball.

If after ten minutes the beach ball is still spinning, check to see whether FCP is the only application being delayed by clicking the Desktop or other open applications and checking if they work normally. (Don't try to launch any unopened applications yet, because that will only compound the problem.)

If other applications respond, let FCP continue to try to work out the delay; you probably aren't experiencing a lockout yet. But if no applications respond, or you still see a beach ball when you click the Desktop, the system is probably hung.

Next, try to force-quit FCP. If you can access the Dock without getting a beach ball, click the Finder icon and choose Apple Menu > Force Quit. You can also try Ctrl-clicking the FCP icon and choosing Force Quit.

If the Dock is unavailable, try to Force Quit FCP by pressing Command-Option-Escape. If all these methods fail, it's time to force-restart the Macintosh.

Don't forget to perform all the maintenance techniques that apply to the complete lockup after restarting from a beach ball, because you are probably creating preferences, cache, and temp-file corruptions when you force-restart. Also make sure to repair permissions immediately, because permissions issues often cause prolonged beach balls.

#3: Kernel Panic, Mac OS Interface Replaced by Restart Error Message

Background

A kernel panic is type of system crash in which the system has enough time to recognize what it is experiencing and let you know about it. Your normal Mac OS interface is replaced by a message in four languages, stating that the Macintosh needs to be restarted.

Kernel panics can be caused by software and third-party device drivers, but most frequently they are caused by hardware, such as USB devices. They can also indicate problems with your motherboard components, such as the processors, RAM chips, or ATA disk interfaces.

Solution

When you encounter a kernel panic, you must restart the computer. As with system hangs, perform system-maintenance steps to clear up any directory damage the crash may have caused.

As soon as the computer restarts, information about the nature of the crash is added to a panic log file in the root-level Library folder (Library > Logs > panic.log). The easiest method of viewing the contents of any log file is using the Console utility.

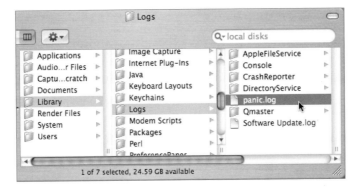

Double-clicking the panic log opens it in the Terminal shell so you can examine this log yourself and glean clues about the cause of the panic. Don't worry if you don't understand what you see; it's mostly code related to memory addresses and the actions of hidden files. But sometimes you might see a clue, such as the name of a file or device.

If you are experiencing frequent kernel panics, even when starting up from a clean backup disk, troubleshoot your system to determine the source. Rule out USB devices by temporarily disconnecting them, check device drivers, and confirm adequate room temperature and ventilation.

Lesson Review

1. What should you do if you get a message saying your scratch disk is missing?

2. What causes audio or video to be missing from your output device?

3. What's the proper way to dismount a FireWire drive so that you avoid disk errors?

4. Is Insert editing possible when using FireWire for device control?

5. What causes 'Unable to Lock Deck Servo' messages?

6. If you get garbled video or no video output at all with a DVCPRO HD 1200A deck, what's likely to be the cause?

7. How do you avoid interruptions to the capture process with DVCPRO HD?

8. If you're capturing 24P clips and FCP can't find pulldown information, what's the likely cause?

Answers

1. Try remounting or resetting the scratch disk.

2. Missing video or audio is usually caused by a settings mix-up or an incorrectly connected device.

3. FireWire drives, like all volumes, must be dismounted by dragging to the Trash before disconnecting.

4. No.

5. These messages could be caused by a Device Control issue or your logging.

6. The DVCPRO HD 1200A deck is particular about its menu settings; make sure you haven't missed any.

7. DVCPRO HD requires significant throughput and storage; in particular, the 1200A FireWire HD deck needs plenty of throughput overhead and unrestricted access to the FireWire bus of the Macintosh.

8. You're using a deck or camera that can't read non-drop frame timecode.

Final Cut Studio Workflows

Apple's family of professional audio and video applications are designed to work together seamlessly, even in the most demanding postproduction workflows. The Final Cut Studio product line—a comprehensive and integrated postproduction package—includes Final Cut Pro 5, Soundtrack Pro, Motion 2, DVD Studio Pro 4, Compressor 2, LiveType 2, Cinema Tools 3. These tools, in conjunction with Shake 4 and Logic Pro 7, provide professional editors with the most comprehensive toolkit in the industry. The appendix on the DVD accompanying this book details the roles of each application in the Final Cut Pro production process. You will also find a sample Final Cut Studio workflow, and information on "roundtripping," the ability to embed and open application project files while working in another application. See **Appendix -Final Cut Studio Workflows**.

Glossary

Look up definitions of terms that you find in this book by going to the glossary on the included DVD.

Index

STRAIGHTEN UP AND FLY RIGHT
IS A SHORT FILM WRITTEN AND
DIRECTED BY JESSE COSTELLO

STARRING   TIM CINNANTE

ALSO STARRING   PETER LINARI

FOR MORE INFORMATION ON FILM DISTRIBUTION RIGHTS OR TO CONTACT THE DIRECTOR, PLEASE VISIT JESSECOSTELLO.COM